Easy to Read
Accurate Literal Translation

of the

HOLY BIBLE

The Complete New Testament
with a Treasure of Old Testament Passages

The New Authorized Version in Present-Day English™

AV7 closely follows the time-honored traditional English text
commonly known as the Authorized Version or KJV,
with recognized errors corrected, obsolete and archaic
words and phrases updated to present-day English,
and with many refinements and enhancements.

AV7 The New Authorized Version
of the New Testament in Present-Day English™

*All Scripture texts contained herein
are the gift of Almighty God to mankind
and may be freely copied for any non-commercial
use* with only three stipulations:*

1. For the benefit of readers, the source of any quotations from this text should be identified as *AV7*.

2. No changes may be made in *AV7* or in any New Authorized Version Foundation text without written consent.

3. *Commercial use is defined as any reproduction of the *AV7* text for which any fee is charged. Commercial use requires an appropriate license from the copyright holder.

Compiled and published by Communication Architects
for the New Authorized Version Foundation

Printed in the USA in cooperation with Barbour Publishing
ISBN numbers:
1-59789-446-X (Burgundy)   1-59789-447-8 (Green)
1-59789-448-6 (Clouds)   1-59789-449-4 (Youth)

For additional information, please visit: www.*AV7*.org

Introduction

The greatest wisdom, truth, and practical guidance for living a successful life are found within the pages of the Bible. It is the most inspiring, the most trustworthy, and the most widely published and distributed source of wisdom and truth ever compiled.

The Bible is the best-selling book of all time. No other best-seller has ever come even close to it. It is, without rival, the most widely read and studied, and the most extensively researched, verified, and validated document in the history of mankind.

Regrettably however, among the great number of different versions of the Bible in print, many use interpretive paraphrasing that may dilute, diminish, or misrepresent the full truth of the Word of God. While a paraphrase may be helpful to some readers, it is important to realize that paraphrasing is not a literally accurate source of truth. Some versions have taken great liberties in the changes they have made. Therefore, readers would be wise to compare any non-literal version to an accurate literal translation.

It is important to understand that there can never be such a thing as different versions of the truth. Every deviation from literal accuracy increases the risk of moving farther and farther away from trustworthy truth. Many Bible publishers have sponsored or created their own unique "All rights reserved" versions and paraphrases of the Bible. All of these very different versions cannot possibly be equally reliable and trustworthy.

AV7 is different. It is not a product of commercial sponsorship or the result of any individual's or committee's interpretation of what the Word of God says. Instead, *AV7* is a present-day English update of the traditional English text that stood for more than 300 years as the most widely accepted, literally accurate English language translation of the Bible. *AV7* closely follows that text.

Therefore, you can now read, study, and rightly divide the Word of Truth with a trustworthy, literally accurate version of the Bible that is easy to read in present-day English.

AV7

The New Authorized Version of the Bible
in Present-Day English ™

1

Table of Contents

Pastoral letters written by some of the first eyewitnesses
to the life and teachings of the Word of God
to encourage new believers in their faith:

The Ten Commandments
are the foundation of all truth

The Ten Commandments are the most readily recognizable of all truths. They are unique in many ways, one of which is that when God established these Ten Commandments, that was the first time that He is reported to have spoken directly to all of mankind, rather than to and through certain individuals one at a time.

The Ten Commandments are further distinguished by the fact that this was the only time in all of recorded history that God ever wrote a message to mankind by His own hand. And it is significant that He wrote this message as an engraving carved in stone.

Ever since that event some 3,300 years ago, the Ten Commandments have been almost universally acknowledged and accepted as the foundation of all truth by people who believe in God.

Very few people who acknowledge that there is a God will ever dispute the relevance, common sense, reasonableness, viability, practicality, and appropriateness of the Ten Commandments as wise words to live by and to govern and be governed by.

Some people have claimed that the Ten Commandments were given only to the Jews, or that they were only meant for the ancient time and place in which they were given. Consequently, they say that only Jews are required to obey them. Some others suggest that God's Ten Commandments are no longer applicable today.

However, as you read these Ten Commandments, it will surely be very apparent that God meant what He said and that He fully intended for these Ten Commandments to remain in effect for all people and for all time.

Please note: The *AV7* Bible text uses reduced-size italics to identify words that have been interpolatively added to otherwise literally translated words to improve clarity, readability, and understandability. For example, in the verse: "I *am* the Lord your God" (see #1 on the facing page), the word "am" is an interpolatively added word. The *AV7* text also uses key word flags to identify significant word revisions from the traditional English text. For example, the word "murder+" (see #6 on the facing page) is a more accurate translation than the traditional translation "kill."

The 10 Commandments

Exodus 20:1-17

#1 [v1-3] God spoke … saying: I *am* the Lord your God … You shall have no other gods before me.

#2 [v4] You shall not make for yourself any graven image or any likeness *of any thing* that *is* in heaven above or that *is* in the earth beneath or that *is* in the water under the earth. [5] You shall not bow yourself down to them nor serve them, for I the Lord your God *am* a jealous God, visiting the iniquity of the fathers upon the children to the third and fourth *generation* of those who hate me [6] and showing mercy to thousands of those who love me and keep my commandments.

#3 [v7] You shall not take the name of the Lord your God in vain, for the Lord will not hold those guiltless who take His name in vain.

#4 [v8] Remember the Sabbath day to keep it holy. [9] Six days shall you labor and do all your work, [10] but the seventh day *is* the Sabbath of the Lord your God. *In it*, you shall not do any work: You nor your son nor your daughter, your servant nor your maid, nor your cattle, nor your visitor+ who *is* within your gates. [11] For *in* six days the Lord made heaven and earth, the sea, and all that *is* in them, and *He* rested *on* the seventh day. Therefore the Lord blessed the Sabbath day and hallowed it.

#5 [v12] Honor your father and your mother *so* that your days may be long upon the land which the Lord your God has given *to* you.

#6 [v13] You shall not murder+.

#7 [v14] You shall not commit adultery.

#8 [v15] You shall not steal.

#9 [v16] You shall not bear false witness against your neighbor.

#10 [v17] You shall not covet your neighbor's house *and* you shall not covet your neighbor's wife nor his manservant nor his maidservant nor his ox nor his ass nor any thing that *is* your neighbor's.

The Most Essential Truth

All of the words and messages presented in the Bible are of great importance and great value, and no part of the Bible should be omitted, ignored, or disregarded. However, all of the words and messages in the Bible are not equal in importance.

Some words and messages, such as the Ten Commandments, establish never-to-be-changed laws as benchmarks of bedrock importance. Other portions include historical narratives, eye-witness accounts of supernatural events, genealogical records, biographical data, personal testimonies, prophetic allegories, and various other types and categories of content.

Interspersed among the 790,391 words in 31,089 verses in the 66 books in the Bible, there are certain key verses — **universal truths and declarative instructions** — that God communicates to mankind. Sometimes He speaks with His own voice, sometimes through the mouths of prophets, and in certain places, God specifically speaks as "**the Word of God**." The first words in the Book of John identify and introduce the Word of God in this way:

> "In the beginning was the Word,
> and the Word was with God,
> and the Word was God."
> *(and then in verse 14)*
> "… and the Word became flesh and lived+ among us."

Only one person in all of recorded history has ever qualified for that name and title. The words that He spoke out of His own mouth are far more significant and more important than any other words ever spoken or written.

A book entitled *The Most Essential Truth in the Bible* (ISBN 978-0-935597-02-7) features 249 passages in which the Word of God proclaims the most essential of all universal truths and declarative instructions. In the 7 pages that follow, you can quickly read 98 of these key passages. While it takes more than 66 hours to read the entire Bible, you can read these key passages in less than 10 minutes. For more information visit: www.MostEssential.com

You can also enjoy refreshing inspiration and encouragement every day by frequently re-reading and meditating on these key passages from the incomparable wisdom of the Word of God.

If anyone has ears that can hear let them listen.

#11 It is written:
Mankind shall not live
by bread alone,
but by every word that proceeds
out of the mouth of God.

#12 Again it is written: You shall not tempt the Lord your God.

#13 You shall worship
the Lord your God
and Him only shall you serve.

#14 Truly, truly, I say to you: Unless a person is born again, they cannot see the kingdom of God.

#15 Truly, truly, I say to you: Unless a person is born of water and *of* the Spirit, they cannot enter into the kingdom of God. *Those* who are born of flesh are flesh, and *those* who are born of the Spirit are spirit. Do not marvel that I said: You must be born again.

#17 God so loved the world,
that He gave
His Only Begotten Son,
so that whoever believes in Him
should not perish,
but have eternal life.

#18 God did not send His Son into the world to condemn the world, but *so* that the world through Him might be saved. *Those* who believe in Him are not condemned, but *those* who do not believe are condemned already, because they have not believed in the name of the Only Begotten Son of God.

#20 *The Word of God said:* Whoever drinks of the water that I give will never thirst. Instead, the water that I give will become a well of water within them springing up into eternal life.

#21 God *is* Spirit. *Those* who worship Him must worship *Him* in spirit and in truth.

#23 Repent. For the kingdom of heaven is *very* near.

#24 Follow me and I will make you fishers of men.

#25 Sin no more, lest a worse thing come to you.

#27 Truly, truly, I say to you: *Those* who hear my Word and believe in Him who sent me have eternal life and will not come into condemnation, but *they* are passed from death to life.

#28 *Those* who have done good will come forth to the resurrection of life, and *those* who have done evil to the resurrection of damnation.

#29 Search the Scriptures.
For in them
you think you have eternal life,
and they testify of me.

#30 Blessed *are* the poor in spirit, for theirs is the kingdom of heaven.

#31 Blessed *are those* who mourn, for they shall be comforted.

#32 Blessed *are* the meek, for they shall inherit the earth.

#33 Blessed *are those* who do hunger and thirst after righteousness, for they shall be filled.

#34 Blessed *are* the merciful, for they shall obtain mercy.

#35 Blessed *are* the pure in heart, for they shall see God.

#36 Blessed *are* the peacemakers, for they shall be called children of God.

#37 Blessed *are those* who are persecuted for righteousness' sake, for theirs is the kingdom of heaven.

#38 Blessed are you when *people* revile you and persecute *you* and say all kinds of evil against you falsely for my sake.

#39 Rejoice and be exceedingly glad. For great *is* your reward in heaven. For so *likewise did* they persecute the prophets who were before you.

#40 You are the salt of the earth, but if salt has lost its savor, with what will it be salted? It is thereafter good for nothing but to be cast out and trampled under foot.

#41 You are the light of the world. A city that is set on a hill cannot be hid. Nor do people light a candle and put it under a bushel, but on a candlestick *so that* it gives light to all who are in the house.

> **#42** Let your light so shine before *people* that they may see your good works and glorify your Father in heaven.

#43 Do not think that I have come to destroy the law or the prophets. I have not come to destroy, but to fulfill. For truly I say to you: Until heaven and earth pass, one jot or one smallest mark shall in no way pass from the law until all is fulfilled.

#44 Whoever therefore shall break one of these least commandments and shall teach people *to do* so shall be called the least in the kingdom of heaven. But whoever shall do *them* and teach *them*, the same shall be called great in the kingdom of heaven.

#53 You have heard that it has been said: You shall love your neighbor and hate your enemy. But I say to you:

> Love your enemies.
> Bless *those* who curse you.
> Do good to *those* who hate you.
> And pray for *those*
> who despitefully use you
> and persecute you
> *so* that you may be the children
> of your Father in heaven.

#57 Pray in this manner:

Our Father in heaven,
Holy is your name.
Your kingdom come.
Your will be done,
on earth as *it is* in heaven.

Give us this day our daily bread.
And forgive us *for* our debts
as we forgive our debtors.

Lead us *so that we will* not
yield to temptation,
but deliver us from evil.

For the kingdom is yours,
and the power and the glory,
forever. Amen.

#58 If you forgive others *for* their trespasses *then* your heavenly Father will also forgive you. But if you do not forgive others *for* their trespasses *then* neither will your Father forgive your trespasses.

#61 Do not lay up for yourselves treasures on earth where moth and rust corrupt and where thieves break through and steal. Lay up for yourselves treasures in heaven where neither moth nor rust corrupt and where thieves do not break through or steal.

#62 Do not be afraid, little flock. For it is your Father's good pleasure to give the kingdom *of God* to you.

#65 No one can serve two masters. For either they will hate the one and love the other, or else they will hold to the one and despise the other.

You cannot serve God
and *worldly* treasures.

#66 Take heed and beware of covetousness. For one's life *is* not *to be found* in the abundance *of things* one possesses.

#73 Seek first the kingdom of God and His righteousness and all these things will be added to you.

#75 Do not judge *so* that you *will* not be judged. For with what judgment you judge, you will be judged. With what gauge you measure, it will be measured to you again.

#76 Give and it will be given to you: Good measure, pressed down, shaken together, and running over. Others will give to your innermost *needs*. For with the same gauge with which you measure it will be measured to you again.

#80 Ask and it will be given *to* you. Seek and you will find.
Knock and it will be
opened to you.
For everyone who asks receives
and *those* who seek *will* find
and to *those* who knock
it will be opened.

#82 - - - *The Golden Rule* - - -

Therefore all things whatsoever you would that others should do to you, you do to them. For this is *the sum of* the law and the prophets.

#84 Beware of false prophets who come to you in sheep's clothing, but inwardly they are greedy wolves. You will know them by their fruits.

#86 Not everyone who says to me: Lord, Lord, will enter into the kingdom of heaven, but *only those* who do the will of my Father in heaven.

#91 Go and learn what *this* means: I will have mercy and not sacrifice. For I have not come to call the righteous but sinners to repentance.

> **#92** Do not be afraid.
> Only believe.

#95 As you go, proclaim *the Word*, say: The kingdom of heaven is *very* near.

#106 … there is nothing covered that will not be revealed and *nothing* hidden that will not be known.

#109 Whoever will confess me before people, I will confess before my Father in heaven. But whoever will deny me before people, I will deny before my Father in heaven.

> **#114** Come to me
> all *you* who labor
> and are heavily burdened.
> I will give you rest.
> Take my yoke upon you
> and learn of me.
> For I am meek and lowly
> in heart. You will find
> rest for your souls.
> For my yoke *is* easy
> and my burden is light.

#115 You are overly anxious and troubled about *too* many things. But one thing is necessary: *giving heed to the Word of God* …

#118 Every kingdom divided against itself is brought to desolation. Every city or house divided against itself will not stand.

#119 *Those* who are not with me are against me. *Those* who do not gather with me scatter.

#122 … out of the abundance of the heart the mouth speaks. A good person out of good treasure of the heart brings forth good things. An evil person out of evil treasure brings forth evil things.

#123 … *for* every idle word that people speak, they will give *an* account of it on the day of judgment.

> For by your words
> you will be justified
> and by your words
> you will be condemned.

#124 … blessed *are those* who hear the Word of God and keep it.

#125 … whoever does the will of my Father in heaven, the same is my brother and sister and mother.

#130 Be of good cheer. I am *with you*. Do not be afraid.

#132 This is the work of God: That you believe in *the one* whom He has sent.

#137 Truly truly I say to you:

> *Those* who believe in me
> have eternal life.

#141 If anyone has ears to hear, let them hear. Out of the heart proceed evil thoughts, murders, adulteries, fornications, thefts, false witness, covetousness, wickedness, deceit, filthiness, an evil eye, blasphemy, pride, *and* foolishness. These are *the things* that defile a person ...

#142 If anyone will come after me, let them deny themselves and take up their cross and follow me. For whoever would save their life will lose it and whoever would lose their life for my sake will find it. For what is anyone to profit if they gain the whole world and lose their own soul? Or what shall anyone give in exchange for their soul?

#143 If you can believe, all things *are* possible to *those* who believe.

#156 If anyone thirsts, let them come to me and drink. As the Scripture has said *of those* who believe in me: Out of their innermost being will flow rivers of living water.

> **#157** If you continue
> in my Word *then*
> you are indeed
> my disciples.
> You shall know the truth
> and the truth
> will make you free.

#159 Truly, truly, I say to you: If anyone keeps my Word, they will never see death.

#161 I am the door. If anyone enters in through me, they will be saved ...

#162 ... I have come *so* that they *might* have life and have *it* more abundantly.

#177 I am the resurrection and the life. *Those* who believe in me, though they were dead, yet shall they live.

> Whoever lives and believes
> in me will never die.
> Do you believe this?

#182 Have you not read that He who made *them* at the beginning made them male and female and said: For this reason a man shall leave father and mother and cleave to his wife and they two shall be one flesh. Therefore they are no longer two but one flesh. Therefore what God has joined together do not let anyone separate.

#186 If you will enter into life, keep the commandments. You shall do no murder. You shall not commit adultery. You shall not steal. You shall not bear false witness. Honor your father and *your* mother. And, you shall love your neighbor as yourself.

> **#189** ... With God
> all things are possible.

#196 Truly I say to you: If you have faith and do not doubt, but say to this mountain: Be removed and be cast into the sea, it will be done. All things whatsoever you ask in prayer believing, you will receive.

#200 You err *by* not knowing the Scriptures or the power of God.

#201 What is written in the law?
How do you read *it*?
You shall love the Lord
your God with all your heart
and with all your soul
and with all your mind.
Do this and you will live.
This is the first
and great commandment.

#202 The second *is* like it:
You shall love your neighbor
as yourself.
On these two commandments
hang all the law and the prophets.

#204 Do not be called Rabbi. For one is your Master, Christ. All *of* you are family.

#205 Do not call any *man* your father on the earth, for one is your Father, who is in heaven. Neither *should* you be called masters. For one is your Master, Christ. But one who is greatest among you shall be your servant.

#206 Whoever exalts themselves will be humbled and *those* who humble themselves will be exalted.

#207 Take heed *so* that no one deceives you.

#211 Heaven and earth will pass away but my words will not pass away.

#223 A new commandment
I give to you:
That you love one another.
As I have loved you,
that you also love one another.
By this all *people* will know
that you are my disciples:
If you have love
toward one another.

#225 Do not let your heart be troubled. You believe in God. Believe also in me.

#226 I am the way,
the truth, and the life.
No one comes to the Father,
but by me.

#229 If you love me,
keep my commandments.

#230 *Those* who have my commandments and keep them are the ones who *truly* love me. *Those* who love me will be loved by my Father and I will love them and will reveal myself to them. If anyone loves me, they will keep my words and my Father will love them and we will come to them and live within them.

#232 Peace I leave with you. My peace I give to you. I do not give to you as the world gives. Do not let your heart be troubled *and do not* let it be afraid.

#235 I have spoken these things to you *so* that my joy might remain in you and *so that* your joy might be full.

#236 This is my commandment:
That you love one another
as I have loved you.

#237 Greater love has no one than this, that one lay down one's *own* life for one's friends.

#242 I have spoken these things to you *so* that in me you might have peace. In the world you will have tribulation. But be of good cheer. I have overcome the world.

#243 Watch and pray *so* that you do not enter into temptation. The spirit indeed *is* willing, but the flesh *is* weak.

#244 Peace to you. As *my* Father has sent me, even so I *now* send you.

#245 Receive *the* Holy Spirit.

#246 Follow me.

#247 Go therefore
and teach all nations,
baptizing them
in the name of the Father
and of the Son
and of the Holy Spirit,
teaching them to observe
all things whatsoever
I have commanded you.
Behold I am with you always,
even to the end of the world.

#248 *Those* who believe and are baptized will be saved, but *those* who do not believe will be damned.

#249

--- *The Invitation* ---

Behold, I stand at the door and knock.

If anyone *will* hear my voice
and open the door,

I will come in to them
and dine[+] with them
and they with me.

The Complete **AV7** New Testament
with the most essential passages highlighted.

Jesus Christ is the most amazing person who ever lived and He is the central figure of the entire Bible. While the Old Testament is very important in setting the stage for and foretelling His arrival, we begin with the New Testament because it presents four accounts of His life on earth and a written record of the most important words that He spoke as the Word of God.

While most Bibles have traditionally presented the first four books of the New Testament (called "The Gospels") in the sequence Matthew, Mark, Luke, and John, this presentation begins with the book of John, followed by Matthew, Mark, and Luke. Some of the reasons for beginning with John should become apparent as you begin to read.

The Gospel of Jesus Christ as written by John

Chapter 1

> 1 In the beginning was the Word and the Word was with God and the Word was God. *Genesis 1:1*

2 He+ was, in the *very* beginning, with God.

3 Everything+ *came into* existence+ through Him. Without Him nothing *would have* come+ into existence.

4 In Him was life and the life was the light of men.

5 The light shines in darkness and the darkness does not overtake+ it.

6 *Now* there was a man sent from God whose name *was* John.

7 *John* came as a witness to testify+ of the Light *so* that through Him everyone might believe.

8 *John* was not that Light, but *was sent* to testify+ of that Light.

9 *This* was the true Light, that enlightens+ everyone+ who comes into the world.

10 He was in the world and the world was made by Him and *yet* the world did not know Him.

11 He came to His own and His own did not receive Him. *Isaiah 53:3*

12 But *to* all+ *who* received Him, He gave authority+ *and power* to become the children+ of God, *even* to *those* who believe on His name,

13 *to those* who were born not of blood nor of the will of the flesh nor of the will of man, but of God.

> 14 And the Word was made flesh and lived+ among us

and we beheld His glory: Glory as of the Only Begotten of the Father, full of grace and truth.

15 John testified+ about Him, and called+ *out* saying: This was He of whom I spoke. He who comes after me is preferred before me because He was before me.

16 Of His fullness we *have* all received, and grace *for everyone* instead+ of grace *for a favored few*.

17 For the law was given by Moses, *but* grace and truth came by Jesus Christ.

18 No one has seen God at any time. The Only Begotten Son who is in the bosom of the Father has declared *Him*.

19 This is the testimony+ of John when the Jews sent priests and Levites from Jerusalem to ask him: Who are you?

20He confessed and did not deny, but confessed: I am not the Christ.
21They asked him: What then? Are you Elijah? He said: I am not. Are you that prophet? He answered: No.
22Then they said to him: Who are you? *Tell us so* that we may give an answer to *those* who sent us. What do you say of yourself?
23He said: I *am* the voice of one crying in the wilderness: Make straight the way of the Lord, as the prophet Isaiah said. *Isaiah 40:3*
24*Those* who were sent *to John* were of the Pharisees.
25They asked him and said to him: Why do you baptize then? If you are not the Christ or Elijah or that prophet?
26John answered them saying: I baptize with water but there stands one among you whom you do not know.
27It is He, who, coming after me, is preferred before me. I am not *even* worthy to loosen His sandal+ straps.+
28These things were done in Bethabara beyond Jordan where John was baptizing.
29The next day John saw Jesus coming to him and *he* said:

> Behold the Lamb of God
> who takes away
> the sin of the world.

30This is He of whom I said: After me comes a man who is preferred before me, because He was before me.
31I did not know Him, but I came baptizing with water*so* that He might be made known+ to Israel.
32*Then* John testified+ saying: I saw the Spirit descending from heaven like a dove, and it *came to* reside+ on Him.
33I did not know Him, but He who sent me to baptize with water said to me:*The one* upon whom you shall see the Spirit descending and remaining on Him is *the One* who baptizes with the Holy Spirit.

> 34I saw and testify+
> that this is the Son of God.

35Again the next day, after John stood with two of his disciples
36looking at Jesus as He walked *by*, he said: Behold the Lamb of God.
37The two disciples heard him say this and they followed Jesus.
38Then Jesus turned, saw them following, and said to them: What are you seeking? They said to Him: Rabbi, meaning+ Master. Where do you live?
39He said to them: Come and see. *So* they went *with Him* and saw where He lived+ and stayed+ with Him that day, for it was about four *in the afternoon.*
40One of the two who heard John *speak* and followed *Jesus* was Andrew, Simon Peter's brother.
41He first found his own brother Simon and said to him: We have found the Messiah who is called+ the Christ.
42*Andrew* brought *his brother* to Jesus and when Jesus saw+ him He said: You are Simon the son of Jonah. You shall be called Cephas. That is translated+ Peter,+ *which means a steadfast stone.*
43The next+ day, Jesus went+ to Galilee, found Philip, and said to him: Follow me.
44Now Philip was from Bethsaida, the *same* city as Andrew and Peter.
45Philip found Nathanael and said to him: We have found Him of whom Moses in the law and the prophets wrote: Jesus of Nazareth, the son of Joseph.
46Nathanael said to him: Can any good thing come out of Nazareth? Philip said to him: Come and see.
47Jesus saw Nathanael coming to Him and said of him: Behold an Israelite indeed in whom is no guile.
48Nathanael said to *Jesus*: From where do you know me? Jesus answered and said to him: Before Philip called you, when you were under the fig tree, I saw you.
49Nathanael answered and said to Him: Rabbi, you are the Son of God. You are the King of Israel.
50Jesus answered and said to him: Because I said to you *that* I saw you under the fig tree you believe? You shall see greater things than these.

[51] *Then Jesus* said to him: Truly,[+] truly, I say to you: Hereafter you will see heaven open and the angels of God ascending and descending upon the Son of man.

John Chapter 2

[1] *On* the third day, there was a marriage in Cana of Galilee and Jesus' mother was there.

[2] Both Jesus and His disciples were invited[+] to the marriage.

[3] When they *ran* out[+] *of* wine, Jesus' mother said to Him: They have no wine.

[4] Jesus said to her: What *is this* to you and to me, woman? My hour has not yet come.

[5] His mother said to the servants: *Do* whatever He may say to you.

[6] *Now* there were six stone water pots standing[+] there of the kind *used* by the Jews for purifying, each[+] *able to* hold[+] *nearly* twenty to thirty gallon.[+]

[7] Jesus said to them: Fill the water pots with water. And they filled them up to the brim.

[8] *Then* He said to them: Draw *some* out now and take[+] *it* to the host[+]. They took[+] *it as Jesus said*.

[9] When the host[+] tasted the water that was made *into* wine, *he* did not understand[+] where it had *come* from. But the servants who drew the water knew. The host[+] called the bridegroom

[10] and said to him: Everyone[+] at the beginning sets forth good wine. When *the guests* have drunk well, then what is lower[+] *quality is set out. But* you have kept the good wine until now.

[11] This beginning of miracles Jesus did in Cana of Galilee, and manifested forth His glory, and His disciples believed in Him.

[12] After this, *Jesus* went to Capernaum, He and His mother and His brothers and His disciples, and they stayed[+] there *though* not many days.

[13] The Jews' Passover was at hand and Jesus went up to Jerusalem.

[14] In the temple, *He* found *those* who sold oxen and sheep and doves, and *also* the money changers sitting *there. Malachi 3:1*

[15] *So* He made a whip[+] of small cords, *and* He drove them all out of the temple, *along with* the sheep and oxen, and *He* poured out the changers' money and overthrew the tables. *Malachi 3:2,3*

[16] To *those* who sold doves, *He* said: Take these things away.[+] Do not make my Father's house a house of merchandise.

[17] And His disciples remembered that it was written: The zeal of your house has eaten me up. *Psalm 69:9*

[18] Then the Jews answered and said to Him: What sign *can* you show us *to demonstrate your authority for* these things that you do?

[19] Jesus answered and said to them: Destroy this temple and in three days I will raise it up.

[20] Then the Jews said: *It took* forty six years to build this temple and you *claim that* you can raise[+] it up in three days?

[21] But *Jesus* was speaking of the temple of His body.

[22] Therefore, when He was risen from the dead, His disciples remembered that He had said this to them, and they believed the Scripture and the Word that Jesus had said.

[23] Now when He was in Jerusalem at the Passover in the feast *day*, many believed in His name when they saw the miracles that He did.

[24] But Jesus did not commit Himself to their *testimony* because He knew all *men*

[25] and *He* did not need any *of them* to testify concerning[+] man, for He knew what was in man.

John Chapter 3

[1] *Now* there was a man of the Pharisees named Nicodemus, a ruler of the Jews.

[2] He came to Jesus by night and said to Him: Rabbi, we know that you are a teacher come from God, for no one can do these miracles that you do, unless[+] God is with them.

[3] Jesus answered and said to him:

> Truly, + truly, I say to you:
> Unless+ a person+ is born again,
> they cannot see
> the kingdom of God.

4 Nicodemus said to Him: How can anyone+ be born when they are old? Can they enter a second time into their mother's womb and be born?

5 Jesus answered: Truly, + truly, I say to you: Unless+ a person+ is born of water and *of* the Spirit, they cannot enter into the kingdom of God.

6 *Those* who are born of flesh are flesh, and *those* who are born of the Spirit are spirit.

7 Do not marvel that I said to you: You must be born again.

8 The wind blows where it will+ and you hear the sound of it, but *you* cannot tell from where it comes and where it goes. So *it* is *with* everyone who is born of the Spirit.

9 Nicodemus answered and said to Him: How can these things be?

10 Jesus answered and said to him: Are you a master of Israel and do not understand+ these things?

11 Truly, + truly, I say to you: We speak what we know and testify *about* what we have seen, but you do not receive our witness.

12 If I have told you earthly things and you do not believe, how will you believe if I tell you *about* heavenly things?

13 No one has ascended up to heaven except+ He who came down from heaven, *even* the Son of man who is in heaven.

14 *Just* as Moses lifted up the serpent in the wilderness, even so the Son of man must be lifted up

15 *so* that whoever believes in Him should not perish, but have eternal life. *Proverbs 8:35*

> 16 For God so loved the world,
> that He gave
> His Only Begotten Son,
> *so* that whoever believes in Him
> should not perish,
> but have eternal+ life.

17 For God did not send His Son into the world to condemn the world, but *so* that the world through Him might be saved.

18 *Those* who believe in Him are not condemned, but *those* who do not believe are condemned already, because they have not believed in the name of the Only Begotten Son of God.

19 And this is the condemnation: That light has come into the world, but people+ *have* loved darkness rather than light, because their deeds were evil.

20 For everyone who does evil hates the light and does not come to the light, lest their deeds should be proved+ *evil*.

21 But *those* who do truth come to the light *so* that their deeds may be made known, + that they are worked+ in God.

22 After these things, Jesus and His disciples went+ into the land of Judea, and He stayed+ there with them and baptized.

23 John was also baptizing in Aenon near Salim, because there was much water there and *the people* came and were baptized.

24 For John had not yet been cast into prison.

25 Then a question arose between *some* of John's disciples and the Jews about purifying.

26 They came to John and said to him: Rabbi, the one who was with you beyond Jordan, to whom you bear witness, behold He is baptizing and everyone+ is going+ to Him.

27 John answered and said: A person+ can receive nothing unless+ it is given *to* them from heaven.

28 You yourselves *can* testify+ that I said: I am not the Christ, but that I am sent before Him.

29 One who has a bride is a bridegroom, but the friend of the bridegroom who stands and hears him, rejoices greatly because of the bridegroom's voice. Therefore, my joy is fulfilled in this.

30 He must increase but I *must* decrease.

31 He who comes from above is above all. *Those* who are of the earth are earthly and speak *about* earthly *things*. He who comes from heaven is above all.

[32] He testifies *about* what He has seen and heard, but no one receives His testimony.

[33] *Those* who have received His testimony have *given their* seal *of affirmation* that God is true.

[34] For He whom God has sent speaks the words of God, for God does not give the Spirit *in a limited* measure. *Matthew 4:4*

[35] The Father loves the Son and has given all things into His hand.

[36] *Those* who believe in the Son have eternal[+] life. *Those* who do not believe the Son shall not see life, but the wrath of God remains[+] on them.

John Chapter 4

[1] Therefore, when the Lord knew that the Pharisees had heard that Jesus made and baptized more disciples than John,

[2] although Jesus Himself did not baptize, but His disciples *did*,

[3] He left Judea and departed again into Galilee.

[4] But He needed to go through Samaria *on the way*.

[5] *So*, He came to a city of Samaria called Sychar, near the parcel of ground that Jacob gave to his son Joseph.

[6] Now Jacob's well was there. Therefore Jesus, being tired[+] from *His* journey, sat *down* on the well. It was about twelve o'clock[+] *noon*.

[7] *Then* a woman from Samaria came to draw water, and Jesus said to her: Give me a drink.

[8] For His disciples had gone to the city to buy food.[+]

[9] Then the woman from Samaria said to Him: How is it that you, being a Jew, ask me, a woman from Samaria, *for a* drink? For the Jews have no dealings with the Samaritans.

[10] Jesus answered and said to her: If you knew the gift of God and who it is that says to you: Give me a drink, you would have asked of Him and He would have given you living water.

[11] The woman said to Him: Sir, you have nothing with *which* to draw and the well is deep. From where then have you

obtained living water?

[12] Are you greater than our father Jacob, who gave us this well and drank from it himself, and his children and his cattle?

[13] Jesus answered and said to her: Whoever drinks of this water will thirst again.

> [14] But whoever drinks
> of the water that I give
> will never thirst.
> However, the water that I give
> will become a well of water
> within[+] them springing up
> into eternal[+] life.

[15] The woman said to Him: Sir, give me this water *so* that I will not thirst nor *need to* come here to draw *water*.

[16] Jesus said to her: Go. Call your husband and come here.

[17] The woman answered and said: I have no husband. Jesus said to her: You have well said: I have no husband.

[18] For you have had five husbands, and he whom you now have is not your husband. In this, you spoke the truth.

[19] The woman said to Him: Sir, I perceive that you are a prophet.

[20] Our fathers worshiped in this mountain, but you say that in Jerusalem is the place where people[+] ought to worship.

[21] Jesus said to her: Woman, believe me. The hour is coming when you will not worship the Father either in this mountain or in Jerusalem.

[22] You do not understand[+] what you worship. We know what we worship, for salvation *comes* through[+] the Jews.

[23] But the hour is coming, and is now *here*, when the true worshipers will worship the Father in spirit and in truth, for the Father seeks such to worship Him.

> [24] God *is* Spirit.
> *Those* who worship Him
> must worship *Him*
> in spirit and in truth.

²⁵The woman said to Him: I know that the Messiah is coming who is called Christ. When He has come, He will tell us everything.⁺

²⁶Jesus said to her: I who speak to you am *He*.

²⁷At this point,⁺ *Jesus'* disciples came, and *they* marveled that He talked with the woman. Yet no one said: What were you seeking? Or: Why were you talking with her?

²⁸*Then* the woman left her water pot and went into the city and said to the people⁺: ²⁹Come *and* see a man who told me everything that I ever did. Is this not the Christ?

³⁰Then *the people* came out of the city and came to Him.

³¹Meanwhile, His disciples urged⁺ Him saying: Master, eat.

³²But He said to them: I have food⁺ to eat that you do not *yet* understand⁺.

³³Therefore the disciples said to one another: Has anyone brought *anything* to Him to eat?

³⁴Jesus said to them: My food⁺ is to do the will of Him who sent me and to finish His work.

³⁵Do you not say: There are yet four months and *then* the harvest *time comes*? Behold I say to you: Lift up your eyes and look at the fields, for they are white, ready to harvest.

³⁶*Those* who reap receive wages and gather fruit to eternal life *so* that both *those* who sow and *those* who reap may rejoice together.

³⁷Herein is that saying true: One sows and another reaps.

³⁸I sent you to reap that on which you bestowed no labor. Others labored and you have *now* entered their labors.

³⁹Many of the Samaritans of that city believed in Him because of the words⁺ of the woman who testified: He told me everything⁺ that I ever did.

⁴⁰So when the Samaritans came to Him, they begged⁺ Him that He would stay⁺ with them, and He stayed⁺ there two days.

⁴¹And many more believed because of His Word.

⁴²*They* said to the woman: Now we believe, not because of *what* you said, but because we have heard *Him* ourselves and *we* know that this is indeed the Christ, the Savior of the world.

⁴³Now after two days, *Jesus* departed from there⁺ and went to Galilee.

⁴⁴For Jesus Himself testified, that a prophet has no honor in his own country.

⁴⁵Then when He had come into Galilee, the Galileans received Him, having seen all the things that He did at Jerusalem at the feast, for they also went to the feast.

⁴⁶So Jesus came again into Cana of Galilee, where He *had* made the water *into* wine. And there was a certain nobleman *there*, whose son was sick in Capernaum.

⁴⁷When he heard that Jesus had come out of Judea into Galilee, he went to *Jesus* and begged⁺ Him that He would come down and heal his son, for he was at the point of death.

⁴⁸Then Jesus said to him: Unless⁺ you see signs and wonders, you will not believe.

⁴⁹The nobleman said to Him: Sir, come down before⁺ my child dies.

⁵⁰Jesus said to him: Go. Your son lives. And the man believed the word that Jesus had spoken to him and he went away.⁺

⁵¹As he was going, his servants met him and told *him* saying: Your son lives.

⁵²Then he inquired of them the hour when *his son* began to recover.⁺ They said to him: Yesterday at one o'clock⁺ *in the afternoon* the fever left him.

⁵³So the father knew that *it was* at the same hour in which Jesus said to him: Your son lives. *Then both* he and his entire⁺ household⁺ believed.

⁵⁴This *was* the second miracle *that* Jesus did when He had come out of Judea into Galilee.

John Chapter 5

¹ After this, there was a feast of the Jews, and Jesus went up to Jerusalem. ² Now there is a pool with five porches near the sheepgate⁺ in Jerusalem. In Hebrew, *this place* is called Bethesda.

³ *Within* these *porches* a large⁺ number⁺ of disabled⁺ people⁺ lay: blind, crippled,⁺ *and* withered, waiting for the water to move.

⁴ From time to time,⁺ an angel went down into the pool and stirred⁺ the water. After this stirring,⁺ whoever stepped into the water first was healed⁺ of whatever disease they had.

⁵ *Now* a certain man there, had an infirmity *for* thirty eight years.

⁶ When Jesus saw him lying *there* and knew that he had been *there* a long time, He said to him: Do you want⁺ to be made whole?

⁷ The disabled⁺ man answered Him: Sir, when the water is stirred,⁺ I have no one to put me into the pool. While I am coming, another steps down before me.

⁸ Jesus said to him: Rise, take up your bed and walk.

⁹ Immediately the man was made whole and took up his bed and walked. And that day was the Sabbath.

¹⁰ Then the Jews said to the one who was cured: It is the Sabbath day. It is not lawful for you to carry *your* bed.

¹¹ He answered them: The one who made me well⁺ said to me: Take up your bed and walk.

¹² Then they asked him: Who is the man who said to you: Take up your bed and walk?

¹³ The *man* who had been healed did not know⁺ who it was, for Jesus had *quietly* moved⁺ away, a multitude being in *that* place.

¹⁴ Afterward Jesus found *the man* in the temple and said to him: Behold, you are made whole.

> Sin no more,
> lest a worse thing come to you.

¹⁵ *Then* the man departed and told the Jews that it was Jesus who had made him whole.

¹⁶ Therefore, the Jews persecuted Jesus and sought to slay Him because He had done these things on the Sabbath day.

¹⁷ But Jesus answered them: My Father is working until now⁺ and I am working.

¹⁸ Therefore the Jews sought *all* the more to kill Him, not only because He had broken the Sabbath, but also *because He* said that God was His Father, making Himself equal with God.

¹⁹ Then Jesus answered and said to them: Truly,⁺ truly, I say to you: The Son can do nothing by Himself, but *only* what He sees the Father do. For what things⁺ He does, these also the Son does in like manner⁺.

²⁰ For the Father loves the Son and shows Him all things that *He* Himself does, and He will show Him greater works than these, *so* that you may marvel.

²¹ For as the Father raises up the dead and gives life⁺ *to them*, even so the Son will give life⁺ *to* whomever He chooses⁺.

²² For the Father judges no one, but has committed all judgment to the Son,

²³ *so* that all *people* should honor the Son, even as they honor the Father. Anyone who does not honor the Son does not honor the Father who has sent Him.

²⁴ Truly,⁺ truly, I say to you:

> *Those* who hear my Word
> and believe in Him who sent me
> have eternal⁺ life and will not
> come into condemnation,
> but are passed from death to life.

²⁵ Truly,⁺ truly, I say to you: The hour is coming, and now is, when the dead will hear the voice of the Son of God, and *those* who hear will live.

²⁶ For as the Father has life in Himself, so *He* also gave to the Son to have life in Himself.

²⁷ *He* has given Him authority to execute judgment also, because He is the Son of man.

²⁸ Do not marvel at this. For the hour is coming in which all who are in the graves will hear His voice

²⁹ and will come forth.

> *Those* who have done good
> to the resurrection of life,
> and *those* who have done evil
> to the resurrection of damnation.

³⁰*By* my own self *alone*, I can do nothing. As I hear, I judge, and my judgment is just because I do not seek my own will but the will of the Father who has sent me.
³¹If I *alone* bear witness of myself, my witness is not *confirmed as* true.
³²There is another who bears witness of me, and *we* know that the testimony *of this* witness for me is true.
³³You sent to John and he testified⁺ to the truth.
³⁴But I do not receive testimony from man, but I say these things *so* that you might be saved.
³⁵*John* was a burning and shining light, and you were willing to rejoice in his light for a season.
³⁶But I have the greater testimony⁺ than *that* of John. For the works that the Father has given me to finish, the same works that I do bear witness of me, that the Father has sent me.
³⁷The Father Himself who sent me has borne witness of me. You have neither heard His voice at any time nor seen His shape.
³⁸You do not have His Word abiding in you. For you do not believe the one whom He has sent.

> ³⁹ Search the Scriptures.
> For in them you think
> you have eternal life,
> and they⁺ testify of me.
> *Jeremiah 29:13*

⁴⁰But you will not come to me *so* that you might have life.
⁴¹I do not receive honor from people⁺.
⁴²But I know you, that you do not have the love of God in you.
⁴³I have come in my Father's name and you do not receive me. If another shall come in his own name, you will receive him.
⁴⁴How can you believe, *you* who receive honor from⁺ one another but⁺ do not seek the honor that *comes* from God alone⁺?
⁴⁵Do not think that I will accuse you to the Father. There is *one* who accuses you, *even* Moses in whom you trust.
⁴⁶*If* you had believed Moses, *then* you would have believed me, because⁺ he wrote about⁺ me.
⁴⁷But if you do not believe his writings, *then* how will you believe my words?

John Chapter 6

¹ After these things, Jesus went over the sea of Galilee *by* Tiberias.
² A great multitude followed Him *because* they saw the miracles that He worked⁺ for the afflicted.⁺
³ Jesus went up on a mountain and sat *down* there with His disciples.
⁴ *Now* the Passover, a feast of the Jews, was near.
⁵ When Jesus lifted up *His* eyes and saw a great multitude⁺ coming to Him, He said to Philip: Where shall we buy bread *so* that these may eat?
⁶ *Jesus* said this to test⁺ *Philip*, for He *already* knew what He was going⁺ to do.
⁷ Philip answered Him: *A half year wages worth*⁺ of bread is not sufficient for them if everyone of them receives⁺ a little.
⁸ One of His disciples, Andrew, Simon Peter's brother, said to Him:
⁹ There is a lad here who has five barley loaves and two small fish, but what are they among so many?
¹⁰Jesus said: Have⁺ the people⁺ sit down. *For* there was much grass in that place. So the people⁺ sat down, about five thousand men *and their families*.
¹¹*Then* Jesus took the loaves and when He had given thanks He distributed to the disciples and the disciples *gave* to those *who were* sitting⁺ *there*. In like manner⁺ *they distributed portions* of the fish, as much as *they* wanted.⁺
¹²When they were filled, He said to His disciples: Gather up the fragments that remain *so* that nothing is lost.
¹³Therefore they gathered together and filled twelve baskets with the fragments of the five barley loaves that remained over and above from *those* who had eaten.
¹⁴When the people⁺ had seen the miracle that Jesus did, *they* said: This truly is the Prophet who is to come into the world.
Psalm 110:4

¹⁵ Therefore, when Jesus perceived that they would come and take Him by force to make Him king, He departed to the mountain again *to be* alone.

¹⁶ When *the* evening came, His disciples went down to the sea,

¹⁷ entered a boat, and went over the sea toward Capernaum. It was now dark and Jesus had not come to them.

¹⁸ *Then* the sea rose up⁺ *because* of a great wind that blew.

¹⁹ When they had rowed about three and a half miles, they saw Jesus walking on the sea and drawing near to the boat, and they were afraid.

²⁰ But He said to them: I Am⁺ *with you*. Do not be afraid.

²¹ Then they willingly received Him into the boat, and immediately the boat *arrived* at the land where they were going.⁺

²² The next day, the people who stood on the other side of the sea saw that there was no other boat there, except⁺ the one in which His disciples had entered, and that Jesus did not leave⁺ with His disciples in the boat, but *that* His disciples had left⁺ alone.

²³ However, other boats had come from Tiberias near the place where they ate bread after the Lord had given thanks.

²⁴ Therefore, when the people saw that Jesus was not there, nor His disciples, they also got into boats and came to Capernaum seeking Jesus.

²⁵ When they found Him on the other side of the sea, they said to Him: Rabbi, when did you come here?

²⁶ Jesus answered them and said: Truly,⁺ truly, I say to you: You seek me, not because you saw the miracles, but because you ate of the loaves and were filled.

²⁷ Do not labor for food⁺ that perishes, but for that food⁺ that endures to eternal⁺ life, which the Son of man will give to you, for God the Father has set *His* seal *on* Him. *Proverbs 9:5*

²⁸ Then they said to Him: What shall we do *so* that we might work the works of God?

²⁹ Jesus answered and said to them:

This is the work of God:
That you believe
in *the one* whom He has sent.

---

³⁰ Therefore, they said to Him: What sign will you show *us* then *so* that we may see and believe you? What work *will you perform*?

³¹ Our fathers ate manna in the desert. As it is written: He gave them bread from heaven to eat. *Exodus 16:4*

³² Then Jesus said to them: Truly,⁺ truly, I say to you: Moses did not give you the bread from heaven, but my Father gives you the true bread from heaven.

³³ For the bread of God is *the One* who comes down from heaven and gives life to the world.

³⁴ Then they said to Him: Lord, give us this bread always⁺ *forevermore*.

³⁵ Jesus said to them: I am the bread of life. *Those* who come to me will never hunger. *Those* who believe in me will never thirst.

³⁶ But *as* I said to you, you have seen me and *yet you* do not believe.

³⁷ All whom⁺ the Father gives *to* me will come to me, and *those* who come to me I will in no way⁺ cast out.

³⁸ For I came down from heaven not to do my own will, but *to do* the will of *the one* who sent me.

³⁹ This is the will of the Father who sent me: That of all He has given me I should not lose any⁺ but should raise them⁺ up again at the last day.

⁴⁰ This is the will of Him who sent me: That everyone who sees the Son and believes in Him may have eternal⁺ life. I will raise them⁺ up at the last day.

⁴¹ Then the Jews complained⁺ about⁺ Him because He said: I am the bread come down from heaven.

⁴² They said: Is this not Jesus the son of Joseph whose father and mother we know? How is it then that He says: I came down from heaven?

⁴³Therefore Jesus answered and said to them:

> Do not complain⁺
> among yourselves.

⁴⁴No one can come to me unless⁺ the Father who has sent me draws them, and I will raise them up at the last day. ⁴⁵It is written in the prophets: And they shall all be taught by God. Therefore everyone who has heard and has learned of the Father comes to me. *cf Isaiah 2:3, Isaiah 54:13, Jeremiah 31:33, and Micah 4:2* ⁴⁶Not that anyone has seen the Father except⁺ *the One* who is from God. He has seen the Father. ⁴⁷Truly⁺ truly I say to you:

> *Those* who believe in me
> have eternal⁺ life.

⁴⁸I am the bread of life. ⁴⁹Your fathers ate manna in the wilderness and are dead. ⁵⁰This is the bread come down from heaven. Anyone⁺ may eat of *this bread* and not die. ⁵¹I am the living bread come down from heaven. If anyone eats of this bread, they will live forever. The bread I will give is my flesh, *and* I will give *myself* for the life of the world. ⁵²Therefore, the Jews argued⁺ among themselves saying: How can this man give us *His* flesh to eat? ⁵³Then Jesus said to them: Truly,⁺ truly, I say to you: Unless⁺ you eat the flesh of the Son of man *which is the bread of life, the Word of God*, and drink His blood *which is to be filled with the Holy Spirit*, you have no life in you. ⁵⁴Whoever eats my flesh and drinks my blood has eternal life, and I will raise them up at the last day. ⁵⁵For my flesh truly is *to* eat⁺ and my blood truly is *to* drink. ⁵⁶*Those* who eat my flesh and drink my blood dwell in me and I in them. ⁵⁷As the living Father has sent me, and

I live by the Father, so also *those* who eat me, *my Word*, shall live by me. ⁵⁸This is that bread come down from heaven: Not as your fathers ate manna and are dead, *but those* who eat of this bread will live forever. ⁵⁹*Jesus* said these things in the synagogue as He taught in Capernaum. ⁶⁰Therefore when His disciples heard *this*, many *of them* said: This is a difficult⁺ saying *to understand*. Who is able⁺ *to* hear *and comprehend* it? ⁶¹When Jesus knew in Himself that His disciples complained⁺ about⁺ this,⁺ He said to them: Does this offend you? ⁶²*What* then⁺ if you see the Son of man ascend up *to* where He was before? ⁶³It is the Spirit who gives life.⁺ The flesh profits nothing. The words that I speak to you are Spirit and *they* are life. ⁶⁴But there are some of you who do not believe. For Jesus knew from the beginning who they were who did not believe, and who would betray Him. ⁶⁵*Then* He said: Therefore I said to you that no one can come to me unless⁺ it is given to them by my Father. ⁶⁶After that, many of His disciples went back and did not walk with Him *any* more. ⁶⁷Then Jesus said to the twelve: Will you also go away? ⁶⁸Simon Peter answered Him: Lord, to whom shall we go? You have the words of eternal life. ⁶⁹We believe and are sure that you are the Christ, the Son of the living God. ⁷⁰Jesus answered them: Have I not chosen you twelve? And *yet* one of you is a devil. ⁷¹He spoke of Judas Iscariot, *the son* of Simon. For it was *Judas* who would betray *Jesus*, *even* being one of the twelve.

John Chapter 7

¹ After these things, Jesus walked in Galilee, for He would not walk in Judea⁺ because the Jews sought to kill Him. ² Now the Jews' Feast of Tabernacles was at hand. ³ Therefore His brothers said to Him: Depart from here⁺ and go into Judea *so*

that your disciples may also see the works that you do.

4 For no one does anything in secret and seeks *thereby* to be *known* openly. If you *are* doing these things, show yourself to the world.

5 For *even* His brothers did not believe in Him.

6 Then Jesus said to them: My time has not yet come, but your time is always ready.

7 The world cannot hate you, but it hates me because I testify about[+] it, that its works are evil.

8 You go *on* to this feast. I am not going to this feast yet because it is not yet my time *to be* fulfilled[+].

9 When He had said these words to them, He stayed[+] in Galilee.

10 But when His brothers had left,[+] then *Jesus* also went up to the feast, not openly, but as in secret.

11 Then the Jews sought Him at the feast and said: Where is He?

12 And there was much murmuring among the people concerning Him. Some said: He is a good man. Others said: No, He deceives the people.

13 However, no one spoke openly about[+] Him for fear of the Jews.

14 Now about midway[+] *through* the feast, Jesus went into the temple and taught.

15 The Jews marveled saying: How does this man know letters, *with* no education[+]?

16 Jesus answered them and said: My doctrine is not mine but His who sent me.

17 If anyone will do *God's* will, they will know about this doctrine, whether it is from God or *whether* I speak *only* from[+] myself.

18 *Those* who speak for[+] themselves seek their own glory. But He who seeks the glory of the one who sent Him is true and *there* is no unrighteousness in Him.

19 Did not Moses give you the law, and *yet* none of you keeps the law? Why do you seek[+] to kill me?

20 The people answered and said: You have a demon.[+] Who is seeking[+] to kill you?

21 Jesus answered and said to them: I have done one work and you all marvel.

22 Moses gave circumcision to you, not that it was from Moses but from the *patriarch* fathers, and therefore you circumcise men *even* on the Sabbath day.

23 If a man receives circumcision on the Sabbath day *so* that the law of Moses should not be broken, *why* are you angry at me, because I have made a man completely[+] whole on the Sabbath day?

24 Do not judge according to appearance, but judge *with* righteous judgment.

25 Then some of them from[+] Jerusalem said: Is this not He whom they seek to kill?

26 But behold, He speaks boldly and they say nothing to Him. Surely[+] the rulers *must* know that this truly[+] is the Christ.

27 However we know this man *and* where He *comes* from, but when Christ comes, no one *will* know where He *has come* from.

28 Then Jesus cried *out* in the temple as He taught saying: You both know me and you know where I am from. And I have not come of myself, but He who sent me is true, *He* whom you do not know.

29 But I know Him for I am from Him and He has sent me.

30 Then they sought to take Him, but no one laid hands on Him because His hour had not yet come.

31 Many of the people believed in Him and said: When Christ comes, will He do more miracles than what this *man* has done?

32 The Pharisees heard that the people murmured such things concerning Him and *so* the Pharisees and the chief priests sent officers to take Him.

33 Then Jesus said to them: Yet a little while *longer* I am *to be* with you, and *then* I *must* go to Him who sent me.

34 You will seek me and will not find *me*, *for* where I am *going* you *will* not be able[+] to come.

35 Then the Jews said among themselves: Where will He go that we will not find Him? Will He go to *those* dispersed among the Greeks[+] and teach the Greeks?

36 *And* what *kind of* saying is this that He said: You will seek me and will not find *me for* where I am *going* you *will* not be able[+] to come.

³⁷Then on the last day, the great *day* of the feast, Jesus stood *up* and cried *out* saying:

> If anyone thirsts,
> let them come to me and drink.
> *Proverbs 8:17*

³⁸As the Scripture has said *of those* who believe in me: Out of their innermost being⁺ will flow rivers of living water. *Isaiah 58:11*

³⁹*Jesus* spoke this about⁺ the Spirit whom those believing in Him were about⁺ to receive. For the Holy Spirit was not yet *being given* because Jesus was not yet glorified.

⁴⁰Therefore, when they heard this Word,⁺ many of the people said: Truly this is the Prophet. *Deuteronomy 18:18*

⁴¹Others said: This is the Christ. But some said: Will Christ come out of Galilee?

⁴²Has the Scripture not said that Christ comes through⁺ the seed of David and from⁺ the town of Bethlehem, where David was? *Jeremiah 23:5 Micah 5:2*

⁴³So, there was a division among the people because of *Jesus*.

⁴⁴Some of them would have taken Him *right then*, but no one laid hands on Him.

⁴⁵Then the officers came to the chief priests and Pharisees who⁺ said to *the officers*: Why have you not brought Him *to us*?

⁴⁶The officers answered: No *one* ever spoke like this man.

⁴⁷Then the Pharisees answered them: Are you also deceived?

⁴⁸Have any of the rulers believed in Him, or *any* of the Pharisees?

⁴⁹But this *crowd of* people who do not know the law are cursed.

⁵⁰*Then* Nicodemus who had come to Jesus by night, being one of them, said to them:

⁵¹Does our law judge *any* man before hearing from Him first⁺ and knowing what He has done?

⁵²They answered and said to him: Are you from⁺ Galilee also? Search and see⁺ that⁺ no prophet arises out of Galilee.

⁵³*Then* everyone went to their own house.

John Chapter 8

¹ Jesus went to the Mount of Olives.

² And early in the morning He came into the temple again, and all the people came to Him, and He sat down and taught them.

³ *Then* the scribes and Pharisees brought a woman to Him *who had been* caught⁺ in adultery. When they had set her in the midst,

⁴ they said to Him: Master, this woman was caught⁺ in adultery, in the very act.

⁵ Now Moses, in the law, commanded us that such *offenders* should be stoned. But what do you say?

⁶ They said this, testing⁺ Him, *so* that they might have *grounds* to accuse Him. But Jesus stooped down and wrote on the ground with *His* finger *as though He had not heard them.*

⁷ When they continued asking Him, He lifted Himself up and said to them: Let whoever is without sin among you cast *the* first stone at her.

⁸ And again, He stooped down and wrote on the ground.

⁹ *Those* who heard *this*, being convicted by *their own* conscience, went out one by one, beginning at the eldest *even* to the last. Jesus was left alone *with* the woman standing in the midst.

¹⁰When Jesus had lifted Himself up and saw no one but the woman, He said to her: Woman, where are those accusers? Has no one condemned you?

¹¹She said: No one Lord. Jesus said to her: Neither do I condemn you. Go and sin no more.

¹²Then Jesus spoke again to them saying: I am the light of the world. *Those* who follow me will not walk in darkness but will have the light of life.

¹³Therefore, the Pharisees said to Him: You bear witness⁺ of yourself. Your witness⁺ *alone* is not true *by itself*.

¹⁴Jesus answered and said to them: *Even though* I bear witness⁺ of myself, my

witness⁺ is true for I know where I came from and where I *am* going, but you cannot tell where I *have* come from and where I *am* going.

¹⁵ You judge after the flesh. I *am* judging no one.

¹⁶ *Yet* if I *should* judge, my judgment *would* be true for I am not alone, but I and the Father who sent me.

¹⁷ It is also written in your law that the testimony of two people⁺ is true.

Deuteronomy 17:6, Deuteronomy 19:15

¹⁸ I am one who bears witness of myself. And the Father who sent me *also* bears witness of me.

¹⁹ Then they said to Him: Where is your Father? Jesus answered: You do not know me or my Father. If you had known me, you would have known my Father also.

²⁰ Jesus spoke these words in the treasury as He taught in the temple. And no one laid hands on Him for His hour had not yet come.

²¹ Then Jesus said to them, *once* again: I am going away,⁺ and you will seek me and *you* will die in your sins, *for* where I am *going*, you cannot come.

²² Then the Jews said: Will He kill Himself? Because He said: Where I am *going*, you cannot come.

²³ He said to them: You are from beneath. I am from above. You are of this world. I am not of this world.

²⁴ Therefore, I said to you that you will die in your sins. For if you do not believe that I am, you will die in your sins.

²⁵ Then they said to Him: Who are you? Jesus said to them: *From* the beginning, I have told you.

²⁶ I have many things to say and to judge of you, but He who sent me is true. I speak to the world those things that I have heard from⁺ Him.

²⁷ They did not understand that He spoke to them of the Father.

²⁸ Then Jesus said to them: When you have lifted up the Son of man, then you will know that I am, and *that* I do nothing of myself, but *only* as my Father has taught me *do* I speak these things.

²⁹ He who sent me is with me. The Father has not left me alone, for I always do those things that please Him.

³⁰ As He spoke these words, many believed in Him.

³¹ Then Jesus said to those Jews who believed in Him:

If you continue in my Word *then* you are indeed my disciples.

---

³² You shall know the truth and the truth will make you free.

³³ They answered Him: We are Abraham's seed and *we* were never in bondage to anyone. How *is it that* you say: You will be made free?

³⁴ Jesus answered them: Truly,⁺ truly I say to you: Whoever commits sin is the servant of sin.

³⁵ The servant does not stay⁺ in the house forever, *but* the Son remains⁺ forever⁺.

³⁶ Therefore, if the Son makes you free, *then* you will truly⁺ be free.

³⁷ I know that you are Abraham's seed, but you seek to kill me because my Word has no place in you.

³⁸ I speak what I have seen with my Father. You do what you have seen with your father.

³⁹ They answered and said to Him: Abraham is our father. Jesus said to them: If you were Abraham's children, you would do the works of Abraham.

⁴⁰ But now you seek to kill me, a man who has told you the truth that I have heard from⁺ God. Abraham did not do this.

⁴¹ You do the deeds of your father. Then they said to Him: We are not born of fornication. We have one Father: God.

⁴² Jesus said to them: If God were your Father, you would love me. For I proceeded forth and came from God. I did not come on my own,⁺ but He sent me.

⁴³ Why do you not understand my speech? Because you are not able⁺ to hear my Word.

⁴⁴ You are of *your* father the devil, and you desire⁺ to do the lusts of your father.

He was a murderer from the beginning and did not abide in the truth because there is no truth in him. When he speaks a lie, he speaks of his own, for he is a liar and the father of it.
⁴⁵And because I speak the truth, you do not believe me.
⁴⁶Who among⁺ you convicts⁺ me of sin? And if I speak⁺ the truth, why do you not believe me?
⁴⁷*Those* who are *transformed* by God hear God's words. You therefore do not hear *them* because you are not *transformed* by God.
⁴⁸Then the Jews answered and said to Him: Do we not say correctly⁺ that you are a Samaritan and have a demon⁺?
⁴⁹Jesus answered: I do not have a demon,⁺ but I honor my Father. And you dishonor me.
⁵⁰I do not seek my own glory. There is one who seeks and judges.
⁵¹Truly, ⁺ truly, I say to you:

> If anyone⁺ keeps my Word,⁺ they will never see death.

⁵²Then the Jews said to Him: Now we know that you have a demon.⁺ Abraham and the prophets are dead. *But* you say: If anyone keeps my Word,⁺ they will *never* taste of death, forever.⁺
⁵³Are you greater than our father Abraham who died? And the prophets *who* died. Whom do you make yourself *to be*?
⁵⁴Jesus answered: If I honor myself, my honor is nothing. It is my Father who honors me. *He* of whom you say that He is your God.
⁵⁵Yet you have not known Him. But I know Him. If I should say I do not know Him, I would⁺ be a liar like you. But I know Him and keep His Word⁺.
⁵⁶Your father Abraham rejoiced to see my day, and he saw *it* and was glad.
⁵⁷Then the Jews said to Him: You are not yet fifty years old and have you seen Abraham?
⁵⁸Jesus said to them: Truly, ⁺ truly, I say to you: Before Abraham was, I Am.

⁵⁹Then they took up stones to throw⁺ at Him, but Jesus hid Himself and went out of the temple, going through the midst of them and passing *right by them*.

John Chapter 9

¹ As *Jesus* passed by, He saw a man *who was* blind from birth.
² His disciples asked Him saying: Master, who sinned? This man or his parents? *Considering* that he was born blind.
³ Jesus answered: *It was* not *that* this man sinned, or his parents. But *this occurred so* that the works of God should be made manifest in him.
⁴ I must work the works of Him who sent me while it is day, *because* the night is coming when no one can work.
⁵ As long as I am in the world, I am the light of the world.
⁶ When He had thus spoken, He spit on the ground, made *some soft* clay with it,⁺ and He anointed the eyes of the blind man with the clay.
⁷ *Then Jesus* said to him: Go. Wash in the pool of Siloam. *The name Siloam* means⁺ sent. Therefore *the man* went away,⁺ washed, and came *back* seeing.
⁸ *Then* the neighbors and *those* who had previously⁺ seen that he was blind said: Is this not the *blind man* who sat and begged?
⁹ Some said: This is he. Others *said*: He is like *the blind man*. *But* he said: I am *the same man*.
¹⁰Therefore they said to him: How were your eyes opened?
¹¹He answered and said: A man who is called Jesus made clay and anointed my eyes and said to me: Go to the pool of Siloam and wash. *So* I went and washed and I received sight.
¹²Then they said to him: Where is He? He said: I do not know.
¹³They brought him who previously⁺ was blind to the Pharisees.
¹⁴*Now* it was the Sabbath day when Jesus made the clay and opened *the blind man's* eyes.

¹⁵ Therefore⁺ the Pharisees *once* again asked him how he had received his sight. He said to them: *Jesus* put clay on my eyes, and I washed and *now I can* see.
¹⁶ Therefore, some of the Pharisees said: This man is not of God, because He does not keep the Sabbath day. Others said: How can a man who is a sinner do such miracles? There was division among them.
¹⁷ Again, they said to the blind man: What do you say about⁺ Him who opened your eyes? He said: He is a prophet.
¹⁸ But the Jews did not believe, concerning him, that he had been blind and received his sight, until they called the parents of him who had received his sight.
¹⁹ They asked *the parents* saying: Is this your son whom you say was born blind? How then does he now see?
²⁰ His parents answered them and said: We know that this is our son and that he was born blind.
²¹ But by what means he now sees, we do not know. Or who has opened his eyes, we do not know. He is of age. Ask him and he will speak for himself.
²² *The blind man's* parents spoke these *words* because they feared the Jews. For the Jews had already agreed that if anyone⁺ confessed that *Jesus* was Christ, they should be put out of the synagogue.
²³ Therefore his parents said: He is of age. Ask him.
²⁴ Then, *yet* again, they called the man who was blind and said to him: Give God the praise. We know that this man is a sinner.
²⁵ He answered and said: Whether He is a sinner *or not* I do not know. One thing I know: That, whereas I was blind, now I see.
²⁶ Then they said to him again: What did He *do* to you? How did He open your eyes?
²⁷ He answered them: I have told you already and you did not hear. Would you therefore hear *it* again? Will you also be His disciples?
²⁸ Then they reviled him and said: You are His disciple, but we are Moses' disciples.

²⁹ We know that God spoke to Moses. *As for* this *fellow*, we do not know where He is from.
³⁰ The man answered and said to them: *Well,* this is marvelous: That you do not know where He is from, and *yet* He has opened my eyes.
³¹ Now we know that God does not hear sinners, but if anyone is a worshiper of God and does His will, He hears them.
³² Since the world began, it has never⁺ *been* heard that anyone opened the eyes of one who was born blind.
³³ If this man were not of God, He could do nothing.
³⁴ They answered and said to him: You were born altogether in sins, and do you teach us? *Then* they cast him out.
³⁵ Jesus heard that they had cast him out, *so* when He found *the man*, He said to him: Do you believe in the Son of God?
³⁶ He answered and said: Who is He Lord, *so* that I might believe in Him?
³⁷ Jesus said to him: You have both seen Him and it is He who talks with you.
³⁸ *Then* he said: Lord I believe. And he worshiped Him.
³⁹ Jesus said: For judgment I have come into this world, *so* that *those* who do not see might see, and *so* that *those* who see might be made blind.
⁴⁰ *Some* of the Pharisees who were with Him heard these words and said to Him: Are we blind also?
⁴¹ Jesus said to them: If you were blind, you would have no sin. But now you say: We see. Therefore your sin remains.

John Chapter 10

¹ Truly, ⁺ truly, I say to you: Anyone who does not enter into the sheepfold by the door, but climbs up some other way, the same is a thief and a robber.
² But one⁺ who enters by the door is the shepherd of the sheep.
³ The doorkeeper⁺ opens to *the shepherd* and the sheep hear his voice and he calls his own sheep by name and leads them out.
⁴ When he puts forth his own sheep, he

goes before them and the sheep follow him, for they know his voice.

5 They will not follow a stranger but will flee from him, for they do not know the voice of strangers.

6 Jesus spoke this parable to them, but they did not understand what it+ was that He spoke to them.

7 Then Jesus said to them again: Truly, + truly, I say to you: I am the door of the sheep.

8 All who ever came before me are thieves and robbers, but the sheep did not hear them.

> 9 I am the door.
> If anyone enters in through+ me,
> they will be saved

and will go in and out and find pasture.

10 The thief does not come, except+ to steal, kill, and destroy.

> I have come
> *so* that they *might* have life
> and have *it* more abundantly.
> *Jeremiah 29:11*

11 I am the good shepherd. The good shepherd gives His life for the sheep.

12 But one who is a hired hand+ and not the shepherd, *in other words* the sheep are not his *very* own, sees the wolf coming and leaves the sheep and runs away. + And the wolf catches *some* and scatters the sheep.

13 The hired hand+ runs away+ because he is a hired hand+ and does not care about the sheep.

14 I am the good shepherd and know my *sheep* and am known by my *own*.

15 As the Father knows me, even so I know the Father and I lay down my life for the sheep.

16 I also have other sheep, not of this fold. I must bring them *in* also. They will hear my voice and there will be one fold *and* one shepherd.

17 For this reason, + my Father loves me. Because I lay down my life *so* that I might take it again.

18 No one takes it from me, but I lay it down of myself. I have authority+ *and power* to lay it down and I have authority+ *and power* to take it again. This commandment I have received from+ my Father.

19 Therefore, there was *once* again, a division among the Jews because+ of these words. +

20 Many of them said: He has a demon+ and is mad. Why do you listen+ *to* Him?

21 Others said: These are not the words of one+ who has a demon. + Can a demon+ open the eyes of the blind?

22 *Now* it was at the Feast of Dedication, and it was winter.

23 And Jesus walked in Solomon's porch in the temple.

24 Then the Jews came around+ Him and said to Him: How long *will you keep* us *in* suspense+? If you are the Christ, tell us plainly.

25 Jesus answered them: I told you and you did not believe. The works that I do in my Father's name, they bear witness of me.

26 But you do not believe because you are not of my sheep, as I said to you.

27 My sheep hear my voice and I know them and they follow me.

28 I give eternal life to them and they will never perish, nor will anyone+ pluck them out of my hand.

29 My Father who gave *them to* me is greater than all. No *one* is able to pluck *them* out of my Father's hand.

30 I and *my* Father are one.

31 Then the Jews took up stones again to stone Him.

32 Jesus answered them: I have shown+ you many good works from my Father. For which of those works do you stone me?

33 The Jews answered Him saying: We do not stone you for a good work, but for blasphemy. Because you, being a man, make yourself God.

34 Jesus answered them: Is it not written in your law: I said: You are gods?

Psalm 82:6

35 If He called them gods to whom the Word of God came, and the Scripture cannot be broken,

[36] do you say of Him whom the Father has sanctified and sent into the world: You blaspheme, because I said: I am the Son of God?
[37] If I do not *do* the works of my Father, *then* do not believe me.
[38] But if I do, *even* though you do not believe me, believe the works *so* that you may know and believe that the Father *is* in me and I *am* in Him.
[39] Therefore they sought again to take Him, but He escaped out of their hand
[40] and went away again beyond Jordan to the place where John at first baptized, and He stayed+ there.
[41] Many came+ to Him and said: John did no miracle, but all things that John spoke of this man were true.
[42] And many believed in Him there.

John Chapter 11

[1] Now a certain *man named* Lazarus was sick *in* Bethany, the town of Mary and her sister Martha.
[2] It was Mary who had anointed the Lord with ointment and wiped His feet with her hair, whose brother Lazarus was sick.
[3] Therefore the sisters sent *word* to *Jesus* saying: Lord, behold *Lazarus* whom you love is sick.
[4] When Jesus heard *that*, He said: This sickness is not to death, but for the glory of God *so* that the Son of God might be glorified by it+.
[5] Now Jesus loved Martha and her sister and Lazarus.
[6] *Yet* when He heard that *Lazarus* was sick, He still stayed+ two days in the same place where He was.
[7] Then, after that, He said to *His* disciples: Let us go to Judea again.
[8] *His* disciples said to Him: Master, the Jews have recently+ sought to stone you. Do you *intend* to go there again?
[9] Jesus answered: Are there not twelve hours in the day? If anyone walks in the day *light*, they will not stumble, because they see the light of this world.
[10] But if people+ walk in the night, they stumble because there is no light in them.
[11] He said these things, and after that He said to them: Our friend Lazarus sleeps, but I *am* going *to him so* that I may awaken him out of sleep.
[12] Then His disciples said: Lord, if he sleeps, he will do well.
[13] However Jesus spoke of *Lazarus's* death. But they thought that He had spoken of rest in *normal* sleep.
[14] Then Jesus said to them plainly: Lazarus is dead.
[15] I am glad for your sakes that I was not there, *so* that you may believe. Nevertheless let us go to him.
[16] Then Thomas who is called Didymus said to his fellow disciples: Let us go also *so* that we may die with *Jesus*.
[17] Then when Jesus came, He found that *Lazarus* had *been* in the grave four days already.
[18] Now Bethany was near Jerusalem, about two miles+ away. +
[19] Many of the Jews had come to Martha and Mary to comfort them concerning their brother.
[20] As soon as Martha heard that Jesus was coming, she went and met Him, but Mary was *still* sitting in the house.
[21] Then Martha said to Jesus: Lord, if you had been here my brother *would* not have died.
[22] But I know that, even now, whatever you will ask of God, God will give *it to* you.
[23] Jesus said to her: Your brother will rise again.
[24] Martha said to Him: I know that he will rise again in the resurrection at the last day.
[25] Jesus said to her:

> I am the resurrection
> and the life.
> *Those* who believe in me,
> though they were dead,
> yet shall they live.

[26] Whoever lives and believes in me will never die. Do you believe this?

27 She said to Him: Yes Lord. I believe that you are the Christ, the Son of God who has come to the world.

28 When she had said this, she went away and called her sister Mary secretly saying: The Master has come and is calling for you.

29 As soon as *Mary* heard *that*, she arose quickly and came to Him.

30 Now Jesus had not yet come into the town, but was in that place where Martha met Him.

31 Then the Jews who were with her in the house and comforted her, when they saw that Mary rose up hastily and went out, *they* followed her saying: She *is* going to the grave to weep there.

32 When Mary came where Jesus was and saw Him, she fell down at His feet saying to Him: Lord, if you had been here, my brother *would* not have died.

33 Therefore, when Jesus saw *Mary* weeping, and the Jews who came with her also weeping, He groaned in the spirit and was troubled.

34 *He* said: Where have you laid *Lazarus*? They said to Him: Lord, come and see.

35 Jesus wept.

36 Then the Jews said: Behold how He loved *Lazarus*.

37 Some of them said: Could not this man who opened the eyes of the blind, also have caused *Lazarus* not to have died?

38 Therefore, Jesus groaned within Himself *and* came to the grave. It was a cave and a stone lay upon it.

39 Jesus said: Take away the stone. Martha, the sister of *Lazarus* who had died, + said to *Jesus*: Lord, by this time he *surely* smells+ *very bad* for he has been *dead* four days.

40 Jesus said to her: Did I not say to you that if you would believe you would see the glory of God?

41 Then they took away the stone *from the place* where the dead *man* was laid, and Jesus lifted up *His* eyes and said: Father, I thank you that you have heard me.

42 I knew that you always hear me, but because of the people who stand by I said *this so* that they may believe that you have sent me.

43 When He had thus spoken, He cried *out* with a loud voice: Lazarus, come forth.

44 *Then Lazarus* who had been dead came forth, bound hand and foot with grave clothes and his face wrapped+ with a cloth.+ Jesus said to them: Loose him and let him go.

45 Then many of the Jews who had come to Mary and had seen the things that Jesus did, believed in Him.

46 But some of them went away+ to the Pharisees and told them what Jesus had done.

47 Then the chief priests and Pharisees gathered a council and said: What *shall* we do? For this man does many miracles.

48 If we leave+ Him alone, all *people* will believe in Him, and the Romans will come and take away both our place and nation.

49 One of them *named* Caiaphas, being the high priest that year, said to them: You know nothing *at all*.

50 Nor *do you* consider that it is expedient for us, that one man should die for the people *so* that the whole nation does not perish.

51 And he did not say+ this from+ himself *only*, but being high priest that year, he *unwittingly* prophesied that Jesus would die for that nation.

52 And not for that nation only, but that He would also gather together in one, the children of God who were scattered.

53 Then from that day forth, they took counsel together to put *Jesus* to death.

54 Therefore, Jesus no longer+ walked openly among the Jews, but went from there+ to a country near the wilderness, to a city called Ephraim, and continued there with His disciples.

55 *Now* the Jews' Passover was *very* near, and many went out of the country *and* up to Jerusalem before the Passover, to purify themselves.

56 *And* they sought Jesus and spoke among themselves as they stood in the temple, *saying*: What do you think? That He will come to the feast *or* not?

57 Now both the chief priests and the Pharisees had given a commandment,

that if anyone knew where He was, they should show *it so* that they might take Him.

John Chapter 12

[1] Six days before the Passover, Jesus came to Bethany where Lazarus was, *the one* who had been dead *but* whom *Jesus* had raised from the dead.
[2] They made a supper *for Jesus* there, and Martha served, and Lazarus was one of *those* who sat at the table with Him.
[3] Then Mary took a pound of ointment of spikenard, very costly, and anointed the feet of Jesus and wiped His feet with her hair. And the house was filled with the aroma[+] of the ointment.
[4] Then one of *Jesus'* disciples, Judas Iscariot, Simon's*son, the one* who would betray *Jesus* said:
[5] Why was this ointment not sold for *a year's wages*[+] and given to the poor?
[6] He said this, not that he cared for the poor, but because he was a thief and had *carried* the *money* bag and *he often* took[+] what was put in it.
[7] Then Jesus said: Let her alone. *It was* for[+] the day of my burial[+] *that* she had kept this.
[8] For you always have the poor with you. But you will not always have me.
[9] Many of the Jews knew that He was there, but they did not come only for Jesus' sake, but *so* that they might see Lazarus also, whom He had raised from the dead.
[10] But the chief priests consulted *so* that they might put Lazarus to death also,
[11] *for it was because of Lazarus* that many of the Jews went *away* and believed in Jesus.
[12] On the next day, many people who had come to the feast, when they heard that Jesus was coming to Jerusalem,
[13] took branches of palm trees and went forth to meet Him, and cried *out*: Hosanna! Blessed*is He* who comes in the name of the Lord, the King of Israel.

[14] When He had found a young donkey,[+] Jesus sat on it. As it is written:
[15] Do not be afraid, daughter of Zion.[+] Behold your King comes sitting on a donkey[+]'s colt. *Zechariah 9:9*
[16] *Jesus'* disciples did not understand these things at first, but when Jesus was glorified, then they remembered that these things were written of Him and *that* they had done these things to Him.
[17] Therefore, the people who were with Him when He called Lazarus out of his grave and raised him from the dead testified[+] *and spread the Word.*
[18] For this reason[+] the people *came to* meet Him, because[+] they heard that He had done this miracle.
[19] Therefore, the Pharisees said among themselves: Do you see[+] that[+] *we are* gaining[+] nothing? Behold the world has gone after Him.
[20] *Now* there were certain Greeks among *those* who came up to worship at the feast.
[21] They came to Philip, who was from Bethsaida in Galilee, and asked[+] him saying: Sir, we would *like to* see Jesus.
[22] Philip came and told Andrew *and* Andrew and Philip told Jesus.
[23] Jesus answered them saying: The hour has come for the Son of man to be glorified.
[24] Truly,[+] truly, I say to you: Unless[+] a grain[+] of wheat falls to the ground and dies, it remains[+] alone. But if it dies, it brings forth much fruit.
[25] *Those* who love their life will lose it, but *those* who hate their life in this world will keep it to eternal life.
[26] If anyone *will* serve me, let them follow me, and where I am, my servant will be there also. If anyone *will* serve me, *my* Father will honor them.
[27] Now my soul is troubled, and what shall I say? Father, save me from this hour? But *it is* for this reason[+] *that* I came to this hour.
[28] Father, glorify your name. Then there came a voice from heaven*saying*: I have glorified *it* and will glorify *it* again.
[29] Therefore the people who stood by and heard *this* said that it thundered.

Others said: An angel spoke to Him.
³⁰Jesus answered and said: This voice did not come because of me, but for your *benefit*.
³¹Now is the judgment of this world. Now the prince of this world will be cast out.
³²*When* I am lifted up from the earth *and exalted*, I will draw all *people* to me.
³³He said this signifying *by* what death He would *soon* die.
³⁴The people answered Him: We have heard out of the law that Christ *will* remain⁺ forever.·How *is it that* you say: The Son of man must be lifted up? Who is this Son of man?
³⁵Then Jesus said to them: Yet a little while is the light with you. Walk *in the light* while you have the light, lest darkness come upon you. For *those* who walk in darkness do not know where they *are* going. *Proverbs 4:19*
³⁶While you have light, believe in the light *so* that you may be the children of light. Jesus spoke these things and *then* departed and hid Himself from them.
³⁷But though He had done so many miracles before them, they *still* did not believe in Him.
³⁸This fulfilled the words of the prophet Isaiah who said: Lord, who has believed our report? And to whom has the arm of the Lord been revealed?
³⁹For this reason⁺ they could not believe. Because Isaiah said again:
⁴⁰He has blinded their eyes and hardened their heart *so* that they would not see with *their* eyes or understand with *their* heart and be converted and I would heal them. *Isaiah 6:9,10*
⁴¹Isaiah said these things when he saw *Jesus* glory and spoke of Him.
⁴²Nevertheless, many among the chief rulers also believed in *Jesus*, but because of the Pharisees they did not confess *Him*, lest they should be put out of the synagogue.
⁴³For they loved the praise of men more than the praise of God.
⁴⁴*Then* Jesus cried *out* and said: *Those* who believe in me do not believe in me, but in Him who sent me.

⁴⁵*Those* who see me see Him who sent me.
⁴⁶I have come *as* a light into the world *so* that whoever believes in me will⁺ not remain⁺ in darkness.
⁴⁷If anyone hears my words, and does not believe, I do not judge them. For I did not come to judge the world, but to save the world.
⁴⁸*Those* who reject me and do not receive my words, have one who judges them. The Word that I have spoken, that⁺ will judge them in the last day.
⁴⁹For I have not spoken from⁺ myself, but the Father who sent me gave me a commandment: What I should say and what I should speak.
⁵⁰I know that His commandment is eternal⁺ life. Therefore, whatever I speak, even as the Father said to me, so I speak.

John Chapter 13

¹ Now before the Feast of the Passover, when Jesus knew that His hour had come that He would depart out of this world to the Father, having loved His own who were in the world, He loved them to the end.
² During⁺ *the last* supper, the devil had already⁺ put *it* into the heart of Judas Iscariot, Simon's *son*, to betray *Jesus*.
³ *Now* Jesus knew that the Father had given all things into His hands and that He had come from God and *would be* returning⁺ to God.
⁴ *So,* He arose from supper, laid aside His garments, took a towel, and wrapped⁺ *it around* Himself.
⁵ After that, He poured water into a basin and began to wash the disciples' feet and to wipe *them* with the towel with which He was wrapped.⁺
⁶ Then He came to Simon Peter, and Peter said to Him: Lord, are you washing my feet?
⁷ Jesus answered and said to him: What I *am* doing, you do not understand⁺ now. But you will understand⁺ after this.
⁸ Peter said to Him: You shall never wash my feet. Jesus answered him: If I do not wash you, you have no part with me.

⁹ Simon Peter said to Him: Lord, *then* not my feet only, but also *my* hands and *my* head.

¹⁰ Jesus said to him: *Those* who are bathed⁺ do not need *more* than to wash the feet, but *they* are completely⁺ clean. You are clean. But not all *of you*.

¹¹ For He knew who would betray Him. Therefore He said: You are not all clean.

¹² So, after He had washed their feet and had taken His garments and sat down again, He said to them: Do you know what I have done to you?

¹³ You call me Master and Lord, and You say well, for *so* I am.

¹⁴ If I then, *your* Lord and Master, have washed your feet, *then* you also ought to wash the feet of one another.

¹⁵ For I have given you an example *so* that you should do as I have done to you.

¹⁶ Truly,⁺ truly, I say to you: The servant is not greater than his lord. Nor *are those* who are sent greater than *one* who sent them.

¹⁷ If you know these things, blessed⁺ are you if you do them.

¹⁸ I do not speak of you all. I know whom I have chosen. But *so* the Scripture may be fulfilled, one⁺ who eats bread with me has lifted up his heel against me.

Psalm 41:9

¹⁹ Now I tell you *this* before it comes, *so* that when it has come to pass, you may believe that I am.

²⁰ Truly,⁺ truly, I say to you: *Those* who receive whomever I send receive me and *those* who receive me receive Him who sent me.

²¹ When Jesus had said these things, He was troubled in spirit and testified and said: Truly,⁺ truly, I say to you that one of you will betray me.

²² Then the disciples looked at one another, perplexed⁺ about whom He spoke.

²³ Now one of Jesus' disciples whom *He* loved was leaning on His chest.⁺

²⁴ Therefore, Simon Peter signaled⁺ to him that he should ask who it might⁺ be of whom He spoke.

²⁵ Then the one⁺ leaning⁺ on Jesus' chest⁺ said to Him: Lord, who is it?

²⁶ Jesus answered: It is *the* one⁺ to whom I shall give a morsel⁺ when I have dipped *it*. And when He had dipped the morsel,⁺ He gave *it* to Judas Iscariot, *the son* of Simon.

²⁷ After the morsel,⁺ Satan entered *Judas*. Then Jesus said to him: What you *must* do, do quickly.

²⁸ But⁺ no one at the table knew why⁺ *Jesus* said this to *Judas*.

²⁹ Some thought *that* since⁺ Judas had the *money* bag, Jesus had said to him: Buy what⁺ *things* we need for⁺ the feast. Or, that He should give something to the poor.

³⁰ Therefore, having received the morsel,⁺ *Judas* immediately went out. And it was night.

³¹ When he was gone, Jesus said: Now is the Son of man glorified and God is glorified in Him.

³² If God be glorified in Him, God will also glorify *the Son of man* in Himself and will glorify Him immediately⁺.

³³ Little children, yet a little while I am with you. *Then* you will seek me and as I said to the Jews: Where I *am* going you cannot come. So now I say to you:

³⁴ A new commandment
I give to you:
That you love one another.
As I have loved you,
that you also love one another.

³⁵ By this all *people* will know that you are my disciples: If you have love toward one another.

³⁶ Simon Peter said to Him: Lord where are you going⁺? Jesus answered him: Where I *am* going you cannot follow me now, but you shall follow me afterwards.

³⁷ Peter said to Him: Lord, why can I not follow you now? I will lay down my life for your sake.

³⁸ Jesus answered him: Will you lay down your life for my sake? Truly,⁺ truly, I say to you: The cock will not crow until you have denied me three times.

John Chapter 14

> ¹ Do not let your heart
> be troubled.
> You believe in God.
> Believe also in me.

² In my Father's house are many mansions. If *it were* not*so*, I would have told you. *Now* I *am* going to prepare a place for you.
³ And if I go and prepare a place for you, I will come again and receive you to myself *so* that where I am, *there* you may be also.
⁴ You know where I *am* going, ⁺ and you know the way.
⁵ Thomas said to Him: Lord, we do not know where you *are* going. How can we know the way?
⁶ Jesus said to him:

> I am the way,
> the truth, and the life.
> No one comes to the Father,
> but by me.

⁷ If you had known me, you would have known my Father also. From henceforth you know Him and have seen Him.
⁸ Philip said to Him: Lord show us the Father and it *will be* sufficient⁺ *for* us.
⁹ Jesus said to him: Have I been so long *a* time with you and yet have you not known me, Philip? *Those* who have seen me have seen the Father. How *is it that* you say *then*: Show us the Father?
¹⁰Do you not believe that I am in the Father and the Father *is* in me? The words that I speak to you I do not speak of myself, but the Father who dwells in me does the works.
¹¹Believe me that I *am* in the Father and the Father *is* in me. Or else believe me because⁺ of the very works themselves⁺.
¹²Truly, ⁺ truly, I say to you: *Those* who believe in me will also do the works that I do, and greater *works* than these will they do because I go to my Father.

¹³Whatever you ask in my name, that I will do *so* that the Father may be glorified in the Son.
¹⁴If you ask anything in my name, I will do *it*.

> ¹⁵ If you love me,
> keep my commandments.

¹⁶I will *pray and* ask⁺ the Father and He will give you another Comforter *so* that He may stay⁺ with you forever.
¹⁷*That comforter is* the Spirit of Truth whom the world cannot receive because it does not see or know Him. But you know Him for He dwells with you and will be in you.
¹⁸I will not leave you orphaned. ⁺ I will come to you. *Deuteronomy 31:6*
¹⁹Yet a little while and the world*will* see me no more. But you *will* see me. Because I live, you will also live.
²⁰At that day, you will know that I *am* in my Father and you *are* in me and I *am* in you.

> ²¹ *Those* who have
> my commandments
> and keep them⁺ are the ones
> who *truly* love me.
> *Those* who love me
> will be loved by my Father
> and I will love them
> and will reveal⁺ myself to them.
> *Proverbs 8:17*

²²*Then* Jude, not *Judas* Iscariot, said to Him: Lord, how is it that you will manifest yourself to us and not to the world?
²³Jesus answered and said to him: If anyone⁺ loves me, they will keep my words and my Father will love them and we will come to them and live⁺ within them.
²⁴*Those* who do not love me do not keep my Word. ⁺ The Word that you hear is not mine, but the Father's who sent me.
²⁵I have spoken these things to you*while I am still* present with you.
²⁶But the Comforter *is* the Holy Spirit

whom the Father will send in my name. *He will* teach you all and remind[+] you *of* all that I have said to you.

> [27] Peace I leave with you.
> My peace I give to you.
> I do not give to you
> as the world gives.
> Do not let your heart be troubled
> *and do not* let it be afraid.

[28] You have heard how I said to you: I *am* going away and *I will* come to you *again*. If you loved me, you would rejoice because I said: I *am* going to the Father. For my Father is greater than I.

[29] Now I have told you before it comes to pass, *so* that when it has come to pass, you might believe.

[30] Hereafter I will not talk with you *very* much *more*. For the prince of this world *is* coming and *he* has nothing in me.

[31] But *so* that the world may know that I love the Father, as the Father has commanded me, even so I do. *Now* arise. Let us go from here.

John Chapter 15

[1] I am the true vine and my Father is the grower[+].

[2] Every branch in me that does not bear fruit He takes away. Every *branch* that bears fruit, He purges *so* that it may bring forth more fruit.

[3] Now you are clean through the Word that I have spoken to you.

[4] Abide in me and I *will abide* in you. Because[+] the branch cannot bear fruit by[+] itself unless[+] it remains[+] *and abides* in the vine. Nor[+] can you, unless[+] you abide in me.

[5] I am the vine. You *are* the branches. *Those* who stay[+] *and abide* in me and I in them bring forth much fruit. For without me you can do nothing.

[6] If anyone[+] does not stay[+] *and abide* in me, *they will be* cast out[+] like[+] a *broken* and withered branch, and these *are* gathered and thrown[+] into a fire and burned.

[7] If you abide in me and my words abide in you, *then you shall* ask whatever[+] you will and it will be done *for* you.

[8] Herein is my Father glorified: That you become[+] my disciples and bear much fruit.

[9] As the Father has loved me, so have I loved you. *Now continue* to abide[+] in my love.

[10] If you keep my commandments, you will abide in my love, even as I have kept my Father's commandments and abide in His love.

> [11] I have spoken these things
> to you *so* that my joy
> might remain in you
> and *so that* your joy
> might be full.

> [12] This is my commandment:
> That you love one another
> as I have loved you.

> [13] Greater love
> has no one than this,
> that one[+] lay down
> one's *own* life for one's friends.

[14] You are my friends if you do whatever I command you.

[15] Henceforth I will not call you servants, for the servant does not understand what his lord does. But I have called you friends, for all things that I have heard from[+] my Father I have made known to you.

[16] You have not chosen me but I have chosen you and ordained you *so* that you should go and bring forth fruit and *so that* your fruit should remain and *so* that whatever you ask of the Father in my name, He may give it *to* you.

[17] *And* these things I command you: That you love one another.

[18] If the world hates you, know that it hated me before *it hated* you.

[19] If you were of the world, the world would love its own. But because you are not of the world, but I have chosen you out of the world, therefore the world hates you.

20Remember the Word that I said to you: The servant is not greater than his lord. If they have persecuted me, they will also persecute you. If they have kept my Word, + they will keep yours also.
21But they will do all these things to you because of my name, because they do not know Him who sent me.
22If I had not come and spoken to them, they *would* not have had sin, but now they have no covering+ for their sin.
23*Those* who hate me hate my Father also.
24If I had not done among them the works that no one+ *else ever* did, they *would* not have had sin, but now *they* have seen *my works* and *even so* hated me and my Father.
25But this fulfills the word written in their law: They hated me without a cause. *Psalm 69:4 Psalm 35:19*
26Yet+ when the Comforter is come, whom I will send to you from the Father, *the one who is* the Spirit of Truth who proceeds from the Father, He will testify of me.
27And you also will bear witness, because you have been with me from the beginning.

John Chapter 16

1 I have spoken these things to you *so* that you would not be offended *and fall away*.
2 They will put you out of the synagogues. Yes, the time *is* coming when+ whoever kills you will think that they do a service *to* God.
3 They will do these things to you because they have not known *either* the Father or me.
4 But I have told you these things *so* that when the time comes, you may remember that I told you of them. I did not say these things to you at the beginning because I was with you.
5 But now I *am* going away+ to Him who sent me, and none of you asks me: Where *are* you going+?
6 But because I have said these things to you, sorrow has filled your hearts.

7 Nevertheless I tell you the truth: It is expedient for you that I go away. For if I do not go away, the Comforter will not come to you. But if I depart, I will send Him to you.
8 When He comes, He will convince+ the world of sin, and of righteousness, and of judgment.
9 Of sin, because they do not believe in me.
10Of righteousness, because I *am* going to my Father and you *will* see me no more.
11Of judgment, because the prince of this world is judged.
12I still+ have many *more* things to say to you, but you cannot bear them now.
13However, when the Spirit of Truth has come, He will guide you into all truth. For He will not speak from+ Himself, but whatever He hears *from God* He will speak, and He will show you things to come.
14He will glorify me, for He will receive of mine and declare+ *that* to you.
15All things that the Father has are mine. Therefore I said that He will take of mine and declare+ *that* to you.
16A little while and you will not see me, and again a little while and you will see me, because I *am* going to the Father.
17Then *some* of *Jesus'* disciples said among themselves: What is this that He says to us: A little while and you will not see me, and again a little while and you will see me. And: Because I go to the Father?
18Therefore, they said: What is this that He says: A little while? We cannot tell what He is saying.
19Now Jesus knew that they desired+ to ask Him *about this*, and *so He* said to them: Do you inquire among yourselves about what I said: A little while and you will not see me, and again a little while and you will see me?
20Truly, + truly, I say to you: That you will weep and mourn, + but the world will rejoice. You will be sorrowful, but your sorrow will be turned into joy.
21When a woman is in labor, + she has grief+ *and pain* because her hour has

come, but as soon as she has delivered the child, she no longer+ remembers the anguish, because+ of *her* joy that a child+ is born into the world.

22 Therefore, you now have grief,+ but I will see you again and your heart will rejoice and no one will take away your joy from you.

23 In that day, you will ask nothing of me. Truly,+ truly, I say to you: Whatever you ask the Father in my name, He will give *it to* you.

24 Before this,+ you have asked nothing in my name. *Now* ask and you shall receive *so* that your joy may be full.

25 I have spoken these things to you in proverbs, but the time is coming when I will no longer+ speak to you in proverbs, but I will show you plainly of the Father.

26 At that day, you shall ask in my name. I do not say to you that I will *pray and* ask+ the Father for you.

27 For the Father Himself loves you because you have loved me and have believed that I came forth+ from God.

28 I came forth from the Father and have come into the world. *Now* I *am* leaving the world again and *I am* going *back* to the Father.

29 His disciples said to Him: Behold, now you speak plainly and speak no proverb.

30 Now are we sure that you know all things and *we* do not need anyone *to* ask you *any more*. By this we believe that you came forth from God.

31 Jesus answered them: Do you now believe?

32 Behold the hour is coming,+ yes *it* has now come, that you will be scattered, everyone+ to their own, and will leave me alone. Yet I am not alone because the Father is with me.

33 I have spoken these things to you *so* that in me you might have peace. In the world you will have tribulation. But

---

Be of good cheer.
I have overcome the world.

John Chapter 17

1 Jesus spoke these things+ and *then* lifted up His eyes to heaven and said: Father, the hour has come. Glorify your Son *so* that your Son may glorify you, also.

2 You have given Him authority+ *and power* over all flesh, *so* that He could give eternal life to all+ whom you have given *to* Him.

3 And this is eternal life: That they might know you, the only true God, and Jesus Christ whom you have sent.

4 I have glorified you on the earth. I have finished the work you gave me to do.

5 Now Father, glorify me *along* with yourself with the glory I had with you before the world was.

6 I have manifested your name to *those* whom you gave *to* me out of the world. They were yours and you gave them *to* me. And they have kept your Word.

7 Now they know that all things whatsoever you have given *to* me are from+ you.

8 For I have given to them the words you gave *to* me and they received *them*. *Now they* truly+ *do* know that I came forth+ from you and they believe that you sent me.

9 I pray for them. I do not pray for the world, but for *those* whom you have given *to* me. For they are yours.

10 All mine are yours and yours are mine. And I am glorified in them.

11 Now, I am *to be* in the world no more, but these are in the world and I *am* coming to you. Holy Father, through your name, keep *those* whom you have given *to* me *so* that they may be one as we *are one*.

12 While I was with them in the world, I kept them in your name. I have kept *those* whom you gave *to* me and not one of them has perished,+ except+ the son of damnation+ *so* the Scripture might be fulfilled. *Psalm 41:9*

13 And now, I am coming to you, and I am speaking these things in the world *so* that they might have my joy fulfilled within+ themselves.

[14]I have given them your Word. The world has hated them because they are not of the world, even as I am not of the world.

[15]I do not pray that you should take them out of the world, but that you keep them from + evil.

[16]They are not of the world, even as I am not of the world.

[17]Sanctify them through your truth. Your Word is truth.

[18]*Just* as you have sent me into the world, I have also sent them into the world.

[19]I *have* sanctified myself for them+ *so* that they might also be sanctified in+ truth.

[20]*And* I do not pray for these alone, but also for *those* who will believe in me through their word.

[21]*I do this so* that all may be one *just* as you, Father, *are* in me and I *am* in you, *so* that they may be one in us also *and so* that the world may believe that you have sent me.

[22]I have given *to* them the glory you gave *to* me, *so* that they may be one even as we are one:

[23]I in them and you in me. *So* that they may be made perfect in one, and *so* that the world may know that you have sent me and have loved them *just* as you have loved me.

[24]Father, *it is my desire and* will that *those* whom you have given *to* me also be with me where I am, *so* that they may behold my glory that you have given *to* me. For you *have* loved me *since* before the foundation of the world.

[25]O righteous Father: The world has not known you, but I have known you and these *now* know that you have sent me.

[26]I have made+ your name known+ to them, and *I* will *make it* known+ that the love with which you have loved me can+ be in them, and I *myself will be* in them.

John Chapter 18

[1] When Jesus had spoken these words, He went forth with His disciples over the brook *of* Kedron, where *there* was a garden into which He and His disciples entered.

[2] Judas who betrayed Him also knew the place, for Jesus often went there with His disciples.

[3] Then Judas, having received a company+ *of soldiers* and officers from the chief priests and Pharisees, went+ there with lanterns and torches and weapons.

[4] Therefore, knowing all things that would come upon Him, Jesus went forth and said to them: Whom do you seek?

[5] They answered Him: Jesus of Nazareth. Jesus said to them: I Am. And Judas who betrayed Him also stood with them.

[6] Then as soon as *Jesus* had said to them: I Am. They went backward and fell to the ground.

[7] Then He asked them again: Whom do you seek? And they said: Jesus of Nazareth.

[8] Jesus answered: I have told you that I Am. Therefore if you seek me, let these *others* go.

[9] *He* said this *so* that the Word+ He *had* spoken would be fulfilled: I have not lost one of those you gave *to* me.

[10]Then Simon Peter, having a sword, drew it and struck+ the high priest's servant and cut off his right ear. The servant's name was Malchus.

[11]Then Jesus said to Peter: Put *away* your sword into the sheath. *This is* the cup that my Father has given *to* me. Shall I not drink it?

[12]Then the company+ *of soldiers* and the captain and officers of the Jews took Jesus, bound Him,

[13]and led Him away to Annas first, for he was father in law to Caiaphas who was the high priest that year.

[14]*Now* it was Caiaphas who had given counsel to the Jews that it was expedient that one man should die for the people.

[15]Simon Peter and another disciple followed Jesus. That *other* disciple was known to the high priest and *he* entered with Jesus into the palace of the high priest.

[16]But Peter stood at the door outside.+ Then that other disciple who was known to the high priest went out and spoke to

the doorkeeper+ and brought in Peter.
17 Then the girl+ who kept the door said
to Peter: Are you not also *one* of this
man's disciples? He said: I am not.
18 The servants and officers who had
made a fire of coals stood there, for it
was cold. They warmed themselves and
Peter stood with them and warmed
himself.
19 The high priest then asked Jesus about+
His disciples and about+ His doctrine.
20 Jesus answered him: I spoke openly
to the world. I always+ taught in the
synagogue and in the temple where
the Jews always come together,+ and
I have said nothing in secret.
21 Why ask me? Ask *those* who heard me
what I have said to them. Behold, they
know what I said.
22 When He had said these things, one of
the officers who stood by struck Jesus
with the palm of his hand saying: Do
you answer the high priest in this way+?
23 Jesus answered him: If I have spoken
evil, testify+ of the evil. But if well,
why do you strike+ me?
24 Now Annas had sent *Jesus* bound to
Caiaphas the high priest.
25 And Simon Peter stood *by the fire*
and warmed himself. Therefore, they
said to him: Are you not also *one* of
Jesus' disciples? *Peter* denied *it* and
said: I am not.
26 *Then* one of the servants of the high
priest, being a relative+ of *the one* whose
ear Peter had cut off, said: Did I not see
you in the garden with Him?
27 Peter then denied again, and immediately the cock crowed.+
28 Then they led Jesus from Caiaphas to
the hall of judgment, and it was early.
They themselves did not go+ into the
judgment hall lest they should be defiled,
but *so* that they might eat the Passover.
29 Pilate then went out to them and said:
What accusation do you bring against
this man?
30 They answered and said to him: If He
were not an evil doer,+ we would not
have delivered Him up to you.
31 Then Pilate said to them: You take

Him and judge Him according to your
law. Then the Jews said to him: It is not
lawful for us to put anyone to death.
32 *They said this so* that the Word+ Jesus
spoke signifying *by* what death He was
about+ to die would be fulfilled.
33 Then Pilate entered the judgment hall
again, called Jesus, and said to Him:
Are you the King of the Jews?
34 Jesus answered him: Do you say this
of yourself or did others tell it *to* you
about+ me?
35 Pilate answered: Am I a Jew? Your own
nation and the chief priests have delivered
you to me. What have you done?
36 Jesus answered: My kingdom is not of
this world. If my kingdom were of this
world, then my servants would fight *so*
that I would not be delivered to the
Jews. But my kingdom is not of this
world+.
37 Therefore, Pilate said to Him: Are
you a king then? Jesus answered: You
say that I am a king. *It is* to this *end and that*
I was born. And, *it is* for this reason+
that I came into the world: That I should
testify+ to the truth. Everyone who is of
the truth hears my voice.
38 Pilate said to Him: What is truth? And
when he had said this, he went out again
to the Jews and said to them: I find no
fault in Him.
39 But you have a custom that I should
release one to you at the Passover.
Therefore, do you want+ me to release
the King of the Jews to you?
40 Then they all cried *out* again saying:
Not this man, but Barabbas. Now
Barabbas was a robber.

John Chapter 19

1 Therefore Pilate then took Jesus and
flogged+ *Him*.
2 And the soldiers made+ a crown of
thorns and put *it* on His head and they
put a purple robe on Him
3 and said: Hail King of the Jews. And
they struck+ Him with their hands.
4 Pilate then+ went out+ to them again
and said: Behold I bring Him out+ to

you *so* that you may know that I find no fault in Him.

5 Then Jesus came out+ wearing the crown of thorns and the purple robe. And *Pilate* said to them: Behold the man.

6 Therefore, when the chief priests and officers saw Him, they cried out saying: Crucify*Him*. Crucify*Him*. Pilate said to them: You take Him and crucify *Him*, for I find no fault in Him.

7 The Jews answered *Pilate*: We have a law, and by our law He ought to die because He made Himself the Son of God.

8 Therefore, when Pilate heard that word, he was *even* more afraid

9 and went into the judgment hall again and said to Jesus: Where are you *from*? But Jesus gave him no answer.

10 Then Pilate said to Him: Do you not speak to me? Do you not know that I have authority+ *and power* to crucify you and authority+ *and power* to release you?

11 Jesus answered: You could have no authority+ *or power at all* against me unless+ it was given*to* you from above. Therefore he who delivered me to you has the greater sin.

12 From that time on+ Pilate sought to release *Jesus*. But the Jews cried out saying: If you let this man go, you are not Caesar's friend. Whoever makes himself a king speaks against Caesar.

13 Therefore, when Pilate heard that word, he brought Jesus out+ and *he* sat on the judgment seat in a place that is called *the* Pavement, or in Hebrew, Gabbatha.

14 It was the *day of* preparation for+ the Passover, and about twelve o'clock+ *noon* He said to the Jews: Behold your King.

15 But they cried out: Away. Away. Crucify Him. Pilate said to them: Shall I crucify your King? The chief priests answered: We have no king but Caesar.

16 Therefore *Pilate* then delivered *Jesus* to them to be crucified. And they took Jesus and led *Him* away.

17 *Then*, bearing His cross, *Jesus* went to a place called *the place* of a skull. In Hebrew, *the place* is called Golgotha.

18 They crucified Him there, and two others with Him, one on either side and Jesus in the middle+ *between them*. *Isaiah 53:12*

19 Pilate wrote a title and put *it* on the cross, and the writing was: Jesus of Nazareth the King of the Jews.

20 Many of the Jews then read this title. For the place where Jesus was crucified was near the city. It was written in Hebrew, Greek, *and* Latin.

21 Then the chief priests of the Jews said to Pilate: Do not write: The King of the Jews, but that He said: I am King of the Jews.

22 Pilate answered: What I have written I have written.

23 When the soldiers had crucified Jesus, they took His garments and made four parts, *giving* a part to each+ soldier. *They* also *took His* coat. *But His* coat was seamless, + woven from the top throughout.

24 Therefore they said among themselves: Let us not tear+ it, but cast lots for it *to decide* whose it shall be. *They did this so* that the Scripture might be fulfilled that says: They divided+ my clothing+ among them and for my coat+ they cast lots. Therefore the soldiers did these things. *Psalm 22:18*

25 Now Jesus' mother stood there by the cross, *along with* His mother's sister Mary, the *wife* of Cleophas, and Mary Magdalene.

26 When Jesus saw His mother and the disciple standing by whom He loved, He said to His mother: Woman behold your son.

27 Then He said to the disciple: Behold your mother. From that hour, that disciple took *Jesus'* mother to *be* his own.

28 After this, knowing that all things were now accomplished *so* the Scripture might be fulfilled, Jesus said: I thirst. *Psalm 22:15*

29 Now a vessel full of vinegar was setting there. *So* they filled a sponge with vinegar and put *it* upon *a* hyssop *branch* and put *it* to His mouth.

³⁰When Jesus had thus[+] received the vinegar, He said: It is finished. And He bowed His head and yielded[+] up *His* spirit.[+]

³¹Because it was *the day of* preparation for that great Sabbath day, *and so* that the bodies might not remain on the cross on the Sabbath, the Jews therefore begged[+] Pilate that their legs might be broken and *the bodies* taken away.

³²*So* the soldiers came and broke the legs of the first *man* and of the other *man* who was crucified with *Jesus*.

³³But when they came to Jesus and saw that He was already dead, they did not break His legs. *Psalm 34:20*

³⁴But one of the soldiers pierced His side with a spear and immediately[+] blood and water came out. *Zechariah 12:10*

³⁵Now, one who saw *this occur has* testified[+] and his record is true. *This witness* knows that *what* he *has* said *is* true, *so* that you might believe.

³⁶For these things were done *so* the Scripture would be fulfilled *that says*: Not *one* of His bones shall be broken. *Psalm 34:20*

³⁷Again another Scripture says: They shall look upon Him whom they pierced. *Zechariah 12:10*

³⁸After this, Joseph of Arimathaea, being a disciple of Jesus but secretly for fear of the Jews, begged[+] Pilate that he might take away Jesus' body. And Pilate allowed[+] *him to do so*. Therefore *Joseph* came and took *away* Jesus' body.

³⁹Nicodemus also came *forward*. *He had* at first come to Jesus by night, *but now he* brought a mixture of myrrh and aloes, about a hundred pound *weight*.

⁴⁰Then they took Jesus' body and wrapped it in linen cloths with the spices, as it is the Jews manner to bury.

⁴¹Now in the place where He was crucified there was a garden, and in the garden a new tomb[+] in which no one[+] had yet been laid.

⁴²So[+] they laid Jesus there because of the Jewish preparation *day*, for the tomb[+] was nearby.[+]

John Chapter 20

¹ *On* the first *of* the week, early *when it was* yet dark, Mary Magdalene came to the tomb[+] and saw *that* the stone *had been* taken away from the tomb.[+]

² Therefore[+] *Mary* ran[+] to Simon Peter and to the other disciple whom Jesus loved and said to them: They have taken the Lord from[+] the tomb and we do not know where they have laid Him.

³ Then Peter [+] and that other disciple went[+] *quickly* to the tomb.[+]

⁴ The two[+] ran together and the other disciple outran Peter and came to the tomb[+] first.

⁵ Stooping down *to look in*, he saw the linen clothes lying *there*, yet he did not go in.

⁶ Then Simon Peter came following him and went into the tomb[+] and saw the linen clothes lying *there*.

⁷ The cloth[+] that had been around[+] *Jesus'* head *was* not lying with the linen clothes, but *was* folded[+] in a place by itself.

⁸ Then the other disciple who came to the tomb[+] first also went in and saw *all these things* and believed.

⁹ For as yet they did not understand[+] the Scripture that *Jesus* must rise again from the dead. *Psalm 16:10*

¹⁰Then the disciples went away again to their *own homes*.

¹¹But Mary stood outside[+] the tomb[+] weeping. As she wept, she stooped down *and looked* into the tomb.[+]

¹²*She* saw two angels in white sitting. One *sat* at the head and the other at the feet where Jesus' body had lain.

¹³They said to her: Woman, why are you weeping? She said to them: Because they have taken away my Lord and I do not know where they have laid Him.

¹⁴When she had thus said, she turned back, and saw Jesus standing, but did not understand[+] that it was Jesus.

¹⁵Jesus said to her: Woman, why do you weep? Whom do you seek? Supposing Him to be the gardener, she said to Him: Sir, if you have moved[+] Him from here,

tell me where you have laid Him and I will take Him away.

¹⁶Jesus said to her: Mary. She turned *and* said to Him: Rabboni. Which is to say, Master.

¹⁷Jesus said to her: Do not touch me *now*. For I have not yet ascended to my Father. But go to my brothers and say to them: I *am now* ascending to my Father and your Father, *to* my God and your God.

¹⁸*Then* Mary Magdalene went⁺ *to* the disciples *and* told *them* that she had seen the Lord and *that* He had spoken these things to her.

¹⁹Therefore, *it* being evening of that day, the first *of* the week, and the doors where the disciples were assembled having been shut for fear of the Jews, Jesus came *forth* and stood in the midst and said to them: Peace to you.

²⁰When He had said this, He showed them His hands and side. Then the disciples were glad when they saw *that it was* the Lord.

²¹Then Jesus said to them again:

> Peace to you.
> As *my* Father has sent me,
> even so I *now* send you.

²²When He had said this, He breathed on *them* and said to them:

> Receive *the* Holy Spirit.

²³Those⁺ sins *you* forgive⁺ are forgiven⁺ *to* them *and* those⁺ you retain, are retained.

²⁴*Now* one of the twelve, Thomas *also* called Didymus, was not with them when Jesus came.

²⁵Therefore, the other disciples said to him: We have seen the Lord. But He said to them: Unless⁺ I see the print of the nails in His hands and put my finger into the print of the nails and thrust my hand into His side, I will not believe.

²⁶After eight days, *Jesus'* disciples were again inside⁺ *the room* and Thomas with them. *Although* the doors were shut, Jesus came and stood in the midst and said: Peace to you.

²⁷Then He said to Thomas: Bring⁺ your finger here and behold my hands. Bring your hand and thrust *it* into my side. Do not be faithless, but believing. *Psalm 22:16*

²⁸Thomas answered and said to Him: My Lord and my God.

²⁹Jesus said to him: Thomas, you have believed because you have seen me. Blessed *are those* who have not seen and *yet* have believed.

³⁰And indeed,⁺ Jesus did many other signs in the presence of His disciples that are not written in this book.

³¹But these are written *so* that you might believe that Jesus is the Christ, the Son of God, *so* that *by* believing you might have life through His name.

John Chapter 21

¹ After *all* these things, Jesus showed Himself to the disciples again at the sea of Tiberias, and He showed *Himself* in this way⁺:

² Simon Peter, Thomas called Didymus, Nathanael of Cana in Galilee, the *sons* of Zebedee, and two others of *Jesus'* disciples were together.

³ And Simon Peter said to them: I am going fishing. They said to Him: We *will* go with you, also. *So* they went forth and entered a boat immediately and that night they caught nothing.

⁴ But when morning came, Jesus stood on the shore, but the disciples did not understand⁺ that it was Jesus.

⁵ Then Jesus said to them: Children, have you any food⁺? They answered Him: No.

⁶ He said to them: Cast the net on the right side of the boat and you will find. Therefore they cast *in their nets* and now they were not able to draw it *in* for the large⁺ *catch* of fish.

⁷ Therefore that disciple whom Jesus loved said to Peter: It is the Lord. Now when Simon Peter heard that it was the Lord, he *put on his* fisher's coat, for he was naked, and threw⁺ himself into the sea.

⁸ The other disciples came in a little boat dragging the net with fish for they were not far from land but *only* about⁺ a hundred yards *out*.

⁹ As soon as they came to land, they saw a fire of coals and fish laying⁺ *on it* and bread.

¹⁰ Jesus said to them: Bring *some* of the fish you just⁺ caught.

¹¹ Simon Peter went over⁺ and pulled⁺ the net full of big⁺ fish to land, a hundred and fifty three *to be exact*, and *although* there were so many, the net was not broken.

¹² Jesus said to them: Come *and* dine. None of the disciples dared⁺ to ask Him: Who are you? *For they* knew that it was the Lord.

¹³ Then Jesus came and took bread and gave *it to* them, and fish likewise.

¹⁴ This is now the third time that Jesus showed Himself to His disciples after He was risen from the dead.

¹⁵ So when they had dined, Jesus said to Simon Peter: Simon *son* of Jonah, do you *truly* love me? More than these? *Peter* said to Him: Yes Lord. You know that I love you. *Jesus* said to him: Feed my lambs.

¹⁶ *Then* He said to *Peter* again the second time: Simon *son* of Jonah, *do* you *truly* love me? *Peter* said to Him: Yes Lord. You know that I love you. *Jesus* said to him: Feed my sheep.

¹⁷ *And* He said to *Peter* the third time: Simon *son* of Jonah, do you ⁺ love me? Peter was grieved because *Jesus had* said to him the third time: Do you⁺ love me? And he said to *Jesus*: Lord, you know all things. You know that I ⁺ love you. Jesus said to him: Feed my sheep.

¹⁸ Truly, ⁺ truly, I say to you: When you were young, you *seized* life⁺ *unto* yourself and walked wherever you wanted⁺ *to go*. But when you become⁺ old, you will stretch forth your hands and another will support⁺ you and carry *you* where you do not want⁺ *to go*.

¹⁹ *Jesus* spoke this *to* signify by what death *Peter* would glorify God. And when He had spoken this, He said to *Peter*: Follow me.

²⁰ Peter then turned around ⁺ *and* saw the disciple whom Jesus loved following. *This was the one* who leaned on *Jesus'* chest⁺ at supper and said: Lord, who is *the one* who betrays you?

²¹ *Upon* seeing *that disciple*, Peter said to Jesus: Lord and what *about* this man?

²² Jesus said to him: If I will that he stay⁺ until I come, what *is that* to you? You follow me.

²³ This word⁺ went among *all* the family⁺ *of believers*, that this disciple would not die. But⁺ Jesus did not say to him: He will not die. *Instead, He said*: If I will that he stay⁺ until I come, what *is that* to you?

²⁴ This *eyewitness* was the *same* disciple who *now* testifies⁺ of these things and *has* written⁺ these things. And we know that his testimony is true.

²⁵ There are also many other things that Jesus did, which, if every⁺ *detail* was written *down*, I suppose that even the world itself could not contain the books that would be written. Amen.

The Gospel of Jesus Christ as written by Matthew

Chapter 1

¹ *This* book *lists* the generations of Jesus Christ the son of David the son of Abraham: *Genesis 12:3*

² Abraham fathered⁺ Isaac. Isaac fathered Jacob. Jacob fathered Judah and his brothers. *Genesis 17:19 Numbers 24:17*

³ Judah fathered Perez and Zerah by Tamar. Perez fathered Hezron. Hezron fathered Ram.

⁴ Ram fathered Amminadab. Amminadab fathered Nahshon. Nahshon fathered Salmon.

⁵ Salmon fathered Boaz by Rahab. Boaz fathered Obed by Ruth. Obed fathered Jesse.

⁶ Jesse fathered David the king. David the king fathered Solomon by *the wife* of Uriah. *Isaiah 11:1*

⁷ Solomon fathered Rehoboam. Rehoboam fathered Abijah. Abijah fathered Asa.

⁸ Asa fathered Jehoshaphat. Jehoshaphat fathered Joram. Joram fathered Uzziah.

⁹ Uzziah fathered Jotham. Jotham fathered Ahaz. Ahaz fathered Hezekiah.

¹⁰ Hezekiah fathered Manasseh. Manasseh fathered Amon. Amon fathered Josiah.

¹¹ Josiah fathered Jeconiah and his brothers, about the time they were carried away to Babylon.

¹² After they were brought to Babylon, Jeconiah fathered Shealtiel. Shealtiel fathered Zerubbabel.

¹³ Zerubbabel fathered Abiud. Abiud fathered Eliakim. Eliakim fathered Azor.

¹⁴ Azor fathered Zadoc. Zadoc fathered Achim. Achim fathered Eliud.

¹⁵ Eliud fathered Eleazar. Eleazar fathered Matthan. Matthan fathered Jacob.

¹⁶ Jacob fathered Joseph the husband of Mary from whom Jesus who is called Christ was born.

¹⁷ So all the generations from Abraham to David *are* fourteen generations. From David until the carrying away into Babylon *are* fourteen generations. From the carrying away into Babylon to Christ *are* fourteen generations. *Isaiah 11:1*

¹⁸ Now the birth of Jesus Christ *came about* this way.⁺ When His mother Mary was espoused to Joseph, before they came together she was found with child by the Holy Spirit.⁺

¹⁹ Then Joseph her husband, being a righteous⁺ *man* and not willing to make her a public example, was of a mind⁺ to put her away privately.⁺

²⁰ But while he thought on these things, behold the angel of the Lord appeared to him in a dream saying: Joseph, son of David, do not fear to take Mary *as* your wife. For what is conceived in her is of the Holy Spirit.

²¹ She will bring forth a son and you shall call His name Jesus, for He will save His people from their sins.

²² Now all this was done to fulfill what was spoken of the Lord by the prophet *who* said:

²³ Behold a virgin shall be with child and shall bring forth a son and they shall call His name Emmanuel, which means⁺: God with us. *Isaiah 7:14*

²⁴ Then Joseph, being raised from sleep, did as the angel of the Lord had directed⁺ him and took *Mary to be* his wife.

²⁵ *However, he* did not know her *as his wife* until she had brought forth her firstborn son. And *they* called His name Jesus.

Matthew Chapter 2

¹ Now when Jesus was born in Bethlehem of Judea in the days of Herod the king, behold wise men came from the east to Jerusalem *Micah 5:2*

² saying: Where is He who is born King of the Jews? For we have seen His star in the east and have come to worship Him. *Psalm 72:10,11*

³ When Herod the king had heard *these things*, he was troubled, and all Jerusalem with him.

⁴ When he had gathered all the chief priests and scribes of the people together, he demanded of them where Christ would be born.

⁵ They said to him: In Bethlehem of Judea, for thus it is written by the prophet:

⁶ You Bethlehem *in* the land of Judah are not the least among the princes of Judah. For out of you will come a Governor who will rule my people Israel. *Micah 5:2*

⁷ Then Herod, when he had privately⁺ called the wise men, inquired of them diligently what time the star appeared.

⁸ He sent them to Bethlehem and said: Go and search diligently for the young child. When you have found *Him*, bring word to me *so* that I may come and worship Him also.

⁹ When they had heard the king, they departed. And behold, the star that they saw in the east went before them until it came and stood over where the young child was.

[10] When they saw the star, they rejoiced with exceedingly great joy.

[11] And when they came into the house, they saw the young child with Mary His mother and *they* fell down and worshiped Him. Then they opened their treasures *and* presented gifts to Him: gold and frankincense and myrrh.

[12] *Then* being warned by God in a dream that they should not return to Herod, they departed to their own country another way.

[13] After they left, behold the angel of the Lord appeared to Joseph in a dream saying: Arise and take the young child and His mother and flee into Egypt and stay there until I bring word to you. For Herod will seek the young child to destroy Him.

[14] Then he arose *and* took the young child and His mother by night and went to Egypt.

[15] *They stayed* there until the death of Herod, thus fulfilling what was spoken of the Lord by the prophet *who* said: Out of Egypt have I called my Son. *Hosea 11:1*

[16] Then Herod, when he saw that he was mocked by the wise men, was exceedingly angry[+] and sent forth and killed[+] all the *male* children in Bethlehem and in all the borders[+] thereof, from two years old and under, according to the time learned[+] from the wise men.

[17] This fulfilled what was spoken by the prophet Jeremiah *who* said:

[18] In Ramah there was a voice heard: lamentation, weeping, and great mourning. Rachel weeping *for* her children and *she* would not be comforted because they are no *more*. *Jeremiah 31:15*

[19] But when Herod was dead, behold an angel of the Lord appeared in a dream to Joseph in Egypt

[20] saying: Arise and take the young child and His mother and go into the land of Israel. For *those* who sought the young child's life are *now* dead.

[21] He arose and took the young child and His mother and came into the land of Israel.

[22] But when he heard that Archelaus reigned in Judea in the room of his father Herod, he was afraid to go there. Even

so,[+] being warned by God in a dream, he turned aside into a part of Galilee.

[23] He came and lived[+] in a city called Nazareth, thus fulfilling what was spoken by the prophets: He shall be called a Nazarene. *Judges 13:5*

Matthew Chapter 3

[1] In those days, John the Baptist came proclaiming[+] in the wilderness of Judea,
[2] saying:

Repent.
For the kingdom of heaven
is *very* near.[+]

---

[3] For this is *the one* who was spoken of by the prophet Isaiah *who* said: The voice of one crying in the wilderness: Prepare the way of the Lord. Make His paths straight. *Isaiah 40:3*

[4] This same John had his clothing[+] of camel's hair and a leather belt[+] around[+] his waist.[+] His food[+] was locusts and wild honey.

[5] Then went out to him Jerusalem and all Judea and all the region around[+] the Jordan.

[6] *They* were baptized by him in *the* Jordan, confessing their sins.

[7] But when he saw many of the Pharisees and Sadducees come to his baptism, he said to them: O generation of vipers, who has warned you to flee from the wrath to come?

[8] Bring forth therefore fruits worthy[+] of repentance.

[9] Do not think to say within yourselves: We have Abraham as *our* father. For I say to you: God is able from these stones to raise up children to Abraham.

[10] Now also the axe is laid to the root of the trees. Therefore, every tree that does not bring forth good fruit is *to be* cut[+] down and cast into the fire.

[11] I indeed baptize you with water for repentance, but He who is coming after me is mightier than I. I am not worthy to carry[+] *His* sandals.[+] He will baptize you with the Holy Spirit and *with* fire.

[12] *His* fan *is* in His hand and He will thoroughly purge His floor and gather His wheat into the barn. [+] But He will burn up the chaff with unquenchable fire.
[13] Then Jesus came from Galilee to Jordan to John, to be baptized by him.
[14] But John forbad Him saying: I need to be baptized by you, and you come to me?
[15] Jesus answering said to him: Allow *it to be so* now. For thus it becomes us to fulfill all righteousness. Then he allowed [+] Him.
[16] When He was baptized, Jesus came up immediately [+] out of the water and lo the heavens were opened to Him and He saw the Spirit of God descending like a dove and coming [+] upon Him. *Isaiah 11:2*
[17] And behold, a voice from heaven said: This is my beloved Son in whom I am well pleased. *Psalm 2:7*

Matthew Chapter 4

[1] Then Jesus was led up by the Spirit into the wilderness to be tempted by the devil.
[2] When He had fasted forty days and forty nights, afterward He was hungry.
[3] And then the tempter came to Him and said: If you are the Son of God, command that these stones be made bread.
[4] But *Jesus* answered and said:

> It is written:
> Mankind [+] shall not live
> by bread alone,
> but by every word that proceeds
> out of the mouth of God.
> *Deuteronomy 8:3*

[5] Then the devil took Him up to the holy city and sat Him on a pinnacle of the temple
[6] and said to Him: If you are the Son of God, cast yourself down. For it is written: He will give His angels charge over [+] you. In *their* hands they will bear you up lest at any time you dash your foot against a stone. *Psalm 91:11,12*

[7] Jesus said to him: Again it is written:

> You shall not tempt
> the Lord your God.
> *Deuteronomy 6:16*

[8] Again, the devil took Him up to an exceedingly high mountain and showed Him all the kingdoms of the world and the glory of them.
[9] And *he* said to Him: All these things will I give you if you will fall down and worship me.
[10] Then Jesus said to him: Get *away* from here Satan. For it is written:

> You shall worship
> the Lord your God
> and Him only shall you serve.
> *Exodus 34:14, Deuteronomy 10:20*

[11] Then the devil left Him and behold angels came and ministered to Him.
[12] Now when Jesus heard that John was cast into prison, He went to Galilee.
[13] Leaving Nazareth, He came and lived [+] in Capernaum on the sea coast in the borders of Zabulon and Nephthalim. *Isaiah 9:1*
[14] This fulfilled what the prophet Isaiah had said:
[15] The land of Zabulon and the land of Nephthalim *by* the way of the sea beyond Jordan, Galilee of the Gentiles. *Isaiah 9:1*
[16] The people who sat in darkness saw great light. To *those* who sat in the region and shadow of death, light is sprung up. *Isaiah 9:2*
[17] From that time *on* Jesus began to proclaim [+] *the Word* and to say:

> Repent. For the kingdom
> of heaven is *very* near [+].

[18] *Then* Jesus, walking by the sea of Galilee, saw two brothers, Simon called Peter and Andrew his brother casting a net into the sea, for they were fishermen. [+]
[19] He said to them: Follow me and I will make you fishers of men.

²⁰Immediately,⁺ they left *their* nets and followed Him.
²¹Going on from there,⁺ He saw another two brothers, James *the son of* Zebedee and John his brother, in a boat with Zebedee their father mending their nets. He called them
²²and immediately they left the boat and their father and followed Him.
²³*Then* Jesus went all around⁺ Galilee teaching in their synagogues, proclaiming⁺ the Gospel of the kingdom, and healing all kinds⁺ of sickness and all kinds⁺ of disease among the people.

Isaiah 35:5

²⁴His reputation⁺ went throughout all Syria. They brought to Him all *kinds of* sick people who were taken with many different⁺ diseases and torments and those *who were* demon⁺ possessed and *those* who were lunatics and *those* who had paralysis⁺ and He healed them. *Isaiah 35:5*
²⁵Great multitudes of people followed Him from Galilee and Decapolis and Jerusalem and Judea and *from* beyond Jordan.

Matthew Chapter 5

¹ Seeing the multitudes, *Jesus* went up into a mountain and when He sat *down* His disciples came to Him.
² And He opened His mouth and taught them saying:

³ Blessed *are* the poor in spirit, for theirs is the kingdom of heaven.
⁴ Blessed *are those* who mourn, for they shall be comforted.
⁵ Blessed *are* the meek, for they shall inherit the earth. *Psalm 37:11*
⁶ Blessed *are those* who do hunger and thirst after righteousness, for they shall be filled.
⁷ Blessed *are* the merciful, for they shall obtain mercy. *Proverbs 11:17*
⁸ Blessed *are* the pure in heart, for they shall see God.
⁹ Blessed *are* the peacemakers, for they shall be called the children of God.

¹⁰ Blessed *are those* who are persecuted for righteousness' sake, for theirs is the kingdom of heaven. *Isaiah 8:12*
¹¹ Blessed are you when *people* revile you and persecute *you* and say all kinds⁺ of evil against you falsely for my sake.
¹² Rejoice and be exceedingly glad. For great *is* your reward in heaven. For so *likewise did* they persecute the prophets who were before you. *2 Chronicles 36:16*

¹³You are the salt of the earth, but if salt has lost its savor, with what will it be salted? It is thereafter⁺ good for nothing but to be cast out and trampled⁺ under foot⁺.
¹⁴You are the light of the world. A city that is set on a hill cannot be hid.
¹⁵Nor do people⁺ light a candle and put it under a bushel, but on a candlestick *so that* it gives light to all who are in the house.

¹⁶ Let your light so shine before *people* that they may see your good works and glorify your Father in heaven.

¹⁷Do not think that I have come to destroy the law or the prophets. I have not come to destroy, but to fulfill.
¹⁸For truly⁺ I say to you: Until heaven and earth pass, one jot or one smallest mark⁺ shall in no way⁺ pass from the law until all is fulfilled.

¹⁹ Whoever therefore shall break one of these least commandments and shall teach people⁺ *to do* so shall be called the least in the kingdom of heaven. But whoever shall do *them* and teach *them*, the same shall be called great in the kingdom of heaven.

²⁰For I say to you: Unless⁺ your righteousness shall exceed *the righteousness* of the scribes and Pharisees, you shall in no case enter into the kingdom of heaven.

[21]You have heard that it was said of old[+]: You shall not kill and whoever shall kill shall be in danger of the judgment. *Exodus 20:13*

[22]But I say to you: Whoever is angry with *one of* the family[+] *of God* without a *just* cause shall be in danger of the judgment. Whoever says to *one of* the family[+]: Raca, *to offend,* shall be in danger of the council. But whoever says: You fool, shall be in danger of hell fire.

[23]Therefore if you bring your gift to the altar and there remember that *one of* your family[+] has anything[+] against you, [24]leave your gift there before the altar and go first*to* be reconciled to your family[+] and then come and offer your gift.

[25]Agree with your adversary quickly while you are on the way with them, lest at any time the adversary deliver you to the judge and the judge deliver you to the officer and you be cast into prison. *Proverbs 25:8* [26]Truly[+] I say to you: You shall by no means come out from there[+] until you have paid the *very* last[+] penny[+].

[27]You have heard that it was said of old[+]: You shall not commit adultery. *Exodus 20:14*

[28]But I say to you that whoever looks upon a woman to lust after her has committed adultery with her already in his heart. *Proverbs 6:25*

[29]If your right eye causes[+] you *to sin,* pluck it out and cast *it* from you. For it is *more* profitable for you that one of your members should perish and not *that* your whole body should be cast into hell.

[30]If your right hand causes[+] you *to sin,* cut it off and cast *it* from you. For it is *more* profitable for you that one of your members should perish and not *that* your whole body should be cast into hell.

[31]It has been said: Whoever shall put away his wife, let him give her a written divorce[+]. *Deuteronomy 24:1*

[32]But I say to you that whoever shall put away his wife, except[+] for the cause of fornication, causes them[+] to commit adultery. And whoever shall marry *one who is thus* divorced commits adultery. *Deuteronomy 24:1*

[33]Again, you have heard that it was said of old[+]: You shall not perjure[+] yourself but shall perform your oaths to the Lord. *Numbers 30:2*

[34]But I say to you: Do not swear *oaths* at all. Not by heaven for it is God's throne [35]nor by the earth for it is His footstool. And not by Jerusalem for it is the city of the great King.

[36]Nor shall you swear by your head, because you cannot make one hair black or white. [37]But let your communication be *simply* yes *for* yes *and* no *for* no. For whatever is more than these comes of evil.

[38]You have heard that it has been said: An eye for an eye and a tooth for a tooth. *Exodus 21:24*

[39]But I say to you: Do not stand against[+] evil *with force,* but whoever shall strike[+] you on your right cheek, turn to them the other also. *Proverbs 24:29*

[40]If anyone will sue you at the law and take away your coat, let them have *your* vest[+] also.

[41]Whoever shall compel you to go a mile, go with them two.

[42]Give to *those* who ask you and from *those* who would borrow from you do not turn away. *Proverbs 19:17*

[43]You have heard that it has been said: You shall love your neighbor and hate your enemy. *Leviticus 19:18*

[44]But I say to you:

> Love your enemies.
> Bless *those* who curse you.
> Do good to *those* who hate you.
> And pray for *those*
> who despitefully use you
> and persecute you
>
> *Proverbs 16:7*

[45]*so* that you may be the children of your Father in heaven. For He makes His sun to rise on the evil and on the good and *He* sends rain on the righteous[+] and on the unrighteous[+].

[46]For if you love *those* who love you, what reward will you have? Do not even worldly[+] people the same?

47 And if you greet+ your family+ only, what do you *do* more*than others*? Do not even worldly+ people so?

48 Therefore be perfect even as your Father in heaven is perfect. *Leviticus 19:2*

Matthew Chapter 6

1 Take heed that you do not give your alms before people+ to be seen by them. Otherwise you *will* have no reward from your Father in heaven.

2 Therefore when you give+ alms, do not sound a trumpet before you as the hypocrites do in the synagogues and in the streets *so* that they may have glory from people.+ Truly+ I say to you: They have their reward.

3 But when you give+ alms, do not let your left hand know what your right hand does

4 *so* that your alms may be in secret and your Father who sees in secret will reward you openly.

> 5 When you pray,
> do not be
> as the hypocrites *are*.

For they love to pray standing in the synagogues and on the corners of the streets *so* that they may be seen by people.+ Truly+ I say to you: They have their reward.

6 But when you pray, enter into your closet and when you have shut your door, pray to your Father in secret and your Father who sees in secret will reward you openly. *Isaiah 26:20*

> 7 When you pray,
> do not use vain repetitions
> as the heathen *do*.

For they think that they will be heard for their much speaking.

8 Therefore do not be like them, for

> your Father knows
> what things you need
> before you ask Him.

9 Therefore pray in this manner:
Our Father in heaven,
Holy+ is your name.
10 Your kingdom come.
Your will be done,
on earth as *it is* in heaven.

11 Give us this day
our daily bread.

12 And forgive us *for* our debts
in which we have done wrong to others
as we forgive our debtors,
those we feel have done wrong to us.

13 Lead us, *so that we will*
not *yield* to temptation,
but deliver us from evil.
For the kingdom is yours,
and the power and the glory,
forever. Amen.

> 14 For if you forgive others
> *for* their trespasses
> *then* your heavenly Father
> will also forgive you.
> 15 But if you do not forgive others
> *for* their trespasses
> *then* neither will your Father
> forgive your trespasses.

16 Moreover when you fast, do not be like the hypocrites of a sad countenance. For they disfigure their faces *so* that they will appear to people+ to fast. Truly+ I say to you: They have their reward.

17 But you, when you fast, anoint your head and wash your face

18 *so* that you do not appear to people+ to fast but*only* to your Father in secret, and your Father who sees in secret will reward you openly.

> 19 Do not lay up for yourselves
> treasures on earth
> where moth and rust corrupt
> and where thieves
> break through and steal.

²⁰ Lay up for yourselves
treasures in heaven
where neither moth nor rust
corrupt and where thieves
do not break through or steal.
²¹ For where your treasure is,
there will your heart be also.

Proverbs 23:7

²²The light of the body is the eye. Therefore if your eye is single *then* your whole body will be full of light.
²³But if your eye is evil, your whole body will be full of darkness. Therefore if the light that is in you is darkness, how great *is* that darkness.

²⁴ No one can serve two masters.
For either they will hate the one
and love the other,
or else they will hold to the one
and despise the other.
You cannot serve
God and *worldly* treasures⁺.

²⁵Therefore I say to you: Take no thought for your life, what you will eat or what you will drink. Nor for your body, what you will put on. Is not life more than food⁺ and the body *more* than clothing⁺?
²⁶Behold the birds⁺ of the air, for they do not sow nor do they reap or gather into barns. Yet your heavenly Father feeds them. Are you not much better than they?
²⁷Who among⁺ you by taking thought can add one cubit to your stature?
²⁸Why do you take thought for clothing⁺? Consider the lilies of the field, how they grow. They do not toil nor do they spin.
²⁹Yet I say to you that even Solomon in all his glory was not arrayed like one of these.
³⁰Therefore if God so clothes the grass of the field, which is *here* today and tomorrow is cast into the oven, *will He* not much more *clothe* you, O you of little faith?

³¹Therefore take no thought saying: What shall we eat? Or what shall we drink? Or how will we be clothed?
³²For after all these things do the Gentiles seek. But your heavenly Father knows that you have need of all these things.

³³ But seek first
the kingdom of God
and His righteousness
and all these things
will be added to you.

³⁴Therefore take no thought for tomorrow, for tomorrow will take thought for the things of itself. Sufficient to the day *is* the evil thereof.

Matthew Chapter 7

¹ Do not judge *so* that
you *will* not be judged.

² For with what judgment you judge, you will be judged. With what gauge⁺ you measure, it will be measured to you again.
³ Why do you notice⁺ the speck⁺ that is in your brother's *or sister's* eye, but do not consider the beam that is in your own eye?
⁴ How can⁺ you say to your brother *or sister*: Let me pull out the speck⁺ from your eye when behold a beam *is* in your own eye?
⁵ You hypocrite. First cast out the beam from your own eye. Then you will see clearly to cast the speck⁺ from your brother's *or sister's*, eye.
⁶ Do not give what is holy to the dogs or cast your pearls before swine lest they trample them under their feet and turn again and tear⁺ you.

⁷ Ask and it will be
given *to* you.
Seek and you will find.
Knock and it will be
opened to you.

8 For everyone who asks receives and *those* who seek *will* find and to *those* who knock it will be opened.

9 Or who is there among you, if *your* son asks *for* bread will give him a stone?

10 Or if he asks *for* a fish will give him a serpent?

11 If you then being wicked+ know how to give good gifts to your children, how much more will your Father in heaven give good things to *those* who ask Him?

- - - *The Golden Rule* - - -
12 Therefore all things whatsoever
you would that others
should do to you,
you do to them.
For this is *the sum*
of the law and the prophets.

13 Enter in at the strait gate, for wide *is* the gate and broad *is* the way that leads to destruction and there are many who go in that way+

14 Because strait *is* the gate and narrow *is* the way that leads to life and there are few who find it.

15 Beware of false prophets
who come to you in sheep's
clothing, but inwardly
they are greedy+ wolves.

16 You will know them by their fruits. Do people+ gather grapes from thorns or figs from thistles? *Proverbs 20:11*

17 Even so, every good tree brings forth good fruit but a corrupt tree brings forth evil fruit.

18 A good tree cannot bring forth evil fruit nor *can* a corrupt tree bring forth good fruit.

19 Every tree that does not bring forth good fruit is cut+ down and cast into the fire.

20 Therefore by their fruits you will know them.

21 Not everyone who says to me: Lord, Lord, will enter into the kingdom of heaven, but *only those* who do the will of my Father in heaven.

22 Many will say to me in that day: Lord, Lord, have we not prophesied in your name? And in your name cast out demons+? And in your name done many wonderful works?

23 Then I will profess to them: I never knew you. Depart from me, you who work iniquity. *Psalm 6:8*

24 Therefore whoever hears these sayings of mine and does them I will compare+ to a wise man who built his house upon a rock.

25 The rain descended and the floods came and the winds blew and beat upon that house, but it did not fall for it was founded upon a rock.

26 Everyone who hears these sayings of mine and does not do them shall be compared+ to a foolish man who built his house on the sand.

27 The rain descended and the floods came and the winds blew and beat upon that house and it fell. And great was the fall of it.

28 *Then* it came to pass, when Jesus had ended these sayings, the people were astonished at His doctrine.

29 For He taught them as *one* having authority and not as the scribes.

Matthew Chapter 8

1 When He had come down from the mountain, great multitudes followed Him.

2 And behold a leper came worshiping Him saying: Lord, if you will, you can make me clean.

3 Jesus put forth *his* hand and touched him saying: I will. Be clean. And immediately his leprosy was cleansed.

4 Jesus said to him: See *that* you tell no one, but go+ *and* show yourself to the priest and offer the gift that Moses commanded as a testimony to them. *Leviticus 14:2*

5 When Jesus entered Capernaum, a centurion came to Him beseeching Him

6 and saying: Lord, my servant lies at home sick with paralysis+ *and* grievously tormented.

7 Jesus said to him: I will come and heal him.

8 The centurion answered and said: Lord, I am not worthy that you should come under my roof, but speak the word only and my servant will be healed.

9 For I am a man under authority having soldiers under me *and* I say to this *man*: Go and he goes, and to another: Come and he comes, and to my servant: Do this and he does *it*.

10 When Jesus heard *this*, He marveled and said to *those* who followed: Truly+ I say to you: I have not found so great *a* faith, no, not in Israel.

11 I say to you that many will come from the east and west and will sit down with Abraham and Isaac and Jacob in the kingdom of heaven,

12 but the children of the kingdom will be cast out into *the* outer darkness *and* there will be weeping and gnashing of teeth.

13 *Then* Jesus said to the centurion: Go.

As you have believed,
so be it done to you.

And his servant was healed in the same hour.

14 When Jesus came to Peter's house, He saw *Peter's* wife's mother laying *down* and sick with a fever.

15 *Jesus* touched her hand and the fever left her and she arose and ministered to them.

16 When the evening+ had come, they brought to Him many *who were* demon+ possessed and He cast out the spirits with *His* word and healed all who were sick.

17 This fulfilled what the prophet Isaiah had said: He took our infirmities and bore *our* sicknesses. *Isaiah 53:4*

18 Now when Jesus saw great multitudes around+ Him, He gave instructions+ to depart to the other side.

19 *Then* a certain scribe came and said to Him: Master, I will follow you wherever you go.

20 Jesus said to him: The foxes have holes and the birds of the air *have* nests, but the Son of man does not have anywhere to lay *His* head.

21 *Then* another of His disciples said to Him: Lord, allow+ me first to go and bury my father.

22 Jesus said to him:

Follow me.

Let the dead bury their dead.

23 *Then* when He entered a boat, His disciples followed Him

24 and behold a great storm+ arose in the sea so that the boat was covered by the waves. But *Jesus* was asleep.

25 His disciples came to *Him* and awoke Him saying: Lord, save us *or* we *will* perish.

26 He said to them: Why are you fearful, O you of little faith? Then He arose and rebuked the winds and the sea and there came a great calm.

27 But the men marveled saying: What kind+ of man is this that even the winds and the sea obey Him.

28 *Then* when He came to the other side, to the country of the Gergesenes, there met Him two *who were* demon+ possessed coming out of the tombs exceedingly fierce so that no one might pass by that way.

29 And behold they cried out saying: What do we have to do with you Jesus, you Son of God? Have you come here to torment us before the time?

30 *Now* there was, a good way off from them, a herd of many swine feeding,

31 so the demons+ begged+ Him saying: If you cast us out, allow+ us to go into the herd of swine.

32 *Jesus* said to them: Go. And when they came out, they went into the herd of swine and behold the whole herd of swine ran violently down a steep place into the sea and perished in the waters.

33 *Those* who kept them fled and went into the city and told everything, and what had befallen the *one who was* demon+ possessed.

34 And behold the whole city came out to meet Jesus. When they saw Him, they begged+ *Him* to depart out of their borders.+

Matthew Chapter 9

¹ *Then* He entered a boat and crossed⁺ over *the sea* and came to His own city.
² And behold they brought to Him a man sick with paralysis⁺ lying on a bed. Seeing their faith, Jesus said to the *one* sick with paralysis⁺: Son, be of good cheer. Your sins are forgiven.
³ And behold some of the scribes said within themselves: This *man* blasphemes.
⁴ Knowing their thoughts, Jesus said: Why do you think evil in your hearts?
⁵ For which⁺ is easier to say: *Your* sins are forgiven. Or to say: Arise and walk.
⁶ But *this is done so* that you may know that the Son of man has authority⁺ *and power* on earth to forgive sins. Then He said to the *one* sick with paralysis⁺: Arise, take up your bed and go to your house.
⁷ And he arose and departed to his house.
⁸ When the multitude saw *this*, they marveled and glorified God who had given such authority⁺ *and power* to men.
⁹ As Jesus passed forth from there, ⁺ He saw a man named Matthew sitting at the tax office⁺ and He said to him: Follow me. And he arose and followed Him.
¹⁰ And it came to pass, as Jesus sat *down* to eat⁺ in the house, behold many worldly⁺ people and sinners came and sat down with Him and His disciples.
¹¹ When the Pharisees saw *this*, they said to His disciples: Why does your Master eat with worldly⁺ people and sinners?
¹² But when Jesus heard *that*, He said to them: *Those* who are whole do not need a physician, but *those* who are sick *do*.

¹³ Go and learn what *this* means:
I will have mercy
and not sacrifice.
For I have not come
to call the righteous
but sinners to repentance.
Hosea 6:6

¹⁴ Then the disciples of John came to Him saying: Why do we and the Pharisees fast often, but your disciples do not fast?
¹⁵ Jesus said to them: Can the children of the bride chamber mourn as long as the bridegroom is with them? But the days will come when the Bridegroom will be taken from them and then they will fast.
¹⁶ No one puts a piece of new cloth onto an old garment, for what is put in to fill it up takes from the garment and the tear⁺ is made worse.
¹⁷ Nor do people⁺ put new wine into old wineskins⁺ *or* else the wineskins⁺ break and the wine runs out and the wineskins⁺ perish. But they put new wine into new wineskins⁺ and both are preserved.
¹⁸ While He spoke these things to them, behold there came a certain ruler and worshiped Him saying: My daughter is even now dead, but come and lay your hand upon her and she will live.
¹⁹ Jesus arose and followed him and *so did* His disciples.
²⁰ And behold a woman who was diseased with an issue of blood *for* twelve years came behind *Him* and touched the hem of His garment.
²¹ For she said within herself: If I may but touch His garment, I will be whole.
²² But Jesus turned around⁺ and when He saw her He said: Daughter, be of good comfort. Your faith has made you whole. And the woman was made whole from that hour.
²³ When Jesus came into the ruler's house and saw the minstrels and the people making a noise,
²⁴ He said to them: Withdraw. ⁺ For the maid is not dead but *is* sleeping. And they laughed *at* Him *scornfully*.
²⁵ But when the people were sent out, ⁺ *Jesus* went in and took her by the hand and the maid arose.
²⁶ The report⁺ of this⁺ went throughout⁺ all that land.
²⁷ When Jesus departed from there, ⁺ two blind men followed Him, crying and saying: Son of David, have mercy on us.

28When He had come into the house, the blind men came to Him and Jesus said to them: Do you believe that I am able to do this? They said to Him: Yes Lord.

29Then He touched their eyes saying: According to your faith be it to you.

30Their eyes were opened *but* Jesus strictly+ charged them saying: See *that* no one knows *about this*.

31But when they went away,+ they spread His reputation+ widely+ *throughout* all that country.

32As they went out, behold they brought to Him a speechless+ demon+ possessed man.

33When the demon+ was cast out, the speechless+ *man* spoke and the multitudes marveled saying: It was never so seen in Israel *before*.

34But the Pharisees said: He casts out demons+ through the prince of the demons.+

35Jesus went to all the cities and villages, teaching in their synagogues, proclaiming+ the Gospel of the kingdom, and healing every sickness and every disease among the people.

36But when He saw the multitudes, He was moved with compassion on them because they fainted and were scattered widely+ like sheep having no shepherd.

37Then He said to His disciples: The harvest truly *is* plentiful, but the laborers *are* few.

38Pray therefore *to* the Lord of the harvest, *so* that He will send forth laborers into His harvest.

Matthew Chapter 10

1 When He had called His twelve disciples, He gave them authority+ *and power against* unclean spirits, to cast them out, and to heal all kinds+ of sickness and all kinds+ of disease.

2 Now the names of the twelve apostles are these: The first, Simon who is called Peter and Andrew his brother, James *the son* of Zebedee and John his brother,

3 Philip and Bartholomew, Thomas and Matthew the worldly+ person, James

the son of Alphaeus, and Lebbaeus whose surname was Thaddaeus,

4 Simon the Canaanite and Judas Iscariot who also betrayed Him.

5 These twelve Jesus sent forth and instructed+ them saying: Do not go into the way of the Gentiles and do not enter into *any* city of the Samaritans,

6 but go instead to the lost sheep of the house of Israel.

> 7 As you go,
> proclaim+ *the Word*, saying:
> The kingdom of heaven
> is *very* near+.
> 8 Heal the sick. Cleanse the
> lepers. Raise the dead.
> Cast out demons.+
> Freely you have received,
> freely give.

9 Provide neither gold nor silver nor brass in your purses,

10nor *a provision* bag+ for *your* journey nor two coats nor sandals+ nor staves. For the worker+ is worthy of his food+.

11Into whatever city or town you enter, inquire who in it is worthy and stay+ there until you go *on* from there+.

12When you come into a house, greet+ it.

13If the house is worthy let your peace come upon it, but if it is not worthy let your peace return to you. *1 Samuel 25:6*

14Whoever will not receive you or hear your words, when you depart out of that house or city, shake off the dust from your feet.

15Truly+ I say to you: It will be more tolerable for the land of Sodom and Gomorrah in the day of judgment than for that city.

16Behold I send you forth like sheep in the midst of wolves. Therefore be *as* wise as serpents and *as* harmless as doves.

17But beware of people,+ for they will deliver you up to the councils and they will flog+ you in their synagogues.

18You will be brought before governors and kings for my sake for a testimony against them and the Gentiles.

¹⁹When they deliver you up, take no thought how or what you shall speak, for it will be given *to* you in that same hour what you shall speak. *Proverbs 16:1*

²⁰For it is not you who *will be* speaking but the Spirit of your Father who speaks in you.

²¹Brother will deliver up brother to death and the father *his* child. Children will rise up against parents and cause them to be put to death. *Micah 7:6*

²²You will be hated by all for my name's sake, but *those* who endure to the end will be saved.

²³But when they persecute you in this city, flee to another. For truly⁺ I say to you: You will not have gone to *all* the cities of Israel until the Son of man has come.

²⁴The disciple is not above *his* master nor the servant above his lord.

²⁵It is enough for the disciple that he be like his master and the servant like his lord. If they have called the master of the house Beelzebub, how much more *will they call* those of his household?

²⁶Therefore do not be afraid of them, for

> there is nothing covered
> that will not be revealed
> and *nothing* hid
> that will not be known.

²⁷What I tell you in darkness, speak in light. What you hear in the ear, proclaim⁺ from the housetops.

²⁸Do not fear *those* who kill the body but are not able to kill the soul. Instead,⁺ fear *Him who* is able to destroy both soul and body in hell.

²⁹Are not two sparrows sold for a penny⁺? And not one of them will fall to the ground without your Father *knowing it*.

³⁰The very hairs of your head are all numbered.

³¹Therefore, do not be afraid. You are of more value than many sparrows.

³²Whoever therefore will confess me before people,⁺ I will confess also before my Father in heaven.

³³But whoever will deny me before people,⁺ I will also deny before my Father in heaven.

³⁴Do not think that I have come to send peace on earth. I did not come to send peace, but a sword.

³⁵For I have come to set a man at contention⁺ against his father and the daughter against her mother and the daughter in law against her mother in law. *Micah 7:6*

³⁶A man's foes *will be* those of his own household.

³⁷*Those* who love father or mother more than me are not worthy of me. *Those* who love son or daughter more than me are not worthy of me.

³⁸*Those* who do not take *up* their cross and follow after me are not worthy of me.

³⁹*Those* who find their life will lose it. *Those* who lose their life for my sake will find it.

⁴⁰*Those* who receive you receive me and *those* who receive me receive Him who sent me.

⁴¹*Those* who receive a prophet in the name of a prophet will receive a prophet's reward. *Those* who receive a righteous man in the name of a righteous man will receive a righteous man's reward.

⁴²Whoever will give a drink to one of these little ones, *even* a cup of cold *water* only in the name of a disciple, truly⁺ I say to you: They shall in no way⁺ lose their reward.

Matthew Chapter 11

¹ Now⁺ it came to pass, when Jesus had made an end of commanding His twelve disciples, He departed from there⁺ to teach and to proclaim⁺ *the Word* in their cities.

² When John, in prison, heard *about* the works of Christ, he sent two of his disciples

³ and said to Him: Are you the *one who was to* come or should⁺ we look for another?

⁴ Jesus answered and said to them: Go and show John again those things that you hear and see.

[5] The blind receive their sight, the lame walk, the lepers are cleansed, the deaf hear, the dead are raised up, and the poor have the Gospel proclaimed+ to them. *Isaiah 35:5*

[6] Blessed are *those* who will not be offended *and disbelieve* in me.

[7] As they departed, Jesus began to say to the multitudes, concerning John: What did you go out into the wilderness to see? A reed shaken with the wind?

[8] But what did you go out to see? A man clothed in soft clothing+? Behold *those* who wear soft *clothing* are in kings' houses.

[9] But what did you go out to see? A prophet? Yes, I say to you, and more than a prophet.

[10] For this is *he* of whom it is written: Behold I send my messenger before your face who will prepare your way before you. *Malachi 3:1*

[11] Truly+ I say to you: Among *those* who are born of women, there has not risen *one* greater than John the Baptist. Even so+ *those* who are least in the kingdom of heaven are greater than he.

[12] From the days of John the Baptist until now the kingdom of heaven suffers violence and the violent take it by force,

[13] for all the prophets and the law prophesied until John.

[14] If you will receive *it*, this is Elijah who was to come.

[15] *Those* who have ears to hear, let them hear.

[16] But to what shall I compare+ this generation? It is like children sitting in the market *places* and calling to their fellows

[17] and saying: We have piped to you and you have not danced. We have mourned to you and you have not grieved+.

[18] For John came neither eating nor drinking and they say: He has a demon+.

[19] The Son of man came eating and drinking and they say: Behold a gluttonous man and a wine drinker,+ a friend of worldly+ people and sinners. But wisdom is justified by her children.

[20] Then He began to upbraid the cities in which most of His mighty works were done because they did not repent.

[21] Woe to you, Chorazin. Woe to you, Bethsaida. For if the mighty works that were done in you had been done in Tyre and Sidon, they would have repented long ago in sackcloth and ashes.

[22] But I say to you: It will be more tolerable for Tyre and Sidon at the day of judgment than for you.

[23] You Capernaum, *being* exalted to heaven, will be brought down to hell. For if the mighty works that have been done in you had been done in Sodom, it would have remained until this day.

[24] But I say to you that it shall be more tolerable for the land of Sodom in the day of judgment than for you.

[25] *Then* at that time, Jesus answered and said: I thank you O Father, Lord of heaven and earth, because You have hid these things from the wise and prudent and have revealed them to babes.

[26] Even so Father, for so it seemed good in your sight.

[27] All things are delivered to me by my Father. No one knows the Son but the Father. Nor does anyone know the Father except+ the Son and *those* to whom the Son will reveal *Him*.

---

[28] Come to me
all *you* who labor
and are heavily burdened+
and I will give you rest.
Jeremiah 31:25

---

[29] Take my yoke upon you and learn from me. For I am meek and lowly in heart, and you will find rest for your souls. *Jeremiah 6:16*

[30] For my yoke *is* easy and my burden is light.

Matthew Chapter 12

[1] At that time, Jesus went through a corn *field* on the Sabbath day. His disciples were hungry and began to pluck the ears of corn and eat.

2 When the Pharisees saw *this*, they said to Him: Behold your disciples do what is not lawful to do on the Sabbath day.

3 But *Jesus* said to them: Have you not read what David did when he was hungry, and *those* who were with him?

4 How he entered the house of God and ate the show bread that was not lawful for him to eat, nor for *those* who were with him, but only for the priests?

5 Or have you not read in the law that on the Sabbath days the priests in the temple profane the Sabbath and are blameless?

6 But I say to you: In this place is *one* greater than the temple.

7 But if you had known what *this* means: I will have mercy and not sacrifice, you would not have condemned the innocent+. *Hosea 6:6*

8 For the Son of man is Lord even of the Sabbath day.

9 When He departed from there,+ He went into their synagogue.

10 And behold there was a man who had *a* withered hand and they asked Him saying: Is it lawful to heal on the Sabbath days? *They did this so* that they might accuse Him.

11 *Jesus* said to them: What man shall there be among you who shall have one sheep and, if it fall into a pit on the Sabbath day, will he not lay hold on it and lift *it* out?

12 *And* how much then is a man better than a sheep? Therefore it is lawful to do good+ on the Sabbath days.

13 Then He said to the man: Stretch forth your hand. And he stretched *it* forth and it was restored whole like the other.

14 Then the Pharisees went out and held a council against Him, *to decide* how they might destroy Him.

15 But when Jesus knew *this*, He withdrew from there.+ Great multitudes followed Him and He healed them all.

16 And *He* charged them to not make Him known.

17 This fulfilled what the prophet Isaiah had said:

18 Behold my servant whom I have chosen, my beloved in whom my soul is well pleased. I will put my spirit upon Him and He will show judgment to the Gentiles. *Isaiah 42:1*

19 He will not strive or cry. Nor will anyone hear His voice in the streets. *Isaiah 42:2*

20 A bruised reed He will not break and smoking flax He will not quench until He sends forth judgment to victory. *Isaiah 42:3*

21 In His name will the Gentiles trust. *Isaiah 42:4*

22 Then one *who was* demon+ possessed was brought to Him, blind and speechless.+ *Jesus* healed him so that the blind and speechless+ *one* both spoke and saw.

23 All the people were amazed and said: Is this not the son of David?

24 But when the Pharisees heard *this* they said: This *fellow* does not cast out demons+ except+ by Beelzebub the prince of the demons.+

25 Jesus knew their thoughts and said to them:

Every kingdom
divided against itself
is brought to desolation.
Every city or house divided
against itself will not stand.
Proverbs 11:29

---

26 If Satan casts out Satan, he is divided against himself. How then will his kingdom stand?

27 And if I cast out demons+ by Beelzebub, *then* by whom do your children cast *them* out? Therefore they shall be your judges.

28 But if I cast out demons+ by the Spirit of God, then the kingdom of God has come to you.

29 Or else how can one enter into a strong man's house and spoil his goods, unless+ he first bind the strong man, and then he will spoil his house.

---

30 *Those* who are not with me
are against me. *Those* who
do not gather with me scatter.

³¹Therefore I say to you: All kinds⁺ of sin and blasphemy will be forgiven to people,⁺ but blasphemy *against* the *Holy* Spirit will not be forgiven to people⁺.
³²Whoever speaks a word against the Son of man, it will be forgiven them. But whoever speaks against the Holy Spirit, it will not be forgiven them. Not in this world or in the *world* to come.
³³Either make the tree good and its fruit good, or else make the tree corrupt and its fruit corrupt. For the tree is known by *its* fruit.
³⁴O generation of vipers, how can you, being evil, speak good things?

> For out of the abundance
> of the heart the mouth speaks.
> ³⁵ A good person⁺
> out of the good treasure
> of the heart
> brings forth good things.
> An evil person⁺
> out of evil treasure
> brings forth evil things.
> *Psalm 19:14, Proverbs 10:11*
>
> ³⁶ But I say to you
> that *for* every idle word
> that people⁺ speak,
> they will give *an* account of it
> on the day of judgment.
> ³⁷ For by your words
> you will be justified
> and by your words
> you will be condemned.

³⁸Then some of the scribes and of the Pharisees answered saying: Master, we would *like to* see a sign from you.
³⁹But He answered and said to them: An evil and adulterous generation seeks after a sign. There shall no sign be given to it but the sign of the prophet Jonah.
⁴⁰For as Jonah was three days and three nights in the belly of the whale, so will the Son of man be three days and three nights in the heart of the earth. *Jonah 1:17*
⁴¹The men of Nineveh will rise in judgment with this generation and will condemn it because they repented at the proclaiming⁺ of Jonah. And behold *one* greater than Jonah *is* here. *Jonah 3:5*
⁴²The queen of the south will rise up in the judgment with this generation and will condemn it. For she came from the ends⁺ of the earth to hear the wisdom of Solomon, and behold *one* greater than Solomon *is* here. *1 Kings 10:1*
⁴³When the unclean spirit is gone out of someone, he walks through dry places seeking rest and finds none.
⁴⁴So he says: I will return to my house from which I came out, and when he comes, he finds *it* empty, swept, and put in order⁺.
⁴⁵Then he goes and takes with him seven other spirits more wicked than himself and they *all* enter in and dwell there. *So* the last *state* of that person⁺ is worse than the first. Even so shall it be also to this wicked generation.
⁴⁶While He yet talked to the people, behold *His* mother and His brothers stood outside⁺ desiring to speak with Him.
⁴⁷Then one said to Him: Behold your mother and your brothers stand outside⁺ desiring to speak with you.
⁴⁸But He answered and said to the one who spoke⁺ *to* Him: Who is my mother? And who are my brothers?
⁴⁹*Then* He stretched forth His hand toward His disciples and said: Behold my mother and my brothers.

> ⁵⁰ For whoever does the will
> of my Father in heaven,
> the same is my brother
> and sister and mother.

Matthew Chapter 13

¹ The same day Jesus went out of the house and sat by the seaside.
² Great multitudes were gathered together to Him so that He went into a boat and sat, and the whole multitude stood on the shore.
³ He spoke many things to them in parables saying: Behold a sower went forth to sow.

4 When he sowed, some fell by the wayside and the birds+ came and devoured them up.

5 Some fell on stony places where they did not have much earth. Immediately+ they sprang up because they had no depth of earth,

6 and when the sun was up, they were scorched, and because they had no root, they withered away.

7 Some fell among thorns and the thorns sprang up and choked them.

8 But other *seed* fell into good ground and brought forth fruit: some a hundredfold, some sixtyfold, *and* some thirtyfold.

9 Who has ears to hear, let them hear.

10 *Then* the disciples came and said to Him: Why do you speak to them in parables?

11 *Jesus* answered and said to them: Because it is given to you to know the mysteries of the kingdom of heaven, but to them it is not given.

12 For whoever has, to them will *more* be given and they will have more abundance. But whoever has nothing, from them will be taken away even what they have. *Proverbs 9:9*

13 Therefore I speak to them in parables, because seeing they do not see and hearing they do not hear, nor do they understand. *Jeremiah 5:21*

14 In them, the prophecy of Isaiah is fulfilled that says: By hearing you will hear and not understand. Seeing you will see and not perceive. *Isaiah 6:9*

15 For the hearts of these people are calloused.+ *Their* ears are dull of hearing and they have closed their eyes, lest at any time they should see with *their* eyes and hear with *their* ears and should understand with *their* hearts and should be converted, and I should heal them. *Isaiah 6:10*

16 But blessed *are* your eyes for they see and your ears for they hear.

17 For truly+ I say to you that many prophets and righteous *people* have desired to see what you see but have not seen *it* and to hear what you hear but have not heard *it*.

18 Hear therefore the parable of the sower:

19 When anyone hears the Word of the kingdom and does not understand *it*, then the wicked *one* comes and catches away what was sown in their heart. This is the one who received seed by the wayside.

20 But the one who received the seed into stony places, the same is *like those* who hear the Word and immediately+ receive it with joy.

21 Yet they have no root in themselves *and therefore they* endure *only* for a while. For when tribulation or persecution arises because of the Word, immediately+ they are offended *and disbelieve*

22 And the one who received seed among the thorns is *like those* who hear the Word but the cares of this world and the deceitfulness of riches choke the Word and they become unfruitful.

23 But the one who received seed into the good ground is *like those* who hear the Word and understand *it* and who also bear fruit and bring forth, some a hundredfold, some sixty, *and* some thirty.

24 *Then* another parable He put forth to them saying: The kingdom of heaven is compared+ to a man who sowed good seed in his field.

25 But while people+ slept, his enemy came and sowed tares among the wheat and went away+.

26 But when the blade was sprung up and brought forth fruit, then the tares appeared also.

27 So the servants of the property owner+ came and said to him: Sir, did you not sow good seed in your field? From where then does it have tares?

28 He said to them: An enemy has done this. The servants said to him: Do you want+ us to go and gather them up?

29 But he said: No, lest while you gather up the tares you also root up the wheat with them.

30 Let both grow together until the harvest. In the time of harvest I will say to the reapers: Gather together first the tares and bind them in bundles to burn them, but gather the wheat into my barn.

³¹Another parable He put forth to them saying: The kingdom of heaven is like a grain of mustard seed that a man sowed in his field.

³²Indeed *it* is the least of all seeds, but when it is grown, it is the greatest among herbs and becomes a tree so that the birds of the air come and lodge in its branches. *Psalm 104:12*

³³*Then* He spoke another parable to them: The kingdom of heaven is like leaven that a woman hid in three measures of meal until the whole was permeated⁺.

³⁴All these things Jesus spoke to the multitude in parables and without a parable He did not speak to them.

³⁵This fulfilled what the prophet had said: I will open my mouth in parables. I will utter things that have been kept secret from the foundation of the world. *Psalm 78:2*

³⁶Then Jesus sent the multitude away and went into the house, and His disciples came to Him saying: Declare to us the parable of the tares of the field. ³⁷He answered and said to them: He who sows the good seed is the Son of man.

³⁸The field is the world and the good seed are the children of the kingdom. But the tares are the children of the wicked *one*.

³⁹The enemy that sowed them is the devil. The harvest is the end of the world and the reapers are the angels.

⁴⁰Therefore as the tares are gathered and burned in the fire, so shall it be in the end of this world.

⁴¹The Son of man will send forth His angels and they will gather out of His kingdom all things that offend *and cause people to sin* and *all those* who do iniquity *Zephaniah 1:3*

⁴²and cast them into a furnace of fire and there will be wailing and gnashing of teeth.

⁴³Then the righteous will shine forth as the sun in the kingdom of their Father. Who has ears to hear, let them hear. *Daniel 12:3*

⁴⁴Again, the kingdom of heaven is like treasure hid in a field. When someone⁺ has found *it*, they hide *it* and with *great* joy go and sell all that they have and buy that field.

⁴⁵Again, the kingdom of heaven is like a merchant seeking fine⁺ pearls.

⁴⁶When he found one pearl of great price, *he* sold all that he had and bought it.

⁴⁷Again, the kingdom of heaven is like a net that was cast into the sea and gathered of every kind.

⁴⁸When it was full, they drew *it* to shore and sat down and gathered the good into vessels but cast the bad away.

⁴⁹So shall it be at the end of the world. The angels will come forth and sever the wicked from among the righteous⁺

⁵⁰and *they* will cast *the wicked* into the furnace of fire and there will be wailing and gnashing of teeth.

⁵¹Jesus said to them: Have you understood all these things? They said to Him: Yes Lord.

⁵²Then He said to them: Therefore every scribe *who is* instructed about the kingdom of heaven is like a property owner⁺ who brings forth out of his treasure *things* new and old.

⁵³And it came to pass when Jesus had finished these parables He departed from there.⁺

⁵⁴And when He had come into His own country, He taught them in their synagogue so that they were astonished and said: From where has this *man* acquired this wisdom and *these* mighty works?

⁵⁵Is this not the carpenter's son? Is not His mother called Mary and His brothers James, Joses, Simon, and Jude?

⁵⁶And His sisters, are they not all with us? From where then has this *man* acquired all these things?

⁵⁷They were offended by Him *and disbelieved*, but Jesus said to them: A prophet is not without honor, save in his own country and in his own house.

⁵⁸*Therefore* He did not *do* many mighty works there because of their unbelief.

Matthew Chapter 14

¹ At that time, Herod the tetrarch heard of the reputation⁺ of Jesus

² and *he* said to his servants: This is John the Baptist. He is risen from the dead and therefore mighty works *are shown* at work by him.

³ For Herod had seized⁺ John and bound him and put *him* in prison for the sake of Herodias, his brother Philip's wife *whom Herod stole and married.*

⁴ For John *had* said to him: It is not lawful for you to have her.

⁵ And when *Herod* would have put *John* to death, *he did not because* he feared the multitude because they counted *John* as a prophet.

⁶ But *then* when Herod's birthday was kept, the daughter of Herodias danced before them and pleased Herod.

⁷ Therefore he promised with an oath to give her whatever she would ask.

⁸ And she, having been instructed by her mother, said: Give me here John the Baptist's head on a platter.⁺

⁹ The king was sorry, nevertheless because of his oath and *those* who sat with him to eat,⁺ he commanded *it* to be given *to her*

¹⁰ and he sent and beheaded John in the prison

¹¹ and *John's* head was brought on a platter⁺ and given to the girl⁺ and she gave⁺ *it* to her mother.

¹² *Then John's* disciples came and took *away* the body and buried it and *then* went and told Jesus.

¹³ When Jesus heard *about it*, He departed from there⁺ by boat to a deserted⁺ place apart. When the people heard *about this*, they followed Him on foot out of the cities.

¹⁴ Jesus went forth and saw a great multitude and was moved with compassion toward them and He healed their sick.

¹⁵ When it was evening, His disciples came to Him saying: This is a deserted⁺ place and the time is now past. Send the multitude away *so* that they may go into the villages and buy food⁺ *for* themselves.

¹⁶ But Jesus said to them: They do not need to go away.⁺ You give them *food* to eat.

¹⁷ They said to Him: We have here only⁺ five loaves and two fish.

¹⁸ He said: Bring them here to me.

¹⁹ *Then* He commanded the multitude to sit down on the grass and *He* took the five loaves and the two fish and looking up to heaven, He blessed and broke *them* and gave the loaves to *His* disciples and the disciples to the multitude.

²⁰ They all ate and were filled and of the fragments that remained they took up twelve baskets full.

²¹ *Those* who had eaten were about five thousand men plus⁺ women and children.

²² Immediately⁺ *after that* Jesus directed⁺ His disciples to get into a boat and go ahead⁺ of Him to the other side while He sent the multitudes away.

²³ And when He had sent the multitudes away, He went up into a mountain apart to pray and when the evening had come He was there alone.

²⁴ But the boat was now in the midst of the sea *and* tossed with waves, for the wind was contrary.

²⁵ *Then* in the fourth watch of the night *sometime after three o'clock in the morning* Jesus went to them, walking on the sea.

²⁶ When the disciples saw Him walking on the sea, they were troubled and said: It is a spirit, and they cried out for fear.

²⁷ But immediately⁺ Jesus spoke to them saying:

> Be of good cheer.
> I am⁺ *with you*.
> Do not be afraid.

²⁸ Peter answered Him and said: Lord, if it is you, bid me come to you on the water.

²⁹ *Jesus* said: Come. And when Peter had come down out of the boat, he walked on the water to go to Jesus.

³⁰ But when he saw the wind boisterous he was afraid and beginning to sink he cried *out* saying: Lord save me.

³¹ Immediately, Jesus stretched forth *His* hand, caught him, and said to him: O you of little faith. Why did you doubt?

[32]When they entered[+] the boat, the wind stopped.[+]

[33]Then *those* who were in the boat came and worshiped Him saying: Truly, you are the Son of God.

[34]When they had crossed[+] over *the sea*, they came to the land of Gennesaret.

[35]When the people[+] of that place recognized[+] Him, they sent *word* all around[+] that country and brought to Him all who were diseased.

[36]*They* begged[+] Him that they might only touch the hem of His garment, and all[+] *who* touched *Him* were made perfectly whole.

Matthew Chapter 15

[1] Then scribes and Pharisees from Jerusalem came to Jesus saying:

[2] Why do your disciples transgress the tradition of the elders? For they do not wash their hands when they eat bread.

[3] But He answered and said to them: Why do you also transgress the commandment of God by your tradition?

[4] For God commanded saying: Honor your father and mother. And: Anyone who curses father or mother, let them die the death. *Exodus 20:12, Exodus 21:17*

[5] But you say: Whoever says to *their* father or mother: *It is* a gift, by whatever you might be profited by me;

[6] and does not honor their father or their mother, *they shall be free*. Thus you have made the commandment of God of no effect by your tradition.

[7] *You* hypocrites. Well did Isaiah prophesy of you saying:

[8] These people draw near to me with their mouths and honor me with *their* lips but their hearts are far from me. *Isaiah 29:13*

[9] However, *it is* in vain *that* they worship me, teaching *as* doctrines the commandments of men. *Isaiah 29:13*

[10]*Then* He called the multitude and said to them: Hear and understand.

[11]*It is* not what goes into the mouth *that* defiles, but what comes out of the mouth that defiles.

[12]Then His disciples came and said to Him: Do you know that the Pharisees were offended after they heard this saying?

[13]But He answered and said: Every plant that my heavenly Father has not planted will be rooted up. *Proverbs 2:22*

[14]Let them alone. They are blind leaders of the blind, and if the blind lead the blind both will fall into the ditch.

[15]Then Peter answered and said to Him: Declare to us this parable.

[16]Jesus said: Are you also yet without understanding?

[17]Do you not yet understand that whatever enters in at the mouth goes into the belly and is then purged[+]?

[18]But the *words* spoken[+] by the mouth come from the heart and they defile a person[+].

[19]For out of the heart proceed evil thoughts, murders, adulteries, fornications, thefts, false witness, *and* blasphemies.

[20]These are *the things* that defile a person,[+] but to eat with unwashed hands does not defile a person[+].

[21]Then Jesus went from there[+] to the borders[+] of Tyre and Sidon.

[22]And behold a woman of Canaan came out of the same borders[+] and cried *out* to Him saying: Have mercy on me O Lord, son of David. My daughter is grievously oppressed[+] with a demon[+].

[23]But He answered her not a word, and His disciples came and begged[+] Him saying: Send her away for she cries *out* after us.

[24]But He answered and said: I was not sent but to the lost sheep of the house of Israel.

[25]Then she came and worshiped Him saying: Lord help me.

[26]But He answered and said: It is not good[+] to take the children's bread and cast *it* to dogs.

[27]And she said: True Lord, yet the dogs eat of the crumbs that fall from their masters' table.

[28]Then Jesus answered and said to her: O woman, great *is* your faith. Be it to

you even as you will. And her daughter was made whole from that very hour.
²⁹ Jesus *then* departed from there, + came near the sea of Galilee, and went up into a mountain and sat down there.
³⁰ Great multitudes came to Him, having with them *those who were* lame, blind, speechless, + maimed, and many others, and cast them down at Jesus' feet and He healed them; *Isaiah 35:5*
³¹ so that the multitude wondered when they saw the speechless+ to speak, the maimed to be whole, the lame to walk, and the blind to see and they glorified the God of Israel. *Isaiah 35:5*
³² Then Jesus called His disciples and said: I have compassion on the multitude because they have continued with me now three days and have nothing to eat. I will not send them away fasting lest they faint on the way.
³³ His disciples said to Him: From where *should we get*+ *so much* bread in the wilderness as to fill so great a multitude?
³⁴ Jesus said to them: How many loaves do you have? They said: Seven and a few little fish.
³⁵ *Then Jesus* commanded the multitude to sit down on the ground
³⁶ and He took the seven loaves and the fish and gave thanks and broke *them* and gave to His disciples and the disciples *gave* to the multitude.
³⁷ They all ate and were filled and they took up, of the broken *pieces* that were left, seven baskets full.
³⁸ *Those* who ate were four thousand men plus+ women and children.
³⁹ *Then Jesus* sent away the multitude and took a boat into the borders+ of Magdala.

Matthew Chapter 16

¹ The Pharisees and Sadducees came testing+ *and* asked Him if He would show them a sign from heaven.
² He answered and said to them: When it is evening, you say: *It will be* fair weather for the sky is red.
³ And in the morning: *It will be* foul weather today for the sky is red and

threatening.+ O *you* hypocrites. You can discern the face of the sky, but can you not *discern* the signs of the times?
⁴ A wicked and adulterous generation seeks after a sign, *but* no sign will be given to it except+ the sign of the prophet Jonah. And He left them and departed.
⁵ When His disciples had come to the other side, they had forgotten to take bread.
⁶ Then Jesus said to them: Take heed and beware of the leaven of the Pharisees and of the Sadducees.
⁷ They reasoned among themselves saying: *It is* because we have taken no bread.
⁸ When Jesus perceived *their thoughts* He said to them: O you of little faith. Why do you reason among yourselves *saying it is* because you have brought no bread?
⁹ Do you not yet understand or remember the five loaves of the five thousand and how many baskets you took up?
¹⁰ Nor the seven loaves of the four thousand and how many baskets you took up?
¹¹ How is it that you do not understand that I did not speak to you concerning bread *but so* that you should beware of the leaven of the Pharisees and of the Sadducees?
¹² Then they understood that He did not tell *them to* beware of the leaven of bread but of the doctrine of the Pharisees and of the Sadducees.
¹³ When Jesus came into the borders+ of Caesarea Philippi, He asked His disciples saying: Who do men say that I the Son of man am?
¹⁴ They said: Some *say that you are* John the Baptist, some *say* Elijah, *and* others *say* Jeremiah+ or one of the prophets.
¹⁵ He said to them: But who do you say that I am?
¹⁶ Simon Peter answered and said: You are the Christ, the Son of the living God.
¹⁷ Jesus answered and said to him: Blessed are you Simon Barjona for flesh and blood have not revealed *this* to you, but my Father in heaven.

18I say also to you that you are *now* Peter and upon this rock I will build my church and the gates of hell will not prevail against it.
19I will give to you the keys of the kingdom of heaven. Whatever you bind on earth will be *already* bound in heaven and whatever you loose on earth will be *already* loosed in heaven.
20Then He charged His disciples that they should tell no one that He was Jesus the Christ.
21From that time forth Jesus began to show His disciples that He must go to Jerusalem and suffer many things by the elders, chief priests, and scribes and be killed and be raised again the third day.
22Then Peter took Him *aside* and began to rebuke Him saying: Far be it from you, Lord. This shall not be to you.
23But *Jesus* turned and said to Peter: Get behind me Satan. You are an offense to me for you do not savor the things that are of God, but those that are of men.
24Then Jesus said to His disciples:

> If anyone+ will come after me,
> let them deny themselves
> and take up their cross
> and follow me.

25For whoever would+ save their life will lose it and whoever would+ lose their life for my sake will find it.
Proverbs 13:7
26For what is anyone to profit if they gain the whole world and lose their own soul? Or what shall anyone give in exchange for their soul?
27For the Son of man will come in the glory of His Father *and* with His angels, and then He will reward everyone+ according to their deeds+.
Jeremiah 17:10
28Truly+ I say to you: There are some standing here who will not taste of death until they see the Son of man coming in His kingdom.

Matthew Chapter 17

1 After six days, Jesus took Peter, James, and John his brother up to a high mountain apart
2 and *He* was transfigured *right there* before them. His face did shine like+ the sun and His clothing+ was *as* white as the light.
3 And behold there appeared to them Moses and Elijah talking with Him.
4 Then Peter answered and said to Jesus: Lord, it is good for us to be here. If you will, let us make three tabernacles here. One for you, one for Moses, *and* one for Elijah.
5 While he spoke, behold a bright cloud overshadowed them and behold a voice out of the cloud said: This is my beloved Son in whom I am well pleased. Hear Him. *Psalm 2:7*
6 When the disciples heard *this* they fell on their faces and were greatly+ afraid.
7 Jesus came and touched them and said: Arise and do not be afraid.
8 When they lifted up their eyes, they saw no one except+ Jesus.
9 *Then* as they came down from the mountain, Jesus charged them saying: Tell the vision to no one until the Son of man is risen from the dead.
10His disciples asked Him saying: Why then do the scribes say that Elijah must come first?
11Jesus answered and said to them: Elijah truly will come first and restore all things. *Malachi 4:6*
12But I say to you that Elijah has already come and they did not know him, but have done to him whatever they desired.+ Likewise will the Son of man also suffer by them. *Malachi 4:5*
13Then the disciples understood that He spoke to them of John the Baptist.
14When they had come to the multitude, a *certain* man came to Him, kneeling down to Him and saying:
15Lord have mercy on my son for he is a lunatic and greatly+ oppressed,+ for often times he falls into the fire and often into the water.

16 I brought him to your disciples and they could not cure him.

17 Then Jesus answered and said: O faithless and perverse generation. How long shall I be with you? How long shall I endure+ you? Bring him here to me.

18 Jesus rebuked the demon+ and he departed out of him and the child was cured from that very hour.

19 Then the disciples came to Jesus privately+ and said: Why could we not cast him out?

20 Jesus said to them: *It was* because of your unbelief. For truly+ I say to you: If you have faith as a grain of mustard seed, you shall say to this mountain: Move from here to there+ and it will move. Nothing will be impossible to you.

21 However this kind does not go out but by prayer and fasting.

22 While they abode in Galilee Jesus said to them: The Son of man will be betrayed into the hands of men.

23 They will kill Him and the third day He will be raised again. And they were exceedingly sorry.

24 When they had come to Capernaum, *those* who received tribute *money* came to Peter and said: Does your master not pay tribute?

25 He said: Yes. And when he had come into the house, Jesus preceded+ him saying: What do you think, Simon? From+ whom do the kings of the earth take custom or tribute? From+ their own children or from+ strangers?

26 Peter said to Him: From+ strangers. Jesus said to him: Then the children are free.

27 Nevertheless, lest we should offend them, go to the sea, throw+ *in* a hook, and take up the first fish that comes up. When you have opened its mouth you will find a piece of money. Take that and give it to them for me and *for* you.

Matthew Chapter 18

1 At the same time the disciples came to Jesus saying: Who is the greatest in the kingdom of heaven?

2 Jesus called a little child to Himself and sat him *down* in the midst of them

3 and said: Truly+ I say to you: Unless+ you be converted and become as little children, you will not enter into the kingdom of heaven.

4 Whoever therefore will humble themselves as this little child, the same is greatest in the kingdom of heaven.

5 Whoever will receive one such little child in my name receives me.

6 But whoever offends *and sins against* one of these little ones who believe in me, it would be better for them if+ a millstone were hung around+ their neck and *if* they were drowned in the depth of the sea.

7 Woe to the world because of offenses. For it must be that offenses come, but woe to those through whom the offenses come.

8 Therefore if your hand or your foot causes+ you *to sin*, cut them off and cast *them* from you. It is better for you to enter into life crippled+ or maimed rather than having two hands or two feet to be cast into everlasting fire.

9 If your eye causes+ you *to sin*, pluck it out and cast *it* from you. It is better for you to enter into life with one eye rather than having two eyes to be cast into hell fire.

10 Take heed that you do not despise one of these little ones. For I say to you: In heaven their angels do always behold the face of my Father in heaven.

11 For the Son of man has come to save *those* who were lost.

12 What do you think? If a man had a hundred sheep and one of them was gone astray, would he not leave the ninety nine and go into the mountains and seek what is gone astray?

13 And if he finds it, truly+ I say to you: He rejoices more over that *one* than over+ the ninety nine that did not go astray.

14 Even so, it is not the will of your Father in heaven that one of these little ones should perish.

15 If *one of* your family+ sins+ against you, go and warn+ them *about their error* between you and them alone. If *they* will hear you, *then* you *will* have rescued+ your family+ *member*.

16But if they will not hear, *then* take with you one or two more *so* that by the mouth of two or three witnesses every word may be established. *Deuteronomy 19:15*

17And if they will neglect to hear them, *then* tell *it* to the church. But if they neglect to hear the church *then* let them be to you as a heathen and a worldly+ person.

18Truly+ I say to you: Whatever you bind on earth will *already* be bound in heaven and whatever you loose on earth will *already* be loosed in heaven.

19Again I say to you: If two of you agree on earth as touching anything that they ask, it will be done for them by my Father in heaven.

20For where two or three are gathered together in my name, there I am in the midst of them.

21Then Peter came to Him and said: Lord, how often shall my brother sin against me and I forgive him? Until seven times?

22Jesus said to him: I do not say to you until seven times but until seventy times seven.

23The kingdom of heaven *may be* compared+ to a certain king who wanted to take account of his servants.

24When he had begun the review,+ one was brought to him who owed him ten thousand talents.

25But since+ he had nothing *with which* to pay, his lord commanded him to be sold and his wife and children and all that he had, and payment to be made.

26The servant therefore fell down and worshiped him saying: Lord have patience with me and I will pay you all.

27Then the lord of that servant was moved with compassion and released+ him and forgave him the debt.

28But the same servant went out and found one of his fellow servants who owed him *four months wages*+ and he laid hands on him and took *him* by the throat saying: Pay me what you owe.

29His fellow servant fell down at his feet and begged+ Him saying: Have patience with me and I will pay you all.

30He would not, but went and cast him into prison until he should pay the debt.

31So when his fellow servants saw what was done, they were very sorry and came and told their lord all that was done.

32Then his lord, after he had called him, said to him: O you wicked servant. I forgave you all that debt because you begged+ me.

33Should you not also have had compassion on your fellow servant even as I had pity on you?

34And his lord was angry+ and delivered him to the torturers+ until he should pay all that was due to him.

35So likewise will my heavenly Father do also to you if you do not, from your hearts, forgive everyone *of the* family+ *of God for* their trespasses.

Matthew Chapter 19

1 It came to pass *that* when Jesus had finished these sayings He departed from Galilee and came into the borders+ of Judea beyond Jordan.

2 Great multitudes followed Him and He healed them there.

3 The Pharisees also came to Him, testing+ Him and saying to Him: Is it lawful for a man to put away his wife for every cause?

4 He answered and said to them: Have you not read that

> He who made *them*
> at the beginning
> made them male and female
> *Genesis 1:27*
>
> 5 and said: For this reason+
> a man shall leave father
> and mother and cleave to his wife
> and they two shall be one flesh.
> *Genesis 2:24*
>
> 6 Therefore they are
> no longer+ two, but one flesh.
> Therefore
> what God has joined *together*,
> mankind+ *must* not separate+.

⁷ They said to Him: Why then did Moses command to give a written divorce⁺ and to put her away? *Deuteronomy 24:1*

⁸ He said to them: Because of the hardness of your hearts Moses allowed⁺ you to put away your wives. But from the beginning it was not *to be* so.

⁹ I say to you: Whoever shall put away his wife, except*it be* for fornication, and shall marry another commits adultery. And whoever marries *one who* is *thus* put away commits adultery. *Matthew 5:32*

¹⁰ His disciples said to Him: If the case of the man be so with *his* wife it is not good to marry.

¹¹ But *Jesus* said to them: All *people* cannot receive this saying, *but* only⁺ *those* to whom it is given.

¹² For there are some eunuchs who were so born from*their* mother's womb. There are some eunuchs who were made eunuchs by men. There are eunuchs who have made themselves eunuchs for the kingdom of heaven's sake.*Those* who are able to receive *this*, let them receive *it*.

¹³ Then *some* little children there were brought to Him *so* that He *might* lay *His* hands on them and pray, but the disciples rebuked them.

¹⁴ But Jesus said: Allow *the* little children and do not forbid them to come to me. For of such is the kingdom of heaven.

¹⁵ He laid *His* hands on them; and *then* departed from there.⁺

¹⁶ Behold one came and said to Him: Good Master what good thing shall I do *so* that I may have eternal life?

¹⁷ *Jesus* said to him: Why do you call me good? *There is* none good but one *who is* God. But

> if you will enter into life,
> keep the commandments.
> *Leviticus 18:5*

¹⁸ *The man* said to Him: Which? Jesus said: You shall do no murder. You shall not commit adultery. You shall not steal. You shall not bear false witness. *Exodus 20:13,14,15,16*

¹⁹ Honor your father and *your* mother. And, you shall love your neighbor as yourself. *Exodus 20:12, Leviticus 19:18*

²⁰ The young man said to Him: All these things have I kept from my youth up. What do I yet lack?

²¹ Jesus said to him: If you will be perfect, go *and* sell your possessions⁺ and give to the poor and you will have treasure in heaven, and come *and* follow me.

²² But when the young man heard that saying, he went away sorrowful for he had great possessions.

²³ Then Jesus said to His disciples: Truly⁺ I say to you that a rich person⁺ shall hardly *be able to* enter into the kingdom of heaven. *Proverbs 11:28*

²⁴ Again I say to you: It is easier for a camel to go through the eye of a needle than for a rich person⁺ to enter into the kingdom of God.

²⁵ When His disciples heard *this* they were exceedingly amazed saying: Who then can be saved?

²⁶ But Jesus looked⁺ at *them and* said to them: With people⁺ this is impossible, but

> with God
> all things are possible.
> *Jeremiah 32:17*

²⁷ Then Peter answered and said to Him: Behold we have forsaken all and followed you. What shall we have therefore?

²⁸ Jesus said to them: Truly⁺ I say to you that you who have followed me, in the regeneration when the Son of man shall sit on the throne of His glory, you also shall sit upon twelve thrones judging the twelve tribes of Israel.

²⁹ Everyone who has forsaken houses or brothers or sisters or father or mother or wife or children or lands for my name's sake shall receive a hundredfold and shall inherit eternal⁺ life.

³⁰ But many *who are* first will be last and the last *will be* first.

Matthew Chapter 20

1 The kingdom of heaven is like a property owner+ who went out early in the morning to hire laborers into his vineyard.

2 When he had agreed with the laborers for a day's wages+ he sent them into his vineyard.

3 *Then* he went out about the third hour, *about nine o'clock*+ in the morning and saw others standing idle in the marketplace

4 and said to them: Go also into the vineyard and whatever is right I will give you. And they went.

5 Again he went out about the sixth and ninth hour and did likewise.

6 And about the eleventh hour he went out and found others standing idle and said to them: Why do you stand here all the day idle?

7 They said to him: Because no one has hired us. He said to them: Go also into the vineyard and whatever is right you will receive.

8 So when evening+ had come, the lord of the vineyard said to his steward: Call the laborers and give them *their* wages+ beginning from the last to the first.

9 When they who *were hired* about the eleventh hour came, everyone+ received a day's wages+.

10 But when the first came, they supposed that they should have received more, but they each+ also+ received a day's wages+.

11 When they had received *it*, they complained+ against the head+ of the house

12 saying: These last have worked+ *but* one hour and you have made them equal to us who have borne the burden and heat of the day.

13 But he answered one of them and said: Friend I do you no wrong. Did you not agree with me for a day's wages+?

14 Take *what is* yours and go. + I will give to this last even as to you.

15 Is it not lawful for me to do what I will with my own? Is your eye evil because I am good?

16 So the last shall be first and the first last, for many are called but few chosen.

17 *Then* Jesus went+ up to Jerusalem *and* He took the twelve disciples aside+ on the way and said to them:

18 Behold we are *now* going up to Jerusalem *where* the Son of man will be betrayed to the chief priests and to the scribes and they will condemn Him to death. *Psalm 22, Isaiah 53*

19 *They* will deliver Him to the Gentiles to mock and to flog+ and to crucify *Him*, and the third day He will rise again.

20 Then the mother of Zebedee's children with her sons came to Him worshiping *Him* and desiring a certain thing of Him.

21 He said to her: What will you *have*? She said to Him: Grant that these my two sons may sit, the one on your right hand and the other on the left, in your kingdom.

22 But Jesus answered and said: You do not know what you ask. Are you able to drink of the cup of which I shall drink and be baptized with the baptism with which I shall be baptized? They said to Him: We are able.

23 He said to them: You shall indeed drink of my cup and be baptized with the baptism with which I shall be baptized, but to sit at my right hand and at my left is not mine to give, but *it shall be given to them* for whom it is prepared by my Father.

24 When the ten heard *this* they were moved with indignation against the two brothers.

25 But Jesus called them *to Himself* and said: You know that the princes of the Gentiles exercise dominion over them and *those* who are great exercise authority upon them.

26 But it shall not be that way+ among you. But whoever will be great among you, let them be your servant+.

27 Whoever will be chief among you, let them be your servant.

28 Even as the Son of man did not come to be ministered to, but to minister and to give His life a ransom for many.

29 As they departed from Jericho, a great multitude followed Him.

30 And behold two blind men sitting by the wayside, when they heard that Jesus passed by, cried out saying: Have mercy on us, O Lord, son of David.
31 The multitude rebuked them *saying* that they should be silent. + But they cried *out all* the more saying: Have mercy on us, O Lord, son of David.
32 Jesus stood still and called them and said: What do you want me to do to you?
33 They said to Him: Lord that our eyes may be opened.
34 So Jesus had compassion *on them* and touched their eyes and immediately their eyes received sight and they followed Him.

Matthew Chapter 21

1 When they drew near to Jerusalem and had come to Bethphage to the Mount of Olives, then Jesus sent two disciples
2 saying to them: Go into the village before + you and immediately + you will find a donkey + tied and a colt with her. Loose *it* and bring *it* to me.
3 If anyone + says anything + to you, you shall say: The Lord has need of them, and immediately + they will send them.
4 All this was done to fulfill what was spoken by the prophet *who* said:
5 Tell the daughter of Zion +: Behold your King comes to you meek and sitting upon a donkey + and a colt, the foal of a donkey. *Isaiah 62:11, Zechariah 9:9*
6 The disciples did as Jesus commanded them.
7 *They* brought the donkey + and the colt and put their clothes on them and *Jesus* sat *on the colt*.
8 A very great multitude spread their garments along + the way. Others cut down branches from the trees and spread + *them* along + the way.
9 The multitudes who went before and *those* who followed cried *out* saying: Hosanna to the son of David. Blessed *is* He who comes in the name of the Lord. Hosanna in the highest. *Psalm 118:26*
10 When He had come into Jerusalem, all the city was moved saying: Who is this?

11 The multitude said: This is Jesus the prophet of Nazareth of Galilee.
12 *Then* Jesus went into the temple of God and cast out all *those* who bought and sold in the temple and *He* overthrew the tables of the money changers and the seats of *those* who sold doves
13 and said to them: It is written: My house shall be called the house of prayer, but you have made it a den of thieves. *Isaiah 56:7, Jeremiah 7:11*
14 The blind and the lame came to Him in the temple and He healed them. *Isaiah 35:5*
15 When the chief priests and scribes saw the wonderful things that He did and the children crying in the temple and saying: Hosanna to the son of David, they were greatly + displeased.
16 *They* said to Him: Hear what these *people* + say? Jesus said to them: Yes. Have you never read: Out of the mouth of babes and nursing infants + you have perfected praise? *Psalm 8:2*
17 *Then* He left them and went out of the city to Bethany and He lodged there.
18 Now in the morning as He returned to the city He was hungry.
19 When He saw a fig tree on the way, He came to it and found nothing on it except + leaves and said to it: Let no fruit grow on you henceforth forever. And immediately + the fig tree withered away.
20 When the disciples saw *this*, they marveled saying: How soon the fig tree has withered away.
21 Jesus answered and said to them: Truly + I say to you:

> If you have faith
> and do not doubt,
> you will not only do this
> to the fig tree, but also
> if you say to this mountain:
> Be removed and be cast
> into the sea, it will be done.

> 22 All things whatsoever
> you ask in prayer believing,
> you will receive.

²³When He had come into the temple, the chief priests and the elders of the people came to Him as He was teaching and said: By what authority do you *do* these things? And who gave you this authority?

²⁴Jesus answered and said to them: I will also ask you one thing. If you tell me, I in like wise will tell you by what authority I do these things.

²⁵The baptism of John, from where was it *authorized*? From heaven, or from⁺ men? They reasoned with themselves saying: If we say: From heaven, He will say to us: Why did you not then believe him?

²⁶But if we say: From men, we fear the people for all hold John as a prophet.

²⁷They answered Jesus and said: We cannot tell. And He said to them: *Then* neither will I tell you by what authority I do these things.

²⁸But what do you think *of this*? A *certain* man had two sons. He came to the first and said: Son, go work today in my vineyard.

²⁹*The son* answered and said: I will not, but afterward he repented and went.

³⁰He came to the second and said likewise. And *the second son* answered and said: I *will go* sir, *but he* did not go.

³¹*Now* which of them did the will of *his* father? They said to Him: The first. Jesus said to them: Truly⁺ I say to you that the worldly⁺ people and harlots *will* go into the kingdom of God before you.

³²For John came to you in the way of righteousness and you did not believe him, but the worldly⁺ people and the harlots believed him. You, when you had seen *it*, did not repent afterward *so* that you might believe him.

³³*Now* hear another parable: There was a certain property owner⁺ who planted a vineyard and built a fence⁺ around it, dug a wine press in it, built a tower, let it out to *tenant* farmers,⁺ and went into a far country. *Isaiah 5:2*

³⁴When the time of the fruit drew near, he sent his servants to the *tenant* farmers⁺ *so* that they might receive the fruits of it.

³⁵*But* the *tenant* farmers⁺ took his servants, beat one, killed another, and stoned another.

³⁶Again, he sent other servants more than the first and they did to them likewise.

³⁷But last of all he sent his son to them saying: *Surely* they will reverence my son.

³⁸But when the *tenant* farmers⁺ saw the son, they said among themselves: This is the heir. Come, let us kill him and let us seize his inheritance.

³⁹*So* they caught him and cast *him* out of the vineyard and killed⁺ *him*.

⁴⁰*Now then* when the lord of the vineyard comes, what will he do to those *tenant* farmers⁺?

⁴¹They said to Him: He will miserably destroy those wicked men and will lease⁺ *his* vineyard to other *tenant* farmers⁺ who will render *to* him the fruits in their seasons.

⁴²Jesus said to them: Did you never read in the Scriptures: The stone that the builders rejected has become the head of the corner. This is the Lord's doing and it is marvelous in our eyes. *Psalm 118:22*

⁴³Therefore I say to you: The kingdom of God will be taken from you and given to a nation bringing forth the fruits thereof.

⁴⁴Whoever falls on this stone will be broken. But on whomever it falls, it will grind them to powder.

⁴⁵When the chief priests and Pharisees had heard His parables, they perceived that He spoke of them.

⁴⁶But when they sought to lay hands on Him, they feared the multitude because they took Him for a prophet.

Matthew Chapter 22

¹ *Now* Jesus answered and spoke to them again by parables and said:

² The kingdom of heaven is like a certain king who made a marriage for his son.

³ *He* sent forth his servants to call *those* who were invited⁺ to the wedding *but* they would not come.

⁴ Again, he sent forth more⁺ servants saying: Tell *those* who are invited⁺: Behold I have prepared my dinner. My oxen and *my* fatted calves⁺ *are* killed and all things *are* ready. Come to the marriage.

⁵ But they made light of *it* and went their *separate* ways: one to his farm, another to his merchandise.

⁶ The rest⁺ took his servants, treated *them* spitefully, and killed⁺ *them*.

⁷ When the king heard *about this*, he was angry.⁺ He sent forth his armies and destroyed those murderers and burned up their city.

⁸ Then he said to his servants: The wedding is ready but *those* who were invited⁺ were not worthy.

⁹ Go therefore into the highways and invite⁺ everyone⁺ you find to the marriage.

¹⁰ So those servants went out into the highways and gathered together everyone,⁺ as many as they *could* find⁺ both good and bad, and the wedding was furnished with guests.

¹¹ *Now* when the king came in to see the guests, he saw there a man who did not have on a wedding garment.

¹² He said to him: Friend, how did you come in here not having a wedding garment? And he was speechless.

¹³ Then the king said to the servants: Bind him hand and foot and take him away and cast *him* into outer darkness and there will be weeping and gnashing of teeth.

¹⁴ For many are called but few *are* chosen.

¹⁵ Then the Pharisees left⁺ and took counsel how they might entangle Him in *His* talk.

¹⁶ They sent their disciples with the Herodians out to Him saying: Master, we know that you are true and teach the way of God in truth. Nor do you *take special* care for any *one person over another*, for you do not regard the positions⁺ people⁺ *hold*.

¹⁷ Tell us therefore: What do you think? Is it lawful to give tribute to Caesar or not?

¹⁸ But Jesus perceived their wickedness and said: Why do you test⁺ me *you* hypocrites?

¹⁹ Show me the tribute money. They brought a coin⁺ to Him.

²⁰ He said to them: Whose image and title⁺ *is* this?

²¹ They said to Him: Caesar's. Then He said to them: Render therefore to Caesar the things that are Caesar's and to God the things that are God's.

²² When they had heard *these words*, they marveled and left Him and went away.⁺

²³ The same day, the Sadducees who say that there is no resurrection came to Him and asked Him

²⁴ saying: Master, Moses said if a man die having no children, *then* his brother shall marry his wife and raise up seed to his brother. *Deuteronomy 25:5*

²⁵ Now there were with us seven brothers and the first, when he had married a wife, died⁺ and having no issue, left his wife to his brother.

²⁶ Likewise the second also and the third to the seventh.

²⁷ Last of all the woman died also.

²⁸ Therefore in the resurrection, of the seven, whose wife will she be? For they all had her.

²⁹ Jesus answered and said to them:

> You err
> *by* not knowing the Scriptures
> or the power of God.

³⁰ For in the resurrection they neither marry nor are given in marriage but are as the angels of God in heaven.

³¹ But as touching the resurrection of the dead, have you not read what was spoken to you by God saying:

³² I am the God of Abraham and the God of Isaac and the God of Jacob. God is not the God of the dead but of the living. *Exodus 3:6*

³³ When the multitude heard *this*, they were astonished at His doctrine.

³⁴ But when the Pharisees had heard that He had put the Sadducees to silence, they were gathered together.

35Then one of them *who was* a lawyer asked *Him a question*, testing+ Him and saying: 36Master, which *is* the great commandment in the law? 37Jesus said to him:

> You shall love the Lord
> your God with all your heart
> and with all your soul
> and with all your mind.
> *Deuteronomy 6:5*
> 38 This is the first
> and great commandment.

> 39 The second *is* like it:
> You shall love your neighbor
> as yourself.
> *Matthew 19:19*

40On these two commandments hang all the law and the prophets. 41While the Pharisees were gathered together, Jesus asked them 42saying: What do you think of Christ? Whose son is He? They said to Him: *The son* of David. 43He said to them: How then does David in spirit call Him Lord saying: 44The Lord said to my Lord: Sit at my right hand until I make your enemies your footstool? *Psalm 110:1* 45If David then called Him Lord, how is He his son? 46No one was able to answer Him a word *and* from that day forth no one+ dared+ ask Him any more *questions*.

Matthew Chapter 23

1 Then Jesus spoke to the multitude and to His disciples 2 saying: The scribes and the Pharisees sit in Moses' seat. 3 Therefore everything+ whatsoever they instruct+ you *to* observe, observe and do *that*, but do not follow+ their works, for they say and do not *do as they say*. 4 They bind heavy burdens grievous to be borne and lay *them* on people's shoulders, but they *themselves* will not *use* one of their fingers *to* move with.

5 But they do all their works to be seen by people.+ They make broad their phylacteries and enlarge the borders of their garments. *Deuteronomy 6:8* 6 *They* love the uppermost rooms at feasts and the chief seats in the synagogues 7 and greetings in the market *places* and to be called Rabbi, Rabbi by people.+

> 8 Do not be called Rabbi.
> For one is your Master, Christ.
> All *of* you are family+.
> 9 Do not call any+ *man*
> your father on the earth,
> for one is your Father,
> who is in heaven.
> 10 Neither *should* you
> be called masters.
> For one is your Master, Christ.
> 11 But one who is greatest
> among you
> shall be your servant.
> 12 Whoever exalts themselves
> will be humbled+ and
> *those* who humble themselves
> will be exalted.
> *Proverbs 25:6*

13But woe to you scribes and Pharisees. Hypocrites. For you shut up the kingdom of heaven against men for you neither go in *yourselves*, nor do you allow+ *those* who are entering to go in. 14Woe to you scribes and Pharisees. Hypocrites. For you devour widows' houses and for a pretence make long prayer. Therefore you will receive the greater damnation. 15Woe to you scribes and Pharisees. Hypocrites. For you travel+ sea and land to make one convert+ and when he is made you make him twofold more the child of hell than yourselves. 16Woe to you blind guides who say: Whoever swears by the temple, *that* is nothing; but whoever swears by the gold of the temple is a debtor. 17*You* fools and blind. Which+ is greater, the gold, or the temple that sanctifies the gold?

[18] And *you say*: Whoever swears by the altar, it is nothing but whoever swears by the gift that is upon it, is guilty.

[19] *You* fools and blind. Which[+] *is* greater, the gift or the altar that sanctifies the gift?

[20] Whoever therefore swears by the altar, swears by it and by all things upon it.

[21] And whoever swears by the temple, swears by it and by Him who dwells therein.

[22] Anyone[+] who swears by heaven, swears by the throne of God and by Him who sits upon it.

[23] Woe to you scribes and Pharisees. Hypocrites. For you pay tithe of mint and anise and cummin and have omitted the weightier *matters* of the law: judgment, mercy, and faith. These *small things* you ought to have done, but not to leave the other undone.

[24] *You* blind guides who strain at a gnat and swallow a camel.

[25] Woe to you scribes and Pharisees. Hypocrites. For you make clean the outside of the cup and of the platter but within they are full of extortion and excess.

[26] *You* blind Pharisee. First clean the inside[+] of the cup and platter, and then the outside of them may be clean also.

[27] Woe to you scribes and Pharisees. Hypocrites. For you are like white-washed[+] tombs[+] that look[+] beautiful *on the* outside[+] but *on the* inside[+] are full of dead *men's* bones and of all uncleanness.

[28] Even so you also appear outwardly *to be* righteous to people[+] but inside[+] you are full of hypocrisy and iniquity.

[29] Woe to you scribes and Pharisees. Hypocrites. Because you build the tombs of the prophets and decorate[+] the tombs[+] of the righteous

[30] and say: If we had lived[+] in the days of our fathers, we would not have been partakers with them in the blood of the prophets.

[31] Therefore you are witnesses to your-selves that you are the children of *those* who killed the prophets.

[32] Fill yourselves[+] up, then, the measure of your fathers.

[33] *You* serpents. *You* generation of vipers. How can you escape the damnation of hell?

[34] Therefore behold I send to you prophets and wise men and scribes. *Some* of them you will kill and crucify and *some* of them you will flog[+] in your synagogues and persecute from city to city.

[35] *So* that upon you may come all the righteous blood shed upon the earth from the blood of righteous Abel to the blood of Zechariah son of Berechiah whom you killed[+] between the temple and the altar. *Genesis 4:8, 2 Chronicles 24:20,21*

[36] Truly[+] I say to you: All these things will come upon this generation.

[37] O Jerusalem, Jerusalem. *You* who kill the prophets and stone *those* who are sent to you. How often would I have gathered your children together even as a hen gathers her chicks[+] under *her* wings, but you would not *come*.

[38] Behold your house is left to you desolate. *Jeremiah 22:5*

[39] For I say to you: You will not see me henceforth until you say: Blessed *is* He who comes in the name of the Lord. *Psalm 118:26*

Matthew Chapter 24

[1] *Then* Jesus went out and departed from the temple and His disciples came to *Him* to show Him the buildings of the temple.

[2] Jesus said to them: Do you not see all these things? Truly[+] I say to you: There will not be left here stone upon stone that will not be thrown down.

[3] As He sat upon the Mount of Olives, the disciples came to Him privately saying: Tell us. When will these things be? And what *will be* the sign of your coming and of the end of the world?

[4] Jesus answered and said to them:

Take heed
so that no one deceives you.
Jeremiah 29:8

⁵ For many will come in my name saying: I am Christ and will deceive many.

⁶ You will hear of wars and rumors of wars. See that you are not troubled for all *these things* must come to pass but the end is not yet.

⁷ For nation will rise against nation and kingdom against kingdom. There will be famines and pestilences and earthquakes in many different⁺ places.
2 Chronicles 15:6, Isaiah 19:2

⁸ All these*are* the beginning of sorrows.

⁹ Then they will deliver you up to be afflicted and *to* kill you. You will be hated by all nations for my name's sake.

¹⁰Then many will be offended *and fall from faith* and will betray one another and hate one another.

¹¹Many false prophets will arise and deceive many.

¹²Because iniquity will abound, the love of many will grow⁺ cold.

¹³But *those* who endure to the end, the same will be saved.

¹⁴And this Gospel of the kingdom will be proclaimed⁺ in all the world for a witness to all nations and then the end will come.

¹⁵Therefore, let whoever reads *this* understand: When you see the abomination of desolation spoken of by Daniel the prophet stand in the holy place *Daniel 11:31*

¹⁶then let *those* who are in Judea flee into the mountains.

¹⁷Let one who is on the housetop not come down to take anything out of their house,

¹⁸nor *those* who are in the field return back to take their clothes.

¹⁹Woe to*those* who are with child and to *those* who are nursing⁺ in those days.

²⁰But pray that your flight not be in the winter or on the Sabbath day.

²¹For then*there* will be great tribulation such as has not *occurred* since the beginning of the world to this time. No, nor ever shall be *again*. *Daniel 12:1*

²²Unless⁺ those days should be shortened, there would no flesh be saved. But for the sake of the elect those days will be shortened.

²³Then if anyone says to you: Lo here*is* Christ or there. Do not believe *it*.

²⁴For there will arise false Christs and false prophets*who* will show great signs and wonders so that, if *it were* possible, they will deceive the very elect.

²⁵Behold I have told you before.

²⁶Therefore if they say to you: Behold He is in the desert, do not go forth and behold *He is* in the secret chambers, do not believe *it*.

²⁷For as the lightning comes out of the east and shines even to the west, so also will the coming of the Son of man be.

²⁸For wherever the carcass is, there will the eagles be gathered together.

²⁹Immediately after the tribulation of those days, the sun will be darkened, the moon will not give her light, the stars will fall from heaven, and the powers of the heavens will be shaken.
Isaiah 13:10, Joel 2:10

³⁰Then the sign of the Son of man will appear in heaven and then all the tribes of the earth will mourn and they will see the Son of man coming in the clouds of heaven with power and great glory.
Daniel 7:13

³¹He will send His angels with a great sound of a trumpet and they will gather together His elect from the four winds, from one end of heaven to the other.
Zechariah 9:14

³²Now learn a parable of⁺ the fig tree. When its branch is yet tender, and puts forth leaves, you know that summer *is* near.

³³So likewise you, when you see all these things, know that it is near at the doors.

³⁴Truly⁺ I say to you: This generation will not pass until all these things are fulfilled.

> ³⁵ Heaven and earth
> will pass away
> but my words
> will not pass away.

³⁶But of that day and hour no*one* knows. No, not *even* the angels of heaven, but only my Father.

³⁷ But as the days of Noah *were*, so also will the coming of the Son of man be.
Genesis 6:5

³⁸ For in the days before the flood, they were eating, drinking, marrying, and giving in marriage until the day that Noah entered the ark. *Genesis 7:7*

³⁹ And *they* did not understand⁺ until the flood came and took them all away. So also will the coming of the Son of man be.

⁴⁰ Then *as* two are in the field, one will be taken and the other left.

⁴¹ *As* two *are* grinding at the mill, one will be taken and the other left.

⁴² Watch, therefore, for you do not know *at* what hour your Lord is coming⁺.

⁴³ But know this: If the head⁺ of the house had known in what watch the thief would come, he would have watched and would not have suffered his house to be broken up.

⁴⁴ Therefore be ready. For the Son of man will come in an hour you do not expect⁺.

⁴⁵ Who then is a faithful and wise servant whom his lord has set⁺ over his household to give them food⁺ in due season?

⁴⁶ Blessed *is* that servant whom his lord will find doing *as instructed* when he comes.

⁴⁷ Truly⁺ I say to you that he will set⁺ *that servant* over all his goods.

⁴⁸ But if that evil servant says in his heart: My lord delays his coming

⁴⁹ and begins to strike⁺ *his* fellow servants and to eat and drink with drunks,

⁵⁰ the lord of that servant will come in a day when he is not looking for *him* and in an unknown⁺ hour.

⁵¹ and shall cut him in half⁺ and appoint his portion with the hypocrites and there will be weeping and gnashing of teeth.

Matthew Chapter 25

¹ Then the kingdom of heaven shall be compared⁺ to ten virgins who took their lamps and went forth to meet the bridegroom.

² Five of them were wise and five *were* foolish.

³ *Those* who *were* foolish took their lamps and took no oil with them.

⁴ But the wise took oil in their vessels with their lamps.

⁵ While the bridegroom tarried, they all slumbered and slept.

⁶ At midnight there was a cry: Behold the Bridegroom is coming.⁺ Go out to meet Him.

⁷ Then all those virgins arose and trimmed their lamps.

⁸ The foolish said to the wise: Give us *some* of your oil for our lamps have gone out.

⁹ But the wise answered saying: *No.* Lest there not be enough for us and you. But rather go to *those* who sell and buy for yourselves.

¹⁰ While they went to buy, the Bridegroom came. *Those* who were ready went in with Him to the marriage and the door was shut.

¹¹ Afterward the other virgins also came saying: Lord, Lord, open to us.

¹² But He answered and said: Truly⁺ I say to you: I do not know you.

¹³ Watch, therefore. For you do not know either the day or the hour in which the Son of man is coming.

¹⁴ For *the kingdom of heaven is* like⁺ a man traveling to a far country *who* called his servants and gave⁺ his goods to them.

¹⁵ To one he gave five talents. To another two. And to another one. To everyone⁺ according to their several abilities, and *then* immediately⁺ took his journey.

¹⁶ Then the one who had received the five talents traded with the same and earned⁺ another five talents.

¹⁷ Likewise the one who *had received* two also gained another two.

¹⁸ But the one who had received one *talent* dug in the earth and hid the lord's money.

¹⁹ After a long time, the lord of those servants came and examined⁺ *their accounts* with them.

²⁰ So the one who had received five talents brought another⁺ five talents saying: Lord, you delivered to me five talents. Behold I have gained five talents more.

²¹His lord said to him: Well done good and faithful servant. You have been faithful over a few things, I will set⁺ you over many things. Enter into the joy of your lord.

²²Likewise, the one who had received two talents said: Lord, you delivered to me two talents. Behold I have gained two more talents.

²³His lord said to him: Well done good and faithful servant. You have been faithful over a few things, I will set⁺ you over many things. Enter into the joy of your lord.

²⁴Then the one who had received one talent said: Lord, I knew that you are a hard man, reaping where you have not sown and gathering where you have not spread⁺.

²⁵I was afraid and hid your talent in the earth. Lo *there* you have *what is* yours.

²⁶The lord answered and said: *You* wicked and lazy⁺ servant. You knew that I reap where I did not sow and gather where I have not spread⁺.

²⁷Therefore you should have put my money with the bankers⁺ and *then* at my coming I should have received my own with interest⁺.

²⁸Therefore take the talent from *the lazy⁺ servant* and give *it* to *the* one who has ten talents.

²⁹For to everyone who has will *more* be given and they will have abundance. But from *those* who have nothing, even what they have will be taken away.

³⁰Cast the unprofitable servant into outer darkness *where* there will be weeping and gnashing of teeth.

³¹When the Son of man comes in His glory and all the holy angels with Him, then He will sit upon the throne of His glory.

³²Before Him will be gathered all nations and He will separate them one from another as a shepherd divides *the* sheep from the goats. *Ezekiel 34:17,20*

³³He will set the sheep at His right hand, but the goats at the left.

³⁴Then the King will say to those at His right hand: Come, you blessed by my Father. Inherit the kingdom prepared for you from the foundation of the world.

³⁵For I was hungry and you gave me food. ⁺ I was thirsty and you gave me drink. I was a stranger, and you took me in. *Isaiah 58:7*

³⁶*I was* naked and you clothed me. I was sick and you visited me. I was in prison and you came to me. *Isaiah 58:7*

³⁷Then the righteous will answer Him saying: Lord, when did we see you hungry and fed *you*? Or thirsty and gave *you* drink?

³⁸When did we see you a stranger and took *you* in? Or naked and clothed *you*?

³⁹Or when did we see you sick or in prison and came to you?

⁴⁰The King will answer and say to them: Truly⁺ I say to you: Inasmuch as you have done *it* to one of the least of these my brothers, you have done *it* to me. *Proverbs 19:17*

⁴¹Then He will also say to them on the left hand: Depart from me you cursed into everlasting fire prepared for the devil and his angels.

⁴²For I was hungry and you gave me no food. ⁺ I was thirsty and you gave me no drink.

⁴³I was a stranger and you did not take me in. Naked and you did not cloth me. Sick and in prison and you did not visit me.

⁴⁴Then they will also answer Him saying: Lord, when did we see you hungry or thirsty or a stranger or naked or sick or in prison and did not minister to you?

⁴⁵Then He will answer them saying: Truly⁺ I say to you: Inasmuch as you did not do *it* to one of the least of these, you did not do *it* to me.

⁴⁶*Therefore* these shall go away into everlasting punishment. But the righteous into eternal life. *Daniel 12:2*

Matthew Chapter 26

¹ Now⁺ it came to pass when Jesus had finished all these sayings, He said to His disciples:

² You know that after two days is *the Feast of* the Passover and the Son of man is betrayed to be crucified.

³ Then the chief priests, the scribes, and the elders of the people assembled together at⁺ the palace of the high priest who was called Caiaphas.

⁴ *They* consulted *so* that they might take Jesus by deceit⁺ and kill *Him*.

⁵ But they said: Not on the feast *day*, lest there be an uproar among the people.

⁶ Now when Jesus was in Bethany in the house of Simon the leper

⁷ A woman having an alabaster box of very precious ointment came to Him and poured it on His head as He sat *to eat*⁺.

⁸ But when His disciples saw *this*, they were indignant and said: To what purpose *is* this waste?

⁹ For this ointment might have been sold for much and given to the poor.

¹⁰ When Jesus understood *it* He said to them: Why do you trouble the woman? For she has done⁺ a good work upon me.

¹¹ For you always have the poor with you, but you will not always have me.

¹² For she has poured this ointment on my body for my burial.

¹³ Truly⁺ I say to you: Wherever this Gospel shall be proclaimed⁺ in the whole world, what this woman has done will also be told as a memorial of her.

¹⁴ Then one of the twelve called Judas Iscariot went to the chief priests

¹⁵ and said *to them*: What will you give me and I will deliver Him to you? And they agreed⁺ with him for thirty pieces of silver. *Zechariah 11:12*

¹⁶ From that time, he sought opportunity to betray Him.

¹⁷ Now the first *day* of the *Feast of* Unleavened Bread, the disciples came to Jesus saying to Him: Where do you want us to prepare for you to eat the Passover? *Exodus 12:14*

¹⁸ He said: Go into the city to such a man and say to him: The Master says: My time is *very* near.⁺ I will keep the Passover at your house with my disciples.

¹⁹ The disciples did as Jesus had directed⁺ them and they made preparations⁺ *for* the Passover.

²⁰ Now when the evening⁺ had come, He sat down with the twelve.

²¹ As they ate He said: Truly⁺ I say to you that one of you will betray me.

²² They were exceedingly sorrowful and began, everyone of them, to say to Him: Lord, is it me?

²³ He answered and said: He who dips *his* hand with me in the dish, the same will betray me.

²⁴ The Son of man goes as it is written of Him. But woe to that man by whom the Son of man is betrayed. It *would* have been good for that man if he had not been born.

²⁵ Then Judas who betrayed Him answered and said: Master, is it me? He said to him: You have said.

²⁶ As they were eating, Jesus took bread and blessed, broke *it*, and gave *it* to the disciples and said: Take. Eat. This is my body.

²⁷ *Then* He took the cup, gave thanks, and gave *it* to them saying: Drink of it, all *of you.*

²⁸ For this is my blood of the new covenant,⁺ which is shed for many for the remission of sins.

²⁹ But I say to you: I will not drink henceforth of this fruit of the vine until that day when I drink it new with you in my Father's kingdom.

³⁰ When they had sung a hymn, they went out to the Mount of Olives.

³¹ Then Jesus said to them: All *of* you will be offended because of me this night. For it is written: I will strike⁺ the shepherd and the sheep of the flock will be scattered. *Zechariah 13:7*

³² But after I am risen again, I will go before you into Galilee.

³³ Peter answered and said to Him: Though all *people* will be offended because of you, I will never be offended.

³⁴ Jesus said to him: Truly⁺ I say to you that this night, before the cock crows, you will deny me three times.

³⁵ Peter said to Him: Though I should die with you, I will not deny you. Likewise all the disciples said *the same* also.

36Then Jesus went+ with them to a place called Gethsemane and said to the disciples: Sit here while I go and pray *over* there+.

37He took Peter with Him, and the two sons of Zebedee, and *He* began to be sorrowful and very heavy.

38Then He said to them: My soul is exceedingly sorrowful, even unto death. Stay+ here and watch with me.

39He went a little farther and fell on His face and prayed saying: O my Father. If it be possible, let this cup pass from me. Nevertheless, not as I will, but as you *will*.

40*Then* He came to the disciples, found them asleep, and said to Peter: What? Could you not watch with me one hour?

---

41 Watch and pray
so that you do not
enter into temptation.
The spirit indeed *is* willing,
but the flesh *is* weak.

42*Then* He went away again the second time and prayed saying: O my Father. If this cup may not pass away from me unless+ I drink it, your will be done.

43And *then* He came and found them asleep again, for their eyes were heavy 44and He left them and went away again and prayed the third time saying the same words.

45Then He came to His disciples and said to them: Sleep on now and take *your* rest. Behold the hour is *very* near+ and the Son of man is betrayed into the hands of sinners.

46Rise. Let us be going. Behold he who betrays me is near+.

47While He spoke, behold, Judas, one of the twelve, came. With him *came* a great multitude with swords and staves, *coming* from the chief priests and elders of the people.

48Now he who betrayed Him gave them a sign saying: Whomever I shall kiss, that same is He. Hold Him fast. *Psalm 41:9*

49Immediately+ he came to Jesus and said: Hail Master, and kissed Him.

50Jesus said to him: Friend, why+ have you come? Then they came and laid hands on Jesus and took Him. *Psalm 41:9*

51And behold one of *those* who were with Jesus stretched out *his* hand and drew his sword and struck a servant of the high priest and cut+ off his ear.

52Then Jesus said to him: Put up your sword into its place, for all *those* who take *up* the sword shall perish by+ the sword.

53Do you think that I cannot now pray to my Father and He would+ immediately+ give me more than twelve legions of angels?

54But how then would+ the Scriptures be fulfilled? So+ it must be *done* in this way.

55In that same hour, Jesus said to the multitudes: Have you come out as against a thief with swords and staves to take me? I sat daily with you teaching in the temple and you laid no hold on me.

56But all this was done *so* the Scriptures of the prophets might be fulfilled. Then all the disciples left+ Him and fled. *Zechariah 13:7*

57*Those* who had seized+ Jesus led *Him* away to Caiaphas the high priest where the scribes and the elders were assembled.

58But Peter followed Him *from* a distance+ to the high priest's palace and went in and sat with the servants to see the end.

59Now the chief priests and elders and all the council sought false testimony+ against Jesus to put Him to death.

60But *they* found none. Yes, though many false witnesses came, *yet* they found none. At last, two false witnesses came *Psalm 27:12, Psalm 35:11*

61and said: This *fellow* said: I am able to destroy the temple of God and to build it in three days.

62The high priest arose and said to Him: Do you answer nothing? What *is it that* these witness against you?

63But Jesus *remained* silent.+ And the high priest answered and said to Him: I beg+ you by the living God that you tell us whether you are the Christ, the Son of God. *Isaiah 53:7*

⁶⁴Jesus said to him: You have said. Nevertheless I say to you: Hereafter you will see the Son of man sitting at the right hand of power and coming in the clouds of heaven. *Psalm 110:1, Daniel 7:13*

⁶⁵Then the high priest tore⁺ his clothes saying: He has spoken blasphemy. What further need do we have of witnesses? Behold, now you have heard His blasphemy.

⁶⁶What do you think? They answered and said: He is guilty of death.

⁶⁷Then they spit in His face and buffeted Him. Others struck⁺ *Him* with the palms of their hands, *Isaiah 50:6*

⁶⁸saying: Prophesy to us, you Christ. Who is he who struck⁺ you?

⁶⁹Now Peter sat outside⁺ in the palace. A girl⁺ came to him saying: You also were with Jesus of Galilee.

⁷⁰But *Peter* denied *it* before *them* all saying: I do not know what you are saying. ⁺

⁷¹*Then* when he went⁺ out to the porch, another saw him and said to *those* who were there: This *fellow* was also with Jesus of Nazareth.

⁷²Again he denied with an oath: I do not know the man.

⁷³After a while *those* who stood by came and said to Peter: Surely you also are *one* of them, for your speech betrays you.

⁷⁴Then he began to curse and to swear *saying*: I do not know the man. And immediately the cock crowed. ⁺

⁷⁵And Peter remembered the words of Jesus who had said to him: Before the cock crows you will deny me three times. And he went out and wept bitterly.

Matthew Chapter 27

¹ When the morning had come, all the chief priests and elders of the people took counsel against Jesus to put Him to death.

² When they had bound Him, they led *Him* away and delivered Him to Pontius Pilate the governor.

³ Then Judas, who had betrayed Him, when he saw that He was condemned, repented and took⁺ the thirty pieces of silver to the chief priests and elders

⁴ saying: I have sinned in that I have betrayed innocent blood. They said: What *is that* to us? You live⁺ *with that*.

⁵ And he threw⁺ down the pieces of silver in the temple and went *out* and hung himself. *Zechariah 11:13*

⁶ The chief priests took the silver pieces and said: It is not lawful to put them into the treasury because it is the price of blood.

⁷ *So* they took counsel and with them bought the potter's field in which to bury strangers.

⁸ Therefore that field was called: The field of blood. *And it is* to this day.

⁹ This fulfilled what was spoken by the prophet Jeremiah *who* said: And they took the thirty pieces of silver, the price *and* value set⁺ by the sons⁺ of Israel, *Jeremiah 32:7, Zechariah 11:12*

¹⁰and gave them for the potter's field, as the Lord directed⁺ me. *Zechariah 11:13*

¹¹*When* Jesus stood before the governor, the governor asked Him saying: Are you the King of the Jews? And Jesus said to him: You say.

¹²When He was accused by the chief priests and elders, He answered nothing.

¹³Then Pilate said to Him: Do you not hear how many things they witness against you?

¹⁴*Jesus* answered not a word; so that the governor marveled greatly. *Isaiah 53:7*

¹⁵Now at *the* feast, it was the custom⁺ for the governor to release a prisoner to the people, whomever⁺ they wanted. ⁺

¹⁶And they had then a notable prisoner called Barabbas.

¹⁷Therefore when they were gathered together, Pilate said to them: Whom do you want⁺ me to release to you? Barabbas or Jesus who is called Christ?

¹⁸For he knew that *it was* for envy they had delivered Him.

¹⁹*Now* when he was seated⁺ on the judgment seat, his wife sent to him saying: Have nothing to do with that righteous⁺ man, for I have suffered many things this day in a dream because of Him.

²⁰But the chief priests and elders persuaded the multitude that they should ask *for* Barabbas and destroy Jesus.

²¹The governor answered and said to them: Which⁺ of the two do you want⁺ me to release to you? They said: Barabbas.

²²Pilate said to them: What shall I do then with Jesus who is called Christ? *They* all said to him: Let Him be crucified.

²³The governor said: Why? What evil has He done? But they cried out *all* the more saying: Let Him be crucified.

²⁴When Pilate saw that he could not prevail, but *that* rather a tumult was made, he took water and washed *his* hands before the multitude saying: I am innocent of the blood of this righteous⁺ person. See *to it*.

²⁵Then all the people answered and said: His blood *be* on us and on our children.

²⁶Then he released Barabbas to them and when he had flogged⁺ Jesus, he delivered *Him* to be crucified.

²⁷Then the soldiers of the governor took Jesus into the common hall and gathered to Him the whole company⁺ *of soldiers*.

²⁸They stripped Him and put a scarlet robe on Him.

²⁹And when they had made⁺ a crown of thorns, they put*it* on His head and a reed in His right hand. *Then* they bowed the knee before Him and mocked Him saying: Hail, King of the Jews.

³⁰They spit on Him and took the reed and struck⁺ Him on the head. *Isaiah 50:6*

³¹After they had mocked Him, they took the robe off of Him and put His own clothing⁺ on Him and led Him away to crucify *Him. Psalm 22:7*

³²As they came out, they found a man of Cyrene by the name of Simon and they compelled him to bear *Jesus'* cross.

³³When they had come to a place called Golgotha, that is to say a place of a skull ³⁴they gave Him vinegar to drink mingled with gall. When He had tasted *it*, He would not drink. *Psalm 69:21*

³⁵*Then* they crucified Him and divided⁺ His garments *by* casting lots, thus fulfilling what was spoken by the prophet:

They divided⁺ my garments among them and upon my coat⁺ they cast lots. *Psalm 22:18*

³⁶And, sitting down, they watched Him there ³⁷and set up over His head *the* written accusation: This is Jesus The King of the Jews.

³⁸There were two thieves crucified with Him: One on the right side⁺ and another on the left. *Isaiah 53:12*

³⁹*Those* who passed by reviled Him, shaking⁺ their heads *Psalm 109:25* ⁴⁰and saying: You who *would* destroy the temple and rebuild⁺ *it* in three days, save yourself. If you are the Son of God, come down from the cross.

⁴¹Likewise also the chief priests mocked *Him* with the scribes and elders, saying: *Psalm 22:7*

⁴²He saved others. He cannot save Himself. If He is the King of Israel, let Him come down from the cross now and we will believe Him.

⁴³He trusted in God, let *God* deliver Him now, if He will have Him, for He said: I Am the Son of God. *Psalm 22:8*

⁴⁴The thieves also, who were crucified with Him, reviled⁺ Him. *Psalm 109:25*

⁴⁵Now from twelve o'clock⁺ *noon*, there was darkness over all the land until⁺ three⁺ *in the afternoon*.

⁴⁶About three⁺ *in the afternoon* Jesus cried *out* with a loud voice saying: Eli, Eli, lama sabachthani. That is to say: My God, my God, why have you forsaken me? *Psalm 22:1*

⁴⁷Some of *those* who stood there, when they heard *that*, said: This *man* calls for Elijah.

⁴⁸Immediately⁺ one of them ran and took a sponge, filled *it* with vinegar, put *it* on a reed, and gave *it to* Him to drink.

⁴⁹The rest said: Let *Him* be. Let us see whether Elijah will come to save Him.

⁵⁰When Jesus had cried *out* again with a loud voice, He yielded up the spirit.⁺

⁵¹And behold the veil of the temple was torn⁺ in two from the top to the bottom, the earth quaked,⁺ and the rocks broke.⁺

⁵²Graves were opened and many bodies of saints who slept arose

⁵³and came out of the graves after His resurrection and went into the holy city and appeared to many.

⁵⁴Now when the centurion and *those* who were with him watching Jesus saw the earthquake and those things that were done, they feared greatly, saying: Truly this was the Son of God.

⁵⁵Many women who *had* followed Jesus from Galilee ministering to Him were there watching⁺ *from* a distance.⁺

⁵⁶Among them were Mary Magdalene, Mary the mother of James and Joses, and the mother of Zebedee's children.

⁵⁷When the evening⁺ had come, there came a rich man of Arimathaea named Joseph, who also himself was Jesus' disciple. *Isaiah 53:9*

⁵⁸He went to Pilate and asked⁺ *for* Jesus' body. Then Pilate commanded the body to be delivered.

⁵⁹When Joseph had taken the body, he wrapped it in a clean linen cloth

⁶⁰and laid it in his own new tomb that he had cut⁺ out in the rock. *Then* he rolled a great stone to the door of the tomb⁺ and departed. *Isaiah 53:9*

⁶¹And there were Mary Magdalene and the other Mary sitting over by⁺ the tomb.⁺

⁶²Now the next day that followed the day of the preparation, the chief priests and Pharisees came together to Pilate

⁶³saying: Sir, we remember that that deceiver said, while He was yet alive: After three days I will rise again.

⁶⁴Therefore command that the tomb⁺ be made sure until the third day, lest His disciples come by night and steal Him away and say to the people *that* He is risen from the dead. So, the last error will be worse than the first.

⁶⁵Pilate said to them: You have guards.⁺ Go *and* make *it* as sure as you can.

⁶⁶So they went and made the tomb⁺ sure, sealing the stone and setting guards.⁺

Matthew Chapter 28

¹ At the end of the Sabbath, as it began to dawn toward the first of the week, Mary Magdalene and the other Mary came to see the tomb.⁺

² And behold there was a great earthquake, for the angel of the Lord descended from heaven, came and rolled back the stone from the door, and sat upon it.

³ His countenance was like lightning and his clothing⁺ white as snow.

⁴ For fear of him, the keepers shook and became like⁺ dead *people*.

⁵ The angel answered and said to the women: Do not be afraid, for I know that you seek Jesus who was crucified.

⁶ He is not here, for He is risen as He said. Come. See the place where the Lord had lain.⁺ *Psalm 16:10, Psalm 49:15*

⁷ Go quickly and tell His disciples that He is risen from the dead, and behold He goes before you into Galilee. You will see Him there. Behold I have told you.

⁸ They departed quickly from the tomb⁺ with fear and great joy and ran to bring word to His disciples.

⁹ As they went to tell His disciples, behold Jesus met them saying: All hail. And they came and held Him by the feet and worshiped Him.

¹⁰Then Jesus said to them: Do not be afraid. Go tell my brothers to go into Galilee and they will see me there.

¹¹Now when they were going, behold some of the guards⁺ came into the city and showed the chief priests all the things that were done.

¹²When they were assembled with the elders and had taken counsel, they gave large *sums of* money to the soldiers,

¹³saying: Say *that* His disciples came by night and stole Him *away* while we slept.

¹⁴If this comes to the governor's ears, we will persuade him and secure you.

¹⁵So they took the money and did as they were taught, and this saying is commonly reported among the Jews *even* until this day.

¹⁶Then the eleven disciples went away into Galilee, to a mountain where Jesus had directed⁺ them *to go*.

¹⁷When they saw Him, they worshiped Him. But some doubted.

¹⁸*Then* Jesus came and spoke to them saying: All authority⁺ is given to me in heaven and in earth.

> ¹⁹ Go therefore
> and teach all nations,
> baptizing them in the name
> of the Father and of the Son
> and of the Holy Spirit,
> ²⁰ teaching them to observe
> all things whatsoever
> I have commanded you.
> Behold I am with you always,
> *even* to the end of the world.
> Amen.

The Gospel of Jesus Christ as surveyed by Mark

Chapter 1

¹ The beginning of the Gospel of Jesus Christ the Son of God.
² As it is written in the prophets: Behold I send my messenger before your face who will prepare your way before you. *Matthew 11:10*
³ The voice of one crying in the wilderness: Prepare the way of *the* Lord. Make His paths straight. *Matthew 3:3*
⁴ John baptized in the wilderness and proclaimed⁺ the baptism of repentance for the remission of sins.
⁵ All *those in* the land of Judea and those of Jerusalem went to him and were all baptized by him in the Jordan river confessing their sins.
⁶ John was clothed with camel's hair with a leather⁺ belt⁺ around⁺ his waist⁺ and he ate locusts and wild honey.
⁷ And *he* proclaimed⁺: One is coming after me *who* is mightier than I, the straps⁺ of whose sandals⁺ I am not worthy to stoop down and loosen.
⁸ I indeed have baptized you with water but He will baptize you with the Holy Spirit.

⁹ Now⁺ it came to pass in those days *that* Jesus came from Nazareth of Galilee and was baptized by John in *the* Jordan *river*.
¹⁰Immediately⁺ *after* coming up out of the water, He saw the heavens opened and the Spirit descending like a dove upon Himself.
¹¹And there came a voice from heaven *saying*: You are my beloved Son in whom I am well pleased.
¹²*Then* immediately *after that* the Spirit drove Him into the wilderness.
¹³He was there in the wilderness forty days tempted by Satan. And *He* was with the *wild* beasts. And the angels ministered to Him.
¹⁴Now after John was put in prison, Jesus came into Galilee proclaiming⁺ the Gospel of the kingdom of God
¹⁵and saying: The time is fulfilled and the kingdom of God is *very* near.⁺ Repent and believe the Gospel.
¹⁶Now as He walked by the sea of Galilee, He saw Simon and Andrew his brother casting a net into the sea, for they were fishermen.⁺
¹⁷Jesus said to them: Come after me and I will make you to become fishers of men.
¹⁸Immediately⁺ they left⁺ their nets and followed Him.
¹⁹When He had gone a little farther from there,⁺ He saw James the *son* of Zebedee and John his brother who also *were* in a boat mending their nets.
²⁰Immediately⁺ He called them and they left their father Zebedee in the boat with the hired servants and followed⁺ Him.
²¹*From there* they went to Capernaum and immediately⁺ on the Sabbath day *Jesus* entered the synagogue and taught.
²²They were astonished at His doctrine for He taught them as one who had authority and not as the scribes.
²³In their synagogue there was a man with an unclean spirit and he cried out ²⁴saying: Let *us* alone. What do we have to do with you Jesus of Nazareth? Have you come to destroy us? I know who you are: the Holy One of God.
²⁵Jesus rebuked him saying: Be still⁺ and come out of him.

²⁶When the unclean spirit had shaken⁺ him and cried *out* with a loud voice, *it* came out of him.

²⁷They were all amazed so that they questioned among themselves saying: What is this? What new doctrine *is* this? For He commands with authority, even the unclean spirits, and they obey Him.

²⁸Immediately His reputation⁺ spread widely⁺ throughout all the region around⁺ Galilee.

²⁹As soon as they came⁺ out of the synagogue, *Jesus* entered the house of Simon and Andrew with James and John.

³⁰Simon's wife's mother lay *sick* with a fever and immediately⁺ they spoke to Him about her.

³¹He came *to her*, took her *by the* hand and lifted her up, and immediately the fever left her and she ministered to them.

³²Evening⁺ having come, when the sun had set, they brought to Him all who were diseased and those *who were* demon⁺ possessed.

³³All the city was gathered together at the door.

³⁴He healed many who were sick *with* various⁺ diseases and cast out many demons.⁺ But *He* did not allow⁺ the demons⁺ to speak because they knew Him.

³⁵In the morning, rising up a great while before day *break*, He went out and departed to a solitary place and prayed there.

³⁶Simon and the others who were with Him followed after Him.

³⁷When they found Him they said to Him: All *the people* are seeking you.

³⁸He said to them: Let us go to the next towns *so* that I can proclaim⁺ *the Word* there also, because *it is* for this *purpose that* I have come.

³⁹*Then* He proclaimed⁺ *the Word* in their synagogues throughout all Galilee and cast out demons.⁺

⁴⁰A leper came to Him beseeching Him, kneeling down to Him, and saying to Him: If you will you can make me clean.

⁴¹Moved with compassion, Jesus put forth *His* hand and touched him and said to him: I will. Be clean.

⁴²As soon as He had spoken, immediately the leprosy departed from him and he was cleansed.

⁴³*Jesus* strictly⁺ warned⁺ him and immediately⁺ sent him away

⁴⁴saying to him: See *that* you say nothing to anyone. But go⁺ and show yourself to the priest and *make an* offering⁺ for your cleansing *according to* those things that Moses commanded, as a testimony to them.

⁴⁵But he went out and began to tell⁺ many⁺ *people* and spread⁺ the matter widely⁺ so that Jesus could no longer⁺ enter the city openly, but was outside⁺ in deserted⁺ places. And *yet the people still* came to Him from everywhere.⁺

Mark Chapter 2

¹After *some* days, *Jesus* entered Capernaum again and it was *quickly* reported⁺ that He was in the house.

²Immediately⁺ many gathered together so that there was no room to receive *them all*. No, not even⁺ near⁺ the door; and He proclaimed⁺ the Word to them.

³They came to Him bringing one sick with paralysis⁺ who was carried⁺ by four *others*.

⁴When they could not get near Him because of the crowd,⁺ they uncovered the roof where He was. When they had broken *it* up, they let down the bed in which the *one* sick with paralysis⁺ lay.

⁵When Jesus saw their faith, He said to the *one* sick with paralysis⁺: Son, your sins are forgiven.

⁶But there were some of the scribes sitting there and reasoning in their hearts:

⁷Why does this *man* speak such blasphemies? Who can forgive sins, but God only?

⁸Immediately when Jesus perceived in His spirit that they so reasoned within themselves, He said to them: Why do you reason these things in your hearts?

⁹ Which⁺ is easier to say to *someone* sick with paralysis⁺: *Your* sins are forgiven; or to say: Arise and take up your bed and walk.

¹⁰But *so* that you may know that the Son of man has authority⁺ *and power* on earth to forgive sins, He said to the *one* sick with paralysis⁺:

¹¹I say to you: Arise. Take up your bed and go⁺ to your house.

¹²Immediately he arose, took up the bed, and went forth before them all so that they were all amazed and glorified God saying: We never saw *anything like this before*.

¹³*Then Jesus* went to the seaside again and all the multitude came⁺ to Him and He taught them.

¹⁴As He passed by, He saw Levi the *son* of Alphaeus sitting at the tax office⁺ and said to him: Follow me. And he arose and followed Him.

¹⁵Now⁺ it came to pass, as *Jesus* sat *down* to eat⁺ in *Levi's* house, many worldly⁺ people and sinners sat with Jesus and His disciples, for there were many and they followed Him.

¹⁶When the scribes and Pharisees saw Him eat with worldly⁺ people and sinners, they said to His disciples: How is it that He eats and drinks with worldly⁺ people and sinners?

¹⁷When Jesus heard *this*, He said to them: *Those* who are whole have no need of a physician but *those* who are sick *do*. I did not come to call the righteous but sinners to repentance.

¹⁸*Now* the disciples of John and of the Pharisees used to fast *so* they came and said to Him: Why do the disciples of John and of the Pharisees fast but your disciples do not fast?

¹⁹Jesus said to them: Can the children of the bride chamber fast while the bridegroom is with them? As long as they have the bridegroom with them, they cannot fast.

²⁰But the days will come when the Bridegroom will be taken away from them and then they will fast in those days.

²¹No one sews a piece of new cloth on an old garment, *or* else the new piece that fills it up takes away from the old and the tear⁺ is made worse.

²²And no one puts new wine into old wineskins,⁺ *or* else the new wine will burst the wineskins⁺ and the wine is spilled and the wineskins⁺ will be destroyed.⁺ But new wine must be put into new wineskins⁺.

²³Now⁺ it came to pass that *Jesus* went through the corn fields on the Sabbath day and His disciples began to pluck the ears of corn as they went.

²⁴The Pharisees said to Him: Behold why do they, on the Sabbath day, *do* what is not lawful?

²⁵*Jesus* said to them: Have you never read what David did when he had need and was hungry, he and *those* who were with him, ²⁶how he went into the house of God in the days of Abiathar the high priest and ate the show bread that is not lawful for *anyone* but the priests to eat, and *he* also gave *some* to *those* who were with him. ²⁷He said to them: The Sabbath was made for people⁺ and not people for the Sabbath.

²⁸Therefore the Son of man is Lord also of the Sabbath.

Mark Chapter 3

¹ *Then Jesus* entered the synagogue again, and there was a man there who had a withered hand.

² *The Pharisees* watched Him *to see* whether He would heal him on the Sabbath day *so* that they might accuse Him.

³ *Jesus* said to the man who had the withered hand: Stand forth.

⁴ And He said to them: Is it lawful to do good on the Sabbath days or to do evil? To save life or to kill? But they *remained* silent.⁺

⁵ When He had looked around⁺ at them with anger, being grieved for the hardness of their hearts, He said to the man: Stretch forth your hand, and he stretched *it* out and his hand was restored whole as the other.

⁶ *Then* the Pharisees went forth and immediately⁺ took counsel with the Herodians against Him, *to decide* how they might destroy Him.

⁷ But Jesus withdrew to the sea with His disciples and a great multitude from Galilee followed Him, and from Judea ⁸ and from Jerusalem and from Idumaea and *from* beyond Jordan. And those from Tyre and Sidon, a great multitude, when they had heard what great things He did, *they also* came to Him.

⁹ He told His disciples that a small boat should wait for Him because of the multitude, lest they should overcrowd⁺ Him.

¹⁰For He had healed many so that all⁺ *who* had plagues pressed *in* upon Him to touch Him.

¹¹Unclean spirits, when they saw Him, fell down before Him and cried *out* saying: You are the Son of God.

¹²And He strictly⁺ charged them to not make Him known.

¹³*Then* He went up into a mountain and called *those* whom He wanted⁺ and they came to Him.

¹⁴He appointed⁺ twelve to⁺ be with Him, *so* that He might send them forth to proclaim⁺ *the Word*

¹⁵and to have authority⁺ *and power* to heal sicknesses and to cast out demons.⁺

¹⁶Simon He surnamed Peter.

¹⁷James the *son* of Zebedee and John the brother of James He surnamed Boanerges, which is: the sons of thunder.

¹⁸*The others were* Andrew, Philip, Bartholomew, Matthew, Thomas, James the *son* of Alphaeus, Thaddaeus, Simon the Canaanite,

¹⁹and Judas Iscariot who also betrayed Him. *Then* they went into a house

²⁰and the multitude came together again so that they could not so much as eat bread.

²¹When His friends heard *about it*, they went out to lay hold on Him, for they said: He is beside Himself.

²²*Then* the scribes who came down from Jerusalem said: He has Beelzebub and by the prince of the demons⁺ He casts out demons.⁺

²³*Jesus* called them *to Himself* and said to them in parables: How can Satan cast out Satan?

²⁴If a kingdom is divided against itself, that kingdom cannot stand.

²⁵If a house is divided against itself, that house cannot stand.

²⁶If Satan rise up against himself and is divided, he cannot stand but has *met his* end.

²⁷No one can enter into a strong man's house and spoil his goods unless⁺ he first bind the strong man. Then he will spoil his house.

²⁸Truly⁺ I say to you: All sins will be forgiven to the children⁺ of people,⁺ and blasphemies with which ⁺ they blaspheme;

²⁹but *those* who blaspheme against the Holy Spirit will have no forgiveness but are in danger of eternal damnation.

³⁰*He said this* because they said: He has an unclean spirit.

³¹Then His brothers and mother came and, standing outside,⁺ *they* sent for Him *by* calling *out to* Him.

³²The multitude sat around⁺ Him and said to Him: Behold your mother and your brothers outside⁺ seek you.

³³He answered them saying: Who are my mother or my brothers?

³⁴And He looked around⁺ at *those* who sat around⁺ Him and said: Behold my mother and my brothers.

³⁵For whoever does the will of God, the same is my brother and my sister and mother.

Mark Chapter 4

¹ *Then Jesus* began again to teach by the seaside. There was gathered to Him a great multitude so that He entered a boat and sat *out* upon the sea, and the whole multitude was on the land by the sea.

² He taught them many things by parables and said to them in His doctrine:

³ Listen.⁺ Behold a sower went out to sow.

⁴ Now⁺ it came to pass as he sowed *that* some fell by the wayside and the birds⁺ of the air came and devoured it up.

5 Some fell on stony ground where it did not have much earth. Immediately it sprang up, because it had no depth of earth.

6 But when the sun was up, it was scorched and because it had no root, it withered away.

7 Some fell among thorns and the thorns grew up and choked it and it yielded no fruit.

8 Other fell on good ground and yielded fruit that sprang up and increased and brought forth: some thirty, some sixty, and some a hundred *times more*.

9 He said to them: *Those* who have ears to hear, let them hear.

10*Later,* when He was alone, *those* who were around+ Him with the twelve asked Him about the parable.

11He said to them: Unto you it is given to know the mystery of the kingdom of God, but for *those* who are outside,+ all *these* things are done in parables

12*so* that seeing they may see and not perceive, and hearing they may hear and not understand, lest at any time they should be converted and *their* sins should be forgiven them. *Matthew 13:14*

13He said to them: Do you not under-stand+ this parable? How then will you understand+ all *the other* parables?

14The sower sows the Word *of God.*

15These are the *ones* by the wayside where the Word is sown, but when they have heard, Satan comes immediately and takes away the Word that was sown in their hearts.

16These are likewise sown on stony ground and when they hear the Word, *they* immediately receive it with gladness

17but *they* have no root in themselves and so *they* endure only for a time. *Then* later,+ when affliction or persecution arises because of the Word, immedi-ately they are caused+ *to sin*.

18These are the *ones* who are sown among thorns, such as hear the Word

19but the cares of this world and the deceitfulness of riches and the lusts of other things enter in and choke the Word and it becomes unfruitful.

20These are the *ones* who are sown on good ground, such as hear the Word and receive *it* and bring forth fruit: some thirtyfold, some sixty, and some a hundred *times more*.

21He said to them: Is a candle brought to be put under a bushel or under a bed and not to be set on a candlestick?

22There is nothing hid that will not be revealed.+ Neither has anything *been* kept secret but that it should *eventually* become known+. *Matthew 10:26*

> 23 If anyone has ears to hear, let them hear.

24He said to them: Take heed what you hear. With what gauge+ you measure, it will be measured to you. To you who hear, more will be given.

25For to *those* who have will *more* be given and from *those* who have nothing, from them will be taken *away* even what they have.

26*Then* He said: The kingdom of God is like this: If a man should cast seed into the ground

27and should sleep and rise night and day and the seed should spring and grow up, he does not understand+ how.

28For the earth brings forth fruit by herself: First the blade, then the stalk,+ *and* after that the full ear of corn.

29But when the fruit is brought forth, *the farmer* immediately puts in the sickle because the harvest *time* has come.

30*Then* He said: To what shall we com-pare+ the kingdom of God? Or with what illustration+ shall we compare it?

31*It is* like a grain of mustard seed which, when it is sown in the earth, is the smallest+ *of* all the seeds in the earth.

32But when it is sown, it grows up and becomes greater than all herbs and shoots out great branches so that the birds+ of the air may lodge under the shadow of it.

33With many such parables He spoke the Word to them, as they were able to hear *it*.

34But without a parable He did not speak to them, and when they were alone, He expounded everything to His disciples.

35 The same day when the evening+ had come, He said to them: Let us go+ over to the other side.

36 When they had sent away the multitude, they took Him as *He* was in the boat. And there were other little boats with Him also.

37 *Then* a great windstorm+ arose and the waves beat into the boat so that it was now full.

38 *Jesus* was in the aft+ of the boat asleep on a pillow. They awakened Him and said to Him: Master, do you not care that we *might* perish?

39 He arose and rebuked the wind and said to the sea: Peace. Be still. And the wind stopped+ and there was a great calm.

40 He said to them: Why are you so fearful? How is it that you have no faith?

41 And they were exceedingly fearful and said to one another: What kind+ of man is this that even the wind and the sea obey Him?

Mark Chapter 5

1 *Then* they came over to the other side of the sea to the country of the Gadarenes.

2 When *Jesus* had come out of the boat, immediately *coming* out of the tombs, a man with an unclean spirit met Him.

3 *This man* had *his* dwelling *place* among the tombs and no one could bind him. No, not with chains.

4 He had often been bound with shackles+ and chains, and the chains had been pulled apart+ by him, and the shackles+ broken in pieces. No one could subdue+ him.

5 Always, night and day, he was in the mountains and in the tombs, crying and cutting himself with stones.

6 But when he saw Jesus *from* a distance,+ he ran and worshiped Him

7 and cried *out* with a loud voice and said: What have I to do with you Jesus, Son of the most high God? I beg+ you by God that you not torment me.

8 For *Jesus* said to him: Come out of the man *you* unclean spirit.

9 *Jesus* asked him: What *is* your name? He answered saying: My name *is* Legion for we are many.

10 And *they* begged+ *Jesus* greatly+ that He would not send them away out of the country.

11 Now a large herd of swine was there on the mountain feeding.

12 And all the demons+ begged+ Him saying: Send us into the swine *so* that we may enter into them.

13 Immediately+ Jesus allowed+ them to go+ and the unclean spirits left+ and entered the swine, and the *entire* herd of about two thousand ran violently down a steep place into the sea and were choked in the sea.

14 *Those* who fed the swine fled and told *all about this* in the city and in the country, and the *people* went out to see what it was that was done.

15 And they came to Jesus and saw the one who had been demon+ possessed and had the legion, dressed+ and sitting *still*, in his right mind, and they were afraid.

16 *Those* who saw *it* told what had happened+ to the one who had been demon+ possessed, and concerning the swine+

17 and they began to beg+ Him to depart out of their borders.+

18 When *Jesus* had come into the boat, the one who had been demon+ possessed begged+ Him that he might stay with Him.

19 However Jesus did not allow him, but said to him: Go home to your *friends* and tell them how much+ the Lord has done for you, *that He* has had compassion on you.

20 *So* he departed and began to tell+ *everyone* in Decapolis how much+ Jesus had done for him, and all *the people* marveled.

21 When Jesus crossed+ over *the sea* again by boat to the other side, many people gathered to Him, and He was near the sea.

22 And behold one of the rulers of the synagogue, Jairus by name, came *to Him*, and when he saw Him, he fell at His feet

²³and begged⁺ Him greatly saying: My little daughter lies at the point of death. *I beg⁺ you to* come and lay your hands on her *so* that she may be healed, and she will live.

²⁴*Jesus* went with him and many people followed Him and crowded⁺ in upon Him.

²⁵*Now* a certain woman had an issue of blood twelve years

²⁶and had suffered many things by many physicians. *She* had spent all that she had and was no better, but rather grew worse.

²⁷*So,* when she heard about Jesus, *she* came in the crowd⁺ *and from* behind touched His garment.

²⁸For she said: If I may touch but His clothes, I will be whole.

²⁹Immediately⁺ the flow⁺ of her blood was dried up and she felt in *her* body that she was healed of that plague.

³⁰Jesus, immediately knowing in Himself that virtue had gone out of Him, turned around⁺ in the crowd⁺ and said: Who touched my clothes?

³¹His disciples said to Him: You see the multitude crowding⁺ *in upon* you and you say: Who touched me?

³²And He looked around⁺ to see who had done this.

³³But the woman, fearful and trembling knowing what was done in her, came and fell down before Him and told Him all the truth.

³⁴He said to her: Daughter, your faith has made you whole. Go in peace and be healed⁺ of your plague.

³⁵While He spoke, someone⁺ came from *the house of* the ruler of the synagogue who said: Your daughter is dead. Why trouble the Master any further?

³⁶As soon as Jesus heard the word that was spoken, He said to the ruler of the synagogue:

> Do not be afraid.
> Only believe.

³⁷He allowed⁺ no one to follow Him except⁺ Peter, James, and John the brother of James.

³⁸He came to the house of the ruler of the synagogue and saw the tumult and *those* who wept and wailed greatly.

³⁹When He had come in, He said to them: Why do you make this fuss⁺ and weep? The girl⁺ is not dead, but sleeps.

⁴⁰They laughed *at* Him *scornfully*, but when He had sent⁺ them all out, He took the father and the mother of the girl⁺ and *those* who were with Him and entered in where the girl⁺ was lying.

⁴¹He took the girl⁺ by the hand and said to her: Talitha cumi, which means⁺: *Little* girl⁺ I say to you: Arise.

⁴²Immediately⁺ the girl⁺ arose and walked for she was twelve years *old.* They were astonished with great amazement.⁺

⁴³*Jesus* charged them strictly⁺ that no one should know *about* this, and commanded that something should be given to her to eat.

Mark Chapter 6

¹ *Then Jesus* went from there⁺ to His own country, and His disciples followed Him.

² When the Sabbath day had come, He began to teach in the synagogue. Many hearing *Him* were astonished saying: From where has this *man acquired* these things? What wisdom *is* this given to Him *so* that even such mighty works are worked⁺ by His hands?

³ Is this not the carpenter, the son of Mary, the brother of James and Joses and of Jude and Simon? Are His sisters not here with us? And they were offended by Him.

⁴ But Jesus said to them: A prophet is not without honor, except in his own country and among his own relatives⁺ and in his own house.

⁵ He could do no mighty works there except that He laid His hands on a few sick people⁺ and healed *them*.

⁶ He marveled beeause of their unbelief. And He went *all* around⁺ the villages teaching.

⁷ *Then* He called the twelve and began to send them forth two *by* two and gave them authority⁺ *and power* over unclean spirits.

[8] *He* commanded them to take nothing for *their* journey except a staff only: No *provision* bag,[+] no bread, *and* no money in *their* purse.

[9] But *to* wear sandals, but not *to* put on two coats.

[10] He said to them: In whatever place [+] you enter into a house, stay[+] there until you depart from that place.

[11] Whoever will not receive you or hear you, when you depart from there[+] shake off the dust under your feet for a testimony against them. Truly[+] I say to you: It will be more tolerable for Sodom and Gomorrah in the day of judgment than for that city.

[12] *So* they went forth[+] and proclaimed[+] that people[+] should repent.

[13] They cast out many demons[+] and anointed many with oil who were sick and healed *them*.

[14] *When* king Herod heard *about Jesus* because His name was spread widely,[+] he said that John the Baptist was risen from the dead and therefore mighty works do show forth themselves in him.

[15] Others said: It is Elijah. And others said: It is a prophet or *someone* like one of the prophets.

[16] But when Herod heard *about it* he said: It is John whom I beheaded. He is risen from the dead.

[17] For Herod himself had sent forth and seized[+] John and bound him in prison for the sake of Herodias, his brother Philip's wife, for he had married her.

[18] For John had said to Herod: It is not lawful for you to have your brother's wife.

[19] Therefore Herodias had a quarrel against *John* and would have killed him. But she could not.

[20] For Herod feared John, knowing that he was a righteous[+] and holy man, *therefore Herod* protected[+] him. When *Herod* heard *John*, he did many things and heard *John* gladly.

[21] When a convenient day had come, Herod made *his* birthday supper for his lords, high captains, and chief *estates* of Galilee.

[22] And when the daughter of Herodias came in and danced and pleased Herod and *those* who sat with him, the king said to the girl[+]: Ask of me whatever you will and I will give *it to* you.

[23] He swore to her: Whatever you ask of me, I will give *it to* you, to the half of my kingdom.

[24] She said to her mother: What shall I ask? Her *mother* said: The head of John the Baptist.

[25] *So* she came in to the king immediately[+] *and* with haste and asked saying: I desire[+] that you give me the head of John the Baptist on a platter[+] immediately.[+]

[26] The king was exceedingly sorry, *but* because of his oath and for the sake of *those* who sat with him, he would not reject her.

[27] *Therefore* the king immediately sent an executioner and commanded *John's* head to be brought, and *the executioner* beheaded him in the prison.

[28] *Then he* brought *John's* head on a platter[+] and gave it to the girl[+] and the girl[+] gave it to her mother.

[29] When *John's* disciples heard *about it*, they came and took *away* his body[+] and laid it in a tomb.

[30] *Then* the apostles gathered themselves together to Jesus and told Him everything, both what they had done and what they had taught.

[31] *Jesus* said to them: Come [+] apart to a deserted[+] place and rest a while. For there were many coming and going and they had no time[+] *even* to eat.

[32] *So* they went to a deserted[+] place by boat privately.

[33] The people saw them departing and many knew Him and ran on foot there out of all cities and outran them and came together to Him.

[34] When Jesus came, He saw many people and was moved with compassion toward them because they were like sheep not having a shepherd. *So* He began to teach them many things.

[35] When the hour[+] was late,[+] *Jesus'* disciples came to Him and said: This is a deserted[+] place and now the hour[+] *is* late.[+]

36Send them away *so* that they may go into the country *all* around+ and into the villages and buy bread *for* themselves, for they have nothing to eat.

37*Jesus* answered and said to them: You give them *food* to eat. And they said to Him: Shall we go and buy *a half a year wages worth*+ of bread and give them to eat?

38He said to them: How many loaves do you have? Go and see. When they knew, they said: Five, and two fish.

39*Then Jesus* directed+ them all *to* sit down group+ *by* group on the green grass.

40And they sat down in groups+ of hundreds and fifties.

41When He had taken the five loaves and the two fish, He looked up to heaven and blessed and broke the loaves and gave *them* to His disciples to set before them and the two fish He *also* divided among them all.

42And they all ate and were filled.

43*Afterward* they took up twelve baskets full of the fragments and of the fish.

44*Those* who ate of the loaves were about five thousand men.

45Immediately+ *after that Jesus* directed+ His disciples to get into the boat and to go before *Him* to the other side, to Bethsaida, while He sent away the people.

46When He had sent them away, He went to a mountain to pray.

47*Then* when evening+ had come, the boat was in the midst of the sea and *Jesus was* alone on the land.

48He saw them toiling in rowing for the wind was contrary to them. About the fourth watch of the night *sometime after three o'clock in the morning Jesus* came to them walking upon the sea, and would have passed by them.

49But when they saw Him walking upon the sea, they supposed it had been a spirit and cried out.

50For they all saw Him and were troubled. And immediately He talked with them and said to them: Be of good cheer. I am+ *with you*. Do not be afraid.

51*Then* He went up to them in the boat and the wind stopped.+ They were greatly+ amazed within themselves beyond measure and wondered.

52For they did not understand+ *the miracle* of the loaves because their heart was hardened.

53When they had crossed+ over *the sea*, they came to the land of Gennesaret and drew to the shore.

54And when they had come out of the boat, immediately+ the *people* recognized+ Him

55and ran through that whole region *all* around+ and began to carry *those* who were sick in bed to where they heard He was.

56Wherever He entered into villages or cities or country, they laid the sick in the streets and begged+ Him that they might touch, if it were *possible*, even *just* the border of His garment. As many as touched Him were made whole.

Mark Chapter 7

1 Then the Pharisees came together to Him, and *also* some+ of the scribes who came from Jerusalem.

2 When they saw some of His disciples eat bread with defiled, that is to say with unwashed hands, they found fault.

3 For holding *to* the tradition of the elders, the Pharisees and all the Jews do not eat unless they wash *their* hands often.

4 And *when they come* from the market, they do not eat unless they wash; and there are many other things that they have received to hold, *such as* the washing of cups and pots, brazen vessels, and tables.

5 Then the Pharisees and scribes asked Him: Why do your disciples not walk according to the tradition of the elders, but eat bread with unwashed hands?

6 He answered and said to them: Well has Isaiah prophesied of you hypocrites, as it is written: This people honors me with *their* lips, but their hearts are far from me. *Matthew 15:8*

⁷ However, in vain do they worship me, teaching *as* doctrines the commandments of men. *Matthew 15:9*

⁸ For laying aside the commandment of God, you hold the traditions of men: *such as* the washing of pots and cups and many other *things* like such you do.

⁹ *Then* He said to them: Full well you reject the commandment of God *so* that you may keep your own tradition.

¹⁰ For Moses said: Honor your father and your mother. And whoever curses father or mother, let them die the death.

¹¹ But you say: If a person⁺ says to their father or mother: Whatever benefit⁺ *you might have received* from me *was given as* Corban, that is a *temple* gift,

¹² and you allow⁺ them to do no more for their father or their mother,

¹³ *by doing this, you are* making the Word of God of no effect through your tradition which you have delivered. Many *things* like such you do.

¹⁴ When He had called all the people, He said to them: Listen⁺ to me everyone *of you* and understand:

¹⁵ There is nothing outside⁺ *of* a person,⁺ which *by* entering into them can defile them. But the things that come out of them, those are the things that defile a person⁺.

¹⁶ If anyone has ears to hear, let them hear.

¹⁷ When *Jesus* went into a house *away* from the people, His disciples asked Him about⁺ the parable.

¹⁸ He said to them: Are you so without understanding also? Do you not perceive that whatever thing from outside⁺ enters into a person⁺ cannot defile them.

¹⁹ Because it does not enter into their heart but into the belly and *then* into the discard⁺ *it* goes, purging all foods⁺.

²⁰ He said: *It is* what comes out of a person⁺ that defiles them.

²¹ For from within, out of the hearts of people⁺ proceed evil thoughts, adulteries, fornications, murders, *Matthew 15:19*

²² thefts, covetousness, wickedness, deceit, filthiness,⁺ an evil eye, blasphemy, pride, *and* foolishness. *Matthew 15:19*

²³ All these evil things come from within and defile a person⁺.

²⁴ From there⁺ *Jesus* arose and went into the borders of Tyre and Sidon. *He* entered a house and wanted⁺ no one *to* know *it*, but He could not be hid.

²⁵ For a *certain* woman whose young daughter had an unclean spirit heard of Him and came and fell at His feet.

²⁶ The woman was a Greek of Syrophenician *or mixed race* nationality.⁺ She begged⁺ *Jesus* to cast the demon⁺ out of her daughter.

²⁷ But Jesus said to her: Let the children first be filled, for it is not good⁺ to take the children's bread and to cast *it* to the dogs.

²⁸ She answered and said to Him: Yes Lord. Yet the dogs under the table eat of the children's crumbs.

²⁹ He said to her: For this saying, Go.⁺ The demon⁺ is gone out of your daughter.

³⁰ When she had come to her house, she found the demon⁺ gone and her daughter laying on the bed.

³¹ *Then* again departing from the borders⁺ of Tyre and Sidon, *Jesus* came to the sea of Galilee, through the midst of the borders⁺ of Decapolis.

³² They brought to Him one who was deaf and had an impediment in his speech and they asked⁺ Him to put His hand upon him.

³³ *Jesus* took him aside from the multitude and put His fingers into his ears and He spit *on His finger* and touched his tongue.

³⁴ *Then* looking up to heaven He sighed and said to him: Ephphatha. That is: Be opened.

³⁵ Immediately⁺ his ears were opened and the string of his tongue was loosed and he spoke plainly.

³⁶ *Jesus* charged him that he should tell no one, but the more He charged them, so much more broadly⁺ they published *it*.

³⁷ *Everyone* was astonished beyond measure saying: He has done all things well. He makes both the deaf to hear and the speechless⁺ to speak.

Mark Chapter 8

¹ In those days, the multitude being very large⁺ and having nothing to eat, Jesus called His disciples and said to them:

² I have compassion on the multitude because they have now been with me three days and have nothing to eat.

³ If I send them away fasting to their own houses, they will faint by the way, for many of them came from far *away*.

⁴ His disciples answered Him: From where can anyone⁺ satisfy these *people* with bread here in the wilderness?

⁵ He asked them: How many loaves do you have? They said: Seven.

⁶ He directed⁺ the people to sit down on the ground. *Then* He took the seven loaves, gave thanks, broke *them* and gave *them* to His disciples to set before *them*. And they sat *them* before the people.

⁷ They also had a few small fish and He blessed and commanded to set them also before *them*.

⁸ So they *all* ate and were filled. And of the broken *pieces* that were left, they took up seven baskets *full*

⁹ *Those* who had eaten were about four thousand. *Then* He sent them away.

¹⁰Immediately⁺ He entered a boat with His disciples and came into the parts of Dalmanutha.

¹¹*Then* the Pharisees came and began to question Him, seeking a sign from heaven from Him, testing⁺ Him.

¹²He sighed deeply in His spirit and said: Why does this generation seek after a sign? Truly⁺ I say to you: No sign will be given to this generation.

¹³*Then* He left them and, entering the boat again, *He* departed to the other side.

¹⁴Now *the disciples* had forgotten to take bread and they did not have in the boat with them more than one loaf.

¹⁵*Jesus* charged them saying: Take heed. Beware of the leaven of the Pharisees and the leaven of Herod.

¹⁶They reasoned among themselves saying: *It is* because we have no bread.

¹⁷Jesus knew *their thoughts and* said to them: Why do you reason because you have no bread? Do you not yet perceive or understand? Have you hardened your hearts, still⁺?

¹⁸Having eyes, do you not see? And having ears, do you not hear? And do you not remember?

¹⁹When I broke the five loaves among five thousand, how many baskets full of fragments did you take up? They said to Him: Twelve.

²⁰When *I broke* the seven among four thousand, how many baskets full of fragments did you take up? They said: Seven.

²¹He said to them: How is it that you do not understand?

²²*Then Jesus* came to Bethsaida and they brought a blind man to Him and begged⁺ Him to touch *the man*.

²³*So,* He took the blind man by the hand and led him out of the town. When He had spit on his eyes and put His hands upon him, He asked him if he saw anything.⁺

²⁴*The man* looked up and said: I see people⁺ like trees walking.

²⁵After that, *Jesus* put *His* hands upon his eyes again and made him look up, and he was restored and saw everyone⁺ clearly.

²⁶*Then Jesus* sent him away to his house saying: Do not go into the town or tell anyone in the town.

²⁷*Then* Jesus and His disciples went to the towns of Caesarea Philippi. Along⁺ the way, He asked His disciples saying to them: Who do people⁺ say that I am?

²⁸They answered: John the Baptist. But some *say* Elijah. *And* others *say* one of the prophets.

²⁹He said to them: But who do you say that I am? Peter answered and said to Him: You are the Christ.

³⁰*But* He charged them that they should tell no one about Him.

³¹He began to teach them that the Son of man must suffer many things and be rejected by the elders and the chief priests and scribes and be killed, and after three days rise again.

³² *Jesus* spoke the Word⁺ openly. *But then* Peter took Him *aside* and began to rebuke Him.

³³ But when He had turned around⁺ and looked at His disciples, He rebuked Peter saying: Get behind me Satan. For you do not savor the things that are of God but the things that are of men.

³⁴ *Then* when He had called the people *together* with His disciples, He said to them: Whoever will come after me, let them deny themselves and take up their cross and follow me.

³⁵ For whoever would⁺ save their life will lose it, but whoever would⁺ lose their life for my sake and *for* the Gospel, the same will save it.

³⁶ For what will it profit anyone if they gain the whole world and lose their own soul?

³⁷ Or what shall anyone⁺ give in exchange for their soul?

³⁸ Whoever therefore is ashamed of me and of my words in this adulterous and sinful generation, the Son of man will be ashamed of them also when He comes in the glory of His Father with the holy angels.

Mark Chapter 9

¹ *Then* He said to them: Truly⁺ I say to you that there are some of *those* who stand here who will not taste of death until they have seen the kingdom of God come with power.

² After six days, Jesus took Peter, James, and John, and led them up into a high mountain apart by themselves and He was transfigured *right there* before them.

³ His clothing⁺ became shining *and* exceedingly white as snow, like no cleaner⁺ on earth could whiten them.

⁴ *Then* Elijah with Moses appeared to them and they were talking with Jesus.

⁵ Peter answered and said to Jesus: Master, it is good for us to be here. Let us make three tabernacles. One for you and one for Moses and one for Elijah.

⁶ For he did not know what to say for they were greatly⁺ afraid.

⁷ There was a cloud that overshadowed them and a voice came out of the cloud saying: This is my beloved Son. Hear Him.

⁸ Suddenly, when they had looked around,⁺ they saw no one any more, except⁺ Jesus *still* with them.

⁹ As they came down from the mountain, *Jesus* charged them that they should tell no one what things they had seen, until the Son of man was risen from the dead.

¹⁰ *So* they kept that word to themselves, questioning with one another what the rising from the dead could⁺ mean.

¹¹ *Then* they asked *Jesus* saying: Why do the scribes say that Elijah must come first?

¹² *Jesus* answered and told them: Elijah truly⁺ comes first *and* restores all things, and how is it written of the Son of man: that He must suffer many things and be rejected⁺. *Matthew 17:11*

¹³ But I say to you that Elijah has indeed come and they have done to him whatever they desired,⁺ as it is written about⁺ him. *Matthew 17:12*

¹⁴ *Then* when *Jesus* came to *His* disciples, He saw a great multitude around⁺ them and the scribes questioning with them.

¹⁵ Immediately⁺ all the people, when they saw⁺ Him, were greatly amazed and running to *Him* greeted⁺ Him.

¹⁶ He asked the scribes: What were you questioning with them?

¹⁷ One of the multitude answered and said: Master, I have brought to you my son who has a spirit *making him* unable to speak.⁺

¹⁸ Wherever he *goes* it tears him and he foams *at the mouth* and gnashes with his teeth and withers⁺ *away*. I spoke to your disciples *to ask* if they could cast it out and they could not.

¹⁹ *Jesus* answered saying: O faithless generation. How long shall I be with you? How long shall I endure⁺ you? Bring him to me.

²⁰ They brought *the boy* to *Jesus* and when he saw Him, immediately⁺ the spirit convulsed⁺ him and he fell on the ground and rolled⁺ *around* foaming *at the mouth*.

21 *Jesus* asked his father: How long ago is it since this came to him? He said: *Since* childhood.

22 Often times it has cast him into the fire and into the water to destroy him. But if you can do anything, have compassion on us and help us.

23 Jesus said to him:

> If you can believe,
> all things *are* possible
> to *those* who believe.

24 Immediately⁺ the father of the child cried out and said with tears: Lord, I believe. Help my unbelief.

25 When Jesus saw that the people came running together, He rebuked the foul spirit saying to it: *You evil* spirit *blocking* speech and hearing, I charge you: Come out of him and enter no more into him.

26 *The spirit* cried *out* and convulsed⁺ him greatly⁺ and came out of him, and *the boy* was like one dead, so that many said: He is dead.

27 But Jesus took him by the hand and lifted him up and he arose.

28 *Then* when *Jesus* had come into the house, His disciples asked Him privately: Why could we not cast him out?

29 He said to them: This kind can come forth by nothing but by prayer and fasting.

30 *Then* they departed from there⁺ and passed through Galilee and He would not *allow* that anyone should know *it*.

31 For He taught His disciples and said to them: The Son of man is delivered into the hands of men and they will kill Him. After He is killed, He will rise the third day.

32 But they did not understand that saying and were afraid to ask Him.

33 *Then* He came to Capernaum and *when they* were⁺ in the house He asked them: What was it that you disputed among yourselves by the way?

34 But they *remained* silent⁺ for on the way they had disputed among themselves who *would be* the greatest.

35 *Then Jesus* sat down and called the twelve and said to them: If anyone desires to be first, *the same* will be last of all and *the* servant of all.

36 He took a child and set him in the midst of them, and when He had taken him in His arms, He said to them:

37 Whoever will receive one of such children in my name receives me. And whoever will receive me does not receive me but Him who sent me.

38 John answered Him saying: Master, we saw someone casting out demons⁺ in your name who does not follow us. *So* we forbad him because he does not follow us.

39 But Jesus said: Do not forbid him, for there is no one who does a miracle in my name who can lightly speak evil of me.

40 For whoever is not against us is for us.

41 For whoever will give you a cup of water to drink in my name because you belong to Christ, truly⁺ I say to you: They will not lose their reward.

42 *But* whoever offends *and sins against* one of *these* little ones who believe in me, it would be better for them if⁺ a millstone were hung around⁺ their neck and they were thrown⁺ into the sea.

43 If your hand causes⁺ you *to sin*, cut it off. It is better for you to enter into life maimed than having two hands to go into hell, into the fire that will never be quenched,

44 where the *flesh eating* worms never die and the fire is never⁺ quenched.

45 If your foot causes⁺ you *to sin*, cut it off. It is better for you to enter crippled⁺ into life, than having two feet to be cast into hell, into the fire that will never be quenched,

46 where the *flesh eating* worms never die and the fire is never⁺ quenched.

47 If your eye causes⁺ you *to sin*, pluck it out. It is better for you to enter into the kingdom of God with one eye, than having two eyes to be cast into hell fire,

48 where the *flesh eating* worms never die and the fire is never⁺ quenched.

49 For everyone will be salted with fire and every sacrifice will be salted with salt.

⁵⁰Salt *is* good, but if the salt has lost its saltness with what will you season it? Have salt in yourselves and have peace with one another.

Mark Chapter 10

¹ *Then Jesus* arose from there⁺ and went⁺ into the borders⁺ of Judea on the other⁺ side of Jordan, and the people went⁺ to Him again. And, as it was His custom, He taught them again.

² The Pharisees came to Him and asked Him: Is it lawful for a man to put away *his* wife? *They said this to* test⁺ Him.

³ He answered and said to them: What did Moses command you?

⁴ They said: Moses allowed⁺ *us* to write a written divorce⁺ to put *them* away.

⁵ Jesus answered and said to them: He wrote this precept because of the hardness of your hearts.

⁶ But from the beginning of the creation God made them male and female. *Matthew 19:4*

⁷ For this reason⁺ a man shall leave his father and mother and cleave to his wife *Matthew 19:5*

⁸ and they two shall be one flesh. So then, they are no longer⁺ two but one flesh. *Matthew 19:6*

⁹ Therefore what God has joined *together*, mankind⁺ *must* not separate⁺. *Matthew 19:6*

¹⁰ *Later*, in the house, *Jesus'* disciples asked Him again about⁺ the same *matter*.

¹¹ He said to them: Whoever shall put away his wife and marry another commits adultery against her.

¹² And if a woman shall put away her husband and be married to another, she commits adultery.

¹³ *Then* they brought young children to Him *so* that He could⁺ touch them, but *His* disciples rebuked *those* who brought *them*.

¹⁴ But when Jesus saw *this*, He was much displeased and said to them: Allow the little children to come to me and do not forbid them, for of such is the kingdom of God.

¹⁵ Truly⁺ I say to you: Whoever will not receive the kingdom of God as a little child will not enter in.

¹⁶ *Then* He took them up in His arms, put *His* hands upon them and blessed them.

¹⁷ When He went forth into the way, one came running, knelt *down* to Him and asked Him: Good Master, what shall I do that I may inherit eternal life?

¹⁸ Jesus said to him: Why do you call me good? No one *is* good but one. God.

¹⁹ You know the commandments: Do not commit adultery. Do not kill. Do not steal. Do not bear false witness. Do not defraud. Honor your father and mother.

²⁰ He answered and said to Him: Master, all these have I observed from my youth.

²¹ Then Jesus, beholding him, loved him and said to him: One thing you lack. Go *and* sell whatever you have and give to the poor, and you will have treasure in heaven. *Then* come, take up the cross and follow me.

²² But at that word he became⁺ sad and went away grieved, for he had great possessions.

²³ *Then* Jesus looked around⁺ and said to His disciples: *Those* who have riches will hardly *be able to* enter into the kingdom of God.

²⁴ The disciples were astonished at His words, but Jesus answered again saying to them: Children, how hard is it for *those* who trust in riches to enter into the kingdom of God.

²⁵ It is easier for a camel to go through the eye of a needle than for a rich person⁺ to enter into the kingdom of God.

²⁶ They were astonished beyond⁺ measure and said among themselves: Who then can be saved?

²⁷ Jesus looking upon them said: With people⁺ *it is* impossible, but not with God. For with God, all things are possible.

²⁸ Then Peter began to say to Him: Behold, we have left all and have followed you.

²⁹ Jesus answered and said: Truly⁺ I say to you: There is no one who has left

house or brothers or sisters or father or mother or wife or children or lands for my sake and the Gospel's

30but will receive a hundredfold now in this time, houses and brothers and sisters and mothers and children and lands, *along* with persecutions; and in the world to come, eternal life.

31But many *who are* first will be last and the last first.

32*Then as* they were on the way *again* going up to Jerusalem, Jesus went before them and they were amazed. As they followed, they were afraid. But *Jesus* took the twelve again and began to tell them what things would happen to Him.

33*He said*: Behold we are going to Jerusalem and the Son of man will be delivered to the chief priests and to the scribes and they will condemn Him to death and deliver Him to the Gentiles. *Matthew 20:18*

34They will mock Him and flog+ Him and spit on Him and kill Him, and the third day He will rise again.

35*Then* James and John the sons of Zebedee came to Him saying: Master, we would *ask* that you do for us whatever we desire.

36He said to them: What do you want me to do for you?

37They said to Him: Grant to us that we may sit, one at your right hand and the other at your left hand, in your glory.

38But Jesus said to them: You do not know what you ask. Can you drink of the cup from which I *shall* drink? And be baptized with the baptism with which I am *to be* baptized?

39They said to Him: We can. And Jesus said to them: You will indeed drink of the cup from which I *shall* drink and with the baptism with which I am baptized, you will be baptized.

40But to sit at my right hand and at my left hand is not mine to give, but *it will be given to them* for whom it is prepared.

41When the ten heard *this*, they began to be much displeased with James and John.

42But Jesus called them and said to them: You know that *those* who are accounted to rule over the Gentiles exercise lordship over them and their great ones exercise authority upon them.

43But it shall not be so among you. But whoever will be great among you, shall be your servant+.

44Whoever of you will be the chief, will be servant of all.

45For even the Son of man did not come to be ministered to, but to minister and to give His life *as* a ransom for many.

46*Then* they came to Jericho, and as *Jesus* went out of Jericho with His disciples and a great number of people, blind Bartimaeus the son of Timaeus, sat by the wayside begging.

47When he heard that it was Jesus of Nazareth, he began to cry out and say: Jesus son of David, have mercy on me.

48Many charged him *saying* that he should be silent.+ But he cried *out all* the more: Son of David, have mercy on me.

49*Then* Jesus stopped+ and asked+ for him to be called. *So* they called the blind man, saying to him: Be encouraged.+ Rise. *Jesus* is calling for you.

50And he, casting away his garment, rose and came to Jesus.

51Jesus answered and said to him: What do you want me to do to you? The blind man said to Him: Lord, that I might receive my sight.

52Jesus said to him: Go. Your faith has made you whole. And immediately he received his sight and followed Jesus in the way.

Mark Chapter 11

1 When they came near to Jerusalem, to Bethphage and Bethany at the Mount of Olives, *Jesus* sent forth two of His disciples

2 and said to them: Go into the village before+ you. As soon as you enter it, you will find a colt tied on which no one has *ever* sat. Loose *it* and bring *it to me*.

3 If anyone says to you: Why are you doing this? Say that the Lord has need of it and immediately+ he will send it here.

4 *So* they went away and found the colt

tied by the door outside⁺ in a cross-way,⁺ and they loose it.

⁵ Certain of *those* who stood there said to them: What are you doing, loosing the colt?

⁶ *The disciples* said to them as Jesus had commanded, and they let them go.

⁷ *Then* they brought the colt to Jesus and cast their garments on it and He sat upon it. *Matthew 21:5*

⁸ Many spread their garments in the way. Others cut down branches off the trees and spread⁺ *them* in the way.

⁹ *Those* who went before and *those* who followed cried *out* saying: Hosanna. Blessed *is* He who comes in the name of the Lord.

¹⁰ Blessed *be* the kingdom of our father David that comes in the name of the Lord. Hosanna in the highest.

¹¹ Jesus entered Jerusalem and *went* into the temple. When He had looked around⁺ upon everything⁺ and *now that* the hour was already late, He went out to Bethany with the twelve.

¹² On the next day, when they had come from Bethany, *Jesus* was hungry.

¹³ Seeing a fig tree with leaves *at a* distance,⁺ He came *closer to see* if perhaps⁺ He might find anything on it. When He came to it, He found nothing but leaves, for the time for figs was not *yet*.

¹⁴ *But* Jesus answered and said to it: No one *shall* eat fruit from you hereafter forever. His disciples heard *this*.

¹⁵ *Then* they came to Jerusalem and Jesus went into the temple and began to cast out *those* who bought and sold in the temple, and overthrew the tables of the money changers and the seats of *those* who sold doves.

¹⁶ *He* would not allow⁺ anyone to carry *any* vessel through the temple.

¹⁷ *Then* He taught them saying: Is it not written: My house shall be called the house of prayer by all nations? But you have made it a den of thieves. *Matthew 21:13*

¹⁸ The scribes and chief priests heard *this* and sought how they might destroy Him, for they feared Him because all the people were astonished at His doctrine.

¹⁹ *Then*, when evening⁺ had come, He went out of the city.

²⁰ In the morning as they passed by, they saw the fig tree dried up from the roots.

²¹ Peter remembering⁺ *what occurred earlier* said to Him: Master, behold the fig tree that you cursed has withered away.

²² Jesus answering said to them: Have faith in God.

²³ For truly⁺ I say to you that whoever says to this mountain: Be removed and be cast into the sea, and does not doubt in their heart, but believes that those things that they said shall come to pass, they shall have whatever they say.

²⁴ Therefore I say to you: What things ⁺ you desire, when you pray, believe that you receive *them* and you shall have *them*.

²⁵ And when you stand praying: Forgive, if you have anything⁺ against anyone⁺ *so* that your Father also who is in heaven may forgive your trespasses.

²⁶ But if you do not forgive, neither will your Father in heaven forgive your trespasses.

²⁷ *Then* they came again to Jerusalem and as He was walking in the temple, the chief priests and the scribes and the elders came to Him

²⁸ and said to Him: By what authority do you *do* these things? And who gave you this authority to do these things?

²⁹ Jesus answered and said to them: I will also ask of you one question. Answer me and I will tell you by what authority I do these things.

³⁰ The baptism of John: Was *it* from heaven or of men? Answer me.

³¹ They reasoned among⁺ themselves saying: If we say: From heaven, He will say: Why then did you not believe him?

³² But if we say: Of men, they feared the people for all *the people* considered⁺ that John was indeed a prophet.

³³ *So* they answered and said to Jesus: We cannot tell. And Jesus answering said to them: *Then* neither will I tell you by what authority I do these things.

Mark Chapter 12

[1] *Then Jesus* began to speak to them in parables: A *certain* man planted a vineyard, set a hedge about *it*, dug *a place for* the wine vat, built a tower, let it out to *tenant* farmers,[+] and went into a far country.

[2] At the season he sent a servant to the *tenant* farmers[+] *so* that he might receive from the farmers[+] of the fruit of the vineyard.

[3] *But* they caught *him* and beat him and sent *him* away empty *handed*.

[4] Again he sent to them another servant but they cast stones at him, wounded *him* in the head, and sent *him* away shamefully treated[+].

[5] Again he sent another, but they killed him and many others, beating some and killing some.

[6] Therefore, having only[+] one son, his beloved, at last he sent *his only son* to them, saying: *Surely* they will reverence my son.

[7] But those *tenant* farmers[+] said among themselves: This is the heir. Come. Let us kill him and the inheritance will be ours.

[8] *So* they took him and killed *him* and cast *him* out of the vineyard.

[9] Therefore what will the lord of the vineyard do? He will come and destroy the *tenant* farmers[+] and will give the vineyard to others.

[10] Have you not read this Scripture: The stone that the builders rejected has become the head of the corner. *Matthew 21:42*

[11] This was the Lord's doing and it is marvelous in our eyes.

[12] *So* they sought to lay hold on Him, but *they* feared the people for they knew that He had spoken the parable against them. *So* they left Him and went away.[+]

[13] *Then* they sent some of the Pharisees and of the Herodians to Him to catch Him in *His* words.

[14] When they had come, they said to Him: Master, we know that you are true and do not *have special* care for any *one person over another*, for you do not regard the positions[+] people[+] hold, but teach the way of God in truth. Is it lawful to give tribute to Caesar or not?

[15] Shall we give or shall we not give? But knowing their hypocrisy, *Jesus* said to them: Why do you test[+] me? Bring a coin[+] to me *so* that I may see *it*.

[16] They brought *it* and He said to them: Whose *is* this image and title[+]? They said to Him: Caesar's.

[17] *So* Jesus answering said to them: Render to Caesar the things that are Caesar's and to God the things that are God's. They marveled at Him.

[18] Then the Sadducees who say there is no resurrection came to Him and they asked Him saying:

[19] Master, Moses wrote to us: If a man's brother die and leave *his* wife and leave no children, that his brother should take his wife and raise up seed to his brother.

[20] Now there were seven brothers. The first took a wife and dying left no seed.

[21] *Then* the second took her and died and he *also* left no seed. And the third likewise.

[22] The seven had her and left no seed. Last of all the woman also died.

[23] Therefore in the resurrection when they rise, whose wife will she be? For the seven had her as *their* wife.

[24] Jesus answering said to them: Do you not therefore err because you do not know the Scriptures or the power of God?

[25] For when they rise from the dead, they neither marry nor are given in marriage but are like[+] the angels in heaven.

[26] And *regarding* the dead, that they rise: Have you not read in the book of Moses, how in the bush God spoke to him saying: I *am* the God of Abraham and the God of Isaac and the God of Jacob.

[27] He is not the God of the dead but the God of the living. You therefore do greatly err.

[28] *Then* one of the scribes came and, having heard them reasoning together and perceiving that He had answered them well, asked Him: Which is the first commandment of all?

²⁹Jesus answered him: The first of all the commandments *is this*: Hear O Israel. The Lord our God is one Lord. *Deuteronomy 6:4*

³⁰You shall love the Lord your God with all your heart and with all your soul and with all your mind and with all your strength. This *is* the first commandment. *Matthew 22:37*

³¹And the second *is* like this: You shall love your neighbor as yourself. There is no other commandment greater than these. *Matthew 19:19*

³²The scribe said to Him: Well *said* Master. You have spoken the truth. For there is one God and there is no other but He.

³³To love Him with all the heart and with all the understanding and with all the soul and with all the strength and to love neighbor as oneself⁺ is more than all burnt offerings and sacrifices.

³⁴When Jesus saw that he answered *with an* understanding mind,⁺ He said to him: You are not far from the kingdom of God. No one after that dared⁺ ask Him *any question*.

³⁵While *He was* teaching in the temple, Jesus answering said: How *is it* that the scribes say that Christ is the son of David?

³⁶For David himself said by the Holy Spirit: The Lord said to my Lord: Sit at my right hand until I make your enemies your footstool.

³⁷Therefore David himself calls Him Lord. How⁺ *then* is He *David's* son? And the common people heard Him gladly.

³⁸*Then* He said to them in His doctrine: Beware of the scribes who love to go in long clothing and *love* salutations in the marketplaces,

³⁹the chief seats in the synagogues and the uppermost rooms at feasts,

⁴⁰who devour widows' houses and for a pretence make long prayers. They will receive greater damnation.

⁴¹*Then* Jesus sat near⁺ the treasury and saw⁺ how the people cast money into the treasury. Many who were rich cast in much.

⁴²*But then* a certain poor widow came and threw in two mites, which were *worth about* a penny.⁺

⁴³*Jesus* called His disciples and said to them: Truly⁺ I say to you that this poor widow has cast more in than all *those* who have cast into the treasury.

⁴⁴For *they* all cast in *out* of their abundance, but she *even out* of her lack⁺ cast in everything⁺ that she had, *even* all her *means of* livelihood⁺.

Mark Chapter 13

¹ As *Jesus* went out of the temple, one of His disciples said to Him: Master, see what manner of stones and what buildings *are here*.

² Jesus answering said to him: See these great buildings? There will not be left stone upon stone that will not be thrown down.

³ *Later* as He sat on the Mount of Olives near⁺ the temple, Peter, James, John, and Andrew asked Him privately:

⁴ Tell us when will these things be? And what *will be* the sign when all these things will be fulfilled?

⁵ Jesus answering them began to say: Take heed lest anyone⁺ deceive you.

⁶ For many will come in my name saying: I am *Christ* and will deceive many.

⁷ When you hear of wars and rumors of wars, do not be troubled for *such things* need to be, but the end *will* not *be* yet.

⁸ For nation will rise against nation and kingdom against kingdom. There will be earthquakes in many different⁺ places and there will be famines and troubles. These *are* the beginnings of sorrows.

⁹ But take heed to yourselves, for they will deliver you up to councils. In the synagogues you will be beaten. You will be brought before rulers and kings for my sake, for a testimony against them.

¹⁰*But* the Gospel must first be published among all nations.

¹¹But when they take⁺ *you away* and deliver you up, take no thought beforehand what you shall speak *and* do not premeditate. But whatever shall be given

to you in that hour, that you *shall* speak. For it is not you who *will be* speaking, but the Holy Spirit.

[12]Now brother will betray brother to death and father *betray* child. Children will rise up against *their* parents and *cause* them *to be* put to death.

[13]You will be hated by all for my name's sake, but *those* who endure to the end, the same will be saved.

[14]Let *those* who read *this* understand: When you see the abomination of desolation spoken of by Daniel the prophet standing where it should not, then let *those* who are in Judea flee to the mountains.

[15]Let *those* who are on the housetop not go down into the house nor enter *there* to take anything out of their house.

[16]Let *those* who are in the field not turn back again to take up their garments.

[17]But woe to *those* who are with child and to *those* who are nursing[+] in those days.

[18]Pray that your flight not be in the winter.

[19]For *in* those days *there* will be affliction *such as* has not *occurred* from the beginning of the creation which God created to this time, nor shall *there* be *ever again*.

[20]Unless[+] the Lord shortened those days, no flesh would be saved. But for the sake of the elect whom He has chosen, He has shortened the days.

[21]Then if anyone says to you: Behold here *is* Christ. Or behold *He is* there, do not believe *them*.

[22]For false Christs and false prophets will arise and will show signs and wonders to deceive,[+] if *it were* possible, even the elect.

[23]But take heed. Behold, I have foretold all *these* things *to* you *before they occur*.

[24]But in those days, after that tribulation, the sun will be darkened and the moon will not give its light.

[25]The stars of heaven will fall and the powers that are in heaven will be shaken.

[26]Then they will see the Son of man coming in the clouds with great power and glory.

[27]And then He will send His angels and gather together His elect from the four winds, from the ends[+] of the earth to the ends[+] of heaven.

[28]Now learn a parable from the fig tree. When its branch is yet tender and puts forth leaves, you know that summer is near.

[29]So in like manner, when you see these things come to pass, know that it is near, *even* at the doors.

[30]Truly[+] I say to you, that this generation will not pass, until all these things are done.

[31]Heaven and earth will pass away, but my words will not pass away.

[32]But of that day and *that* hour no one knows. No, not *even* the angels in heaven nor the Son, but the Father *only*.

[33]Take heed, watch, and pray. For you do not know when the time is *to be*.

[34]*For the Son of man is* like[+] a man taking a far journey who left his house and gave authority to his servants, to every person[+] their work, and *then* commanded the doorkeeper[+] to watch.

[35]Watch, therefore. For you do not know when the master of the house is coming: In the evening,[+] at midnight, at the cock crowing, or in the morning,

[36]lest coming suddenly, he find you sleeping.

[37]And what I say to you, I say to all: Watch.

Mark Chapter 14

[1] After two days was *to be the Feast of* the Passover and of unleavened bread. The chief priests and the scribes sought how they might take Him by craft and put *Him* to death.

[2] But they said: Not on the feast *day*, lest there be an uproar of the people.

[3] *Now* as *Jesus* sat *down* to eat[+] in the house of Simon the leper in Bethany, a woman came *to Him* with an alabaster box of ointment of spikenard, very precious. And she broke the box and poured *the contents* on His head.

[4] *But* there were some who had indignation within themselves and said: Why was this waste of the ointment made?

⁵ For it might have been sold for more than *a year's wages*⁺ and given to the poor. And they complained⁺ against her.

⁶ Jesus said: Let her alone. Why do you trouble her? She has done⁺ a good work on me.

⁷ For you have the poor with you always, and whenever you will you may do good *to them*. But you will not always have me.

⁸ She has done what she could. She has come beforehand to anoint my body for burial⁺.

⁹ Truly⁺ I say to you: Wherever this Gospel shall be proclaimed⁺ throughout the whole world, *this* also that she has done will be spoken of for a memorial of her.

¹⁰ *Then* Judas Iscariot, one of the twelve, went to the chief priests to betray Him to them.

¹¹ When they heard *this*, they were glad and promised to give him money. *So Judas* sought how he might conveniently betray Him.

¹² The first day of *the Feast of* Unleavened Bread when they killed the Passover *lamb*, His disciples said to Him: Where do you want us to go and prepare *so* that you may eat the Passover?

¹³ He sent forth two of His disciples and said to them: Go into the city and there a man bearing a pitcher of water will meet you. Follow him.

¹⁴ Wherever he goes in, say to the head⁺ of the house: The Master asks: Where is the guest chamber where I shall eat the Passover with my disciples?

¹⁵ He will show you a large upper room furnished *and* prepared. Make ready for us there.

¹⁶ *So* His disciples went forth and came into the city and found as He had said to them, and they made preparations⁺ *for* the Passover.

¹⁷ *Then* in the evening, He came with the twelve.

¹⁸ As they sat and ate, Jesus said: Truly⁺ I say to you: One of you who eats with me will betray me.

¹⁹ They began to be sorrowful and to say to Him one by one: *Is* it me? And another *said: Is* it me?

²⁰ He answered and said to them: *It is* one of the twelve who dips with me in the dish.

²¹ The Son of man indeed goes as it is written of Him. But woe to that man by whom the Son of man is betrayed. It would be good for that man if he had never been born.

²² As they ate, Jesus took bread, blessed, broke *it*, gave to them, and said: Take. Eat. This is my body.

²³ *Then* He took the cup, and when He had given thanks, He gave *it* to them and they all drank of it.

²⁴ He said to them: This is my blood of the new covenant,⁺ which is shed for many.

²⁵ Truly⁺ I say to you: I will drink no more of the fruit of the vine until the day that I drink it new in the kingdom of God.

²⁶ *Then* when they had sung a hymn, they went out to the Mount of Olives.

²⁷ And Jesus said to them: All *of* you will be offended because of me this night. For it is written: I will strike⁺ the shepherd and the sheep will be scattered. *Matthew 26:31*

²⁸ But after I am risen, I will go before you into Galilee.

²⁹ But Peter said to Him: Although all will be offended, yet I *will* not.

³⁰ Jesus said to him: Truly⁺ I say to you: That this day, *even* in this night before the cock crows twice, you will deny me three times.

³¹ But *Peter* spoke *all* the more forcefully⁺: If I should die with you, I will not deny you in any way.⁺ And they all spoke⁺ in the same manner.⁺

³² *Then* they came to a place named Gethsemane and He said to His disciples: Sit here while I pray.

³³ And He took Peter, James, and John with Him and began to be greatly⁺ amazed and to be very heavy.

³⁴ He said to them: My soul is exceedingly sorrowful unto death. Stay⁺ here and watch.

35 *Then* He went forward a little, fell on the ground, and prayed that, if it were possible, the hour might pass from Him. 36 He said: Abba, Father, all things *are* possible to you. Take away this cup from me. Nevertheless not what I will but what you will.

37 *Then* He came and found them sleeping and said to Peter: Simon, are you sleeping? Could you not watch one hour?

38 Watch and pray lest you enter into temptation. The spirit truly *is* ready but the flesh *is* weak.

39 Again He went away and prayed and spoke the same words.

40 When He returned, He found them asleep again, for their eyes were heavy. *And* they did not know how+ to answer Him.

41 *Then* He came the third time and said to them: Sleep on now and take *your* rest. It is enough. The hour has come. Behold the Son of man is betrayed into the hands of sinners.

42 Rise up. Let us go. Behold, he who betrays me is near+.

43 Immediately, while He spoke, Judas, one of the twelve, came. With him *came* a great multitude with swords and staves, *coming* from the chief priests and the scribes and the elders.

44 He who betrayed *Jesus* had given them a token saying: Whomever I kiss, that same is He. Take Him and lead *Him* away safely.

45 As soon as *Judas* had come, he went to *Jesus* immediately+ and said: Master, Master. And kissed Him. *Matthew 26:48*

46 *Then* they laid their hands on Him and took Him.

47 One of *those* who stood by drew a sword and struck+ a servant of the high priest and cut off his ear.

48 Jesus answered and said to them: Have you come out as against a thief with swords and *with* staves to take me? 49 I was with you daily in the temple teaching and you did not take me. But the Scriptures must be fulfilled.

50 *Then* they all left+ Him and fled.

51 Now a certain young man followed *Jesus. He had only* a linen cloth around+ *his* naked *body*. The young men seized+ him 52 *but* he left the linen cloth and fled from them naked.

53 *So* they led Jesus away to the high priest. With Him were assembled all the chief priests and the elders and the scribes. 54 Peter followed Him *from* a distance,+ even into the palace of the high priest. He sat with the servants and warmed himself at the fire.

55 The chief priests and all the council sought *a* witness against Jesus to put Him to death, *but they* found none. 56 For many bore false testimony+ against Him, but their testimonies+ did not agree.

57 *Then* certain *ones* arose and bore false testimony+ against Him saying: 58 We heard Him say: I will destroy this temple that is made with hands and within three days I will build another made without hands. *Matthew 26:61*

59 But neither did their testimonies+ agree.

60 *Then* the high priest stood up in the midst and asked Jesus saying: Do you not answer? What *is it that* these witness against you?

61 But *Jesus remained* silent+ and answered nothing. Again the high priest asked Him and said to Him: Are you the Christ, the Son of the Blessed?

62 Jesus said: I Am. You will see the Son of man sitting at the right hand of power and coming in the clouds of heaven.

63 Then the high priest tore+ his clothes and said: What need do we have for any further witnesses?

64 You have heard the blasphemy. What do you think? And they all condemned Him to be guilty of death.

65 Some began to spit on Him and to cover His face and to buffet Him and to say to Him: Prophesy. And the servants struck Him with the palms of their hands.

66 *Meanwhile* Peter was in the court+ below.+ One of the maids of the high priest came

⁶⁷and when she saw Peter warming himself, she looked at him and said: And you also were with Jesus of Nazareth.

⁶⁸But *Peter* denied *it* saying: I do not know or understand what you say. *Then* he went out into the porch and the cock crowed.⁺

⁶⁹*Then* a maid saw him again and began to say to *those* who stood by: This is *one* of them.

⁷⁰*Peter* denied it again. And a little after, *those* who stood by said again to Peter: Surely you are *one* of them for you are a Galilaean and your speech is like⁺ *that*.

⁷¹But *Peter* began to curse and to swear *saying*: I do not know this man of whom you speak.

⁷²*Then* the second time the cock crowed,⁺ Peter called to mind the word that Jesus said to him: Before the cock crows twice, you will deny me three times. When he thought about this, he wept.

Mark Chapter 15

¹ Immediately⁺ in the morning, the chief priests held a consultation with the elders and scribes and the whole council. *Then* *they* bound Jesus, carried *Him* away, and delivered *Him* to Pilate.

² Pilate asked Him: Are you the King of the Jews? And He answering said to him: You say *it*.

³ The chief priests accused Him of many things, but He answered nothing.

⁴ Pilate asked Him again saying: Do you not answer? Behold how many things they witness against you.

⁵ But Jesus still⁺ answered nothing, so that Pilate marveled. *Matthew 27:14*

⁶ Now at *the* feast Pilate *was* to release one prisoner to them, whomever they desired.

⁷ And there was *one* named Barabbas *who laid* bound with *those* who had made insurrection with him, *and Barabbas* had committed murder in the insurrection.

⁸ Now the multitude began to cry aloud asking⁺ *Pilate to do* as he had always⁺ done for them.

⁹ But Pilate answered them saying: Do you want me *to* release the King of the Jews to you?

¹⁰For he knew that the chief priests had delivered *Jesus* because⁺ of envy.

¹¹But the chief priests stirred *up* the people *so* that *Pilate* would release Barabbas to them instead.

¹²Pilate answered and said to them again: Then what do you want me to do *to Him* whom you call the King of the Jews?

¹³They cried out again: Crucify Him.

¹⁴Then Pilate said to them: Why? What evil has He done? And they cried out *all* the more exceedingly: Crucify Him.

¹⁵*So* Pilate, choosing⁺ to satisfy⁺ the people, released Barabbas to them and delivered Jesus, when he had flogged⁺ *Him*, to be crucified.

¹⁶The soldiers led Him away into the hall called Praetorium, and they called together the whole company⁺ *of soldiers*.

¹⁷They clothed Him with purple and made⁺ a crown of thorns and put it around⁺ His *head*.

¹⁸And *they* began to salute Him *saying*: Hail, King of the Jews.

¹⁹They struck⁺ Him on the head with a reed and spit on Him and bowing *their* knees worshiped Him.

²⁰When they had mocked Him, they took the purple off of Him, put His own clothes on Him, and led Him out to crucify Him.

²¹*Then* they compelled one *called* Simon, a Cyrenian who passed by coming out of the country, the father of Alexander and Rufus, to bear His cross.

²²They brought Him to the place *called* Golgotha, which means⁺: The place of a skull.

²³They gave Him wine mingled with myrrh to drink, but He did not accept⁺ *it*.

²⁴When they had crucified Him, they divided⁺ His garments, casting lots upon them *to decide* what each one⁺ would⁺ take. *Matthew 27:35*

²⁵It was nine o'clock⁺ *in the morning* when⁺ they crucified Him.

²⁶The title⁺ of His accusation was written over *Him*: The King of the Jews.

²⁷And they crucified two thieves with Him: One at His right hand and the other at His left. *Matthew 27:38*

²⁸*Thus* the Scripture was fulfilled that says: He was numbered with the transgressors. *Isaiah 53:12*

²⁹*Those* who passed by railed at Him, shaking⁺ their heads and saying: Ah, you who *would* destroy the temple and build *it again* in three days: *Matthew 27:41*

³⁰Save yourself and come down from the cross.

³¹Likewise also the chief priests, mocking, said among themselves with the scribes: He saved others, *but* He cannot save Himself. *Matthew 27:42*

³²Let Christ the King of Israel descend now from the cross *so* that we may see and believe. And *those* who were crucified with Him reviled Him.

³³When twelve o'clock⁺ *noon* came, there was darkness over the whole land until three *in the afternoon*.

³⁴At three o'clock⁺ *in the afternoon*, Jesus cried *out* with a loud voice saying: Eli, Eli, lama sabachthani. That means⁺: My God, my God. Why have you forsaken me?

³⁵Some of *those* who stood by, when they heard *this*, said: Behold He calls Elijah.

³⁶One ran and filled a sponge full of vinegar and put *it* on a reed and gave *it* to Him to drink saying: Let *Him* alone. Let us see whether Elijah will come to take Him down.

³⁷*Then* Jesus cried *out* with a loud voice and expired.⁺

³⁸And the veil of the temple was torn⁺ in two from the top to the bottom.

³⁹When the centurion who stood near⁺ Him saw that He cried out and expired,⁺ he said: Truly this man was the Son of God.

⁴⁰There were also women looking on *from* a distance.⁺ Among them were Mary Magdalene, Mary the mother of James the less and of Joses, and Salome.

⁴¹*This Salome was* the one who, when He was in Galilee, followed Him and ministered to Him, *along with* many other women who came up with Him to Jerusalem.

⁴²Now when the evening⁺ had come, because it was the preparation, that is, the day before the Sabbath,

⁴³Joseph of Arimathaea, an honorable counselor who also waited for the kingdom of God, went in boldly to Pilate and asked⁺ *for* Jesus' body.

⁴⁴Pilate wondered⁺ if *Jesus* was already dead and, calling the centurion, he asked him whether He had been dead for long.⁺

⁴⁵When he knew *it* from the centurion, he gave the body to Joseph.

⁴⁶*Joseph* bought fine linen, took *Jesus* down and wrapped Him in the linen, laid Him in a tomb⁺ cut⁺ out of a rock, and rolled a stone to the door of the tomb.⁺

⁴⁷And Mary Magdalene and Mary *the mother* of Joses saw⁺ where He was laid.

Mark Chapter 16

¹ When the Sabbath was past, Mary Magdalene and Mary the *mother* of James and Salome bought sweet spices *so* that they might come and anoint Him.

² Very early⁺ *on* the first *of the* week, they came to the tomb⁺ at the rising of the sun.

³ They said among themselves: Who will roll away the stone from the door of the tomb⁺ *for* us?

⁴ *But* when they looked, they saw that the stone was rolled away, for it was very large.⁺

⁵ Entering the tomb,⁺ they saw a young man sitting on the right side clothed in a long white garment, and they were frightened.⁺

⁶ He said to them: Do not be frightened.⁺ You seek Jesus of Nazareth who was crucified. He is risen. He is not here. Behold the place where they laid Him. *Matthew 28:6*

⁷ But go⁺ *and* tell His disciples and Peter that He has gone before you into Galilee. There you will see Him, as He said to you.

⁸ *So* they went out quickly and fled from

the tomb, + for they trembled and were amazed. Nor did they say anything to anyone, + for they were afraid.

⁹ *Now* having risen early, *the* first *of the* week *Jesus* appeared first to Mary Magdalene out of whom He had cast seven demons. +

¹⁰ She went and told *those* who had been with Him as they mourned and wept.

¹¹ When they heard that He was alive and had been seen by her, they did not believe.

¹² After that, He appeared in another form to two of them as they walked and went into the country.

¹³ They went and told *it* to the rest+ and *they* did not believe them either.

¹⁴ Afterward He appeared to the eleven as they sat *down* to eat+ and *He* upbraided them for their unbelief and hardness of heart because they did not believe *those* who had seen Him after He was risen.

¹⁵ He said to them: Go into all the world and proclaim+ the Gospel to all creation+.

> ¹⁶ *Those* who believe
> and are baptized will be saved,
> but *those* who do not believe
> will be damned.

¹⁷ These signs will follow *those* who believe: In my name they will cast out demons. + They will speak with new tongues.

¹⁸ They will take up serpents and if they drink any deadly thing it will not hurt them. And they will lay hands on the sick and they will recover.

¹⁹ So then after the Lord had spoken to them, He was received up into heaven and sat at the right hand of God. *Psalm 68:18*

²⁰ And they went forth and proclaimed+ *the Word* everywhere, the Lord working with*them* and confirming the Word with signs following. Amen.

The Gospel of Jesus Christ as surveyed by Luke

Chapter 1

¹ Having observed+ *that* many *others* have taken *it* upon themselves+ to set forth a declaration of those things that are most surely believed among us,

² as *those* who were eyewitnesses and ministers of the Word have delivered *those things* to us,

³ it seemed good to me also, having diligently+ *sought* understanding of everything+ from the very first, to write to you an orderly+ *account*, most excellent Theophilus,

⁴ *so* that you might know the certainty of those things in which you have been instructed.

⁵ *Now* there was, in the days of Herod the king of Judea, a certain priest named Zacharias of the course of Abijah. His wife *was* of the daughters of Aaron and her name *was* Elisabeth.

⁶ They were both righteous before God, walking in all the commandments and ordinances of the Lord, blameless.

⁷ They had no child because Elisabeth was barren, and*now* they were both well advanced+ in years.

⁸ Now+ it came to pass, that while *Zacharias* executed the priest's office before God in the order of his course,

⁹ according to the custom of the priest's office, his lot was to burn incense when he went into the temple of the Lord.

¹⁰ The whole multitude of the people were praying outside+ at the time of incense.

¹¹ *Then* an angel of the Lord appeared to him standing on the right side of the altar of incense.

¹² When Zacharias saw *this*, he was troubled and fear fell upon him.

¹³ But the angel said to him: Do not be afraid Zacharias, for your prayer is heard. Your wife Elisabeth will bear a son to you and you shall call his name John.

¹⁴And you will have joy and gladness, and many will rejoice at his birth.

¹⁵For he will be great in the sight of the Lord. *He* will not drink either wine or strong drink, and he will be filled with the Holy Spirit, even from his mother's womb.

¹⁶He will turn many of the children of Israel to the Lord their God.

¹⁷He will go before *the Lord* in the spirit and power of Elijah, to turn the hearts of the fathers to the children and the disobedient to the wisdom of the righteous,⁺ to make ready a people prepared for the Lord.

¹⁸Zacharias said to the angel: How⁺ can I understand⁺ this? For I am an old man and my wife *is* well advanced⁺ in years.

¹⁹The angel answering said to him: I am Gabriel who stands in the presence of God. *I* am sent to speak to you and to show you these glad tidings.

²⁰And behold *now* you shall be speechless⁺ and not able to speak until the day that these things shall be performed, because you did not believe my words that *surely* will be fulfilled in their season.

²¹*Meanwhile* the people waited for Zacharias and marveled that he stayed⁺ so long in the temple.

²²*Then* when he came out he could not speak to them. They perceived that he had seen a vision in the temple, for he signaled⁺ to them, but remained speechless.

²³Now⁺ it came to pass that as soon as the days of his service⁺ were fulfilled,⁺ he departed to his own house.

²⁴After those days his wife Elisabeth conceived and hid herself five months saying:

²⁵Thus has the Lord dealt with me in the days in which He looked upon *me* to take away my reproach among men.

²⁶*Meanwhile* in *Elisabeth's* sixth month, the angel Gabriel was sent from God to a city of Galilee named Nazareth

²⁷to a virgin espoused to a man whose name was Joseph of the house of David. The virgin's name *was* Mary.

²⁸The angel came to her and said: Hail, *O highly* favored, the Lord *is* with you. Blessed *are* you among women.

²⁹When *Mary* saw *him*, she was troubled by what he said and wondered⁺ in her mind what kind⁺ of greeting⁺ this might⁺ be.

³⁰The angel said to her: Do not be afraid Mary, for you have found favor with God.

³¹Behold you will conceive in your womb and bring forth a son, and shall call His name Jesus. *Isaiah 7:14*

³²He will be great and will be called the Son of the Highest and the Lord God will give to Him the throne of His father David,

³³and He will reign over the house of Jacob forever. Of His kingdom there will be no end. *Isaiah 9:7*

³⁴Then Mary said to the angel: How shall this be since⁺ I have not known⁺ a man?

³⁵The angel answered and said to her: The Holy Spirit will come upon you and the power of the Highest will overshadow you. And therefore, that Holy One⁺ who will be born of you shall be called the Son of God.

³⁶And behold your cousin Elisabeth has also conceived a son in her old age and this is the sixth month with her who was called barren.

³⁷For with God nothing will be impossible.

³⁸Mary said: Behold the handmaid of the Lord. Be it to me according to your word. And the angel departed from her.

³⁹*Then* Mary arose in those days and went with haste into the hill country to a city of Judah.

⁴⁰*She* entered the house of Zacharias and greeted⁺ Elisabeth.

⁴¹And it came to pass that when Elisabeth heard Mary's greeting, the babe in her womb leaped and Elisabeth was filled with the Holy Spirit.

⁴²*Then* she spoke out with a loud voice and said: Blessed *are* you among women and blessed *is* the fruit of your womb.

⁴³Why *has* this *honor come* to me, that the mother of my Lord should come to me?

⁴⁴For behold, as soon as the voice of your greeting⁺ sounded in my ears, the babe in my womb leaped for joy.

⁴⁵Blessed *is* she who believed, for there will be a performance of those things that were told *to* her from the Lord.

⁴⁶Mary said: My soul magnifies the Lord.

⁴⁷My spirit rejoices in God my Savior.

⁴⁸For He has regarded the low estate of His handmaiden. For behold, from henceforth all generations will call me blessed.

⁴⁹For He who is mighty has done great things to me. Holy *is* His name.

⁵⁰His mercy *is* on *those* who fear Him from generation to generation.

⁵¹He has shown strength with His arm. He has scattered the proud in the imagination of their hearts.

⁵²He has put down the mighty from *their* seats and exalted those of low degree.

⁵³He has filled the hungry with good things and He has sent *the* rich away empty.

⁵⁴He has helped⁺ His servant Israel in remembrance of *His* mercy,

⁵⁵as He spoke to our fathers, to Abraham and to his seed forever.

⁵⁶Mary stayed⁺ with *Elisabeth* about three months and *then* returned to her own house.

⁵⁷Now Elisabeth fulfilled⁺ the time *in* which⁺ she should give birth⁺ and she brought forth a son.

⁵⁸Her neighbors and her cousins heard how the Lord had shown great mercy upon her and they rejoiced with her.

⁵⁹And it came to pass that on the eighth day they came to circumcise the child and they called him Zacharias after the name of his father.

⁶⁰But⁺ his mother answered and said: No. He shall be called John.

⁶¹They said to her: *But* there is no one in your family⁺ who is called by this name,

⁶²and they made signs to his father *asking* what he would have *the child* called.

⁶³*Zacharias* asked for a writing table and wrote saying: His name is John. And they all marveled.

⁶⁴Immediately, his mouth was opened and his tongue *loosed* and he spoke and praised God.

⁶⁵Fear came upon all who lived⁺ around⁺ them and all these things⁺ were reported⁺ throughout all the hill country of Judea.

⁶⁶All who heard *these things* laid *them* up in their hearts saying: What kind⁺ of child will this be? And the hand of the Lord was with him.

⁶⁷Now *John's* father Zacharias was filled with the Holy Spirit and prophesied saying:

⁶⁸Blessed *be* the Lord God of Israel, for He has visited and redeemed His people.

⁶⁹*He* has raised up a horn of salvation for us in the house of His servant David,

⁷⁰*just* as He spoke by the mouth of His holy prophets who have been *with us* since the world began,

⁷¹*so* that we should be saved from our enemies and from the hand of all who hate us,

⁷²to perform the mercy *promised* to our fathers and to remember His holy covenant.

⁷³*Remember* the oath that He swore to our father Abraham,

⁷⁴that He would grant *deliverance* to us *so* that we, *by* being delivered out of the hand of our enemies, might serve Him without fear,

⁷⁵in holiness and righteousness before Him all the days of our life.

⁷⁶*Then Zacharias said:* You, child, shall be called the prophet of the Highest. For you shall go before the face of the Lord to prepare His ways,

⁷⁷to give knowledge of salvation to His people by the remission of their sins

⁷⁸through the tender mercy of our God from whom the Dayspring from on high has visited us,

⁷⁹to give light to *those* who sit in darkness and *in* the shadow of death *and* to guide our feet into the way of peace.

⁸⁰The child grew and *became* strong in spirit, and was in the deserts until the day of his showing to Israel.

Luke Chapter 2

¹ Now⁺ it came to pass in those days *that* a decree went out from Caesar Augustus that all the world should be registered.⁺ *Daniel 9:25*

² This census⁺ was first made when Cyrenius was governor of Syria

³ and all went to be registered,⁺ everyone to their own city.

⁴ Joseph also went up from Galilee out of the city of Nazareth to Judea to the city of David called Bethlehem, because he was of the house and family⁺ of David. *Micah 5:2*

⁵ *He went* to be registered⁺ with Mary his espoused wife *who was great* with child.

⁶ So it was that, while they were there, the days were fulfilled⁺ that she should give birth,⁺

⁷ and she brought forth her firstborn son and wrapped Him in swaddling clothes and laid Him in a manger, because there was no room for them in the inn.

⁸ Now⁺ in the same country, there were shepherds abiding in the field, keeping watch over their flock by night.

⁹ And behold, the angel of the Lord came upon them and the glory of the Lord shone around⁺ them and they were greatly⁺ afraid.

¹⁰The angel said to them: Do not be afraid, for behold I bring to you good tidings of great joy that will be *for* all people.

¹¹For unto you is born this day in the city of David, a Savior who is Christ the Lord.

¹²This *shall be* a sign to you: You will find the babe wrapped in swaddling clothes, lying in a manger.

¹³And suddenly there was with the angel a multitude of the heavenly host praising God and saying:

¹⁴Glory to God in the highest. And on earth peace *and* good will toward all mankind.⁺

¹⁵*Now* it came to pass, as the angels had gone away from them into heaven, the shepherds said to one another: Let us now go to Bethlehem and see the *fulfill-*

ment of this word that the Lord has made known to us.

¹⁶*So* they went⁺ with haste and found Mary and Joseph, and the babe lying in a manger.

¹⁷When they had seen *this*, they made widely⁺ known the things⁺ that were told *to* them concerning this child.

¹⁸All *those* who heard *this* wondered at those things that were told *to* them by the shepherds.

¹⁹But Mary kept all these things in her heart and pondered *them*.

²⁰*Then* the shepherds returned, glorifying and praising God for all the things that they had heard and seen, as it was told to them.

²¹When eight days were fulfilled⁺ *and the time came* for circumcising the little⁺ child, His name was called Jesus, which is the name *He* was called⁺ by the angel before He was conceived in the womb.

²²When the days of *Mary's* purification were accomplished, according to the law of Moses, they took Him to Jerusalem to present *Him* to the Lord.

²³As it is written in the law of the Lord: Every male who opens the womb shall be called holy to the Lord. *Exodus 13:2, Exodus 13:12, Exodus 22:29, Numbers 3:13, Numbers 8:16-17, Numbers 18:15*

²⁴*So* the child *was brought* to offer a sacrifice according to what is said in the law of the Lord: A pair of turtledoves or two young pigeons.

²⁵And behold, there was a man in Jerusalem whose name *was* Simeon. *He was* righteous⁺ and devout, waiting for the consolation of Israel, and the Holy Spirit was upon him.

²⁶It was revealed to him by the Holy Spirit that he should not see death before he had seen Christ⁺ the Lord.

²⁷*So* He came by the Spirit into the temple. When the parents brought in the child Jesus to do for Him according *to* the custom of the law,

²⁸*Simeon* took *Jesus* up in his arms and blessed God and said:

²⁹Lord, now let your servant depart in peace, according to your Word.

30 For my eyes have seen your salvation 31 that you have prepared in the presence+ of all the people,

32 a light for *the* revelation+ *of* the Gentiles and *for* the glory of your people Israel.

33 Joseph and His mother marveled at those things that were spoken of Him.

34 Simeon blessed them and said to Mary His mother: Behold this *child* is appointed+ for the fall and rising again of many in Israel and *also for* a sign *that will be* spoken against.

35 Yes. A sword will pierce through your own soul also *so* that the thoughts of many hearts may be revealed.

36 *Then came* one *called* Anna, a prophetess, the daughter of Phanuel of the tribe of Asher. She was *well* advanced+ *in years* and had lived with a husband seven years from her virginity

37 but+ *then had been* a widow for about eighty four years. *During that time* she had not departed from the temple but served *God* with fastings and prayers night and day.

38 Now she also came in that same hour *and* gave thanks to the Lord and spoke about *Jesus* to all *those* who looked for redemption in Jerusalem.

39 When they had performed all things according to the law of the Lord, they returned to Galilee, to their own city Nazareth.

40 And the child grew and became+ strong in spirit *and* filled with wisdom, and the grace of God was upon Him.

41 Now every year at the Feast of the Passover, His parents went to Jerusalem.

42 And when He was twelve years old, they went up to Jerusalem according+ *to* the custom of the feast.

43 And when they had fulfilled the days, as they returned, the young+ Jesus stayed+ behind in Jerusalem, but+ Joseph and His mother did not know *about this*.

44 But supposing Him to be in the company, they went a day's journey, and sought Him among *their* relatives+ and acquaintance.

45 When they did not find Him, they returned+ to Jerusalem seeking Him.

46 Now+ it came to pass that after three days they found Him in the temple, sitting in the midst of the teachers, + both hearing them and asking them questions.

47 All who heard Him were astonished at His understanding and answers.

48 When *Joseph and His mother* saw Him, they were amazed and His mother said to Him: Son, why have you done+ this to us? Behold your father and I have *been much* distressed+ seeking+ you.

49 He said to them: How is it that you sought me? Did you not know that I must be about my Father's business?

50 But+ they did not understand the words He spoke to them.

51 *Then* He went down with them and came to Nazareth and was subject to them, but His mother kept all these things+ in her heart.

52 And Jesus increased in wisdom and stature and in favor with God and *with* people. + *Isaiah 11:2*

Luke Chapter 3

1 Now in the fifteenth year of the reign of Tiberius Caesar, Pontius Pilate was governor of Judea, Herod was tetrarch of Galilee and his brother Philip tetrarch of Ituraea and of the region of Trachonitis, and Lysanias *was* the tetrarch of Abilene.

2 Annas and Caiaphas were the high priests. *Then* the Word of God came to John the son of Zacharias in the wilderness.

3 And *John* went+ into all the country around+ Jordan proclaiming+ the baptism of repentance for the remission of sins.

4 As it is written in the book of the words of the prophet Isaiah *who* said: The voice of one crying in the wilderness: Prepare the way of the Lord. Make His paths straight. *Matthew 3:3*

5 Every valley shall be filled and every mountain and hill shall be brought low. The crooked shall be made straight and the rough ways *shall be* made smooth.

6 All flesh will see the salvation of God.

7 Then he said to the multitude that came forth to be baptized by him: O generation of vipers, who has warned you to flee from the wrath to come?

8 Bring forth therefore fruits worthy of repentance and do not begin to say within yourselves: We have Abraham as *our* father. For I say to you that God is able to raise up children to Abraham from these stones.

9 Now also the axe is laid to the root of the trees. Therefore, every tree that does not bring forth good fruit is *to be* cut+ down and cast into the fire.

10*Then* the people asked him saying: What shall we do then?

11 He answered saying to them:*If* anyone has two coats, let them give+ to one who has none. And *those* who have food,+ let them do likewise.

12 Then worldly+ people also came to be baptized and said to him: Master, what shall we do?

13 He said to them: Exact no more than what is appointed *to* you.

14 The soldiers also+ asked+ him saying: And what shall we do? He said to them: Do violence to no one. Do not accuse *anyone* falsely. And be content with your wages.

15 Since+ all the people were in expectation, everyone+ reasoned+ in their hearts about+ John, *wondering* whether he might+ be the Christ or not.

16 John answered saying to *them* all: I indeed baptize you with water, but one is coming *who is* mightier than I, the straps+ of whose sandals+ I am not worthy to loosen. He will baptize you with the Holy Spirit and with fire.

17*His* fan *is* in His hand and He will thoroughly purge His floor and will gather the wheat into His barn,+ but the chaff He will burn with unquenchable fire.

18 And *John* proclaimed+ many other things in his exhortation to the people.

19 But Herod the tetrarch, having been reproved by *John* because+ of Herodias his brother Philip's wife *whom Herod stole and married* and for all the evils Herod had done,

20 added yet this above all, that he shut up John in prison.

21 Now when all the people were baptized, it came to pass that Jesus also being baptized and praying, the heaven was opened

22 and the Holy Spirit descended upon Him in a bodily shape like a dove and a voice came from heaven saying: You are my beloved Son. In you I am well pleased.

23*Then* Jesus Himself began *His ministry when He was* about thirty years of age. *It* was supposed *that He was* the son of Joseph *who was the descendant* of Heli

24 of Matthat of Levi of Melchi of Janna of Joseph

25 of Mattathiah of Amos of Nahum of Esli of Naggai

26 of Maath of Mattathiah of Semei of Joseph of Judah

27 of Johanan of Rhesa of Zerubbabel of Shealtiel of Neri

28 of Melchi of Addi of Cosam of Elmodam of Er

29 of Jose of Eliezer of Jorim of Matthat of Levi

30 of Simeon of Judah of Joseph of Jonan of Eliakim

31 of Melea of Menan of Mattatha of Nathan of David

32 of Jesse of Obed of Boaz of Salmon of Nahshon

33 of Amminadab of Ram of Hezron of Perez of Judah *Genesis 49:10*

34 of Jacob of Isaac of Abraham of Terah of Nahor *Genesis 17:19*

35 of Saruch of Ragau of Phalec of Heber of Sala

36 of Cainan of Arphaxad of Sem of Noah of Lamech

37 of Methuselah of Enoch of Jared of Mahalaleel of Cainan

38 of Enos of Seth of Adam of God.

Luke Chapter 4

1 Now+ Jesus, being full of the Holy Spirit, returned from Jordan and was led by the Spirit into the wilderness.

2 *For* forty days, *He was* tempted by the

devil. In those days, He ate nothing and after they were ended, He was hungry.

3 *Then* the devil said to Him: If you are the Son of God, command this stone that it be made bread.

4 Jesus answered him saying: It is written that mankind+ shall not live by bread alone, but by every Word of God.

Matthew 4:4

5 *Then* the devil took+ *Jesus* up to a high mountain *and* showed to Him all the kingdoms of the world in a moment of time.

6 And the devil said to Him: I will give you authority+ *and power over* all these, and the glory of them, for that is delivered to me and to whomever I will, I *can* give it.

7 Therefore, if you will worship me, all *this* shall be yours.

8 Jesus answered and said to him: Get behind me Satan. For it is written: You shall worship the Lord your God and Him only shall you serve. *Matthew 4:10*

9 *Then* Satan took *Jesus* to Jerusalem, sat Him on a pinnacle of the temple, and said to Him: If you are the Son of God, cast yourself down from here.

10 For it is written: He will give His angels charge over you to keep you.

Matthew 4:6

11 In *their* hands they will bear you up, lest at any time you dash your foot against a stone. *Matthew 4:6*

12 Jesus answering said to him: It is said: You shall not tempt the Lord your God.

Matthew 4:7

13 When the devil had ended all the temptation, he departed from *Jesus* for a season.

14 *Then* Jesus returned in the power of the Spirit to Galilee, and His reputation+ went all around+ the region.

15 He taught in their synagogues, being honored+ by everyone.+

16 *Then* He came to Nazareth where He had been brought up. And, as His custom was, He went into the synagogue on the Sabbath day and stood up to read.

17 The book of the prophet Isaiah was delivered to Him, and when He had opened the book, He found the place where it was written:

18 The Spirit of the Lord *is* upon me because He has anointed me to proclaim+ the Gospel to the poor. He has sent me to heal the broken hearted, to proclaim+ deliverance to the captives and recovering of sight to the blind, to set at liberty *those* who are bruised, *Isaiah 61:1*

19 to proclaim+ the acceptable year of the Lord ... *Isaiah 61:2*

20 *Then* He closed the book, gave *it* back to the attendant, + and sat down. And the eyes of all who were in the synagogue were fastened on Him.

21 He began to say to them: This day this Scripture is fulfilled in your ears.

22 All bore witness *to* Him and wondered at the gracious words that came out of His mouth. And they said: Is this not Joseph's son?

23 He said to them: You will surely say to me this proverb: Physician, heal yourself. Whatever we have heard done in Capernaum, do also here in your country.

24 He said: Truly+ I say to you: No prophet is accepted in his own country.

25 But truly I say to you: Many widows were in Israel in the days of Elijah when the heaven was shut up three years and six months, when great famine was throughout all the land.

26 But Elijah was not sent to any of them except+ to Sarepta, *a city* of Sidon, to a woman *who was* a widow.

27 Many lepers were in Israel in the time of Elisha the prophet and none of them was cleansed except+ Naaman the Syrian.

28 When they heard these things, all those in the synagogue were filled with wrath

29 and rose up and thrust Him out of the city and led Him to the brow of the hill on which their city was built *so* that they might cast Him down headlong.

30 But passing through the midst of them, *Jesus* went away+

31 and came down to Capernaum, a city of Galilee, and taught them on the Sabbath days.

³²They were astonished at His doctrine, for His Word was with authority⁺ *and power*.

³³Now⁺ there was a man in the synagogue who had a spirit of an unclean demon⁺ and cried out with a loud voice

³⁴saying: Let *us* alone. What do we have to do with you Jesus of Nazareth? Have you come to destroy us? I know who you are: The Holy One of God.

³⁵Jesus rebuked him saying: Be still⁺ and come out of him. And when the demon⁺ had thrown him in the midst, he came out of him and did not hurt him.

³⁶They were all amazed and spoke among themselves saying: What a Word this *is*. For He commands the unclean spirits with authority and power and they come out.

³⁷*So* His reputation⁺ went into every place in the country *all* around.⁺

³⁸*Then* He arose out of the synagogue and entered Simon's house *where* Simon's wife's mother was taken with a great fever, and they prayed *to* Him for her.

³⁹He stood over her and rebuked the fever *and* it left her and immediately she arose and ministered to them.

⁴⁰Now when the sun was setting, all *those* who had any sick *ones* with many different⁺ diseases brought them to Him and He laid His hands on everyone of them and healed them.

⁴¹Demons⁺ also came out of many, crying out and saying: You are Christ the Son of God. But⁺ He rebuked *them* and did not allow them to speak, for they knew that He was Christ.

⁴²When it was day, He departed and went into a deserted⁺ place. But⁺ the people sought Him *out* and came to Him and detained⁺ him *so* that He could⁺ not depart from them.

⁴³He said to them: I must proclaim⁺ the kingdom of God to other cities also, because *it is* for that *purpose* I have been sent.

⁴⁴And He proclaimed⁺ *the Word* in the synagogues of Galilee.

Luke Chapter 5

¹ Now⁺ it came to pass that as the people pressed *in* upon *Jesus* to hear the Word of God, He stood by the lake of Gennesaret

² and saw two boats standing by the lake. But the fishermen were gone out of them and were washing *their* nets.

³ *So,* He entered one of the boats, which was Simon's, and asked⁺ him if he would thrust out a little from the land, and *then* He sat down and taught the *whole* crowd⁺ *of people* from⁺ the boat.

⁴ When He finished⁺ speaking *to them*, He said to Simon: Launch out into the deep and let down your nets for a catch⁺.

⁵ Simon answering said to Him: Master, we have toiled all night and have taken nothing. Nevertheless at your word I will let down the net.

⁶ When they had done this, they caught⁺ a large⁺ number⁺ of fish, *so many that* their net broke.

⁷ *So* they signaled⁺ to *their* partners who were in the other boat that they should come and help them, and they came and filled both the boats so that they began to sink.

⁸ When Simon Peter saw *this*, he fell down at Jesus' knees saying: Depart from me for I am a sinful man, O Lord.

⁹ For *Peter* and all who were with him were astonished at the catch⁺ of the fish they had taken.

¹⁰So also *were* James and John the sons of Zebedee who were partners with Simon. But⁺ Jesus said to Simon: Do not be afraid. From henceforth you will catch men.

¹¹And when they had brought their boats to land, they left⁺ everything⁺ *behind* and followed Him.

¹²Now⁺ it came to pass when *Jesus* was in a certain city, behold a man full of leprosy *came to Him. Upon* seeing Jesus he fell upon *his* face and begged⁺ Him saying: Lord, if you will you can make me clean.

¹³*Jesus* put forth*His* hand and touched him saying: I will. Be clean. And immediately the leprosy departed from him.

¹⁴*But then Jesus* charged him to tell no one but*He said:* Go and show yourself to the priest and *make an* offering⁺ for your cleansing as Moses commanded, for a testimony to them.

¹⁵But *because of this, all* the more His reputation⁺ went *all* around,⁺ and great multitudes came together to hear and to be healed of their infirmities by Him.

¹⁶*Then* He withdrew into the wilderness and prayed.

¹⁷Now⁺ it came to pass on a certain day as He was teaching, that there were Pharisees and teachers⁺ of the law sitting by, who had come from⁺ every town of Galilee, Judea, and Jerusalem. And the power of the Lord was *present* to heal them.

¹⁸And behold men brought a man in a bed who was paralyzed⁺ and they sought to bring him in and lay *him* before *Jesus.*

¹⁹When they could not find by what *way* they might bring him in because of the multitude, they went upon the housetop and let him down through the *roof* tiles⁺ with *his* bed⁺ into the midst before Jesus.

²⁰When *Jesus* saw their faith, He said to *the sick man*: Man, your sins are forgiven.

²¹*Then* the scribes and the Pharisees began to reason saying: Who is this who speaks blasphemies? Who can forgive sins but God alone?

²²But when Jesus perceived their thoughts, He answering said to them: What are you thinking⁺ in your hearts?

²³Which⁺ is easier to say: Your sins are forgiven. Or to say: Rise up and walk.

²⁴But *so* that you may know that the Son of man has authority⁺ *and power* on earth to forgive sins,*Jesus* said to the *one* sick with paralysis⁺: I say to you: Arise and take up your bed⁺ and go to your house.

²⁵Immediately he rose up before them and took up that on which he *had been* laying⁺ and departed to his own house, glorifying God.

²⁶They were all amazed and glorified God and were filled with fear saying: We have seen astonishing⁺ things today.

²⁷After these things *Jesus* went forth and saw a worldly⁺ person named Levi sitting at the tax office⁺ and He said to him: Follow me.

²⁸Therefore,⁺ he left everything,⁺ rose up, and followed *Jesus.*

²⁹Levi made a great feast *for Jesus* in his own house and there was a great multitude⁺ of worldly⁺ people and of others who sat down with them.

³⁰But their scribes and Pharisees complained⁺ against His disciples saying: Why do you eat and drink with worldly⁺ people and sinners?

³¹Jesus answering said to them: *Those* who are whole do not need a physician, but *those* who are sick *do*.

³²I did not come to call the righteous but sinners to repentance.

³³*Then* they said to Him: Why do the disciples of John fast often and make prayers, and likewise *the disciples* of the Pharisees, but yours eat and drink?

³⁴He said to them: Can you make the children of the bride chamber fast while the bridegroom is with them?

³⁵But the days will come when the Bridegroom will be taken away from them and then they will fast in those days.

³⁶Then He spoke a parable to them: No one puts a piece of a new garment on an old garment, or else the new makes a tear⁺ and the piece that was *taken* out of the new does not agree with the old.

³⁷No one puts new wine into old wineskins⁺ *or* else the new wine will burst the wineskins⁺ and be spilled and the wineskins⁺ will perish.

³⁸But new wine must be put into new wineskins⁺ *so* both are preserved.

³⁹No one having drunk old *wine* immediately⁺ desires new, for he says: The old is better.

Luke Chapter 6

¹ Now⁺ it came to pass on the second Sabbath after the first, that *Jesus* walked⁺ through the corn fields, and His disciples plucked the ears of corn and ate, rubbing *them* in *their* hands.
² Certain of the Pharisees said to them: Why do you *do* what is not lawful to do on the Sabbath days?
³ Jesus answering them said: Have you not even read what David did when he himself and *those* who were with him were hungry?
⁴ How he went into the house of God and took and ate the show bread, which it is not lawful for anyone⁺ except⁺ the priests alone *to eat*? And *he* also gave *some* to *those* who were with him.
⁵ *Then Jesus* said to them: The Son of man is Lord also of the Sabbath.
⁶ Now⁺ it came to pass on another Sabbath that *Jesus* entered the synagogue and taught, and there was a man whose right hand was withered.
⁷ The scribes and Pharisees watched *Jesus to see* whether He would heal on the Sabbath day *so* that they might find an accusation against Him.
⁸ But He knew their thoughts and said to the man who had the withered hand: Rise up and stand forth in the midst. And he arose and stood forth.
⁹ Then Jesus said to them: I will ask you one thing: Is it lawful on the Sabbath days to do good or to do evil? To save life or to destroy *it*?
¹⁰ Looking around⁺ upon them all, He said to the man: Stretch forth your hand. And he did so and his hand was restored whole as the other.
¹¹ *The scribes and Pharisees* were filled with rage⁺ and conferred⁺ with one another *to decide* what they might do to Jesus.
¹² *Then* it came to pass in those days that *Jesus* went to a mountain to pray and continued all night in prayer to God.
¹³ When it was day, He called His disciples, and from⁺ *among* them He chose twelve whom He also named apostles:

¹⁴ Simon, whom He also named Peter, and Andrew his brother, James and John, Philip and Bartholomew,
¹⁵ Matthew and Thomas, James the *son* of Alphaeus and Simon called Zelotes,
¹⁶ Jude *the brother* of James, and Judas Iscariot, who also became⁺ the traitor.
¹⁷ *Jesus* came down with them and stood in the plain *with* a multitude⁺ of His disciples and *also* a great multitude of people out of all Judea and Jerusalem and from the sea coast of Tyre and Sidon, who came to hear Him and to be healed of their diseases,
¹⁸ *including those* who were oppressed⁺ with unclean spirits, and they were healed.
¹⁹ The whole multitude sought to touch Him, for virtue went out of Him and healed *them* all.
²⁰ He lifted up His eyes to His disciples and said: Blessed *are you who are* poor for the kingdom of God is yours.
²¹ Blessed *are you* who hunger now for you shall be filled. Blessed *are you* who weep now for you shall laugh.
²² Blessed are you when people⁺ shall hate you and when they shall separate you *from their company* and reproach *you* and cast out your name as evil, because⁺ of the Son of man.
²³ Rejoice in that day and leap for joy, for behold, your reward *will be* great in heaven, for in like manner did their fathers *treat* the prophets.
²⁴ But woe to you who are rich, for you have received your consolation.
²⁵ Woe to you who are full, for you shall hunger. Woe to you who laugh now, for you shall mourn and weep.
²⁶ Woe to you, when everyone⁺ speaks well of you, for so did their fathers *speak* to the false prophets.
²⁷ But I say to you who hear: Love your enemies. Do good to *those* who hate you. *Matthew 5:44*
²⁸ Bless *those* who curse you. And pray for *those* who use you despitefully.
²⁹ To one who strikes⁺ you on the cheek offer also the other, and *if* anyone takes away your vest⁺ do not forbid *them to take your* coat also.

³⁰Give to everyone⁺ who asks of you. Of anyone who takes away your goods, do not ask to take *them* back.

³¹As you would *have* others⁺ do to you, you also do to them likewise.

³²For if you love *those* who love you, what grace⁺ have you *shown*? For sinners also love *those* who love them.

³³And if you do good to *those* who do good to you, what grace⁺ have you *shown*? For sinners also do the same.

³⁴And if you lend *to those* from whom you hope to receive, what grace⁺ have you *shown*? For sinners also lend to sinners to receive as much again.

³⁵*Instead, I say to you:* Love your enemies and do good and lend, hoping for nothing again, and your reward will be great and you shall be the children of the Highest. For He is kind to the unthankful and *to* the evil.

³⁶Therefore, be merciful as your Father also is merciful.

³⁷Do not judge and you will not be judged. Do not condemn and you will not be condemned. Forgive and you will be forgiven.

---

³⁸ Give and it will be given to you: Good measure, pressed down, shaken together, and running over, others⁺ will give to your innermost⁺ *needs*. For with the same gauge⁺ with which you measure⁺ it will be measured to you again.

---

³⁹*Then Jesus* spoke a parable to them: Can the blind lead the blind? Will they not both fall into the ditch?

⁴⁰The disciple is not above his master, but everyone who is perfect will be like⁺ their master.

⁴¹Why do you notice⁺ the speck⁺ that is in your brother's *or sister's* eye, but do not notice⁺ the beam that is in your own eye?

⁴²How can you say to your brother: Brother, let me pull out the speck⁺ that is in your eye, when you yourself do not notice⁺ the beam that is in your own eye? You hypocrite. First cast the beam out of your own eye and then you will see clearly to pull out the speck⁺ that is in your brother's eye.

⁴³For a good tree does not bring forth corrupt fruit. Nor does a corrupt tree bring forth good fruit.

⁴⁴For every tree is known by its own fruit. People⁺ do not gather figs from thorn *bushes*. Nor do they gather grapes from a thorn⁺ bush.

⁴⁵A good person brings forth what is good out of the good treasure in their heart. An evil person brings forth what is evil out of the evil treasure *that is in* their heart. For the mouth speaks *out* of the abundance of the heart.

⁴⁶Why do you call me: Lord, Lord, and do not *do* the things that I say?

⁴⁷Whoever comes to me and hears my sayings and does them: I will show you to whom they are *to be* compared⁺:

⁴⁸They are like a person who built a house and dug deep and laid the foundation on a rock. When the flood arose, the stream beat forcefully⁺ upon that house, and could not shake it for it was founded upon a rock.

⁴⁹But *those* who hear and do not *follow through* are like a person⁺ who built a house upon the earth without a foundation, against which the stream beat forcefully⁺ and immediately it fell, and the ruin of that house was great.

Luke Chapter 7

¹Now when *Jesus* had ended all His words⁺ to the people, He entered Capernaum.

²*There* a certain centurion's servant who was dear to him, was sick and ready to die.

³When *the centurion* heard about Jesus, he sent the elders of the Jews to Him, beseeching Him that, having come, He would heal his servant.

⁴When *the elders* came to Jesus, they begged⁺ Him diligently,⁺ saying that *the centurion* for whom He should do this was worthy.

⁵ For *they said:* He loves our nation and he has built a synagogue *for* us.

⁶ Then Jesus went with them and when He was not far from the house, the centurion sent friends to Him saying: Lord, do not trouble yourself. For I am not worthy that you should come⁺ under my roof.

⁷ Nor, for that reason⁺ did I think myself worthy to come to you. But *if you would just* speak a word, my servant will be healed.

⁸ For I also am a man set under authority, having soldiers under me. I say to one: Go. And he goes. To another: Come. And he comes. To my servant: Do this. And he does *it.*

⁹ When Jesus heard these things, He marveled at him and *He* turned around⁺ and said to the people who followed Him: I say to you: I have not found such⁺ great faith *before,* even in Israel.

¹⁰*Upon* returning to the house, *those* who had been sent found the servant who had been sick *now* well.⁺

¹¹And it came to pass on the next⁺ *day* that *Jesus* went to a city called Nain, and many of His disciples went with Him and many people *followed.*

¹²Now when He came near to the gate of the city, behold a dead man was being carried out, the only son of his mother, and she was a widow. Many people from the city were with her.

¹³When the Lord saw her, He had compassion on her and said to her: Do not weep.

¹⁴*Then* He came and touched the casket⁺ and *those* who carried⁺ *it* stopped.⁺ He said: Young man, I say to you: Arise.

¹⁵The dead *man* sat up and began to speak. And *Jesus* gave⁺ him to his mother.

¹⁶Fear seized⁺ everyone⁺ and they glorified God saying: A great prophet has risen up among us. And, God has visited His people.

¹⁷The report⁺ of this went throughout all Judea and throughout the region all around.⁺

¹⁸The disciples of John told⁺ him about⁺ all these things,

¹⁹and John called two of his disciples *and* sent *them* to Jesus saying: Are you the *one who was to* come, or should we look for another?

²⁰When the men had come to *Jesus*, they said: John the Baptist has sent us to you saying: Are you the *one who was to* come, or should we look for another?

²¹In that same hour, *Jesus* cured many of *their* infirmities and plagues, and of evil spirits. And to many *who were* blind He gave sight.

²²Then Jesus answering said to *John's disciples*: Go and tell John what things you have seen and heard: That the blind see, the lame walk, the lepers are cleansed, the deaf hear, the dead are raised, *and* the Gospel is proclaimed⁺ to the poor.

²³Blessed are *those* who will not be offended *and disbelieve* in me.

²⁴*After* the messengers from John departed, *Jesus* began to speak to the people concerning John: What did you go out into the wilderness to see? A reed shaken with the wind?

²⁵But what did you go out to see? A man clothed in soft clothing⁺? Behold *those* who are gorgeously appareled and live luxuriously⁺ are in kings' courts.

²⁶But what did you go out to see? A prophet? Yes, I say to you, and much more than a prophet.

²⁷This is *the one* of whom it is written: Behold I send my messenger before your face, who shall prepare your way before you. *Matthew 11:10*

²⁸For I say to you: Among *all* those born of women, there is not a greater prophet than John the Baptist, but *those* who are least in the kingdom of God are greater than he.

²⁹All the people who heard *Jesus*, and the worldly⁺ people, justified God, being baptized with the baptism of John.

³⁰But the Pharisees and lawyers rejected the counsel of God against themselves, not being baptized by him.

³¹*Then* the Lord said: To what then shall I compare⁺ the people⁺ of this generation? What are they like?

³²They are like children sitting in the marketplace, calling to one another, and saying: We have piped to you and you have not danced. We have mourned to you and you have not wept.

³³For John the Baptist came neither eating bread nor drinking wine, and you say: He has a demon⁺.

³⁴*Now*, the Son of man has come eating and drinking, and you say: Behold a gluttonous man, a wine drinker,⁺ a friend of worldly⁺ people and sinners.

³⁵But wisdom is justified by all her children.

³⁶*Then* one of the Pharisees asked⁺ *Jesus* to eat with him. *So* He went to the Pharisee's house and sat down to eat.

³⁷And behold a woman in the city who was a sinner, when she knew that *Jesus* sat *down* to eat⁺ in the Pharisee's house, brought an alabaster box of ointment

³⁸and stood at His feet behind *Him* weeping and began to wash His feet with tears and wipe *them* with the hair of her head and kissed His feet and anointed *them* with the ointment.

³⁹Now when the Pharisee who had invited⁺ Him saw *this*, he spoke within himself saying: If this man was a prophet, He would have known who and what kind⁺ of woman *this is* who touches Him, for she is a sinner.

⁴⁰Jesus answering said to him: Simon, I have something⁺ to say to you. He said: Master, say on.

⁴¹There was a certain creditor who had two debtors. One owed *nearly two year's wages*⁺ and the other *two month's wages*⁺.

⁴²When they had nothing *with which* to pay, he frankly forgave them both. Tell me therefore: Which of them will love him most?

⁴³Simon answered and said: I suppose that *the one* to whom he forgave most. *Jesus* said to him: You have judged correctly⁺.

⁴⁴*Then* He turned to the woman and said to Simon: See this woman? I entered your house *and* you gave me no water for my feet, but she has washed my feet with tears and wiped *them* with the hair of her head.

⁴⁵You gave me no kiss, but since the time I came in, this woman has not stopped⁺ kissing my feet.

⁴⁶You did not anoint my head with oil, but this woman has anointed my feet with ointment.

⁴⁷Therefore I say to you: Her sins, which are many, are forgiven. For she loved much. But *those* to whom little is forgiven, love *but* little.

⁴⁸*Then Jesus* said to her: Your sins are forgiven.

⁴⁹*Those* who sat *down* to eat⁺ with Him began to say within themselves: Who is this that forgives sins also?

⁵⁰He said to the woman: Your faith has saved you. Go in peace.

Luke Chapter 8

¹Now⁺ after *this*, it came to pass that *Jesus* went throughout every city and village, proclaiming⁺ *the Word* and showing the glad tidings of the kingdom of God. And the twelve *disciples went* with Him.

²Also, certain women who had been healed of evil spirits and infirmities, Mary called Magdalene out of whom went seven demons,⁺

³Joanna the wife of Chuza, Herod's steward, Susanna, and many others ministered to Him from their substance.

⁴When many people had gathered together, having come to Him out of every city, He spoke *to them* by a parable:

⁵A sower went out to sow his seed. As he sowed, some fell by the wayside and it was trampled⁺ down and the birds⁺ of the air devoured it.

⁶Some fell upon a rock and as soon as it had sprung up, it withered away because it lacked moisture.

⁷Some fell among thorns and the thorns sprang up with it and choked it.

⁸Other *seed* fell on good ground and sprang up and bore fruit a hundredfold. And when He had said these things, He cried *out*: *Those* who have ears to hear, let them hear.

9 *Then* His disciples asked Him saying: What might this parable be?

10 *Jesus* said: Unto you it is given to know the mysteries of the kingdom of God. But to others *I speak* in parables, that seeing they might not see and hearing they might not understand.

11 Now the parable is this: The seed is the Word of God.

12 Those by the wayside are *those* who hear, *and* then the devil comes and takes away the Word out of their hearts, lest they should believe and be saved.

13 Those on the rock *represent those* who, when they hear, receive the Word with joy *but* they have no root *and so* they believe *only* for a time,+ and in *a* time of trials+ *they* fall away.

14 *The seed* that fell among thorns are *those* who, when they have heard, go forth and are choked with *the* cares and riches and pleasures of *this* life, and bring no fruit to perfection.

15 But that on the good ground are *those* who, in an honest and good heart, having heard the Word, keep *it* and bring forth fruit with patience.

16 No one, having lit a candle, covers it with a vessel or puts *it* under a bed, but sets *it* on a candlestick *so* that *those* who enter in may see the light.

17 For nothing is secret, that will not be made manifest. Nor *is anything* hid, that will not come to light+ and become known+.

18 Therefore, take heed how you hear, for whoever has, to them *more* will be given, and whoever has nothing, from them will be taken even what they seem to have.

19 Then His mother and brothers came to Him, but were not able to get *close to* Him because of the crowd.+

20 *Someone* told Him *about this*, saying: Your mother and your brothers are standing outside+ desiring to see you.

21 He answered and said to them: My mother and my brothers *and sisters* are these who hear the Word of God and do it.

22 Now it came to pass on a certain day

that *Jesus* got into a boat with His disciples, and He said to them: Let us go over to the other side of the lake. And they launched forth.

23 But as they sailed, *Jesus* fell asleep. *Then* a windstorm+ came down on the lake and they were filled *with water* and were in jeopardy.

24 *His disciples* came to Him and awoke Him saying: Master, master, we *are* perishing. Then He arose and rebuked the wind and the raging of the water, and they stopped+ and there was a calm.

25 He said to them: Where is your faith? They were afraid, and wondered, and said to one another: Who is this *man*? For He commands even the winds and water and they obey Him.

26 *Then* they arrived in the country of the Gadarenes near+ Galilee.

27 When He went forth to land, a certain man out of the city met Him. *This man* had demons+ for a long time and wore no clothes *and* did not live+ in *a* house but among the tombs.

28 When he saw Jesus, he cried out and fell down before Him and with a loud voice said: What do I have to do with you Jesus, Son of God most high? I beseech you, do not torment me.

29 For *Jesus* commanded the unclean spirit to come out of the man, for often times it had seized+ him. He had been kept bound with chains and shackles,+ but he broke the bands and was driven into the wilderness by the demon.+

30 Jesus asked him saying: What is your name? He said: Legion. Because many demons+ had entered him.

31 *The demons* begged+ *Jesus* to not command them to go into the bottomless pit.+

32 *Now* there was a herd of many swine there feeding on the mountain and they begged+ Him that He allow them to enter into the *swine*, and He allowed+ them *to do so*.

33 Then the demons+ went out of the man and entered the swine and the herd ran violently down a steep place into the lake and were choked.

³⁴When *those* who fed *them* saw what was done, they fled and told *it* in the city and in the country.

³⁵Then the *people* went out to see what was done. *They* came to Jesus and found the man out of whom the demons⁺ had departed, sitting at the feet of Jesus, clothed and in his right mind. And they were afraid.

³⁶*Those* who had seen *it* told *the others who came later* how *Jesus* healed the man⁺ who had been demon⁺ possessed.

³⁷Then the whole multitude from the country around⁺ the Gadarenes begged⁺ *Jesus* to depart from them, for they were taken with great fear. *So Jesus* got into the boat and returned back again.

³⁸Now the man from⁺ whom the demons⁺ were gone⁺ begged⁺ *Jesus* to be *taken* with Him, but Jesus sent him away saying:

³⁹Return to your own house and declare⁺ all⁺ *the great things* God has done to you. *So* he went away⁺ and published throughout the whole city all⁺ *the great things* Jesus had done *for* him.

⁴⁰And it came to pass that when Jesus returned, the people *gladly* received Him, for they were all waiting for Him.

⁴¹Behold a man named Jairus, a ruler of the synagogue, came and fell down at Jesus' feet and begged⁺ Him to come to his house,

⁴²for he had only one daughter, about twelve years of age, and she was⁺ dying. As *Jesus* went, the people crowded⁺ *in upon* Him,

⁴³and a woman *who* had been bleeding *for* twelve years and had spent all her *means of* livelihood⁺ on physicians, but could not be healed by any *of them*

⁴⁴came behind *Him* and touched the border of His garment. Immediately her bleeding stopped.⁺

⁴⁵Jesus said: Who touched me? When everyone⁺ denied *it*, Peter and *those* who were with Him said: Master, the multitude is overcrowding⁺ you and pressing *you* and do you say: Who touched me?

⁴⁶Jesus said: Somebody touched me, for I perceive that virtue has gone out of me.

⁴⁷When the woman saw that she was not hidden,⁺ she came trembling. Falling down before Him, she declared to Him, before all the people, the reason⁺ she had touched Him and how she was immediately healed.

⁴⁸*Jesus* said to her: Daughter, be of good comfort. Your faith has made you whole. Go in peace.

⁴⁹While He spoke, one came from *the house of* the ruler of the synagogue, saying to him: Your daughter is dead. Do not trouble the Master.

⁵⁰But when Jesus heard *this*, He answered him saying: Do not be afraid. Only believe and she will be made whole.

⁵¹When *Jesus* went⁺ into the house, He allowed⁺ no one to go in except⁺ Peter, James, John, and the father and mother of the girl.⁺

⁵²Everyone wept and mourned for her, but *Jesus* said: Do not weep. She is not dead but *is* sleeping.

⁵³They laughed at Him *scornfully*, knowing that she was dead.

⁵⁴*Then* Jesus sent⁺ them all out and took her by the hand and called *to her* saying: Child, arise.

⁵⁵Her spirit came again and she arose immediately,⁺ and *Jesus* directed⁺ *them* to give her *something* to eat.

⁵⁶Her parents were astonished, but He charged them that they should tell no one what was done.

Luke Chapter 9

¹ Then *Jesus* called His twelve disciples together and gave them power and authority over all demons,⁺ and to cure diseases.

² And He sent them to proclaim⁺ the kingdom of God and to heal the sick.

³ He said to them: Take nothing for *your* journey: not staves nor *provision* bag⁺ nor bread nor money. And do not have two coats apiece.

4 Whatever house you enter, stay⁺ there, and from there⁺ depart.

5 Whoever will not receive you, when you go out of that city, shake off the very dust from your feet for a testimony against them.

6 *So* they departed and went through the towns, proclaiming⁺ the Gospel and healing everywhere.

7 Now Herod the tetrarch heard about⁺ all that was done by *Jesus* and he was perplexed. Because, it was said by some that John had been raised from the dead,

8 by some that Elijah had appeared, and by others that one of the old prophets was risen again.

9 Herod said: I have beheaded John, but who is this of whom I hear such things? And he desired to see Him.

10 When the apostles returned, they told *Jesus* all that they had done. *Then* He took them away⁺ privately to a deserted⁺ place belonging to the city called Bethsaida.

11 When the people knew *about this*, they followed Him and He received them and spoke to them about⁺ the kingdom of God, and *He* healed *those* who had need of healing.

12 When the day began to wear away, the twelve came and said to Him: Send the multitude away *so* that they may go into the towns and country *all* around⁺ to lodge and get food,⁺ for we are in a deserted⁺ place.

13 But He said to them: You give them *food* to eat. They said: We have no more than five loaves and two fish, unless⁺ we go and buy food⁺ for all these people.

14 Now there were about five thousand men. *Jesus* said to His disciples: Make them sit down in groups⁺ of fifty.

15 They did so and made them all sit down.

16 Then He took the five loaves and the two fish, and looking up to heaven, He blessed them and broke and gave to the disciples to set before the multitude.

17 They all ate and were filled, and of the fragments that remained, they took up twelve baskets.

18 *Now* it came to pass, as He was alone praying, His disciples came⁺ *to* Him and He asked them saying: Who do the people say that I am?

19 They answering said: John the Baptist. But some *say* Elijah. Others *say* that one of the old prophets is risen again.

20 He said to them: But who do you say that I am? Peter answering said: The Christ of God.

21 And He strictly⁺ charged and directed⁺ them to tell this *to* no one,

22 saying: The Son of man must suffer many things and be rejected by the elders and chief priests and scribes, and be slain, and be raised the third day.

23 *Then* He said to *them* all: If anyone⁺ will come after me, let them deny themselves and take up their cross daily and follow me.

24 For whoever would⁺ save their life will lose it, but whoever would⁺ lose their life for my sake, will save it.

25 For what is a person⁺ benefited⁺ if they gain the whole world and lose themselves or be destroyed⁺?

26 For whoever is ashamed of me and of my words, of them will the Son of man be ashamed when He comes in His own glory and *in His* Father's and of the holy angels.

27 But in truth I say to you: There are some standing here who will not taste death until they see the kingdom of God.

28 *Then* it came to pass about eight days after these sayings, *Jesus* took Peter, John, and James, and went up into a mountain to pray.

29 As He prayed, the appearance of His face changed⁺ and His clothing⁺ *became* white *and* radiant.⁺

30 And behold two men talked with Him, ⁺ Moses and Elijah,

31 who appeared in glory and spoke of His exodus⁺ that would *soon* be accomplished in Jerusalem.

32 But Peter and *those* who were with him were heavy with sleep. When they were awake, they saw His glory and the two men who stood with Him.

[33] *Then* it came to pass as *Moses and Elijah* departed from *Jesus*, Peter said to Him: Master, it is good for us to be here. Let us make three tabernacles. One for you, one for Moses, and one for Elijah. *Peter* did not know what he was saying.

[34] As *Peter* spoke, a cloud came and overshadowed them and they *became* fearful as they entered the cloud.

[35] *Then* a voice came out of the cloud saying: This is my beloved Son. Hear Him.

[36] As the voice occurred,[+] Jesus was found alone. And they kept *this matter* silent[+] and told no one in those days any of those things that they had seen.

[37] It came to pass on the next day, when they had come down from the mountain,[+] many people met Him.

[38] And behold a man in the multitude[+] cried out saying: Master I beseech you: Look upon my son for he is my only child.

[39] And behold, a spirit takes him and he suddenly cries out. It convulses[+] him *so* that he foams *at the mouth*, bruising him *and it will* hardly leave[+] him.

[40] I begged[+] your disciples to cast him out and they could not.

[41] Jesus answering said: O faithless and perverse generation. How long shall I be with you and endure[+] you? Bring your son here.

[42] Even[+] as *the boy* was coming, the demon[+] threw him down and convulsed[+] *him*. Jesus rebuked the unclean spirit and healed the child and gave[+] him to his father.

[43] They were all amazed at the mighty power of God. While everyone marveled[+] at everything Jesus did, He said to His disciples:

[44] Let these words[+] sink down into your ears, for the Son of man will *soon* be delivered into the hands of men.

[45] But they did not understand this saying. It was hidden from them *so* that they did not perceive it, and they were afraid to ask Him about[+] that saying.

[46] Then a discussion[+] arose among them *as to* who might[+] be *the* greatest.

[47] Perceiving the thoughts in their hearts, Jesus took a child and sat *the child* down by Him

[48] and said to them: Whoever will receive this child in my name receives me. Whoever will receive me receives Him who sent me. For *those* who are least among you all, the same shall be great.

[49] John answered and said: Master, we saw one casting out demons[+] in your name and we forbad him because he does not follow us.

[50] Jesus said to *John*: Do not forbid him. For whoever is not against us is for us.

[51] *Then* it came to pass that the time had come when *Jesus* was to be received up, and He steadfastly set His face to go to Jerusalem.

[52] *He* sent messengers before His *own* presence[+] and they entered a village of the Samaritans to make ready for Him.

[53] But they did not receive Him because His face was *set* to go to Jerusalem.

[54] When His disciples James and John saw *this*, they said: Lord, do you want us to command fire to come down from heaven and consume them even as Elijah did?

[55] But *Jesus* turned and rebuked them and said: You do not understand[+] what *manner of* spirit you are *to be*.

[56] For the Son of man did not come to destroy people's[+] lives, but to save *them*. *Then* they went to another village.

[57] *Now* it came to pass that as they went in the way, a certain *man* said to *Jesus*: Lord, I will follow you wherever you go.

[58] Jesus said to him: Foxes have holes and birds of the air *have* nests, but the Son of man does not have anywhere to lay *His* head.

[59] *Then* He said to another: Follow me. But he said: Lord, allow me to go and bury my father first.

[60] Jesus said to him: Let the dead bury their dead. You go and proclaim[+] the kingdom of God.

[61] Another also said: Lord, I will follow you, but first let me bid farewell to *those* who are at my house.

⁶²Jesus said to him: No one, having put their hand to the plow and *then* looking back, is fit for the kingdom of God.

Luke Chapter 10

¹ After these things, the Lord appointed another seventy also and sent them by twos⁺ before His *own* presence⁺ into every city and place where He Himself would come.

² He said to them: The harvest truly *is* great but the laborers *are* few. Therefore, pray *to* the Lord of the harvest *so* that He will send forth laborers into His harvest.

³ *Now* go. Behold I send you forth as lambs among wolves.

⁴ Do not carry a purse nor *provision* bag⁺ nor sandals,⁺ and do not *stop to* salute anyone along⁺ the way.

⁵ Into whatever house you enter, first say: Peace to this house.

⁶ If a son of peace is there, your peace shall rest upon *that house*. If not, it shall return⁺ to you.

⁷ Remain in the same house, eating and drinking such things as they provide,⁺ for workers⁺ are worthy of their wages.⁺ Do not go from house to house.

⁸ Into whatever city you enter and they receive you, eat such things as are set before you.

⁹ Heal the sick who are there and say to them: The kingdom of God has come near to you.

¹⁰But into whatever city you enter and they do not receive you, go⁺ out into the streets of the same and say:

¹¹Even the very dust of your city that clings⁺ on us, we wipe off against you. Even so⁺ know that the kingdom of God has come near to you.

¹²But I say to you, that it will be more tolerable for Sodom in that day *of judgment*, than for that city.

¹³Woe to you Chorazin. Woe to you Bethsaida. For if the mighty works that have been done in you had been done in Tyre and Sidon, they would have repented a great while ago, sitting in sackcloth and ashes.

¹⁴But it shall be more tolerable for Tyre and Sidon at the judgment, than for you.

¹⁵You Capernaum, *being* exalted to heaven, will be thrust down to hell.

¹⁶*Those* who hear you, hear me. *Those* who despise you, despise me. *Those* who despise me, despise Him who sent me.

¹⁷*Later,* the seventy returned again with joy saying: Lord, even the demons⁺ are subject to us through your name.

¹⁸He said to them: I saw⁺ Satan fall from heaven like⁺ lightning.

¹⁹Behold I give you authority⁺ *and power* to tread on serpents and scorpions and over all the power of the enemy. Nothing shall by any means hurt you.

²⁰Even so, do not rejoice that the spirits are subject to you, but rather rejoice because your names are written in heaven.

²¹In that hour, Jesus rejoiced in spirit and said: I thank you, O Father, Lord of heaven and earth, that you have hid these things from the wise and prudent and have revealed them to babes. Even so, Father, for so it seemed good in your sight.

²²All things are delivered to me by my Father. No one knows who the Son is but the Father, and who the Father is but the Son and *those* to whom the Son will reveal *Him*.

²³*Then* He turned to *His* disciples and said privately: Blessed *are* the eyes that see the things that you see.

²⁴For I tell you that many prophets and kings have desired to see what you see but have not seen *it*, and to hear what you hear but have not heard *it*.

²⁵*Then* behold, a certain lawyer stood up and tested⁺ *Jesus* saying: Master, what shall I do to inherit eternal life?

²⁶*Jesus* said to him: What is written in the law? How do you read *it*?

²⁷ *The lawyer* answering said: You shall love the Lord your God with all your heart and with all your soul and with all your strength and with all your mind; and your neighbor as yourself.
Matthew 22:37

²⁸ *Jesus* said to him: You have answered correctly.⁺ Do this and you will live.

[29] But *the lawyer*, wanting to justify himself, said to Jesus: And who is my neighbor?

[30] Jesus answering said: A certain *man* went down from Jerusalem to Jericho and fell among thieves who stripped him of his clothing,[+] wounded *him*, and departed, leaving *him* half dead.

[31] *About the same time* a certain priest came down that way, and when he saw *the injured man*, he passed by on the other side.

[32] Likewise a Levite came by the *same* place, looked *at the injured man*, and passed by on the other side.

[33] But *then* a certain Samaritan, as he was traveling[+] by, saw *the injured man*, had compassion *on him*,

[34] went to *him*, bound up his wounds, poured *soothing* oil *on him, gave him* wine, set him on his own beast, *and* brought him to an inn and took care of him.

[35] On the next day when he departed, *the Samaritan* took out two coins[+] and gave *them* to the host and said to him: Take care of him. Whatever more you spend, I will repay you when I come again.

[36] Which now of these three do you think, was *a good* neighbor to the one who fell among the thieves?

[37] *The lawyer* said: He who showed mercy on him. Then Jesus said to him: Go and do likewise.

[38] Now it came to pass as they went, that *Jesus* entered a certain village and a certain woman named Martha received Him into her house.

[39] *Martha* had a sister named[+] Mary who sat at Jesus' feet and heard His Word.

[40] But Martha was distracted[+] by much *busyness in* serving, and *she* came to Him and said: Lord, do you not care that my sister has left me to serve alone? Speak[+] to her *so* that she *will* help me.

[41] Jesus answered and said to her: Martha, Martha.

You are overly anxious[+] and troubled about *so* many things. [42] But one thing is necessary[+]

---

and Mary has chosen that good part *and* that will not be taken from her.

Luke Chapter 11

[1] *Now* it came to pass that as *Jesus* was praying in a certain place, when He stopped,[+] one of His disciples said to Him: Lord, teach us to pray, as John also taught His disciples.

[2] *Jesus* said to them: When you pray, say: Our Father in heaven, Holy[+] is your name. Your kingdom come. Your will be done, on earth as *it is* in heaven.

[3] Give us each[+] day our daily bread.

[4] And forgive us *for* our sins, for we also forgive everyone *who is* indebted to us. And lead us *so that we* not *yield* to temptation, but deliver us from evil.

[5] *Then* He said to them: Who among[+] you shall have a friend and shall go to him at midnight and say to him: Friend, lend me three loaves.

[6] For a friend of mine in his journey has come to me and I have nothing to set before him.

[7] And from inside[+] *your friend* shall answer and say: Do not trouble me *now, for* the door is shut and *both I and* my children are in bed *and* I cannot arise *now* and give you *anything*.

[8] I say to you: Though he will not arise and give *anything to* him because he is his friend, yet because of his persistence[+] he will rise and give him all[+] he needs.

[9] I say to you: Ask and it will be given *to* you. Seek and you will find. Knock and it will be opened to you.

[10] For everyone who asks receives, and *those* who seek *will* find, and to *those* who knock it will be opened.

[11] If a son asks *for* bread from[+] any of you who are fathers, will *you* give him a stone? Or if *he* asks *for* a fish, will *you* give him a serpent?

[12] Or if he asks *for* an egg, will *you* offer him a scorpion?

[13] If you then, being wicked,[+] know how to give good gifts to your children, how much more shall *your* heavenly Father give the Holy Spirit to *those* who ask Him?

[14]*Later on, Jesus* was casting out a demon[+] *that had caused a man to be* speechless.[+] And it came to pass, when the demon[+] was gone out, the speechless[+] *man* spoke. And the people marveled.[+]

[15]But some of them said: He casts out demons[+] through Beelzebub the chief of the demons.[+]

[16]Others, testing[+] *Him*, sought from[+] Him a sign from heaven.

[17]But knowing their thoughts, He said to them: Every kingdom divided against itself is brought to desolation. A house *divided* against a house falls.

[18]If Satan also is divided against himself, how shall his kingdom stand? Because you say that I cast out demons[+] through Beelzebub,

[19]*well* if I cast out demons[+] by Beelzebub, *then* by whom do your sons cast *them* out? Therefore shall they be your judges.

[20]But if I cast out demons[+] with the finger of God, *then* no doubt the kingdom of God has come upon you.

[21]When an armed strong man keeps his palace *guarded*, his possessions[+] are in peace.

[22]But when *one* stronger than he comes upon him and overcomes him, *the overcomer* takes from *the strong man* all his armor in which he trusted, and divides his spoils.

[23]*Those* who are not with me are against me. *Those* who do not gather with me scatter.

[24]When the unclean spirit is gone out of a person,[+] *that unclean spirit* walks through dry places seeking rest. Finding none, he says: I will return to my house from which I came.

[25]When he comes, he finds *it* swept and put in order[+].

[26]Then he goes and takes seven other spirits more wicked than himself and they enter in and dwell there. And the last *state* of that person[+] is worse than the first.

[27]*Now* it came to pass, as *Jesus* spoke these things: A certain woman in the crowd[+] lifted up her voice and said to Him: Blessed *is* the womb that bore you and the breasts[+] that nursed[+] you.

[28]But He said: Yes rather,

> Blessed *are those* who hear the Word of God and keep it.
> *Proverbs 8:32*

[29]When the people were gathered close[+] together, He began to say: This is an evil generation. They seek a sign, but there shall not be *any* sign given *to* it except[+] the sign of Jonah the prophet. *Matthew 12:39*

[30]For as Jonah was a sign to the Ninevites, so also will the Son of man be to this generation. *Matthew 12:40*

[31]The queen of the south will rise up in the judgment with the people[+] of this generation and condemn them. For she came from the ends[+] of the earth to hear the wisdom of Solomon. And behold *one* greater than Solomon *is* here. *Matthew 12:42*

[32]The men of Nineveh shall rise up in the judgment with this generation and shall condemn it, for they repented at the proclaiming[+] of Jonah. And behold, *one* greater than Jonah *is* here.

[33]No one, having lit a candle, puts *it* in a secret place or under a bushel, but on a candlestick *so* that *those* who come in may see the light.

[34]The light of the body is the eye. Therefore when your eye is single *then* your whole body is also full of light. But when *your eye* is evil, *then* your body also *is* full of darkness.

[35]*Therefore*, take heed that the light *that is* in you is not darkness.

[36]If your whole body therefore *is filled with* light, having no part dark, *then* the whole *truly* will be light as when a brightly *truly* shining light[+] illuminates[+] you.

[37]As He spoke, a certain Pharisee asked[+] *Jesus* to dine with him. *So*, He went in and sat down to eat.

[38]When the Pharisee saw that *Jesus* did not wash first, before dinner, he wondered[+] *at that*.

[39]The Lord said to him: Now you Pharisees make the outside of the cup and platter clean, but your inward part is full of greed[+] and wickedness.

40 _You_ fools. Did not He who made what is outside[+] also make what is inside[+]?
41 But _rather_ give alms _of_ lasting[+] _value_ and behold, all things are clean to you.
42 But woe to you Pharisees. For you tithe _of_ mint and rue and all kinds[+] of herbs, but _you_ bypass[+] justice[+] and the love of God. These you ought to do, but not to leave the other undone.
43 Woe to you Pharisees. For you love the uppermost seats in the synagogues and greetings in the market _places_.
44 Woe to you scribes and Pharisees. Hypocrites. For you are like[+] unmarked[+] graves and those[+] who walk over _them_ are not aware _of them_.
45 Then one of the lawyers answered and said to Him: Master, saying these things, you insult[+] us, also.
46 He said: Woe to you lawyers, also. For you saddle[+] people[+] with grievous burdens and you yourselves do not touch the burdens with one of your fingers.
47 Woe to you. For you build the tombs[+] of the prophets, and your fathers killed them.
48 Truly you bear witness that you consent[+] _to_ the deeds of your fathers. For they indeed killed them, and you build their tombs[+].
49 Therefore the wisdom of God _has_ also said: I will send prophets and apostles _to_ them, and they will persecute and slay _some_ of them,
50 _so_ that the blood of all the prophets that was shed from the foundation of the world, may be required of this generation,
51 from the blood of Abel to the blood of Zacharias, who perished between the altar and the temple. Truly[+] I say to you: It shall be required of this generation.
52 Woe to you lawyers. For you have taken away the key of knowledge. You did not enter in yourselves and you hindered _those_ who were entering.
53 As He said these things to them, the scribes and the Pharisees began to forcefully[+] press and provoke Him to speak of many things,

54 laying in wait for Him, seeking to catch some _statement_ out of His mouth so that they might accuse Him.

Luke Chapter 12

1 Meanwhile,[+] _as_ a large[+] crowd[+] gathered so _close together_ that they stepped[+] on one another, _Jesus_ began to say to His disciples: First, beware of the leaven of the Pharisees, which is hypocrisy.
2 For there is nothing covered that will not be revealed, nor hid that will not become[+] known. _Matthew 10:26_
3 Therefore, whatever you have spoken in darkness will be heard in the light and what you have spoken in the ear in closets will be proclaimed from[+] the housetops.
4 I say to you my friends: Do not be afraid of _those_ who kill the body and after that have no more that they can do.
5 But I will forewarn you whom you shall fear: Fear Him who, after He has killed, has authority[+] _and power_ to cast into hell. Yes, I say to you: Fear Him.
6 Are not five sparrows sold for two pennies,[+] and not one of them is forgotten before God?
7 But even the very hairs of your head are all numbered. Therefore, do not be afraid. You are of more value than many sparrows.
8 I also say to you:

> Whoever will confess me before people,[+] the Son of man will also confess them before the angels of God.

9 But _those_ who deny me before people[+] will be denied before the angels of God.
10 Whoever speaks a word against the Son of man may be forgiven. But _anyone_ who blasphemes against the Holy Spirit will not be forgiven.
11 When they bring you to the synagogues and highest officials[+] and powers, take no thought how or what you shall answer or what you shall say.

¹²For the Holy Spirit will teach you in that same hour what you ought to say.
¹³Someone⁺ in the crowd⁺ said to Him: Master, tell⁺ my brother *to* divide the inheritance with me.
¹⁴*Jesus* said to him: Man, who made me a judge or a divider over you?
¹⁵And He said to them:

> Take heed
> and beware of covetousness.
> For one's life *is* not *to be found*
> in the abundance *of things*
> one possesses.

¹⁶*Then* He spoke a parable to them saying: The ground of a certain rich man brought forth plentifully.
¹⁷He thought within himself saying: What shall I do, because I have no room to store⁺ *all* my fruits?
¹⁸*Then* he said: This *is what* I will do: I will pull down my barns and build larger⁺ *ones*, and there I will store⁺ all my fruits and my possessions⁺. *Proverbs 27:1*
¹⁹I will say to my soul: Soul, you have many goods stored⁺ up for many years. *Now* take your ease: Eat, drink, *and* be merry.
²⁰But God said to him: *You* fool. This night your soul will be required of you. Then whose shall those things be that you have prepared⁺ *for yourself*?
²¹So *it is with those* who lay up treasure for themselves and are not rich toward God.
²²He said to His disciples: Therefore I say to you: Take no thought for your life *and* what you shall eat, nor what *clothes* to put on *your* body.
²³Life is more than food⁺ and the body *more* than clothes⁺.
²⁴Consider the ravens. They neither sow nor reap nor have storehouses or barns, and God feeds them. *Yet* how much more value⁺ you *are* than the birds⁺.
²⁵Who among you, by taking thought, can add one cubit to their stature?
²⁶Therefore, if you are not able *to do even the* smallest⁺ *thing*, why give thought to the rest?

²⁷Consider how the lilies grow. They do not toil. They do not spin. Yet I say to you that Solomon in all his glory was not arrayed like one of these.
²⁸Therefore, if God so clothes the grass, which is in the field today and tomorrow is cast into the oven, how much more *will he clothe* you, O you of little faith?
²⁹Do not seek what you shall eat or what you shall drink, and do not be of *a* doubtful mind.
³⁰For all the nations of the world seek after these things, and your Father knows that you have need of these things.
³¹But rather, you *just* seek the kingdom of God, and all these things will be added to you.

> ³² Do not be afraid, little flock.
> For it is your Father's
> good pleasure to give
> the kingdom *of God* to you.

³³Sell what you have and give alms. Make⁺ *provision* bags *for* yourselves that will not grow⁺ old, a treasure in the heavens that will not fail, where no thief approaches nor moth corrupts.
³⁴For where your treasure is, there will your heart be also. *Matthew 6:21*
³⁵Let your waist⁺ be belted⁺ up and *your* lights burning.
³⁶*Be* like people waiting⁺ for their lord, *so that* whenever he returns from the wedding, when he comes and knocks, *you* may open to him immediately.
³⁷Blessed *are* those servants whom the lord, when he comes, finds watching. Truly⁺ I say to you that he will prepare⁺ himself and seat⁺ them *to be served* and *he* will come forth and serve them.
³⁸Blessed are those servants if he comes in the second watch or in the third watch and finds *them watching*.
³⁹And know this: If the head⁺ of the house had known what hour the thief would come, he would have watched and not allowed⁺ his house to be broken through.
⁴⁰Therefore, you also *must be* ready. For the Son of man will come at an hour when you do not expect⁺ Him.

⁴¹Then Peter said to Him: Lord, are you speaking this parable to us, or to everyone⁺?

⁴²The Lord said: Who then is that faithful and wise steward whom *the* lord will set over his household to give *them their* portion⁺ in due season?

⁴³Blessed *is* that servant whom the lord shall find working⁺ when he comes.

⁴⁴Truly I say to you, that he will set *such a servant* over all that he has.

⁴⁵But if that servant says within their heart: My lord delays his coming, and begins to beat the servants and maids and to eat and drink and to be drunk,

⁴⁶*then* the lord of that servant will come in a day when not expected⁺ and in an unknown⁺ hour, and will cut him in two⁺ and will appoint *that servant's* portion *to be* with the unbelievers.

⁴⁷That servant who knew the lord's will and did not prepare nor do according to his will shall be beaten with many *stripes*.

⁴⁸But *those* who do not *know his will* and did commit things worthy of stripes shall be beaten with few *stripes*. For to whomever much is given, much will be required from them; and to whom much was committed, more will be asked of them.

⁴⁹I have come to send fire on the earth and what I desire⁺ *is* if it already be started⁺.

⁵⁰But I have a baptism with which to be baptized and how constrained⁺ I am until it be accomplished.

⁵¹Did you think⁺ that I came to give peace on earth? I tell you: No, but rather division.

⁵²For from henceforth, there will be five in one house divided three against two and two against three.

⁵³The father will be divided against the son and the son against the father. The mother against the daughter and the daughter against the mother. The mother in law against her daughter in law and the daughter in law against her mother in law.

⁵⁴*Then* He said to the people: When you see a cloud rise out of the west, immediately⁺ you say: A *rain* shower is coming, and so it is.

⁵⁵When *you see* the south wind blow you say: There will be heat, and it comes to pass.

⁵⁶*You* hypocrites. You can discern the face of the sky and of the earth, but how is it that you do not discern this time?

⁵⁷Yes, and why even of yourselves do you not judge what is right?

⁵⁸When you go with your adversary to the magistrate, *as you are* on the way, diligently *do everything you can so* that you may be freed⁺ from him, lest he drag⁺ you to the judge and the judge deliver you to the officer and the officer cast you into prison.

⁵⁹I tell you: You will not depart from there⁺ until you have paid the *very* last penny⁺.

Luke Chapter 13

¹ At that same time,⁺ some who were there told Him about the Galilaeans, whose blood Pilate had mingled with their sacrifices.

² Jesus answering said to them: Do you suppose that these Galilaeans were sinners above all the Galilaeans, because they suffered such things?

³ I tell you: No. But unless⁺ you repent, you will all likewise perish.

⁴ Or *consider* those eighteen upon whom the tower in Siloam fell and killed⁺ them. Do you think that they were sinners above all *other* people⁺ who lived⁺ in Jerusalem?

⁵ I tell you: No. But unless⁺ you repent, you will all likewise perish.

⁶ *Then Jesus* spoke this parable also: A certain *man* had a fig tree planted in his vineyard. He came and sought fruit upon it and found none.

⁷ Then he said to the dresser of his vineyard: Behold *for* three years I have come seeking fruit on this fig tree and have found none. Cut it down. Why *allow it* to burden⁺ the ground?

⁸ *The vine dresser* answering said to *his master*: Lord, let it alone this year also until I can dig around⁺ it and fertilize⁺ *it*.

⁹ If it bears fruit, *good*. If not, *then* after that cut it down.

¹⁰*Later on, Jesus* was teaching in one of the synagogues on the Sabbath.

¹¹And behold there was a woman who had a spirit of infirmity eighteen years and was bent over⁺ and unable⁺ to lift up *herself*.

¹²When Jesus saw her, He called *to her* and said: Woman, you are loosed from your infirmity.

¹³He laid *His* hands on her and immediately she was made straight and glorified God.

¹⁴Since⁺ Jesus had healed on the Sabbath day, the ruler of the synagogue answered with indignation and said to the people: There are six days in which people⁺ ought to work. Therefore, come in those *days* and be healed, and not on the Sabbath day.

¹⁵Then the Lord answered him and said: *You* hypocrite. Does not each one of you on the Sabbath loose his ox or *his* donkey⁺ from the stall and lead *it* to water?

¹⁶Should not this woman, being a daughter of Abraham whom Satan has bound, behold, eighteen years, be loosed from this bond on the Sabbath day?

¹⁷When He had said these things, all His adversaries were ashamed and all the people rejoiced for all the glorious things that were done by Him.

¹⁸Then He said: What is the kingdom of God like? To what shall I compare⁺ it?

¹⁹It is like a grain of mustard seed that a man cast into his garden, and it grew and became⁺ a large⁺ tree and the birds⁺ of the air lodged in its branches.

²⁰Again He said: To what shall I compare⁺ the kingdom of God?

²¹It is like leaven that a woman hid in three measures of meal until the whole was permeated⁺.

²²*Then* He went throughout the cities and villages, teaching, and journeying toward Jerusalem.

²³Then someone said to Him: Lord, are there few who are being⁺ saved? He said to them:

²⁴*Earnestly* endeavor⁺ to enter in through⁺ the strait gate. For I say to you *that* many will seek to enter in and will not be able.

²⁵Once the master of the house has risen and shut the door, and you begin to stand outside⁺ and to knock at the door saying: Lord, Lord, open to us. He will answer and say to you: I do not know you where you are.

²⁶Then you will begin to say: We ate and drank in your presence and you taught in our streets.

²⁷But He will say: I tell you, I do not know you where you are. Depart from me all you workers of iniquity.

²⁸And there will be weeping and gnashing of teeth when you see Abraham, Isaac, Jacob, and all the prophets in the kingdom of God, and you *yourselves* thrust out.

²⁹They will come from the east and west and from the north and south and will sit down in the kingdom of God.

³⁰And behold, there are *some who come in* last who will be first and there are *some who came in* first who will be last.

³¹The same day some of the Pharisees came and said to Him: Get out and depart from here, for Herod will kill you.

³²*Jesus* said to them: Go and tell that fox: Behold I cast out demons⁺ and I do cures today and tomorrow, and the third *day* I will be perfected.

³³Nevertheless, I must proceed⁺ today and tomorrow and the *day* following, for it cannot be that a prophet shall perish outside⁺ of Jerusalem.

³⁴O Jerusalem, Jerusalem, you kill the prophets and stones *those* who are sent to you. How often would I have gathered your children together as a hen *gathers* her brood under *her* wings, and you would not *come*.

³⁵*Now* behold your house is left to you desolate. Truly⁺ I say to you: You will not see me until *the time* comes when you will say: Blessed *is* He who comes in the name of the Lord.

Luke Chapter 14

[1] *Now* it came to pass, as *Jesus* went into the house of one of the chief Pharisees to eat bread on the Sabbath day, that they watched Him.

[2] And behold, there was a certain man before Him who had a serious illness.[+]

[3] Jesus answering spoke to the lawyers and Pharisees saying: Is it lawful to heal on the Sabbath day?

[4] They *remained* silent.[+] *So Jesus* took hold[+] *of him*, healed him, and released[+] him.

[5] *Then He* answered them saying: Who among[+] you shall have a donkey[+] or an ox fall into a pit and will not immediately[+] pull it out on the Sabbath day?

[6] Again, they could not answer Him about these things.

[7] *So, Jesus* put forth a parable to *those* who were invited,[+] remarking[+] how they chose out the chief rooms *for themselves*, and saying to them:

[8] When you are invited[+] to a wedding, do not sit down in the highest place[+] lest someone[+] more honorable than you be invited[+] by *the host*,

[9] and *then the host* who invited[+] you *both might* come and say to you: Give *your* place to this man, and you then, with shame, must[+] take the lowest place[+].

[10] But when you are invited,[+] go and sit down in the lowest place[+] *so* that when *the one* who invited you comes, he might say to you: Friend, go up higher. Then you shall be honored[+] in the presence of *those* who sit *down* to eat[+] with you.

[11] For whoever exalts themselves will be humbled[+] and *those* who humble themselves will be exalted. *Matthew 23:12*

[12] Then He said to the one who invited[+] Him: When you make a dinner or a supper, do not call your friends or your brothers or your relatives[+] or *your* rich neighbors lest they also invite[+] you *back* again and repayment[+] be made *to* you.

[13] But when you make a feast, call the poor, the maimed, the lame, *and* the blind

[14] and you will be blessed, for they cannot repay[+] you. You will be repaid[+] at the resurrection of the righteous[+].

[15] When one of *those* who sat *down* to eat[+] with Him heard these things, *Jesus* said to him: Blessed *are those* who shall eat bread in the kingdom of God.

[16] Then *Jesus* said to him: A certain man made a great supper and invited[+] many *people*.

[17] *Then he* sent his servant at supper time to say to *those* who were invited[+]: Come. For all things are now ready.

[18] But they all with one *consent* began to make excuses. The first said to him: I have bought a piece of ground and I need to go and see it. I beg[+] you *to* excuse me.

[19] Another said: I have bought five yoke of oxen and I am going to examine[+] them. I ask[+] you *to* excuse me.

[20] Another said: I have married a wife and therefore I cannot come.

[21] So that servant came and reported[+] these things to his lord. Then the master of the house, being angry, said to his servant: Go out quickly into the streets and lanes of the city and bring in the poor, the maimed, the crippled,[+] and the blind.

[22] The servant said: Lord, it has been done as you have commanded, and yet there is room.

[23] The lord said to the servant: Go out into the highways and hedges and compel *them* to come in *so* that my house may be filled.

[24] For I say to you, that none of *those* who were invited[+] shall taste of my supper.

[25] Great multitudes went with *Jesus* and He turned and said to them:

[26] If anyone[+] comes to me and does not hate father and mother and wife and children and brothers and sisters and yes, *even* their own life also, they cannot be my disciple. *Matthew 10:37*

[27] Whoever does not bear their cross and come after me cannot be my disciple.

[28] For who among[+] you, intending to build a tower, does not sit down first and count the cost, *to see* whether *you* have *sufficient* to finish *it*?

²⁹Lest perhaps⁺ after having laid the foundation and not being able to finish *it*, all who see⁺ *this* begin to mock ³⁰saying: This person⁺ began to build and was not able to finish.
³¹Or what king, going to make war against another king, does not sit down first and take counsel *to know* whether he *might* be able, with ten thousand, to meet one who comes against him with twenty thousand?
³²Otherwise,⁺ while the *enemy* is yet a great way off, he *might* send an ambassador *to* ask for peace.
³³So likewise, whoever does not forsake all that they have cannot be my disciple.
³⁴Salt *is* good. But if salt has lost its savor, with what shall it be seasoned?
³⁵*Otherwise* it is not fit for the land or for the dunghill, *but just* to be cast out. *Those* who have ears to hear, let them hear.

Luke Chapter 15

¹ Then all the worldly⁺ people and sinners drew near to *Jesus* to hear Him.
² But the Pharisees and scribes complained⁺ saying: This man receives sinners and eats with them.
³ *Then Jesus* spoke this parable to them saying:
⁴ What man among⁺ you having a hundred sheep, if he lost one of them, would not leave the ninety nine in the wilderness and go after what is lost, until he finds it?
⁵ And when he has found *it*, lays *it* on his shoulders, rejoicing;
⁶ and coming home, calls together friends and neighbors saying to them: Rejoice with me, for I have found my sheep that was lost.
⁷ I say to you, that likewise *there* will be *more* joy in heaven over one sinner who repents than over ninety nine righteous⁺ persons who do not need repentance.
⁸ Or, what woman, having ten pieces of silver, if she loses one piece, does not light a lamp,⁺ sweep the house, and seek diligently until she finds *it*?

⁹ And when she has found *it*, *does she not* call *her* friends and neighbors together saying: Rejoice with me, for I have found the piece that I had lost.
¹⁰Likewise, I say to you: there is joy in the presence of the angels of God over one sinner who repents.
¹¹*Then* He said: A certain man had two sons.
¹²The younger of them said to *his* father: Father, give me the portion of *your* property⁺ that will fall *to me*. So, *his father* divided *his worldly* possessions⁺ to *his sons*.
¹³Not many days later,⁺ the younger son gathered everything⁺ together and went away⁺ to a far country and there wasted *all* his possessions⁺ with riotous living.
¹⁴*After* he had spent everything⁺ *he had*, a mighty famine arose in that land and he began to be in want.
¹⁵*So,* he joined a citizen of that country *who* sent him into his fields to feed swine.
¹⁶*The foolish son* would gladly⁺ have filled his belly with the husks that the swine ate but no one gave him *any*.
¹⁷When he came to himself, he said: How many of my father's hired servants have bread enough and to spare, and I *am* perishing with hunger.
¹⁸I will arise and go to my father and will say to him: Father, I have sinned against heaven and before you.
¹⁹*I* am no longer⁺ worthy to be called your son. Make me as one of your hired servants.
²⁰*So* he arose and went⁺ to his father, but when he was yet a great distance⁺ away, his father saw him, had compassion, ran *to him*, embraced⁺ his neck, and kissed him.
²¹The son said to him: Father, I have sinned against heaven and in your sight and am no longer⁺ worthy to be called your son.
²²But the father said to his servants: Bring forth the best robe and put *it* on him. Put a ring on his hand and sandals⁺ on *his* feet.
²³Bring the fatted calf here and kill *it*. Let us eat and be merry.

²⁴ For this my son was dead but *now* is alive again. He was lost but *now* is found. And they began to be merry.

²⁵ Now *the father's* elder son was in the field, and as he came near the house, he heard music and dancing.

²⁶ *So,* he called one of the servants and asked what these things meant.

²⁷ *The servant* said to him: Your brother has come *home* and your father has killed the fatted calf because he has received him safe and sound.

²⁸ *The older brother* was angry and would not go in. Therefore his father came out and pleaded⁺ *with* him.

²⁹ He answering said to *his* father: Behold, these many years I have served you *and* not at any time transgressed your commandment. Yet you never gave me a *young* goat *so* that I might make merry with my friends.

³⁰ But *now,* when this son *of* yours has come, *one* who has devoured your livelihood⁺ with harlots, you have killed the fatted calf for him.

³¹ *The father* said to him: Son, you are always⁺ with me and all that I have is yours.

³² It was fitting⁺ that we should make merry and be glad, for this your brother was dead and *now* is alive again. *He* was lost, but *now* is found.

Luke Chapter 16

¹ *Then Jesus* said to His disciples: There was a certain rich man who had a steward. The same was accused to him that he had wasted his goods.

² *So, the man* called *his steward* and said to him: How is it that I hear this of you? Give an account of your stewardship, for you cannot⁺ be *my* steward *any* longer.

³ Then the steward said within himself: What shall I do? For my lord *now* takes the stewardship away from me. I cannot dig and I am ashamed to beg.

⁴ I know⁺ what I will do, *so* that when I am removed⁺ from the stewardship *position*, they may receive me into their houses.

⁵ So he called everyone of his lord's debtors and said to the first: How much do you owe to my lord?

⁶ He said: A hundred measures of oil. *The steward* said to him: Take your bill and sit down quickly and write fifty.

⁷ Then he said to another: How much do you owe? He said: A hundred measures of wheat. *The steward* said to him: Take your bill and write eighty.

⁸ The lord commended the unrighteous⁺ steward because he had done shrewdly.⁺ For the children of this world are, in their generation, *more* shrewd⁺ than the children of light.

⁹ I say to you: *If you* make yourselves friends with the *worldly* treasures⁺ of unrighteousness, *then* when you fail, *they will* receive you into *their* eternal⁺ dwellings⁺.

¹⁰ *Those* who are faithful in the smallest⁺ *matters* are also faithful in much and *those* who are unrighteous⁺ in the smallest⁺ *matters* are also unrighteous in much.

¹¹ Therefore, if you have not been faithful in the unrighteous *worldly* treasures,⁺ who will commit to your trust the true *riches*?

¹² If you have not been faithful in what is another's, who will give you your own?

¹³ No servant can serve two masters. For either *a servant* will hate the one and love the other, or else hold to the one and despise the other. You cannot serve God and *worldly* treasures⁺. *Matthew 6:24*

¹⁴ Now the Pharisees, who were covetous, also heard all these things and they ridiculed⁺ Him.

¹⁵ He said to them: You ⁺ justify yourselves before people,⁺ but God knows your hearts. For what is highly esteemed among people⁺ is *an* abomination in the sight of God.

¹⁶ The law and the prophets *were* until John. Since that time, the kingdom of God is proclaimed⁺ and everyone⁺ presses into it.

¹⁷ It is easier for heaven and earth to pass, than one smallest mark⁺ of the law to fail.

¹⁸Whoever puts away his wife and marries another, commits adultery. Whoever marries one who is put away from *her* husband commits adultery. *Matthew 19:9*
¹⁹There was a certain rich man who was clothed in purple and fine linen and *lived in* luxury⁺ and merrymaking⁺ every day.
²⁰And, there was a certain beggar named Lazarus who laid at *the rich man's* gate, full of sores,
²¹desiring to be fed with the crumbs that fell from the rich man's table. Moreover the dogs came and licked his sores.
²²*Now* it came to pass that the beggar died and was carried by the angels into Abraham's bosom. *Then* the rich man also died and was buried.
²³In hell, being in torments, *the rich man* lifted up his eyes and saw Abraham *at a* far distance,⁺ and Lazarus in his bosom.
²⁴And he cried *out* and said: Father Abraham, have mercy on me and send Lazarus *so* that he may dip the tip of his finger in water and cool my tongue, for I am tormented in this flame.
²⁵But Abraham said: Son, remember that in your lifetime you received your good things and likewise Lazarus evil things. But now he is comforted and you are tormented.
²⁶Above⁺ all this, there is a great chasm⁺ fixed between you and us so that whoever *might* want⁺ to go⁺ from here⁺ to you cannot. Nor *can* anyone⁺ from there come⁺ to us.
²⁷Then *the rich man* said: I beg⁺ you therefore, father, that you would send him to my father's house.
²⁸For I have five brothers, *and I pray* that he might testify to them, lest they also come into this place of torment.
²⁹Abraham said to him: They have Moses and the prophets. Let them hear them.
³⁰He said: No, father Abraham, but if one went to them from the dead, they will repent.
³¹*Abraham* said to him: If they do not hear Moses and the prophets, neither will they be persuaded, *even* though one rose from the dead.

Luke Chapter 17

¹ Then *Jesus* said to the disciples: It is impossible but that offenses will come. But woe *to those* through whom they come.
² It would be better for them if⁺ a millstone were hung around⁺ their neck and they were cast into the sea, than that they should offend *or cause sin to come to* one of these little ones.
³ Take heed to yourselves. If *one of* your family⁺ trespasses against you, rebuke them. If they repent, forgive them.
⁴ If *one* trespasses against you seven times in a day, and seven times in a day turn again to you saying: I repent, you shall forgive them.
⁵ The apostles said to the Lord: Increase our faith.
⁶ The Lord said: If you had faith as a grain of mustard seed, you might say to this fig⁺ tree: Be plucked up by the root and be planted in the sea, and it should obey you.
⁷ Who among⁺ you, having a servant plowing or feeding cattle, will say to him immediately⁺ when he comes *in* from the field: Go and sit down to eat?
⁸ Will *you* not rather say to him: Make ready *that* with which I may dine⁺ and prepare⁺ yourself *to* serve me until I have eaten and drunk, and afterward you shall eat and drink.
⁹ Does he thank that servant because he did the things that were commanded *to* him? I think not.
¹⁰So likewise you, when you have done all those things that you are commanded *to do*, say: We are unprofitable servants. We have done what was our duty to do.
¹¹*Now* it came to pass, as *Jesus* went to Jerusalem, that He passed through the midst of Samaria and Galilee.
¹²As He entered a certain village, ten men who were lepers met Him, standing⁺ *at* a distance.⁺
¹³They lifted up *their* voices and said: Jesus, Master, have mercy on us.
¹⁴When He saw *them*, He said to them:

Go *and* show yourselves to the priests. And it came to pass that as they went, they were cleansed.

¹⁵ One of them, when he saw that he was healed, turned back and with a loud voice glorified God.

¹⁶ *He* fell face *down* at *Jesus'* feet, giving Him thanks. And he was a Samaritan.

¹⁷ Jesus answering said: Were there not ten cleansed? But where *are* the nine?

¹⁸ There are none found that returned to give glory to God, except⁺ this stranger.

¹⁹ *Jesus* said to him: Arise and go. Your faith has made you whole.

²⁰ When the Pharisees asked Him when the kingdom of God should come, He answered them and said: The kingdom of God does not come with observation.

²¹ Nor shall they say: Behold here. Or, behold there. For behold, the kingdom of God is within you.

²² *Then* He said to the disciples: The days will come when you will desire to see one of the days of the Son of man and you will not see *it*.

²³ They will say to you: See here. Or: See there. Do not go after *them* or follow *them*.

²⁴ For as the lightning that illuminates⁺ out of one *part* under heaven shines to the other *part* under heaven, so also will the Son of man be in His day.

²⁵ But first He must suffer many things and be rejected by this generation.

²⁶ As it was in the days of Noah, so will it also be in the days of the Son of man.

²⁷ They ate, they drank, they married wives, and they were given in marriage until the day that Noah entered the ark and the flood came and destroyed them all.

²⁸ Likewise also as it was in the days of Lot. They ate, they drank, they bought, they sold, they planted, and they built.

²⁹ But the same day that Lot went out of Sodom, it rained fire and brimstone from heaven and destroyed *them* all.

³⁰ Even thus shall it be in the day when the Son of man is revealed.

³¹ In that day, *if* someone is up on the housetop with their goods⁺ in the house, let them not come down to take it away.

And *those* who are in the field, let them likewise not return back.

³² Remember Lot's wife.

³³ Whoever will seek to save their life will lose it, and whoever would⁺ lose their life will preserve it.

³⁴ I tell you: In that night there will be two *people* in one bed. The one will be taken and the other will be left.

³⁵ Two will be grinding together. One will be taken and the other left.

³⁶ *Two will be in the field. One will be taken and the other left.*

³⁷ They answered and said to Him: Where Lord? And He said to them: Wherever the body *is*, there the eagles will be gathered together.

Luke Chapter 18

¹ *Then Jesus* spoke a parable to them *to this end*: That people⁺ should always pray, and not faint *or give up*.

² *He* said: There was a judge in a city who did not fear God or regard anyone⁺.

³ There was also a widow in that city, and she came to *the judge* saying: Avenge me of my adversary.

⁴ For a while, *the judge* would not *respond*. But afterward he said within himself: Although I do not fear God or regard man,

⁵ yet because this widow troubles me, I will avenge her, lest by her continual coming she weary me.

⁶ The Lord said: Hear what the unrighteous⁺ judge said.

⁷ Will God not *also* avenge His own elect who cry day and night to Him, *even* though He bear with them *for* a long *while*.

⁸ I tell you: He will avenge them speedily. Nevertheless when the Son of man comes, will He find faith on the earth?

⁹ *Jesus* spoke this parable to certain *ones* who trusted in themselves, *believing* that they were righteous, and despised others:

¹⁰ Two men went up into the temple to pray. The one a Pharisee and the other a worldly⁺ person.

¹¹The Pharisee stood and prayed thus with himself: God, I thank you that I am not as other men *are*: extortioners, unrighteous, + adulterers, or even as this worldly+ person.

¹²I fast twice in the week *and* I give tithes of all that I possess.

¹³The worldly+ person, standing *at a* distance+ *away*, would not so much as lift up *his* eyes to heaven, but beat+ upon his *own* breast saying: God be merciful to me a sinner.

¹⁴I tell you: This man went down to his house justified *rather* than the other. For everyone who exalts themselves will be humbled+ and *those* who humble themselves will be exalted. *Matthew 23:12*

¹⁵*Then* they brought infants to *Jesus*, *so* that He would touch them. But when *His* disciples saw *this*, they rebuked them.

¹⁶But Jesus called *to* them and said: Allow little children to come to me and do not forbid them. For of such is the kingdom of God.

¹⁷Truly+ I say to you: Whoever will not receive the kingdom of God as a little child shall in no way+ enter therein.

¹⁸A certain ruler asked Him saying: Good Master, what shall I do to inherit eternal life?

¹⁹Jesus said to him: Why do you call me good? No one *is* good except+ one. God.

²⁰You know the commandments: Do not commit adultery. Do not kill. Do not steal. Do not bear false witness. Honor your father and your mother.

²¹*The ruler* said: All these I have kept from my youth.

²²Now when Jesus heard these things, He said to him: Yet you lack one thing. Sell all *the things* that you have and distribute to the poor and you shall have treasure in heaven. And come, follow me.

²³When he heard this, he was very sorrowful, for he was very rich.

²⁴When Jesus saw that he was very sorrowful, He said: How hard+ *it is for those* who have riches *to* enter into the kingdom of God.

²⁵It is easier for a camel to go through an eye of a needle than for a rich man to enter into the kingdom of God.

²⁶*Those* who heard *this* said: Who then can be saved?

²⁷*Jesus* said: The things that are impossible with people+ are possible with God.

²⁸Then Peter said: Behold, we have left all and followed you.

²⁹*Jesus* said to them: Truly+ I say to you: There is no one who has left house or parents or brothers or wife or children for the sake of the kingdom of God *Matthew 19:29*

³⁰who will not receive many times+ more in this present time, and in the world to come, eternal+ life.

³¹Then *Jesus* took the twelve and said to them: Behold, we *shall now* go up to Jerusalem and all things that are written by the prophets concerning the Son of man will be accomplished. *Matthew 20:18*

³²For He will be delivered to the Gentiles *to* be mocked and spitefully treated and spit on.

³³They will flog+ *Him* and put Him to death, and the third day He will rise again.

³⁴*The disciples* did not understand these things. This saying was hid from them and they did not know *the meaning of* the things that *Jesus now* spoke *to them*.

³⁵*Now* it came to pass that as *Jesus* had come near Jericho, a certain blind man sat by the wayside begging.

³⁶Hearing the multitude pass by, *the blind man* asked what it meant.

³⁷They told him that Jesus of Nazareth is passing by.

³⁸*So* he cried *out* saying: Jesus son of David, have mercy on me.

³⁹*Those* who went before rebuked him, *saying* that he should be silent. + But he cried *out* so much the more: Son of David, have mercy on me.

⁴⁰Jesus stopped+ and directed+ *the blind man* to be brought to Him. When he had come near, *Jesus* asked him

⁴¹saying: What do you want me to do to you? He said: Lord, that I may receive my sight.

⁴²Jesus said to him: Receive your sight. Your faith has saved you.

⁴³Immediately he received his sight and followed *Jesus*, glorifying God. And when they saw *this*, all the people gave praise to God.

Luke Chapter 19

¹ *Then Jesus* entered and passed through Jericho.

² And behold *there was* a man named Zacchaeus who was a chief among the worldly+ people, and he was rich.

³ He sought to see Jesus, *to see* who He was, but *he* could not *see* because of the crowd,+ because he was small+ in stature.

⁴ *So* he ran ahead+ and climbed up into a sycamore tree to see *Jesus*, for He was to pass that *way*.

⁵ When Jesus came to the place, He looked up and saw him and said to him: Zacchaeus, come down quickly.+ For today I must stay+ at your house.

⁶ *So* he came down quickly+ and received *Jesus* joyfully.

⁷ When they saw *this* everyone+ complained+ saying: He has gone to stay+ with a man who is a sinner.

⁸ *Then* Zacchaeus stood and said to the Lord: Behold Lord, half of my goods I *am* giving to the poor, and if I have taken anything from anyone by false accusation, I *will* restore *them* fourfold.

⁹ Jesus said to him: This day salvation has come to this house, since+ *Zacchaeus* also is a son of Abraham.

¹⁰ For the Son of man has come to seek and to save *those* who were lost.

¹¹ As they heard these things, *Jesus* spoke another+ parable *to them* because He was near Jerusalem and because they thought that the kingdom of God *was going to* appear immediately.

¹² Therefore He said: A certain nobleman went into a far country to receive for himself a kingdom, and *then* to return.

¹³ He called his ten servants, gave+ ten pounds to them, and said to them: Occupy until I come.

¹⁴ But his citizens hated him and sent a message after him saying: We will not have this *man* to reign over us.

¹⁵ *Now* it came to pass that when he had returned, having received the kingdom, he then commanded those servants to be called to him to whom he had given the money *so* that he might know how much each one+ had gained+.

¹⁶ The first came saying: Lord, your pound has gained ten pounds.

¹⁷ *The nobleman* said to him: Well *done* good servant. Because you have been faithful in a very little, you *shall now* have authority over ten cities.

¹⁸ The second came saying: Lord, your pound has gained five pounds.

¹⁹ *The nobleman* likewise said to him: You also *shall* be over five cities.

²⁰ *Then* another came saying: Lord, behold *here is* your pound that I have kept wrapped+ up in a cloth+.

²¹ For I feared you because you are an austere man. You take up what you have not laid down and reap what you did not sow.

²² *The nobleman* said to him: Out of your own mouth I will judge you, *you* wicked servant. You knew that I was an austere man, taking up what I did not lay down and reaping what I did not sow.

²³ Why then did you not give my money to the bank *so* that at my coming I might have received+ *what was mine* with interest+?

²⁴ *Then* he said to *those* who stood by: Take the pound from him and give *it* to the one who has ten pounds.

²⁵ They said to him: Lord, he has ten pounds.

²⁶ I say to you, that to everyone who has will *more* be given, but from *those* who have nothing, even what they have will be taken away from them.

²⁷ But those *who were* my enemies, *those* who were unwilling+ *for* me to reign over them, bring here and slay *them* before me.

²⁸ After+ *Jesus* had said these things, He went, *as He had started* before, going+ up to Jerusalem.

²⁹ *Now* it came to pass, when He had come near Bethphage and Bethany at the mount called *the Mount* of Olives, He sent two of His disciples

³⁰ saying: Go into the village near+ *you*. Upon+ entering, you will find a colt tied, on which no one has ever sat. Loosen it and bring *it here*.

³¹If anyone asks you: Why do you loosen *it*? You shall say this: Because the Lord has need of it.

³²*Those* who were sent went and found *it* just⁺ as He had said to them.

³³As they were loosing the colt, the owners said to them: Why are you loosening the colt?

³⁴They said: The Lord has need of it.

³⁵*Then* they brought it to Jesus and they cast their garments upon the colt and sat Jesus upon⁺ *it*.

³⁶And as He went, they spread their clothes in the way. *Zechariah 9:9*

³⁷When He had come near, even now at the descent of the Mount of Olives, the whole multitude of the disciples began to rejoice and praise God with a loud voice for all the mighty works that they had seen,

³⁸saying: Blessed *be* the King who comes in the name of the Lord. Peace in heaven and glory in the highest. *Psalm 118:26*

³⁹Some of the Pharisees from among the multitude said to Him: Master, rebuke your disciples.

⁴⁰He answered and said to them: I tell you that if these should *remain* silent⁺ the stones would *immediately* cry out.

⁴¹As *Jesus* came near, He saw⁺ the city and wept over it

⁴²saying: If you had *only* known, even you, at least in this your day, the things *that are* for your peace. But now they are hid from your eyes.

⁴³For the days will come upon you *in which* your enemies will cast a blockade⁺ around⁺ you and surround⁺ you and keep you in on every side

⁴⁴and *knock you* to the ground, and your children within you. They will not leave in you stone upon stone because you did not understand⁺ the time of your visitation.

⁴⁵*Then Jesus* went into the temple and began to cast out *those* who bought and sold therein,

⁴⁶saying to them: It is written: My house is the house of prayer. But you have made it a den of thieves. *Matthew 21:13*

⁴⁷*Jesus* taught in the temple daily, but the chief priests and the scribes and the chief of the people sought to destroy Him.

⁴⁸But *they* could not find what they might do, for all the people were very attentive to hear Him.

Luke Chapter 20

¹ *Now* it came to pass, *that* on one of those days as *Jesus* taught the people in the temple and proclaimed⁺ the Gospel, the chief priests and the scribes came with the elders

² and spoke to Him saying: Tell us. By what authority do you *do* .these things? Or who is He who gave you this authority?

³ *Jesus* answered and said to them: I will also ask you one thing. Answer me.

⁴ The baptism of John, was it from heaven, or of men?

⁵ They reasoned with themselves saying: If we say: From heaven, He will say: Why then did you not believe him?

⁶ But if we say: Of men. All the people will stone us for they are persuaded that John was a prophet.

⁷ They answered that they could not tell from where *it came*.

⁸ Jesus said to them: *Then* neither will I tell you by what authority I do these things.

⁹ Then He began to speak this parable to the people: A certain man planted a vineyard, leased⁺ it to *tenant* farmers, ⁺ and went into a far country for a long time.

¹⁰At the *harvest* season, he sent a servant to the *tenant* farmers⁺ *so* that they should give him *his portion* of the fruit of the vineyard. But the farmers⁺ beat him and sent *him* away empty *handed*.

¹¹Again he sent another servant, and they beat him also and treated *him* shamefully and sent *him* away empty *handed*.

¹²Again he sent a third, and they wounded him also and cast *him* out.

¹³Then the lord of the vineyard said: What shall I do? I will send my beloved son. Perhaps⁺ when they see *him* they will respect⁺ him.

[14] But when the *tenant* farmers[+] saw him, they reasoned among themselves saying: This is the heir. Come, let us kill him *so* that the inheritance may be ours.
[15] So they cast him out of the vineyard, and killed *him*. What therefore will the lord of the vineyard do to them?
[16] He will come and destroy these *tenant* farmers[+] and give the vineyard to others. When they heard *this*, they said: *God* forbid.
[17] *Then Jesus* looked[+] at them and said: What is this then that is written: The stone that the builders rejected has become the head of the corner. *Matthew 21:42*
[18] Whoever falls upon that stone will be broken, but on whomever it falls, it will grind them to powder.
[19] *In* that same hour, the chief priests and the scribes sought to lay hands on Him, but they feared the people, for they perceived that He had spoken this parable against them.
[20] *So* they watched *Him* and sent forth spies who pretended[+] *to be* righteous[+] men *so* that they might take hold of Him *as He* was speaking, to deliver Him to the power and authority of the governor.
[21] They asked Him saying: Master, we know that you say and teach rightly *and* you do not accept *any other* person's *authority*, but teach the way of God truly.
[22] Is it lawful for us to give tribute to Caesar, or not?
[23] But He perceived their craftiness and said to them: Why are you testing[+] me?
[24] Show me a coin.[+] Whose image and title[+] does it have? They answered and said: Caesar's.
[25] *Then* He said to them: Therefore, render to Caesar the things that are Caesar's and to God the things that are God's.
[26] *So* they could not catch[+] Him in His words before the people, but *instead* they marveled at His answer and *remained* silent.[+]
[27] Then some of the Sadducees who deny that there is any resurrection came and asked Him,
[28] saying: Master, Moses wrote to us: If any man's brother die having a wife and he die without children, that his brother

should take his wife and raise up *children as* seed to his brother.
[29] *Once* there were seven brothers. The first took a wife and died without children.
[30] The second took her as *his* wife and he died childless.
[31] The third took her and in like manner the seven also, and they *all* left no children and died.
[32] Last of all the woman died also.
[33] Therefore, in the resurrection whose wife of them is she? For seven had her as *their* wife.
[34] Jesus answering said to them: The children of this world marry and are given in marriage,
[35] but *those* who shall be accounted worthy to obtain that world and the resurrection from the dead, neither marry nor are given in marriage.
[36] Nor can they die any more, for they are equal to the angels and are the children of God, being the children of the resurrection,
[37] now that the dead are raised, even *as* Moses showed at the bush when he called the Lord the God of Abraham and the God of Isaac and the God of Jacob.
[38] For He is not a God of the dead, but of the living, for all live to Him.
[39] Then some of the scribes answering said: Master, you have well said.
[40] After that they did not dare[+] ask Him any *more questions*.
[41] *Then Jesus* said to them: How can they say that Christ is David's son?
[42] In the book of Psalms, David himself said: The Lord said to my Lord: Sit at my right hand
[43] until I make your enemies your footstool.
[44] Therefore, if David calls Him Lord, how is He then his son?
[45] Then in the audience of all the people He said to His disciples:
[46] Beware of the scribes who desire to walk in long robes and love greetings in the market *places* and the highest seats in the synagogues and the chief room at feasts,

⁴⁷who devour widows' houses and for a show make long prayers. These shall receive greater damnation.

Luke Chapter 21

¹ *Then Jesus* looked up and saw the rich men casting their gifts into the treasury. ² And He also saw a certain poor widow casting in there two mites, *worth about a penny*.
³ He said: Truly I say to you, that this poor widow has cast in more than all *of* them.
⁴ For all these have cast into the offerings of God *out* of their abundance, but she, *even out* of her poverty, ⁺ has cast in all the *means of* livelihood⁺ that she had.
⁵ *Later* as some spoke about the temple, how it was adorned with fine⁺ stones and gifts, *Jesus* said:
⁶ *As for* these things that you behold, the days will come in which there will not be left stone upon stone that will not be thrown down.
⁷ *Then* they asked Him saying: Master, but when shall these things be? And what sign *will there be* when these things shall come to pass?
⁸ He said: Take heed *so* that you are not deceived. For many will come in my name saying: I am *Christ*, and the time draws near. Do not go after them.
⁹ When you hear about wars and commotions, do not be terrified. For these things must come to pass first, but the end *is* not immediately⁺.
¹⁰Then He said to them: Nation will rise against nation and kingdom against kingdom.
¹¹Great earthquakes will be in many different⁺ places, and famines and pestilences. Fearful sights and great signs from heaven will occur⁺.
¹²But before all these, they will lay their hands on you and persecute *you*, delivering *you* up to the synagogues and into prisons, *and* bringing *you* before kings and rulers for my name's sake.
¹³But this will turn to you for a testimony.

¹⁴Therefore, *be* settled in your hearts to not meditate before *hand* what *or how* you will answer.
¹⁵For I will give you a mouth and wisdom that all your adversaries will not be able to speak against⁺ nor stand against⁺.
¹⁶You will be betrayed by both parents and brothers and *close* relatives⁺ and friends, and they will *even* put to death *some* from among⁺ you.
¹⁷You will be hated by all because of my name.
¹⁸But not a hair of your head will perish.
¹⁹In your patience, possess your souls.
²⁰When you see Jerusalem surrounded⁺ with armies, then know that *its* desolation is near.
²¹Then let *those* who are in Judea flee to the mountains. Let *those* who are in the midst of it depart. And do not let *those* who are in *other* countries enter into there.
²²For these are the days of vengeance *so* that all *the* things that are written may be fulfilled. *Isaiah 61:2*
²³But woe to *those* who are with child and to *those* who are nursing⁺ in those days. For there will be great distress in the land and wrath upon this people.
²⁴They will fall by the edge of the sword and be led away captive into all nations. Jerusalem will be trampled⁺ down by the Gentiles until the times of the Gentiles are fulfilled.
²⁵There will be signs in the sun and in the moon and in the stars. And upon the earth, distress of nations, with perplexity. The sea and the waves *will* roar.
²⁶Men's hearts *will* fail them for fear and for expectation⁺ of those things that are coming upon the world. ⁺ For the powers of heaven will be shaken.
²⁷Then they will see the Son of man coming in a cloud with power and great glory.
²⁸When these things begin to come to pass, look up and lift up your heads. For your redemption draws near.
²⁹*Then Jesus* spoke a parable to them: Behold the fig tree and all the trees.

³⁰When they shoot forth, you see and know of yourselves that summer is now *very* near⁺.

³¹So likewise when you see these things come to pass, know that the kingdom of God is *very* near.

³²Truly⁺ I say to you: This generation will not pass away until all be fulfilled.

³³Heaven and earth will pass away, but my words will not pass away.

³⁴Take heed to yourselves, lest at any time your hearts be overburdened⁺ with excesses⁺ and drunkenness and *the* cares of this life *so* that *judgment* day comes upon you unexpectedly⁺.

³⁵For it will come like⁺ a snare upon all *those* who dwell on the face of the whole earth.

³⁶Therefore watch and pray always *so* that you may be accounted worthy to escape all these things that will come to pass and to stand before the Son of man.

³⁷In the daytime *Jesus* taught in the temple. At night He went out and stayed⁺ on the mountain that is called *the Mount* of Olives.

³⁸And all the people came to Him early in the morning to hear Him in the temple.

Luke Chapter 22

¹ Now the Feast of Unleavened Bread called the Passover drew near.

² And the chief priests and scribes sought how they might kill *Jesus*, because they feared the people.

³ Then Satan entered into Judas surnamed Iscariot *who* was *one* of the twelve.

⁴ *Judas* went away⁺ and conferred⁺ with the chief priests and captains *to determine* how he might betray *Jesus* to them.

⁵ They were delighted⁺ and agreed⁺ to give him money.

⁶ *So Judas* promised and sought opportunity to betray *Jesus* to them, in the absence of the multitude.

⁷ Then the day of unleavened bread came, when the Passover *lamb* must be killed.

⁸ *Jesus* sent Peter and John saying: Go and prepare the Passover *for* us *so* that we may eat.

⁹ They said to Him: Where do you want us to prepare?

¹⁰He said to them: Behold, when you have entered the city, there a man will meet you bearing a pitcher of water. Follow him into the house where he enters.

¹¹Say to the head⁺ of the house: The Master says to you: Where is the guest chamber where I shall eat the Passover with my disciples?

¹²He will show you a large, furnished upper room. Make ready there.

¹³*So* they went and found *it* as *Jesus* had said to them, and they made preparations⁺ *for* the Passover.

¹⁴When the hour had come, *Jesus* sat down and the twelve apostles *sat* with Him.

¹⁵He said to them: *It is* with *a burning* desire *that* I have desired to eat this Passover with you before I suffer.

¹⁶For I say to you: I will not any more eat thereof, until it is fulfilled in the kingdom of God.

¹⁷*Then Jesus* took the cup, gave thanks, and said: Take this and divide *it* among yourselves.

¹⁸For I say to you: I will not drink of the fruit of the vine until the kingdom of God comes.

¹⁹*Then Jesus* took *the* bread, gave thanks, broke *it*, and gave *it* to them saying: This is my body, given for you. Do this in remembrance of me.

²⁰Likewise, after supper *He took* the cup and said: This cup *represents* the new covenant⁺ in my blood, shed for you.

²¹But, behold, the hand of the one who betrays me *is* with me on the table.

²²Truly the Son of man goes as it was determined. But woe to that man by whom He is betrayed.

²³*Then* they began to inquire among themselves who among them it was that should do this thing.

²⁴And there was also a dispute⁺ among them *regarding* who among them should be considered⁺ the greatest.

²⁵*But Jesus* said to them: The kings of the Gentiles exercise lordship over them, and *those* who exercise authority upon them are called benefactors.

²⁶But you *shall* not *be* that way.⁺ Let *those* who are *to be* greatest among you be like the younger, and *those* who lead⁺ *be* as *those* who serve.

²⁷For who⁺ *is* greater? *Those* who sit *down* to eat⁺ or *those* who serve? *Is it* not *those* who sit *down* to eat⁺? But I am among you as one who serves.

²⁸You are the ones who have continued with me in my trials⁺.

²⁹And I appoint to you a kingdom, as my Father has appointed to me.

³⁰*So* that you may eat and drink at my table in my kingdom and sit on thrones judging the twelve tribes of Israel.

³¹*Then* the Lord said: Simon, Simon. Behold, Satan has desired *to have* you *so* that he may sift *you* as wheat.

³²But I have prayed for you, that your faith not fail. When you are converted, strengthen the family⁺ *of God.*

³³*Peter* said to Him: Lord, I am ready to go with you, both into prison and to death.

³⁴*Jesus* said: I tell you Peter, the cock will not crow this day before you deny three times that you know me.

³⁵He said to them: When I sent you without purse and *provision* bag⁺ and sandals,⁺ did you lack anything? They said: Nothing.

³⁶Then He said to them: But now, let *those* who have a purse take *it*, and likewise *take a provision* bag.⁺ Let *those* who have no sword sell their clothes and buy one.

³⁷For I say to you, that this that is written must yet be accomplished in me: He was numbered⁺ among the transgressors. For the things concerning me have an end. *Isaiah 53:12*

³⁸They said: Lord, behold here *are* two swords. He said to them: It is enough.

³⁹*Then* going forth, as it was *His* custom,⁺ He went to the Mount of Olives, and His disciples also followed Him.

⁴⁰When He was at the place, He said to them: Pray *so* that you do not enter into temptation.

⁴¹*Then Jesus* withdrew about a stone's throw⁺ *away* from them and knelt down and prayed

⁴²saying: Father, if you are willing, remove this cup from me. Nevertheless not my will, but yours be done.

⁴³*Then* an angel appeared to Him from heaven, strengthening Him.

⁴⁴Being in agony, *Jesus* prayed *even* more earnestly, and His sweat became⁺ like⁺ great drops of blood falling down to the ground.

⁴⁵When He rose up from prayer and had come to His disciples, He found them sleeping, *exhausted* from sorrow.

⁴⁶*Jesus* said to them: Why are you sleeping? Rise and pray lest you enter into temptation.

⁴⁷While He spoke, behold a multitude *came forth*, and the one who was called Judas, one of the twelve, went before them. And *Judas* drew near to Jesus to kiss Him.

⁴⁸But Jesus said to him: Judas, are you betraying the Son of man with a kiss? *Matthew 26:48*

⁴⁹When *those* who were around⁺ *Jesus* saw what would follow, they said to Him: Lord, shall we strike⁺ with the sword?

⁵⁰And one of them struck⁺ the servant of the high priest and cut off his right ear.

⁵¹Jesus answered and said: Do you *really* condone⁺ this? And He touched *the* servant's ear and healed him.

⁵²Then Jesus said to the chief priests, captains of the temple, and the elders who had come to Him: Have you come out as against a thief with swords and staves?

⁵³When I was with you daily in the temple, you stretched forth no hands against me. But this is your hour and the power of darkness.

⁵⁴Then they took *Jesus*, led *Him away*, and brought Him to the high priest's house. And Peter followed *from* a distance.⁺

⁵⁵When they had started⁺ a fire in the midst of the courtyard⁺ and *everyone* sat down together, Peter sat among them.

⁵⁶*Then* a certain maid saw⁺ *Peter* as he sat by the fire, peered⁺ *intently* at him, and said: This man was also with *Jesus*.

⁵⁷*But Peter* denied *Jesus* saying: Woman, I do not know Him.

⁵⁸After a little while another noticed⁺ *Peter* and said: You are also of them. And Peter said: Man, I am not.

⁵⁹About one hour later,⁺ another confidently affirmed saying: Truly this *fellow* also was with Him, for he is a Galilaean.

⁶⁰Peter said: Man, I do not know what you say. And immediately, while *Peter* spoke, the cock crowed.⁺

⁶¹*Then* the Lord turned and looked upon Peter, and Peter remembered the word of the Lord, how He had said to him: Before the cock crows, you will deny me three times.

⁶²And Peter went out and wept bitterly.

⁶³*Then* the men who held Jesus mocked Him and struck⁺ *Him*.

⁶⁴When they had blindfolded Him, they struck Him on the face and asked Him saying: *Now* prophesy. Who is it that struck⁺ you?

⁶⁵And they spoke many other things to Him blasphemously.

⁶⁶As soon as it was day, the elders of the people and the chief priests and the scribes came together and led *Jesus* into their council *chambers*, saying:

⁶⁷Are you the Christ? Tell us. He said to them: If I tell you, you will not believe.

⁶⁸If I also ask *you*, you will not answer me or let *me* go.

⁶⁹Hereafter the Son of man will sit at the right hand of the power of God.

⁷⁰Then they all said: Are you then the Son of God? And He said to them: You say that I am.

⁷¹And they said: What further witness do we need? For we ourselves have heard *Him* from⁺ His own mouth.

Luke Chapter 23

¹ *Then* the whole multitude of them arose and led *Jesus* to Pilate.

² And they began to accuse Him saying: We found this *fellow* corrupting⁺ the nation and forbidding to give tribute to Caesar, saying that He Himself is Christ a King.

³ Pilate asked Him saying: Are you the King of the Jews? *Jesus* answered *Pilate* and said: You say *it*.

⁴ Then Pilate said to the chief priests and *to* the people: I find no fault in this man.

⁵ But they were more *fiercely* insistent,⁺ saying: He stirred up the people, teaching throughout all Judea,⁺ beginning from Galilee to this place.

⁶ When Pilate heard *the name* Galilee, he asked if the man was a Galilaean.

⁷ As soon as he knew that *Jesus* belonged to Herod's jurisdiction, he sent Him to Herod, who was in Jerusalem at that time.

⁸ When Herod saw Jesus, he was exceedingly glad, for he had desired to see Him for a long *time* because he had heard many things about Him and he hoped to see some miracle done by Him.

⁹ Then *Herod* questioned with Him in many words, but *Jesus* answered nothing.

¹⁰The chief priests and scribes *then* stood and forcefully⁺ accused *Jesus*.

¹¹*Then* Herod, with his soldiers,⁺ belittled⁺ *Jesus* and mocked *Him* and dressed⁺ Him in a gorgeous robe and sent Him back⁺ to Pilate.

¹²*That* same day, Pilate and Herod were made friends together, for before *that* they had been at enmity between themselves.

¹³*Then* Pilate, when he had called together the chief priests and the rulers and the people,

¹⁴said to them: You have brought this man to me as one who corrupts⁺ the people. But behold, I have examined *Him* before you *and I* have found no fault in this man touching those things of which you accuse Him.

¹⁵No, nor yet Herod. For I sent you to him and behold, *Herod and I agree that* nothing worthy of death is done by Him.

¹⁶Therefore, I will chastise Him and release *Him*.

¹⁷For *tradition had made it* necessary that *Pilate* must release one *prisoner* to them at the feast.

18 *Then* they all cried out at once saying: Away with this *man*, and release to us Barabbas.

19 *It was* for a certain sedition made in the city and for murder *that Barabbas* had been cast into prison.

20 Therefore Pilate, *being* willing to release Jesus, spoke again to them.

21 But *the people* cried *out* saying: Crucify *Him*. Crucify Him.

22 *Pilate* said to them the third time: Why? What evil has He done? I have found no cause of death in Him. Therefore, I will chastise Him and let *Him* go.

23 But they were insistent+ with loud voices, requiring that *Jesus* be crucified, and their voices, and *those* of the chief priests prevailed.

24 *So* Pilate gave *the* sentence that it should be as they required,

25 and he released to them *Barabbas* who, for sedition and murder was cast into prison, whom they had desired. But he delivered Jesus *according* to their will.

26 As they led Him away, they laid hold upon one Simon, a Cyrenian coming out of the country, and they laid the cross on him *so* that he might carry+ *it* for Jesus.

27 A great multitude+ of people followed *Jesus*, *including many* women who cried+ and grieved+ *for* Him.

28 But Jesus turning to them said: Daughters of Jerusalem, do not weep for me but weep for yourselves and for your children.

29 For behold the days are coming in which they will say: Blessed *are* the barren and the wombs that never gave birth+ and the breasts+ that never nursed+.

30 Then they will begin to say to the mountains: Fall on us. And to the hills: Cover us.

31 For if they do these things in a green tree, what will be done in the dry?

32 *Now* there were also two others, criminals,+ led *away* with *Jesus* to be put to death.

33 When they had come to the place called Calvary, there they crucified Him and the criminals,+ one on the right side+ and the other on the left. *John 19:18*

34 Then Jesus said: Father, forgive them. For they do not know what they *are* doing. *The soldiers then* divided+ up His clothing+ and cast lots *for it*. *Psalm 109:4, Matthew 27:35*

35 And the people stood beholding, and the rulers also with them ridiculed+ *Him* saying: He saved others. Let Him save Himself, if He is Christ, the chosen of God. *Matthew 27:41*

36 The soldiers also mocked Him, coming to Him and offering Him vinegar,

37 saying: If you are the king of the Jews, save yourself.

38 A title+ was also written over Him in letters of Greek and Latin and Hebrew *reading*: This is the king of the Jews.

39 One of the criminals+ who was hung *there beside Jesus* railed at Him saying: If you are Christ, save yourself and us.

40 But the other answering rebuked him saying: Do you not fear God, seeing you are in the same condemnation?

41 We indeed justly *deserve this*, for we receive the due reward of our deeds. But this man has done nothing amiss.

42 And he said to Jesus: Lord, remember me when you come into your kingdom.

43 Jesus said to him: Truly+ I say to you: Today you will be with me in paradise.

44 *When* it was about twelve o'clock+ *noon*, there was a darkness over all the earth *in the afternoon*.

45 The sun was darkened and the veil of the temple was torn+ *down* the middle.+

46 And when Jesus had cried *out* with a loud voice, He said: Father, into your hands I commend my spirit. And having said that, He expired.+

47 Now when the centurion saw what was done, he glorified God saying: Certainly this was a righteous man.

48 And all the people who came together to that sight, beholding the things that were done, beat+ *on* their breasts, and returned.

49 All *those* who knew+ *Jesus*, and the women who followed Him from Galilee, stood *at a* distance+ *away*, beholding these things.

⁵⁰And behold, *there was* a man named Joseph, a counselor *and* a good and righteous⁺ man,

⁵¹*one who* had not consented to the counsel and deed *of the rest* of them. Joseph *was* from Arimathaea, a city of the Jews *and* he himself also was waiting for the kingdom of God.

⁵²This *Joseph* went to Pilate and asked⁺ *for* Jesus' body.

⁵³He took it down, wrapped it in linen, and laid it in a tomb⁺ that was cut⁺ in stone, *one* in which no one before had *ever* been laid.

⁵⁴That day was the preparation and the Sabbath drew on.

⁵⁵The women also who came with Him from Galilee, followed after and saw⁺ the tomb⁺ and how His body was laid *in it*.

⁵⁶*Then* they returned and prepared spices and ointments and rested the Sabbath day according to the commandment.

Luke Chapter 24

¹ *Now* upon the first of the week *at* early twilight,⁺ they came to the tomb⁺ bringing the spices they had prepared, and certain *others came* with them.

² They found the stone rolled away from the tomb.⁺

³ *Upon* entering *the tomb*, they did not find the body of the Lord Jesus.

⁴ *Now* it came to pass, as they were much perplexed about this,⁺ behold two men in shining garments stood by them.

⁵ *The women* were frightened⁺ and bowed down *their* faces to the earth. *But the men in shining garments* said to them: Why do you seek the living among the dead?

⁶ *Jesus* is not here, but *He* is risen. Remember how He spoke to you when He was yet in Galilee

⁷ saying: The Son of man must be delivered into the hands of sinful men and be crucified, and the third day rise again.

⁸ *Then* they remembered His words

⁹ and returned from the tomb⁺ and told all these things to the eleven and to all the rest.

¹⁰It was Mary Magdalene, Joanna, Mary *the mother* of James, and other *women who were* with them who told these things to the apostles.

¹¹But their words seemed to *the apostles* like⁺ idle tales and they did not believe them.

¹²Then Peter got up⁺ and ran to the tomb⁺ and, stooping down, he saw⁺ the linen clothes laid by themselves. *Then he* left,⁺ wondering within himself at what had come to pass.

¹³And behold, on that *same* day, two of them went to a village called Emmaus, which was *about* seven miles⁺ from Jerusalem.

¹⁴And they talked together about all these things that had taken place.⁺

¹⁵*Now* it came to pass that, while they conversed and reasoned *together*, Jesus Himself drew near *to them* and went *along* with them.

¹⁶But their eyes were held⁺ *so* that they should not know Him.

¹⁷*Then Jesus* said to them: What kind of conversation⁺ *is* this that you have with one another as you walk and are sad?

¹⁸One of them, whose name was Cleopas, answering said to Him: Are you only a stranger in Jerusalem and have not known the things that have come to pass there in these *last few* days?

¹⁹*Jesus* said to them: What things? And they said to Him: Concerning Jesus of Nazareth, who was a prophet mighty in deed and word before God and all the people.

²⁰*Have you not heard* how the chief priests and our rulers delivered Him to be condemned to death and have crucified Him?

²¹We trusted that it was *Jesus* who would have redeemed Israel. But yet today is the third day since these things were done.

²²Yes, and certain women also of our company made us astonished, having been to the tomb⁺ early.

²³When they did not find His body, they came saying that they had also seen a vision of angels who said that *Jesus* is alive.

²⁴Some of *those* who were with us went to the tomb⁺ and found *it just* as the women had said, but they did not see *Jesus*.

²⁵Then *Jesus* said to them: O fools and slow of heart to believe all that the prophets have spoken.

²⁶Was it not necessary⁺ *that Christ should* suffer these things and *then* to enter into His glory?

²⁷*Then*, beginning with Moses and all the prophets, *Jesus* expounded to them in all the Scriptures the things concerning Himself.

²⁸*As* they drew near to the village, where they were going,⁺ *Jesus* appeared⁺ as though He would have gone further.

²⁹But they constrained Him saying: Stay⁺ with us, for it is toward evening and the day is far spent. *So Jesus* went in to stay⁺ with them.

³⁰*Now* it came to pass, as He sat *down* to eat⁺ with them, He took bread and blessed, broke *it*, and gave *it* to them.

³¹*Then* their eyes were opened and they knew Him, and He vanished out of their sight.

³²And they said to one another: Did our hearts not burn within us while He talked with us on the way and while He opened the Scriptures to us?

³³*Then* they got up⁺ that same hour and returned to Jerusalem and found the eleven gathered together, and *those* who were with them,

³⁴saying: The Lord is risen indeed and has appeared to Simon.

³⁵They told what things *were done* in the way and how He was known by them in *the* breaking of bread.

³⁶*Then* as they spoke *of* these *things*, Jesus Himself stood in the midst of them and said to them: Peace to you.

³⁷But they were terrified and frightened⁺ and supposed that they had seen a spirit.

³⁸*Jesus* said to them: Why are you troubled? And why do thoughts arise in your hearts?

³⁹Behold my hands and my feet, that it is I myself. Touch⁺ me and see. For a spirit does not have flesh and bones as you see me have.

⁴⁰After⁺ *Jesus* had said these things, He showed them *His* hands and *His* feet.

⁴¹While they yet did not believe, for joy, and wondered, He said to them: Do you have anything to eat⁺.

⁴²They gave Him a piece of a broiled fish and a honeycomb.

⁴³He took *it* and ate before them.

⁴⁴*Then* He said to them: These *are* the words that I spoke to you while I was yet with you: All things must be fulfilled that were written in the law of Moses and *in* the prophets and *in* the psalms, concerning me.

⁴⁵Then He opened their understanding *so* that they might understand the Scriptures.

⁴⁶He said to them: Thus it is written and thus it was essential⁺ for Christ to suffer and to rise from the dead the third day,

Psalm 22:12-18, Isaiah 50:6

⁴⁷so that repentance and remission of sins should be proclaimed⁺ in His name among all nations, beginning at Jerusalem.

⁴⁸You are witnesses of these things.

⁴⁹And behold I send the promise of my Father upon you. But stay⁺ in the city of Jerusalem until you are endowed⁺ with power from on high.

⁵⁰*Then* He led them out as far as to Bethany and He lifted up His hands and blessed them.

⁵¹And it came to pass while He blessed them *that* He was taken⁺ from them and carried up to heaven.

⁵²And they worshiped Him and returned to Jerusalem with great joy.

⁵³And *they* continued praising and blessing God in the temple. Amen.

This concludes the four Gospel accounts of the life and teachings of Jesus Christ, the Word of God.

*Following are 23
letters and accounts
written by early followers
of Jesus Christ
to encourage faith in Him.*

Acts Chapter 1

[1] The first[+] record[+] *that* I made, Theophilus, *was about all* that Jesus began to do and teach

[2] until the day in which He was taken up. After that, through the Holy Spirit, *He* gave instructions[+] to the apostles whom He had chosen.

[3] After He had suffered[+] *death*, He also showed Himself to *them* alive by many infallible proofs. *For* forty days, He was seen by them and spoke *to them* about the things pertaining to the kingdom of God.

[4] Being assembled together with *them*, *He* commanded them to not depart from Jerusalem, but *to*: Wait for the promise of the Father that you have heard me *proclaim*.

[5] For John indeed[+] baptized with water, but you shall be baptized with the Holy Spirit, not many days from now.

[6] Therefore, when they came together, they asked of Him saying: Lord, will you at this time restore again the kingdom to Israel?

[7] He said to them: It is not for you to know the times or the seasons the Father has put under[+] His own authority[+].

> [8] Yet after the Holy Spirit
> has come upon you,
> you shall receive power

and you shall be witnesses to me both in Jerusalem and in all Judea and in Samaria and to the ends[+] of the earth.

[9] When He had spoken these things, while they observed,[+] He was taken up and a cloud received Him out of their sight.

[10] While they looked steadfastly toward heaven as He went up, behold, two men stood by them in white apparel.

[11] *They* said: Men of Galilee, why do you stand gazing up into heaven? This same Jesus who is taken up from you into heaven, will come *back* in like manner as you have seen Him go into heaven.

[12] Then they returned to Jerusalem from the mountain called Olivet, which is a Sabbath day's journey from Jerusalem.

[13] When they entered[+] *the city*, they went into an upper room where *they* were staying[+]: Peter, James, John, Andrew, Philip, Thomas, Bartholomew, Matthew, James *the son* of Alphaeus, Simon Zelotes, and Jude *the brother* of James.

[14] These all continued with one accord in prayer and supplication, *along* with the women and Mary the mother of Jesus, and with His brothers.

[15] In those days, Peter stood up in the midst of the disciples and spoke. [+] The number of names together was about a hundred and twenty.

[16] *Peter said:* Men *and* family[+]: This Scripture needed to be fulfilled. The Holy Spirit spoke through the mouth of David before concerning Judas *Iscariot* who was *the* guide to *those* who took Jesus. *Psalm 109:7*

[17] For he was numbered with us and had obtained part of this ministry.

[18] Now this man purchased a field with the reward of iniquity, and falling headlong, he burst apart[+] in the midst and all his insides[+] gushed out.

[19] *This fact* became[+] known to all who live in Jerusalem, so that field is *now* called in their own language[+]: Aceldama. That is: The Field of Blood.

[20] For it is written in the book of Psalms: Let his habitation be desolate and let no one dwell therein. Let another take his office.[+] *Psalm 109:8*

[21] Therefore, *from among* these men who have joined[+] with us all the time that the Lord Jesus went in and out among us,

[22] beginning from the baptism of John to

that day *in* which He was taken up from us, one *must be selected* to be a witness with us of *Jesus'* resurrection.

²³*So* they put forth⁺ two *names*: Joseph called Barsabas, who was surnamed Justus, and Matthias.

²⁴*Then* they prayed and said: You Lord, know the hearts of all *people*. Show which⁺ of these two you have chosen

²⁵*so* that he may take part of this ministry and apostleship from which Judas *Iscariot* fell by transgression*so* that he might go to his own place.

²⁶And they gave forth their lots and the lot fell upon Matthias, and he was numbered with the*other* eleven apostles.

Acts Chapter 2

¹ When the day of Pentecost had come, they were all with one accord in one place.

² Suddenly there came a sound from heaven, like a rushing mighty wind, and it filled all the house where they were sitting.

³ And there appeared to them divided⁺ tongues like fire, both⁺ *of which* sat down upon each of them,

⁴ and they were all filled with the Holy Spirit and began to speak with other tongues as the Spirit gave them utterance.

⁵ Now *at that time* there were Jews living⁺ in Jerusalem, devout men from every nation under heaven.

⁶ And when this was reported,⁺ the multitude came together and were confounded, because everyone⁺ heard them speaking in their own language.

⁷ They were all amazed and marveled, saying to one another: Behold, are these who speak not all Galileans?

⁸ How *is it that* we hear everyone⁺ in our own tongue in which we were born?

⁹ Parthians, Medes, Elamites, and *those who* live in Mesopotamia, Judea, Cappadocia, Pontus, Asia,

¹⁰Phrygia, Pamphylia, Egypt, and in the parts of Libya around Cyrene, also strangers of Rome, Jews and proselytes,

¹¹Cretans, and Arabians. *We all* hear them speaking in our tongues *about* the wonderful works of God.

¹²They were all amazed and perplexed⁺ *and* said to one another: What does this mean?

¹³Others, mocking, said: These men are full of new wine.

¹⁴But Peter, standing with the eleven, raised⁺ his voice and said to them: You men of Judea and all *of you* who dwell in Jerusalem: Let this be known to you and listen carefully⁺ to my words:

¹⁵These *people* are not drunk as you suppose, since it is *only* about nine o'clock⁺ *in the morning*.

¹⁶But this is what was spoken by the prophet Joel:

¹⁷God has declared⁺: It will come *to pass* in the last days *that* I will pour out of my Spirit upon all flesh. Your sons and your daughters will prophesy. Your young men will see visions. And your old men will dream dreams. *Joel 2:28*

¹⁸In those days, I will pour out of my Spirit on my servants and on my handmaidens and they will prophesy. *Joel 2:29*

¹⁹I will show wonders in heaven above and signs on the earth below,⁺ *with* blood and fire and vapor of smoke. *Joel 2:30*

²⁰The sun will be turned into darkness and the moon to *the color of* blood before that great and notable day of the Lord comes. *Joel 2:31*

---

²¹ And it will come *to pass that* whoever will call on the name of the Lord will be saved. *Joel 2:32*

---

²²Men of Israel, hear these words: Jesus of Nazareth *was* a man proved⁺ by God among you, by miracles and wonders and signs that God did through Him in the midst of you, as you yourselves also know.

²³*Jesus* was delivered by the predetermined⁺ purpose⁺ and foreknowledge of God *and* you have taken *Him* by wicked hands *and* crucified and slain *Him*.

[24] *But* God raised *Him* up, having loosed the pains of death, because it was not possible that He could be held[+] by it.

[25] For David spoke concerning Him: I foresaw the Lord continuously[+] before me. For He is at my right hand *so that* I would not be shaken.[+] *Psalm 16:8*

[26] Therefore my heart rejoiced and my tongue was glad. Moreover, my flesh will rest in hope. *Psalm 16:9*

[27] Because, you will not leave my soul in Hades. Nor will you allow[+] your Holy One to see corruption. *Psalm 16:10*

[28] You have made the ways of life known to me. You will make me full of joy with your countenance. *Psalm 16:11*

[29] Men *and* family,[+] let *me* speak freely to you about the patriarch David. He is dead and buried, and his tomb[+] is with us to this day.

[30] Therefore, being a prophet, he knew that God had sworn to him with an oath that, from the fruit of his loins according to the flesh, He would raise up Christ to sit on his throne.

[31] *David* foresaw[+] this *and* spoke about the resurrection of Christ: That His soul was not left in Hell nor did His flesh see corruption. *Psalm 16:10*

[32] God has raised up this Jesus, *and* we all are witnesses of this *fact*.

[33] Therefore, being exalted to the right hand of God, and having received the promise of the Holy Spirit from the Father, He has poured[+] out this that you now see and hear.

[34] For David is not ascended into the heavens. But he himself said: The Lord said to my Lord: Sit at my right hand *Psalm 110:1*

[35] until I make your enemies[+] your footstool. *Psalm 110:1*

[36] Therefore, let all *of* the house of Israel know assuredly, that God has made that same Jesus whom you have crucified, both Lord and Christ.

[37] Now when they heard *this*, they were pierced[+] in their hearts and said to Peter and to the rest of the apostles: Men *and* family,[+] what shall we do?

[38] Then Peter said to them:

> Repent and be baptized,
> everyone of you,
> in the name of Jesus Christ
> for the remission of sins,
> and you will receive
> the gift of the Holy Spirit.

[39] For the promise is to you and to your children and to all who are far away,[+] *to* all[+] *whom* the Lord our God calls.

[40] With many other words *Peter* testified and exhorted saying: Be saved from this corrupt[+] generation.

[41] Then *those* who gladly received his word were baptized. The same day there were added, about three thousand souls.

[42] And they continued steadfastly in the apostles' doctrine and fellowship and in breaking bread and in prayers.

[43] Fear came upon every soul and many wonders and signs were done by the apostles.

[44] All who believed were together and had everything[+] common.

[45] *They* sold their possessions and goods and divided[+] them to all as everyone[+] had need.

[46] And they continued daily in one accord, in the temple and breaking bread from house to house. *They* ate their food[+] with gladness and singleness of heart,

[47] praising God and having favor with all the people. And the Lord added to the assembly[+] daily *those* who were being saved.

Acts Chapter 3

[1] Now Peter and John went together into the temple at the hour of prayer, the ninth *hour, or three o'clock in the afternoon.*

[2] A certain man *who had been* lame from his mother's womb was carried *and* laid daily at the gate of the temple called Beautiful to ask for alms from *those* who entered the temple.

[3] *Upon* seeing Peter and John about to go into the temple, *the lame man* asked *them* for alms.

⁴ Fastening his eyes upon *the man* Peter, with John, said: Look at us.

⁵ *The man* gave heed to them, waiting⁺ *expectantly* to receive something from them.

⁶ Then Peter said: Silver and gold I do not have. But such as I have, I give to you. In the name of Jesus Christ of Nazareth, rise up and walk.

⁷ *Then Peter* took *the lame man* by the right hand and lifted *him* up, and immediately his feet and ankle bones received strength.

⁸ *The man* jumped⁺ up, stood and walked and entered with them into the temple, walking and leaping and praising God.

⁹ All the people saw him walking and praising God.

¹⁰They knew that it was *the lame man* who *had* sat *asking* for alms at the Beautiful gate of the temple and they were filled with wonder and amazement at what had happened to him.

¹¹As the lame man who was healed held Peter and John, all the people ran together to them in the porch called Solomon's, greatly wondering.

¹²When Peter saw *this*, he answered the people: Men of Israel, why *do* you marvel at this? Why *do* you look so earnestly at us as though by our own power or holiness we had made this man to walk?

¹³The God of Abraham and of Isaac and of Jacob, the God of our fathers has glorified His Son Jesus whom you delivered up and denied in the presence of Pilate when *Pilate* was determined to let *Jesus* go.

¹⁴But you denied the Just and Holy One and desired a murderer be granted to you.

¹⁵*You* killed the Prince of life, whom God has raised from the dead, of which we are witnesses.

¹⁶*It is Jesus* name, through faith in His name, *that* has made this man, whom you see and know, strong. Yes, faith *in Jesus* has given *this man* perfect soundness in the presence of you all.

¹⁷Now family,⁺ I know⁺ that *it was* through ignorance *that* you *and* your rulers *did what you did.*

¹⁸But those things that God *long* before had shown by the mouths of all His prophets that Christ would suffer, *Jesus* has *indeed* fulfilled.

¹⁹ Therefore, repent and be converted *so* that your sins may be blotted out *and so* that times of refreshing will come from the presence of the Lord.

²⁰*God* will send Jesus Christ who was proclaimed⁺ to you before.

²¹*Meanwhile, Jesus* must *be* received *in* heaven until the times of restoration⁺ of all things that God has spoken by the mouth of all His holy prophets since the world began.

²²For Moses truly said to the fathers: The Lord your God will raise up a prophet to you, like me, from *among* your family.⁺ You shall hear Him in everything⁺ He shall say to you. *Deuteronomy 18:15*

²³And it shall come to pass, *that* every soul who will not hear that prophet will be destroyed from among the people. *Deuteronomy 18:19*

²⁴Yes, and all the prophets from Samuel and *all* those *who* followed after, all⁺ *who* have spoken have likewise foretold of these days.

²⁵You are the children of the prophets and of the covenant that God made with our fathers, saying to Abraham: And in your descendants,⁺ all the families⁺ of the earth will be blessed. *Genesis 18:18*

²⁶To you first, God raised up His Son Jesus *and* sent Him to bless you in turning everyone of you away from your iniquities.

Acts Chapter 4

¹ As *Peter and John* spoke to the people, the priests and the captain of the temple and the Sadducees came upon them.

² They were upset⁺ that they taught the people and proclaimed⁺ through Jesus the resurrection from the dead.

³ *So* they laid hands on them and put *them* in holding until the next day. For it was now evening.

[4] However, many of *those* who heard the Word believed. The number of the men was about five thousand.

[5] On the next day, the rulers, elders, and scribes,

[6] Annas the high priest, Caiaphas, John, Alexander, and all[+] *who* were of the family[+] of the high priest, gathered together at Jerusalem.

[7] They stood[+] *Peter and John* before them *and* asked, By what power or by what name have you done this?

[8] Then Peter, filled with the Holy Spirit, said to them: You rulers of the people and elders of Israel,

[9] If we this day are *being* examined for the good deed done to the disabled[+] man, by what means he is made whole,

[10] *May* it be known to you all and to all the people of Israel that *it is* by the name of Jesus Christ of Nazareth whom you crucified *and* whom God raised from the dead, *it is* by Him that this man stands here before you whole.

[11] This is the stone that was rejected[+] by you builders and *it* has become the head of the corner. *Psalm 118:22*

[12] There is no salvation in any other, for there is no other name under heaven given among men by which we must be saved.

[13] When they saw the boldness of Peter and John and perceived that they were uneducated[+] and unsophisticated[+] men, they marveled, for they knew that they had been with Jesus.

[14] Seeing the man who was *now* healed standing with them, they could say nothing against it.

[15] But then they commanded them to go aside *away* from the council *and* they conferred among themselves.

[16] *They* said: What shall we do to these men? For indeed a notable miracle has been done by them. *It is* known[+] to all who dwell in Jerusalem and we cannot deny *it*.

[17] But *so* that it spreads no further among the people, let us strictly[+] threaten them *so* that they *will* not speak, hereafter, to anyone in this name.

[18] *So* they called them and commanded them to not speak at all or teach in the name of Jesus.

[19] But Peter and John answered and said to them: Whether it is right in the sight of God to listen to you more than to God, you judge.

[20] For we cannot but speak the things that we have seen and heard.

[21] So, after they further threatened them, they let them go, finding no *basis* for punishing them. For all *people* glorified God for what had been done.

[22] For the man on whom this miracle of healing was shown was more than forty years old.

[23] Being let go, they went to their own company and reported all that the chief priests and elders had said to them.

[24] When they heard that, they raised[+] their voices to God with one accord and said: Lord, you *are* God who has made heaven and earth and the sea and all that in them is.

[25] By the mouth of your servant David, you have said: Why did the heathen rage and the people imagine vain things? *Psalm 2:1*

[26] The kings of the earth stood up and the rulers were gathered together against the Lord and against His Christ. *Psalm 2:2*

[27] For truly against your holy child Jesus, whom you have anointed, both Herod and Pontius Pilate, with the Gentiles and the people of Israel were gathered together

[28] to do whatever your hand and your counsel determined before to be done.

[29] Now Lord, behold their threatenings. Grant to your servants that with all boldness they may speak your Word.

[30] Stretch forth your hand to heal *so* that signs and wonders may be done by the name of your holy child Jesus.

[31] When they had prayed, the place was shaken where they were assembled together. They were all filled with the Holy Spirit and they spoke the Word of God with boldness.

[32] The multitude of *those* who believed were of one heart and of one soul. None

of them said that any of the things that they possessed was their own, but they had everything+ in common.

33With great power, the apostles gave witness of the resurrection of the Lord Jesus. Great grace was upon them all.
34Neither was there any among them who lacked, for all+ who were possessors of lands or houses sold them and brought the prices of the things that were sold
35and laid them down at the apostles' feet, and distribution was made to everyone+ as they had need.
36Joses, who was surnamed Barnabas by the apostles, as that name means+ son of consolation, a Levite from the country of Cyprus,
37had some land, sold it, and brought the money and laid it at the apostles' feet.

Acts Chapter 5

1 Then a certain man named Ananias, with Sapphira his wife, sold a possession 2 and kept back part of the price. His wife was also aware+ of this. Ananias brought a certain part and laid it at the apostles' feet.
3 Peter said: Ananias, why has Satan filled your heart to lie to the Holy Spirit and to keep back part of the price of the land?
4 While it remained unsold, was it not your own? And even after it was sold, was it not still under your own author-ity+? Why have you conceived this thing in your heart? You have not lied to people,+ but to God.
5 Upon hearing these words, Ananias fell down and died+ and great fear came upon all who heard these things.
6 The young men arose, covered+ him up, carried him out, and buried him.
7 It was about three hours later when his wife also came in, not knowing what had been done.
8 Peter answered her: Tell me if you sold the land for so much? She said: Yes, for so much.
9 Then Peter said to her: How is it that you have agreed together to test+ the

Spirit of the Lord? Behold the feet of those who have buried your husband are at the door and will now carry you out.
10Then she immediately+ fell down at his feet and died.+ Then the young men came in, found her dead, and carried her out and buried her by her husband.
11Great fear came upon all the assembly+ and upon all+ who heard these things.
12By the hands of the apostles, many signs and wonders were worked+ among the people and they were all with one accord in Solomon's porch.
13Among the rest, no one dared+ to join them, but the people highly regarded+ them.
14Many more believers were added to the Lord, multitudes of both men and women.
15So much so that they brought forth the sick into the streets and laid them on beds and couches so that at the least shadow of Peter passing by might overshadow some of them.
16There also came a multitude from the cities all around+ to Jerusalem, bringing sick folks and those who were oppressed+ with unclean spirits and they healed everyone.
17Then the high priest and all those of the sect of the Sadducees who were with him rose up, filled with indignation.
18They laid their hands on the apostles and put them into the common prison.
19But the angel of the Lord came at night, opened the prison doors, brought them forth, and said:
20Go, stand and speak all the words of life to the people in the temple.
21When they heard that, they entered the temple early in the morning and taught, but the high priest and those who were with him came and called the council and all the senate of the children of Israel together, and sent to the prison to have Peter and John brought to them.
22But when the officers did not find them in the prison, they returned and told of this
23saying: We found the prison shut with all safety and the keepers standing

outside⁺ before the doors. But when we opened *the doors*, we found no one inside. ²⁴Now when the high priest and the captain of the temple and the chief priests heard these things, they they wondered⁺ how *big* this *story* would grow.

²⁵Then someone came and told them: Behold the men you put in prison are standing in the temple and teaching the people.

²⁶Then the captain went with the officers and brought *Peter and John* without violence, for they feared the people, lest they should be stoned.

²⁷When they had brought them, they set *them* before the council and the high priest asked them:

²⁸Did we not strictly⁺ command you to not teach in this name? And behold you have filled Jerusalem with your doctrine and intend to bring this man's blood upon us.

²⁹Then Peter and the *other* apostles answered and said: We must⁺ obey God rather than men.

³⁰The God of our fathers raised up Jesus, whom you killed⁺ and hung on a tree.

³¹This *is the one* whom God exalted *to be* Prince and Savior *having* the right to give repentance to Israel and forgiveness *of* sins.

³²We are His witnesses of these things. *So* also *is* the Holy Spirit, whom God has given to *those* who obey Him.

³³When they heard *this*, they were cut *to the heart* and took counsel to slay them.

³⁴Then in the council a Pharisee named Gamaliel stood up, a teacher⁺ of the law *who* had a *good* reputation among all the people. *He* commanded *them* to allow⁺ the apostles a little space.

³⁵*He* said to them: Men of Israel, take heed to yourselves what you intend to do concerning these men.

³⁶Before these days *one named* Theudas rose up, boasting himself to be somebody. A number of men, about four hundred, joined themselves to him. *But eventually* he was killed⁺ *and* all, as many as obeyed him, were scattered and brought to nothing.

³⁷After this a man *named* Judas of Galilee rose up in the days of the taxing and drew away many people after him. He also perished and all, as many as obeyed him, were dispersed.

³⁸Now I say to you: Refrain from these men and let them alone. For if this counsel or this work be of men, it will come to nothing.

³⁹But if it be of God, you cannot overthrow it lest perhaps⁺ you be found even to fight against God.

⁴⁰*So* they *all* agreed with *Gamaliel*. Then they called the apostles, beat *them*, commanded that they should not speak in the name of Jesus, and let them go.

⁴¹*The apostles* then departed from the presence of the council, rejoicing that they were counted worthy to suffer shame for His name.

⁴²*After that* every day in the temple and in every house, they did not stop⁺ teaching and proclaiming⁺ Jesus Christ.

Acts Chapter 6

¹ In those days, when the number of the disciples was multiplied, there arose complaints⁺ from the Greeks against the Hebrews because their widows were neglected in the daily distribution.⁺

² Therefore the twelve called the multitude of the disciples *together* and said: It is not reasonable⁺ that we should leave the Word of God and serve tables.

³ Therefore family,⁺ select⁺ seven men of honest report, full of the Holy Spirit and wisdom, from among you whom we may appoint over these needs,⁺

⁴ and we will give ourselves continually to prayer and to the ministry of the Word.

⁵ The saying pleased the whole multitude. They chose Stephen, a man full of faith and of the Holy Spirit, and Philip, and Prochorus, and Nicanor, and Timon, and Parmenas, and Nicolas a convert⁺ from Antioch.

⁶ These they set before the apostles, and when they had prayed, they laid *their* hands on them *to commission them.*

⁷ The Word of God increased and the number of the disciples greatly multiplied in Jerusalem, and a great multitude⁺ of the priests were obedient to the faith.

⁸ Stephen, full of faith and power, did great wonders and miracles among the people.

⁹ Then there arose certain *detractors* from the synagogue of the Libertines, and Cyrenians, and Alexandrians, and of those of Cilicia and of Asia, disputing with Stephen.

¹⁰They were not able to stand against⁺ the wisdom and the Spirit by which he spoke.

¹¹So they *secretly* induced⁺ men to say: We have heard Him speak blasphemous words against Moses and *against* God.

¹²They stirred up the people and the elders and the scribes, and came upon *him* and caught him and brought *him* to the council.

¹³*They* set up false witnesses who said: This man does not stop⁺ speaking blasphemous words against this holy place and the law.

¹⁴For we have heard him say that this Jesus of Nazareth will destroy this place and will change the customs that Moses delivered *to* us.

¹⁵All who sat in the council looked steadfastly at him *and* saw his face *become radiant* as *though* it had become⁺ the face of an angel.

Acts Chapter 7

¹ Then the high priest said: Are these things so?

² *In reply, Stephen* said: Men, family,⁺ and fathers, listen carefully.⁺ The God of glory appeared to our father Abraham when he was in Mesopotamia, before he lived⁺ in Haran,

³ and said to him: Get out of your country and from your family⁺ and come into the land that I will show you. *Genesis 12:1*

⁴ Then *Abraham* came out of the land of the Chaldeans and lived⁺ in Haran. From there,⁺ when his father was dead,

he moved into this land in which you now dwell.

⁵ *God* gave *Abraham* no inheritance in it. No, not *so much as* to set his foot on. Yet He promised that He would give it to him for a possession, and to his seed after him, *even* when he did not *yet* have a child.

⁶ God spoke in this way *knowing* that *Abraham's* seed would journey⁺ into a strange land that would bring them into bondage and mistreat⁺ *them with* evil *for* four hundred years.

⁷ The nation to whom they shall be in bondage I will judge, said God. After that, they shall come forth and serve me in this place. *Genesis 15:14*

⁸ *Then God* gave the covenant of circumcision *to Abraham* and *he* fathered⁺ Isaac and circumcised him *on* the eighth day. *Then* Isaac *fathered* Jacob and Jacob *fathered* the twelve patriarchs.

⁹ The patriarchs, moved with envy, sold Joseph into Egypt. But God was with him.

¹⁰*God* delivered *Joseph* out of all his afflictions and gave him favor and wisdom in the sight of Pharaoh, king of Egypt, *who* made *Joseph* governor over Egypt and all his house.

¹¹Now a famine⁺ came over all the land of Egypt and Canaan, a great affliction, and our fathers found no sustenance.

¹²But when Jacob heard that there was corn in Egypt, *at* first, he sent out our fathers.

¹³At a second *time*, Joseph was made known to his family⁺ and Joseph's family⁺ was made known to Pharaoh.

¹⁴Then Joseph summoned⁺ *and* sent *for* his father Jacob and all his family,⁺ seventy five souls.

¹⁵So Jacob went down into Egypt and died. He and our fathers

¹⁶were carried into Sychem and laid in the tomb⁺ that Abraham bought for a sum of money from the sons of Emmor *the father of* Sychem.

¹⁷But when the time of the promise that God had sworn to Abraham drew near, the people grew and multiplied in Egypt,

[18] until another king arose who did not know Joseph.

[19] That *king* oppressed[+] our ancestors[+] and treated our fathers wickedly so that they cast out their young children, to the end they might not live.

[20] During this time, Moses was born and *he* was *very* fair to God. *He was* nurtured[+] in his father's house *for* three months.

[21] When he was cast out, Pharaoh's daughter took him and nurtured[+] him as her own son.

[22] Moses was educated[+] in all the wisdom of the Egyptians and *he* was mighty in words and deeds.

[23] When he was forty years old, it came into his heart to visit his family,[+] the children of Israel.

[24] Seeing one *of them* suffer wrong, he defended and avenged *the one* who was oppressed and struck[+] *down* an Egyptian.

[25] *Moses* thought[+] *that* his brothers would have understood that God, by his hand, would deliver them. But they did not understand.

[26] The next day, he appeared[+] to them as they argued[+] and *he* tried to set them at peace[+] saying: Sirs, you are brothers. Why do you *do* wrong to one another?

[27] But *the one* who did his neighbor wrong, pushed[+] *Moses* away saying: Who made you a ruler and a judge over us? *Exodus 2:14*

[28] Will you kill me as you did the Egyptian yesterday? *Exodus 2:14*

[29] At this saying, Moses fled and became a stranger in the land of Midian where he fathered[+] two sons.

[30] After forty years passed,[+] an angel of the Lord appeared to him in the wilderness of Mount Sinai in a flame of fire in a bush.

[31] When Moses saw *this*, he wondered at the sight. As he drew near to behold *it*, the voice of the Lord came to him

[32] *saying*: I *am* the God of your fathers, the God of Abraham and the God of Isaac and the God of Jacob. Then Moses trembled and did not dare[+] *to* behold. *Exodus 3:6*

[33] Then the Lord said to him: Take your sandals[+] off of your feet, for the place where you stand is holy ground. *Exodus 3:5*

[34] I have seen the suffering[+] of my people in Egypt and I have heard their groaning and *I* have come down to deliver them. Now come, I will send you into Egypt. *Exodus 2:24*

[35] This Moses whom they refused saying: Who made you a ruler and a judge? The same did God send *to be* a ruler and a deliverer by the hand of the angel who appeared to him in the bush.

[36] He brought them out after he had shown wonders and signs in the land of Egypt, and in the Red sea, and in the wilderness forty years.

[37] This is that Moses who said to the children of Israel: The Lord your God will raise up for you a prophet from *among* your brothers, like me. You shall hear Him. *Deuteronomy 18:15*

[38] This is *the man* who was in the assembly[+] in the wilderness with the angel who spoke to him on Mount Sinai, and *with* our fathers. *It was he* who received the living[+] oracles to give to us.

[39] *But* our fathers would not obey *him*. *Instead, they* thrust *him away* from them and in their hearts turned back again to Egypt.

[40] *They* said to Aaron: Make gods *for* us to go before us. For *as for* this Moses who brought us out of the land of Egypt, we do not know[+] what has become of him. *Exodus 32:23*

[41] They made a calf in those days and offered sacrifice to the idol and rejoiced in the works of their own hands.

[42] But God turned and gave them up to worship the host of heaven. As it is written in the book of the prophets: *O* house of Israel, did you offer to me slain beasts and sacrifices *for* forty years in the wilderness? *Amos 5:25*

[43] And you *also* took up the tabernacle of Moloch and the star of your god Remphan, *with* figures that you made to worship. I will carry you away beyond Babylon. *Amos 5:26,27*

⁴⁴Our fathers had the tabernacle of witness in the wilderness, as *God* who spoke to Moses instructed,⁺ *so* he would make it according to the pattern⁺ he had seen. ⁴⁵Our fathers who came after brought *this* in with Joshua⁺ into the possession of the Gentiles whom God drove out before the face of our fathers, until the days of David. ⁴⁶*But then David* found favor before God and desired to find a tabernacle for the God of Jacob. ⁴⁷But *then it was* Solomon *who* built a house *for God*. ⁴⁸However the most High does not dwell in temples made with hands. As the prophet said: ⁴⁹Heaven *is* my throne and earth *is* my footstool. What house will you build *for* me? says the Lord. Or what place of my rest? *Isaiah 66:1* ⁵⁰Has not my hand made all these things? *Isaiah 66:2* ⁵¹You stiffnecked and uncircumcised in heart and ears. You always resist the Holy Spirit. As your fathers *did*, so you *do*. ⁵²Which of the prophets have your fathers not persecuted? And they have slain *those* who foretold⁺ of the coming of the Just One of whom you have now been the betrayers and murderers. ⁵³You have received the law by the disposition of angels but have not kept *it*. ⁵⁴When they heard these things, they were cut to the heart and gnashed their teeth at him. ⁵⁵But *Stephen*, being full of the Holy Spirit, looked up steadfastly into heaven and saw the glory of God and Jesus standing at the right hand of God. ⁵⁶*He* said: Behold I see the heavens opened and the Son of man standing at the right hand of God. ⁵⁷Then they cried out with a loud voice and stopped their ears and ran upon him with one accord. ⁵⁸*They* cast *Stephen* out of the city and stoned *him* and the witnesses laid down their clothes at the feet of a young man whose name was Saul.

⁵⁹They stoned Stephen *as he* called upon *God* saying: Lord Jesus, receive my spirit. ⁶⁰Then he knelt down and cried *out* with a loud voice: Lord, do not lay this sin to their charge. When he had said this, he fell asleep.

Acts Chapter 8

¹ Saul consented to *Stephen's* death. At that time there was a great persecution against the assembly⁺ at Jerusalem and all except the apostles were scattered throughout the regions of Judea and Samaria. ² Devout men carried Stephen *to his burial* and grieved⁺ greatly over him. ³ As for Saul, he made havoc of the assembly,⁺ entering every house and dragging⁺ *away* men and women, committing *them* to prison. ⁴ *Those* who were scattered went everywhere proclaiming⁺ the Word. ⁵ Then Philip went down to the city of Samaria, and proclaimed⁺ Christ to them. ⁶ With one accord, the people gave heed to the things that Philip spoke, hearing and seeing the miracles that he did. ⁷ For unclean spirits crying *out* with loud voices came out of many who were possessed *with them* and many afflicted⁺ with palsies and *many* who had been lame were healed. ⁸ There was great joy in that city. ⁹ But there was a man called Simon who in the past⁺ in the same city used sorcery and bewitched the people of Samaria, suggesting⁺ that *he* himself was great. ¹⁰All from the least to the greatest gave heed to him, saying: This man is the great power of God. ¹¹They *highly* regarded *this Simon* because for a long time he had bewitched them with sorceries. ¹²But now they believed Philip *who was* proclaiming⁺ the things concerning the kingdom of God and the name of Jesus Christ, and both men and women were baptized.

[13] Then Simon himself also believed and when he was baptized, he continued with Philip and *was* amazed[+] as he saw the miracles and signs that were done.

[14] Now when the apostles in Jerusalem heard that Samaria had received the Word of God, they sent Peter and John to them.

[15] So they came down and prayed for them, *so* that they might receive the Holy Spirit.

[16] For as yet, *the Holy Spirit* had not come upon any of them but only *upon* those who had been baptized in the name of the Lord Jesus.

[17] So Peter and John laid *their* hands upon *the new believers* and then they received the Holy Spirit.

[18] When Simon saw that *it was* through *the* laying on of the apostles' hands *that* the Holy Spirit was given, he offered them money,

[19] saying: Give me also this authority[+] *so* that on whomever I lay hands, they may receive the Holy Spirit.

[20] But Peter said to him: *May* your money perish with you, because you have thought that the gift of God could be purchased with money.

[21] You have no part or share[+] in this, for your heart is not right in the sight of God.

[22] Therefore, repent of your wickedness and pray *to* God that the thoughts in your heart may be forgiven.

[23] For I perceive that you are in the gall of bitterness and *in* the bond of iniquity.

[24] Then Simon answered and said: Pray to the Lord for me, that none of these things that you have spoken *will* come upon me.

[25] After *Peter and John* had testified and proclaimed[+] the Word of the Lord, they returned to Jerusalem and proclaimed[+] the Gospel in many villages of the Samaritans.

[26] Then the angel of the Lord spoke to Philip saying: Arise and go toward the south on the desert road[+] that goes from Jerusalem to Gaza.

[27] *So Philip* arose and went and behold *he met* a man from Ethiopia, a eunuch with great authority under Candace queen of the Ethiopians who had the charge of all her treasure. *He* had come to Jerusalem to worship.

[28] *Now, he* was returning and sitting in his chariot reading the prophet Isaiah.

[29] Then the Spirit said to Philip: Go near and join yourself to this chariot.

[30] *So* Philip ran to *the eunuch*, heard him reading the prophet Isaiah, and said: Do you understand what you *are* reading?

[31] *The eunuch* said: How can I, unless someone should guide me? And he asked Philip to come up and sit with him.

[32] The place in the Scripture that he read was this: He was led like a sheep to the slaughter *and* like a lamb silent[+] before its shearer, He did not open His mouth. *Isaiah 53:7*

[33] In *Jesus'* humiliation, justice[+] was taken away *and denied to Him*. Who *then* shall declare His generation? *Who can count how long it will last?* For His life has been taken from the earth. *Isaiah 53:8*

[34] The eunuch answered Philip and said: I beg[+] you: About whom is the prophet speaking *in* this? About himself? Or about some other man?

[35] Then Philip opened his mouth and began at the same Scripture and proclaimed[+] Jesus to him.

[36] As they went on *their* way, they came to a certain *body of* water and the eunuch said: See, *here is* water. What hinders me from being baptized?

[37] Philip said: If you believe with all your heart, you may. *The eunuch* answered and said: I believe that Jesus Christ is the Son of God.

[38] *Then the eunuch* commanded the chariot to stop[+] and Philip and the eunuch both went down into the water and *Philip* baptized him.

[39] When they came up out of the water, the Spirit of the Lord caught Philip away *so* that the eunuch no longer[+] saw him, *but* he went on his way rejoicing.

[40] Philip was *later* found at Azotus. Passing through *there* he proclaimed[+] *the Gospel* in all the cities until he came to Caesarea.

Acts Chapter 9

¹ While *Saul was still* breathing out threatenings and slaughter against the disciples of the Lord, he went to the high priest

² and requested⁺ letters from him to the synagogues in Damascus *so* that if he found any of this way, *followers of Christ*, whether they were men or women, he might bring them bound to Jerusalem.

³ As he journeyed, he came near Damascus and suddenly a light from heaven shined *down* on⁺ him.

⁴ He fell to the ground and heard a voice saying to him: Saul, Saul, why do you persecute me?

⁵ He said: Who are you, Lord? The Lord said: I am Jesus whom you persecute. *It is* hard for you to kick against the pricks.

⁶ Trembling and astonished, *Saul* said: Lord, what will you have me to do? The Lord *said* to him: Arise and go into the city and it will be told *to* you what you must do.

⁷ The men who traveled with him stood speechless, hearing a voice, but seeing no one.

⁸ Saul arose from the ground and when he opened his eyes he saw no one, *for he was blind* but they led him by the hand and took *him* to Damascus.

⁹ He was three days without sight and neither ate nor drank.

¹⁰There was a certain disciple at Damascus named Ananias. In a vision, the Lord said to him: Ananias. And he said: Behold I *am here*, Lord.

¹¹The Lord *said* to him: Arise, and go to the street called Straight and inquire in the house of Judas for *one* called Saul of Tarsus. For behold, he is praying *there*.

¹²In a vision, *he* has seen a man named Ananias coming in and putting *his* hand on him *so* that he might receive his sight.

¹³Then Ananias answered: Lord, I have heard from many *people* about this man, how much evil he has done to your saints at Jerusalem.

¹⁴Here he has authority from the chief priests to bind all who call on your name.

¹⁵But the Lord said to him: Go *to him*, for he is a chosen vessel to me, to bear my name before the Gentiles and kings and the children of Israel.

¹⁶For I will show him what *great things* he must suffer for my name's sake.

¹⁷*So,* Ananias went away⁺ and entered the house. Putting his hands on *Saul, he* said: Brother Saul, the Lord Jesus who appeared to you on the way as you came has sent me *so* that you might receive your sight and be filled with the Holy Spirit.

¹⁸Immediately *something like* scales fell from *Saul's* eyes and he received sight immediately⁺ and arose and was baptized.

¹⁹Then he received *some* food⁺ and was strengthened and *he remained* a few days with the disciples at Damascus.

²⁰Immediately⁺ he proclaimed⁺ Christ in the synagogues, *confidently declaring* that *surely Jesus* is the Son of God.

²¹But all who heard *him* were amazed and said: Is this not the one who destroyed *those* who called on *Jesus* name in Jerusalem? And *did he not* come here intending to take them bound to the chief priests?

²²Yet Saul increased *all* the more in strength and confounded the Jews who lived⁺ at Damascus, *thus* proving that this *surely* is *the work of the* very Christ.

²³After many days were fulfilled, the Jews took counsel *together* to kill *Saul*.

²⁴Saul knew that they were waiting and *that* they watched the gates day and night *for an opportunity* to kill him.

²⁵So the disciples took *Saul* by night and let *him* down by the wall in a basket.

²⁶When Saul had *first* come to Jerusalem, he tried⁺ to join himself to the disciples, but they were all afraid of him and did not believe that he was a disciple.

²⁷But Barnabas brought *Saul* to the apostles, and declared to them how he had seen the Lord in the way and that He had spoken to him and how he had boldly proclaimed⁺ the name of Jesus in Damascus.

²⁸He was with them coming in and going out at Jerusalem.

²⁹He spoke boldly in the name of the Lord Jesus and disputed against the Greeks, but they went about to slay him.

³⁰When the brothers knew *about* this, they brought *Saul* down to Caesarea and sent him forth to Tarsus.

³¹Then the assemblies⁺ throughout all Judea and Galilee and Samaria were *at* rest and edified. Walking in the fear of the Lord, and in the comfort of the Holy Spirit, were multiplied.

³²*Now* it came to pass, as Peter passed throughout all *quarters*, he came to the saints who lived⁺ at Lydda.

³³There he found a certain man named Aeneas who had stayed in bed *for* eight years and was sick with paralysis.⁺

³⁴Peter said to him: Aeneas, Jesus Christ makes you whole. Arise and make your bed. And he arose immediately.

³⁵All who lived⁺ at Lydda and Saron saw him, and turned to the Lord.

³⁶Now at Joppa, there was a certain disciple named Tabitha who was *also* known⁺ *as* Dorcas. This woman was full of good works and alms deeds that she did.

³⁷*But* it came to pass in those days that she *became* sick and died. After they washed *her*, they laid *her* in an upper chamber.

³⁸Since⁺ Lydda was near to Joppa, and the disciples had heard that Peter was there, they sent two men to him to ask that he come to them without delay.

³⁹Then Peter arose and went with them. When he arrived, they took him into the upper chamber. All the widows stood by him weeping and showing the coats and garments that Dorcas made while she was with them.

⁴⁰But Peter sent them all out *of the room* and knelt down and prayed. Turning to the body *he* said: Tabitha, arise. She opened her eyes and when she saw Peter, she sat up.

⁴¹He gave her *his* hand and lifted her up, and when he had called the saints and widows, *he* presented her alive.

⁴²*All* this was *made* known throughout all Joppa and many believed in the Lord.

⁴³*Then* it came to pass that he stayed many days in Joppa with Simon, a tanner.

Acts Chapter 10

¹ There was a certain man in Caesarea called Cornelius, a centurion of the company⁺ *of soldiers* called the Italian *company*.

² *Cornelius was a* devout *man* who revered⁺ God, with all his house. *He* gave many alms to the people and prayed to God always.

³ About three o'clock⁺ *in the afternoon*, in a vision he clearly⁺ saw an angel of God coming in to him and saying to him: Cornelius.

⁴ When *Cornelius* looked at *the angel*, he was afraid and said: What is it, Lord? *The angel* said to him: Your prayers and your alms have come up for a memorial before God.

⁵ Now send men to Joppa and call for Simon whose surname is Peter.

⁶ He is staying⁺ with Simon the tanner whose house is by the seaside. He will tell you what you ought to do.

⁷ After the angel who spoke to Cornelius departed, he called two of his household servants and a devout soldier *who faithfully* served him.

⁸ After he explained all *these* things to them, he sent them to Joppa.

⁹ On the next day as they went on their journey and drew near to the city, Peter went up on the housetop to pray about twelve o'clock⁺ *noon*.

¹⁰He became very hungry and would have eaten, but while they made ready, he fell into a trance.

¹¹*He* saw heaven opened and a vessel like a large sheet knit at the four corners descending to him and let down to the ground.

¹²In this *sheet* were all kinds⁺ of four footed beasts of the earth and wild beasts and creeping things and birds⁺ of the air.

¹³Then a voice came to him *saying*: Rise, Peter. Kill and eat.

[14]But Peter said: *Surely* not, Lord, for I have never eaten anything that is common or unclean.

[15]The voice *spoke* to him again a second time, *saying*: What God has cleansed, you *must* not call common.

[16]This was done three times and the vessel was received up again into heaven.

[17]Now while Peter pondered[+] what this vision that he had seen should mean, behold the men who were sent from Cornelius had made inquiry for Simon's house and stood before the gate.

[18]*They* called and asked if Simon who was surnamed Peter was staying[+] there.

[19]While Peter thought about this vision, the Spirit said to him: Behold three men seek you.

[20]Therefore arise. Get down and go with them, doubting nothing. For I have sent them.

[21]Then Peter went down to the men who were sent to him from Cornelius and said: Behold I am *he* whom you seek. What*is* the reason[+] *that* you have come?

[22]They said: Cornelius the centurion, a righteous[+] man, one who fears God and *is* of good report among all the nation of the Jews, was warned from God by a holy angel to send for you *and ask you to come* to his house and to hear words from you.

[23]Then *Peter* invited[+] them in and lodged *them*. On the next day, Peter went away with them and certain brothers from Joppa accompanied him.

[24]The next day,[+] they entered Caesarea. Cornelius *was* waiting for them and *he* had called together his relatives[+] and close friends.

[25]As Peter was coming in, Cornelius met him and fell down at his feet and worshiped *him*.

[26]But Peter lifted[+] him up saying: Stand up. I myself am also a man.

[27]As *Peter* talked with *Cornelius*, he went in and found many who had come together.

[28]He said to them: You know that it is an unlawful thing for a man who is a Jew to keep company or come to one of another nation. But God has shown me that I should not call anyone common or unclean.

[29]Therefore I came *to you* without dispute[+] as soon as I was sent for. I ask therefore, for what intent have you sent for me?

[30]Cornelius said: Four days ago, I was fasting until this hour. At three o'clock[+] *in the afternoon*, I prayed in my house and behold, a man stood before me in bright clothing.

[31]*He* said: Cornelius, your prayer is heard and your alms are remembered in the sight of God.

[32]Therefore, send to Joppa and call Simon whose surname is Peter *to come* here. He is staying at the house of Simon the tanner by the seaside. When he comes, *he* will speak to you.

[33]Therefore, I immediately sent for you. You have done well *to* have come. Therefore we are now all here, present before God, to hear all things that are commanded *to* you by God.

[34]Then Peter opened *his* mouth and said: Truly I perceive that God is not *a discriminating* respecter of persons.

[35]But in every nation, *those* who fear Him and work righteousness are accepted by Him.

[36]The Word that *God* sent to the children of Israel proclaiming[+] peace by Jesus Christ who is Lord of all,

[37]that Word you know. It was published throughout all Judea, beginning in Galilee after the baptism that John proclaimed[+]:

[38]God anointed Jesus of Nazareth with the Holy Spirit and with power. *He* went about doing good and healing all who were oppressed by the devil. For God was with Him. *Matthew 3:16*

[39]We are witnesses of everything[+] *that* He did, both in the land of the Jews and in Jerusalem. *It was this Jesus* they killed[+] and hung on a tree.

[40]*But* God raised Him up the third day and showed Him openly.

[41]Not to all the people, but to witnesses chosen before by God, *even* to *those of* us

who ate and drank with Him after He rose from the dead.

⁴²He commanded us to proclaim⁺ *the Word* to the people and to testify that it is He who was ordained by God *to be* the Judge of *the* quick and *the* dead.

⁴³All the prophets gave witness to Him, that through His name, whoever believes in Him shall receive remission of sins.

⁴⁴While Peter spoke these words, the Holy Spirit fell on all who heard the Word.

⁴⁵Those of the circumcision who believed were astonished, *including* all⁺ *who* came with Peter, because the gift of the Holy Spirit was poured out on the Gentiles also.

⁴⁶For they heard them speak with tongues and magnify God. Then Peter answered:

⁴⁷Can anyone forbid water, *so* that these who have received the Holy Spirit as well as we *have* should not be baptized?

⁴⁸And he commanded them *all* to be baptized in the name of the Lord. Then they asked⁺ him to stay⁺ *with them for* a few days.

Acts Chapter 11

¹ The apostles and family⁺ in Judea *soon* heard that the Gentiles had also received the Word of God.

² *So* when Peter came up to Jerusalem, *those* of the circumcision contended with him,

³ saying: You went in to uncircumcised men and ate with them.

⁴ But Peter reviewed *the matter with them* from the beginning and explained⁺ *it* to them in detail⁺ saying:

⁵ I was in the city of Joppa praying. In a trance I saw a vision *of* a certain vessel like a great sheet descend, let down from heaven by four corners. It came *directly* to me.

⁶ When I fastened my eyes on it, I looked⁺ *inside* and saw four footed beasts of the earth and wild beasts and creeping things and birds⁺ of the air.

⁷ *Then* I heard a voice say to me, Arise, Peter. Slay and eat.

⁸ But I said: *Surely* not, Lord, for nothing common or unclean has *ever* entered my mouth at any time.

⁹ But the voice answered again from heaven, *saying*: What God has cleansed, do not call common.

¹⁰This was done three times. *Then* everything⁺ was drawn up again into heaven.

¹¹And behold immediately there were three men *who had* already come to the house where I was *staying*, sent from Caesarea to me.

¹²The Spirit told me *to* go with them, not doubting *anything*. These six brothers also accompanied me and we entered the man's house.

¹³He told⁺ us how he had seen an angel in his house, who stood and said to him: Send men to Joppa and call for Simon whose surname is Peter.

¹⁴*Peter* will tell you words by which you and all your house will be saved.

¹⁵As I began to speak, the Holy Spirit fell upon them, as *it did* upon us at the beginning.

¹⁶Then I remembered the Word of the Lord, that He said: John indeed baptized with water, but you shall be baptized with the Holy Spirit.

¹⁷Since⁺ God gave them the same⁺ gift as *He did* to us who believed on the Lord Jesus Christ, who was I that I could withstand God?

¹⁸When they heard these things, they *remained* silent⁺ and glorified God saying: Then God has also granted repentance to *eternal* life to the Gentiles.

¹⁹Now *those* who were scattered *because* of the persecution that arose about Stephen traveled as far as Phoenicia, Cyprus, and Antioch, proclaiming⁺ the Word, but only to the Jews *and* to no one *else*.

²⁰Some of them were men of Cyprus and Cyrene, who, when they had come to Antioch, spoke to the Greeks, proclaiming⁺ the Lord Jesus.

²¹The hand of the Lord was with them and a great number believed and turned to the Lord.

²²Then news⁺ of *all* this came to the assembly⁺ in Jerusalem and they sent forth Barnabas to go as far as Antioch.
²³When he came and saw the grace of God, *he* was glad and exhorted them all, that with purpose of heart they should *be* joined⁺ *close* to the Lord.
²⁴For *Barnabas* was a good man, full of the Holy Spirit and faith and many people were added to the Lord.
²⁵Then Barnabas went to Tarsus to look for Saul.
²⁶When he found him, he brought him *back* to Antioch, and it came to pass that *for* a whole year they joined⁺ with the assembly⁺ *of believers* there and taught many people. And the disciples were called Christians first *there* in Antioch.
²⁷In these days, prophets came from Jerusalem to Antioch.
²⁸One of them named Agabus stood up and signified by the Spirit that there would be *a* great famine⁺ throughout all the world. This *soon* came to pass in the days of Claudius Caesar.
²⁹Therefore, the disciples determined *that* everyone, according to their ability, should send relief to the family⁺ who lived⁺ in Judea.
³⁰*So* they did *this* and sent it to the elders by the hands of Barnabas and Saul.

Acts Chapter 12

¹ Now about that time, Herod the king stretched forth *his* hands to harass⁺ some of the assemblies⁺ *of believers*.
² He killed James the brother of John with the sword.
³ When he saw *that* this pleased the Jews, he proceeded further to take Peter also. This *occurred during* the days *known as the Feast* of Unleavened Bread. *Exodus 12:18*
⁴ After *Herod* apprehended *Peter*, he put *him* in prison and sent four squads⁺ of soldiers to keep him *there*, intending to bring him forth to the people after Passover.⁺
⁵ While Peter was kept in prison, the assembly⁺ *of believers* prayed to God without ceasing for him.

⁶ *On* the night when Herod *had intended* to bring him forth, Peter was sleeping between two soldiers, bound with two chains *and* keepers by the door kept the prison *secure*.
⁷ But *then* behold, the angel of the Lord came upon *Peter* and a light shined in the prison. *The angel* touched⁺ Peter on the side and raised him up saying: Arise up quickly. *Instantly*, *Peter's* chains fell from *his* hands.
⁸ The angel said to him: Prepare⁺ yourself and put⁺ on your sandals. And so he did. *Then the angel* said to *Peter*: Put⁺ on your garment and follow me.
⁹ *Peter* followed *the angel*, but *he* did not understand⁺ that what was done by the angel was real.⁺ *He* thought *that* he had seen a vision.
¹⁰After they went past the first and the second ward, they came to the iron gate that leads to the city. It opened for them of its own accord and they went out and passed by one street. Then⁺ the angel departed from him.
¹¹When Peter came to himself, he said: Now I know with certainty⁺ that the Lord sent His angel and delivered me out of the hand of Herod and *from* all the expectations of the Jews.
¹²After he had considered *this*, he went to the house of Mary the mother of John, whose surname was Mark where many *believers* had gathered together praying.
¹³As Peter knocked at the door of the gate, a girl⁺ named Rhoda came to listen carefully⁺ *to see who was there*.
¹⁴When she recognized⁺ Peter's voice, she did not open the gate but in *her* excitement⁺ *she* ran in and told *the others* that Peter was standing at the gate.
¹⁵They said to her: You *must be* mistaken.⁺ But she constantly affirmed that it was true.⁺ Then they said: It is his angel.
¹⁶But Peter continued knocking *and* when they opened *the door* and saw him, they were astonished.
¹⁷*Peter* signaled⁺ to them with his hand to *remain* silent⁺ *and he* described⁺ to them how the Lord had brought him out of the prison. Then he said: Go *and*

report[+] these things to James and to the family.[+] And he departed and went to another place.

[18] Now as soon as it was day, there was no small stir among the soldiers, *wondering* what had become of Peter.

[19] When Herod sought *Peter* and did not find him, he questioned[+] the keepers and *then* commanded that *they* should be put to death. *Then* he went from Judea down to Caesarea and stayed *there*.

[20] Now, *during this time* Herod was highly displeased with the *people* of Tyre and Sidon. But they came to him with one accord and sought[+] peace *with him*. They had *already* made Blastus the king's chamberlain their friend because their country was supplied[+] *with food* by the king's *country*.

[21] *Therefore* on the appointed[+] day, Herod dressed[+] in *his* royal apparel, sat upon his throne, and made an oration to them.

[22] The people gave a shout, *saying: It is* the voice of *a* god and not *of a* man.

[23] Immediately, the angel of the Lord struck[+] *Herod down* because he did not give God the glory, and he died[+] and was eaten by worms.

[24] But the Word of God grew and multiplied.

[25] *Meanwhile*, when Barnabas and Saul had fulfilled *their* ministry, they returned from Jerusalem and *they* took John, whose surname was Mark, with them.

Acts Chapter 13

[1] In the assembly[+] *of believers* at Antioch, there were certain prophets and teachers *including* Barnabas, Simeon who was called Niger, Lucius of Cyrene, Manaen, who had been brought up with Herod the tetrarch, and Saul.

[2] As they ministered to the Lord and fasted, the Holy Spirit said: Separate Barnabas and Saul for the work to which I have called them.

[3] *Therefore*, after they fasted and prayed, *they* laid hands on them *and* sent *them on* their way.

[4] Being *thus* sent forth by the Holy Spirit, they departed to Seleucia, *and* from there[+] they sailed to Cyprus.

[5] While they were in Salamis, they proclaimed[+] the Word of God in the synagogues of the Jews. They also had John as *their* minister *there*.

[6] As they went through the island[+] of Paphos, they encountered[+] sorcerer *and* a false prophet, a Jew whose name *was* Barjesus.

[7] *He* was with the deputy of the country, Sergius Paulus, a prudent man who called for Barnabas and Saul and desired to hear the Word of God.

[8] But Elymas the sorcerer as his name is interpreted, opposed[+] them, seeking to turn the deputy away from the faith.

[9] Then Saul, who *is now also called* Paul, filled with the Holy Spirit, set his eyes on him,

[10] and said: *You* child of the devil, *you* enemy of righteousness, *you are* full of deceit[+] and mischief. Will you not stop[+] perverting the right ways of the Lord?

[11] Now behold, the hand of the Lord *is* upon you and you shall be blind *and you will* not see the sun for a season. Immediately a mist and a darkness fell on him *and* he went around seeking some to lead him by the hand.

[12] When the deputy saw what was done, *he* believed *and* was astonished at the doctrine of the Lord.

[13] Now when Paul and his company left[+] Paphos, they went to Perga in Pamphylia *and* John left[+] them *and* returned to Jerusalem.

[14] When they left[+] Perga, they went to Antioch in Pisidia, and went into the synagogue on the Sabbath day and sat down.

[15] After the reading of the law and the prophets, the rulers of the synagogue said to them: Men *and* family,[+] if you have any word of exhortation for the people, speak *freely*.

[16] Then Paul stood up and, signaling[+] with *his* hand, *he* said: Men of Israel and you who fear God, *please* listen.

[17] The God of this people of Israel chose our fathers and exalted the people when

they lived[+] as strangers in the land of Egypt, and with a high arm He brought them out of it.

[18]For forty years, He endured[+] their behavior[+] in the wilderness.

[19]After He destroyed seven nations in the land of Canaan, He divided that land to them by lot.

[20]After that He gave *them* judges for four hundred and fifty years, until Samuel the prophet.

[21]Then they wanted a king, *so* God gave God gave to them Saul the son of Kish, a man of the tribe of Benjamin, for forty years. *1 Samuel 9:17*

[22]When *God* removed *Saul*, He *then* raised up David for them to be their king. And to *David* He gave *this* testimony and said: I have found David the *son* of Jesse *to be* a man after my own heart, *someone* who will fulfill all *of* my will. *1 Samuel 13:14*

[23]From this man's seed, God has raised *up* to Israel a Savior, Jesus *Christ* according to *His* promise. *Psalm 132:11*

[24]Before *Christ* came, John first proclaimed[+] the baptism of repentance to all the people of Israel. *Matthew 3:2*

[25]As John fulfilled his course, he said: Who do you think that I am? I am not *the Messiah*. But behold, one is coming after me the sandals[+] of whose feet I am not worthy to loosen. *Matthew 3:11*

[26]Men *and* family,[+] children of the stock of Abraham, and whoever among you fears God: The Word of this salvation is *now* sent to you.

[27]But *those* who live in Jerusalem and their rulers, because they did not know *Jesus* or the voices of the prophets who are read every Sabbath day, they fulfilled *those prophets' words* by condemning *Him*.

[28]Although they found no cause *in Him* for death, yet *even so* they wanted Pilate to execute[+] Him.

[29]*Then* when they had fulfilled all that was written about Him, they took *Him* down from the tree and laid *Him* in a tomb.[+]

[30]But God raised Him from the dead.

[31]He was seen *for* many days by *those* who came up with Him from Galilee to Jerusalem *and* they are His witnesses to the people.

[32]*Now* we declare to you *the* glad tidings, that the promise that was made to the fathers,

[33]God has fulfilled to us, their children, in that He has raised up Jesus again, as it is also written in the second psalm: You are my Son. This day I have begotten you. *Psalm 2:7*

[34]Now concerning *the fact* that *God* raised *Jesus* up from the dead, no longer[+] to return to *the decay and* corruption *of this world*, *God* said this: I will give you the sure mercies of David. *Isaiah 55:3*

[35]And, in another *psalm* He also said: You will not allow[+] your Holy One to see corruption *and decay*. *Psalm 16:10*

[36]After David had served his own generation according[+] to the will of God, *he* fell asleep and was laid to *rest with* his fathers, and saw corruption *and decay*.

[37]But *Jesus* whom God raised again saw no corruption *or decay*.

[38]Therefore be it known to you, men *and* family,[+] that through this man, forgiveness of sins is proclaimed[+] to you.

[39]All who believe *in Jesus* are justified from all things. From *all of this*, you could not be justified by the law of Moses.

[40]*Therefore* take heed[+] so that what was spoken by the prophets does not come upon you.

[41]Behold you despisers and wonder and perish. For I *will* work a work in your days, a work that you will not[+] believe, *even* though a man declare it to you. *Habakkuk 1:5*

[42]After the Jews left the synagogue, the Gentiles begged[+] that these words might be proclaimed[+] to them the next Sabbath.

[43]When the congregation was concluded,[+] many of the Jews and worshiping[+] converts[+] followed Paul and Barnabas, speaking with them *and* encouraging[+] them to continue in the grace of God.

[44]*On* the next Sabbath day almost the whole city came together to hear the Word of God.

[45]But when the Jews saw the multitudes,

they were filled with envy and spoke against those things that were spoken by Paul, contradicting and blaspheming.

⁴⁶Then Paul and Barnabas grew⁺ bold and said: It was necessary that the Word of God should first have been spoken to you, but since you put it *away* from you and judge yourselves unworthy of eternal⁺ life, behold, we turn to the Gentiles.

⁴⁷For the Lord has commanded us, *saying*: I have set you to be a light to the Gentiles, *so* that you should be *proclaiming* salvation to the ends of the earth.

Isaiah 49:6

⁴⁸When the Gentiles heard this, they were glad and glorified the Word of the Lord. And many believed *and were* ordained to eternal life.

⁴⁹The Word of the Lord was *then* published throughout all the region.

⁵⁰But the Jews stirred up the prominent⁺ religious⁺ women and chief men of the city and inflamed⁺ persecution against Paul and Barnabas and expelled them out of their borders.⁺

⁵¹But they shook off the dust from their feet against them and went to Iconium.

⁵²*And* the disciples were filled with joy and with the Holy Spirit.

Acts Chapter 14

¹ *While* in Iconium, *Paul and Barnabas* went into the synagogue of the Jews and spoke so that a great multitude of both Jews and Greeks believed.

² But the unbelieving Jews stirred up the Gentiles and *caused them to have* evil thoughts⁺ against *Paul and Barnabas*.

³ Yet they stayed⁺ *there for* a long time, speaking boldly in the Lord. This testified to the Word of *God's* grace and *He* granted signs and wonders to be done by their hands.

⁴ But the multitude of the city was divided. Part held with the Jews and part with the apostles.

⁵ Then an assault *was planned* by both the Gentiles and the Jews *and* their rulers, to mistreat⁺ *them* and stone them.

⁶ *Paul and Barnabas* were aware of *this*

and *so they* fled to Lystra and Derbe, cities of Lycaonia, and to the surrounding⁺ region

⁷ *and* proclaimed⁺ the Gospel there.

⁸ In Lystra, a disabled⁺ man sat *by the way*. His feet had been crippled from his mother's womb *and he* had never walked.

⁹ As this *man* heard Paul speak, *Paul* looked at him steadfastly and perceived that he had faith to be healed.

¹⁰*So* Paul said with a loud voice: Stand upright on your feet. And *the crippled man* leaped *up* and walked.

¹¹When the people saw what Paul had done, they raised⁺ their voices, saying in the speech of Lycaonia: The gods have come down to us in the likeness of men.

¹²They called Barnabas, Jupiter *and* Paul, Mercurius, because he was the chief speaker.

¹³Then the priest of Jupiter, *whose temple* was near⁺ their city, brought oxen and garlands to the gates, and wanted⁺ to make⁺ a sacrifice with the people.

¹⁴When the apostles Barnabas and Paul, heard *this*, they tore⁺ their clothes and ran in among the people, crying out,

¹⁵saying: Sirs, why do you *do* these things? We also are men of like passions with you, and *we* proclaim⁺ to you to turn *away* from these vain *things* to the living God who made heaven and earth and the sea and everything that is therein.

¹⁶In times past, *God* allowed⁺ all nations to walk in their own ways.

¹⁷Nevertheless He did not leave Himself without a witness in that He did good and gave us rain from heaven and fruitful seasons, filling our hearts with food and gladness.

¹⁸But saying these *things* scarcely restrained the multitudes⁺ *to* not *make a* sacrifice to them.

¹⁹Then *certain* Jews from Antioch and Iconium came and persuaded the people, and after *they* stoned Paul, *they* dragged⁺ *him* out of the city, supposing *that* he was dead.

²⁰However, as the disciples stood around⁺ *Paul*, he rose up and went *back*

into the city. The next day he departed with Barnabas to Derbe.

²¹After they had proclaimed⁺ the Gospel to that city and taught many, they returned again to Lystra and *to* Iconium and Antioch.

²²*They* reassured⁺ the souls of the disciples *and* exhorted them to continue in the faith, *telling them* that *often* we must *go* through much tribulation *in order to* enter into the kingdom of God.

²³After they had ordained elders in every assembly⁺ *of believers* and prayed with fasting, they commended them to the Lord in whom they believed.

²⁴*And then*, after they had passed throughout Pisidia, they came to Pamphylia.

²⁵When they had proclaimed⁺ the Word in Perga, they went down into Attalia.

²⁶From there⁺ *they* sailed *back* to Antioch, from where they had been recommended to the grace of God for the work that they fulfilled.

²⁷When they returned,⁺ they gathered the assembly⁺ together *and* reviewed⁺ all that God had done through⁺ them and how He had opened the door of faith to the Gentiles.

²⁸And they stayed⁺ with the disciples there *for* a long time.

Acts Chapter 15

¹ Certain men *then* came down from Judea *and* taught the family⁺ *saying*: Unless⁺ you are circumcised after the manner of Moses, you cannot be saved.

² *This brought great* dissension and therefore Paul and Barnabas had no small dispute with them. *So*, they decided⁺ that Paul and Barnabas and certain others of them should go to Jerusalem to the apostles and elders about this question.

³ *So*, the assembly⁺ *of believers* sent them on. *As* they passed through Phoenicia and Samaria, *they* described the conversion of the Gentiles *and this* caused great joy to all the family.⁺

⁴ When they arrived⁺ at Jerusalem, they were received by the assembly⁺ and *by* the apostles and elders, and they reported⁺ all *the* things that God had done through⁺ them.

⁵ But some of the Pharisees who *had become* believers stood⁺ *up* and said that *they believed that* it was necessary⁺ to circumcise them and to instruct⁺ *them* to keep the law of Moses.

⁶ *So* the apostles and elders came together to consider this matter.

⁷ After there had been much disputing, Peter rose up and said to them: Men *and* family,⁺ you know that a good while ago God made *a* choice among us, that from my mouth, the Gentiles should hear the Word of the Gospel and believe.

⁸ God, who knows the hearts, bore witness *of* them *by* giving them the Holy Spirit, even as *He did* to us.

⁹ *He* made no difference between them and us, purifying their hearts by faith.

¹⁰Therefore, why do you now test⁺ God, by putting a yoke upon the neck of the disciples, which neither our fathers nor we were able to bear?

¹¹But we believe that *it is* through the grace of the Lord Jesus Christ *that* we will be saved, even as they *surely have been*.

¹²Then all the multitude kept silent and gave *their* attention⁺ to Barnabas and Paul *who* described⁺ *the many* miracles and wonders *that* God had worked⁺ among the Gentiles through them.

¹³After they stopped⁺ speaking,⁺ James answered saying: Men *and* family,⁺ listen carefully⁺ to me.

¹⁴Simon *Peter* has declared how God first visited the Gentiles to take from *among* them a people for His name.

¹⁵To this the words of the prophets agree. As it is written:

¹⁶After this I will return and will build again the tabernacle of David, which is fallen down. I will build again from those ruins and I will set it up. *Amos 9:11*

¹⁷Thereby *all* the rest⁺ of mankind⁺ might *also* seek the Lord, *including* all the Gentiles who are called by my name. *Thus* spoke the Lord *Himself* who does all these things. *Amos 9:12*

¹⁸*Surely* God knows *about* all His works from the beginning of the world.

¹⁹ Therefore my judgment⁺ is that we should not trouble *those* who have turned to God from among the Gentiles.

²⁰ But we *should* write to *instruct* them that they *must* abstain from *the* pollutions of idols and *from* fornication and *from* things strangled and *from* blood.

²¹ For *many* long generations,⁺ Moses has had in every city *those* who proclaim⁺ his *writings as they are* read in the synagogues every Sabbath day.

²² Then it seemed good⁺ to the apostles and elders *and* with the whole assembly⁺ to send chosen men of their own company to Antioch with Paul and Barnabas, *namely* Jude surnamed Barsabas and Silas, *who were* leading⁺ men in the family.⁺

²³ They wrote this *letter to send with them: The apostles, elders, and family*⁺ *here send* greetings to the family⁺ of Gentiles in Antioch, Syria, and Cilicia.

²⁴ Since⁺ we have heard, that certain *ones* who came *to you* from us have troubled you with *their* words, subverting your souls *by* saying *that you must* be circumcised and keep the law, *we want to inform you that* we gave no *such* commandment.

²⁵ It seemed good to us, being assembled with one accord, to send *these* chosen men to you *along* with our beloved Barnabas and Paul.

²⁶ *These* men have risked⁺ their lives for the name of our Lord Jesus Christ.

²⁷ Therefore we have sent Jude and Silas who will also tell *you* the same things by *their own* mouths.

²⁸ For it seemed good to the Holy Spirit and to us to lay upon you no greater burden than these necessary things:

²⁹ Abstain from meats offered to idols and from blood and from things strangled and from fornication. If you keep yourselves from these, you will do well. Fare well.

³⁰ So when they were dismissed, they went to Antioch *and* when they had gathered the multitude together, they delivered the epistle.

³¹ When it was read, they *all* rejoiced for the consolation.

³² Jude and Silas, also being prophets, exhorted the family⁺ with many words, and confirmed *them*.

³³ After they stayed *there for* a while, they returned⁺ in peace to the apostles.

³⁴ *But* Silas decided⁺ to remain there.

³⁵ Paul and Barnabas also continued teaching and proclaiming⁺ the Word of the Lord in Antioch, *along* with many others.

³⁶ Some days later, Paul said to Barnabas: Let us go again and visit our family⁺ in every city where we have proclaimed⁺ the Word of the Lord, *and see* how they are doing.

³⁷ Barnabas decided⁺ to take John, whose surname was Mark, with them.

³⁸ But Paul thought *it would* not *be* good to take *Mark* with them, *because* he had left⁺ them in Pamphylia and did not go with them to *finish* the work.

³⁹ The disagreement⁺ between them was so sharp that they parted⁺ from one another. So Barnabas took Mark and sailed to Cyprus.

⁴⁰ Paul chose Silas and left,⁺ being recommended by the family⁺ to the grace of God.

⁴¹ He went through Syria and Cilicia, confirming the assemblies⁺ *of believers*.

Acts Chapter 16

¹ Then *Paul* went to Derbe and Lystra. And behold a certain disciple named Timothy was there. *Timothy* was the son of a Jewish woman who was a believer *and* a Greek father

² who was well thought⁺ of by the family⁺ at Lystra and Iconium.

³ Paul wanted⁺ *Timothy* to go with him, *so* he took him *to be* circumcised because of the Jews who were in that area,⁺ for they all knew that his father was a Greek.

⁴ As they went through the cities, they delivered *to* them the decrees to *be* kept that had been ordained by the apostles and elders in Jerusalem.

⁵ *In this way* the assemblies⁺ *of believers* were established in the faith, and *they* increased in number daily.

⁶ When they went throughout Phrygia and the region of Galatia, *they* were forbidden by the Holy Spirit to proclaim⁺ the Word in Asia.

⁷ After they came to Mysia, they tried⁺ to go into Bithynia, but the Spirit did not allow⁺ them *to go*.

⁸ *So* they passed by Mysia and went to Troas.

⁹ *Then* a vision appeared to Paul in the night *in which* a man of Macedonia begged⁺ him saying: Come over to Macedonia and help us.

¹⁰ After seeing the vision, we immediately endeavored to go to Macedonia, assuredly gathering that the Lord had called us to proclaim⁺ the Gospel to them.

¹¹ Therefore sailing⁺ from Troas, we went with a straight course to Samothracia and the next *day* to Neapolis.

¹² From there⁺ *we went* to Philippi, which is the chief city in that part of Macedonia *and* a colony. We stayed⁺ in that city *for* several⁺ days.

¹³ On the Sabbath, we went out of the city by a river side *and* prayed, as was our custom,⁺ and we sat down and spoke to the women *there*.

¹⁴ A certain woman named Lydia, a seller of purple from the city of Thyatira, who worshiped God, heard *us*. The Lord opened *her* heart *so* that she *was very* attentive⁺ *to* the things that Paul said.

¹⁵ Therefore she and *all of* her household were baptized *and* she begged⁺ *us* saying: If you have judged me to be faithful to the Lord, come to my house and stay⁺ *there*. And *so* she convinced⁺ us.

¹⁶ *Now,* it came to pass, as we went to prayer, *that* a certain girl⁺ possessed with a spirit of divination met us. *This* girl brought her masters much gain by soothsaying.

¹⁷ The *girl* followed Paul and us and cried *out* saying: These men are servants of the most high God who show the way of salvation to us.

¹⁸ She did this *for* many days. But Paul, being grieved, turned and said to the spirit: I command you in the name of Jesus Christ to come out of her. And *the* spirit came out *of the girl* that same hour.

¹⁹ When *the girl's* masters saw that their hope of gains was gone, they caught Paul and Silas and took⁺ them to the marketplace to the rulers.

²⁰ *They* took⁺ them to the highest officials⁺ saying: These men, being Jews, exceedingly trouble our city.

²¹ *They* teach customs that are not lawful for us to receive or observe *since we are* Romans.

²² *Therefore* the crowd⁺ rose up against them *and* the highest officials⁺ tore⁺ off their clothes and commanded *that they be* beaten.

²³ After they laid many whippings⁺ on them, they cast *them* into prison, *and* charged the jailer to keep them secured.⁺

²⁴ Having received *this* charge, *he* threw⁺ them into the inner prison and fastened their feet in the stocks.

²⁵ At midnight Paul and Silas prayed and sang praises to God *so that all* the *other* prisoners heard them.

²⁶ Suddenly there was a great earthquake so that the foundations of the prison were shaken. Immediately all the doors were opened, and everyone's chains⁺ were loosed.

²⁷ *When* the keeper of the prison awoke out of his sleep and saw the prison doors open, he drew out his sword and would have killed himself, supposing that the prisoners had fled.

²⁸ But Paul cried *out* with a loud voice saying: Do yourself no harm, for we are all here.

²⁹ *So the jailer* called for a light, got up,⁺ came trembling, and fell down before Paul and Silas.

³⁰ *Then he* brought them out and said: Sirs, what must I do to be saved?

³¹ They said: Believe on the Lord Jesus Christ and you will be saved, *you* and your *entire* household.⁺

³² They spoke the Word of the Lord to him and to all who were in his house.

³³ *Then the jailer* took them, *at* that same hour of the night, and washed *their* wounds⁺ *and* he and all his *family* were baptized immediately.⁺

³⁴Then he took them into his house, sat food⁺ before them, and rejoiced, believing in God *along* with all *the rest of* his household.
³⁵When it was day, the highest officials⁺ sent the sergeants saying: Let those men go.
³⁶The keeper of the prison *then* reported⁺ this to Paul, saying: The highest officials⁺ have sent *instructions* to let you go. Therefore, *you may* now leave⁺ and go in peace.
³⁷But Paul said to them: They have beaten us openly uncondemned, being Romans, and have cast *us* into prison. Now do they thrust us out privately⁺? No truly,⁺ but let them come themselves and fetch us out.
³⁸The sergeants reported⁺ these words to the highest officials⁺ *and* they *became very* fearful when they heard that *Paul and Silas* were Roman *citizens*.
³⁹*So the officials then personally* came and begged⁺ them and brought *them* out and asked⁺ *them* to leave⁺ their city.
⁴⁰*Then Paul and Silas* left the prison and went⁺ *to* Lydia's *house*. When they saw the family,⁺ they comforted them, and *then* departed.

Acts Chapter 17

¹ After *Paul and Silas* passed through Amphipolis and Apollonia, they came to Thessalonica where was a synagogue of the Jews.
² *Keeping* his *usual* custom,⁺ Paul went in to them and *for* three Sabbath days *he* reasoned with them from the Scriptures.
³ *He* opened *the Scripture* and showed⁺ *them* that *it was* necessary⁺ *for* Christ to suffer and rise again from the dead. *And he said:* This Jesus I proclaim⁺ to you, is Christ.
⁴ Some of them believed and joined⁺ with Paul and Silas, *including* a large⁺ number⁺ of the devout Greeks and not a few of the prominent⁺ women.
⁵ But the Jews who did not believe *were* moved with envy. *So they* took *some* evil⁺ fellows *who could be* bought⁺ and gathered a mob⁺ and set all the city in an uproar. *Then they* assaulted the house of Jason and sought to bring out *Paul and Silas* to the people.
⁶ When *the mob* did not find them, they dragged⁺ Jason and certain brothers to the rulers of the city, crying *out*: Those who have turned the world upside down have *now* come here also.
⁷ *And* Jason has received *them*. They all do *things that are* contrary to the decrees of Caesar *by* saying that there is another king, *one called* Jesus.
⁸ This troubled the people and the rulers of the city, when they heard these things.
⁹ *So* when they had taken security from Jason and from the others, they let them go.
¹⁰The family⁺ immediately sent Paul and Silas away by night to Berea. *Upon* arriving,⁺ *they* went into the synagogue of the Jews.
¹¹These *Jews* were more noble than those in Thessalonica, in that they received the Word with all readiness of mind and *they* searched the Scriptures daily *to see* if those things *claimed* were so.
¹²Therefore many of these *Jews* believed *as well as many* prominent⁺ Greek women and not a few *Greek* men.
¹³But when the Jews of Thessalonica learned⁺ that the Word of God was proclaimed⁺ by Paul at Berea, they came there also and stirred up the people.
¹⁴Then immediately the family⁺ urged⁺ Paul to go *on his* way by sea. But Silas and Timothy stayed *at Berea*.
¹⁵*Those* who escorted⁺ Paul took⁺ him to Athens. *And then, after* receiving *instructions* for Silas and Timothy to come to *Paul* with all speed, they departed.
¹⁶While Paul waited for them in Athens, his spirit was stirred in him when he saw the city wholly given to idolatry.
¹⁷Therefore he contended⁺ with the Jews and religious⁺ people in the synagogue and in the market daily with *those* who met with him.
¹⁸Then certain Epicurean and Stoick philosophers confronted⁺ him and said: What is this babbler saying? Others said: He seems to be a proposer⁺ of

strange gods, because he proclaimed[+] Jesus and the resurrection to them.

[19] *So* they took him to *the* Areopagus saying: We *would like to* know what this new doctrine is of which you speak?

[20] For you bring certain strange things to our ears. Therefore, we would *like to* know what these things mean.

[21] For all the Athenians and strangers there spent their time doing nothing else but to tell or hear *about* some new thing.

[22] So Paul stood in the midst of Mars' hill and said: *You* men of Athens, I perceive that in all things you are too superstitious.

[23] For as I passed by and saw[+] *the objects of* your worship,[+] I saw[+] an altar with this inscription: *To the* Unknown God. Therefore, I *now* declare to you *the God whom* you worship *as* unknown.

[24] God who made the world and everything[+] in it, since He is Lord of heaven and earth, does not dwell in temples made by *human* hands.

[25] Neither *is* any worship *or service* needed from human[+] hands. For *God* gives all life and breath *to* all *things*.

[26] *God* has made all nations of mankind to dwell on all the face of the earth from one blood, and *He* has determined *long* ago[+] the times appointed and the boundaries[+] of their habitation.

[27] *God desires* that *all mankind* should seek the Lord. Even *hoping* perhaps[+] *that some will* feel *His presence* and find Him, although He is not far from each of us.

[28] For in Him we live and move and have our being. And as some of your own poets have said: For we also are His offspring.

[29] Since[+] we are the offspring of God, we should not to think that the Godhead is like gold or silver or stone, engraved like art *by* man's devices.

[30] The times of ignorance *in the past* God overlooked,[+] but now *He* commands everyone[+] everywhere to repent.

[31] Because He has appointed a day in which He will judge the world in righteousness by *the* man whom He has ordained. He has given assurance to everyone[+] in that He raised *Jesus* from the dead.

[32] When they heard of the resurrection of the dead, some mocked. Others said: We will hear you again on this *matter*.

[33] So Paul departed from among them.

[34] However certain men joined[+] to him, and believed. Among them *were* Dionysius the Areopagite and a woman named Damaris and others with them.

Acts Chapter 18

[1] After these things Paul left[+] Athens and went to Corinth.

[2] *There, he* found a certain Jew named Aquila, born in Pontus *and* recently[+] come from Italy with his wife Priscilla, because Claudius had commanded all Jews to leave Rome. *Paul* went to them

[3] because he was of the same craft. He stayed[+] and worked[+] with them for in their occupation they were tent makers.

[4] Every Sabbath, *Paul* reasoned in the synagogue, persuading the Jews and the Greeks.

[5] When Silas and Timothy came from Macedonia, Paul was pressed *in the* spirit *to* testify to the Jews *that* Jesus *was indeed the* Christ.

[6] When they opposed *this* and blasphemed, *Paul* shook *his* clothing[+] and said to them: Your blood *be* upon your own heads. I *am* clean. From now on, I will go to the Gentiles.

[7] *So* he departed from there[+] and entered a certain *man's* house, *one* named Justus who worshiped God *and* whose house adjoined[+] the synagogue.

[8] Crispus, the chief ruler of the synagogue *along* with all his household also believed on the Lord. And many other Corinthians *who* heard *also* believed and were baptized.

[9] Then the Lord spoke to Paul by a vision at night, *saying*: Do not be afraid, but speak *out*. Do not keep silent[+].

[10] For I am with you and no one shall set upon you to hurt you, for I have many people in this city.

[11] *Paul* continued *there for* a year and six months, teaching the Word of God among them.

¹²*Then* when Gallio was the deputy of Achaia, the Jews, with one accord, made insurrection against Paul and brought him to the judgment seat.

¹³*They* said: This *man* persuades people+ to worship God contrary to the law.

¹⁴When Paul was about to open *his* mouth, Gallio said to the Jews: If it were a matter of wrong or wicked lewdness, O Jews, *it* would *be* reasonable that I bear with you.

¹⁵However, if it is *merely* a question of words and names and *of* your law, *then* you look *after it*. For I will not judge such *matters*.

¹⁶And he drove them *away* from the judgment seat.

¹⁷Then all the Greeks took Sosthenes, the chief ruler of the synagogue, and beat *him* before the judgment seat. But Gallio did not care *about* these things.

¹⁸*After this*, Paul stayed *there for* many days+ but then *he* left the family+ and sailed to Syria *with* Priscilla and Aquila with him. *Paul* shaved+ *his* head in Cenchrea, for he had *made* a vow.

¹⁹He *then* went to Ephesus and left *Priscilla and Aquila* there while he himself entered the synagogue and reasoned with the Jews.

²⁰When they asked+ *him* to stay+ *a* longer time with them, he did not consent,

²¹but bid them farewell saying: I must by all means keep this feast that comes in Jerusalem. But I will return to you again, if *it is* God's will. Then he sailed from Ephesus.

²²After he landed at Caesarea, he went up and greeted+ the assembly,+ *and then* he went down to Antioch.

²³After he had spent some time *there*, he departed and went over *all* the country of Galatia and Phrygia in order, strengthening all the disciples.

²⁴*Then* a certain Jew named Apollos *who was* born at Alexandria *and who was* an eloquent man *and* mighty in the Scriptures, came to Ephesus.

²⁵*Apollos* was *well* instructed in the way of the Lord. *He was* fervent in the spirit *and* he spoke and taught diligently the things of the Lord. *But he* only knew the baptism of John.

²⁶*As* he began to speak boldly in the synagogue, when Aquila and Priscilla heard *him*, they took him *aside* and expounded the way of God to him more perfectly.

²⁷*After that* when *Apollos* was disposed to pass into Achaia, the family+ wrote *a letter*, exhorting the disciples to receive him. When he came, *he* helped those who had believed through grace.

²⁸For he mightily refuted+ the Jews, *and that* publicly, showing by the Scriptures that Jesus was *the* Christ.

Acts Chapter 19

¹ It came to pass that while Apollos was in Corinth, Paul passed through the upper region+ *and* came to Ephesus. Finding certain disciples *there*,

² he said to them: Have you received *the* Holy Spirit since you believed? And they said to him: We have not even heard that there is a Holy Spirit.

³ *Paul* said to them: Into what then were you baptized? They said: Into John's baptism.

⁴ Then Paul said: John truly+ baptized with the baptism of repentance, saying to the people that they should believe in *the One* who would come after him, that is, in Christ Jesus.

⁵ When they heard *this*, they were baptized in the name of the Lord Jesus.

⁶ And when Paul laid *his* hands on them, the Holy Spirit came upon them and they spoke with tongues and prophesied.

⁷ All the men *there* numbered+ about twelve.

⁸ *Then Paul* went into the synagogue and spoke boldly for three months, advocating+ and persuading *those who heard him about* the things concerning the kingdom of God.

⁹ But when many *of* different+ *persuasions* were hardened *against him* and did not believe, but spoke evil about the way *of Christ* before the multitude, *Paul* left them and separated the disciples *away*

from them, now reasoning[+] daily in the school of Tyrannus.

[10]This continued for two years, so that all who lived[+] in Asia heard the Word of the Lord Jesus, both Jews and Greeks.

[11]And God worked[+] special miracles through Paul's hands.

[12]So *much so* that handkerchiefs and aprons were taken[+] from *Paul's* body to the sick and diseases left[+] them and evil spirits went out of them.

[13]Then some vagabond Jews *who were* exorcists took *it* upon themselves to call *out* the name of the Lord Jesus over *those* who had evil spirits, saying: We beg[+] you by Jesus whom Paul proclaims.[+]

[14]There were seven sons of Sceva, a Jew *and* chief of the priests, who did this.

[15]But the evil spirit answered and said: Jesus I know and Paul I know, but who are you?

[16]*Then* the man who had the evil spirit leaped on them and overcame them and prevailed against them so that they fled out of that house naked and wounded.

[17]All the Jews and Greeks *who* lived[+] in Ephesus knew *about* this *so that* fear fell on them all and the name of the Lord Jesus was magnified.

[18]Many who believed came and confessed and reported[+] their deeds.

[19]Many of those who used *curious* arts also brought their books together and burned them before all *people.* They counted the value[+] of *those books* and found *it to be* fifty thousand *pieces* of silver.

[20]Therefore, the Word of God grew mightily and prevailed.

[21]After these things were fulfilled,[+] in *his* spirit, Paul *decided* to pass through Macedonia and Achaia *and* go to Jerusalem, saying: After I have been there, I must also see Rome.

[22]So he sent *word* to Macedonia *to* two of *those* who *had* ministered to him, Timothy and Erastus, but he himself stayed in Asia for a season.

[23]*At* the same time, there arose no small stir about *this faith called* the Way *meaning believing in Christ and His resurrection.*

[24]For a certain *man* named Demetrius, a silversmith, made silver shrines for Diana, *and this* brought no small gain to the craftsmen.

[25]*So, Demetrius* called the workmen of this occupation together and said: Sirs, you know that by this craft we have our wealth.

[26]Moreover you see and hear that not only[+] at Ephesus, but almost throughout all Asia, this Paul has persuaded and turned many people away, saying that there are no gods that are made with hands.

[27]Therefore, not only is our craft in danger of being rejected,[+] but also the temple of the great goddess whom all *of* Asia and the world worships could be despised and her magnificence destroyed.

[28]When they heard *this*, they were full of anger[+] and cried out saying: Great *is* Diana of the Ephesians.

[29]*So* the whole city was filled with confusion. *But* with one accord *the mob* ran into the theater *and* caught Gaius and Aristarchus *of* Macedonia *who were* Paul's companions.

[30]When Paul wanted[+] *to* go in to the people, the disciples did not allow[+] him *to do so.*

[31]Some of the chiefs of Asia who were *Paul's* friends, sent *word* to him asking[+] *him* to not venture[+] into the theater.

[32]Some therefore cried *out* one thing and some another for the assembly was confused. Most[+] did not *even* understand[+] why[+] they had come together.

[33]They pulled[+] Alexander out of the crowd[+] *and* the Jews put him forward. Alexander signaled[+] with the hand and would have made his defense to the people,

[34]But when they knew that he was a Jew, all with one voice cried out for two hours: Great *is* Diana of the Ephesians.

[35]Then the town clerk appeased the people *when* he said: *You* men of Ephesus, what man is there that does not understand[+] that the city of the Ephesians is a worshiper of the great goddess Diana and of the *image* that fell down from Jupiter?

³⁶ Since these things cannot be *successfully* spoken against, you ought to be quiet and to do nothing rashly.

³⁷ For you have brought these men here who are neither robbers of assemblies⁺ nor blasphemers of your goddess.

³⁸ Therefore if Demetrius and the craftsmen who are with him have a matter against anyone, the law is open and there are deputies. Let them accuse⁺ one another.

³⁹ And if you *have* any *other* inquiry concerning other matters, it should⁺ be determined in a lawful assembly.

⁴⁰ For we are in danger of being called in question for this day's uproar. *For* there is no *justifiable* cause that we can give to account for this *unruly* concourse.

⁴¹ When he had thus spoken, he dismissed the assembly.

Acts Chapter 20

¹ After the uproar was stopped,⁺ Paul called the disciples *to* embrace *them* and *then he* left⁺ to go to Macedonia.

² *Then* after he had gone through those regions⁺ and given them much exhortation, he went *on* to Greece.

³ *He* stayed⁺ *there for* three months. When the Jews *were* plotting⁺ *against* him as he was about to sail to Syria, he decided⁺ to return through Macedonia.

⁴ Accompanying him to Asia were Sopater from Berea, Aristarchus and Secundus from Thessalonica, Gaius from Derbe, Tychicus and Trophimus from Asia, and Timothy.

⁵ *All* these going before, waited for us at Troas.

⁶ After *celebrating* the days of unleavened bread, we sailed from Philippi *and* met⁺ them in Troas in five days *and* stayed⁺ *with them* there *for* seven days.

⁷ On the first *day* of the week, when the disciples came together to break bread, Paul proclaimed⁺ *the* Word to them, ready to depart on the next day, *and he* continued his speech until midnight.

⁸ There were many lights in the upper chamber where they were gathered together.

⁹ In a window *sill*, a certain young man named Eutychus sat *and* began to fall into a deep sleep as Paul *continued* speaking⁺ *for a* long *time. The young man* slumped⁺ down in sleep, fell from the third loft, and was taken *as* dead.

¹⁰ Paul went downstairs and fell upon him *to* embrace him *and* said: Do not *be* troubled, for his life is *still* in him.

¹¹ Therefore, after *Paul* came *back* upstairs again and broke bread and ate and talked a long while, even until *the* break of day, he *then* departed.

¹² They took⁺ the young man *with them*, *very much* alive, and *they* were not a little comforted *by this*.

¹³ *So* we went to *the* ship and sailed to Assos. There *we* had intended to take Paul onto *the ship*. For he had appointed himself to go *this far* on foot.

¹⁴ *Therefore*, when he met us in Assos, we took him in and went *on* to Mitylene.

¹⁵ From *Assos*, we sailed *on* and the next *day* came near⁺ Chios. The next *day* we arrived at Samos and stayed at Trogyllium. *And* the next *day* we came to Miletus.

¹⁶ Paul had determined to sail by Ephesus because he would not spend the time in Asia. For he hurried,⁺ *so that* if it were possible, he *wanted* to be in Jerusalem *for* the day of Pentecost.

¹⁷ From Miletus, he sent *word* to Ephesus to call *together* the elders of the assemblies.⁺

¹⁸ When they came to him, he said to them: You know, from the first day that I came to Asia, how⁺ I have been with you at all times.⁺

¹⁹ *I have* served the Lord with all humility of mind and with many tears and trials⁺ that befell me from the plotting⁺ of the Jews.

²⁰ I have kept back nothing that would be beneficial⁺ *to you*. But *I* have shown you and taught you *both* publicly and from house to house.

²¹ *I have* testified to both the Jews and also to the Greeks, *proclaiming* repentance to God and faith in our Lord Jesus Christ.

22*And* now behold, I *am* going bound in the spirit to Jerusalem, not knowing what things will befall me there.

23Except[+] *I know* that the Holy Spirit testifies[+] *to me* in every city saying that chains[+] and afflictions *will* stay[+] *with* me.

24But none of these things deter[+] me. Nor *do* I count my life dear to myself, so that I might finish my course with joy, and*complete* the ministry that I have received from the Lord Jesus: To testify *to* the Gospel of the grace of God.

25Now, behold I know that you all, among whom I have gone proclaiming[+] the kingdom of God, will see my face no longer.[+]

26Therefore I ask[+] you to record this day, that I *am* pure from the blood of all *people.*

27For I have not shunned *the responsibility* to declare the counsel of God to all *of* you.

28Therefore, take heed to yourselves and to all the flock over which the Holy Spirit has made you overseers. Feed the assembly[+] of God that He purchased with His own blood.

29For I know this, that after I leave,[+] grievous wolves will enter in among you *and* will not spare the flock.

30Also from *among* yourselves, *certain* men will rise *up and* speak perverse things to draw away disciples after themselves.

31Therefore watch and remember that for three years I did not stop[+] warning everyone night and day with tears.

32Now family,[+] I commend you to God and to the Word of His grace, which is able to build you up and give you an inheritance among all who are sanctified.

33I have coveted no one's silver or gold or apparel.

34Yes, you yourselves know that these hands have ministered to my *own* needs[+] and *to the needs of those* who were with me.

35I have shown you everything[+] *so* that, laboring in this way,[+] you ought to support the weak and remember the words of the Lord Jesus, how He said:

It is more blessed to give
than to receive.

36When he had thus spoken, he knelt down and prayed with them all.

37They all wept greatly[+] and fell on Paul's neck and kissed him.

38Of all the words that *Paul* spoke, *what caused them* the most sorrow was that they would see his face no longer.[+] But *then* they accompanied him to the ship.

Acts Chapter 21

1 It came to pass, that after we left[+] them and launched, we came with a straight course to Coos and the *day* following to Rhodes and from there[+] to Patara.

2 Finding a ship *that was* sailing to Phoenicia, we went aboard and set forth.

3 When we sighted[+] Cyprus, we passed[+] *by* it on the left and sailed to Syria and landed at Tyre, for the ship was to unload its cargo[+] there.

4 Finding disciples there, we stayed *with them for* seven days. Through the Spirit, they said to Paul that he should not go to Jerusalem.

5 When we completed[+] those days, we departed and went *on* our way. They all accompanied[+] us with *their* wives and children until *we were* out of the city. *Then* we knelt down on the shore and prayed.

6 After we left[+] each other, we boarded[+] *the* ship *and* they returned home again.

7 When we finished *our* course from Tyre, we came to Ptolemais and greeted[+] the family[+] *there* and stayed[+] with them *for* one day.

8 The next *day*, we who were in Paul's company left[+] and went *on* to Caesarea. *There*, we entered the house of Philip the evangelist who was *one* of the seven and stayed[+] with him.

9 *Philip* had four daughters *who were* virgins *and who* prophesied.

10As we continued[+] *there for* many days, a prophet named Agabus came from Judea.

11When he arrived,[+] he took Paul's belt[+] and bound his own hands and feet and said: The Holy Spirit *has* said *this to me*: *In this same way*, the Jews in

Jerusalem will bind the man who owns this belt+ and deliver *him* into the hands of the Gentiles.

12 When we heard these things, both we and those in that place begged+ *Paul* to not go to Jerusalem.

13 But Paul answered: Why do you weep and break my heart? For I am ready not only to be bound, but also to die in Jerusalem for the name of the Lord Jesus.

14 When he would not be persuaded, we stopped+ *protesting and* said: *May* the Lord's will be done.

15 After those days we took our baggage+ and went to Jerusalem.

16 *Some* of the disciples in Caesarea also went with us and *they* brought Mnason from Cyprus, an old disciple with whom we *had* lodged.

17 When we arrived+ in Jerusalem, the family+ received us gladly.

18 The next+ *day*, Paul *and the rest of* us went to James, and all the elders were present.

19 After we greeted+ them, *Paul* described+ *in* detail+ what *great* things God had worked+ among the Gentiles through his ministry.

20 When they heard *this*, they glorified the Lord and said to *Paul*: You see, brother, how many thousands of Jews there are who believe, but they are all zealous *for* this law *of* substance.

21 They have been told+ about you, that you teach all the Jews who are among the Gentiles to forsake Moses saying that they should not circumcise *their* children or follow+ the *traditional Jewish* customs.

22 What should *we* do? Surely a crowd *will* come together, for they will hear that you have come.

23 Therefore do this that we say to you. We have four men who have *taken* a vow.

24 Take them and purify yourself with them and pay+ *the* costs+ for them *so* that they can shave *their* heads. *Then* all may know that those things *that have been* told+ about+ you are nothing, but *that* you yourself also walk orderly and keep the law.

25 Concerning the Gentile believers, we have written *and* concluded that they observe no such things, except+ that they keep themselves from *things* offered to idols and from blood and from *things* strangled and from fornication.

26 So Paul took the men and the next day *after* purifying himself with them *he* entered the temple to signify the accomplishment of the days of purification until an offering could be offered for everyone of them.

27 When the seven days were· almost ended, the Jews from Asia saw *Paul* in the temple *and they* stirred up all the people and laid hands on him.

28 *They* cried out: Men of Israel help *us*. This is the man who teaches all *people* everywhere *things that are* against the people and the law and this place. Furthermore, *he* also took Greeks into the temple and polluted this holy place.

29 For in the city Trophimus, they had seen an Ephesian with *Paul and* they assumed+ that *he* had taken *the Ephesian* into the temple.

30 *Therefore* all the city was riled+ *up* and the people ran together and took Paul and dragged+ him out of the temple and immediately+ shut the doors.

31 As *the mob* was about to kill *Paul*, a message+ came to the chief captain of the company+ *of soldiers saying* that all Jerusalem was in an uproar.

32 *So the captain* immediately took soldiers and centurions and ran down to them. When they saw the chief captain and the soldiers, they stopped+ beating Paul.

33 Then the chief captain came near and took him and commanded *him* to be bound with two chains. *The captain* demanded *to know* who *Paul* was and what he had done.

34 Some *people* in the crowd+ cried *out* one thing *and* some another. When *the captain* could not know *with* certainty *what the cause was* for the tumult, he commanded *that Paul* be carried into the castle.

35 When *they* came to the stairs, *Paul* was carried+ by the soldiers *because* of the violence of the people.

³⁶The crowd⁺ followed after *them*, crying *out*: Away with him.

³⁷As Paul was *about* to be led into the castle, he said to the chief captain: May I speak to you? *The captain* said: Can you speak Greek?

³⁸Are you not that Egyptian who before these days made an uproar and led four thousand men who were murderers out into the wilderness?

³⁹But Paul said: I am a Jew from Tarsus, *a city* in Cilicia, a citizen of no mean city. I urge you, allow me to speak to the people.

⁴⁰When *the captain* gave *Paul* permission,⁺ *he* stood on the stairs and signaled⁺ to the people with his hand. When there was silence, he spoke to *them* in the Hebrew tongue.

Acts Chapter 22

¹ Men, family,⁺ and fathers: Now hear my defense to you.

² When they heard that he spoke to them in the Hebrew tongue, they kept *all* the more silent. *Then* he said:

³ I am truly⁺ a Jew, born in Tarsus, *a city* in Cilicia. *I was* brought in this city at the feet of Gamaliel, taught according to the strict⁺ *letter* of the law of the fathers, and zealous toward God as you all are this day.

⁴ *Therefore*, I persecuted this *faith known as* The Way *even* to the death, binding and delivering both men and women into prisons.

⁵ The high priest and all of the council⁺ of elders testify⁺ *to this fact*. And from them, I received letters to the family⁺ and *I* went to Damascus to bring *those* who were bound there to Jerusalem to be punished.

⁶ It came to pass that, as I made my journey and came near Damascus about noon, suddenly there shone from heaven a great light around⁺ me.

⁷ I fell to the ground and heard a voice saying to me: Saul, Saul, why do you persecute me?

⁸ I answered: Who are you Lord? He said to me: I am Jesus of Nazareth whom you persecute.

⁹ *Those* who were with me also saw the light and were afraid but they did not hear the voice of Him who spoke to me.

¹⁰I said: What shall I do, Lord? And the Lord said to me, Arise, and go into Damascus. There you will be told about all the things that are appointed for you to do.

¹¹When I could not see because of the brightness⁺ of that light, *I was* led by the hand of *those* who were with me *and* I came to Damascus.

¹²*After I arrived there, a man named* Ananias, *who was* a devout man according to the law, *and who* had a good report from all the Jews who lived⁺ *there*,

¹³came to me and stood *by me* and said to me: Brother Saul, receive your sight. And the same hour I looked up *and saw* him.

¹⁴He said: The God of our fathers has chosen you, that you should know His will and see that Just One and hear the voice of His mouth.

¹⁵For you shall be His witness to every-one⁺ of what you have seen and heard.

¹⁶*Therefore* why *do* you delay⁺ now? Arise and be baptized and wash away your sins, calling on the name of the Lord.

¹⁷*Now* it came to pass, that when I had come again to Jerusalem, as I prayed in the temple, I went into a trance.

¹⁸*And I* saw Him *and heard Him* say to me: Hurry and quickly get out of Jerusalem, for they will not receive your testimony concerning me.

¹⁹I said: Lord, they know that I imprisoned and beat *some* in every synagogue who believe in you.

²⁰When the blood of your martyr Stephen was shed, I also was standing by and consenting to his death and held⁺ the coats⁺ of *those* who killed⁺ him.

²¹He said to me: Leave⁺ *now*, for I will send you far from here to the Gentiles.

²²They listened⁺ to *Paul's* words and *then* raised⁺ their voices and said: Away with such a *fellow* from the earth, for it is not proper⁺ that he should live.

²³ As they cried out, *they* tore⁺ off *their* clothes and threw dust into the air.

²⁴ *Then* the chief captain commanded *that* Paul be brought into the castle and ordered⁺ that he should be examined by scourging *so* that he might know why⁺ they cried *out* so against him.

²⁵ As they bound him with thongs, Paul said to the centurion who stood by: Is it lawful for you to flog⁺ a man who is a Roman and *has not been* convicted⁺ *of anything*?

²⁶ When the centurion heard *that*, he went *away* and told the chief captain saying: Take heed what you do, for this man is a Roman.

²⁷ Then the chief captain came and said to *Paul*: Tell me: Are you a Roman? He said: Yes.

²⁸ The chief captain answered: I obtained this freedom at a great cost.⁺ And Paul said: But I was born *free*.

²⁹ Then immediately⁺ *he* who had been *about* to examine *Paul* left.⁺ The chief captain was also afraid after he knew that *Paul* was a Roman, because he *was the one who* had bound him.

³⁰ On the next day, because he wanted to know for certain why *Paul* had been accused by the Jews, he released⁺ him from *his* chains⁺ and commanded the chief priests and all their council to appear, and *then he* brought Paul down and stood⁺ him before them.

Acts Chapter 23

¹ Paul looked⁺ earnestly *at* the council *and* said: Men *and* family,⁺ I have lived in all good conscience before God to this day.

² Ananias the high priest Ananias *then* commanded *those* who stood by *Paul* to strike⁺ him on the mouth.

³ Then Paul said to him: God will strike⁺ you, *you* whitewashed⁺ wall. For you sit to judge me by the law but *then* command me to be struck⁺ contrary to the law?

⁴ *Those* who stood by said: Do you revile God's high priest?

⁵ Then Paul said: I did not understand,⁺ family,⁺ that he was the high priest. For it is written: You shall not speak evil about the ruler of your people. *Exodus 22:28*

⁶ But when Paul perceived that one part *of the audience* were Sadducees and the other Pharisees, he cried out in the council: Men *and* family,⁺ I am a Pharisee, the son of a Pharisee. *Am* I *being* judged⁺ *because of the* hope and resurrection of the dead?

⁷ When he said *this*, dissension arose between the Pharisees and the Sadducees and the crowd⁺ was divided.

⁸ For the Sadducees say that there is no resurrection, neither angel nor spirit, but the Pharisees confess both.

⁹ *And so* a great cry arose. The scribes *who were* Pharisees rose *up* and argued⁺ saying: We find no evil in this man, but if a spirit or an angel has spoken to him, let us not fight against God.

¹⁰ When this great dissension arose, the chief captain, fearing lest Paul might be pulled to pieces by them, commanded the soldiers to go down and take him by force from them and take *him* into the castle.

¹¹ The following night, the Lord stood by *Paul* and said: Be of good cheer, Paul. For as you have testified about me in Jerusalem, so also, you must testify⁺ in Rome.

¹² When it was day, some of the Jews banded together and bound themselves under a curse saying that they would neither eat nor drink until they had killed Paul.

¹³ More than forty *of them* made this conspiracy.

¹⁴ They came to the chief priests and elders and said: We have bound ourselves under a great curse that we will eat nothing until we have killed⁺ Paul.

¹⁵ Now therefore you and the council signal⁺ to the chief captain to bring *Paul* down to you tomorrow as though you want *to* question⁺ *him* further.⁺ And before⁺ he comes near, we are ready to kill him.

¹⁶ When Paul's sister's son heard about

their plot,+ he entered the castle and told Paul.

17Then Paul called one of the centurions and said: Take this young man to the chief captain, for he has something to tell him.

18So *the centurion* took *the young man* to the chief captain and said: Paul the prisoner called me and asked+ me to bring this young man to you. *He* has something to say to you.

19Then the chief captain took him by the hand and went *with him* aside privately and asked *him*: What is that you have to tell me?

20He said: The Jews have agreed to ask+ that you bring Paul down to the council tomorrow, as though they would question+ him further.+

21But do not yield to them, for they *are* plotting+ *against* him. More than forty men have bound themselves with an oath, that they will neither eat nor drink until they have killed him. Now are they ready, looking for a promise from you.

22So the chief captain let the young man leave+ and charged *him*: Tell no one that you have shown these things to me.

23*Then the captain* called two centurions saying: Make ready two hundred soldiers and seventy horsemen and two hundred spearmen to go to Caesarea at nine o'clock+ *at* night.

24Provide *a* beast *for* Paul *to ride to* take *him* safely to Felix the governor.

25*Then* he wrote a letter in this manner.

26*From* Claudius Lysias to the most excellent governor Felix. Greetings.

27This man *Paul* was taken by the Jews and would have been killed by them. But I came with an army and rescued him, having understood that he was a Roman.

28When I wanted to know the reason+ why+ they accused him, I brought him forth into their council.

29I perceived *him* to be accused regarding+ questions in their law, but to have nothing laid to his charge worthy of death or of chains.+

30When I was told that the Jews *were* plotting+ against this man, I immedi-

ately+ sent *him* to you and gave instructions+ to his accusers also to say before you what *they had* against him. Farewell.

31Then as it was commanded *to* them, the soldiers took Paul by night to Antipatris.

32The next day, the *soldiers* left the horsemen to go with *Paul* and *they* returned to the castle.

33When the *horsemen* came to Caesarea, *they* delivered the epistle to the governor *and* presented Paul to him.

34When the governor read *the letter*, he asked what province *Paul* was from. When he understood that *he was* from Cilicia,

35he said: I will hear your *case* when your accusers have also come. Then he commanded *that Paul* be kept in Herod's judgment hall.

Acts Chapter 24

1 After five days, Ananias the high priest arrived+ with the elders and *with* a certain orator *named* Tertullus, who informed the governor *of the charges* against Paul.

2 When he was called forth, Tertullus began to accuse *Paul* saying: Since+ *it is* by you, *governor*, *that* we enjoy great quietness, and that very worthy deeds are done to this nation by your providence,

3 we accept *this* always and in all places with all thankfulness most noble Felix.

4 Nevertheless, *hoping* that I *may* not be tedious to you, I ask+ that by your patience+ you *might* hear a few words *from* us.

5 For we have found this man *Paul to be a* pestilent *fellow*, a mover of sedition among all the Jews throughout the world, and a ringleader of the sect of the Nazarenes.

6 He has gone about profaning the temple. *So* we took *him* and would have judged *him* according to our law.

7 But the chief captain Lysias came and with great violence took *him* away out of our hands.

8 *He* commanded *us, Paul's* accusers, to come to you. By examining him yourself, *you will* know about all the things about which we accuse him.

9 The Jews *all* agreed+ *by* saying that these things were so.

10 Then, the governor signaled+ for Paul to speak, *and he* answered: Since+ I know that you have been a judge in this nation for many years, I gladly answer for myself.

11 *So* you may understand, it *has been* twelve days since I went to Jerusalem to worship.

12 They *did* not find me in the temple disputing with anyone. Nor *did anyone find me* stirring+ up people in the synagogues or in the city.

13 Neither can they prove the things about which they now accuse me.

14 But I confess this to you: That *in* following+ The Way, which they call *a* heresy, I also worship the God of my fathers *and I* believe everything+ that is written in the law and in the prophets.

15 I have hope in God, as *do all* who accept+ this, that there will be a resurrection of the dead, both of the righteous+ and unrighteous.+

16 In this *hope* I strive+ to always have a conscience void of offense toward God and *toward* men.

17 Now after many years I came to bring alms to my nation and offerings.

18 At that time,+ certain Jews from Asia found me purified in the temple *and* not with *a* mob+ or tumult.

19 *Those people* ought to have been here before you *to* object if they had something against me.

20 Or else let these *accusers* say *so* if they found any evil doing in me while I stood before the council.

21 *It is* for this one sound+ that I cried *out while* standing among them, touching *on* the resurrection of the dead, *that* I am called in *for* questioning by you this day.

22 When Felix heard these things, having straighter+ knowledge about *the* way *from Paul,* he deferred *the matter* and said: When Lysias the chief captain comes down, I will *further* consider+ your matter.

23 *Then Felix* commanded a centurion to keep Paul and to let *him* have liberty and that he should not forbid any of his acquaintances to minister or come to him.

24 After several+ days, Felix came with his wife Drusilla, who was a Jew,+ *and* he sent for Paul and *wanted to* hear *from* him concerning faith in Christ.

25 As *Paul* spoke+ about righteousness, temperance, and judgment to come, Felix trembled and answered: Go away for this time. When I have a convenient season, I will call for you.

26 *Felix* also hoped that Paul might give him money *so* that he could release him. Therefore he sent for *Paul* more often and conversed+ with him.

27 But after two years, Porcius Festus came into Felix' office+ *and* Felix, wanting+ to show the Jews a favor,+ left Paul bound.

Acts Chapter 25

1 Now when Festus came to the province, after three days he went up+ from Caesarea to Jerusalem.

2 Then the high priest and the chief of the Jews informed *Festus* about Paul and begged+ him

3 *for a* favor, *asking Festus* to send *Paul* to Jerusalem *so they could* wait along the way to kill him.

4 But Festus answered that Paul should be kept at Caesarea and that he himself would soon+ go+ *there.*

5 Therefore *Festus* said: Let *those* among you who are able go with *me* and accuse this man *to see* if there is any wickedness in him.

6 After he stayed+ *there* among them *for* ten days, he went down to Caesarea. The next day sitting on the judgment seat, *he* commanded Paul to be brought.

7 When *Paul* came *in,* the Jews who came down from Jerusalem stood around+ and made many grievous complaints against Paul that they could not prove.

8 When *Paul* answered for himself, *he said:* I have not offended *anyone in* anything at all, not against the law of the Jews or

against the temple or against Caesar.
⁹ But Festus, wanting⁺ to do the Jews a favor,⁺ answered Paul and said: Will you go up to Jerusalem and be judged by me there about these things?
¹⁰Then Paul said: I stand at Caesar's judgment seat where I ought to be judged. I have done no wrong to the Jews, as you very well know.
¹¹For if I am an offender or have committed anything worthy of death, I do not refuse to die. But if none of these things are *true* of which these *Jews* accuse me, no one *should be* able to deliver me to them. I appeal to Caesar.
¹²Then Festus, when he had conferred with the council, answered: *Since* you have appealed to Caesar, to Caesar you shall go.
¹³After several⁺ days, King Agrippa and Bernice came to Caesarea to greet⁺ Festus.
¹⁴When they had been there many days, Festus described⁺ Paul's case⁺ to the king saying: There is a certain man *who was* left in prison⁺ by Felix.
¹⁵When I was in Jerusalem, the chief priests and the elders of the Jews informed *me* about him *and* wanted⁺ *a* judgment against him.
¹⁶I answered them, *by saying*: It is not the Roman way⁺ to deliver anyone to die before *the one* who is accused has the accusers face to face with license to answer for himself concerning the crime laid against him.
¹⁷Therefore when they came here, without any delay, on the *very* next day I sat on the judgment seat and commanded the man to be brought forth.
¹⁸When the accusers stood up, they brought no accusation of such things as I supposed.
¹⁹But from their own superstition *they* had certain questions against him and about one *called* Jesus, who was dead, *but* whom Paul affirmed to be alive.
²⁰Because I *was* doubtful about such questions, I asked *Paul* if he would go to Jerusalem and be judged there about these matters.
²¹But when Paul appealed to be heard by Augustus, I commanded him to be kept until I might send him to Caesar.
²²Then Agrippa said to Festus: I would also *like to* hear the man myself. Tomorrow, *Festus* said, you shall hear him.
²³The next day, when Agrippa and Bernice came with great pomp and entered the place of hearing *along* with the chief captains and principal men of the city, at Festus' commandment Paul was brought forth.
²⁴Festus said: King Agrippa and everyone⁺ here present with us: You see this man about whom all the multitude of Jews have petitioned⁺ me, both at Jerusalem and *also* here, crying *out* that he should not live any longer.
²⁵But when I found that he had committed nothing worthy of death and that he himself appealed to Augustus, I decided⁺ to send him *there*.
²⁶*However*, I have no certain thing to write *about him* to my lord *Caesar*. Therefore I have brought him forth before you, and especially before you, O king Agrippa, *so* that after *you have* examined *him*, I might have something to write.
²⁷For it seems unreasonable to me to send a prisoner and not *send* with *him a* significant⁺ *description* of the crimes *laid* against him.

Acts Chapter 26

¹ Then Agrippa said to Paul: You are permitted to speak for yourself. Then Paul stretched forth his hand and answered for himself.
² I think myself blessed,⁺ king Agrippa, because I shall answer for myself this day before you, touching *upon* all the things about which I am accused by the Jews.
³ Especially *because I know* you to be expert in all *of the* customs and questions that are *debated* among the Jews. Therefore I urge you to hear me patiently.
⁴ From my youth, my life from the *very* beginning was formed⁺ among my own nation in Jerusalem. The Jews all know *this*.
⁵ *They all* knew me from the beginning.

If they would testify, *they would say* that I lived following⁺ the strictest⁺ sect of our religion as a Pharisee.

⁶ *Yet* now I stand and am judged for the hope of the promise made to our fathers by God.

⁷ For this *promise* our twelve tribes earnestly⁺ served *God* day and night, hoping to attain⁺ it. *It is* because⁺ *of this* hope, King Agrippa, *that* I am accused by the Jews.

⁸ Why should it be thought incredible that God could raise the dead?

⁹ I myself truly⁺ thought that I ought to do many things contrary to the name of Jesus of Nazareth.

¹⁰ And I *actually* did these things in Jerusalem. Having received authority from the chief priests, I shut up many of the saints in prison. When they were put to death, I gave my voice against *them*.

¹¹ I often punished them in all the synagogues and compelled *them* to blaspheme. Being exceedingly furious⁺ against them, I persecuted *them* even to outlying⁺ cities.

¹² But then, as I went to Damascus with authority and commission from the chief priests,

¹³ At midday, O king, I saw a light from heaven on the way. *It was* brighter than the sun *and* shining *all* around⁺ me. *Those* traveling⁺ with me also *saw it*.

¹⁴ When we all fell to the ground,⁺ I heard a voice speaking to me and saying in the Hebrew tongue: Saul, Saul, why do you persecute me? *It is* hard for you to kick against the pricks.

¹⁵ I said: Who are you, Lord? He said: I am Jesus whom you persecute.

¹⁶ But rise and stand up on your feet. For I have appeared to you for this purpose, to make you a minister and a witness both of these things that you have seen and of those things in which I will appear to you.

¹⁷ *I will* deliver you from the people and *from* the Gentiles, to whom now I send you,

¹⁸ to open their eyes *and* to turn *them* from darkness to light and *from* the authority⁺ of Satan to God *so* that they may receive forgiveness of sins and inheritance among *those* who are sanctified by faith that is in me.

¹⁹ Therefore, O King Agrippa, I was not disobedient to the heavenly vision.

²⁰ But *I* declared⁺ *it* first to those in Damascus and in Jerusalem and throughout all the borders⁺ of Judea, and *then* to the Gentiles *so* that they could repent and turn to God and do works worthy⁺ of repentance.

²¹ For these causes the Jews caught me in the temple and went about to kill *me*.

²² Therefore, having obtained help from God, I continue to this day, witnessing both to small and great saying no other things than what the prophets and Moses said would come:

²³ That Christ would suffer *and* that He would be the first who would rise from the dead and show light to the people and to the Gentiles.

²⁴ As he thus spoke for himself, Festus said with a loud voice: Paul, you are beside yourself. *Too* much learning has made you mad.

²⁵ But *Paul* said: I am not mad, most noble Festus, but *I* speak forth the words of truth and soberness.

²⁶ For the king knows *all* about these things. Before him, I *can* speak freely. For I am persuaded that none of these things are hidden from him. For this thing was not done *hidden* in a corner.

²⁷ King Agrippa, do you believe the prophets? I know that you believe.

²⁸ Then Agrippa said to Paul: You almost persuade me to be a Christian.

²⁹ *Then* Paul said: I wish⁺ to God that not only you, but also all who hear me this day, were both almost and entirely⁺ as I am, except these chains.⁺

³⁰ When he had thus spoken, the king rose up,. and the governor and Bernice and *those* who sat with them.

³¹ After they had gone aside, they talked among themselves saying: This man does nothing worthy of death or of chains.⁺

³² Then Agrippa said to Festus: This man might have been released⁺ if he had not appealed to Caesar.

Acts Chapter 27

[1] When they decided[+] that we would sail to Italy, they delivered Paul and certain other prisoners to *one* named Julius, a centurion of Augustus' company[+] *of soldiers*.

[2] *After* entering a ship from Adramyttium, we launched, intending[+] to sail passed[+] the borders[+] of Asia. Aristarchus, a Macedonian from Thessalonica was with us.

[3] The next *day* we stopped[+] *briefly* at Sidon. Julius treated Paul courteously and gave *him* liberty to go to his friends to refresh himself.

[4] When we launched from there,[+] we sailed under Cyprus because the winds were against[+] *us*.

[5] After we sailed over the sea *near* Cilicia and Pamphylia, we came to Myra, *a city* of Lycia.

[6] There, the centurion found a ship from Alexandria sailing to Italy *and* he put us on it.

[7] When we had sailed slowly *for* many days and barely[+] came near[+] to Cnidus *because* the wind did not allow[+] us *closer*, we *then* sailed under Crete near[+] Salmone.

[8] Barely[+] passing *by* it, *we* came to a place called The Fair Havens near the city *of* Lasea.

[9] After[+] much time had passed and sailing was now dangerous because the fast *conditions* had past, Paul cautioned *them*.

[10] *He* said to them: Sirs, I perceive that this voyage will be with much injury[+] and damage, not only to the ship and cargo,[+] but also to our lives.

[11] Nevertheless, the centurion believed the master and the owner of the ship more than the things that Paul said.

[12] And, because the harbor[+] was not well suited[+] to winter in, most[+] advised *them* to leave[+] from there[+] if they could by any means make[+] *it* to Phoenix to winter *there*. *The* harbor[+] in Crete faces[+] to *both* the southwest and northwest.

[13] *Therefore* when the south wind blew softly, they supposed that this suited[+] *their* purpose *so* they left[+] *there and* sailed close by Crete.

[14] But not long after, a tempestuous wind called Euroclydon arose *like a hurricane* against *the ship*.

[15] When the ship was caught and could not bear up into the wind, we let *it* run adrift.[+]

[16] *As we* ran under an island called Clauda, we had much work *to do* by the lifeboat

[17] that was used to help undergird the ship. But, fearing lest they might fall into the quicksands, *they* struck sail and *thus* were driven *along*.

[18] Being exceedingly tossed by the storm,[+] the next *day* they lightened the ship.

[19] *On* the third *day*, we cast out the ship's tackle with our own hands.

[20] For many days, neither sun nor stars appeared and *as* no small storm[+] lay on *us*, all hope that we might be saved was taken away.

[21] Then, after long abstinence, Paul stood forth in the midst of them and said: Sirs, you should have listened[+] to me and not sailed[+] from Crete and *you would not* have received[+] this harm and loss.

[22] *But* now I exhort you to be of good cheer, for there will be no loss of *any man's* life among you, but *only* the ship *will be lost*.

[23] For an angel of God, whose I am and whom I serve, stood by me this night

[24] saying: Do not be afraid Paul. You must be brought before Caesar. And behold, God is giving *to* you all who *are* sailing with you.

[25] Therefore sirs, be of good cheer, for I believe God, that it will *indeed* be as it was told *to* me.

[26] However, we must *first* be cast onto a certain island.

[27] Therefore, when the fourteenth night came, as we were driven up and down in *the* Adriatic *sea*, about midnight the ship's men thought[+] that they were drawing near to some country.

²⁸ *So they* sounded *the depth* and found *it to be* twenty fathoms. After they went a little further, they sounded again and found *it to be* fifteen fathoms.

²⁹ Then fearing lest we might fall upon rocks, they cast four anchors out of the stern, and wished for daylight.

³⁰ As the ship's men were about to flee out of the ship, they let down the lifeboat under the pretense⁺ that they were casting anchors out of the bow⁺ *of the* ship.

³¹ Paul said to the centurion and to the soldiers, Unless⁺ these *men* stay⁺ in the ship, you cannot be saved.

³² Then the soldiers cut the ropes to the lifeboat and let it fall.

³³ *Then* as day was coming, Paul begged⁺ *them* all to take *some* food⁺ saying: This is the fourteenth day that you have expectantly⁺ continued fasting *and* taken nothing *to eat.*

³⁴ Therefore I beg⁺ you to take *some* food.⁺ For this is *so that* you *can be* saved.⁺ For *not one* hair shall fall from the head of any of you.

³⁵ After *Paul* had spoken this, he took bread and gave thanks to God in presence of them all. When he had broken *it*, he began to eat.

³⁶ Then they were all of good cheer and they also took *some* food.⁺

³⁷ In all, there were two hundred *and* seventy six souls on the ship.

³⁸ When they had eaten enough, they lightened the ship *by* casting out the wheat *that was left* into the sea.

³⁹ When it was daylight, they did not recognize⁺ the land, but they discovered a certain creek with a shore into which they were of a mind⁺ to drive⁺ in the ship, if possible.

⁴⁰ After they had taken away⁺ the anchors, they committed *themselves* to the sea. *Then they* loosened the rudder ropes,⁺ hoisted⁺ up the mainsail to the wind, and headed⁺ toward shore.

⁴¹ *They* fell into a place where two seas met *and* ran the ship aground. The fore part stuck fast and remained immovable but the stern⁺ was broken by the violence of the waves.

⁴² The soldiers' counsel was to kill the prisoners, lest any of them should swim out and escape.

⁴³ But the centurion wanted to save Paul *so he* kept them from *their* purpose. *He* commanded that *those* who could swim should cast *themselves* first *into the sea* and get to land.

⁴⁴ The rest *followed*, some on boards and some on *broken pieces* of the ship. And so it came to pass that they all escaped safely to land.

Acts Chapter 28

¹ After they escaped, they learned⁺ that the island was called Malta.

² The natives⁺ showed us no little kindness. They started⁺ a fire and accepted⁺ everyone because of the rain and cold.

³ When Paul gathered a bundle of sticks and laid *them* on the fire, a came viper out of the heat and fastened on his hand.

⁴ When the natives⁺ saw the *venomous* beast hang on his hand, they said among themselves: No doubt this man is a murderer *and* though he has escaped the sea, yet vengeance does not allow⁺ *him* to live.

⁵ *But* Paul shook the beast off *and* into the fire and felt no harm.

⁶ When they looked *at the place* where he should have swollen, *if not* suddenly fallen down dead, after they had looked *for* a great while and saw no harm had come to him, they changed their minds and said that he was a god.

⁷ In that same area⁺ was the home⁺ of the chief man of the island whose name was Publius. He received us courteously and lodged us *for* three days.

⁸ *Now* it came to pass that the father of Publius lay sick with a fever and dysentery. Paul went to him, prayed, laid his hands on him, and healed him.

⁹ After this, others on the island who had diseases also came *to Paul* and were healed.

¹⁰ *Therefore* they honored us with many honors *and* when we departed, they provided⁺ *for us* such things as were necessary.

¹¹After three months we left⁺ in a ship from Alexandria that had wintered *there* on that island.⁺ *That ship's* sign was Castor and Pollux.

¹²*Upon* landing at Syracuse, we stayed⁺ *there for* three days.

¹³From there⁺ we fetched a compass and came to Rhegium. After one day *there*, the south wind blew, and the next day we went to Puteoli.

¹⁴There, we found family⁺ who invited⁺ us to stay⁺ with them seven days. Then, we went toward Rome.

¹⁵When the family⁺ there heard about us, they came *from* as far *away* as *the* Appii Forum and *the* Three Taverns to meet us. When Paul saw *them*, he thanked God and was encouraged.

¹⁶When we came to Rome, the centurion delivered the prisoners to the captain of the guard. But Paul was allowed⁺ to live⁺ by himself with a soldier to guard⁺ him.

¹⁷Now it came to pass that after three days, Paul called the chief of the Jews together. When they had come together, he said to them: Men *and* family,⁺ though I have committed no *wrong* against the people or customs of our fathers, yet I was delivered *as a* prisoner from Jerusalem into the hands of the Romans.

¹⁸After they examined me, *they* would have let *me* go because there was no *just* cause *to put* me to death.

¹⁹But when the Jews spoke against *me*, I was compelled⁺ to appeal to Caesar, *because* my nation did not have any⁺ *just* accusation *against me*.

²⁰For this reason⁺ therefore I have called for you to see *you* and to speak with *you*. *It is* because of the hope of Israel *that* I am bound with this chain.

²¹They said to him: We did not receive *any* letters from Judea concerning you, nor *did* any of the family⁺ who came *here* report⁺ or speak of any harm *by* you.

²²But we desire to hear your thoughts concerning this sect. For we know that *people* everywhere are speaking against it.

²³So they appointed a day *and* many came to *hear* him at *his* lodging. From morning until evening, he testified and expounded *about* the kingdom of God *to* persuade them about Jesus from both the law of Moses and *from* the prophets.

²⁴Some believed the things that he said and some did not believe.

²⁵When they did not agree among themselves, they left⁺ after Paul spoke one *final* word: Through the prophet Isaiah the Holy Spirit spoke well to our fathers

²⁶saying: Go to this people and say: Hearing, you will hear and not understand. Seeing, you will see and not perceive. *Matthew 13:14*

²⁷For the hearts of these people are calloused⁺ and their ears are dull of hearing and they have closed their eyes, lest they should see with *their* eyes and hear with *their* ears and understand with *their* heart and be converted and *I would* heal them. *Matthew 13:15*

²⁸Therefore, let it be known to you that the salvation of God has been sent to the Gentiles and they will hear it.

²⁹After *Paul* said these words, the Jews left⁺ and had a great debate⁺ among themselves.

³⁰Paul then lived⁺ *for* two whole years in his own rented⁺ house and welcomed⁺ all who came to him.

³¹*He* proclaimed⁺ the kingdom of God and taught those things that pertain⁺ *to* the Lord Jesus Christ with all confidence *and* no one forbid him.

Romans Chapter 1

¹ *From* Paul, a servant of Jesus Christ, called *to be* an apostle *and* separated to the Gospel of God.

² *God* promised *this Gospel* before,⁺ through His prophets in the Holy Scriptures.

³ *This Gospel* concerns His Son Jesus Christ, our Lord, who was made from the seed of David according to the flesh. *John 7:42*

⁴ *Jesus was* declared *to be* the Son of God, with power according to the spirit of holiness, from⁺ the resurrection from the dead.

5 From *Him* we have received grace and apostleship for obedience to the faith among all the nations, for His name.

6 You also are called by Jesus Christ *to be* among *the nations*.

7 To all who are in Rome, loved by God, *and* called *to be* saints. Grace to you and peace from God our Father and Lord Jesus Christ.

8 First *of all*, I thank my God through Jesus Christ for you all. Your faith is spoken of throughout the whole world.

9 For God is my witness, whom I serve in my spirit in the Gospel of His Son: Without ceasing, I make mention of you always in my prayers,

10 asking+ if now *or* when I might have a prosperous *journey*, by the will of God, to come to you.

11 For I long to see you *so* that I may impart to you *some* spiritual gift to which you may be established:

12 That is, comforted together with you through the mutual faith of both you and me.

13 Now I do not want you to lack understanding,+ family.+ Often times I intended+ to come to you *so* that I might have *some* fruit among you also, even as among other nations.+ But until now, *I* was prevented.+

14 I am obligated+ to both the Greeks and the Barbarians, to both the wise and the unwise.

15 So, *with all that is* in me, I am ready to proclaim+ the Gospel to you who are in Rome also.

16 For I am not ashamed of the Gospel of Christ. For it is the power of God unto salvation for everyone who believes. Both to *the* Jew, first, and also to *the* Greek.

17 For the righteousness of God is revealed from *believing* faith to faith *fully persuaded*. As it is written: The righteous+ shall live by faith. *Hab. 2:4*

18 For the wrath of God is revealed from heaven against all *the* ungodly and unrighteous who hold *back* the truth by unrighteousness.

19 Because what may be known of God is revealed+ within them, for God has shown *it* to them.

20 For the invisible things of Him from the creation of the world are clearly seen *and* understood through the things that are made, *even* His eternal power and Godhead, *so* *unbelievers* are without excuse.

21 Because, *even though* they knew God, they did not glorify *Him* as God, nor were *they* thankful. But *they* became vain in their imaginations and their foolish hearts were darkened.

22 Professing themselves to be wise, they became fools

23 and changed the glory of the incorruptible God into an image made like corruptible man and birds and four footed *beasts* and creeping things.

24 Therefore, God gave them up to uncleanness in the lusts of their hearts, to dishonor their bodies between themselves.

25 *They* changed the truth of God into a lie and worshiped and served the creature more than the Creator who is blessed forever. Amen.

26 For this reason,+ God gave them up to vile passions.+ For even their women did change the natural use into what is against nature.

27 Likewise the men also abandoned+ natural joining+ *together* with a woman *and* burned in their lust toward one another, men with men, doing+ shameful+ *things* and receiving in themselves the fitting+ repayment+ for their error.

28 And accordingly,+ since+ they did not like to acknowledge+ God, God gave them over to a reprobate mind, to do those things that are not proper.+

29 *Therefore,* being filled with all unrighteousness, fornication, wickedness, covetousness, *and* maliciousness, *they were also* full of envy, murder, strife,+ deceit, *and* ill will.+ *And they were* whisperers, *Matthew 15:19*

[30]backbiters, haters of God, despiteful, proud, boasters, inventors of evil things, disobedient to parents,

[31]without understanding, covenant breakers, *given to* unnatural[+] affections, unforgiving,[+] *and* unmerciful.

[32]*Yet even* knowing the judgment of God, that *those* who commit such things are worthy of death, *they* not only do them, but *also* consent[+] to *those* who do them.

Romans Chapter 2

[1] Therefore you are inexcusable, people,[+] whoever you are who judge. For *in those things* in which you judge another, you condemn yourself. For you who judge do the same things.

[2] But we are sure that the judgment of God is according to truth against *those* who commit such things.

[3] Do you think this, *you* people who judge *those* who do such things and do the same, that you shall escape the judgment of God?

[4] Or do you despise the riches of His goodness and forbearance and long-suffering, not understanding[+] that the goodness of God leads you to repentance?

[5] But according[+] to your hardness and impenitent heart, *you* treasure up to yourself wrath in the day of wrath and revelation for

> the righteous judgment of God
> [6] will render to everyone[+]
> according to their deeds:
> *Matthew 16:27*
> [7] To *those* who,
> by patient continuance
> in well doing, seek for glory
> and honor and immortality,
> eternal life. *Proverbs 11:23*

[8] But to *those* who are contentious and do not obey the truth, but obey unrighteousness, indignation and wrath, *Proverbs 11:23*

[9] tribulation and anguish upon every soul of people who do evil. Of the Jew first and also of the Gentile. *Proverbs 11:23*

[10]But glory, honor, and peace, to everyone[+] who works good. To the Jew first and also to the Gentile.

[11]For there is no partiality[+] with God.

[12]For all[+] *who* have sinned without law will also perish without law, and as many as have sinned in the law shall be judged by the law.

[13]For *it is* not the hearers of the law *who are* righteous[+] before God, but the doers of the law shall be justified.

[14]For when the Gentiles who do not have the law, do by nature the things contained in the law, they, not having the law, are a law to themselves.

[15]This shows the work of the law written in their hearts, their conscience also bearing witness and *their* thoughts *in* the mean-while accusing or else excusing one another

[16]in the day when God will judge the *inner* secrets of people's *hearts* by Jesus Christ according to my Gospel.

[17]Behold you *who* are called a Jew and rest in the law and make your boast of God,

[18]*you who* know *His* will and approve the things that are more excellent, being instructed out of the law,

[19]*you who* are confident that you your-self are a guide to the blind, a light to *those* who are in darkness,

[20]an instructor of the foolish, a teacher of babes, *you* who have the form of knowledge and of the truth in the law.

[21]Therefore you who teach another, do you not teach yourself? You who preach *that* people[+] should not steal, do you steal?

[22]You who say a man should not commit adultery, do you commit adultery? You who abhor idols, do you commit sacrilege?

[23]You who make your boast of the law, do you dishonor God through breaking the law?

[24]For the name of God is blasphemed among the Gentiles through you, as it is written. *Isaiah 52:5*

[25]For circumcision truly[+] benefits[+] if you keep the law. But if you are a breaker of the law, *then* your circumcision is made uncircumcision.

26 Therefore if *those of* the uncircumcision keep the righteousness of the law, shall not their uncircumcision be counted for circumcision?

27 Shall not *those of the* uncircumcision which is by nature, if they fulfill the law, judge you, who by the letter and circumcision transgress the law?

28 For they are not outwardly Jews. *But* neither *is* circumcision in the flesh *an* outward *matter*.

29 But *they are* Jews who are *so* inwardly. *True* circumcision *is* of the heart, in the spirit, *and* not in the letter. Their praise *is* not of men, but of God.

Romans Chapter 3

1 What advantage then has the Jew? Or what benefit[+] *is there* in circumcision?

2 Much *in* every way. Chiefly because, to them were committed the oracles of God.

3 For what if some did not believe? Shall their unbelief make the faith of God without effect?

4 *That* cannot be.[+] Yes, let God be true but everyone *else* a liar. As it is written: That you might be justified in your sayings and might overcome when you are judged. *Psalm 51:4*

5 But if our unrighteousness commend the righteousness of God, what shall we say? *Is* God unrighteous who takes vengeance? *Paul says, aside:* I speak as a man.

6 *It* cannot be[+] *that God would be unrighteous.* For then how shall God judge the world?

7 For if the truth of God has more abounded through my lie to His glory, *then* why am I yet also judged as a sinner?

8 Not *rather*, as we *have been slanderously* accused,[+] and as some have affirmed that we say: Let us do evil *so* that good may come. Their judgment[+] is just.

9 What then? Are we better *than they*? No, in no way.[+] For we have before proved both Jews and Gentiles, that they are all under sin.

10 As it is written: There are none righteous, no not one. *Psalm 14:3*

11 There are none who understand. There are none who seek after God. *Psalm 14:2*

12 They have all gone out of the way and they together have become unprofitable. There are none who do good. No not one. *Psalm 14:1*

13 Their throats *are* an open tomb.[+] With their tongues they have used deceit. The poison of asps *is* under their lips. *Psalm 5:9*

14 Their mouth *is* full of cursing and bitterness. *Psalm 10:7*

15 Their feet *are* swift to shed blood. *Isaiah 59:7*

16 Destruction and misery *are* in their ways. *Isaiah 59:7*

17 They have not known the way of peace. *Isaiah 59:8*

18 There is no fear of God before their eyes. *Psalm 36:1*

19 Now we know what things the law declares. It says to *those* who are under the law that every mouth may be stopped and all the world may become guilty before God.

20 Therefore by the deeds of the law no flesh will be justified in His sight. For by the law *is* the knowledge of sin.

21 But now the righteousness of God without the law is revealed,[+] being witnessed by the law and the prophets.

22 The righteousness of God *comes* by faith *in* Jesus Christ to all and upon all who believe. For there is no difference.

> 23 For all have sinned
> and come short
> of the glory of God.

24 *All are* being justified freely by His grace through the redemption that is in Christ Jesus.

25 God has set *Jesus* forth *to be* a *means of* reconciliation[+] through faith in His blood, to declare His righteousness for the remission of sins that are past, through the forbearance of God,

26 to declare His righteousness at this time *so* that He might be just and the justifier of *those* who believe in Jesus.

27 Where *is* boasting then? It is excluded. By what law? Of works? No, but by the law of faith.

28 Therefore we conclude that a person[+]

is justified by faith without the deeds of the law.

²⁹*Is God* the God of the Jews only? *Is He* not also of the Gentiles? Yes, of the Gentiles also.

³⁰Seeing *it is* one God who will justify the circumcision by faith and *the* uncircumcision through faith,

³¹do we then make void the law through faith? *That* cannot be.⁺ Yes *rather*, we establish the law.

Romans Chapter 4

¹ What shall we say then that Abraham, our father as pertaining to the flesh, has found?

² For if Abraham were justified by works, *then* he has *something in which* to rejoice,⁺ but not before God.

³ For what do the Scriptures say? Abraham believed God and it was counted to him for righteousness. *Genesis 15:6*

⁴ Now to *those* who work, the reward is not counted⁺ as grace, but as debt.

⁵ But to *those* who do not work, but believe in Him who justifies the ungodly, their faith is counted for righteousness.

⁶ Even as David also described the blessedness of those⁺ to whom God credits⁺ righteousness without works,

⁷ *he said*: Blessed *are* those whose iniquities are forgiven and whose sins are covered. *Psalm 32:1*

⁸ Blessed *are* those⁺ whom the Lord does not make accountable⁺ *for their* sin. *Psalm 32:2*

⁹ *Is* this blessedness, then, *only* upon the circumcision, or upon the uncircumcision also? For we say that faith was credited⁺ to Abraham as righteousness.

¹⁰How was it then credited⁺? When he was in circumcision or in uncircumcision? Not in circumcision, but in uncircumcision.

¹¹He received the sign of circumcision, a seal of the righteousness of the faith *he had while still* uncircumcised *so* that he might be the father of all who believe, *even* the uncircumcised, *so* that righteousness might be credited⁺ to them also,

¹²and the father of circumcision to *those* who are not of the circumcision only, but also *to those* who walk in the steps of that faith of our father Abraham, which *he had while he was still* uncircumcised.

¹³For the promise, that he would be the heir of the world, *was* not to Abraham or to his seed through the law, but through the righteousness of faith.

¹⁴For if *only those* who are of the law *are* heirs, *then* faith is made void and the promise *is* made of no effect.

¹⁵Because the law works wrath. For where no law is, *there is* no transgression.

¹⁶Therefore *it is* by faith, *and* that by *God's* grace, *that* the promise is assured⁺ to all descendants,⁺ not only to those who are of the law, but also to those who are of the faith of Abraham who is the father of us all.

¹⁷As *it is* written: *I have* made you the father of many nations. *For you* believed God who gives life⁺ *to* the dead and calls the not *existing into* what is *existing*. *Genesis 17:5*

¹⁸Who against hope believed in hope that he might become the father of many nations according to what *God had* spoken: So shall your seed be. *Genesis 15:5*

¹⁹Not being weak in faith, *Abraham* did not consider his own body already⁺ dead when he was about a hundred years old, nor the deadness of Sarah's womb.

²⁰He did not stagger at the promise of God through unbelief. But *he* was strong in faith, giving glory to God,

²¹being fully persuaded that what *God* had promised, He was also able to perform.

²²Therefore it was credited⁺ to him for righteousness. *Genesis 15:6*

²³Now this was not written for *Abraham's* sake alone, that it was credited⁺ to him.

²⁴But also for us to whom it shall be credited,⁺ if we believe in Him who raised up Jesus our Lord from the dead,

²⁵who was delivered for our transgressions⁺ and was raised again for our justification.

Romans Chapter 5

[1] Therefore, being justified by faith, we have peace with God through our Lord Jesus Christ.

[2] And through *Jesus*, we have access by faith to this grace in which we stand. And *we* rejoice in *the* hope of the glory of God.

[3] Not only *this*, but we rejoice[+] in tribulations also, knowing that

> tribulation produces[+] patience,
> [4] patience *produces* experience,
> and experience *produces* hope.

[5] And *it is* hope, not shame, *so* that the love of God is shed abroad in our hearts by the Holy Spirit who is given to us.

[6] For when we were yet without strength, in due time Christ died for the ungodly.

[7] For scarcely will one die for a righteous man. Yet perhaps[+] for a good man some would even dare to die.

> [8] But God commends His love toward us, in that, while we were yet sinners, Christ died for us.
> *Isaiah 53:5, John 3:16*

[9] Much more then, now being justified by His blood, we will be saved from wrath through Him.

[10] For if, when we were enemies, we were reconciled to God by the death of His Son, much more, being reconciled, we will be saved by His life.

[11] Not only *this*, but we also rejoice[+] in God through our Lord Jesus Christ from whom we have now received atonement.

[12] Therefore, as by one man sin entered the world and death by sin, so death *is* passed upon all people[+] because[+] all have sinned.

[13] For until the law, sin was in the world, but sin is not chargeable[+] when there is no law.

[14] Nevertheless, death reigned from Adam until Moses, even over *those* who had not sinned after the manner[+] of the transgression of Adam, who is symbolic[+] of *Him who was* to come.

[15] But the gift *is* not like the transgression[+] *of Adam*. For if, through the transgression[+] of one, many are dead, much more the grace of God and the gift by grace, through one man, Jesus Christ, has abounded to many.

[16] The gift *is* not like *what came by* the one who sinned. For the judgment *was* by one to condemnation, but the free gift *is* for many transgressions[+] to justification.

[17] For if by the transgression[+] of one death reigned through[+] *that* one, *then* much more shall *those* who receive abundance of grace and the gift of righteousness reign in life through[+] one: Jesus Christ.

[18] Therefore, as by the transgression[+] of one *judgment came* upon all mankind[+] to condemnation, even so by the righteousness of one *the free gift came* upon all people[+] to justification of life.

[19] For as by one man's disobedience many were made sinners, so *also* by the obedience of one many will be made righteous.

[20] Moreover the law entered *so* that the transgression[+] might abound. But where sin abounded, grace did much more abound,

[21] *so* that as sin has reigned to death, even so might grace reign through righteousness to eternal life by Jesus Christ our Lord.

Romans Chapter 6

[1] What shall we say then? Shall we continue in sin *so* that grace may abound?

[2] *That* cannot be.[+] How shall we who are dead to sin, live any longer in it?

[3] Do you not know that as many of us as were baptized into Jesus Christ were baptized into His death?

[4] Therefore we are buried with Him by baptism into death *so* that, as Christ was raised up from the dead by the glory of the Father, even so we also should walk in newness of life.

[5] For if we have been planted together in the likeness of His death, *then* we will

also be *in the likeness* of *His* resurrection.
[6] Know this: That our old self[+] is crucified with *Him* *so* that the body of sin might be destroyed, *so* that from now on we would not serve sin.
[7] For *those* who are dead are freed from sin.
[8] Now if we are dead with Christ, *then* we believe that we will also live with Him.
[9] *We* know that Christ, being raised from the dead, dies no longer.[+] Death no longer[+] has dominion over Him.
[10] For in that He died, He died to sin once. But in that He lives, He lives to God.
[11] Likewise count[+] yourselves to be dead indeed to sin but alive to God through Jesus Christ our Lord.
[12] Therefore do not let sin reign in your mortal body *so* that you obey it in its lusts.
[13] Do not submit[+] your members *to be* instruments of unrighteousness to sin. But submit[+] yourselves to God, as *people who are* alive from the dead. *Make* your members instruments of righteousness to God.
[14] For sin will not have dominion over you, for you are not under the law, but under grace.
[15] What then? Shall we sin because we are not under the law but under grace? *That* cannot be.[+]
[16] Do you not know that to whomever you submit[+] yourselves *as* servants to obey, you are *indeed* servants of whomever you obey: Whether sin unto death or obedience unto righteousness?
[17] But thanks *be* to God that *even though* you were the servants of sin, you have obeyed from the heart the example[+] of doctrine that was delivered *to* you.
[18] Therefore, being *set* free from sin, you became servants of righteousness.
[19] I speak after the manner of men because of the weakness[+] of your flesh. For as you have yielded your members *as* servants to uncleanness and to iniquity unto iniquity, even so now submit[+] your members *to be* servants to righteousness unto holiness.

[20] For when you were the servants of sin, you were free from righteousness.
[21] What fruit did you have then in those things about which you are now ashamed? For the end of those things *is* death.
[22] But now, being made free from sin and *having* become servants to God, you have your fruit to holiness, and the end: eternal[+] life.

> [23] For the wages of sin *is* death, but the gift of God *is* eternal life through Jesus Christ our Lord.
> *Proverbs 11:19*

Romans Chapter 7

[1] Do you not know, family,[+] for I speak to *those* who know the law, that the law has dominion over people[+] as long as *they* live?
[2] For the woman who has a husband is bound by the law to *her* husband as long as he lives. But if the husband is dead, she is loosed from the law of *her* husband.
[3] So then if while *her* husband lives, she is married to another man, *then* she shall be called an adulteress. But if her husband is dead, she is free from that law, so she is no adulteress *even* though she is married to another man.
[4] Therefore my family,[+] you also have become dead to the law by the body of Christ *so* that you should be married to another, *even* to *Christ* who is raised from the dead, *so* that we would bring forth fruit to God.
[5] For when we were in the flesh, the motions of sins *as exposed* by the law, worked in our members to bring forth fruit unto death.
[6] But now we are delivered from the law, being dead *to that* in which we were held *so* that we might serve in newness of spirit and not *in* the oldness of the letter.
[7] What shall we say then? *Is* the law sin? *That* cannot be.[+] No, I would not have known *about* sin, except[+] by the law.

For I would not have known *about* lust, except the law said: You shall not covet.
[8] But sin, taking occasion by the commandment, produced[+] in me all kinds[+] of abnormal appetites.[+] For without the law, sin *was* dead.
[9] For I was alive without the law once. But when the commandment came, sin revived, and I died.
[10] and found[+] that the commandment that was *intended* for life, *could lead* to death.
[11] For sin, taking occasion by the commandment, deceived me and by it, killed[+] *me*.
[12] Therefore the law *is* holy and the commandment holy and just and good.
[13] Then *was* what *is* good *a cause of* death to me? *That* cannot be.[+] But sin, *so* that it might appear*as* sin, produced[+] death in me by what is good, *so* that sin, by the commandment, might become exceedingly sinful.
[14] For we know that the law is spiritual, but I am worldly,[+] sold under sin.
[15] For what I do, I allow not. For what I would *do*, that I do not. But what I hate, that do I.
[16] Then if I do what I would not *approve*, I consent to the law that *it is* good.
[17] Now then it is no longer[+] I *myself* doing it, but sin that dwells in me.
[18] For I know that good does not dwell in me, that is in my flesh. For to will *to do good* is present within me but *how* to perform what is good I do not find.
[19] For the good that I want[+] *to do*, I do not do. But the evil that I do not *want to do*, that I do.
[20] Now if I do what I would not *want to do, then* it is no longer[+] I *myself* doing it, but sin that dwells in me.
[21] I find then a law: That when I would *want to* do good, evil is present with me.
[22] For I delight in the law of God according[+] *to* the inward man.
[23] But I see another law in my members, warring against the law of my mind and bringing me into captivity to the law of sin that is *lurking* in my members.
[24] O wretched man that I am. Who shall deliver me from the body of this death?
[25] I thank God through Jesus Christ our Lord. So then with the mind I myself serve the law of God, but with the flesh the law of sin.

Romans Chapter 8

[1] Now *there is* no condemnation to *those* who are in Christ Jesus, who do not walk according[+] *to* the flesh but according[+] *to* the Spirit. *John 3:18*

[2] For the law of the Spirit of life in Christ Jesus has made me free from the law of sin and death.
[3] For what the law could not do, in that it was weak through the flesh, God *by* sending His own Son in the likeness of sinful flesh and for sin, condemned sin in the flesh,
[4] *so* that the righteousness of the law might be fulfilled in us, who do not walk according[+] *to* the flesh, but according[+] *to* the Spirit.
[5] For *those* who are after the flesh do mind the things of the flesh. But *those* who are after the Spirit *mind* the things of the Spirit.
[6] To be worldly[+] minded *is* death. But to be spiritually minded *is* life and peace.
[7] Because the worldly[+] mind *is* enmity against God, for it is not subject to the law of God, nor indeed can *it* be.
[8] So then, *those* who are in the flesh cannot please God.
[9] But you are not in the flesh, but in the Spirit, if indeed[+] the Spirit of God dwells in you. Now if anyone does not have the Spirit of Christ, they are not His.
[10] If Christ *is* in you, *then* the body *is* dead because of sin but the Spirit *is* life because of righteousness.
[11] But if the Spirit of Him who raised up Jesus from the dead dwells in you, *then* He who raised up Christ from the dead will also give life[+] *to* your mortal bodies by His Spirit who dwells in you.
[12] Therefore family,[+] we are debtors, not to the flesh to live after the flesh,

[13] for if you live after the flesh you shall die. But if you, through the Spirit, put to death[+] the deeds of the body, you shall live.

[14] For all[+] *who* are led by the Spirit of God are the children[+] of God.

[15] For you have not received the spirit of bondage again to fear, but you have received the Spirit of adoption through whom we cry *out*: Abba Father.

[16] The Spirit bears witness with our spirit that we are the children of God.

[17] If *we are* children, then *we are also* heirs: Heirs of God and joint heirs with Christ. If indeed[+] we suffer with *Him so* that we may also be glorified together.

[18] For I reckon that the sufferings of this present time *are* not worthy *to be compared* with the glory that will be revealed in us.

[19] For the earnest expectation of the creation[+] waits for the manifestation of the children[+] of God.

[20] For the creation[+] was made subject to vanity, not willingly, but by reason of Him who has subjected *it* in hope.

[21] Because the creation[+] itself will also be delivered from the bondage of corruption into the glorious liberty of the children of God.

[22] For we know that the whole creation groans and labors[+] in pain together until now.

[23] Not only *they*, but *we* ourselves also, who have the first fruits of the Spirit, even we ourselves groan within ourselves, waiting for the adoption, the redemption of our body.

[24] For we are *being* saved by hope. But hope that is seen is not hope. For what anyone *already* sees, why would they still[+] hope for *it*?

[25] But if we hope for what we do not see, *then* with patience we wait for *it*.

[26] Likewise the Spirit also helps our weaknesses.[+] For we do not know how to pray as we should. But the Spirit intercedes for us with groanings more profound[+] *than words*.

[27] *He* who searches the hearts knows the mind of the Spirit because He makes intercession for the saints according to *the will of* God.

> [28] We know that
> all things work together for good
> to *those* who love God,
> to *those* who are called
> according to *His* purpose.
> *Matthew 6:33*

[29] For whom He did foreknow, He also predestined *to be* conformed to the image of His Son *so* that He might be the firstborn among many others.[+]

[30] Moreover *those* whom He predestined, He also called. *Those* whom He called, He also justified. *And those* whom He justified, He also glorified.

[31] What shall we then say to these things?

> If God *is* for us,
> who *can be* against us?

[32] He did not spare His own Son, but gave[+] Him up for us all. How shall He not with Him also freely give all things *to* us?

[33] Who will lay anything to the charge of God's elect? *It is* God who justifies.

[34] Who condemns *us*? *It is* Christ who died, and more *important* is risen again, who is at the right hand of God and who also makes intercession for us.

[35] Who shall separate us from the love of Christ? *Shall* tribulation or distress or persecution or famine or nakedness or peril or sword?

[36] As it is written: For your sake we are killed all the day long. We are accounted as sheep for the slaughter. *Psalm 44:22*

[37] No, in all these things we are more than conquerors through Him who loved us.

[38] For I am persuaded that

> neither death nor life
> nor angels nor principalities
> nor powers nor things present
> nor things to come
> [39] nor height nor depth
> nor any other creature
> will be able to separate us
> from the love of God that is
> in Christ Jesus our Lord.

Romans Chapter 9

[1] I speak the truth in Christ. I do not lie. My conscience *is* also bearing witness to me in the Holy Spirit

[2] that I have great heaviness and continual sorrow in my heart.

[3] For I could wish that *I* myself were accursed from Christ for *the sake of* my family[+] *and* my relatives[+] according to the flesh

[4] who are Israelites to whom *was given* the adoption and the glory and the covenants and the giving of the law and the service *of God* and the promises

[5] whose *are* the fathers, and of whom, as concerning the flesh, Christ who is over all, God blessed forever. Amen.

[6] Not as though the Word of God has taken no effect. For they *are* not all Israel who are from Israel.

[7] Nor *are they*, because they are *from* the seed of Abraham, all children. But in Isaac shall your seed be called. *Genesis 21:12*

[8] That is *to say*: Those *who are* children of the flesh *are* not children of God. But the children of the promise are counted to *be* the seed.

[9] For this *was* the word of promise: At this time I will come and Sarah will have a son. *Genesis 17:21*

[10] Not only *that*, but Rebecca also conceived by one, by our father Isaac.

[11] For *the children* not yet born nor having done any good or evil, that the purpose of God according to election might stand, not of works, but of Him who calls,

[12] it was said to her: The elder shall serve the younger. *Genesis 25:23*

[13] As it is written: Jacob I have loved, but Esau I have hated. *Malachi 1:2*

[14] What shall we say then? *Is there* unrighteousness with God? *That* cannot be.[+]

[15] For He said to Moses: I will have mercy on whom I will have mercy, and I will have compassion on whom I will have compassion. *Exodus 33:19*

[16] So then, *it is* not of him who wills or of him who runs, but of God who shows mercy. *Exodus 33:19*

[17] For the Scriptures said to Pharaoh: Even for this same purpose I have raised you up *so* that I might show my power in you and *so* that my name might be declared throughout all the earth. *Exodus 9:16*

[18] Therefore *God* has mercy on whomever He will *have mercy* and He *also* hardens whomever He will.

[19] Then you will say to me: Why does He yet find fault? For who has resisted His will?

[20] Indeed,[+] people,[+] who are you to reply against God? Shall the thing formed say to the one who formed *it*: Why have you made me thus?

[21] Does the potter not have authority[+] over the clay, of the same lump to make one vessel to honor and another to dishonor?

[22] *What* if God, willing to show *His* wrath and to make His power known, endured with much longsuffering vessels of wrath fitted for destruction?

[23] Then He might make known the riches of His glory on the vessels of mercy He prepared for glory,

[24] *even* us, whom He has called, not only of the Jews, but also of the Gentiles?

[25] As He also said in Hosea: I will call them my people who were not my people and *call* her beloved who was not beloved. *Hosea 2:23*

[26] It shall come to pass *that* in the place where it was said to them: You *are* not my people, there they shall be called the children of the living God. *Hosea 1:10*

[27] Isaiah also cried *out* concerning Israel: Though the number of the children of Israel be as the sand of the sea, a remnant will be saved. *Isaiah 10:22*

[28] For He will finish the work and cut *it* short in righteousness, because the Lord will make a short work upon the earth. *Matthew 24:22*

[29] As Isaiah said before: Except the Lord of Sabaoth had left us a seed, we *would have* been like Sodom and been made like Gomorrah. *Isaiah 1:9*

[30] What shall we say then? That the Gentiles, who did not follow after

righteousness, have attained righteousness, even the righteousness that is by faith,

³¹but Israel, which followed after the law of righteousness, has not attained to the law of righteousness.

³²Why? Because *it was* not by faith but by the works of the law. For they stumbled at that stumbling stone. *Isaiah 8:14*

³³As it is written: Behold I lay in Zion⁺ a stumbling stone and rock of offense. Whoever believes in Him will not be ashamed. *Isaiah 28:16*

Romans Chapter 10

¹ Family,⁺ my heart's desire and prayer to God for Israel is that they might be saved.

² For I testify⁺ that they have a zeal for God, but not according to knowledge.

³ For they, being ignorant about God's righteousness and going about to establish their own righteousness, have not submitted themselves to the righteousness of God.

⁴ For Christ *is* the end of the law for righteousness to everyone who believes.

⁵ For Moses described the righteousness that is *attained* by *obedience to* the law: That those who do those things shall live by them. *Leviticus 18:5*

⁶ But the righteousness of faith speak in this way: Do not say in your heart: Who shall ascend into heaven? *For* that is to bring Christ down *from above*. *Deuteronomy 30:12*

⁷ Or *do not say:* Who shall descend into the deep? *For* that is to bring Christ up from the dead. *Deuteronomy 30:13*

⁸ But what does it say? The Word is near you, *even* in your mouth and in your heart. That is the Word of faith we proclaim⁺: *Deuteronomy 30:14*

⁹ If you confess with your mouth the Lord Jesus and believe in your heart that God has raised Him from the dead, you will be saved. *Matthew 10:32*

¹⁰For with their hearts, people⁺ believe unto righteousness, *and* with their mouths confession is made unto salvation.

¹¹For the Scriptures declare: Whoever believes in Him will not be ashamed. *Isaiah 28:16*

¹²For there is no difference between the Jew and the Greek. For the same Lord over all is rich toward all who call upon Him.

¹³For whoever will call upon the name of the Lord will be saved. *Joel 2:32*

¹⁴How then will they call on Him in whom they have not believed? And how will they believe in Him of whom they have not heard? And how will they hear without *someone* proclaiming *the Word?*

¹⁵And how will they proclaim⁺ *the Word* unless they are sent? As it is written: How beautiful are the feet of *those* who proclaim⁺ the Gospel of peace and bring glad tidings of good things. *Isaiah 52:7*

¹⁶But they have not all obeyed the Gospel. For Isaiah says: Lord, who has believed our report? *Isaiah 53:1*

> ¹⁷ So then, faith *comes* by hearing and hearing by the Word of God.

¹⁸But I say: Have they not heard? Yes truly,⁺ the sound of their *voices* went into all the earth and their words to the ends of the world. *Psalm 19:4*

¹⁹But I say: Did Israel not know? First Moses says: I will provoke you to jealousy by *those who are* no people *and* by a foolish nation I will anger you. *Deuteronomy 32:21*

²⁰Isaiah boldly said: I was found by *those* who did not seek me. I was revealed⁺ to *those* who did not ask for me. *Isaiah 65:1*

²¹But to Israel He says: All day long I have stretched forth my hands to a disobedient and rebellious⁺ people. *Isaiah 65:2*

Romans Chapter 11

¹ I say then: Has God cast away His people? *That* cannot be.⁺ For I also am an Israelite, of the seed of Abraham, *of* the tribe of Benjamin.

² God has not cast away His people whom He foreknew. Do you not know⁺ what the Scripture says about Elijah?

How He makes intercession to God against Israel saying:

³ Lord, they have killed your prophets and torn⁺ down your altars. I am left alone and *now* they seek my life. *1 Kings 19:10*

⁴ But what does the answer of God say to him? I have reserved to myself seven thousand men who have not bowed the knee to Baal. *1 Kings 19:18*

⁵ Even so then, at this present time also, there is a remnant according to the election of grace.

⁶ If by grace, then *is it* no longer⁺ of works. Otherwise grace is no longer⁺ grace. But if *it is* from works, then is it no longer⁺ grace. Otherwise work is no longer⁺ work.

⁷ What then? Israel has not obtained what it sought.⁺ Except the elect⁺ obtained it and the rest were blinded.

⁸ As it is written: God has given the spirit of slumber *to* them, eyes that *do* not see and ears that *do* not hear, *even* to this day. *Isaiah 29:10*

⁹ And David said: Let their table be made a snare and a trap and a stumbling block and a repayment⁺ to them. *Psalm 69:22*

¹⁰ Let their eyes be darkened *so* that they may not see and bow down their back always. *Psalm 69:23*

¹¹ I say then: Have they stumbled *so* that they should fall? *That* cannot be.⁺ But *rather* through their transgressions,⁺ salvation *has come* to the Gentiles to provoke them to jealousy.

¹² Now if their transgressions⁺ *bring about* the riches of the world, and the diminishing of them *bring* riches to the Gentiles, how much more *shall* their fullness *be*?

¹³ For I speak to you Gentiles, inasmuch as I am the apostle to the Gentiles *and* I delight⁺ in serving⁺ *you*.

¹⁴ If by any means I may provoke to jealousy⁺ *those who are of* my *own* flesh and *thereby* rescue⁺ some of them.

¹⁵ For if the casting away of them *produce* the reconciling of the world, what *will* the receiving *of them be*, but life from the dead?

¹⁶ For if the first fruit *is* holy, the lump *is* also *holy*. If the root *is* holy, so *are* the branches.

¹⁷ If some of the branches are broken off, and you, being a wild olive tree, were grafted in among them, and with them partake of the root and fatness of the olive tree,

¹⁸ do not boast against the branches. But if you boast, *remember* you do not bear the root, but the root *bears* you.

¹⁹ Then you may say: The branches were broken off *so* that I might be grafted in.

²⁰ Well, *it was* because of unbelief *that* they were broken off, and by faith *that* you stand. Do not be high minded, but fear.

²¹ For if God did not spare the natural branches, *take heed* lest He also not spare you.

²² Behold therefore the goodness and *the* severity of God. Severity on *those* who fell, but goodness toward you if you continue in *His* goodness. Otherwise you also will be cut off.

²³ They also, if they do not abide still in unbelief, will be grafted in again. For God is able to graft them in again.

²⁴ For if you were cut out of the olive tree that is wild by nature and were grafted into a good olive tree, contrary to nature, *then* how much more shall these who are the natural *branches* be grafted *back* into their own olive tree?

²⁵ For I would not, family,⁺ want you to be ignorant of this mystery, lest you should be wise in your own conceits: That, in part, blindness is happened to Israel until the fullness of the Gentiles has come in.

²⁶ So, all Israel will be saved. As it is written: There shall come out of Zion⁺ the Deliverer, and turn ungodliness away from Jacob. *Isaiah 59:20*

²⁷ For this *is* my covenant to them, when I shall take away their sins. *Isaiah 27:9*

²⁸ As concerning the Gospel, *they are* enemies for your sakes. But concerning the elect,⁺ *they are* beloved for the fathers' sakes.

²⁹ For the gifts and calling of God *are* not to be repented.⁺

[30]For as you in times past have not believed God, yet now *you* have received+ mercy through their unbelief. [31]Now these also have not believed *so* that through your mercy they also may receive+ mercy. [32]For God has determined+ them all *to be* in unbelief *so* that He might have mercy upon *them* all. [33]O the depth of the riches in both the wisdom and knowledge of God. How unsearchable *are* His judgments and His ways past finding out. [34]For who has known the mind of the Lord? Or who has been His counselor?

Isaiah 40:13

[35]Or who has first given to Him and it shall be repaid+ to them again? *Job 41:11* [36]For from Him and through Him and to Him *are* all things. To Him *be* glory forever. Amen.

Romans Chapter 12

[1] Therefore I urge+ you family,+ by the mercies of God to present your bodies *as* a living sacrifice, holy *and* acceptable to God, *as* your reasonable service.

> [2] Do not be conformed to this world.
> But be transformed
> by the renewing of your mind
> *so* that you may prove
> what *is* that good and acceptable
> and perfect will of God.

[3] For through the grace given to me, I say to everyone+:

> Do not think *of yourselves*+
> more highly than you+ ought to
> think, but think soberly,
> as God has divided+ to everyone+
> *a* measure of faith.

[4] For as we have many members in one body, and all members do not have the same work+ *to do,* [5] so *also* we, *being* many, are one body in Christ, and everyone members one of *one* another.

[6] But *we* have different gifts according to the grace that is given to us. If+ *our gift is* prophecy, *let us prophesy* according to the proportion of faith. [7] Or *if* ministry, in ministering. Or *those* who teach, in teaching. [8] Or *those* who exhort, in exhortation. *Those* who give, *let them do it* with simplicity. *Those* who rule, with diligence. *Those* who show mercy, with cheerfulness.

> [9] *Let* love be
> without dissimulation.
> Abhor what is evil.
> Cleave to what is good.
> [10] *Be* kindly affectionate+
> to one another, with brotherly love,
> in honor preferring one another.

[11]*Do* not *be* lazy+ in diligence.+ *But be* fervent in spirit in the time+ of serving. [12]Rejoice in hope. *Be* patient in tribulation. Continue *steadfastly* in prayer. [13]Distribute to the necessity of *the* saints. *And be* given to hospitality. [14]Bless *those* who persecute you. Bless and do not curse. *Matthew 05:44* [15]Rejoice with *those* who do rejoice and weep with *those* who weep. [16]*Be* of the same mind toward one another. Do not mind high things, but condescend to people+ of low estate. Do not be wise in your own conceits. *Proverbs 3:7* [17]Repay+ evil for evil to no one. *Rather* provide *what is* honest in the sight of everyone.+ *Matthew 5:39* [18]If possible, as much as lies in you, live peaceably with everyone.+ *Proverbs 12:18* [19]Beloved, do not avenge yourselves, but *rather* yield+ *the* place *of* wrath *to* God. For it is written: Vengeance *is* mine. I will repay, says the Lord. *Deuteronomy 32:35, Proverbs 20:22* [20]Therefore, if your enemy *is* hungry, feed him. If he *is* thirsty, give him *a* drink. For in so doing you will heap coals of fire on his head. *Proverbs 25:21* [21]Do not be overcome by evil, but overcome evil with good.

Romans Chapter 13

¹ Let every soul be subject to the higher authorities⁺ *and powers*. For there is no authority⁺ *or power* but *what comes from*⁺ God. The authorities that exist⁺ are ordained by God.

² Therefore, whoever resists authorities⁺ *and powers*, resists the ordinance of God and *those* who resist will receive judgment⁺ upon themselves.

³ For rulers are not a terror to good works, but to evil. *So*, do you want⁺ to be unafraid of the authorities⁺? *Then* do what is good and you will have praise from *them*.

⁴ For they are ministers of God to you for good. But if you do what is evil, *then* be afraid. For they do not bear the sword in vain. They are ministers of God and avengers⁺ to *execute* wrath upon *those* who do evil.

⁵ Therefore *you* need to be subject *to them*, not only because⁺ of *fear of their* wrath, but also for conscience sake.

⁶ *It is* for this reason⁺ *that* you pay tribute, also. For they are God's ministers, attending continually upon this very thing.

⁷ Therefore, render to all their dues: Tribute to whom tribute *is due*. Custom to whom custom. Fear to whom fear. Honor to whom honor.

> ⁸ Owe no one anything,
> but to love one another.
> For *those* who love *one* another
> have fulfilled the law. *John 13:34*

⁹ For these *commandments*: You shall not commit adultery, you shall not kill, you shall not steal, you shall not bear false witness, you shall not covet, *and if there is* any other commandment, *all* are briefly summarized⁺ in this saying: You shall love your neighbor as yourself. *Matthew 19:18,19, Exodus 20:13-17*

¹⁰ *True* love works no ill toward one's neighbor. Therefore *true* love *is* the fulfilling of the law.

¹¹ Also, knowing the time, *know* that now *is the* time to awake out of sleep, for now our salvation *is* nearer than when we *first* believed.

¹² The night is far spent. The day is *very* near.⁺ Therefore, let us cast off the works of darkness and let us put on the armor of light.

> ¹³ Let us walk honestly, as in the day.
> Not in rioting and drunkenness.
> Not in chambering and wantonness.
> Not in strife and envying.

¹⁴ But put on the Lord Jesus Christ and do not make provision for the flesh, to *fulfill* the lusts *thereof*.

Romans Chapter 14

¹ Receive *those* who are weak in the faith, *but* not to doubtful disputations.

² For some believe that they may eat everything. Others, who are weak, eat *only* herbs.

³ Do not let *those* who eat despise *those* who do not eat. Do not let *those* who do not eat judge *those* who eat. For God has received them.

⁴ Who are you to judge another's servants? To their own masters they stand or fall. Yes, they shall be held⁺ up, for God is able to make them stand.

⁵ One person⁺ esteems one day above another. Others esteem every day *alike*. Let everyone⁺ be fully persuaded in their own mind.

⁶ *Those* who regard the day, regard *it* to the Lord. *Those* who do not regard the day, *it is* to the Lord *that* they do not regard *it*. *Those* who eat, eat to the Lord, for they give God thanks. *Those* who do not eat, *it is* to the Lord *that* they do not eat, and give God thanks.

⁷ For none of us lives to ourselves, and no one dies to themselves.

⁸ For if we live, we live to the Lord *and* if we die, we die to the Lord. Therefore, whether we live or die, we are the Lord's.

⁹ For to this end Christ both died and rose and revived *so* that He might be

Lord of both the dead and *the* living.

¹⁰But why do you judge your brother? Or why do you belittle⁺ your brother? For we shall all stand before the judgment seat of Christ.

¹¹For it is written: *As* I live, says the Lord, every knee shall bow to me, and every tongue shall confess to God. *Isaiah 45:23*

¹²So then everyone of us shall give account of themselves to God.

¹³Therefore, let us not judge one another any more. But judge this instead⁺: That no one put a stumbling block or an occasion to fall in another's way.

¹⁴I know and am persuaded by the Lord Jesus, that *there is* nothing unclean of itself. But to *those* who consider⁺ anything to be unclean, to them *it is* unclean.

¹⁵But if another⁺ is grieved because of *your* food, ⁺ *then* you are not walking *in true* love. Do not destroy one for whom Christ died because of your food.⁺

¹⁶Do not let your good be evil spoken of.

¹⁷For the kingdom of God is not food⁺ and drink, but righteousness and peace and joy in the Holy Spirit.

¹⁸For *those* who serve Christ in these things *are* acceptable to God and approved by mankind.⁺

---

¹⁹ Therefore, let us follow after the things that make for peace and things with which one may edify another.

---

²⁰Do not destroy the work of God for *the sake of* food.⁺ All things indeed *are* pure, but evil for that person⁺ who stumbles⁺ by eating.

²¹*It is* good to not eat flesh or drink wine or *do anything* by which another⁺ stumbles or is offended *and caused to sin* or is made weak.

²²Do you have faith? Have *it* to yourself before God. Blessed *are those* who do not condemn themselves in what they allow.

²³*Those* who doubt are damned if they eat because *they do* not *eat* in faith. For whatever *is* not of faith is sin.

Romans Chapter 15

¹ We who are strong ought to bear the infirmities of the weak and not *live* to please ourselves.

² Let everyone of us please *their* neighbor for *their* good to edification.

³ For even Christ did not please Himself, but as it is written: The reproaches of *those* who reproached you fell on me. *Psalm 69:9*

⁴ For whatever things were written previously⁺ were written for our learning *so* that we, through patience and comfort of the Scriptures, might have hope.

⁵ Now the God of patience and consolation grant you to be like minded toward one another according to Christ Jesus

⁶ *so* that you may with one mind *and* one mouth glorify the God and Father *of* our Lord Jesus Christ.

⁷ Therefore receive one another as Christ also received us, to the glory of God.

⁸ Now I say that Jesus Christ was a minister of the circumcision for the truth of God to confirm the promises *made* to the fathers

⁹ *so* that the Gentiles might glorify God for *His* mercy. As it is written: For this reason⁺ I will confess to you among the Gentiles and sing to your name. *Psalm 18:49*

¹⁰Again he said: Rejoice you Gentiles, with His people. *Deuteronomy 32:43*

¹¹And again: Praise the Lord all you Gentiles. Praise⁺ Him, all you people. *Psalm 117:1*

¹²Again, *as* Isaiah said: There will be a root of Jesse who will rise to reign over the Gentiles. The Gentiles will trust in Him. *Isaiah 11:10*

¹³Now the God of hope fill you with all joy and peace in believing *so* that you may abound in hope through the power of the Holy Spirit.

¹⁴I myself am also persuaded about you, my family,⁺ that you also are full of goodness, filled with all knowledge, and able to admonish one another.

¹⁵Nevertheless, family, ⁺ I have written more boldly to you in some sort, as

putting you in mind, because of the grace that is given to me from God,

[16] that I should be the minister of Jesus Christ to the Gentiles, ministering the Gospel of God *so* that the offering up of the Gentiles might be acceptable, being sanctified by the Holy Spirit.

[17] Therefore, I have reason+ to rejoice+ through Jesus Christ in those things that pertain to God.

[18] For I do not dare to speak *about* anything *other than* what Christ accomplished+ *using* me to *make the* Gentiles obedient, by word and deed,

[19] through mighty signs and wonders by the power of the Spirit of God so that, from Jerusalem and *all* around+ to Illyricum, I have fully proclaimed+ the Gospel of Christ.

[20] And so, I have endeavored+ to proclaim+ the Gospel, not where Christ was *already* named, lest I should build upon another's foundation,

[21] but as it is written: To whom He was not spoken of, they shall see. *Those* who have not heard shall understand. *Isaiah 52:15*

[22] For this cause also I have been much hindered from coming to you.

[23] But now, having no more place *to go* in these parts, and having a great desire these many years to come to you,

[24] whenever I take my journey into Spain, I will come to you. For I trust to see you on my journey, and to be brought to you on my way there, if I *may* be somewhat filled by your *company* first.

[25] But *for* now I *am* going to Jerusalem to minister to the saints *there*.

[26] For it has pleased those of Macedonia and Achaia to make a certain contribution for the poor saints who are at Jerusalem.

[27] It has truly+ pleased them. They are indebted to them. For if the Gentiles have been made partakers of their spiritual things, *then it* is their duty also to minister to them in *their needs in the* flesh. +

[28] Therefore, when I have performed this and have sealed this fruit to them, I will come to you *on the way* to Spain.

[29] I am sure that when I come to you, I will come in the fullness of the blessing of the Gospel of Christ.

[30] Now I urge you, family, + for the sake of the Lord Jesus Christ and for the love of the Spirit, that you strive together with me in *your* prayers to God for me

[31] *so* that I may be delivered from *those* who do not believe in Judea, *so* that my service for Jerusalem may be accepted by the saints,

[32] *and so* that I may come to you with joy by the will of God and may be refreshed with you.

[33] Now the God of peace *be* with you all. Amen.

Romans Chapter 16

[1] I commend to you Phebe our sister, who is a servant of the assembly+ at Cenchrea.

[2] Receive her in the Lord, as becomes saints, and assist her in whatever business she has need of you. For she has been a helper+ of many and of me also.

[3] Greet Priscilla and Aquila, my helpers in Christ Jesus

[4] who have laid down their own necks for my life. Not only *do* I give thanks to them, but so *do* all the assemblies+ of the Gentiles.

[5] Likewise *greet* the assembly+ that is in their house. Greet+ my beloved Epaenetus, who is the first fruits of Achaia to Christ.

[6] Greet Mary, who bestowed much labor on us.

[7] Greet+ Andronicus and Junia, my relatives+ and my fellow prisoners who are of note among the apostles *and* who also were in Christ before me.

[8] Greet Amplias my beloved in the Lord.

[9] Greet+ Urbane, our helper in Christ, and Stachys my beloved.

[10] Greet+ Apelles *who is* approved in Christ. Greet+ *those* who are of *the household of* Aristobulus.

[11] Greet Herodion, my kinsman. Greet *those* who are of the *household* of Narcissus who are in the Lord.

¹²Greet⁺ Tryphena and Tryphosa who labor in the Lord. Greet⁺ the beloved Persis who labored much in the Lord.

¹³Greet⁺ Rufus, chosen in the Lord, and his mother and mine.

¹⁴Greet⁺ Asyncritus, Phlegon, Hermas, Patrobas, Hermes, and the *members of the* family⁺ who are with them.

¹⁵Greet⁺ Philologus and Julia, Nereus and his sister, Olympas, and all the saints who are with them.

¹⁶Greet⁺ one another with a holy kiss. The assemblies⁺ of Christ *all* greet⁺ you.

¹⁷Now I urge you, family⁺: Note⁺ *those* who cause divisions and offenses contrary to the doctrine you have learned. Avoid them.

¹⁸For such *people* do not serve our Lord Jesus Christ, but their own belly. By good *sounding* words and *a pretense of speaking* blessings⁺ *they* deceive the hearts of the simple,

¹⁹for your obedience has become known⁺ to everyone. ⁺ Therefore, I rejoice⁺ about you. But yet, I would have you *be* wise to what is good and simple concerning evil.

²⁰The God of peace will bruise Satan under your feet soon.⁺ The grace of our Lord Jesus Christ *be* with you. Amen.

²¹Timothy my fellow worker and Lucius and Jason and Sosipater, my relatives,⁺ greet⁺ you.

²²I Tertius who wrote *this* epistle greet⁺ you in the Lord.

²³Gaius, my host, and of the whole assembly⁺ greets⁺ you. Erastus the chamberlain of the city greets⁺ you, and *also* Quartus, a brother.

²⁴The grace of our Lord Jesus Christ *be* with you all. Amen.

²⁵Now unto Him who has the power to strengthen⁺ you according to my Gospel and *my* proclaiming⁺ of Jesus Christ according to the revelation of the mystery *that was previously* silent⁺ *since* time⁺ began

²⁶but is now revealed⁺ by the Scriptures of the prophets *and* according to the commandment of the eternal⁺ God *to* make *this* known to all nations for the obedience of faith:

²⁷To God only wise, *be* glory through Jesus Christ forever. Amen.

This epistle was written at Corinth and was sent to the Romans by Phebe, a servant of the church at Cenchrea.

1 Corinthians Chapter 1

¹ *From* Paul, called *to be* an apostle of Jesus Christ through the will of God, and *from* Sosthenes *our* brother.

² To the assembly⁺ of God at Corinth. To *those* who are sanctified in Christ Jesus *and* called *to be* saints, *along* with everyone in every place who calls upon the name of Jesus Christ our Lord, both their *Lord* and ours.

³ Grace to you and peace from God our Father and Lord Jesus Christ.

⁴ I thank my God always for you, for the grace of God that is given *to* you by Jesus Christ,

⁵ *knowing* that in everything you are enriched by Him, in all utterance and *in* all knowledge,

⁶ even as the testimony of Christ was confirmed in you,

⁷ so that you are not lacking⁺ in any gift *while* waiting for the coming of our Lord Jesus Christ.

⁸ And *Christ* will confirm you to the end *so that you may be* blameless in the day of our Lord Jesus Christ.

⁹ God *is* faithful *and* you were called by *Him* into fellowship with His Son Jesus Christ our Lord.

¹⁰Now I urge you, family,⁺ by the name of our Lord Jesus Christ, that you all speak the same thing and *that* there be no divisions among you, but *that* you

> be perfectly joined together
> in the same mind
> and in the same judgment.

¹¹For it has been declared to me about you, my family,⁺ by those *who are of the house* of Chloe, that there are contentions among you. *Proverbs 6:19*

¹²Now I say this, *noting* that each of you

says: I am of Paul, or I of Apollos or I of Cephas or I of Christ.

¹³Is Christ divided? Was Paul crucified for you or were you baptized in the name of Paul?

¹⁴I thank God that I baptized none of you except⁺ Crispus and Gaius,

¹⁵lest anyone should say that I had baptized in my own name.

¹⁶I also baptized the household of Stephanas, *but* besides *that*, I do not know if I baptized any others.

¹⁷For Christ did not send me to baptize, but to proclaim⁺ the Gospel. *Yet* not with *the* wisdom of words, lest the cross of Christ should be made of no effect.

¹⁸For the proclaiming⁺ of the cross is foolishness to *those* who *will* perish. But to *those of* us who are being saved it is the power of God.

¹⁹For it is written: I will destroy the wisdom of the wise and bring to nothing the understanding of the prudent. *Isaiah 29:14*

²⁰Where *are* the wise? Where *is* the scribe? Where *is* the disputer of this world? Has God not made the wisdom of this world foolishness?

²¹Because, in the wisdom of God, the world *would* not know *or understand* God through *human* wisdom. *Instead*, it pleased God to save *those* who *would* believe *through* the simpleness⁺ of proclaiming⁺ *the Word*.

²²For the Jews require a sign and the Greeks seek after wisdom.

²³But we proclaim⁺ Christ crucified. To the Jews *He is* a stumbling block and to the Gentiles *He is* foolishness.

²⁴But to *those* who are called, both Jews and Greeks, Christ *is* the power of God and the wisdom of God.

²⁵Because the foolishness of God is wiser than men, and the weakness of God is stronger than men.

²⁶For you see *in* your *being* called, family,⁺ that not many wise according⁺ to the flesh, not many mighty, *and* not many noble *are called*.

²⁷But God has chosen the foolish things of the world to confound the wise. God has chosen the weak things of the world to confound the things that are mighty.

²⁸God has chosen *the* lowly⁺ of the world and the despised and things that are not *mighty and noble*, *in order* to bring to nothing the things that are *thought by the world to be mighty and noble*,

²⁹*so* that no flesh would boast⁺ in His presence.

³⁰But from Him, you are in Christ Jesus who by God was made wisdom and righteousness and sanctification and redemption to us,

³¹*so* that, as it is written: *Those* who *would* boast,⁺ let them boast⁺ *only* in the Lord. *Psalm 105:3*

1 Corinthians Chapter 2

¹ When I came to you, family,⁺ I did not come with excellent speech or wisdom, declaring to you the testimony of God.

² For I determined to not know anything among you except Jesus Christ, and Him crucified.

³ I was with you in weakness and fear and much trembling.

⁴ My speech and my proclaiming⁺ *was* not with enticing words of man's wisdom, but in demonstration of Spirit and of power,

⁵ *so* that your faith would not stand on the wisdom of men, but in the power of God.

⁶ However we speak wisdom among *those* who are perfect, but *it is* not the wisdom of this world or of the princes of this world who come to nothing.

⁷ But we speak the wisdom *that* God hid in mystery. *And* God predetermined⁺ *all this* for our glory before the world *began*.

⁸ None of the princes of this world understood⁺ this. For if they had understood *it*, they would not have crucified the Lord of glory.

⁹ But as it is written: Eye has not seen nor ear heard nor has *it* entered the heart of mankind,⁺ the things that God has prepared for *those* who love Him. *Isaiah 64:4*

¹⁰But God has revealed *them* to us by His Spirit, for the Spirit searches all things. Yes, the deep things of God.

[11]For who understands[+] the things of mankind,[+] except[+] the spirit within them? Likewise, no one understands the things of God but the Spirit of God.

[12]Now we have not received the spirit of the world, but the Spirit of God, *so* that we might know the things that are freely given to us by God.

[13]*We* do not speak in the words taught *by the* wisdom of mankind, but *in words* taught *by the* Holy Spirit, *considering and* comparing spiritual *concepts with* spiritual *words*.

> [14] For natural man
> does not comprehend[+]
> the things of the Spirit of God,
> for they are foolishness to them.
> Neither can they know *them*,
> because they are
> spiritually discerned.

[15]But *those* who are spiritual judge all things. Yet they themselves are judged by no one.

[16]For who has known the mind of the Lord, that they might *presume to* instruct Him? But we have the mind of Christ.

Isaiah 40:13,14

1 Corinthians Chapter 3

[1] Family,[+] I have not spoken to you as to spiritual *people*, but as to worldly[+] *people*, *even* as to babes in Christ.

[2] I have fed you with milk and not with *solid* food.[+] Because until now,[+] you have not been able *to bear it*, nor are you able now.

[3] For you are still[+] worldly.[+] For among you *there is* envying and strife and divisions. Are you not *still* worldly[+] and walking in fleshly[+] *desires*?

[4] For while one says: I am of Paul, and another: I *am* of Apollos. Are you not worldly[+]?

[5] Who then is Paul and who *is* Apollos, but ministers through whom you believed, even as the Lord gave to everyone[+]?

[6] I have planted and Apollos watered. But God gave the increase.

[7] So then, *those* who plant are not anything *special*, nor are *those* who water. But *it is* God who gives the increase.

[8] Now *those* who plant and *those* who water are one. Everyone will receive their own reward according to their own labor.

[9] For we are laborers together with God. You are God's husbandry. *You are* God's building.

[10]According to the grace of God that is given to me as a wise master builder, I have laid the foundation and another builds *upon it*. But let everyone[+] take heed how they build.

[11]For no other foundation can anyone lay than the *one already* laid, *and* that is Jesus Christ.

[12]Now if anyone builds upon this foundation: Gold, silver, precious stones, wood, hay, *or* stubble,

[13]everyone's work will be revealed.[+] For the *judgment* day will declare it because it will be revealed by fire.

> Fire will test[+]
> everyone's[+] work
> *to see* of what sort it is.

[14]If anyone's work builds *something that will* last,[+] *they* will receive a reward.

[15]If anyone's work shall be burned*up*, *then they* will suffer loss, but they *themselves* will be saved, even though through fire.

[16]Do you not know that you are the temple of God and *that* the Spirit of God dwells in you?

[17]If anyone defiles the temple of God, God will destroy them. For the temple of God is holy *and* you are *one of those temples*.

[18]Let no one deceive themselves. If anyone among you seems to be wise in this world, let them become a fool *so* that they may become wise.

[19]For the wisdom of this world is foolishness with God. For it is written: He frustrates[+] the wise in their own craftiness. *Job 5:13*

[20]Again, The Lord knows the thoughts of the wise, that they are vain. *Psalm 94:11*

[21] Therefore let no one boast[+] in mankind.[+] For all things are yours. [22] Whether Paul or Apollos or Cephas or the world or life or death or things present or things to come: All are yours [23] and you are Christ's and Christ *is* God's.

1 Corinthians Chapter 4

[1] Let mankind[+] count us as ministers of Christ and stewards of the mysteries of God.
[2] Now, it is required in stewards that they be found faithful.
[3] As for me, it is a very small thing that I should be judged by you or by the judgment of mankind.[+] Nor do I judge myself.
[4] For I know nothing in myself, and *it is* not in this *that* I am justified, but *it* is the Lord who will judge me.
[5] Therefore, do not judge anything before the time, until the Lord comes who will bring to light the hidden things of darkness and reveal[+] the counsels of the hearts. Then shall everyone[+] have praise from God.
[6] Now family,[+] I have applied these *things* to myself and *to* Apollos *as an example* for you *so* that you might learn from us to not think *that you know* more than what has been written. None of you should be puffed up against one another.
[7] For who makes you different *from another*? And what do you have that you did not receive? Now if you received *it*, *then* why do you boast[+] as if you had not received *it*?
[8] Now you are full. Now you are rich. You have reigned as kings without us. I wish[+] to God *that* you did reign *so* that we might also reign with you.
[9] For I think that God has set us forth as apostles last appointed to death. For we are made a spectacle to the world and to angels and to people.[+]
[10] We *are* fools for Christ's sake, but you *are* wise in Christ. We *are* weak, but you *are* strong. You *are* honored, but we *are* despised.

[11] Even to this present hour we both hunger and thirst and are naked and are buffeted and have no certain dwelling place.
[12] *We* labor working with our own hands. Being reviled, we bless. Being persecuted, we suffer it.
[13] Being defamed, we entreat. We are made like the filth of the world *and* the rubbish[+] of all things to this day.
[14] I do not write these things to shame you, but as my beloved children,[+] I warn *you*.
[15] For though you have ten thousand instructors in Christ, yet *you do* not *have* many fathers. For in Christ Jesus I have fathered[+] you through the Gospel.
[16] Therefore I urge[+] you: Be followers *of* me.
[17] For this reason[+] I have sent Timothy to you. *He* is my beloved son and faithful in the Lord. He will remind you about my way *of life* in Christ as I teach everywhere in every assembly.[+]
[18] Now some *of you* are puffed up as though I would not come to you.
[19] But I will come to you soon,[+] if the Lord will *allow it*, and *then I* will know, not the speech of *those* who are puffed up, but the power.
[20] For the kingdom of God *is* not in *mere* words but in power.
[21] What will you *have me do*? Shall I come to you with a rod or in love and *in* the spirit of meekness?

1 Corinthians Chapter 5

[1] It is commonly reported *that there is* fornication among you, and such fornication as is not even[+] named among the Gentiles: That one should have his father's wife.
[2] And you are puffed up, instead[+] of mourning *so* that *the one* who has done this deed might be taken *out* from among you.
[3] For truly, [+] *even though* I am absent in body, but present in *the* spirit, *I* have already judged *this* as though I were present, *concerning the one* who has done this deed.

⁴ In the name of our Lord Jesus Christ, when you are gathered together, and my spirit *with you*, with the power of our Lord Jesus Christ,

⁵ deliver such a one to Satan for the destruction of the flesh *so* that the spirit might be saved in the day of the Lord Jesus.

⁶ Your boasting⁺ *is* not good. Do you not know that a little leaven permeates⁺ the whole lump?

⁷ Therefore, purge out the old leaven *so* that you may be a new lump, as you are, unleavened. For Christ our Passover is sacrificed for us.

⁸ Therefore let us keep the feast, not with old leaven or with the leaven of malice and wickedness, but with the unleavened *bread* of sincerity and truth.

⁹ I wrote to you in an epistle to not *keep* company with fornicators.

¹⁰ Yet *that does* not *mean* entirely⁺ *isolated* from the fornicators of this world or from the covetous or extortioners or from idolaters. For then you must need *to* go out of the world.

> ¹¹ But now I have written to you to not keep company *with them* if anyone who is called a believer⁺ is a fornicator or covetous or an idolater or a railer or a drunkard or an extortioner. Do not *even* eat with such a one.
>
> ¹² Should I judge *those* who are outside⁺ *the faith*? *No.* But do you not judge *those* who are within?

¹³ God judges *those* who are outside.⁺ Therefore, put away from among yourselves that wicked person.

1 Corinthians Chapter 6

¹ Dare any of you, having a matter against another, go to law before the unrighteous⁺ and not before the saints?

Matthew 5:25

² Do you not know that the saints will judge the world? And if the world will be judged by you, are you unworthy to judge the smallest matters?

³ Do you not know that we will judge angels? How much more *then, the* things that pertain to this life?

⁴ *So* then, if you have judgments of things pertaining to this life, set them to judge who are least esteemed in the assembly.⁺

⁵ I speak *this* to your shame. Is it so that there is not a wise person⁺ among you? Not one who is able to judge between believers⁺?

⁶ But believer⁺ goes to law with believer,⁺ and that before unbelievers.

⁷ Now therefore, there is utterly a fault among you because you go to law with one another. Why do you not instead⁺ *just* accept⁺ *the* wrong? Why do you not instead⁺ *allow yourselves to* be defrauded?

⁸ No. You do wrong and defraud, and that *among* believers.⁺

> ⁹ Do you not know that the unrighteous will not inherit the kingdom of God? Do not be deceived. Neither fornicators nor idolaters nor adulterers nor effeminate *persons* nor defilers⁺ of themselves
>
> ¹⁰ nor thieves nor covetous nor drunks nor revilers nor extortioners will inherit the kingdom of God.

¹¹ Such were some of you. But *now* you are washed. But *now* you are sanctified. But *now* you are justified in the name of the Lord Jesus and by the Spirit of our God.

¹² All things are lawful to me. But all things are not expedient. All things are lawful for me. But I will not be brought under the power of anything.

¹³ Food⁺ for the belly and the belly for food.⁺ But God will destroy both it and them. Now the body *is* not for fornication, but for the Lord. And the Lord for the body.

¹⁴ God has both raised up the Lord and will also raise up us by His own power.

¹⁵ Do you not know that your bodies are the members of Christ? Shall I then take the members of Christ and make *them* the members of a harlot? *That* cannot be.⁺

[16]What? Do you not know that anyone who is joined to a harlot becomes[+] one body *with them*? For two, He says, shall be one flesh. *Matthew 19:5*

[17]But *those* who are joined to the Lord are one *in* spirit *with Him*.

[18]Flee fornication. Every *other* sin that anyone does is outside[+] the body. But *those* who commit fornication sin against their own bodies.

[19]What? Do you not know that your body is the temple of the Holy Spirit in you, whom you have *received* from God? You are not your own.

[20]You are bought with a price. Therefore glorify God in your body and in your spirit, which are God's.

1 Corinthians Chapter 7

[1] Now concerning the things about which you wrote to me: *It is* good *for a* man *and* woman not to touch.

[2] But because of *the temptation of* fornication, let every man have his own wife and let every woman have her own husband.

[3] Let the husband render to the wife due benevolence. Likewise also *let* the wife to the husband.

[4] The wife does not have authority[+] over her own body, but the husband. Likewise also the husband does not have authority[+] over his own body, but the wife.

[5] Do not deprive[+] one another, except *it be* with consent for a time *so* that you may give yourselves to fasting and prayer. *Then* come together again *so* that Satan will not tempt you for your inability to restrain.[+]

[6] But I say this as a permission *and* not as a commandment.

[7] For I would *prefer* that all mankind[+] was even as I myself. But everyone[+] has their proper gift from God: One after this manner, and another after that.

[8] Therefore, I say to the unmarried and *to* widows, it is good for them if they remain even as I *am*.

[9] However, if they cannot restrain[+] *themselves*, *then* let them marry. For it is better to marry than to burn *with passion*.

[10]To the married I charge,[+] not I but the Lord: Do not let *a* wife separate[+] from *her* husband.

[11]But if she separate,[+] let her remain unmarried or be reconciled to *her* husband. And do not let *a* husband put away *his* wife.

[12]But to the rest I, not the Lord, speak: If any brother has a wife who does not believe and she is pleased to live[+] with him, *then* let him not put her away.

[13]And if a woman has a husband who does not believe and he is pleased to dwell with her, *then* let her not leave him.

[14]For the unbelieving husband is sanctified by the wife. And the unbelieving wife is sanctified by the husband. Otherwise,[+] your children would be *considered* unclean, but now they are holy.

[15]But if the unbelieving depart, let them go.[+] A brother or a sister is not under bondage in such *cases*, but God has called us to peace.

[16]For how do you know, O wife, if you *might* save *your* husband? Or how do you know, O man, if you *might* save *your* wife?

[17]But as God has distributed to everyone[+] *and* as the Lord has called everyone, so let them walk. And so I *also* ordain in all *the* assemblies.[+]

[18]Was anyone called *after* being circumcised? *Then* let them not become uncircumcised. Has anyone been called *while yet* in uncircumcision? *Then* let them not be circumcised.

[19]Circumcision is nothing and uncircumcision is nothing, but keep the commandments of God.

[20]Let everyone[+] abide in the same calling in which they were called.

[21]Were you called *while* a servant? Do not be concerned[+] about it. But if you may be made free, *then* use *that* instead.[+]

[22]For *those* who are called in the Lord, *while being* servants, are the Lord's free[+] *people*. And likewise *those* who are called, *being* free, are Christ's servants.

[23]You are bought with a price. Do not become the servants of men.

[24]Family,[+] let each one[+] abide with God in *that* state in which they were called.

²⁵Now concerning virgins I have no commandment from the Lord. Yet I *will* give my judgment as one who has received⁺ mercy from the Lord to be faithful.

²⁶I suppose therefore that this *assessment* is good for the present conditions,⁺ that *it is* good for a man to *remain as he* is.

²⁷Are you bound to a wife? Do not seek to be loosed. Are you loosed from a wife? Do not seek a wife.

²⁸But if you have married, you have not sinned and if a virgin marries, she has not sinned. But such will have trouble in the flesh and I *would* spare you *of that*.

²⁹But this I say, family⁺: The time *is* short. It remains, that *those* who have wives *should* be as though they had none ³⁰and *those* who weep as *though they* did not weep and *those* who rejoice as *though they* did not rejoice and *those* who buy as *though they* did not possess *things* ³¹and *those* who use this world as not misusing⁺ *it*. For the fashion of this world passes away.

³²But I would have you to be *free from anxious* cares.⁺ *Those* who are unmarried care *about* the things of the Lord *and* how to please the Lord. *Matthew 6:25*

³³But *those* who are married care *about* the things of the world *such as* how to please *a* wife.

³⁴*And there is a* difference between a wife and a virgin. The unmarried care about the things of the Lord, to be holy in both body and in spirit. But *the* married care about the things of the world, *such as* how to please *a* husband.

³⁵I say this for your own benefit.⁺ Not *so* that I might cast a snare upon you, but for what is desirable⁺ and *so* that you may attend upon the Lord without distraction.

³⁶But if anyone thinks *that they might* behave improperly⁺ *with regard* to *preserving* virginity, *and* if *they are* beyond *the appropriate* age, and so it ought to be, *then* let them do what they will *for* they do not sin *if* they marry.

³⁷Nevertheless, one does well who stands steadfast in their heart, having no necessity, but having authority⁺ over their own will and having decreed in their heart to preserve⁺ virginity.

³⁸So then, one who enters⁺ into marriage does well. But one who does not enter⁺ into marriage does better.

³⁹A wife is bound by the law as long as her husband lives. But if her husband dies, she is at liberty to be married to whomever she will, *yet* only in the Lord.

⁴⁰But in my judgment, she *will be* happier if she remains⁺ *unmarried*, and I think that I have the Spirit of God.

1 Corinthians Chapter 8

¹ Now concerning⁺ things offered to idols, we know that we all have knowledge, *yet* knowledge puffs up. But *true* love edifies.

² If anyone thinks that they know anything, they know nothing yet as they ought to know.

³ But if anyone *truly* loves God, *then* they are *also* known by Him.

⁴ Therefore, as concerning the eating of those things that are offered in sacrifice to idols, we know that an idol *is* nothing in the world and that *there is* no other God but one.

⁵ For though there are *some* who are called gods, whether in heaven or in earth, as there are many *so called* gods and many lords,

⁶ yet to us *there is only* one God who *is the* Father, from whom everything *has come*, and we *are* His. And *there is* one Lord Jesus Christ through whom everything *has come*. And we *have come* through Him.

⁷ However everyone⁺ does not *yet* have this understanding.⁺ But some still⁺ have a concern⁺ *about* sacrifices offered to idols, and their conscience, being weak, *would thus be* defiled.

⁸ But food⁺ does not commend us to God. For if we eat we are not better, nor if we do not eat are we worse.

⁹ But take heed lest by any means this liberty of yours becomes a stumbling block to *those* who are weak.

¹⁰For if anyone sees you who have understanding⁺ sit to eat⁺ in the idol's temple, will not the conscience of *those*

who are weak be made bold+ to eat those things that are offered to idols?
¹¹ And *so* through your knowledge, will *you cause* the weak brother for whom Christ *also* died *to* perish?
¹² When you sin against the family+ and wound their weak conscience, you sin against Christ.
¹³ Therefore if *certain* foods+ cause+ another to sin, I will not eat *such* flesh ever,+ lest I offend another *and cause them to sin.*

1 Corinthians Chapter 9

¹ Am I not an apostle? Am I not free? Have I not seen Jesus Christ our Lord? Are you not *the fruit of* my work in the Lord?
² If I am not an apostle to others, yet doubtless I am to you. For you are the seal of my apostleship in the Lord.
³ *Therefore* my answer to *those* who examine me is this:
⁴ Do we not have authority+ to eat and to drink?
⁵ Do we not have authority+ to go around+ *with* a sister *or* a wife, as well as *the* other apostles and the brothers of the Lord and Cephas?
⁶ Or *is it* only Barnabas and I *who* do not have authority+ to forgo+ *temporal* work *in order to minister.*
⁷ Who ever+ soldiers+ at his own expense+? Who plants a vineyard and does not eat of its fruit? Or who feeds a flock and does not eat of the milk of the flock?
⁸ Do I say these things as a man? Or does the law not say the same also?
⁹ For it is written in the law of Moses: You shall not muzzle the mouth of the ox that treads out the corn. Does God care about oxen? *Deuteronomy 25:4*
¹⁰ Or does He say *this* entirely+ for our sakes? *No doubt this* is written for our sakes *so* that *those* who plow should plow in hope, *and those* who thresh in hope should be partakers of their hope.
¹¹ If we have sown spiritual things to you, *is it* a great thing *to you* if we reap *some of* your worldly+ things?

¹² If others are partakers of *this* authority+ over you, *should* we not *just as* much+? Nevertheless we have not used this authority,+ but *we* suffer all things lest we should hinder the Gospel of Christ.
¹³ Do you not know that *those* who minister about holy things live *from the things* of the temple? And *those* who attend+ at the altar are partakers *of* the altar?
¹⁴ Even so, the Lord has ordained that *those* who proclaim+ the Gospel should live from *the fruit of* the Gospel.
¹⁵ But I have used none of these things. Nor have I written these things *so* that it should be so done for me. For *it is* better for me to die than that anyone should make my rejoicing+ void.
¹⁶ For although I proclaim+ the Gospel, I have nothing to boast+ about, for *this* necessity is laid upon me. Yes, woe is me if I do not proclaim+ the Gospel.
¹⁷ For if I do this willingly, I *will* have a reward *in it.* But *even* if *it was* not willingly, the administration+ *of the Gospel* is entrusted+ to me.
¹⁸ What is my reward then? *Truly*+ it is that when I proclaim+ the Gospel, I may make the Gospel of Christ without charge *so* that I do not abuse my authority+ in the Gospel.
¹⁹ For though I am free from all *people*, yet I have made myself *a* servant to all *so* that I might gain *that many* more.
²⁰ To the Jews I became like a Jew *so* that I might gain the Jews. To *those* who are under the law *I became* as *though* under the law *so* that I might gain *those* who are under the law.
²¹ To those outside+ *the* law *I became* as *though I was* outside+ *the* law. Not outside+ *of* God's law, but *under* the law of Christ, *so* that *I might* gain *those who are* outside+ *the* law.
²² To the weak I became weak *so* that I might gain the weak. I have become+ all things to all *people so* that I might by all means rescue+ some.
²³ I do this for the sake of the Gospel *so* that I might be *a* partaker of it with *you.*
²⁴ Do you not know that *those* who run in

a race all run, but one receives the prize? *Therefore,* run so that you may obtain *it.*

²⁵Everyone⁺ who strives *for victory* is temperate in all things. Now some⁺ *strive* to obtain a worldly⁺ crown. But we *do it to obtain* an incorruptible *crown.* ²⁶Therefore, I so run, *but* not with uncertainty. I do not fight as one who beats the air *aimlessly.*

²⁷But I keep my body under *control* and bring *it* into subjection, lest by any means, when I have proclaimed⁺ *the Word* to others, I myself should become a reprobate.⁺

1 Corinthians Chapter 10

¹ Now I do not want you to be ignorant, family.⁺ All *of* our fathers were under the cloud and all passed through the sea. ² *They* were all baptized into Moses in the cloud and in the sea.

³ *They* all ate the same spiritual food.⁺ ⁴ *They* all drank the same spiritual drink. For they drank of that spiritual Rock that followed them *and* that Rock was Christ.

⁵ But God was not well pleased with many of them. For they were overthrown in the wilderness.

⁶ Now these things are our examples to the intent we should not lust after evil things as they lusted.

⁷ Do not be idolaters as some of them *were.* As it is written: The people sat down to eat and drink and rose up to play. *Exodus 32:6*

⁸ Do not let us commit fornication as some of them committed and in one day twenty three thousand fell.

⁹ Do not let us test⁺ Christ as some of them tested⁺ *God* and were destroyed by serpents.

¹⁰Do not complain⁺ as some of them complained⁺ and were destroyed by the Destroyer.

¹¹Now all these things happened to them for examples *to us.* They were written for our admonition. *For* upon *us* the end of the world has come.

¹²Therefore let *those* who think *that* they stand take heed lest they fall.

¹³ There has no trial⁺ taken you but such as is common to man. But God *is* faithful. *He* will not allow⁺ you to be tested⁺ beyond⁺ what you are able *to withstand.* But *He* will, with the trial, ⁺ also make a way to escape *so* that you may be able to bear *it.*

¹⁴Therefore my beloved, flee from idolatry.

¹⁵I speak as to wise men. Judge what I say.

¹⁶The cup of blessing that we bless, is it not the communion of the blood of Christ? The bread that we break, is it not the communion of the body of Christ? ¹⁷For we, *being* many, are one bread *and* one body. For we are all partakers of that one bread.

¹⁸Behold Israel according⁺ to the flesh. Are not *those* who eat of the sacrifices partakers of the altar?

¹⁹What shall I say, then? That the idol is anything or what is offered in sacrifice to idols is anything?

²⁰Rather, I *say* that the things that the Gentiles sacrifice, they sacrifice to demons⁺ and not to God. I would not *allow* that you should have fellowship with demons.⁺

²¹You cannot drink the cup of the Lord and the cup of demons.⁺ You cannot be partakers of the Lord's table and of the table of demons.⁺

²²Do we provoke the Lord to jealousy? Are we stronger than He?

²³All things are lawful for me, but all things are not expedient. All things are lawful for me, but all things do not edify. ²⁴Let no one seek their own, but *let* each one⁺ *seek* other's *well being.*

²⁵Whatever is sold in the market, ⁺ eat *it* asking no question for conscience sake. ²⁶For the earth *is* the Lord's and the fullness thereof. *Psalm 24:1*

²⁷If any of *those* who do not believe invite⁺ you *to a feast* and you are inclined⁺ to go, *then* eat whatever is set before

you, asking no questions for conscience sake.

²⁸But if anyone says to you: This was offered *in sacrifice* to an idol, *then* do not eat *it* because of that *one who* declared⁺ *this* and *for their* conscience. For the earth *is* the Lord's and the fullness thereof. *Psalm 24:1*

²⁹*By* conscience, I do not speak *of* your own but of others'. For why is my liberty judged by another's conscience?

³⁰For if by grace I am a partaker, *then* why am I blasphemed⁺ for that for which I give thanks?

³¹Therefore, if you eat or drink or whatever you do, do all to the glory of God.

³²Do not offend⁺ *anyone*, not *the* Jews or the Gentiles or those called⁺ by God.

³³*Do* even as *I do*. Please all *people* in all *things*, not seeking my own benefit⁺ but the *benefit* of many *so* that they may be saved.

1 Corinthians Chapter 11

¹ Be followers of me, even as I also *am* of Christ.

² Now I praise you, family,⁺ that you remember me in everything⁺ and keep the traditions⁺ as I delivered *them* to you.

³ And I want you to know that *for* every man the head is Christ. And *the* head *for* woman *is* man. And *the* head *for* Christ *is* God.

⁴ Every man praying or prophesying, having *his* head covered, dishonors his head.

⁵ But every woman who prays or prophesies with *her* head uncovered dishonors her head. For that is one and the same as if she were shaven.

⁶ For if the woman is not covered, *then* let her *head* also be sheared.⁺ But if it is a shame for a woman to be sheared or shaved *then* let her be covered.

⁷ For a man indeed should not cover *his* head, since⁺ he is the image and glory of God. But the woman is the glory of the man.

⁸ For the man is not from the woman, but the woman from the man.

⁹ Nor was the man created for the woman, but the woman for the man.

¹⁰For this reason⁺ the woman ought to have authority⁺ over⁺ *her* head because of the angels.

¹¹Nevertheless man *is* not *complete* without woman nor woman *complete* without man in the Lord.

¹²For as the woman *is* from the man, so also *is* the man from the woman. But everything⁺ *is* from God.

¹³Judge within yourselves: Is it fitting⁺ that a woman pray to God uncovered?

¹⁴Does not even nature itself teach you that if a man has long hair, it is a shame to him?

¹⁵But if a woman has long hair, it is a glory to her, for *her* hair is given *to* her for a covering.

¹⁶But if anyone seems to be contentious, we have no such custom *and* not *in* the assemblies⁺ of God.

¹⁷Now in this I declare that I do not praise *you because* you come together not for the better but for the worse.

¹⁸For first of all, when you come together in the assembly,⁺ I hear that there are divisions among you, and I partly believe it.

¹⁹For there must also be heresies among you *so* that *those* who are approved may be revealed⁺ among you.

²⁰Therefore, when you come together in one place, *it* is not to eat the Lord's supper.

²¹For in eating, everyone takes their own supper before *others*, one hungry and another drunk.

²²What? Do you not have houses *in which* to eat and to drink? Or *do you* despise the assembly⁺ of God and *put to* shame *those* who do not have *very much*? What shall I say to you? Shall I praise you in this? I do not praise *you*.

²³For I have received from the Lord what also I delivered to you: That the Lord Jesus, *on* the *same* night in which He was betrayed, took bread

²⁴and when He had given thanks, He broke *it* and said: Take, eat. This is my body, broken for you. Do this in remembrance of me. *John 6:53*

25In the same manner also *He took* the cup after supper+ and said: This cup is the new covenant+ in my blood. Do this, as often as you drink, in remembrance of me.

26For as often as you eat this bread and drink this cup, you proclaim+ *remembrance of* the death of the Lord, until He comes.

27Therefore, whoever eats this bread and drinks *this* cup of the Lord unworthily, shall be guilty of the body and blood of the Lord.

28But let everyone+ examine themselves and accordingly+ eat of the bread and drink of the cup.

29For *those* who eat and drink unworthily, eat and drink judgment+ unto themselves *for* not discerning the Lord's body.

30For this reason+ many *are* weak and sickly among you, and many sleep.

31For if we would judge ourselves, *then* we would not be judged.

32But when we are judged, we are disciplined+ by the Lord *so* that we *will* not be condemned with the world.

33Therefore my family, + when you come together to eat, wait+ for one another.

34If any *are* hungry, *let them* eat at home *so* that you do not come together to condemnation. And the rest I will set in order when I come.

1 Corinthians Chapter 12

1 Now concerning spiritual *gifts*, family, + I do not want you to be ignorant.

2 You know that you were Gentiles, carried away to these speechless+ idols, even as you were led.

3 Therefore I give you to understand that no one speaking by the Spirit of God calls Jesus accursed. No one can say that Jesus *is* Lord, but by the Holy Spirit.

4 Now there are diversities of gifts but the same Spirit.

5 There are differences of administrations but the same Lord.

6 There are diversities of operations but it is the same God who works all in all.

7 But the manifestation of the Spirit is given to everyone+ to *receive its* benefit. +

8 For to one, from the Spirit, is given the word of wisdom. To another, the word of knowledge from the same Spirit.

9 To another, faith from the same Spirit. To another, the gifts of healing from the same Spirit.

10To another, the working of miracles. To another, prophecy. To another, discerning of spirits. To another, *different*+ kinds of tongues. To another, the interpretation of tongues.

11But all these *gifts* operate+ *through* one and the same Spirit, dividing to everyone+ individually+ as He will.

12For as the body is one and has many members, and all the members of that one body, being many, are one body, so *it is* also *with* Christ.

13For by one Spirit we are all baptized into one body. Whether *we are* Jews or Gentiles. Whether *we are* slaves+ or free. All have been made to drink from one Spirit.

14For the body is not one member, but many.

15If the foot says: Because I am not the hand I am not of the body, is it therefore not of the body?

16If the ear says: Because I am not the eye I am not of the body, is it therefore not of the body?

17If the whole body *was* an eye, where *is* hearing? If the whole *was* hearing, where *is* smelling?

18But now God has placed+ everyone of the members in the body as it has pleased Him.

19If they were all one member, where *is* the body?

20But now *there are* many members, but in one body.

21The eye cannot say to the hand: I have no need of you. Nor again the head to the feet: I have no need of you.

22No, much more those members of the body that seem to be more feeble, are necessary.

23And those *members* of the body that we think to be less honorable, upon these we bestow more abundant honor. Our unattractive[+] *parts* have more abundant attractiveness.[+]

[24] For our attractive[+] *parts* have no need. But God has tempered the body together, giving more abundant honor to that *part* which lacked

[25] *so that* there should be no division[+] in the body, but *so that* the members should have the same care for one another.

[26] If one member suffers, *then* all the members suffer with it. Or *if* one member is honored, *then* all the members rejoice with it.

[27] Now you are the body of Christ and members in particular.

[28] God has placed[+] some in the assembly[+] *thus*: First apostles, second prophets, third teachers. After that miracles, then gifts of healings, helps, governments, *and* diversities of tongues.

[29] *Are* all apostles? *Are* all prophets? *Are* all teachers? *Are* all workers of miracles?

[30] Do all have the gifts of healing? Do all speak with tongues? Do all interpret?

[31] Zealously[+] *desire* the better gifts. *And* yet I *will* show you a more excellent way.

1 Corinthians Chapter 13

[1] If[+] I speak with the tongues of men and of angels but do not have *true* love, I become *like* sounding brass or a tinkling cymbal.

[2] And if[+] I have *the gift of* prophecy and understand all mysteries and all knowledge, and though I have all faith so that I could remove mountains, but do not have *true* love, I am nothing.

[3] And if[+] I bestow all my goods to feed *the poor* and though I give my body to be burned, but do not have *true* love, nothing *is* gained.[+] *Matthew 9:13*

[4] *True* love *patiently* suffers long *and* is kind. *True* love does not envy. *True* love does not vaunt itself *and* is not puffed up. *Matthew 5:44*

[5] *It* does not behave shamefully.[+] *It* does not seek *its* own *way*. *It* is not easily provoked. *And* it does not think evil. *Matthew 5:22*

[6] *True love* does not rejoice in iniquity, but rejoices in the truth. *Matthew 5:8*

[7] *True love* bears all things, believes all things, hopes all things, *and* endures all things. *Matthew 10:22*

[8] *True* love never fails.

But where *there are* prophecies, they will fail. Where *there are* tongues, they will cease. Where *there is* knowledge, it will vanish away. *John 15:9*

[9] For we know in part and we prophesy in part.

[10] But when what is perfect has come, then what is in part will be done away.

[11] When I was a child, I spoke as a child. I understood as a child. I thought as a child. But when I became a man, I put away childish things.

[12] For now we see through a glass darkly, but then face to face. Now I know in part, but then I shall know even as also I am known.

[13] Now abide faith, hope, *and true* love, these three. But the greatest of these *is* *true* love.

1 Corinthians Chapter 14

[1] Pursue[+] *true* love zealously[+] and *desire* the spiritual *gifts*, especially[+] that of prophecy.

[2] For *those* who speak in an *unknown* tongue do not speak to people[+] but to God. For no one understands *them*. However in the spirit *they* speak mysteries.

[3] But *those* who prophesy speak to people[+] *for* edification, exhortation, and comfort.

[4] *Those* who speak in tongues edify themselves. But *those* who prophesy edify the assembly.[+]

[5] I would *have* you all speak with tongues, but more[+] that you prophesied. For *those* who prophesy *are* greater than *those* who speak with tongues, unless they interpret *so* that the assembly[+] receives edification.

[6] Now family,[+] if I come to you speaking with tongues, what will I

benefit[+] you? Unless[+] I speak to you either by revelation or by knowledge or by prophesying or by doctrine?

[7] Even *when* things without life *are* giving sound, whether *it be a* pipe or harp, unless they give a distinction in the sounds, how will it be known what is piped or harped?

[8] For if the trumpet gives an uncertain sound, who will prepare themselves for battle?

[9] So likewise you, unless[+] you utter words easy to be understood by the tongue, how will it be known what is spoken? For *otherwise* you speak into the air.

[10]There are many kinds of voices in the world and none of them *is* without distinctive[+] *character*.

[11]Therefore, if I do not know the meaning of the voice, I will be to *those* who speak a barbarian and *those* who speak *will be* a barbarian to me.

[12]Even so you, since[+] you are zealous for spiritual *gifts*, seek *them so* that you may excel in edifying the assembly.[+]

[13]Therefore, let *those* who speak in an *unknown* tongue pray that they may interpret.

[14]For if I pray in an *unknown* tongue, my spirit prays, but my understanding is unfruitful.

[15]What is it *to be* then? I will pray with the spirit and I will pray with understanding also. I will sing with the spirit and I will sing with understanding also.

[16]Otherwise[+] when you bless with the spirit, how will *those* who occupy the room of the uninformed[+] say Amen at your giving of thanks, since they do not understand what you say?

[17]For you truly[+] give thanks well, but the other is not edified.

[18]I thank my God *that* I speak with tongues more than all *of* you.

[19]Yet in the assembly[+] I would rather speak five words with my understanding, *so* that *by my voice* I might teach others also, than ten thousand words in an *unknown* tongue.

[20]Family,[+] do not be children in *your* understanding. However in malice, be children. But in understanding, be mature.[+]

[21]In the law it is written: With other tongues and other lips I will speak to this people. And yet for all that, they will not hear me, says the Lord. *Isaiah 28:11*

[22]Therefore tongues are for a sign, not to *those* who believe, but to *those* who do not believe. But prophesying does not *serve those* who do not believe, but *those* who believe.

[23]Therefore if the whole assembly[+] has come together into one place and all speak with tongues, and *those who are* uninformed[+] or unbelievers come in, will they not say that you are mad?

[24]But if all prophesy and *some* who do not believe or *who are* uninformed[+] come in, they will be convinced by all *and* judged by all.

[25]Thus are the secrets of their hearts revealed.[+] So falling down on *their* face they will worship God and report that God is truly in you.

[26]How is it *to be* then, family[+]? When you come together, everyone of you has a psalm, a doctrine, a tongue, a revelation, *and* an interpretation. And let all things be done for edifying.

[27]If any speak in a tongue, *allow* two or *at* the most three, in succession,[+] and *with* one *to* interpret.

[28]But if there is no interpreter, keep silence in the assembly,[+] *each* speaking to themselves and to God.

[29]Allow two or three prophets to speak and the others discern.[+]

[30]If *anything* is revealed to another who sits by, let the first *remain* silent.[+]

[31]For against[+] one *in error*, you may all prophesy *so* that all may learn and all may be exhorted.[+]

[32]For[+] the spirits of the prophets are subject to the prophets.

[33] For God is not *the author* of confusion, but of peace,

as in all assemblies[+] of the saints.

[34] Let your women keep silence in the assemblies.+ For it is not permitted *for* them to speak, but to be under obedience as the law also says.

[35] If they will learn anything, let them ask their husbands at home. For it is a shame for women to speak in the assembly.+

[36] *What?* Did the Word of God originate+ from you? Or did it come to you only?

[37] If anyone thinks themselves to be a prophet or spiritual, let them acknowledge that the things that I write to you are the commandments of the Lord.

[38] But if anyone is ignorant, let them be ignorant.

[39] Therefore family,+ zealously+ *desire* to prophesy. And do not forbid *anyone* to speak with tongues.

[40] Let all things be done decently and in order.

1 Corinthians Chapter 15

[1] Family,+ I *now* declare to you the Gospel that I *have already* proclaimed+ to you and which you have received and in which you stand

[2] *and* by which you are also being saved, if you keep in memory what I *have* proclaimed+ to you, unless you have believed in vain. *Psalm 119:11*

[3] For I delivered to you first of all what I also received: That Christ died for our sins according to the Scriptures, *Isaiah 53:5*

[4] that He was buried and that He rose again the third day, according to the Scriptures, *Psalm 68:18*

[5] that He was seen by Cephas *and* then by the twelve.

[6] After that, He was seen by more than five hundred *of the* family+ at once, of whom the greater part remain to this present *time*. But some have fallen asleep.

[7] After that, He was seen by James *and* then by all the apostles.

[8] Last of all, He was seen by me also, as one unnaturally+ born.

[9] For I am the least of the apostles, not *even* suitable+ to be called an apostle because I persecuted the assembly+ of God.

[10] But by the grace of God, I am what I am. His grace to me was not in vain, but I labored more abundantly than all of them. Yet not I, but *it was* the grace of God with me.

[11] Therefore whether *it were* I or they, we thus proclaim+ *the Word*, and you thus believed.

[12] Now if Christ is proclaimed,+ that He rose from the dead, how *do* some among you say that there is no resurrection of the dead?

[13] But if there is no resurrection of the dead, then Christ is not risen.

[14] And if Christ is not risen, then our proclaiming+ *is in* vain and your faith *is* also vain.

[15] Yes, and we are found false witnesses of God because we have testified of God that He raised up Christ, whom He did not raise up if *it* be so that the dead do not rise.

[16] For if the dead do not rise, then Christ is not raised.

[17] And if Christ is not raised, *then* your faith *is* vain *and* you are yet in your sins.

[18] Then also those who fell asleep in Christ perished.

[19] If *it is* only in this life *that* we have hope in Christ, *then* we, of all people, are most miserable.

[20] But now Christ is risen from the dead *and* become the first fruits of *those* who slept.

[21] For since death *came* by man, *Adam*, *then* the resurrection of the dead also *came* by man, *Jesus Christ*.

[22] For *just* as in Adam all die, even so in Christ shall all be made alive.

[23] But everyone+ in their own order: Christ the first fruits, and afterward *those* who are Christ's at His coming.

[24] Then the end *will come*, when *Jesus* will have delivered up the kingdom to *our* God and Father, *and* when He will have put down all rule and all authority and power.

[25] For *Christ* must reign until He has put all enemies under His feet.

[26] *And* the last enemy *to be* destroyed *is* death.

27For He has put all things *in subjection* under His feet. But when it is said that all things are put *in subjection* under *Him*, *it is* obvious+ *that He is* excepted who put all things under Him. *Psalm 8:6*

28For when all things have been subdued to Him, then the Son will Himself also be subject to *God* who put all things under Him *so* that God may be all in all.

29Otherwise+ what shall those do who are baptized for the dead, if the dead do not rise at all? Why then are they baptized for the dead?

30And why do we stand in jeopardy every hour?

31Every day, *I risk* dying. Our rejoicing is in having Christ Jesus our Lord.

32If according+ to the *way* of men I have fought with beasts at Ephesus, *then* what benefit+ *is* it *to* me. If the dead are not raised, *then* let us eat and drink for tomorrow we die. *Isaiah 22:13*

33Do not be deceived. Evil companions+ corrupt good behavior.+

34Awaken to righteousness and do not sin. For some do not have the knowledge of God. I speak *this* to your shame.

35But someone will say: How are the dead raised up? And with what body do they come?

36*You* fool. What you sow is not given life+ unless+ it dies.

37What you sow *is this*: You do not sow the body that will be, but bare grain. It may be+ of wheat or of some other *grain*.

38But God gives it a body as it pleases Him, and to every seed its own body.

39All flesh *is* not the same flesh. *There is* one *kind of* flesh for men, another flesh for beasts, another for fish, *and* another for birds.

40*There are* also celestial bodies and terrestrial bodies, and the glory of the celestial *is* one and the *glory* of the terrestrial *is* another.

41*There is* one glory of the sun and another glory of the moon and another glory of the stars. For *one* star differs from *another* star in glory.

42So also *is* the resurrection of the dead. It is sown in corruption *and* it is raised in incorruptibility.+

43It is sown in dishonor. It is raised in glory. It is sown in weakness. It is raised in power.

44It is sown *as* a natural body. It is raised *as* a spiritual body. There is a natural body and there is a spiritual body.

45So it is written: The first man, Adam, was made a living soul. *And* the last Adam *was made* a life giving+ spirit. *Genesis 2:7*

46However the first was not spiritual but the natural. Then *afterward came* the spiritual.

47The first man *came* out of the earth, *made of* dust.+ The second man *came as* the Lord out of heaven.

48Just as *God made the first man out of the* earth,+ of such also *are all* those *made out of the* earth. And just as one+ *was* heavenly, of such also *is* heavenly *regeneration.*

49As we have borne the image of the earthly, we will also bear the image of the heavenly.

50Now family,+ I say this: That flesh and blood cannot inherit the kingdom of God. Nor does corruption inherit incorruptibility.+

51Behold I *will* tell+ you a mystery: We will not all sleep, but we will all be changed.

52In a moment. In the twinkling of an eye. At the last trumpet. For a trumpet will sound and the dead will be raised incorruptible, and we will be changed.

53For this corruptible *being* must put on incorruptibility+ and this mortal *must* put on immortality.

54So when this corruptible shall have put on incorruptibility+ and this mortal shall have put on immortality, then shall *it* be brought to pass that saying that is written: Death is swallowed up in victory. *Isaiah 25:8*

55O death, where *is* your sting? O grave, where *is* your victory?

56The sting of death *is* sin and the strength of sin *is* the law.

57But thanks *be* to God who gives us the victory through our Lord Jesus Christ.

⁵⁸Therefore my beloved⁺:

> Be steadfast, immovable,
> always abounding
> in the work of the Lord,
> because⁺ you know
> that your labor in the Lord
> is not in vain. *Matthew 4:10*

1 Corinthians Chapter 16

¹ Now concerning the collection for the saints, as I have directed⁺ the assemblies⁺ of Galatia, so also you *should* do.
² Every⁺ first *of the* week, let everyone of you put⁺ *aside* in store, as *God* has prospered, *so* that there *need* be no collections⁺ when I come.
³ When I come, whomever you approve by *your* letters, I will send to take⁺ your liberal *gifts* to Jerusalem.
⁴ If it is fitting⁺ that I go also, *then* they shall go with me.
⁵ Now I will come to you when I pass through Macedonia, for I do pass through Macedonia.
⁶ It may be that I will stay⁺ and winter with you *so* that you may *then* take⁺ me on my journey wherever I go.
⁷ For I will not see you now, on the way, but I trust to stay⁺ a while with you, if the Lord permits.
⁸ But I will stay⁺ at Ephesus until Pentecost.
⁹ For a great and effective door is opened to me but *there are* many adversaries.
¹⁰Now if Timothy comes, see that he may be with you without fear. For he works the work of the Lord, as I also *do.*
¹¹Therefore let no one despise him, but conduct him forth in peace *so* that he may come to me. For I look for him with the brothers.
¹²Concerning *our* brother Apollos, I greatly desired him to come to you with the brothers. But his will was not at all to come at this time, but he will come when he has convenient time.
¹³Watch. Stand fast in the faith. Be courageous.⁺ Be strong.

¹⁴Let all things be done with *true* love.
¹⁵I urge you, family.⁺ You know the house of Stephanas, that it is *the* first fruit of Achaia, and *that* they have applied⁺ themselves to the ministry of the saints.
¹⁶*See* that you submit yourselves to such *as them* and to everyone who helps with *us* and labors.
¹⁷I am glad for the coming of Stephanas and Fortunatus and Achaicus, for what you were lacking, they supplied.
¹⁸They have refreshed my spirit and yours. Therefore acknowledge *those* who are such.
¹⁹The assemblies⁺ of Asia greet⁺ you. Aquila and Priscilla greet⁺ you much in the Lord, *along* with the assembly⁺ that is in their house.
²⁰All the family⁺ greet you. Greet one another with a holy kiss.
²¹The salutation of Paul *I make* with my own hand.
²²If anyone does not delight⁺ *in* the Lord Jesus Christ, let them be accursed.⁺ Maranatha. *Oh Lord come.*
²³The grace of our Lord Jesus Christ *be* with you.
²⁴My love *be* with you all in Christ Jesus. Amen.

The first epistle to the Corinthians was transcribed at Philippi by Stephanas, Fortunatus, Achaicus, and Timothy.

2 Corinthians Chapter 1

¹ *From* Paul, an apostle of Jesus Christ by the will of God, and Timothy *our* brother. To the assembly⁺ of God at Corinth with all the saints who are in all *of* Achaia.
² Grace to you and peace from God our Father and Lord Jesus Christ.
³ Blessed *is* the God and Father *of* our Lord Jesus Christ, the Father of mercies and the God of all comfort.
⁴ *He* comforts us in all our tribulation *so* that we may be able to comfort *those* who are in any trouble with the *same* comfort with which we ourselves are comforted by God.

⁵ For *just* as the sufferings of Christ abound in us, so also our consolation abounds through Christ.

⁶ If we are afflicted, *it is* for your consolation and salvation, which is effective in enduring the same sufferings that we also suffer. Or if we are comforted, *that also is* for your consolation and salvation.

⁷ Our hope in you *is* steadfast, knowing that as you are partakers of the sufferings, so also *you will be partakers* of the consolation.

⁸ For we would not, family,⁺ have you uninformed⁺ about our trouble that came to us in Asia. We were pressed out of measure, beyond strength, so that we despaired even of life.

⁹ But we have *already* had the judgment⁺ of death within ourselves, *so* that we would not trust in ourselves but in God who raises the dead.

¹⁰*He* delivered us from so great a death, and *He still* does deliver. *And* we trust that He will *even* yet deliver *us*.

¹¹You also labor⁺ together for us by prayer, *so* that thanks may be given by many on our behalf for the gifts *bestowed* upon us by *so* many people.

¹²This is the reason for our rejoicing: The testimony of our conscience is that we have had our conversation and conduct in the world, and especially⁺ toward you, in simplicity and godly sincerity and not with fleshly wisdom, but *simply* by the grace of God.

¹³For we write no other things to you than what you read or acknowledge. I trust you will acknowledge *this* even to the end.

¹⁴And, as you have acknowledged us in part *so* that we are your *means of* rejoicing, even so you also *will be* ours in the day of the Lord Jesus.

¹⁵In this confidence, I was of a mind⁺ to come to you before *so* that you might have a second benefit.

¹⁶*I intended* to pass by you to *on the way to* Macedonia, and to come again to you out of Macedonia and be brought by you on my way to Judea.

¹⁷When I was thus minded, did I use lightness *to decide*? Or are the things that I purpose done according to the flesh *so* that there might be *an uncertain* yes yes and no no?

¹⁸*As* God *is* true, our word to you was not *an uncertain* yes and no.

¹⁹For the Son of God, Jesus Christ who was proclaimed⁺ among you by us, *both* by me and *by* Silvanus and Timothy, was not yes and no, but in Him *it* was *consistently* yes.

²⁰For all the promises of God in Him *are* yes, and in Him Amen, for the glory of God through us.

²¹Now He who establishes us with you in Christ and has anointed us, *is* God.

²²*He* has also sealed us and given *us* the Spirit *as* the guarantee⁺ in our hearts.

²³But I call upon God to testify⁺ upon my soul, that *it was to* spare you *that* I did not yet come to Corinth.

²⁴Not that we have dominion over your faith, but *we* are helpers of your joy. For *it is* by faith *that* you stand.

2 Corinthians Chapter 2

¹ I determined within myself that I would not come to you again in sorrow.⁺

² For if I grieve⁺ you, then who will make me glad, if not those who *might otherwise* be grieved by me?

³ I wrote this to you lest when I came, I might have sorrow from those *in* whom I ought to rejoice. *But I* have confidence in you all that my joy is *in* all of you *also*.

⁴ For out of much suffering⁺ and anguish of heart, I wrote to you with many tears. Not *so* that you would be grieved, but *so* that you might know the love that I have for you more abundantly.

⁵ But if any have caused grief, *it is* not me *that* they have grieved, but in part *it is* all of you, *so* that I may not be overcharged.

⁶ Sufficient to such a one *is* this rebuke,⁺ which *has been* expressed by many.

⁷ On the contrary, you *should* instead⁺ forgive and comfort, lest perhaps such a one be swallowed up with too much sorrow.

[8] Therefore I urge you to confirm *your* love toward them.

[9] *It was* for this *purpose* also that I wrote *to you*, *so* that I might know the proof of you, if you are obedient in everything.[+]

[10] To *those* whom you forgive anything, I also *forgive*. For if I have forgiven anything, it is for your sakes that I have forgiven it in the person of Christ.

[11] *We do this* lest Satan should get an advantage over us. For we are not ignorant about his devices.

[12] Furthermore, when I came to Troas to *proclaim*[+] Christ's Gospel, a door was opened to me by the Lord.

[13] I had no rest in my spirit because I did not find my brother Titus. But upon leaving them, I went from there[+] to Macedonia.

[14] Now thanks *be* to God who always causes us to triumph in Christ and reveals[+] the savor of His knowledge through us in every place.

[15] For we are to God a sweet savor of Christ in *those* who are being saved, and *even* in those *who are* perishing.

[16] To the one, *we are* the savor of death to death. To the other, the savor of life to life. And who *is* sufficient for these things?

[17] For we are not like many who corrupt the Word of God. But from sincerity and as from God in the sight of God, we speak in Christ.

2 Corinthians Chapter 3

[1] Do we begin again to commend ourselves? Or do we need, as some *others*, epistles of commendation to you, or *letters* of commendation from you?

[2] You are our epistle written in our hearts, known and read by everyone.[+]

[3] *You are* manifestly declared to be the epistle of Christ ministered by us, not written with ink but with the Spirit of the living God. Not in tables of stone, but in fleshy tables of the heart.

[4] Such trust do we have through Christ toward God.

[5] Not that we are sufficient in ourselves to think anything of ourselves, but our sufficiency *is* from God.

[6] *God* has also made us able ministers of the new covenant.[+] Not of the letter, but of the spirit. For the letter kills, but the spirit gives life.

[7] But if the administration of death written *and* engraved[+] in stones was glorious, so *much so* that the children of Israel could not steadfastly behold the face of Moses for the glory of his countenance, which *glory* was to be done away,

[8] *then* how shall the administration of the spirit not be rather *more* glorious?

[9] For if the administration of condemnation *is* glory, *then* much more does the administration of righteousness exceed in glory.

[10] For even what was made glorious had no glory in this respect, by reason of the glory that excels.

[11] For if what is done away *was* glorious, *even* much more so *is* what remains glorious.

[12] Therefore, seeing that we have such hope, we use great plainness of speech.

[13] *We are* not like Moses, *who* put a veil over his face *so* that the children of Israel could not steadfastly look to the end of what is abolished.

[14] But their minds were blinded. For until this day, the same veil remains. *It is* not taken away in the reading of the old covenant,[+] but *the veil* is done away in Christ.

[15] Even to this day when Moses is read, the veil is upon their hearts.

[16] Nevertheless, when it shall turn to the Lord, the veil will be taken away.

[17] Now the Lord is that Spirit, and where the Spirit of the Lord *is*, there *is* liberty.

[18] But with *an* open face beholding the glory of the Lord as in a mirror,[+] we are all changed by the Spirit of the Lord into the same image, from glory *shining upon us* to glory *reflected in us*.

2 Corinthians Chapter 4

[1] Therefore, since we have this ministry, as we have received mercy, we do not faint.
[2] But *we* have renounced the hidden things of dishonesty, not walking in craftiness or handling the Word of God deceitfully, but by *the* manifestation of the truth *we* commend ourselves to everyone's[+] conscience in the sight of God.
[3] But if our Gospel is hid, it is hid to *those* who are lost.
[4] The god of this world has blinded the minds of *those* who do not believe, lest the light of the glorious Gospel of Christ, who is the image of God, should shine *forth* to them.
[5] For we do not proclaim[+] ourselves, but Christ Jesus the Lord. *We are* your servants for Jesus' sake.
[6] For God, who commanded the light to shine out of darkness, has shown in our hearts the light of the knowledge of the glory of God, in the face of Jesus Christ.
[7] But we have this treasure in earthen vessels *so* that the excellency of the power may be of God and not of us.
[8] *We are* troubled on every side, yet not distressed. *We are* perplexed but not in despair.
[9] *We are* persecuted but not forsaken, cast down but not destroyed.
[10] *We* always bear the dying of the Lord Jesus in the body *so* that the life of Jesus might be revealed[+] in our body.
[11] For we who live are always *being* delivered to death for Jesus' sake *so* that the life of Jesus might also be revealed[+] in our mortal flesh.
[12] So then, death is working in us, but life in you.
[13] We have the same spirit of faith. As it is written: I believed and therefore I have spoken. We also believe, and therefore speak, *Psalm 116:10*
[14] knowing that He who raised up the Lord Jesus will also raise us up by Jesus and present *us* with you.
[15] For all things *are* for your sakes, *so* that the abundant grace might, through the thanksgiving of many, abound[+] to the glory of God.
[16] For this reason, [+] we do not faint, but though our outward person *may* perish, yet the inward is renewed day by day.
[17] For our light suffering, [+] which is but for a moment, works for us a far more exceeding *and* eternal weight of glory.
[18] We do not look at the things that are seen, but at the things that are not seen. For the things that are seen *are* temporal. But the things that are not seen *are* eternal.

2 Corinthians Chapter 5

[1] We know that if our earthly house *in this* tabernacle is destroyed, [+] we have *another* building from God. *It is* a house not made with hands, *but* eternal in the heavens.
[2] In this we groan, earnestly desiring to be clothed with our house that is from heaven.
[3] Indeed, [+] being *thus* clothed, we will not be found naked.
[4] For *we* who are in *this temporary* tabernacle groan, being burdened. Not that we wish to be unclothed, but clothed upon *so* that mortality might be swallowed up by life.
[5] Now *He* who has prepared[+] us for this *is* God. *And He* has also given to us the guarantee[+] of the Spirit.
[6] Therefore *we are* always confident, knowing that while we are at home in the body, we are absent from the Lord.
[7] For we walk by faith *and* not by sight.
[8] We are confident, *I say*, and willing instead[+] to be absent from the body and to be present with the Lord.
[9] Therefore we labor *so* that, whether present or absent, we may be accepted by Him.
[10] For we must all appear before the judgment seat of Christ *so* that everyone may receive the things *done* in body, according to what they have done, whether good or bad.
[11] Therefore, knowing the terror of the Lord, we persuade people. [+] And we are

revealed+ to God. I trust also *that we* are revealed+ in your consciences.

¹² For we do not commend ourselves to you again. But *we* give you occasion to rejoice+ on our behalf *so* that you may have something to *answer to those* who glory in *outward* appearance and not in *their* hearts.

¹³ For if we are beside ourselves, *it is for* God. Or if we are sober, *it is* for you.

¹⁴ For the love of Christ compels+ us. *Because* we have concluded this: That if one died for all, then all *are destined* to die.

¹⁵ *Jesus* died for all *so* that *those* who live would no longer live for themselves but for Him who died for them and rose again.

¹⁶ Therefore, from now on we *will* know no one in the flesh. Yes, though we have known Christ in the flesh, yet from now on we know *Him that way* no longer.+

¹⁷ Therefore if any *are* in Christ, *they are* a new creation.+ Old things are passed away. Behold all things are become new.

¹⁸ All things *are* from God who has reconciled us to Himself by Jesus Christ and has given to us the ministry of reconciliation.

¹⁹ As God was, in Christ, reconciling the world to Himself, not imputing their trespasses to them, *He* has committed to us the Word of reconciliation.

²⁰ Therefore, we are ambassadors for Christ. As God has exhorted+ *you* through us, we urge+ *you* in Christ's place+: Be reconciled to God.

²¹ For *God* made *Jesus* who knew no sin *to be* sin for us *so* that we might be made the righteousness of God in Him.

2 Corinthians Chapter 6

¹ *As* workers together *with Christ*, we exhort+ *you* also *so* that you do not receive the grace of God in vain.

² For He says: I have heard you in a time accepted, and in the day of salvation I have helped+ you. Behold now *is* the accepted time. Behold now *is* the day of salvation. *Isaiah 49:8*

³ *We* give no offense in anything *so* that the ministry *will* not be blamed.

⁴ But in everything+ *we* prove ourselves as ministers of God: In much patience, in sufferings,+ in necessities, in distresses,

⁵ in whippings,+ in imprisonments, in tumults, in labors, in sleepless+ *nights*, in fasting,

⁶ *and* by pureness, by knowledge, by longsuffering, by kindness, by the Holy Spirit, by sincere+ love,

⁷ by the Word of Truth, by the power of God, by the armor of righteousness at the right hand and at the left,

⁸ by honor and dishonor, by evil report and good report, as *called* deceivers and *yet* true,

⁹ as unknown and *yet* well known, as dying and *yet* behold we live, as chastened but not killed,

¹⁰ as in sorrow yet always rejoicing, as poor yet making many rich, as having nothing and *yet* possessing everything.+

¹¹ O Corinthians. Our mouth is open to *bless* you. Our heart is enlarged.

¹² You are not constrained+ by us, but you are constrained in your own innermost being.+

¹³ But I urge+ you children to respond+ the same *as us*: with enlarged *hearts*.

¹⁴ Do not be unequally yoked together with unbelievers. For what fellowship has righteousness with unrighteousness? And what communion has light with darkness?

¹⁵ What concord has Christ with Belial? Or what part have *those* who believe with an infidel?

¹⁶ What agreement has the temple of God with idols? For you are the temple of the living God. As God said: I will dwell among them and walk among *them*. I will be their God and they shall be my people. *Exodus 29:45, Leviticus 26:12*

¹⁷ Therefore come out from among them and be separate, says the Lord. Do not touch the unclean *and* I will receive you *Isaiah 52:11, Numbers 16:21*

¹⁸ *and* I will be a Father to you and you shall be my sons and daughters, says the Lord Almighty. *2 Samuel 7:14*

2 Corinthians Chapter 7

[1] Therefore, having these promises, beloved, let us cleanse ourselves from all filthiness of the flesh and spirit, perfecting holiness in the fear of God.
[2] Receive us. We have wronged no one. We have corrupted no one. We have defrauded no one.
[3] I do not speak *this* to condemn *you*, for I have said before that you are in our hearts to live and die with *you*.
[4] Great *is* my boldness of speech toward you. Great *is* my rejoicing+ in you. I am filled with comfort. I am exceedingly joyful in all our tribulation.
[5] For when we had come to Macedonia, our flesh had no rest, but we were troubled on every side. Fighting *on the* outside,+ fearful *on the* inside.+
[6] Nevertheless God who comforts *those* who are cast down, comforted us by the coming of Titus.
[7] Not only by his coming, but by the consolation with which he was comforted by you. When he told us *about* your earnest desire, your mourning, *and* your fervent mind toward me, I rejoiced *all* the more.
[8] For though I made you sorry with a letter, I do not repent, though I did repent *at first*. For I perceive that the same epistle made you sorry, although *that was* only for a season.
[9] Now I rejoice, not that you were made sorry, but that you sorrowed unto repentance. For you were made sorry in a godly manner *so* that you might receive no damage from us in anything.
[10] For godly sorrow produces+ repentance unto salvation *and that is* not to be regretted.+ But the sorrow of the world produces+ death.
[11] For behold this: That you sorrowed according+ *to* God *and* what diligence+ it produced+ in you, *what* answers,+ *what* indignation, *what* fear, *what* intense+ desire, *what* zeal, *what* vindication.+ In everything+ you have proved+ yourselves to be clear in this matter.

[12] Therefore, although I wrote to you, *it was* not for *the one* who did wrong nor for *the one* who suffered wrong, but *so* that our care for you in the sight of God might be evident+ to you.
[13] Therefore we were comforted in your comfort. Yes, and we rejoiced+ exceedingly more over the joy of Titus because his spirit was refreshed by you all.
[14] For if I have boasted to him about you in anything, I am not ashamed. But as we spoke everything+ to you in truth, even so our boasting, which *I did* before Titus, is found *to be* truth.
[15] His inward affection is more abundant toward you as he remembers the obedience of you all *and* how you received him with fear and trembling.
[16] Therefore I rejoice that I *can* have confidence in you in everything.+

2 Corinthians Chapter 8

[1] Family,+ understand+ the grace of God *that has been* bestowed in the assemblies+ of Macedonia.
[2] In a great trial of suffering,+ the abundance of their joy and their deep poverty abounded to the riches of their liberality.
[3] I testify+ to *their* power. Yes and *they were* willing *even* beyond *their* power.
[4] With much encouragement+ *they* urged+ us to receive *their* gracious+ *gift* in fellowship to serve the saints.
[5] And not *only this*, according *as we* had hoped, but *they* themselves gave first to the Lord and to us, by the will of God.
[6] In *view of* this, we urged+ Titus, that as he had begun, so also he would finish with you *in the same* grace.
[7] Therefore, as you abound in everything+: *In* faith and utterance and knowledge and all diligence and *in* your love to us, *see* that you abound in this grace also.
[8] I do not speak *this* as a commandment, but by the diligent+ *example* of others also proving the sincerity of your love.
[9] For you know the grace of our Lord Jesus Christ, that although He was rich, yet for your sakes He became

poor *so* that through His poverty you might be rich.

[10] In this *example* I give *you my* advice. For this is beneficial[+] for you who have *already* begun, not only to do *these things*, but also to have been *so* willing *to do them, even* before a year ago.

[11] Now therefore, perform the doing. As *there was* a ready will, so *may there be* a performance also out of what you have.

[12] For if there is first a willing mind, *it is* accepted according to what one has *and* not according to what one does not have.

[13] For *I* do not *mean* that others be eased and you burdened.

[14] But *in the interest* of equality in this present time, *may* your abundance be *a supply for their* deficiency[+] *so* that their abundance *may* also be *a supply* for your deficiency *later*.

[15] As it is written: *Those* who *had gathered* much had nothing over, and *those* who *had gathered* little had no lack. *Exodus 16:18*

[16] But thanks *be* to God who put the same earnest care into the heart of Titus for you.

[17] For indeed, he accepted the exhortation. But being diligent,[+] he went to you of his own accord.

[18] We sent with him that brother whose praise in the Gospel *has gone* throughout all the assemblies.[+]

[19] Not only *that*, but *he* was also chosen by the assemblies[+] to travel with us *in* this grace *that is* administered by us to the glory of the Lord and *to show* your readiness *to serve*.

[20] *We are exercising* caution[+] *so* that no one should blame us *in the way* in which this abundance is administered by us.

[21] *We are* providing for honest things, not only in the sight of the Lord, but also in the sight of *people*.

[22] We have sent our brother with them, *one* whom we have repeatedly[+] proved diligent in many things, but now much more diligent, *reflecting* upon the great confidence that *I have* in you.

[23] If *any ask* about Titus, *he is* my partner and fellow helper concerning you. Or *if* they ask about our brothers, *they are* the messengers from the assemblies[+] *and* the glory of Christ.

[24] Therefore show to them and before the assemblies[+] the proof of your love and of our rejoicing[+] in you.

2 Corinthians Chapter 9

[1] Concerning the ministering to the saints, it is superfluous for me to write to you.

[2] For I know the forwardness of your mind, for which I boast about you to those of Macedonia, that Achaia was ready a year ago. Your zeal has provoked very many.

[3] Yet I have sent the brothers *so* that our rejoicing[+] in you might not be in vain in some respect, *but so* that you *may indeed* be ready, as *has been* said.

[4] Lest *perhaps* if they of Macedonia come with me and find you unprepared, we should not be ashamed that we spoke *with such* confident boasting *about* you.

[5] Therefore I thought it necessary to exhort the family[+] *so* that they would go to you before and make up your *gift of* blessing[+] that you previously[+] announced[+] beforehand *so* that it might be ready as *a* blessing[+] and not as covetousness.

[6] *Those* who sow sparingly will also reap sparingly and *those* who sow bountifully will also reap bountifully,

[7] everyone *giving* as they purpose in their hearts, not complaining[+] or *out* of necessity.

> God loves a cheerful giver.
> [8] God *is* able to make
> all grace abound to you
> *so* that you always have sufficient
> *and* abound in every good work.

[9] As it is written: He has dispersed abroad. He has given to the poor. His righteousness remains forever. *Psalm 112:9*

[10] Now He who supplies[+] seed to the sower and bread for *your* food, *may He also* multiply your seed sown and increase the fruits of your righteousness.

[11]*May you* be enriched in everything to all bountifulness, *thereby* causing us *even greater* thanksgiving to God.

[12]For the administration of this service not only supplies the needs[+] of the saints, but is abundantly *overflowing* also in many thanksgivings to God.

[13]Through the experience of this service, God *is* glorified *by* submissiveness[+] that proclaims the Gospel of Christ *by* giving[+] to Him and to all.

[14]And their prayer for you longs *for* you *to have* the exceeding grace of God upon you.

[15]Thanks *be* to God for His indescribable[+] gift.

2 Corinthians Chapter 10

[1] Now I Paul urge you with the meekness and gentleness of Christ. In *your* presence *I am* small[+] among you, but being absent *I* am bold toward you.

[2] But I exhort[+] *you*, that I may not be bold when I am present with that confidence, with which I think to be bold against some, who think of us as if we walked according to the flesh.

[3] For though we walk in the flesh, we do not war after the flesh.

[4] For the weapons of our warfare *are* not worldly,[+] but mighty through God to the pulling down of strong holds,

[5] casting down imaginations and every high thing that exalts itself against the knowledge of God, bringing into captivity every thought to the obedience of Christ, *and*

[6] having in a readiness to revenge all disobedience when your obedience is fulfilled.

[7] Are you looking at things according to *their outward* appearance? If any trust themselves that they are Christ's *then* let them think *about* this again: As they *are* Christ's, so also *are* we Christ's.

[8] For *even* though I boast more about the authority that the Lord has given *to* us for edification, and not for your destruction, I should not be ashamed.

[9] May *it* not seem as if I would terrify you by *my* letters.

[10]For they say letters *are* weighty and powerful, but bodily presence weak and speech contemptible.

[11]*Rather* let one think that as we are in word by letters when we are absent, such *will we be* also in deed when we are present.

[12]For we dare not make ourselves of the number or compare ourselves with some who commend themselves. Those who measure themselves by themselves and comparing themselves among themselves, are not wise.

[13]But we will not boast of things without measure, but *rather* according to the measure of the rule that God has distributed to us, a measure to reach even to you.

[14]For we do not stretch ourselves beyond *our measure* as though we did not reach to you, for we have come as far as to you also in *proclaiming*[+] the Gospel of Christ.

[15]*We are* not boasting of things without measure. *But our measure is not* from other men's labors, but having hope that when your faith is increased, we shall be abundantly enlarged by you according to our rule.

[16]*We desire* to proclaim[+] the Gospel in the *regions* beyond you, *and* not to boast in another man's line of things made ready to our hand.

[17]But whoever rejoices,[+] let *them* rejoice[+] in the Lord.

[18]For *it is* not *those* who commend themselves *who* are approved, but *those* whom the Lord commends. *Proverbs 27:2*

2 Corinthians Chapter 11

[1] I wish[+] you could bear with me a little in *my* folly and *just* endure.

[2] For I am jealous over you with godly jealousy, for I have pledged[+] you to one husband *so* that I may present *you as* a chaste virgin to Christ.

[3] But I fear, lest by any means, as the serpent deceived[+] Eve through his deceit,[+] so your minds could become corrupted *away* from the simplicity that is in Christ.

4 For if one comes proclaiming+ another Jesus whom we have not proclaimed,+ or *if* you receive another spirit, not *the same* as you had received or another Gospel not *the same* as you had accepted, you might well bear with *it*.

5 For *I* consider+ *that I am* no less+ *useful than* the very chief apostles.

6 Though *I am* unrefined+ in speech, *I am* not *lacking* in knowledge, but in all things, thoroughly revealed+ among you.

7 Have I committed an offense in abasing myself *so* that you might be exalted, because I have freely proclaimed+ the Gospel of God to you?

8 I robbed other assemblies,+ taking wages *from them*, to serve you.

9 When I was present with you and *in* need,+ I was chargeable to no one. For what I was lacking, the family+ from Macedonia supplied. In everything,+ I have kept myself from being burdensome to you, and *so* I will keep *myself*.

10 As the truth of Christ is in me, no one in the regions of Achaia shall stop me from boastful+ *rejoicing*.

11 Why? Because I do not love you? God knows *I do*.

12 But I will *continue to* do what I do *so* that I may cut off the occasion from *those* who desire occasion *to* glory *in* that in which they may be found even as we.

13 For such *are* false apostles, deceitful workers, transforming themselves into the apostles of Christ.

14 No marvel, for Satan himself is transformed into an angel of light.

15 Therefore *it is* no great thing if his ministers also *seem to* be transformed as the ministers of righteousness. Their end shall be according to their works.

16 I say again, Let no one think me a fool. Or otherwise, *just* receive me as a fool *so* that I may boast a little.

17 What I speak, I do not speak according+ to the Lord, but foolishly, in this confident boasting.

18 Seeing that many glory after the flesh, I glory also.

19 For *you* endure+ fools gladly, since you *yourselves* are wise.

20 For you suffer, if *someone* brings you into bondage, or devours *you*, or takes *something from you*, or exalts themselves, or strikes+ you on the face.

21 *I am* ashamed+ to say that *sometimes* we were weak. However, whenever anyone *else* is bold *even* foolishly, *I am* bold, also.

22 Are they Hebrews? So *am* I. Are they Israelites? So *am* I. Are they the seed of Abraham? So *am* I.

23 Are they ministers of Christ? *Now* I speak like a fool. I *am even* more in labor, in whippings+ above measure, in prison more frequently, often *near* death.

24 From the Jews, five times I received forty *lashes*, less one.

25 Three *times* I was beaten with rods. Once was I stoned. Three times I suffered shipwreck. A night and a day I have been in the deep.

26 *In* journeys often, *in* perils of waters, *in* perils of robbers, *in* perils by *my own* countrymen, *in* perils by the heathen, *in* perils in the city, *in* perils in the wilderness, *in* perils in the sea, *in* perils among false brothers.

27 In weariness and painfulness, in watchings often, in hunger and thirst, in fastings often, in cold and nakedness.

28 Beside those things that come upon me daily from the outside, *I have* the care of all the assemblies.+

29 Who is weak and I am not weak? Who is offended *and caused to sin* and I do not burn?

30 If I need to boast,+ I will boast about those things *that reveal* my weaknesses.+

31 The God and Father *of* our Lord Jesus Christ who is blessed forever, knows that I do not lie.

32 In Damascus the governor under Aretas the king kept the city of the Damascenes with a garrison, desirous to apprehend me.

33 But I was let down in a basket through a window by the wall and escaped his hands.

2 Corinthians Chapter 12

[1] It is *surely* not beneficial for me to boast.[+] *Instead*, I will come to *the* visions and revelations of the Lord.

[2] About fourteen years ago, I knew a man in Christ *who had been* caught up to the third heaven. I do not know whether *this was* in the body or out of the body. *Only* God knows *that*.

[3] But I did know such a man. *Again*, whether *this was* in body or out of body, I do not know. God knows.

[4] He was caught up into paradise and heard indescribable[+] words that are not lawful for a man to utter.

[5] Of such a one I will boastfully[+] *rejoice*. Yet of myself I will not boast, except in my infirmities.

[6] For though I would desire to boast,[+] I shall not be a fool. But I will speak the truth. But *now* I hesitate,[+] lest anyone should think more[+] of me than what is seen or heard from me.

[7] Lest I be exalted above measure through the abundance of revelations, a thorn in the flesh was given to me, a messenger of Satan to buffet me, lest I be exalted above measure.

[8] Three times, I begged[+] the Lord that this might depart from me.

[9] He said to me:

> My grace is sufficient for you.
> For my strength is made perfect
> in weakness.

Therefore I will most gladly rejoice[+] in my infirmities *so* that the power of Christ may rest upon me.

[10] Therefore I take pleasure in infirmities, in reproaches, in necessities, in persecutions, in distresses for Christ's sake, for when I am weak, then am I strong.

[11] I am made[+] a fool *by my* boasting.[+] You have compelled me. I ought to have been commended by you. For I am not *lacking* behind the very chief apostles, *even* though I am nothing.

[12] Truly the signs of an apostle were produced[+] among you in all patience, in signs, and wonders, and mighty deeds.

[13] For what is it in which you were inferior to other assemblies,[+] except that I was not a burden to you? Forgive me *for* this wrong.

[14] Behold *now for* the third time I am ready to come to you. I will not be a burden to you. For I do not seek *what is* yours, but you. For children should not *need* to lay up *reserves* for parents, but parents for the children.

[15] I will very gladly spend and be spent for you. Though the more abundantly I love you, the less I *seem to* be loved.

[16] But so be it. I did not burden you. *However* being crafty, guile caught you.

[17] Did I make a gain from you by any of *those* I sent to you?

[18] I encouraged[+] Titus and sent a brother with *him*. Did Titus make a gain from you? Did we not walk in the same spirit? Did we not *walk* in the same steps?

[19] Again, do you think that we excuse ourselves to you? We speak before God in Christ, but *we do* all things, beloved, for your edification.

[20] For I fear lest when I come, *that* I will not find you as I wish[+] *you would be*, and *that* I will be found *by* you as you would not *wish*, lest *there be* debates, envyings, wraths, strifes, backbitings, whisperings, swellings, tumults;

[21] *and* lest, when I come again, my God will humble me among you, and I shall mourn[+] for many who have sinned and not repented of the uncleanness and fornication and filthiness[+] that they have committed.

2 Corinthians Chapter 13

[1] This *now, is* the third *time that* I am coming to you. By the mouth of two or three witnesses, every word shall be established. *Matthew 18:16*

[2] I *have* told you before, and *now I am* forewarning[+] you a second time as though I were present *with you*. Being absent *from you* now, I *am* writing to *those* who have sinned before[+] and to all

others *to say* that if I come again, I will not spare *you*.

³ Since you seek proof in me, *I am* speaking of Christ who is not weak toward you, but is mighty in you.

⁴ For though *Christ* was crucified through weakness, yet He lives by the power of God. For we also are weak in Him, but we shall live with Him by the power of God toward you.

> ⁵ Examine yourselves
> *to see* if you are in the faith.
> Prove yourselves.
> Do you yourselves not know
> that Jesus Christ is in you,
> unless⁺ you are reprobates.

⁶ But I trust that you will know that we are not reprobates.

⁷ Now I pray to God that you do no evil. Not *so* that we *may* appear *as* approved, but *so* that you would do what is honest, *even* if we are rejected.⁺

⁸ For we can do nothing against the truth, but *only* for the truth.

⁹ We are glad when we are weak and you are strong. This also we wish, *even* your perfection.

¹⁰Therefore, being absent *from you*, I write these things *to you* lest *by* being present I should use sharp *words* according to the authority⁺ that the Lord has given *to* me for edification and not for destruction.

¹¹ Finally, family⁺: Farewell. Be perfect. Be of good comfort.

> Be of one mind. Live in peace,
> and the God of love and peace
> will be with you.

¹² Greet one another with a holy kiss.

¹³ All the saints greet⁺ you.

¹⁴ The grace of the Lord Jesus Christ and the love of God and the communion of the Holy Spirit *be* with you all. Amen.

The second epistle to the Corinthians was transcribed at Philippi, a city of Macedonia, by Titus and Lucas.

Galatians Chapter 1

¹ *From* Paul, an apostle, not of men nor by man, but by Jesus Christ and God the Father who raised Him from the dead,

² and *from* all the family⁺ who are with me. To the assemblies⁺ of Galatia.

³ Grace to you and peace from God *the* Father and our Lord Jesus Christ

⁴ who gave Himself for our sins *so* that He might deliver us from this present evil world, according to the will of our God and Father,

⁵ to whom *be* glory forever and ever. Amen.

⁶ I marvel that you so quickly⁺ turned⁺ *away* from Him who called you into the grace of Christ, to a different⁺ Gospel.

⁷ There is not another *valid Gospel*. Yet there are some who trouble you and would pervert the Gospel of Christ.

⁸ But if we or an angel from heaven proclaim⁺ any Gospel to you, *different* than what we have *already* proclaimed⁺ to you, *let them* be accursed.

⁹ As we have said before, I now say again: If anyone⁺ proclaims⁺ any Gospel to you other than what you have *already* received, *let them* be accursed.

¹⁰For do I now persuade men, or God? Or do I seek to please men? For if I yet pleased men, I should not be the servant of Christ.

¹¹But I certify *to* you, family,⁺ that the Gospel that was proclaimed⁺ by me is not from man.

¹²For I did not receive it from man, nor was I taught *it by man*. But *it came to me* by the revelation of Jesus Christ.

¹³For you have heard about my conversation *and conduct* in *the* past, in Judaism.⁺ *You know* that I excessively⁺ persecuted the assembly⁺ of God beyond measure, and ravaged⁺ it.

¹⁴And *I* advanced⁺ in the Jews' religion beyond⁺ many *of* my peers⁺ in my own nation, being more exceedingly zealous of the traditions of my fathers.

¹⁵But when it pleased God, who separated me from my mother's womb and called *me* by His grace,

¹⁶to reveal His Son in me *so* that I might proclaim⁺ Him among the heathen, immediately I conferred, not with flesh and blood,

¹⁷nor did I go up to Jerusalem to *those* who were apostles before me, but I went to Arabia. *Then, I* returned again to Damascus.

¹⁸Then after three years, I went to Jerusalem to see Peter and stayed⁺ with him fifteen days.

¹⁹But I did not see the other apostles, except⁺ James the brother of the Lord.

²⁰Now behold what I write to you. Before God, I do not lie.

²¹Then, I went into the regions of Syria and Cilicia.

²²I was unknown, in person,⁺ to the assemblies⁺ of Judea that were in Christ.

²³But they had heard only *this*: That *he* who once⁺ persecuted us, now proclaims⁺ the faith that he once ravaged.⁺

²⁴And they glorified God in me.

Galatians Chapter 2

¹ Fourteen years later,⁺ I again went to Jerusalem with Barnabas and *also* took Titus with *me.*

² I went according to *the* revelation *I received* and communicated to them the Gospel that I proclaim⁺ among the Gentiles. But *I spoke* privately to those of *lofty* reputation, lest by any means I should be running or had run, in vain.

³ But *even* Titus who was with me, being Greek, was not compelled to be circumcised.

⁴ *Even though* false brothers came⁺ *in* secretly⁺ to spy out our liberty that we have in Christ Jesus *so* that they might bring us into bondage.

⁵ We did not yield⁺ in subjection *to them,* even for an hour, *so* that the truth of the Gospel might continue with you.

⁶ But from those thought⁺ to be somebody⁺ *important,* what they were makes no difference⁺ to me. God does not receive *one* person *above another.* To me *also,* those of *lofty* reputation⁺ conveyed⁺ nothing *special.*

⁷ On the contrary, *they* saw that the Gospel *to* the uncircumcision was committed to me *just* as *the Gospel to* the circumcision *was* to Peter.

⁸ For He who worked⁺ *in* Peter for apostleship *to* the circumcision *also* worked⁺ *in* me for the Gentiles.

⁹ When James, Cephas, and John, who seemed to be pillars, perceived the grace that was given to me, they gave to me and *to* Barnabas the right hand of fellowship *so* that we *might go* to the Gentiles⁺ and they to the circumcision.

¹⁰Only *they* urged that we remember the poor, which I also was diligent⁺ to do.

¹¹However, when Peter came to Antioch, I challenged⁺ him to *his* face, because he was to be blamed.

¹²Because, before certain *ones* came from James, *Peter* ate with the Gentiles. But when they came, he withdrew and separated himself, fearing those of the circumcision.

¹³The other Jews also *joined in putting on a false* pretense⁺ with *Peter* so that Barnabas was also carried away with their hypocrisy.⁺

¹⁴When I saw that they did not walk uprightly according to the truth of the Gospel, I said to Peter before *them* all: If you, being a Jew, live after the manner of Gentiles and not like the Jews, *then* why do you compel the Gentiles to live like the Jews?

¹⁵By nature, we *are* Jews and not sinners from the Gentiles.

¹⁶*We* know that a man is not justified by the works of the law, but by faith *in* Jesus Christ. We have believed in Jesus Christ *so* that we might be justified by faith *in* Christ and not by the works of the law. For no flesh will be justified by the works of the law.

¹⁷But if, while we seek to be justified by Christ, we ourselves are also found sinners, *is* Christ therefore a minister of sin? *That* cannot be.⁺

¹⁸For if I build again the things that I *had* destroyed, *then* I make myself a transgressor.

¹⁹For through *the* law, I died *to the* law *so* that I might live *for* God.
²⁰*I* have been crucified *with* Christ, *and* yet⁺ I live. *However, it is* no longer I, but Christ living in me. And *the life* that I now live in the flesh, I live by faith *in* the Son of God who loved me and gave Himself for me.
²¹I do not reject⁺ the grace of God. For if righteousness *is* through *the* law, then Christ died in vain.

Galatians Chapter 3

¹ O foolish Galatians, who has bewitched you to not obey the truth? Before *your* eyes, Jesus Christ was set forth *and* crucified among you.
² This only would I learn from you: Did you receive the Spirit from works of the law or by hearing of faith?
³ Are you so foolish? Having begun in the Spirit, are you now made perfect by the flesh?
⁴ Have you suffered so many things in vain? If *it was* in vain.
⁵ Therefore, *does* He who supplies⁺ the Spirit to you and works miracles among you *do it* by works of the law or by hearing of faith?
⁶ As Abraham believed God, it was credited⁺ to him as righteousness. *Genesis 15:6*
⁷ Know, therefore, that *those* who are of faith, the same are the children of Abraham.
⁸ The Scripture, foreseeing that God would justify the heathen through faith, proclaimed⁺ the Gospel to Abraham before, *saying*: In you, all the nations will be blessed. *Genesis 12:3*
⁹ So, *those* who are of faith are *being* blessed with the faith⁺ *of* Abraham.
¹⁰For all⁺ *who* endure⁺ by works of the law are under a curse. For it is written: Cursed *is* everyone who does not continue in all things that are written in the book of the law, to do them. *Deuteronomy 27:26*
¹¹However⁺ *it is* evident that no one is justified by the law in the sight of God. For the righteous⁺ shall live by faith.

¹²However,⁺ law is not by faith. But, those of mankind⁺ who make them shall live in them. *Leviticus 18:5*
¹³Christ has redeemed us from the curse of the law *by* becoming⁺ cursed for us. For it is written: Cursed *is* everyone who hangs on a tree. *Deuteronomy 21:23*
¹⁴*This occurred so* that the blessing of Abraham might come to the Gentiles through Jesus Christ, *so* that we might receive the promise of the Spirit through faith.
¹⁵Family,⁺ *I am* speaking after the manner of men. Even so, no one *can* nullify⁺ or add to a man's confirmed covenant.
¹⁶Now the promises were made to Abraham and *to* his seed. He did not say: And to seeds, as of many, but as of one. And *specifically* to your seed, who is Christ.
¹⁷I say this: The covenant *pertaining* to Christ was confirmed before by God. The law that *came into* being⁺ four hundred and thirty years later,⁺ cannot nullify⁺ *it so* that it would make the promise of no effect.
¹⁸For if the inheritance *is* from the law, *then it is* no longer⁺ from *the* promise. But God gave *it* to Abraham by promise.
¹⁹Why then *was* the law *given*? It was added because of transgressions, until the seed should come *for* whom the promise was made. *It was* ordained in *the* hand *of a* mediator by angels.
²⁰But the mediator is not *the* one *who made the promise*, but God is.
²¹Then *is* the law against the promises of God? *That* cannot be.⁺ For if a law had been given that was able to give life, *then* truly⁺ righteousness could have been *achieved* by law.
²²But the Scripture established⁺ all things under sin *so* that the promise of Jesus Christ might be given by faith to *those* who believe.
²³But before faith came, under law we were guarded⁺ *while* closed⁺ to the faith that was about to be revealed.
²⁴Therefore the law was our tutor⁺ *to bring us* to Christ *so* that we might be justified by faith.

²⁵But after faith has come, we are no longer under an instructor.⁺

> 26 You are all children of God by faith in Christ Jesus.

²⁷For all⁺ *who* have been baptized into Christ have put on Christ.
²⁸There is neither Jew nor Greek. There is neither bond nor free. There is neither male nor female. For you are all one in Christ Jesus.
²⁹And if you *are* Christ's, then you are Abraham's seed and heirs according to the promise.

Galatians Chapter 4

¹ Now I say: For as long a time as an heir is a child, *there* is no difference⁺ *from* a servant, *even though that heir* will be lord *over* all.
² But *a child* is under tutors and guardians⁺ until the *time* appointed *by* the father.
³ And so when we were children, we were *held* in bondage under the elements of the world.
⁴ But when the fullness of time came, God sent forth His Son, made from a woman *and* made under *the* law, *Genesis 3:15*
⁵ to redeem *those* who were under *the* law *so* that we might receive adoption.
⁶ But because *you* are children⁺ *of God*, God has sent forth the Spirit of His Son into your hearts, crying *out*: Abba Father.
⁷ Therefore you are no longer⁺ a servant, but a child⁺ *of God*. And as a child⁺ *of God*, also an heir of God through Christ.
⁸ However, when you did not know God, you were in bondage⁺ to *those* who are not by nature gods.
⁹ But now, having known God, or rather having been known by God, how *can you* turn again to the weak and contemptible⁺ elements, to which you *seem to* desire to be in bondage again?
¹⁰You observe days and months and times and years.
¹¹I am afraid *for* you, lest *somehow* I have labored for you in vain.

¹²Family,⁺ I urge you: Be as I *am*. For I *am* like you. You have not wronged⁺ me at all.
¹³You know how, *even* through *my* weakness⁺ in the flesh, I proclaimed⁺ the Gospel to you *from* the first.
¹⁴And you did not despise or reject *me for* my trials⁺ in my flesh, but *you* received me like an angel of God, *even* as Christ Jesus.
¹⁵What then was *the source of* your blessedness? For I testify⁺ that, if *it had been* possible, you would have plucked out your own eyes and given them to me.
¹⁶Have I become your enemy because I speak the truth to you?
¹⁷*Certain things* zealously affect you, *but* not *for* good. But *rather* they desire⁺ that you be zealous⁺ *for them* to draw⁺ you *away*.
¹⁸*It is* good to be zealous in good *things* always, and not only when I am present with you.
¹⁹My little children *for* whom I labor⁺ again until Christ be formed in you,
²⁰I desire to be present with you now and to change my voice. For I stand in doubt *about* you.
²¹Tell me, you who desire to be under the law: Do you not hear the law?
²²For it is written: Abraham had two sons. One by a servant⁺ *woman*. The other by a free woman. *Genesis 21:10*
²³But one was born of the servant⁺ woman by the flesh. And one of the free woman through the promise.
²⁴This is an allegory. For these are *representative of* the two covenants: One from Mount Sinai that brings forth⁺ bondage is Hagar.
²⁵Hagar is *representative of* Mount Sinai in Arabia and corresponds⁺ to Jerusalem now, and *she* is in bondage with her children.
²⁶But *the* Jerusalem *that is* above is free *and* this is the mother of us all.
²⁷For it is written: Rejoice, *you* barren who do not bear. Break forth and cry *out*, you who do not labor⁺ *in childbirth*. For the desolate has many more children than she who has a husband. *Isaiah 54:1*

28 Now we, family,+ are children of *the* promise *just* as Isaac was.

29 But *just* as one born by the flesh persecuted one *born* by the Spirit, so also *is it* now.

30 Nevertheless, what does the Scripture say? Cast out the servant+ woman and her son. For the son of the servant+ woman will not be *the* heir with the son of the free woman. *Genesis 21:10, John 8:35*

31 So then, family,+ we are not children of the servant+ woman, but of the free.

Galatians Chapter 5

1 Stand fast therefore in the liberty with which Christ has made us free, and do not become entangled again with the yoke of bondage.

2 Behold I Paul say to you, that if you become+ circumcised *out of obedience to the law*, Christ will *bring* you no benefit.+

3 For I testify again to everyone+ who is *thus* circumcised, that *in so doing* one becomes+ obligated+ to do the whole law.

4 Whoever *among you* are *endeavoring to be* justified within the law are deprived+ of any benefit+ from Christ. *Rather, such as these* have fallen from grace.

5 For we, through the Spirit, by faith, wait for the hope of righteousness.

6 For in Christ Jesus, neither circumcision nor uncircumcision avails anything, but *only* faith working through love.

7 You have run well. Who hindered you *and caused you* to not obey the truth?

8 This persuasion does not *come* from Him who calls you.

9 A little leaven leavens the whole lump.

10 I have confidence in you through the Lord, that you will not be otherwise minded. But whoever has troubled you will bear the judgment, whoever it may be.

11 But I, family,+ if I still proclaim+ circumcision, *then* why do I still suffer persecution *from the Jews*? Then the offense of the cross has ceased.

12 I wish+ *those* who trouble you were cut off.

13 For, family,+ you have been called to liberty. Only do not *use* liberty for an occasion *for weakness in* the flesh, but by love serve one another.

14 For the whole+ law is fulfilled in one word, in this: Love your neighbor as yourself. *Matthew 19:19*

15 But if you bite and devour one another, take heed *so* that you are not consumed by one another.

16 *This* I say then: Walk in the Spirit and you will not fulfill the lust of the flesh.

17 For the flesh lusts against the Spirit, and the Spirit against the flesh. These are contrary the one to the other so that you cannot do the things that you should do.

18 But if you are led by the Spirit *then* you are not under the law.

19 Now the works of the flesh are revealed+ as *these*: Adultery, fornication, uncleanness, filthiness,+ *Matthew 15:19*

20 idolatry, witchcraft, hatred, contentiousness,+ jealousy,+ wrath, strife, rebellion,+ heresies,

21 envies, murders, drunkenness, riots,+ and such like. I told you about *all* this before *and* as I have also told *you* in time past: *Those* who do such things will not inherit the kingdom of God.

> 22 But the fruit of the Spirit is love, joy, peace, longsuffering, gentleness, goodness, faith, 23 meekness, *and* temperance.

There is no law against these things.

24 *Those* who are Christ's have crucified the flesh with its passions+ and lusts.

25 If we live in the Spirit, let us also walk in the Spirit.

26 Let us not be *overtaken by selfcentered* pride,+ provoking one another, *or* envying one another.

Galatians Chapter 6

1 Family,+ if someone+ is overtaken in a fault, you who are spiritual *ought to try to* restore such a one in the spirit of meekness, considering yourself, lest you also be tested.+ *Matthew 18:15*

² Bear one another's burdens and thereby⁺ fulfill the law of Christ.

³ For if anyone thinks themselves to be something when they are nothing, they deceive themselves.

⁴ But let everyone⁺ prove their own work and then they will have rejoicing in themselves alone and not in another.

⁵ For everyone⁺ shall bear their own burden.

⁶ Let *those* who are taught in the Word share with *those* who teach in all good things.

⁷ Do not be deceived. God is not mocked.

> For whatever anyone sows,
> that they shall also reap.

⁸ For *those* who sow to their flesh will reap corruption from the flesh. But *those* who sow to the Spirit will reap eternal⁺ life from the Spirit. *Proverbs 11:18*

⁹ Let us not be weary in well doing. For in due season we will reap, if we do not faint.

¹⁰Therefore, as we have opportunity, let us do good to everyone.⁺ Especially to *those* who are of the household of faith. *Proverbs 3:27*

¹¹See *in* what large letters I have written to you with my own hand.

¹²As many as desire to make a fair appearance⁺ in the flesh, they constrain you to be circumcised. *But this is* only so that they might not suffer persecution for the cross of Christ.

¹³For they themselves who are circumcised do not keep the law, but *they* desire to have you circumcised *so* that they might boast⁺ in your flesh.

¹⁴But *as for* me, *may it* not be⁺ that I should boast⁺ *in anything* except⁺ in the cross of our Lord Jesus Christ through whom, to me, the world has been crucified and I to the world.

¹⁵For in Christ Jesus neither circumcision nor uncircumcision avails anything, but *only being* a new creation⁺ *in Christ*.

¹⁶And *to* as many as walk according to this rule: Peace *be* upon them and mercy, and upon the Israel of God.

¹⁷From now on, let no one trouble me. For I bear in my body the marks of the Lord Jesus.

¹⁸Family,⁺ the grace of our Lord Jesus Christ *be* with your spirit. Amen.

This epistle was written at Rome.

Ephesians Chapter 1

¹ *From* Paul, an apostle of Jesus Christ by the will of God. To the saints at Ephesus and to the faithful in Christ Jesus.

² Grace to you and peace from God our Father and Lord Jesus Christ.

³ Blessed *is* the God and Father *of* our Lord Jesus Christ who has blessed us with all spiritual blessings in heavenly *places*, in Christ.

⁴ He chose us *to be* in Him before *the* foundation of *the* world *so* that we should be holy and without blame before Him in love.

⁵ *He* predestined us for adoption through Jesus Christ to Himself, according to the good pleasure of His will,

⁶ to the praise of the glory of His grace, in which He has made us accepted in the Beloved.

⁷ In *Jesus*, we have redemption through His blood *and* the forgiveness of sins according to the riches of His grace

⁸ that He has *made to* abound to us in all wisdom and prudence.

⁹ He has made the mystery of His will known to us, according to His good pleasure that He purposed in Himself,

¹⁰so that in the administration⁺ of the fullness of times He might gather together in one all things in Christ, both *those* in heaven and *those* on earth, *all gathered* in Him.

¹¹*For* in *Jesus*, we also have obtained an inheritance, being predestined according to the purpose of Him who works all things after the counsel of His own will,

¹²so that we who first trusted in Christ should be to the praise of His glory.

¹³You also *trusted* in *Him* after you heard the Word of Truth, the Gospel of your salvation. In *Him* also, after you

believed, you were sealed with the Holy Spirit of promise.

[14] *The Holy Spirit* is the guarantee[+] of our inheritance until the redemption of the purchased possession, to the praise of His glory.

[15] Therefore I also, after I heard of your faith in the Lord Jesus and love to all the saints,

[16] did not cease to give thanks for you, making mention of you in my prayers,

[17] *and asking* that the God *of* our Lord Jesus Christ, the Father of glory, might give *to* you the spirit of wisdom and revelation in the knowledge of Him.

[18] *I also ask that* the eyes of your understanding be enlightened *so* that you might know what is the hope of His calling and what *are* the riches of the glory of His inheritance in the saints,

[19] what *is* the exceeding greatness of His power toward us who believe, according to the working of His mighty power

[20] that He worked[+] in Christ when He raised Him from the dead and seated *Him* at His own right hand in the heavenly *places*,

[21] far above all principality and authority[+] and power and dominion and every name that is named, not only in this world, but also in what is to come.

[22] *God* has put all *things* under His feet and gave Him *to be* the head over all *things* to the assembly[+]

[23] that is His body, the fullness of Him who fills all in all.

Ephesians Chapter 2

[1] *In the past,* you were[+] dead in trespasses and sins.

[2] *In the past,* you walked according to the course of this world, according to the prince of the power of the air, the spirit that now works in the children of disobedience.

[3] *In the past,* we all had our conversation *and conduct* in the lusts of our flesh, fulfilling the desires of the flesh and of the mind. *We* were, by nature, the children of wrath, even as others.

[4] But God *is* rich in mercy because of His great love with which He loved us.

[5] Even when we were dead in sins, *He* gave us life[+] with Christ. By grace, you are *being* saved.

[6] *He* has raised *us* up together and made *us* sit together in heavenly *places* in Christ Jesus,

[7] *so* that in the ages to come He might show the exceeding riches of His grace in *His* kindness toward us through Christ Jesus.

> [8] For *it is* by grace *that* you are
> *being* saved through faith,
> and that not of yourselves.
> *It is* the gift of God.
> [9] *It is* not of works,
> lest anyone should boast.

[10] For we are His workmanship, created in Christ Jesus to *do the* good works that God has before ordained *so* that we should walk in them.

[11] Therefore remember that you *were*, in time past, Gentiles in the flesh *and* called uncircumcision by *those* who are called the circumcision in the flesh made by hands.

[12] At that time, you were without Christ, being aliens from the commonwealth of Israel and strangers from the covenants of promise, having no hope, and without God in the world.

[13] But now in Christ Jesus, you who sometimes were far off, are made near by the blood of Christ.

[14] For He is our peace, who made both one and broke down the middle wall of partition *between us*.

[15] *He* abolished, in His flesh, the enmity, the law of commandments *contained* in ordinances, to make in Himself one new man *out* of two, *thereby* making peace,

[16] *so* that He might reconcile both to God in one body by the cross, having slain the enmity thereby.

[17] *He* came and proclaimed[+] peace to you who were far off and to *those* who were near.

[18] For through Him we both have access

to the Father by one Spirit.

¹⁹Now therefore, you are no longer strangers and foreigners, but fellow citizens with the saints, and of the household of God.

²⁰*You* are being built upon the foundation of the apostles and prophets, Jesus Christ Himself being the chief corner *stone*.

²¹In *Jesus*, all the building fitly framed together grows to a holy temple in the Lord.

²²In *Jesus*, you are also built together for a habitation of God through the Spirit.

Ephesians Chapter 3

¹ For this reason,⁺ I Paul, *am* the prisoner of Jesus Christ for you Gentiles.

² *Now* indeed, you have heard of the administration⁺ of the grace of God that was given *to* me for you.

³ By revelation, *God* made the mystery known to me, as I wrote before⁺ in a few words.

⁴ When you read *this*, you may understand my knowledge in the mystery of Christ.

⁵ In other ages, *this* was not made known to the children⁺ of mankind⁺ as it is now revealed to His holy apostles and prophets by the Spirit.

⁶ *But now* the Gentiles can be fellow heirs and of the same body and partakers of His promise in Christ by the Gospel.

⁷ For this, I was made a minister according to the gift of the grace of God. *This was* given to me by the effective working of His power.

⁸ This grace has been given to me, *one* who is less than the least of all saints, *so* that I might proclaim⁺ the unsearchable riches of Christ among the Gentiles,

⁹ to make all see what *is* the fellowship of the mystery, which from the beginning of the world has been hid in God who created all things by Jesus Christ.

¹⁰*This* to the intent that now the manifold wisdom of God might be *made* known by the assembly⁺ to the principalities and powers in heavenly *places*,

¹¹according to the eternal purpose that He purposed in Christ Jesus our Lord.

¹²In *Him* we have boldness and access with confidence through faith in Him.

¹³Therefore, I urge⁺ that you not faint at my tribulations for you, which is your glory.

¹⁴For this reason,⁺ I bow my knees to the Father *of* our Lord Jesus Christ,

¹⁵after whom the whole family in heaven and earth is named,

¹⁶*so* that He would grant *to* you, according to the riches of His glory, to be inwardly⁺ strengthened with might by His Spirit,

¹⁷*so* that Christ may dwell in your hearts by faith, *and so* that you, being rooted and grounded in love,

¹⁸might be able to comprehend with all saints what*is* the breadth and length and depth and height *of His love*:

¹⁹To know the love of Christ that surpasses⁺ knowledge *so* that you might be filled with all the fullness of God.

²⁰Now unto Him who is able to do exceedingly abundant above all that we ask or think according to the power that works in us,

²¹unto Him *be* glory in the assembly⁺ by Christ Jesus throughout all ages, world without end. Amen.

Ephesians Chapter 4

¹ Therefore I, the prisoner of the Lord, urge you to walk worthy of the vocation into which you are called,

² with all lowliness and meekness *and* with longsuffering, forbearing one another in love.

³ Endeavor to keep the unity of the Spirit in the bond of peace.

⁴ *There is* one body and one Spirit, even as you are called in one hope of your calling.

⁵ One Lord, one faith, one baptism.

⁶ One God and Father of all, who *is* above all and through all and in you all.

⁷ But to everyone of us, grace is given according to the measure of the gift of Christ.

⁸ Therefore He said: When He ascended up on high, He led captivity captive and gave gifts to people.⁺ *Psalm 68:18*

⁹ *Knowing* that He ascended, what is *to be understood* but that He also descended first into the lower parts of the earth?

¹⁰ He who descended is the same also who ascended up far above all heavens *so* that He might fill all things.

¹¹ He gave some *to be* apostles, some *to be* prophets, some *to be* evangelists, *and* some *to be* pastors and teachers

¹² for the perfecting of the saints, for the work of the ministry, *and* for the edifying of the body of Christ,

¹³ until we all come in the unity of the faith and in the knowledge of the Son of God to a perfect man, to the measure of the stature of the fullness of Christ.

¹⁴ *Therefore* we *must* no longer⁺ be *like* children tossed to and fro and carried away⁺ with every wind of doctrine, by the sleight *and* cunning craftiness of *those* who lie in wait to deceive.

¹⁵ But *we must* speak the truth in love *and* grow up into *Him* who is the head, Christ, in all things.

¹⁶ Through *Christ*, the whole body *is* fitly joined together and connected⁺ by what every joint supplies. Accordingly, the effective working together⁺ of every part increases the body edifying itself in love.

¹⁷ Therefore this I say and testify in the Lord: You *must* no longer⁺ walk as other Gentiles walk, in the vanity of their mind,

¹⁸ having the understanding darkened, *and* being alienated from the life of God through the ignorance that is in them, because of the blindness of their heart.

¹⁹ Being past feeling, they have given themselves over to filthiness,⁺ to work all uncleanness with greediness.

²⁰ But you have not so learned Christ.

²¹ If indeed⁺ you have heard Him and have been taught by Him, as the truth is in Jesus,

²² then you *will* put off the old self,⁺ concerning the former conversation *and* conduct that is corrupt according to the deceitful lusts,

²³ and be renewed in the spirit of your mind,

²⁴ and put on the new man, which, after God, is created in righteousness and true holiness.

²⁵ Therefore put away lying. Everyone⁺ *must* speak truth with their neighbor. For we are members of one another.

²⁶ *If you* become⁺ angry, do not sin. Do not let the sun go down upon your wrath. *Psalm 37:8*

²⁷ Do not give place to the devil.

²⁸ Let *those* who stole, steal no longer.⁺ But rather let them labor, working with *their* hands *in* the things that are good *so* that they may have *sufficient* to give to *those* who *have* needs. *Proverbs 21:26*

²⁹ Do not let corrupt communication
proceed out of your mouth,
but what is good to the use
of edifying *so* that it may
minister grace to the hearers.
Matthew 12:35

³⁰ Do not grieve the Holy Spirit of God, by whom you are sealed to the day of redemption.

³¹ Let all bitterness, wrath,
anger, clamor, and evil speaking
be put away from you,
along with all malice.
³² Be kind to one another,
tenderhearted,
forgiving one another,
even as God for Christ's sake
has forgiven you.

Ephesians Chapter 5

¹ Therefore, be followers of God, as dear children.

² Walk in love as Christ also has loved us and has given Himself for us, an offering and a sacrifice to God for a sweet smelling savor.

³ Do not let fornication and all uncleanness or covetousness be named among you *even* once, as becomes saints.

⁴ *Do not allow* filthiness or foolish talking or jesting, which is not proper, + but rather give thanks.

⁵ For this you know: That no fornicator+ or unclean person or covetous person who is an idolater has any inheritance in the kingdom of Christ and of God.

⁶ Let no one deceive you with vain words. For because of these things the wrath of God *will* come upon the children of disobedience.

⁷ Therefore do not be partakers with them.

⁸ For you were sometimes darkness. But now *you are* light in the Lord. Walk as children of light.

⁹ For the fruit of the Spirit *is* in all goodness and righteousness and truth,

¹⁰proving what is acceptable *and pleasing* to the Lord.

¹¹Do not have fellowship with the unfruitful works of darkness, but rather admonish+ *them*.

¹²For it is a shame to even speak of those things that are done by them in secret.

¹³But all *who* are admonished+ by the light are revealed.+ For whatever reveals+ *truth and error* is light.

¹⁴Therefore He says: Awake, you who sleep. Arise from the dead, and Christ will give you light. *Isaiah 60:1*

¹⁵See then that you walk circumspectly, not as fools, but as wise. *Proverbs 15:21*

¹⁶Redeem the time, because the days are evil.

¹⁷Therefore do not be unwise but understand what the will of the Lord *is*.

¹⁸Do not be drunk with wine in which is excess, but be filled with the Spirit.

¹⁹Speak to yourselves in psalms and hymns and spiritual songs, singing and making melody in your heart to the Lord.

²⁰Always give thanks for all things to God the Father in the name *of* our Lord Jesus Christ.

²¹Submit yourselves to one another in the fear of God.

²²Wives, submit yourselves to your own husbands, as to the Lord.

²³For the husband is the head of the wife, even as Christ is the head of the church, and He is the Savior of the body.

²⁴Therefore as the assembly+ is subject to Christ, so *let* the wives *be* to their own husbands in everything.

²⁵Husbands love your wives, even as Christ also loved the assembly+ and gave Himself for it,

²⁶*so* that He might sanctify and cleanse it with the washing of water by the Word,

²⁷*so* that He might present it to Himself a glorious assembly,+ not having spot or wrinkle or any such thing, but *so* that it should be holy and without blemish.

²⁸So *also* men ought to love their wives as their own bodies. He who loves his wife loves himself.

²⁹For no one ever yet hated their own flesh, but nourishes and cherishes it, even as the Lord *nourishes and cherishes* the church.

³⁰For we are members of His body, of His flesh, and of His bones.

³¹For this reason+ a man shall leave his father and mother and shall be joined to his wife and they two shall be one flesh. *Matthew 19:5*

³²This is a great mystery, but I speak concerning Christ and the church.

³³Nevertheless, let everyone of you in particular so love his wife, even as himself. And the wife *see* that she reverence *her* husband.

Ephesians Chapter 6

¹ Children, obey your parents in the Lord, for this is right.

² Honor your father and mother, which is the first commandment with *a* promise, *Matthew 15:4*

³ *so* that it may be well with you and you may live long on the earth. *Exodus 20:12*

⁴ And you fathers: Do not provoke your children to anger,+ but bring them up in the nurture and admonition of the Lord. *Proverbs 22:6*

⁵ Servants, be obedient to *those* who are *your* masters according to the flesh, with fear and trembling, in singleness of your heart, as to Christ.

⁶ Not for appearance⁺ *sake*, as pleasing people,⁺ but as the servants of Christ, doing the will of God from the heart.

⁷ With good will, do *your* service as to the Lord and not to people.⁺

⁸ Know that whatever good thing anyone does, they will receive the same from the Lord, whether *they are* bond or free.

⁹ And you masters: Do the same things to them, forgoing⁺ threatening, knowing that your Master also is in heaven, and there is no partiality⁺ with Him.

¹⁰ Finally, my family,⁺ be strong in the Lord and in the power of His might.

¹¹ Put on the whole armor of God *so* that you may be able to stand against the traps⁺ of the devil.

¹² For we do not wrestle against flesh and blood but against principalities, against powers, against the rulers of the darkness of this world, *and* against spiritual wickedness in high *places*.

¹³ Therefore, take up⁺ the whole armor of God *so* that you may be able to stand against⁺ *evil* in the evil day. And having done all *you can*, stand *firm*.

¹⁴ Therefore stand, having your waist⁺ belted⁺ *strong* with truth, and having on the breastplate of righteousness,

¹⁵ and your feet shod with the preparation of the Gospel of peace.

¹⁶ Above all, take the shield of faith with which you will be able to quench all the fiery darts of the wicked.

¹⁷ And take the helmet of salvation and the sword of the Spirit, which is the Word of God,

¹⁸ praying always with all prayer and supplication in the Spirit and watching to this with all perseverance and supplication for all the saints.

¹⁹ *Pray also* for me *so* that utterance may be given to me *so* that I may open my mouth boldly to make known the mystery of the Gospel,

²⁰ for which I am an ambassador in chains⁺ *so* that *even* in that *state*, I may speak boldly as I ought to speak.

²¹ *So* that you may also know my affairs *and* how I am doing, Tychicus, a beloved brother and faithful minister in the Lord,

will make everything⁺ known to you.

²² I have sent *him* to you for the same purpose, *so* that you might know our affairs and *so that* he might comfort your hearts.

²³ Peace to the family⁺ and love in faith, from God *our* Father and Lord Jesus Christ.

²⁴ Grace to all who love our Lord Jesus Christ in sincerity. Amen.

This epistle was transcribed at Rome by Tychicus.

Philippians Chapter 1

¹ *From* Paul and Timothy, servants of Jesus Christ. To all the saints in Christ Jesus who are at Philippi, with the bishops and deacons.

² Grace to you and peace from God our Father and Lord Jesus Christ.

³ I thank my God upon every remembrance of you.

⁴ Always, in every prayer of mine for you all, *I* ask⁺ with joy

⁵ for your fellowship in the Gospel, from the first day until now.

⁶ *I* am confident of this: That

> He who has begun
> a good work in you
> will perform *it*
> until the day of Jesus Christ.

⁷ It is right⁺ for me to think this of you all, because I have you in my heart. Inasmuch as both in my chains⁺ and in the defense and confirmation of the Gospel, you are all partakers *with* me *of* grace.

⁸ For God is my witness,⁺ how greatly I long for you all in the tender⁺ *mercies* of Jesus Christ.

⁹ This I pray: That your love may abound yet more and more in knowledge and *in* all judgment,

¹⁰ *so* that you may approve things that are excellent *and so* that you may be sincere and without offense until the day of Christ.

¹¹Be filled with the fruit of righteousness that *comes* through Jesus Christ, to the glory and praise of God.

¹²I want you to understand, family,⁺ that the things *that have happened* to me have turned⁺ out instead⁺ to the advancement⁺ of the Gospel,

¹³so that my chains⁺ in Christ are known⁺ in all the palace and in all other *places*.

¹⁴Many of the family⁺ in the Lord, growing⁺ more confident *because of* my chains,⁺ are much more bold to speak the Word without fear.

¹⁵Indeed, some proclaim⁺ Christ from envy and strife, but some also from good will.

¹⁶*Those* who proclaim⁺ Christ from contention *and* not sincerely *are* supposing to add suffering⁺ to my chains.⁺

¹⁷But the others *do so* out of love, knowing that I am set for the defense of the Gospel.

¹⁸What then? Even so,⁺ *in* every way, whether in pretence or in truth, Christ is proclaimed,⁺ and I rejoice in this. Yes, and I will *continue to* rejoice.

¹⁹For I know that this will turn to my salvation through your prayer and the supply of the Spirit of Jesus Christ.

²⁰According to my earnest expectation and hope, I will be ashamed in nothing. But with all boldness, now, as always, Christ shall be magnified in my body, whether by life or by death.

²¹For to me, to live *is* Christ and to die *is* gain.

²²If I live in the flesh, this *is* the fruit of my labor. Yet I do not know⁺ what I shall choose.

²³For I am in a strait between⁺ two *desires*. Having a desire to depart and to be with Christ, which is far better.

²⁴Nevertheless, *desiring* to remain⁺ in the flesh *is* more necessary⁺ for you.

²⁵*But I* have this confidence: I know that I shall remain⁺ and continue with you all for your advancement⁺ and joy of faith,

²⁶so that your rejoicing may be more abundant in Jesus Christ for me by my coming to you again.

²⁷Only *let your* conversation *and conduct* be worthy⁺ of the Gospel of Christ, *so* that whether I come and see you or else *must* be absent, I may hear that you stand fast in one spirit, with one mind striving together for the faith of the Gospel.

²⁸Do not be frightened⁺ by your adversaries. That will be, to them, an evidence of *their* damnation,⁺ and of your salvation, and that from God.

²⁹For it is given to you, on the behalf of Christ, to not only believe in Him, but also to suffer for His sake.

³⁰*You may* have conflicts *just* as you saw in mine and now hear *about* in mine.

Philippians Chapter 2

¹ Therefore, if *there be* any consolation in Christ, if any comfort in love, if any fellowship of the Spirit, if any tender⁺ mercies,

² fulfill my joy: That you

---

be like minded,
having the same love,
being of one accord *and* of one mind.
³ *Let* nothing *be done* through strife
or *selfcentered* pride,⁺
but in lowliness of mind
let each esteem others
better than themselves.

---

⁴ Do not consider⁺ *only those* things of your own⁺ *concern* but also the things of others.

⁵ Let this mind be in you, which was also in Christ Jesus.

⁶ *Christ* being in the form of God did not think it robbery to be equal with God.

⁷ But *He* made Himself of no reputation and took upon Himself⁺ the form of a servant and was made in the likeness of men.

⁸ And being found in fashion as a man, *Christ* humbled Himself and became obedient unto death, even the death of the cross.

⁹ Therefore God also has highly exalted Him and given Him a name that is above every name,

¹⁰ *so* that at the name of Jesus, every knee should bow, of *things* in heaven and *things* in *the* earth and *things* under the earth.

¹¹ Every tongue should confess that Jesus Christ *is* Lord, to the glory of God the Father.

¹² Therefore my beloved, as you have always obeyed, not as in my presence only but now much more in my absence, work out your own salvation with fear and trembling.

¹³ For it is God who works in you both to will and to do of *His* good pleasure.

¹⁴ Do all things without complaining and disputing

¹⁵ *so* that you may be blameless and harmless, the children⁺ of God, without rebuke, in the midst of a crooked and perverse nation, among whom you shine as lights in the world.

¹⁶ Hold forth the Word of life *so* that I may rejoice in the day of Christ, *so* that I have not run in vain nor labored in vain.

¹⁷ Yes, and if I be offered upon the sacrifice and service of your faith, I *have* joy and rejoice with you all.

¹⁸ For the same cause also, you *should have* joy and rejoice with me.

¹⁹ But I trust in the Lord Jesus to send Timothy to you soon⁺ *so* that I may also be of good comfort when I know your condition. ⁺

²⁰ For I have no one like minded who will naturally care for your condition. ⁺

²¹ For all seek their own *objectives*, not the things that are Jesus Christ's.

²² But you know the proof of Him, that, like a son with *his* father, *Timothy* has served with me in the Gospel.

²³ Therefore I hope to send him *to you* immediately, ⁺ as soon as I see how it will go with me.

²⁴ But I trust in the Lord that I myself will also come *to you* soon. ⁺

²⁵ Yet I supposed it necessary to send Epaphroditus to you, my brother, companion in labor, and fellow soldier, but your messenger and one⁺ who ministered to my wants.

²⁶ For he longed after you all and was full of sorrow⁺ because you had heard that he had been sick.

²⁷ For indeed he was sick, near death. But God had mercy on him. Not on him only, but on me also, lest I should have sorrow upon sorrow.

²⁸ I sent him therefore *all* the more carefully *so* that, when you see him again, you may rejoice and *so* that I may be less sorrowful.

²⁹ Therefore, receive him in the Lord with all gladness. Hold such *as him* in *high* reputation.

³⁰ Because of the work of Christ, he was near death, not regarding his *own* life, *in order* to supply your lack of service toward me.

Philippians Chapter 3

¹ Finally my family⁺: Rejoice in the Lord. To write the same things to you *is* indeed not grievous to me. But for you *it is* safe.

² Beware of dogs. Beware of evil workers. Beware of division. ⁺

³ For we are the circumcision, who worship God in the spirit and rejoice in Christ Jesus and have no confidence in the flesh.

⁴ Though I might also have confidence in the flesh. If anyone⁺ *else* thinks that they have reason⁺ *to* trust in the flesh, I *have* more.

⁵ *I was* circumcised *on* the eighth day, of the stock of Israel, *of* the tribe of Benjamin, a Hebrew of the Hebrews, *and* concerning the law, a Pharisee.

⁶ *As* concerning zeal, *I was* persecuting the church. *As* touching the righteousness that is in the law, *I was* blameless.

⁷ But what things were gain to me, those I counted loss for *the sake of* Christ.

⁸ Yes doubtless. And I count all things *but* loss for the excellency of the knowledge of Christ Jesus my Lord for whom I have suffered the loss of all things and do count them *but* dung *so* that I may win Christ

⁹ and be found in Him. *For I do* not have *any* righteousness *of* my own

from *obedience to* the law, but *only* through faith in Christ, righteousness from God by faith.

[10]*so* that I may know Him and the power of His resurrection and the fellowship of His sufferings, being made conformable to His death.

[11]If by any means I might attain to the resurrection of the dead,

[12]not as though I had already attained or had already *become* perfect, but I follow after *so* that I may attain[+] that for which I am claimed[+] by Christ Jesus.

[13]Family,[+] I do not count myself to have attained[+] *everything*, but *this* one thing *I do*: Forgetting those things that are behind and reaching forth to those things that are before,

[14]I press toward the mark for the prize of the high calling of God in Christ Jesus.

[15]Therefore let us, as many as be perfect, be thus minded. If, in anything, you are otherwise minded, God will reveal this to you.

[16]Nevertheless, in what we have already attained, let us walk by the same rule. Let us mind the same thing.

[17]Family,[+] be followers together *with* me. Note[+] *those* who walk *in this way*, as you have us for an example.

[18]For many walk, of whom I have often told you, and now *I* tell you weeping, *that they are* the enemies of the cross of Christ.

[19]Their end *will be* destruction. Their God *is their* belly. And *those* who mind earthly things glory in their shame.

[20]For our conversation *and conduct* is in heaven. From there we also look for the Savior, the Lord Jesus Christ

[21]who will change our vile body *so* that it may be fashioned like His glorious body, according to the work by which He is able even to subdue all things to Himself.

Philippians Chapter 4

[1] Therefore my family,[+] beloved and longed for, my joy and crown, so stand fast in the Lord, *my* beloved.

[2] I urge[+] Euodias and Syntyche that they be of the same mind in the Lord.

[3] I entreat you also, *my* true yokefellow: Help those women who labored with me in the Gospel *and* with Clement also and *with* my other fellow laborers whose names *are* in the Book of Life.

---

[4] Rejoice in the Lord always.
And again I say: Rejoice.

Matthew 5:12

[5] Let your moderation
be known to everyone.[+]
The Lord *is very* near.[+]

Luke 12:15

[6] Do not be anxious[+] about[+] anything,
but in everything by prayer
and supplication with thanksgiving
let your requests
be made known to God.

Matthew 6:25

[7] And the peace of God
that surpasses[+] all understanding
will keep your hearts and minds
through Christ Jesus. *John 14:27*

---

[8] Finally family[+]: Whatever things are true, whatever things *are* honest, whatever things *are* righteous,[+] whatever things *are* pure, whatever things *are* lovely, whatever things *are* of good report, if *there be* any virtue and if *there be* any praise, think on these things. *Matthew 5:8*

---

[9] Do those things that you have both learned and received and heard and seen in me, and the God of peace will be with you.

[10]But I rejoiced in the Lord greatly that now at the last your care for me has flourished again in which you were also careful but you lacked opportunity.

[11]Not that I speak in respect of want, for I have learned, in whatever state I am, *there* to be content.

[12]I know both how to be humbled[+] and I know how to abound. Everywhere and in all things I am instructed both to be full and to be hungry, both to abound and to suffer need.

> ¹³ I can do all things
> through Christ
> who strengthens me.

¹⁴ Nevertheless, you have done well *in* that you shared⁺ in my suffering.⁺
¹⁵ Now you Philippians also know, that in the beginning of the Gospel, when I departed from Macedonia, no assembly⁺ shared⁺ with me as concerning giving and receiving, but only you.
¹⁶ For even in Thessalonica, you sent once and again to my necessity.
¹⁷ Not because I desire a gift, but I desire fruit that may abound to your account.
¹⁸ But I have everything⁺ *I need* and abound. I am full, having received from Epaphroditus the things *that were sent* from you. An aroma⁺ of a sweet smell, a sacrifice acceptable, well pleasing to God.

> ¹⁹ God will supply all you need
> according to His riches in glory
> by Christ Jesus.

²⁰ Now to God our Father, *be* glory forever and ever. Amen.
²¹ Greet⁺ every saint in Christ Jesus. The family⁺ who are with me greet you.
²² All the saints greet⁺ you, chiefly *those* who are of Caesar's household.
²³ The grace of our Lord Jesus Christ *be* with you all. Amen.

This epistle was transcribed at Rome by Epaphroditus.

Colossians Chapter 1

¹ *From* Paul, an apostle of Jesus Christ by the will of God, and Timothy *our* brother.
² To the saints and faithful believers⁺ in Christ who are at Colosse. Grace to you and peace from God our Father and Lord Jesus Christ.
³ We give thanks *to our* God and Father *and* our Lord Jesus Christ, praying for you continually.⁺

⁴ We have heard of your faith in Christ Jesus and of the love *that you have* for all the saints.
⁵ Hope *is* laid up for you in heaven. You heard about this before, in the Word of Truth, in the Gospel
⁶ that has come to you, as to all the world. *It* brings forth fruit, as *it has* in you since the day you heard *of it* and knew the grace of God in truth.
⁷ *Just* as you learned from Epaphras, our dear fellow servant who is a faithful minister of Christ for you.
⁸ *He* also declared to us your love in the Spirit.
⁹ For this reason,⁺ since the day we heard *about this*, we have not stopped⁺ praying for you and desiring that you might be filled with the knowledge of His will in all wisdom and spiritual understanding,
¹⁰ *so* that you might walk worthy of the Lord to all pleasing, being fruitful in every good work and increasing in the knowledge of God,
¹¹ strengthened with all might according to His glorious power, to all patience and longsuffering with joyfulness.
¹² Give thanks to the Father who has made us suitable⁺ to be partakers of the inheritance of the saints in light.
¹³ *God* has delivered us from the power of darkness and translated *us* into the kingdom of His dear Son.
¹⁴ In *Him*, we have redemption through His blood, *even* the forgiveness of sins.
¹⁵ *He* is the *very* image of the invisible God, the firstborn of all creation.⁺
¹⁶ By Him, all things were created, that are in heaven and that are in earth, visible and invisible, whether *they be* thrones or dominions or principalities or powers. All things were created by Him and for Him.
¹⁷ He is before all things and by Him all things consist.
¹⁸ He is the head of the body, the assembly.⁺ He is *the* beginning, the firstborn from the dead, *so* that in all *things* He might have preeminence.
¹⁹ For it pleased *the Father* that all fullness should dwell in Him.

[20]And by Him, having made peace through the blood of His cross, to reconcile all things to Himself. By Him, *I say*, whether *they be* things in earth or things in heaven.

[21]And you, who were at one time alienated and enemies in *your* mind by wicked works, yet now He has reconciled [22]in the body of His flesh through death, to present you holy and blameless[+] and unreprovable in His sight.

[23]Continue in the faith, grounded and settled and not moved away from the hope of the Gospel that you have heard as *it is* proclaimed[+] to all creation[+] under heaven. For this, I Paul am made a minister.

[24]Now *I* rejoice in my sufferings for you, and fill up what is lacking[+] through the sufferings[+] of Christ in my *own* flesh, for the sake of His body, which is the *whole* assembly[+] *of believers*.

[25]I have become[+] a minister according to the administration[+] of God. *This assignment was* given to me *for* you, to fulfill the Word of God.

[26]The mystery *that had been* hidden for ages and for generations is now revealed[+] to His saints.

[27]To *His saints*, God wants[+] *to* make known the riches of the glory of this mystery among the Gentiles. *It* is Christ in you, the hope of glory

[28]whom we proclaim,[+] warning everyone[+] and teaching everyone[+] in all wisdom *so* that we may present everyone[+] perfect in Christ Jesus.

[29]To *this cause* I also labor, striving according to His working, which works in me mightily.

Colossians Chapter 2

[1] I wish[+] that you knew what great conflict I have *endured* for you, and *for* those at Laodicea and *for* all[+] *who* have not *even* seen my face in the flesh,

[2] *so* that their hearts might be comforted, being knit together in love and *enjoying* all *the* riches of the full assurance of understanding, *even* to the acknowledgment of the mystery of God, and of the Father and of Christ

[3] in whom all the treasures of wisdom and knowledge are hid.

[4] I say *all* this, lest anyone should deceive[+] you with enticing words.

[5] For *even* though I *may* be absent in the flesh, yet am I with you in the spirit, rejoicing[+] and beholding your order and the steadfastness of your faith in Christ.

[6] Therefore, as you have received Christ Jesus the Lord,
so also walk in Him.
[7] *Be* rooted and built up in Him and established in the faith, as you have been taught, abounding therein with thanksgiving.

[8] Beware lest anyone spoil you through philosophy and vain deceit, after the traditions of men *and* after the things[+] of the world, and not after Christ.

[9] For in Him dwells all the fullness of the Godhead bodily.

[10]You are complete in Him who is the head of all principalities and authorities[+] *and powers*.

[11]In *Him* also you are circumcised with the circumcision made without hands, in putting off the body of the sins of the flesh by the circumcision of Christ.

[12]*You were* buried with Him in baptism, in which you are also risen with *Him* through faith in the operation of God who has raised Him from the dead.

[13]And *to* you, being dead in your sins and in the uncircumcision of your flesh, He has given life[+] together with Him, having forgiven you *for* all trespasses,

[14]blotting out the handwriting of ordinances that was against us, which was contrary to us. *He* took it out of the way, nailing it to His cross.

[15]*And* having spoiled principalities and powers, He made a show of them openly, triumphing over them in it.

[16]Therefore, do not let anyone judge you in food[+] or in drink or in respect of

a holy day or of the new moon or of the Sabbath *days*.

¹⁷ *These* are a shadow of things to come. But the body *is* of Christ.

¹⁸ Do not let anyone deceive⁺ you into selfwilled⁺ humility *of your own pretense* and worshiping angels, intruding into things that have not been seen *but* vainly puffed up by the fleshly mind,

¹⁹ not holding *fast* the Head from which all the body, by joints and bands having nourishment ministered *to them* and knit together, increases *by* the increase of God.

²⁰ Therefore, if you are dead with Christ from the things⁺ of the world, *then* why, as though living in the world, are you subject to ordinances:

²¹ Do not touch. Do not taste. Do not handle.

²² All *this* is *subject* to corruption according *to* the use, commandments, and doctrines of men.

²³ *These* things indeed have the appearance⁺ of wisdom in selfwilled⁺ worship and humility and neglecting of the body *but they are* not of any honor for *they* satisfy the flesh.

Colossians Chapter 3

¹ If you then are risen with Christ, seek those things that are above, where Christ sits at the right hand of God.

² Set your affection on things above, not on things on the earth.

³ For you are dead, and your life is hid with Christ in God.

⁴ When Christ, *who is* our life, appears, then you will also appear with Him in glory.

⁵ Therefore, put to death⁺ your members which are upon the earth: fornication, uncleanness, inordinate affection, evil abnormal appetites,⁺ and covetousness, which is idolatry.

⁶ Because of these things, the wrath of God will come upon the children of disobedience.

⁷ You also walked in *these things for* some time, when you lived among⁺ them.

⁸ But now you also put off all these: Anger, wrath, malice, blasphemy, *and* filthy communication out of your mouth.

⁹ Do not lie to one another, since you have put off the old self⁺ with its *self centered* deeds.

¹⁰ *You* have put on the new *quality of character* that is renewed in knowledge after the image of Him who created *the new person that you now are.*

¹¹ *Now* there is neither Greek nor Jew, circumcision nor uncircumcision, Barbarian, Scythian, bond *nor* free. But Christ *is* all and in all.

¹² Therefore, as the elect of God, holy and beloved, put on a heart⁺ of mercies, kindness, humbleness of mind, meekness, *and* longsuffering.

¹³ Forbear one another and forgive one another. If anyone has a quarrel against another,⁺ *just* as Christ forgave you, so also you *do likewise*.

¹⁴ Above all these things *put on true* love, which is the bond of perfection.⁺

¹⁵ Let the peace of God rule in your hearts, to which you also are called in one body. Be thankful.

¹⁶ Let the Word of Christ dwell in you richly in all wisdom. Teach and admonish one another in psalms and hymns and spiritual songs, singing with grace in your hearts to the Lord.

¹⁷ Whatever you do in word or deed, *do* all in the name of the Lord Jesus, giving thanks to God and Father by Him.

¹⁸ Wives, submit yourselves to your own husbands as it is proper⁺ in the Lord.

¹⁹ Husbands, love *your* wives and do not be bitter against them.

²⁰ Children, obey *your* parents in everything. For this is well pleasing to the Lord.

²¹ Fathers, do not provoke your children *to anger*, lest they become⁺ discouraged.

²² Servants obey *your* masters in everything according to the flesh. Not for appearance,⁺ as pleasing people,⁺ but in singleness of heart, fearing God.

> ²³ Whatever you do,
> do *it* heartily as to the Lord
> and not to people.⁺

²⁴Know that from the Lord you will receive the reward of the inheritance, for you serve the Lord Christ.

²⁵But *those* who do wrong will receive *accordingly* for the wrongs they have done. There will be no partiality⁺ *shown*.

Colossians Chapter 4

¹ Masters, give to *your* servants what is just and equal, knowing that you also have a Master in heaven.

² Continue in prayer, watching in it with thanksgiving.

³ Pray for us also, that God would open a door of utterance for us to speak the mystery of Christ, for which I am also in chains,⁺

⁴ *so* that I might make it manifest, as I ought to speak.

⁵ Walk in wisdom toward *those* who are outside,⁺ redeeming the time.

⁶ Let your speech always *be* with grace *and* seasoned with salt *so* that you may know how you ought to answer everyone.⁺

⁷ Tychicus, *who is* a beloved brother and a faithful minister and fellow servant in the Lord, will declare to you everything concerning my condition.⁺

⁸ I have sent *him* to you for that purpose, *and so* that he might know your condition⁺ and comfort your hearts.

⁹ *Along* with Onesimus, a faithful and beloved brother who is *one* of you, they will make known to you all things that *are being done* here.

¹⁰Aristarchus, my fellow prisoner, greets⁺ you, *along with* Mark whose cousin *is* Barnabas. Concerning⁺ *Mark*, you have received instructions,⁺ *that* if he comes to you, *you are to* receive him.

¹¹Also Jesus who is called Justus *sends greetings*. *All of them* are of *the* circumcision *and* they alone⁺ *are my* fellow workers for the kingdom of God who have been a comfort to me.

¹²Epaphras who is of you, a servant of Christ, greets⁺ you. *He is* always laboring fervently for you in prayers *so* that you may stand perfect and complete in all the will of God.

¹³For I testify⁺ that he has a great zeal for you and *for* those *who are* in Laodicea and *for* those in Hierapolis.

¹⁴Luke, the beloved physician, and Demas greet you.

¹⁵Greet⁺ the family⁺ who are in Laodicea and Nymphas and the assembly⁺ in his house.

¹⁶When this epistle is read among you, cause *it* to be read in the assembly⁺ of the Laodiceans also, *so* that you likewise *might* read the *epistle* from Laodicea.

¹⁷Say to Archippus: Take heed to the ministry you have received in the Lord *so* that you fulfill it.

¹⁸*I* Paul, *now close with* the salutation of my own hand. Remember my chains. Grace *be* with you. Amen.

This epistle was transcribed at Rome by Tychicus and Onesimus.

1 Thessalonians Chapter 1

¹ *From* Paul, Silvanus, and Timothy. To the assembly⁺ of the Thessalonians in God *the* Father and Lord Jesus Christ. Grace to you and peace from God our Father and Lord Jesus Christ.

² We always give thanks to God for you all, making mention of you in our prayers.

³ *We* remember without ceasing your work of faith and labor of love and patient hope in our Lord Jesus Christ, in the sight of our Father God.

⁴ *We* know, beloved family,⁺ *that* you were chosen⁺ by God.

⁵ For our Gospel did not come to you in word only, but also in power and in *the* Holy Spirit and in much assurance, as you know what *kind of people* we were among you for your sake.

⁶ You became followers of us and of the Lord, having received the Word with joy in the Holy Spirit, *even* in much suffering,⁺

⁷ so that you became⁺ examples to all who believe in Macedonia and Achaia.

⁸ For *it was* from you *that* the Word of the Lord sounded forth,⁺ not only in

Macedonia and Achaia, but also in every place *where* your faith toward God was widely[+] spread, so that we did not need *to* say anything.

9 For *they* themselves declared[+] *to* us what *an* entrance[+] we had to you and how you turned to God from idols, to serve the living and true God

10 and to wait for His Son from heaven, whom He raised from the dead: Jesus, who delivers us from the wrath to come.

1 Thessalonians Chapter 2

1 For *you* yourselves know, family,[+] that our entrance in to you was not in vain.

2 But *even after* we had suffered and were shamefully treated at Philippi, as you know, we were bold in our God to speak the Gospel of God to you, *even* in much contention.

3 For our exhortation *was* not from error[+] nor of uncleanness, nor in deceitfulness.[+]

4 But as we were allowed by God to be entrusted[+] with the Gospel, even so we speak. Not as pleasing men, but God, who proves[+] our hearts.

5 For as you know, we did not at any time use flattering words or a cloak of covetousness. God *is our* witness.

6 We did not seek glory from people or from you or from others, *even though* as apostles of Christ we could have *placed* a burden *on you*.

7 But we were gentle among you, *just* as a nurse cherishes her children.

8 So, *because of our* deep affection for you, we were willing to have imparted to you, not only the Gospel of God, but also our *very* own souls, because you were *so* dear to us.

9 For you remember, family,[+] our labor and toil,[+] for working[+] night and day to not be a burden[+] to any of you, we proclaimed[+] the Gospel of God to you.

10 You *are our* witnesses, and God *also*, how holy[+] and righteously[+] and blamelessly[+] we behaved ourselves among you who believe.

11 As you know how we exhorted and comforted and charged everyone of you, as a father *does* his *own* children,

12 so that you would walk worthy of God who has called you to His kingdom and glory.

13 For this reason[+] also, we thank God without ceasing. Because, *even though* you received the Word of God that you heard from us, you did not receive *it as* the word of men, but as it is in truth, the Word of God that works effectively in you who believe.

14 For you, family,[+] became followers of the assemblies[+] of God in Judea that are in Christ Jesus. For you also have suffered like things from your own countrymen, even as they *have* from the Jews.

15 *For the Jews* killed their own prophets and the Lord Jesus and *they* persecuted us. They do not please God and *they* are contrary to all people,[+]

16 forbidding us to speak to the Gentiles *so* that they might be saved, *thus* to fill up their sins always. But the wrath *of God* is coming upon them to the uttermost.

17 But we, family,[+] being taken from you for a short time in presence *though* not in heart, have endeavored *all* the more abundantly *and* with great desire, to see you *in* person.[+]

18 Therefore, we, even I Paul, would have come to you once and again, but Satan hindered us.

19 For what *is* our hope or joy or crown of rejoicing? *Is it* not *to see* you in the presence of our Lord Jesus Christ at His coming?

20 For you are our glory and joy.

1 Thessalonians Chapter 3

1 When we could no longer endure[+] *waiting*, we thought it good to be left alone at Athens,

2 and sent Timothy, our brother and servant[+] of God and our fellow laborer in the Gospel of Christ, to establish you and to comfort you concerning your faith,

3 so that no one would be moved by these afflictions. For *you* yourselves know that we are appointed to this.

4 For truly+ when we were with you, we told you before that we would suffer tribulation, even as it has come to pass and you know *it*.

5 For this reason,+ when I could no longer endure+ *waiting*, I sent to know *the condition of* your faith, lest by some means the tempter had tempted you and our labor had been in vain.

6 But now, Timothy has come to us from you and brought us good tidings of your faith and *true* love. *He tells us* that you have a good remembrance of us always *and* greatly desire to see us, as we also *desire to see* you.

7 Therefore family,+ we were comforted over you in all our affliction and distress by your faith.

8 For now we live, if you stand fast in the Lord.

9 For what thanks can we render to God again for you, for all the joy with which we rejoice+ for your sakes before our God.

10 Night and day *we* pray exceedingly that we might see you *in* person+ and might perfect what is lacking in your faith.

11 Now *may* God Himself, our Father and our Lord Jesus Christ direct our way to you.

12 *And may* the Lord make you to increase and abound in love toward one another and toward all *people*, even as we *do* toward you,

13 to the end *that* He may strengthen+ your hearts *to be* blameless+ in holiness before our God and Father at the coming *of* our Lord Jesus Christ with all His saints.

1 Thessalonians Chapter 4

1 Furthermore then, we urge and exhort you family,+ by the Lord Jesus, that as you have received *instruction* from us *as to* how you ought to walk and please God, that you should abound more *in this*.

2 For you know what instructions+ we gave you by the Lord Jesus.

3 For this is the will of God *for* your sanctification: That you should abstain from fornication.

4 Everyone of you should know how to possess their own vessels in sanctification and honor,

5 not in the lust of abnormal appetites+ like the Gentiles who do not know God,

6 *so* that no one goes beyond and defrauds another in *any* matter. Because the Lord *is* the avenger of all such, as we also have forewarned you and testified.

7 For God has not called us to uncleanness, but to holiness.

8 Therefore, *those* who despise do not despise people,+ but God who has also given His Holy Spirit to us.

9 But concerning brotherly love, you do not need me *to* write to you. For you yourselves are taught by God to love one another.

10 Indeed, you *already* do this toward all the family+ who are in all Macedonia. But we urge you, family,+ that you increase more and more.

11 *Earnestly* endeavor+ to be quiet and to do your own *things* and to work with your own hands as we have instructed+ you

12 *so* that you may walk honestly toward *those* who are outside+ *of the faith* and *so that* you may lack nothing.

13 But I do not want you to lack understanding+ family,+ concerning *those* who are asleep, *so* that you are not grieved+ as others *are* who have no hope.

14 For if we believe that Jesus died and rose again, *then* so also will God bring *those* who sleep in Jesus with Him.

15 For this we say to you by the Word of the Lord: That we who are alive *and* remain until the coming of the Lord will not precede+ *those* who are asleep.

16 For the Lord Himself will descend from heaven with a shout, with the voice of the archangel, and with the trumpet of God. *And* the dead in Christ will arise first.

17 Then we who are alive *and* remain will be caught up together with them in the clouds to meet the Lord in the air. Thus we will be forever+ with the Lord.

18 Therefore, comfort one another with these words.

1 Thessalonians Chapter 5

¹ Family,⁺ you have no need that I write to you about the times and the seasons.

² For *you* yourselves know perfectly *well* that the day of the Lord will come like a thief in the night.

³ For when they say: Peace and safety, then sudden destruction *will* come upon them like labor⁺ upon a woman with child. And they will not escape.

⁴ But you, family,⁺ are not in darkness *so* that that day should overtake you like a thief.

⁵ You are all children of light and children of the day. We are not of the night or darkness.

⁶ Therefore let us not sleep as others *do*, but let us watch and be sober.

⁷ For *those* who sleep, sleep in the night. And *those* who get drunk, *get* drunk in the night.

⁸ But let us who are of the day be sober, putting on the breastplate of faith, and love *and* for a helmet, the hope of salvation.

⁹ For God has not appointed us to wrath, but to obtain salvation through our Lord Jesus Christ.

¹⁰ *Jesus* died for us *so* that, whether we *are* awake or asleep, we should live together with Him.

¹¹ Therefore, comfort yourselves together and edify one another, *just* as you are *already* doing.

¹² We urge you family,⁺ to know *those* who labor among you and are over you in the Lord and admonish you.

¹³ Esteem them very highly in love for the sake of their work. *And* be at peace among yourselves.

¹⁴ Now we exhort you family⁺: Warn *those* who are unruly, comfort the feebleminded, support the weak, *and* be patient toward all *people*.

¹⁵ See that no one renders evil for evil to anyone,⁺ but always⁺ follow what is good, both among yourselves and toward all *people*.

¹⁶ Rejoice forever.

¹⁷ Pray without ceasing.

¹⁸ In everything, give thanks. For this is the will of God in Christ Jesus concerning you.

¹⁹ Do not quench the Spirit.

²⁰ Do not despise prophecies.

> ²¹ Prove all things.
> Hold fast what is good.

²² Abstain from all appearance of evil.

²³ The God of peace Himself will sanctify you wholly *so that* your whole spirit and soul and body *will* be preserved blameless for the coming *of* our Lord Jesus Christ.

²⁴ He who calls you *is* faithful and *He* will perform⁺ *it*.

²⁵ Family,⁺ pray for us.

²⁶ Greet all the family⁺ with a holy kiss.

²⁷ I charge you by the Lord that this epistle be read to all the holy family.⁺

²⁸ The grace of our Lord Jesus Christ *be* with you. Amen.

This first epistle to the Thessalonians was written at Athens.

2 Thessalonians Chapter 1

¹ *From* Paul, Silvanus, and Timothy. To the assembly⁺ of the Thessalonians in God our Father and the Lord Jesus Christ.

² Grace to you and peace from God our Father and Lord Jesus Christ.

³ We are bound to thank God for you always, family,⁺ as it is right⁺ *to do*. Because your faith grows exceedingly, and the *true* love of everyone of you all toward each other abounds

⁴ so that we ourselves rejoice⁺ in you in the assemblies⁺ of God for your patience and faith in all your persecutions and tribulations that you endure.

⁵ *This is* a revealed⁺ evidence⁺ of the righteous judgment of God for you to be counted worthy of the kingdom of God for which you also suffer.

⁶ If *it is* to be the righteousness of God

to repay[+] tribulation to *those* who oppress[+] you,

[7] and *to give* you who are oppressed[+] rest with us when the Lord Jesus shall be revealed from heaven with His mighty angels,

[8] *then* in flaming fire, *He* will take vengeance on *those* who do not know God and who do not obey the Gospel of our Lord Jesus Christ.

[9] *They* will be punished with everlasting destruction, *taken away* from the presence of the Lord and from the glory of His power.

[10]In that day, He will come to be glorified in His saints and to be admired by all who believe because our testimony among you was believed.

[11]Therefore, we always pray for you, also, that our God would count you worthy of *this* calling and fulfill all the good pleasure of *His* goodness and the work of faith with power

[12]*so* that the name of our Lord Jesus Christ may be glorified in you and you in Him, according to the grace of our God and Lord Jesus Christ.

2 Thessalonians Chapter 2

[1] Now we urge you, family,[+] *regarding* the coming of our Lord Jesus Christ and our gathering to Him,

[2] that you not be soon shaken in mind or troubled, not by spirit or by word or by letter as from us, *regarding the fact* that the day of Christ is *very* near.[+]

[3] Let no one deceive you by any means. For *that day will not come* until[+] there first come a falling away, and the man of sin, the son of damnation,[+] becomes revealed.

[4] *That man will* oppose *God* and exalt himself above all *that is* called God or is worshiped as God, so that he sits in the temple of God, showing himself *in a pretense* that he is God.

[5] Do you not remember that I told you *about* these things while I was still[+] with you?

[6] And now you know what *it is that* is

holding[+] *back* for *that man* to be revealed in his time.

[7] For the mystery of iniquity is already working. *It is* only *being* restrained[+] now until *the restraint is* taken out of the way.

[8] Then that wicked *one* will be revealed, whom the Lord will consume with the breath[+] of His mouth and nullify[+] with the brightness of His coming.

[9] *That wicked one* whose coming is according[+] *to* the work of Satan with all power and signs and false[+] wonders

[10]and with every unrighteous deceit in *those* who perish because they did not receive the love of the truth *so* that they might be saved.

[11]Because[+] of this, God will send *a* strong delusion upon them for[+] believing a lie

[12]*so* that all who did not believe the truth but *took* pleasure in unrighteousness might be damned.

[13]But we are bound to give thanks to God always for you, family,[+] beloved of the Lord. Because from the beginning, God has chosen you to *receive* salvation through sanctification of the Spirit and belief *of the* truth.

[14]To this, He called you *through* our *proclaiming of the* Gospel to *the* obtaining of *the* glory of our Lord Jesus Christ.

[15]Therefore family[+]: Stand fast and hold the traditions you have been taught, whether by Word or *by* our epistle.

[16]Now our Lord Jesus Christ Himself and God our Father who has loved us and given *us* everlasting consolation and good hope through grace

[17]comfort your hearts and strengthen[+] you in every good word and work.

2 Thessalonians Chapter 3

[1] Finally, family,[+] pray for us: That the Word of the Lord may have *free* course and be glorified, even as *it is* with you.

[2] *Pray* that we may be delivered from unreasonable and wicked men, for all do not have faith.

[3] But the Lord is faithful, who will strengthen[+] you and keep *you* from evil.

[4] We have confidence in the Lord

touching you, that you both do and will *continue to* do the things that we charged+ you *to do.*

> ⁵ *May* the Lord direct your hearts
> in the love of God
> and in waiting patiently for Christ.

---

⁶ Now we charge+ you family,+ in the name of our Lord Jesus Christ, that you withdraw yourselves from every *member of the* family+ who walks disorderly and not according+ to the tradition received from us.

⁷ For *you* yourselves know how you ought to follow us. For we did not behave ourselves disorderly among you.

⁸ Nor did we eat anyone's bread for nothing. But *we* worked+ with labor and toil+ night and day *so* that we might not be a burden+ to any of you,

⁹ not because we do not have authority,+ but to make ourselves an example to you to follow us.

¹⁰For even when we were with you, we instructed+ you that if any would not work, neither should *they* eat.

¹¹For we hear *that* some among you are walking disorderly *and* not working at all, but are busybodies.

¹²Now *those* who are such we instruct+ and exhort by our Lord Jesus Christ to work with quietness and eat their own bread.

¹³But family,+ do not be weary in well doing.

¹⁴If anyone does not obey our word by this epistle, note that person and have no company with them *so* that they may be ashamed.

¹⁵Yet do not count *them* as an enemy, but admonish *them* as a *member of the* family.+

¹⁶Now the Lord of peace Himself give you peace always, by all means. The Lord *be* with you all.

¹⁷The salutation Paul by my own hand is *my* signature+ on every epistle I write.

¹⁸The grace of our Lord Jesus Christ *be* with you all. Amen.

The second epistle to the Thessalonians was written at Athens.

1 Timothy Chapter 1

¹ *From* Paul, an apostle of Jesus Christ by the commandment of God our Savior and Lord Jesus Christ *who is* our hope.

² To Timothy, *my* own son in the faith: Grace, mercy, *and* peace from God our Father and Jesus Christ our Lord.

³ I urged+ you to remain+ at Ephesus *when I* went to Macedonia *so* that you might charge them to teach no other doctrine

⁴ *and to* not give heed to fables and endless genealogies that bring+ questions rather than godly edifying in faith.

⁵ Now the objective+ of this instruction+ is *true* love out of a pure heart and a good conscience and sincere+ faith.

⁶ *Yet* some have erred+ *by* turning aside to vain talking.+

⁷ *They* desire to be teachers of the law, *but they* do not understand what they are saying or what they affirm.

⁸ Now we know that the law *is* good if it is used lawfully,

⁹ Know this: That the law is not made for the righteous, but *for the* lawless and disobedient, ungodly sinners, unholy and worldly,+ murderers of fathers and mothers *and all* murderers,+

¹⁰*for* fornicators,+ *for those who* defile themselves, *for* slave traders,+ liars, perjurers, and any other *thing* that is contrary to sound teaching.+

¹¹*This is* according to the glorious Gospel of the blessed God that was committed to my trust.

¹²I thank Christ Jesus our Lord who has enabled me because He counted me faithful to put *me* into the ministry.

¹³*Because* before, *I* was a blasphemer, a persecutor, and injurious *to others.* But I received+ mercy because I did *it* ignorantly in unbelief.

¹⁴The grace of our Lord was exceedingly abundant with the faith and love that are in Christ Jesus.

¹⁵This *is* a faithful saying and worthy of all acceptance: That Christ Jesus came into the world to save sinners, of whom I am chief.

[16]However for this purpose[+] I received[+] mercy, *so* that in me first Jesus Christ might show forth all longsuffering as a pattern to *those* who would hereafter believe in Him for eternal[+] life.

[17]Now to the King eternal, immortal, invisible, the only wise God, *be* honor and glory forever and ever. Amen.

[18]This charge I commit to you, son Timothy, according to the earlier[+] prophecies about you, *so* that by them you might fight[+] a good warfare,

[19]holding faith and a good conscience. *For* some have put away *their conscience* so as to make *their* faith shipwreck.

[20]*Among them* are Hymenaeus and Alexander whom I have delivered to Satan *so* that they may learn to not blaspheme.

1 Timothy Chapter 2

[1] *I* urge[+] *you*, therefore, first *of* all: Make supplications, prayers, intercessions, *and* thanksgiving for everyone,

[2] *including* for kings and all who are in authority, *so* that we may lead a quiet and peaceable life in all godliness and honesty.

[3] For this *is* good and acceptable in the sight of God our Savior

[4] who desires[+] all people[+] to be saved and to come to the knowledge of the truth.

> [5] For *there is* one God
> and one mediator
> between God and mankind[+]:
> the man Christ Jesus

[6] who gave Himself *as* a ransom for all *with the* testimony *of this to come* in due time.

[7] To this *purpose*, I am ordained a preacher and an apostle. I speak the truth in Christ. *As* a teacher of the Gentiles in faith and truth[+] *I* do not lie.

[8] Therefore, I desire[+] that people[+] everywhere pray, lifting up holy hands, without wrath and doubting.

[9] In like manner also, *I urge* that women adorn themselves in modest apparel, with humility[+] and moderation,[+] not with *elaborately* braided hair or gold or pearls or costly array,

[10]but *with* what becomes women professing godliness: With good works.

[11]Let the woman learn in silence with all subjection.

[12]I do not allow[+] women to teach or usurp authority over men, but to be in quietness.[+]

[13]For Adam was formed first, then Eve.

[14]Adam was not deceived, but the woman, being deceived, went into transgression.

[15]Nevertheless *women* will be saved in child bearing if they continue in faith and *true* love and holiness with moderation.[+]

1 Timothy Chapter 3

[1] This *is* a true saying: If a man desires the office of bishop, he desires a good work.

[2] A bishop then must be blameless, the husband of one wife, vigilant, sober, of good behavior, given to hospitality, *able* to teach,

[3] not given to wine, no striker, *and* not greedy of filthy gain,[+] but patient, not a brawler, *and* not covetous.

[4] *He must be* one who governs[+] his own house well, having his children in subjection with all gravity.

[5] For if a man does not know how to govern[+] his own house, *then* how can he take care of the assembly[+] of God?

[6] *He must* not *be* a novice, lest being lifted up with pride he *may* fall into the condemnation of the devil.

[7] Moreover, he must have a good report from *those* who are outside[+] *of the faith*, lest he fall into reproach and the snare of the devil.

[8] Likewise, deacons *must be* honest,[+] not double tongued, not given to much wine, *and* not greedy for filthy gain.[+]

[9] *They must* hold the mystery of the faith in a pure conscience.

[10]Also, let these *candidates* be proved, first. Then let them serve[+] *after* being *found* blameless.

[11]Even so *their* wives *must also be* honest,[+]

not slanderers, sober, *and* faithful in all things.

¹²Deacons *must be* husbands of one wife, governing⁺ their children and their own houses well.

¹³For *those* who have served⁺ well in the office of a deacon acquire⁺ a good degree for themselves and much boldness in faith in Christ Jesus.

¹⁴I write these things to you hoping to come to you soon.⁺

¹⁵But if I *am* delayed⁺ *then by this* you will know how you ought to behave yourself in the house of God, which is the assembly⁺ of the living God, the pillar and base⁺ of the truth.

¹⁶*We* confess⁺ *that* the mystery of godliness is great *indeed*. God was revealed⁺ in the flesh, justified by the Spirit, seen by angels, proclaimed⁺ to the Gentiles, believed in the world, *and* received up in glory. *John 1:14*

1 Timothy Chapter 4

¹ Now the Spirit speaks expressly that in the latter times some will depart from the faith, giving heed to seducing spirits and doctrines of demons.⁺

² *Some will* speak lies in hypocrisy, having their conscience seared with a hot iron.

³ *Some will* forbid to marry *and require you to* abstain from *certain* foods⁺ that God has created to be received with thanksgiving by *those* who believe and know the truth.

⁴ Every creature *created by* God *is* good, and nothing *is* to be refused if it is received with thanksgiving,

⁵ for it is sanctified by the Word of God and prayer.

⁶ If you remind the family⁺ about these things, you will be a good servant⁺ of Jesus Christ, nourished with the words of faith and good doctrine that you have *closely* followed.⁺

⁷ But refuse the worldly⁺ and old wives' fables, and *instead* exercise yourself toward godliness.

⁸ For bodily exercise is of little benefit.⁺ But godliness is beneficial⁺ for every-

thing,⁺ having *both* the promise of life now and *eternal life* to come.

⁹ This *is* a faithful saying and worthy of all acceptance.

¹⁰And for this, we labor and suffer reproach because we trust in the living God who is the Savior of everyone,⁺ especially believers.⁺

¹¹Prescribe⁺ and teach these things.

¹²Do not let anyone despise your youth. But be an example *to* the believers, in word, in conversation *and conduct*, in *true* love, in spirit, in faith, *and* in purity.

¹³Until I come, give attention⁺ to reading, to exhortation, *and* to doctrine.

¹⁴Do not neglect the gift that is in you, which was given *to* you by prophecy with laying on of hands by the elders.⁺

¹⁵Meditate upon these things. Give yourself wholly to them *so* that your advancement⁺ *may be* evident⁺ to everyone.

¹⁶Take heed to yourself and to the doctrine. Continue in them, for in doing this both *you* yourself and *those* who hear you will be saved.

1 Timothy Chapter 5

¹ Do not rebuke an elder, but exhort⁺ *him* as a father. *Exhort* the younger men as family,⁺

² the elder women as mothers, *and* the younger *women* as sisters, with all purity.

³ Honor widows who truly⁺ are widows.

⁴ But if any widow has children or nephews, let them learn to show piety at home first, and to reciprocate⁺ *care for* their parents. For that is good and acceptable before God.

⁵ Now *one who is* truly⁺ a widow and desolate trusts in God and continues in supplications and prayers night and day.

⁶ But *one who* lives in pleasure is dead while she lives.

⁷ *Give* instruction⁺ in these *matters so* that *all* may be blameless.

⁸ But if any do not provide for their own, and especially for those of their own house, *then* they have denied the faith and are worse than an infidel.

⁹ Do not let a widow be taken into the number *for assistance who is* less *than* sixty years *old*, having been the wife of one man, ¹⁰and *who is* well reported for *her* good works: *For example:* If she has brought up children, if she has lodged strangers, if she has washed the feet of the saints, if she has relieved the afflicted, *and* if she has diligently followed every good work.
¹¹But refuse the younger widows. For when they have begun to grow⁺ wanton against Christ, they will *want to* marry.
¹²*In this, they will receive* judgment,⁺ because they have cast off their first faith.
¹³And with all this, they learn *to be* idle, wandering about from house to house. Not only idle, but tattlers also and busybodies, speaking things that they should not. *Proverbs 11:13*
¹⁴Therefore, I will that the younger women marry, bear children, guide the house, *and* give no occasion to the adversary to speak reproachfully.
¹⁵For some are already turned aside after Satan.
¹⁶If any man or woman who is a believer has widows *in their family*, let them relieve them and not let the assembly⁺ be burdened⁺ *so* that it may relieve *those* who are truly⁺ widows.
¹⁷Let the elders who govern⁺ well be counted worthy of double honor, especially *those* who labor in the Word and doctrine.
¹⁸For the Scriptures declare: You shall not muzzle the ox that treads out the corn. And: The laborer *is* worthy of his reward. *Deuteronomy 25:4*
¹⁹Do not receive an accusation against an elder unless⁺ *it is* from two or three witnesses.
²⁰Rebuke *those* who sin, before everyone,⁺ *so* that others may also *have* fear.
²¹I charge *you* before *our* God and Lord Jesus Christ and the elect angels, that you observe these things without preferring one before another, doing nothing by partiality.
²²Do not lay hands too quickly⁺ on anyone, nor be a partaker in the sins of others. Keep yourself pure.

²³Do not drink *polluted* water, but use a little wine for your stomach and your frequent⁺ infirmities.
²⁴The sins of some men are *clearly* revealed⁺ before *they go* to judgment, and some follow after.
²⁵Likewise also, the good works *of some* are *clearly* evident,⁺ but *those* that are otherwise cannot be hid.

1 Timothy Chapter 6

¹ As many servants as are under *the* yoke *should* count their own masters worthy of all honor *so* that the name of God and *His* doctrine *is* not blasphemed.
² *Those* who have believing masters *must* not despise *them* because they are family.⁺ But rather, do *them* service because they are faithful and beloved partakers of the benefit. Teach and exhort these things.
³ If anyone teaches otherwise and does not consent to wholesome words, *even* the words of our Lord Jesus Christ and to the doctrine according to godliness,
⁴ *then* they are proud *and* know nothing. Rather, *they have* sick⁺ *minds full* of questions and strifes of words from which comes envy, strife, reviling,⁺ evil accusations,⁺
⁵ *and* perverse disputings by people of corrupt minds and destitute of the truth *who* suppose that gain is godliness. Withdraw yourself from such.
⁶ But godliness with contentment is great gain.
⁷ For we brought nothing into *this* world *and it is* certain we can carry nothing out.
⁸ Having food and clothing,⁺ let us be content with that.
⁹ *Those* who desire⁺ to be rich fall into temptation and a snare and *into* many foolish and hurtful lusts that drown *people* in destruction and damnation.⁺

¹⁰ The love of money
is the root of all evil.
While some *have* coveted after *it*,
they have erred from the faith
and pierced themselves through
with many sorrows.

[11] But you, O people[+] of God, flee *from* these things. Follow after righteousness, godliness, faith, love, patience, *and* meekness.

[12] Fight the good fight of faith. Lay hold on eternal life to which you are also called and have professed a good profession before many witnesses.

[13] I charge you in the sight of God who quickens all things, and *before* Christ Jesus who witnessed a good confession before Pontius Pilate,

[14] that you keep the commandment without spot *and* unrebukable until the appearing of our Lord Jesus Christ.

[15] He will show, in *due* time, *who is* the blessed and only Potentate, the King of kings, and Lord of lords.

[16] *He* alone has immortality, dwelling in light unapproachable,[+] whom no one has seen nor can see. To *Him* be honor and power everlasting. Amen.

[17] Charge *those* who are rich in this world, that they not be high minded nor trust in uncertain riches, but *only* in the living God who gives us richly all things to enjoy.

[18] *Do this so* that they *may* do good, *so* that they be rich in good works, ready to distribute, willing to share,[+]

[19] laying up in store for themselves a good foundation against the time to come *so* that they may lay hold on eternal life.

[20] O Timothy, keep what is committed to your trust. Avoid worldly[+] *and* vain babblings and *the* oppositions of science, falsely so called.

[21] *By* professing *these things*, some have erred concerning the faith. Grace *be* with you. Amen.

The first epistle to Timothy was written at Laodicea, which is the chief city of Phrygia Pacatiana.

2 Timothy Chapter 1

[1] *From* Paul, an apostle of Jesus Christ by the will of God, according to the promise of life that is in Christ Jesus.

[2] To Timothy, *my* beloved son: Grace, mercy, *and* peace from God *the* Father and Christ Jesus our Lord.

[3] I *am* thankful to God, whom I serve from *my* forefathers' *example* with *a* pure conscience, as I remember you in my prayers night and day without ceasing.

[4] I greatly desire to see you *so* that I may be filled with joy. I remember[+] your tears

[5] *and* I remember the sincere[+] faith that is in you that lived[+] first in your grandmother Lois and *in* your mother Eunice. And I am persuaded that *it is* in you also.

[6] Therefore I remind[+] you to stir up the gift of God that is in you by the laying[+] on of my hands.

[7] For God has not given us the spirit of fear, but of power and love and a sound mind.

[8] Therefore, do not be ashamed of the testimony of our Lord nor of me His prisoner. But endure[+] the hardships[+] *that come* with the Gospel according to the power of God.

[9] *He* saves[+] us and calls[+] *us* with a holy calling, not according to our works, but according to His own purpose and grace that was given *to* us in Christ Jesus before the world began.

[10] But now, *it* is revealed[+] by the appearing of our Savior Jesus Christ who has abolished death and has brought life and immortality to light through the Gospel.

[11] To this *purpose* I am appointed a preacher and an apostle and a teacher of the Gentiles.

[12] *It is* for this reason[+] *that* I also suffer these things. Nevertheless, I am not ashamed. For I know whom I have believed and *I* am persuaded that He is able to keep what I have committed to Him against that day.

[13] Hold fast the example[+] of sound words that you have heard from me, in the faith and love that are in Christ Jesus.

[14] Keep *safe* that good deposit[+] that was entrusted[+] to you by the Holy Spirit who dwells in us.

[15] You know this, that all who are in Asia turned away from me, *among* whom are Phygellus and Hermogenes.

¹⁶*May* the Lord give mercy to the house of Onesiphorus, for he often refreshed me and was not ashamed of my chains. ¹⁷When he was in Rome, he diligently sought and found me. ¹⁸*May* the Lord grant *to* him to find mercy from the Lord in that day, *for* you know how well he served⁺ me at Ephesus.

2 Timothy Chapter 2

¹ Therefore my son, be strong in the grace that is in Christ Jesus.
² Entrust⁺ the things that you heard from me among many witnesses to faithful men who will be able to teach others also.
³ Therefore, you *must* endure hardship⁺ as a good soldier of Jesus Christ.
⁴ No warrior⁺ *becomes* entangled with the affairs of *this* life, *so* that *the one who* chose the soldier might be pleased.
⁵ If anyone competes⁺ *in something*, *they* cannot be crowned *as a winner* unless⁺ they competed⁺ lawfully.
⁶ *Moreover*, the grower⁺ who labors must be *the* first partaker of the fruits.
⁷ Consider what I say. *May* the Lord give you understanding in everything.⁺
⁸ Remember that Jesus Christ, *who was* from the seed of David, was raised from the dead, according to my *understanding of the* Gospel.
⁹ In *proclaiming* this, I suffer hardship⁺ like an evil doer, *even* to chains.⁺ But the Word of God is not bound.
¹⁰Therefore I endure all things for the sake of the elect *so* that they may also obtain the salvation that is in Christ Jesus, with eternal glory.
¹¹*This is* a faithful saying. For if we have died with *Him*, *then* we will also live with *Him*. *Romans 6:5*
¹²If we suffer, we will also reign with *Him*. *But* if we deny *Him*, *then* He will also deny us. *Matthew 10:33*
¹³If we do not believe, *Jesus* remains⁺ faithful, *nevertheless*. He cannot deny Himself.
¹⁴Remind *everyone* about these things,

charging *them* before the Lord that they not argue⁺ over words to no benefit⁺ *or* to the subverting of the hearers.

> ¹⁵ Study to show yourself approved to God, a worker⁺ who does not need to be ashamed, rightly dividing the Word of truth.

¹⁶Shun worldly⁺ *and* vain babblings. For they will increase to more ungodliness.
¹⁷Their word will spread⁺ like cancer.⁺ *Consider* Hymenaeus and Philetus
¹⁸who, concerning the truth, have erred *by* saying that the resurrection is already past. *This* overthrows the faith of some.
¹⁹Nevertheless, the foundation of God stands sure, having this seal: The Lord knows *those* who are His. And: Let everyone who names the name of Christ depart from iniquity.
²⁰But in a great house there are not only vessels of gold and of silver, but also of wood and of earth. Some to honor, and some to dishonor.
²¹Therefore, if anyone purges themselves from these *wicked things*, *they* will be a vessel to honor, sanctified and fitting⁺ for the master's use *and* prepared for every good work.

> ²² Flee youthful lusts. But follow righteousness, faith, *true* love, *and* peace with *all* who call on the Lord out of a pure heart.
>
> ²³ Avoid foolish and uninstructive⁺ questions, knowing that they provoke⁺ strife.

²⁴The servant of the Lord must not strive, but *must* be gentle toward everyone,⁺ *able* to teach, patient,
²⁵in meekness instructing *those* who oppose *so that* perhaps⁺ God will give them repentance to the acknowledging of the truth.
²⁶*Thus* they might awaken⁺ out of the snare of the devil, *after* being taken captive by him to *do* his will.

2 Timothy Chapter 3

¹ Know this also: That in the last days, perilous times will come.
² For people⁺ will be lovers of themselves, covetous, boasters, proud, blasphemers, disobedient to parents, unthankful, unholy,
³ without affection, unforgiving,⁺ false accusers, unrestrained,⁺ fierce, hateful,⁺
⁴ disloyal,⁺ headstrong,⁺ arrogant,⁺ *and* lovers of pleasure rather⁺ than lovers of God.
⁵ *They* have a form of piety,⁺ but deny the power of it. Turn away from these.
⁶ For *among* them are *some* who enter⁺ into houses and lead *into* captivity naive⁺ women burdened⁺ with sins, led away with many different⁺ lusts.
⁷ *They are* ever learning, but never able to come to knowledge of truth.
⁸ *Just* as Jannes and Jambres opposed⁺ Moses, so do these also resist the truth. *They are* people⁺ of corrupt minds, reprobate concerning the faith.
⁹ But they will progress⁺ no further, for their folly will be revealed⁺ to everyone,⁺ as it was *with Jannes and Jambres*.
¹⁰You, however, have fully known my doctrine, manner of life, purpose, faith, longsuffering, *true* love, patience,
¹¹persecutions, *and* afflictions that came to me at Antioch, at Iconium, *and* at Lystra. What persecutions I endured. But out of *them* all the Lord delivered me.
¹²Yes, and all who live godly *lives* in Christ Jesus will suffer persecution.
¹³But evil men and imposters⁺ will grow⁺ worse and worse, deceiving and being deceived.
¹⁴But you *must* continue in the things that you have learned and have been assured of, knowing from whom you have learned *them*.
¹⁵From childhood you have known the holy Scriptures that are able to make you wise unto salvation through faith in Christ Jesus.

> ¹⁶ All Scripture
> *is* given by inspiration of God
> and *is* beneficial⁺ for doctrine,
> for proof,⁺ for correction, *and*
> for instruction in righteousness,

¹⁷*so* that God's people may become perfect, thoroughly equipped to all good works.

2 Timothy Chapter 4

¹ I charge *you*, therefore, before God and the Lord Jesus Christ who will judge the living⁺ and the dead at His appearing and His kingdom:

> ² Proclaim⁺ the Word.
> Be attentive⁺ *to duty*
> in season *and* out of season.

Prove,⁺ rebuke, *and* exhort with all longsuffering and doctrine.
³ For the time will come when they will not endure sound doctrine, but according to their own lusts, they look⁺ for teachers to satisfy⁺ their hearing.
⁴ They turn away *their* ears from the truth and are turned to fables.
⁵ But you *must* watch in all things, endure afflictions, do the work of an evangelist, *and* make full proof of your ministry.
⁶ For I am now ready to be offered and the time of my departure is *very* near.⁺
⁷ I have fought a good fight. I have finished *my* course. *And* I have kept the faith.
⁸ Hereafter, there is a crown of righteousness laid up for me, which the Lord, the righteous judge, will give *to* me on that day. And not only to me, but also to all who love His appearing.
⁹ Be diligent to come to me soon.⁺
¹⁰For Demas has forsaken me, having loved this present world. *He* has departed to Thessalonica, Crescens to Galatia, *and* Titus to Dalmatia.
¹¹Only Luke is with me. *Therefore* bring Mark with you, for he is useful⁺ to me for *this* ministry.

¹²I have sent Tychicus to Ephesus.

¹³When you come, bring the cloak that I left at Troas with Carpus, and the books, especially the parchments.

¹⁴Alexander the coppersmith did much evil *to* me. The Lord *will* reward him according to his works.

¹⁵You beware⁺ of him also, for he has greatly opposed⁺ our words.

¹⁶In my first defense,⁺ no one stood with me, but everyone⁺ left⁺ me. *I pray that this* will not be charged to them.

¹⁷Nevertheless, the Lord stood with me and strengthened me *so* that, by me, the proclaiming⁺ might be fully known and all the Gentiles might hear. I was delivered out of the mouth of the lion.

¹⁸The Lord will deliver me from every evil work and will preserve *me* to His heavenly kingdom. *To Him be the* glory forever and ever. Amen.

¹⁹Greet⁺ Priscilla and Aquila and the household of Onesiphorus.

²⁰Erastus stayed⁺ at Corinth, but I have left Trophimus at Miletum sick.

²¹Be diligent to come before winter. Eubulus greets you, and Pudens and Linus and Claudia and all the family.⁺

²²The Lord Jesus Christ *be* with your spirit. Grace *be* with you. Amen.

The second epistle to Timothy, who was ordained the first bishop of the church of the Ephesians, was written at Rome when Paul was brought before Nero the second time.

Titus Chapter 1

¹ *From* Paul, a servant of God and an apostle of Jesus Christ according to the faith of God's elect and knowledge of the truth in godliness,

² in *the* hope of eternal life, which God, who cannot lie, promised before the world began.

³ *He* has in due times manifested His Word through proclaiming⁺ *it. And it* is committed to me according to the commandment of God our Savior.

⁴ To Titus, *my* own son after the common faith: Grace, mercy, *and* peace from God *our* Father and Lord Jesus Christ our Savior.

⁵ For this reason,⁺ I left you in Crete *so* that you should set in order the things that are wanting and ordain elders in every city as I had appointed you *to do*,

⁶ if any are blameless, the husband of one wife, *and* have faithful children *who are* not accused of excesses⁺ or unruly *rebellion*.

⁷ For bishops must be blameless as the stewards of God. Not selfwilled. Not soon angry. Not given to wine. No striker. Not given to filthy gain.⁺

⁸ But a lover of hospitality. A lover of good people.⁺ Sober, just, holy, *and* temperate.

⁹ *They must* hold fast the faithful Word as they have been taught *so* that they may be able, by sound doctrine, both to exhort and to convince *those* who doubt.⁺

¹⁰For there are many unruly and vain talkers and deceivers, especially *among* those of the circumcision.

¹¹*Their* mouths must be stopped. Some⁺ subvert whole houses, teaching things that they should not, for *the* sake *of* filthy lucre.

¹²One of them, *one* of their own prophets said: The Cretians *are* always liars, evil beasts, *and* slow bellies.

¹³This witness is true. Therefore rebuke them sharply *so* that they may become sound in the faith,

¹⁴not giving heed to Jewish fables and commandments of men who turn from the truth.

¹⁵Unto the pure, everything⁺ *is* pure. But to *those* who are defiled and unbelieving nothing *is* pure. Even their minds and conscience are defiled.

¹⁶They profess that they know God. But in works, they deny *Him*, being abominable and disobedient and reprobate to every good work.

Titus Chapter 2

¹ Speak the things that become sound doctrine,

² *so* that older⁺ men become sober,

honest,[+] temperate, sound in faith, in *true* love, *and* in patience.

[3] Likewise *speak to* the older[+] women *so* that *they become* in behavior as becomes holiness. Not false accusers. Not given to much wine. Teachers of good things,

[4] *so* that they may teach the young women to be sober, to love their husbands, to love their children,

[5] *to be* discreet, chaste, keepers at home, good, *and* obedient to their own husbands *so* that the Word of God is not blasphemed.

[6] Likewise, exhort *the* young men to be sober minded.

[7] In all things, show *in* yourself a pattern of good works in doctrine, uncorruptness, gravity, sincerity,

[8] and sound speech. None *of this* can be condemned. *Therefore, those* who are contrary may be ashamed and have no evil thing to say about you.

[9] *Exhort* servants to be obedient to their own masters *and* to please *them* well in all *things,* not contradicting[+] *them,*

[10] not stealing[+] *from them,* but showing all good fidelity *so* that they may adorn the doctrine of God our Savior in everything.

[11] For the grace of God who brings salvation has appeared to everyone,[+]

[12] teaching us to deny ungodliness and worldly lusts *and* live soberly, righteously, and godly in this present world,

[13] looking for that blessed hope and the glorious appearing of the great God and our Savior Jesus Christ

[14] who gave Himself for us *so* that He might redeem us from all iniquity and purify *for* Himself a unique[+] people, zealous *for* good works.

[15] Speak and exhort these things and rebuke with all authority. Let no one despise you.

Titus Chapter 3

[1] Remind[+] *people* to be subject to rulers[+] and authorities,[+] to obey highest officials,[+] to be ready to every good work,

[2] speaking evil of no one *and* not to be brawlers, *but to be* gentle, showing meekness to everyone.[+]

[3] For we ourselves also were sometimes foolish, disobedient, deceived, serving many different[+] lusts and pleasures, living in malice and envy, hateful, *and* hating one another.

[4] But after the kindness and love of our Savior God toward mankind[+] appeared,

[5] *we saw that it was* not by works of righteousness that we practice[+] but according to His mercy *that* He saves[+] us, by the washing of regeneration and renewing of the Holy Spirit

[6] that He shed on us abundantly through Jesus Christ our Savior,

[7] *so* that being justified by His grace, we should be made heirs according to the hope of eternal life.

[8] *This is* a faithful saying and these things I urge[+] that you affirm constantly *so* that *those* who have believed in God might be careful to maintain good works. These things are good and beneficial[+] to people.[+]

[9] But avoid foolish questions and genealogies and contentions and fighting[+] about the law. For they are vain and not beneficial.[+] *Proverbs 17:14*

[10] Reject anyone who is *still* a heretic, after the first and second admonition. *Matthew 18:17*

[11] Know that anyone like that is subverted and sins *and is* condemned by themselves.

[12] When I send Artemas or Tychicus to you, be diligent to come to me at Nicopolis, for I have decided[+] to winter there.

[13] Send[+] Zenas the lawyer and Apollos diligently on their journey *so* that nothing *will* be lacking[+] to them.

[14] Let our *people* also learn to maintain good works for necessary uses *so* that they *will* not be unfruitful.

[15] All who are with me greet[+] you. Greet *those* who delight[+] *in* us in the faith. Grace *be* with you all. Amen.

This epistle was written at Nicopolis in Macedonia to Titus who was ordained the first bishop of the church of the Cretians.

Philemon Chapter 1

[1] *From* Paul, a prisoner of Jesus Christ, and Timothy *our* brother. To Philemon our beloved and fellow laborer.

[2] And to *our* beloved Apphia and Archippus our fellow soldier and to the assembly+ in your house.

[3] Grace to you and peace from God our Father and Lord Jesus Christ.

[4] I thank my God, making mention of you always in my prayers,

[5] hearing of your love and faith that you have toward the Lord Jesus and toward all *the* saints.

> [6] May the communication of your faith become effective by acknowledging every good thing that is in you in Christ Jesus.

[7] For we have great joy and consolation in your love, because the hearts+ of the saints are refreshed by you, brother.

[8] Therefore, *even* though I could be very+ bold in Christ to command+ you *to do* what is proper,+

[9] *now*, because+ of love, I appeal+ *to you* as Paul the aged and now also a prisoner of Jesus Christ.

[10] I appeal+ *to* you for my son Onesimus whom I fathered+ *while* in my chains.+

[11] In times past, *he* was not beneficial+ to you. But now *he is* beneficial+ to you and to me.

[12] *Therefore* I am sending *him* back *to you*. Receive him as my own heart.+

[13] I would have retained him with me *so* that in your place+ he might have ministered to me in the bonds of the Gospel.

[14] But without your agreement+ I would not do anything, *so* that your good+ *works* would not be from obligation,+ but willingly.

[15] For perhaps this was the reason+ he departed for a season, *so* that you might receive him forever.

[16] Now, not as a servant, but above a servant *as* a beloved brother, especially to me but how much more to you, both in the flesh and in the Lord?

[17] Therefore if you count me a partner, *then* receive him as *you would receive* me.

[18] If he has wronged you or owes *you* anything,+ put that on my account.

[19] I Paul have written *this* with my own hand: I will repay. *In* that, I do not say to you how *much* you owe to me, even your own self besides.

[20] Yes brother, let me have joy of you in the Lord. Refresh my heart+ in the Lord.

[21] Having confidence in your obedience, I wrote to you knowing that you will also do more than I say.

[22] But with the same prepare a lodging *for* me also. For I trust that through your prayers I will be given to you.

[23] Greet+ Epaphras, my fellow prisoner in Christ Jesus.

[24] *Also* Mark, Aristarchus, Demas, *and* Lucas, my fellow laborers.

[25] The grace of our Lord Jesus Christ *be* with your spirit. Amen.

This epistle was transcribed at Rome by Onesimus a servant.

Hebrews Chapter 1

[1] At various+ times and in many different+ ways+ in the past, God spoke to the fathers through+ the prophets.

[2] *Now,* in these last days *He has* spoken to us through+ *His* Son whom He has appointed heir of all things *and* by whom also He made the worlds.

[3] *The Son*, being the brightness of *God's* glory and the express image of His person and upholding all things by the Word of His power, when He had by Himself purged our sins, sat down at the right hand of the Majesty on high.

[4] He, being made so much better than the angels, has by inheritance obtained a more excellent name than they.

[5] For to which of the angels did *God* say at any time: You are my Son. This day I have begotten you? And again: I will be to Him a Father and He shall be to me a Son? *Psalm 2:7, 2 Samuel 7:14*

⁶ Moreover,⁺ when He brought in *His* firstborn⁺ into the world, He said: Let all the angels of God worship Him.

⁷ And as to the angels He says: Who makes His angels spirits and His ministers a flame of fire? *Psalm 104:4*

⁸ But to the Son *He says*: Your throne, O God, *is* forever and ever. A scepter of righteousness *is* the scepter of your kingdom. *Psalm 45:6*

⁹ You have loved righteousness and hated iniquity. Therefore God, your God, has anointed you with the oil of gladness above your fellows. *Psalm 45:7*

¹⁰ And you Lord, in the beginning, have laid the foundation of the earth. The heavens are the works of your hands. *Psalm 102:25*

¹¹ They will perish, but you *will* remain. They will all grow⁺ old as a garment does. *Psalm 102:26*

¹² Like a robe,⁺ you will fold them up and they will be changed. But you are the same and your years will not fail. *Psalm 102:27*

¹³ But to which of the angels did He at any time say: Sit at my right hand until I make your enemies your footstool? *Psalm 110:1*

¹⁴ Are they not all ministering spirits, sent forth to minister for *those* who will be heirs of salvation?

Hebrews Chapter 2

¹ Therefore we ought to give more earnest heed to the things that we have heard, lest at any time we should let *them* slip *away.*

² For if the word spoken by angels was steadfast and every transgression and disobedience received a just repayment⁺ of reward,

³ *then* how shall we escape, *if we* neglect so great *a* salvation, which at first began to be spoken by the Lord and was confirmed to us by *those* who heard *Him.*

⁴ God also testified⁺ *about this*, both with signs and wonders and with many different⁺ miracles and gifts of the Holy Spirit according to His will.

⁵ For He has not put the world to come, about which we speak, in subjection to the angels.

⁶ But in a certain place, one testified saying: What is mankind⁺ that you are mindful of them? Or the children of mankind⁺ that you visit them? *Psalm 8:4*

⁷ You made mankind⁺ a little lower than the angels. You crowned them with glory and honor and set them over the works of your hands. *Psalm 8:5*

⁸ You have put all things in subjection under their feet. For in that He put everything in subjection under them, He left nothing *that is* not put under them. But now we do not yet see everything *that is* put under them. *Psalm 8:6*

⁹ But we *do* see Jesus, who was made a little lower than the angels for the suffering of death *and* crowned with glory and honor *so* that He, by the grace of God, would taste death for everyone.⁺

¹⁰ For it was fitting⁺ *for* Him, for whom everything *was made* and by whom everything *was made* in bringing many children⁺ to glory to make the Captain of their Salvation perfect through sufferings.

¹¹ For both He who sanctifies and *those* who are sanctified *are* all of one, for which reason⁺ He is not ashamed to call them family,⁺

¹² saying: I will declare your name to my family.⁺ In the midst of the assembly⁺ I will sing praise to you. *Psalm 22:22*

¹³ And again: I will put my trust in Him. And again: Behold, I Am,⁺ and *behold* the children that God has given *to* me. *2 Samuel 22:3, Isaiah 8:18*

¹⁴ Since⁺ the children are partakers of flesh and blood, He also Himself likewise took part of the same *so* that through death He might destroy him who had the power of death, that is the devil,

¹⁵ and deliver *those* who, through fear of death, were all their lifetime subject to bondage.

¹⁶ For truly⁺ He did not take upon *Himself the nature of* angels, but He took upon *Himself* the seed of Abraham.

[17]Therefore, in all things it was essential[+] for Him to be made like mankind[+] *so* that He might be a merciful and faithful high priest in things *pertaining* to God, to make reconciliation for the sins of the people.

[18]For in that He Himself has suffered, being tempted, He is able to help[+] *those* who are tempted.

Hebrews Chapter 3

[1] Therefore holy believers,[+] partakers of the heavenly calling, consider the Apostle and High Priest of our profession: Christ Jesus.

[2] He was faithful to *God* who appointed Him, as also Moses *was faithful* in all *God's* house.

[3] For this *Jesus* was counted worthy of more glory than Moses, inasmuch as He who has built the house has more honor than the house.

[4] For every house is built by someone, but He who built all things *is* God.

[5] Moses truly[+] *was* faithful in all *God's* house as a servant, for a testimony of those things that were to be spoken *later*.

[6] But Christ *is faithful* as a Son over His own house, whose house we are if we hold fast the confidence and the rejoicing of the hope, firm to the end.

[7] Therefore, as the Holy Spirit says: Today, if you will, hear His voice. *Psalm 95:7*

[8] Do not harden your hearts as in the rebellion[+] in the day of trials[+] in the wilderness *Psalm 95:8*

[9] when your fathers tested[+] me, proved me, and saw my works *for* forty years. *Psalm 95:9*

[10]Therefore, I was grieved with that generation and said: They always err in *their* heart *because* they have not known my ways. *Psalm 95:10*

[11]So I swore in my wrath: They shall not enter into my rest. *Psalm 95:11*

[12]Take heed, family,[+] lest there be in any of you an evil heart of unbelief in departing from the living God.

[13]But exhort one another daily while it is called today, lest any of you be hardened through the deceitfulness of sin.

[14]For we are made partakers of Christ if we hold the beginning of our confidence steadfast to the end.

[15]In *this* it is said: Today, if you will, hear His voice. Do not harden your hearts as in the rebellion.[+] *Psalm 95:7,8*

[16]For some, when they had heard, did provoke, however not all who came out of Egypt by Moses.

[17]But with whom was *God* grieved *for* forty years? *Was it* not with *those* who had sinned, whose carcasses fell in the wilderness?

[18]And to whom did He swear *that* they would not enter into His rest, but to *those* who did not believe?

[19]So we see that they could not enter in because of unbelief.

Hebrews Chapter 4

[1] Therefore, let us fear lest being left a promise of entering into His rest, any of you might[+] come short of it.

[2] For the Gospel was proclaimed[+] to us as well as to them, but the Word proclaimed[+] did not benefit[+] them, not being mixed with faith in *those* who heard *it*.

[3] For *only* we who have believed do enter into rest. As He said: As I have sworn in my wrath: They shall not[+] enter into my rest. *Even* though the works were finished from the foundation of the world. *Psalm 95:11*

[4] For He spoke in a certain place of the seventh *day* in this way: And God rested *on* the seventh day from all His works. *Genesis 2:2*

[5] And in this again: They shall not[+] enter into my rest. *Psalm 95:11*

[6] Therefore it remains *for* some to enter into it. Those to whom it was first proclaimed[+] did not enter in because of unbelief.

[7] Again, He specifies[+] a certain day, saying in David: Today. After so long a time, it is *still* said: Today, if you will, hear His voice. Do not harden your hearts. *Psalm 95:7,8*

⁸ For if Joshua⁺ had given them rest, *it* would not have been spoken about another after those days.
⁹ Therefore, there remains a rest to the people of God.
¹⁰ For *those* who have entered rest have also stopped⁺ from their own works, as God *did* from His.
¹¹ Therefore, let us labor to enter that rest, lest anyone fall after the same example of unbelief.

> ¹² The Word of God *is* quick and powerful and sharper than any two edged sword, piercing even to the dividing apart⁺ of soul and spirit and of the joints and marrow. *It is* a discerner of the thoughts and intents of the heart.

¹³ Nor is there any creature that is not revealed⁺ in His sight. But everything⁺ *is* naked and opened to the eyes of Him with whom we have to do. *Matthew 10:26*
¹⁴ Since⁺ we have a Great High Priest who is passed into the heavens, Jesus the Son of God, let us hold fast *our* profession.
¹⁵ For we do not have a high priest who cannot be touched with the feeling of our weaknesses,⁺ but *He* was in all points tempted as *we are, yet* without sin.
¹⁶ Let us therefore come boldly to the throne of grace *so* that we may receive⁺ mercy and find grace to help in time of need.

Hebrews Chapter 5

¹ For every high priest taken from among men is ordained by men in things *pertaining* to God *so* that he may offer both gifts and sacrifices for sins.
² *He* has compassion on the uninformed⁺ and on *those* who are erring, ⁺ because he himself is also surrounded⁺ with infirmity.
³ For this⁺ reason, he should⁺ *make an* offering⁺ for sins for the people as for himself.
⁴ No one takes this honor unto himself, but *only* one who is called by God as Aaron *was*.
⁵ So also Christ did not glorify Himself to be made a high priest, but *God* said to Him: You are my Son. Today I have fathered⁺ you. *Psalm 2:7*
⁶ As He said also in another *place*: You *are* a priest forever after the order of Melchisedec. *Psalm 110:4*
⁷ In the days of His flesh, when *Christ* had offered up prayers and supplications with strong crying and tears to *God the Father* who was able to save Him from death, *He* was heard because⁺ He revered⁺ God.
⁸ *Even* though He was *the* Son, He learned obedience through⁺ the things that He suffered.
⁹ And being made perfect, He became the Author of Eternal Salvation to all who obey Him.
¹⁰ *Christ was* called by God *to be* High Priest after the order of Melchisedec. *Psalm 110:4*
¹¹ About *Him* we have many things to say *that are* hard to explain⁺ because⁺ you are dull of hearing.
¹² By this time you ought to be teachers *yet* you have need of one *to* teach you *again* the first principles of the oracles of God, and *you* have become *in* need of having milk and not solid⁺ food. ⁺
¹³ For all who take milk *are* unskillful in the Word of righteousness, for *they* are babes.
¹⁴ But solid⁺ food⁺ belongs to *those* who are of full age, *those* who by reason of use have their senses exercised to discern both good and evil.

Hebrews Chapter 6

¹ Therefore, leaving the first⁺ *principles* of the doctrine of Christ, let us go on to perfection, not laying again the foundation of repentance from dead works and of faith toward God,
² of the doctrine of baptisms and of laying on of hands and of resurrection of the dead and of eternal judgment.
³ This we will do, if God permits.

⁴ For *it is* impossible for *those* who were once enlightened and have tasted of the heavenly gift and were made partakers of the Holy Spirit

⁵ and have tasted the good Word of God and the powers of the world to come,

⁶ if they shall fall away, to renew them again to repentance, since they themselves crucify the Son of God *all over again* and put *Him* to an open shame.

⁷ For the earth that drinks in the rain that often comes upon it and brings forth herbs fit⁺ for those by whom it is dressed, receives blessing from God.

⁸ But *the land* that bears thorns and briers *is* rejected and *is* near to *being* cursed, *and* the end of that *is* to be burned.

⁹ But, beloved, we are persuaded *of* better things about you, things that accompany salvation. And *it is about* that, we speak.

¹⁰For God *is* not unrighteous to forget your work and labor of love that you have shown toward His name in that you have ministered to the saints and *still* do minister to *them*.

¹¹We desire that everyone of you show the same diligence to the full assurance of hope to the end.

---

¹² Do not be lazy,⁺
but *be* followers of *those* who,
through faith and patience,
inherit the promises.

---

¹³For when God made *His* promise to Abraham, because He could swear by no greater, He swore by Himself.

¹⁴*He* said: Surely blessing I will bless you and multiplying I will multiply you.
Genesis 22:17

¹⁵Therefore, after *Abraham* had patiently endured, he obtained the promise.

¹⁶For indeed,⁺ men swear with a great oath to confirm an end to all their strife.

¹⁷In this, God *was* willing, more abundantly, to show to the heirs of promise the unchangeableness⁺ of His counsel *and He* confirmed *it* by an oath.

¹⁸*Now*, by two unchangeable⁺ things in

which *it was* impossible for God to lie, we have a strong consolation, *those of us* who have fled for refuge to lay hold upon the hope set before us.

¹⁹*In this hope* we have an anchor for the soul *that is* both sure and steadfast and enters into that *area* within the veil.

²⁰There, the forerunner has entered for us: Jesus, made a high priest forever after the order of Melchisedec.

Hebrews Chapter 7

¹ For this Melchisedec, king of Salem *and* priest of the most high God, met Abraham returning from the slaughter of the kings and blessed him.

² Abraham gave a tenth *part* of all *the spoils* to *Melchisedec. For Melchisedec* was known⁺ first as the King of righteousness and after that also as King of Salem, which is King of peace.

³ *Melchisedec was* without father, without mother, *and* without *family* history,⁺ having no *known* beginning of days nor end of life, but *he was made as one* resembling⁺ the Son of God, abiding as a priest without end.⁺

⁴ Now consider how great this man *was*, to whom even the patriarch Abraham gave a tenth of the spoils.

⁵ Truly⁺ *those* who are of the sons of Levi, who receive the office of the priesthood, have a commandment to take tithes from the people according to the law, that is from their family,⁺ though they have come out of the loins of Abraham.

⁶ But *Melchisedec*, whose genealogy⁺ is not counted from them, received tithes from Abraham and blessed him who had the promises.

⁷ *Now* without any⁺ contradiction, the lesser was blessed by the greater.⁺

⁸ Here, men who die *as mere mortals* receive tithes. But there, *one received tithes* of whom it is witnessed that he lives.

⁹ And, if I may say so, Levi who receives tithes, also paid tithes in Abraham.

[10] For *Levi* was still in the loins of his father *Abraham* when Melchisedec met him.

[11] Therefore if perfection were *attained* through the Levitical priesthood under which the people received the law, *then* what further need *was there* that another priest should rise *up* after the order of Melchisedec and not be called after the order of Aaron?

[12] For the priesthood being changed, makes[+] *it* necessary also *for* a change *in* the law.

[13] For He about whom these things are spoken belongs[+] to another tribe from which no man has given attention[+] at the altar.

[14] For *it is* evident that our Lord arose[+] out of Judah, *and* Moses spoke nothing about that tribe concerning priesthood.

[15] It is yet far more evident, because after the likeness[+] of Melchisedec there arises another priest

[16] who is made, not after the law of a worldly[+] commandment, but after the power of an endless life.

[17] For He testifies: You *are* a priest forever after the order of Melchisedec. *Psalm 110:4*

[18] For there is truly[+] a nullifying[+] of the commandment going before for the weakness and unprofitableness of it.

[19] For the law made nothing perfect. But the bringing in of a better hope *did*. By this, we draw near to God.

[20] *It was* not without an oath *that He was made priest*.

[21] For those priests were made without an oath. But this *priest was made* with an oath by *God* who said to Him: The Lord swore and will not repent: You *are* a priest forever after the order of Melchisedec. *Psalm 110:4*

[22] By so much was Jesus made a guarantee[+] of a better covenant.[+]

[23] Truly, there had been many priests, because they were not allowed[+] to continue because of death.

[24] But this *one* continues forever because He has an unchangeable priesthood.

[25] Therefore, He is able also to save them to the uttermost who come to God through Him since[+] He lives continually[+] to make intercession for them.

[26] For such a high priest came *to* us *who is* holy, harmless, undefiled, separate from sinners, and made higher than the heavens.

[27] *Jesus* does not need to offer sacrifices daily as the high priests, first for His own sins and then for the people's. For this He did once, when He offered up Himself.

[28] For the law makes men high priests who have weaknesses.[+] But the word of the oath, which *came* after[+] the law, *made* the Son consecrated forever.

Hebrews Chapter 8

[1] Now, *here is a* summary of the things being spoken: We have such a high priest, who is set at the right hand of the throne of the Majesty in the Heavens.

[2] *He is* a minister of the sanctuary and of the true tabernacle that the Lord built,[+] and not man.

[3] For every high priest is ordained to offer gifts and sacrifices. Therefore *it is* necessary that this man have something to offer, also.

[4] For if He were on earth, He would not be a priest, since there are priests who offer gifts according to the law,

[5] who serve *the* example and shadow of heavenly things, as Moses was admonished by God when he was about to make the tabernacle. For He said: See *that* you make all things according to the pattern shown to you on the mountain. *Exodus 25:40*

[6] But now He has obtained a more excellent ministry, as He is also the mediator of a better covenant established upon better promises.

[7] For if that first were faultless, *then* no place would *have been* sought *for the* second.

[8] Because *in* finding fault *with* them, He says: Behold the days are coming, says the Lord, when I will make a new covenant with the house of Israel and with the house of Judah, *Jeremiah 31:31*

[9] not according to the covenant that I made with their fathers in the day when I took them by the hand to lead them out of the land of Egypt. Because they did not continue in my covenant, I ignored[+] them, says the Lord. *Jeremiah 31:32*

[10]For this *is* the covenant that I will make with the house of Israel after those days, says the Lord: I will put my laws into their mind and write them in their hearts. I will be to them God. And they shall be my people. *Jeremiah 31:33*

[11]They shall not teach every[+] neighbor and every[+] brother saying: Know the Lord. For everyone will know me, from the least to the greatest. *Jeremiah 31:34*

[12]For I will be merciful to their unrighteousness and their sins and their iniquities I will remember no longer.[+] *Jeremiah 31:34*

[13]In that He said: A new, He has made the first old. Now what *is* decaying and growing[+] old *is* ready to vanish away.

Hebrews Chapter 9

[1] Truly[+] then, the first *covenant* also had ordinances of divine service and a worldly sanctuary.

[2] In the first tabernacle, *there was* a table prepared *with* a candlestick and showbread *in an area* called the sanctuary.

[3] Then, after the second veil, *was* the tabernacle called the Holiest of all.

[4] It had the golden censer and the ark of the covenant overlaid *all* around[+] with gold. In it *was* the golden pot that had manna and Aaron's rod that budded and the tables of the covenant.

[5] Over it *were* the cherubims of glory shadowing the mercy seat. About this, we cannot now speak in detail.[+]

[6] Now when these things were thus ordained, the priests always went into the first tabernacle *to* accomplish the service *of God*.

[7] But into the second, the high priest *went* alone once every year, *and* not without blood that he offered for himself and *for* the errors of the people.

[8] This signified, *by* the Holy Spirit, that the way into the holiest of all was not yet revealed[+] while the first tabernacle was yet standing.

[9] This *was* symbolic[+] for the time then present in which both gifts and sacrifices were offered that could not make *those* who did the service perfect, as pertaining to the conscience.

[10]*For it concerned* only food[+] and drink and many different[+] washings and worldly[+] ordinances imposed *on them* until the time of reformation.

[11]But Christ came *as* a high priest of good things to come, by a greater and more perfect tabernacle not made with hands. That is to say, not of this building.

[12]*It is* not by the blood of goats and calves, but by His own blood *that* He entered once *for all* into the holy place, *thereby* obtaining eternal redemption *for us*.

[13]For if the blood of bulls and goats and the ashes of a heifer sprinkling the unclean sanctifies to the purifying of the flesh,

[14]how much more shall the blood of Christ, who, through the eternal Spirit offered Himself without spot to God, purge your conscience from dead works to serve the living God?

[15]For this reason,[+] *Christ* is the mediator of the new covenant[+] *so* that, by means of death for the redemption of the transgressions *that were* under the first covenant,[+] *those* who are called might receive the promise of eternal inheritance.

[16]For where a testament *is*, there must, of necessity, also be the death of the testator.

[17]For a testament *is* of force after one[+] is dead. Otherwise, it is of no strength at all while the testator lives.

[18]Therefore, the first *covenant* was not dedicated without blood.

[19]For when Moses had spoken every precept to all the people according to the law, he took the blood of calves and goats with water and scarlet wool and a hyssop *branch* and sprinkled both the book and all the people,

[20]saying: This *is* the blood of the

covenant[+] that God commanded[+] to you. *Exodus 24:7-8, Matthew 26:28*

[21] Moreover he sprinkled with blood both the tabernacle and all the vessels of the ministry.

[22] Almost all things are, by the law, purged with blood. Without *the* shedding of blood, *there* is no remission.

[23] Therefore *it was* necessary that the patterns of things in the heavens should be purified with these, but the heavenly things themselves with better sacrifices than these.

[24] For Christ has not entered the holy places made with hands, *that are* symbolic[+] of the true. But into heaven itself *He* now appears in the presence of God for us.

[25] Nor *was it* that He should offer Himself often, as the high priest enters into the holy place every year with blood of others.

[26] For then He must often have suffered since the foundation of the world. But now once in the end of the world He has appeared to put away sin by the sacrifice of Himself.

[27] As it is appointed to *all* humans[+] once to die and after that judgment,

[28] so *also* Christ was offered once to bear the sins of many, *and to* appear second, without *bearing* sins, to those who wait *for* Him for salvation.

Hebrews Chapter 10

[1] For the law, having *only* a shadow of *the* good things to come *and* not the very image of those things, can never, with those sacrifices that they offered year by year continually, make those *who* come to that perfect.

[2] For then would they not have stopped[+] being offered? Because the worshipers, once purged, would have had no more conscience of sins.

[3] But in those *sacrifices, there is* a remembrance of sins *made* again every year.

[4] For *it is* not possible that the blood of bulls and of goats should take away sins.

[5] Therefore, when *Christ* came into the world, He said: Sacrifice and offering you did not desire,[+] but you have prepared a body *for* me. *Psalm 40:6*

[6] In burnt offerings and *sacrifices* for sin you have had no pleasure. *Malachi 1:10*

[7] Then I said: Behold, I *have* come. *As* it is written in the pages[+] of the book about me: *I delight* to do your will, O God. *Psalm 40:7,8*

[8] Above saying: Sacrifice and offering and burnt offerings and *offering* for sin you would not *desire* nor have pleasure *in*, such as were offered according to the law, *Matthew 9:13*

[9] *He* then said: Behold, I come to do your will O God. *In this,* He takes away the first *so* that He may establish the second.

[10] By this will we are sanctified through the offering of the body of Jesus Christ once *for all*.

[11] Every priest stands daily ministering and repeatedly[+] offering the same sacrifices that can never take away sins.

[12] But after *Jesus* had offered one sacrifice for sins forever, He sat down at the right hand of God,

[13] thereafter waiting[+] *expectantly* until His enemies be made His footstool.

[14] For by one offering He has perfected forever *those* who are sanctified.

[15] The Holy Spirit is also a witness to us. For after He had said before:

[16] This *is* the covenant that I will make with them after those days, says the Lord: I will put my laws into their hearts, and in their minds I will write them. *Jeremiah 31:33*

[17] Their sins and iniquities I will remember no longer.[+] *Jeremiah 31:34*

[18] Now where remission of these *sins is, there is* no more *need for sacrificial* offering for sin.

[19] Therefore family,[+] having boldness to enter into the holiest by the blood of Jesus,

[20] by a new and living way that He has consecrated for us through the veil, that is to say His flesh,

[21] *having* a high priest over the house of God:

²²Let us draw near with a true heart in full assurance of faith, having our hearts sprinkled from an evil conscience and our bodies washed with pure water.

²³Let us hold fast the profession of *our* faith without wavering. For He who promised *is* faithful.

²⁴Let us consider one another to provoke *one another* to love and to good works.

²⁵*Let us* not forsake the assembling of ourselves together, as the manner of some *is*, but exhort *one another*. So much the more, as you see the day approaching.

²⁶For if we sin willfully after we have received the knowledge of the truth, there remains no more sacrifice for sins.

²⁷But *there will be* a certain fearful expectation⁺ of judgment and fiery indignation that will devour the adversaries.

²⁸*Those* who despised Moses' law died without mercy under *the testimony of* two or three witnesses.

²⁹Of how much greater⁺ punishment do you suppose one⁺ shall be thought worthy who has trampled⁺ the Son of God under foot and has counted the blood of the covenant with which they were sanctified an unholy thing and has done dishonor⁺ to the Spirit of grace?

³⁰For we know Him who said: Vengeance *belongs* to me. I will repay,⁺ says the Lord. And again: The Lord will judge His people. *Deuteronomy 32:35-36*

³¹*It is* a fearful thing to fall into the hands of the living God.

³²But remember the former days in which, after you were enlightened,⁺ you endured a great fight of afflictions.

³³Partly while you were made a subject of stares⁺ both by reproaches and afflictions and partly while you became companions of *those* who were abiding⁺ *in them.*

³⁴For you had compassion for me in my chains⁺ and took joyfully the spoiling of your goods, knowing in yourselves that you have in heaven a better and an enduring substance.

³⁵Therefore do not cast away your confidence that has great repayment⁺ of reward.

³⁶For you have need of patience *so* that after you have done the will of God, you might receive the promise.

³⁷For *it will be* only⁺ a little while and He who is coming will *indeed* come and will not delay.⁺ *Habakkuk 2:3, John 16:16*

³⁸Now the just shall live by faith. But if *anyone* draws back, my soul will not delight⁺ in them. *Habakkuk 2:4*

³⁹We are not drawing back to damnation,⁺ but *we have* faith⁺ *in* the saving *of the* soul.

Hebrews Chapter 11

> ¹ Faith is the substance
>   of things hoped for,
> the evidence of things not seen.

² For by it the elders obtained a good report.

³ Through faith we understand that the worlds were framed by the Word of God, so that things that are seen were not made of things that do appear.

⁴ By faith Abel offered to God a more excellent sacrifice than Cain. By this, he obtained *a* witness that he was righteous, God testifying of his gifts. By it he, being dead, yet speaks.

⁵ By faith Enoch was translated *so* that he would not see death. *He* was not found because God had translated him. For before his translation, he had this testimony: That he pleased God.

> ⁶ Without faith *it is* impossible to please *God.* For *those* who come to God must believe that He is and *that* He is a rewarder of *those* who diligently seek Him.

⁷ By faith Noah, being warned by God of things not yet seen, moved with fear *and* prepared an ark for the saving of his house. In this, he condemned the world and became *an* heir of the righteousness that *comes* by faith.

⁸ By faith Abraham, when he was called

to go to a place that he would later[+] receive as an inheritance, obeyed. He went, not knowing where he was going.
[9] By faith he sojourned to the land of promise, as *in* a strange country, dwelling in tabernacles with Isaac and Jacob, the heirs with him of the same promise.
[10] He was looking for the city having foundations, whose builder and maker *is* God.
[11] Through faith Sarah herself also received strength to conceive seed and gave birth[+] when she was past *childbearing* age, because she judged Him faithful who had promised.
[12] Therefore there arose,[+] even from one as good as dead, *many descendants* like the multitude of stars in the sky and innumerable as the sand on the sea shore.
[13] These all died in faith, not having received the promises, but having seen them a far *distance away*. *They* were persuaded about *them* and embraced *them* and confessed that they were strangers and sojourners[+] on the earth.
[14] For *those* who say such things declare plainly that they are seeking a homeland.[+]
[15] Truly, if they had been mindful of that *country* from where they came, they might have had opportunity to have returned.
[16] But now they desire a better *country*, that is a heavenly *homeland*. Therefore, God is not ashamed to be called their God for He has prepared a city for them.
[17] By faith Abraham, when he was tested,[+] offered up Isaac. He who had received the promises offered up his only begotten *son*.
[18] It was said of him that in Isaac your descendants[+] shall be called *forth*.
Genesis 21:12
[19] *Abraham* concluded[+] that God *was* able to raise *anyone* up, even from the dead. And in this, he also received a *prophetic* example.[+]
[20] By faith Isaac blessed Jacob and Esau concerning things to come.
[21] By faith Jacob, when he was dying,

blessed both the sons of Joseph, and *he still* worshiped, *even leaning* on the top of his staff.
[22] By faith Joseph, when he died, made mention of the departing of the children of Israel and gave instructions[+] concerning his bones.
[23] By faith Moses, when he was born, was hid *for* three months by his parents because they saw *he was* a beautiful[+] child. They were not afraid of the king's edict.[+]
[24] By faith Moses, when he had come of age,[+] refused to be called the son of Pharaoh's daughter.
[25] *He* chose rather to suffer affliction with the people of God, than to enjoy the pleasures of sin for a season.
[26] *He* esteemed the reproach of Christ greater riches than the treasures in Egypt. For he had respect for the repayment[+] of the reward.
[27] By faith he left[+] Egypt, not fearing the wrath of the king. For seeing the invisible, he endured.
[28] Through faith he kept the Passover and the sprinkling of blood, lest he who destroyed the firstborn should touch them.
[29] By faith they passed through the Red sea as on dry *land*. When the Egyptians tried[+] to do *that, they* were drowned.
[30] By faith the walls of Jericho fell down after they were surrounded[+] about seven days.
[31] By faith the harlot Rahab did not perish with *those* who did not believe when she had received the spies with peace.
[32] What more shall I say? For time would fail me to tell of Gideon and Barak and Samson and Jephthae, *of* David and Samuel and *of all* the prophets.
[33] Through faith *they* subdued kingdoms, worked[+] righteousness, obtained promises, stopped the mouths of lions,
[34] quenched the violence of fire, *and* escaped the edge of the sword. Out of weakness *they* were made strong, grew[+] valiant in fight, *and* turned the armies of the aliens to flight.

[35]Women received their dead raised to life again. Others were tortured, not accepting deliverance *so* that they might obtain a better resurrection.

[36]Others received[+] trials by *cruel* mockings and scourgings *and* even[+] chains[+] and imprisonment.

[37]They were stoned, sawn apart,[+] tested,[+] *and* slain with the sword. They wandered about in sheepskins and goat skins, being destitute, afflicted, *and* tormented.

[38]The world was not worthy of them. They wandered in deserts and mountains and *in* dens and caves in the earth.

[39]*And yet* all of them, *even* having obtained a good report through faith, did not receive the promise.

[40]God anticipated[+] something better for us *so* that, without us, *everything would not be* fulfilled.[+]

Hebrews Chapter 12

[1] Therefore, since we also are surrounded[+] with so great a cloud of witnesses, let us lay aside every weight and the sin that does so easily beset *us*, and let us run the race that is set before us with patience, [2] looking to Jesus, the Author and Finisher of *our* faith. *He*, for the joy that was set before Him, endured the cross, despising the shame, and *He* is *now* set down at the right hand of the throne of God.

[3] Consider Him who endured such contradictions of sinners against Himself, lest you be wearied and faint in your minds.

[4] You have not yet resisted to *the point of* blood *in* striving against sin.

[5] You have forgotten the exhortation that speaks to you as to children: My child, do not despise the discipline[+] of the Lord nor faint when you are rebuked by Him. *Proverbs 3:11*

[6] For *those* the Lord loves, He chastens and *He* disciplines[+] every child whom He receives. *Proverbs 3:12*

[7] If you endure discipline,[+] God deals *with* you as His *own* children.[+] For who is *the* child whom the father does not discipline[+]?

[8] But if you are without chastisement, of which all are partakers, then you are illegitimate[+] *children* and not children *of the Father*.

[9] Furthermore we have had fathers in the flesh who corrected *us* and we gave *them* reverence. Shall we not much rather be in subjection to the Father of spirits and live?

[10]For indeed[+] they chastened *us* for a few days as they think[+] *best*. But He *chastens* for *our own* benefit[+] *so* that *we* might be partakers of His holiness.

[11]Now, no discipline[+] for the present seems to be joyous, but grievous. Nevertheless afterward it yields the peaceable fruit of righteousness to *those* who are exercised thereby.

[12]Therefore lift up the hands that hang down and the feeble knees.

[13]Make straight paths for your feet, lest what is lame be turned out of the way. But rather, let it be healed.

> [14] Follow peace with all *people*, and holiness without which no one will see the Lord.

> [15] Watch[+] diligently lest anyone fail of the grace of God *and* lest any root of bitterness spring up *and* trouble *you*. For by that[+] many become defiled.

[16]*Watch*, lest there *be* any fornicator or worldly[+] person like Esau who, for one serving[+] of food,[+] sold his birthright.

[17]For you know that afterward, when he would have inherited the blessing, he was rejected, for he found no place of repentance, though he sought it carefully with tears.

[18]For you have not come to the mountain being touched and burned with fire and blackness and darkness and storm[+]

[19]and sound of trumpet and voice of words *at* which *those* who heard *it* *begged* that the word not be spoken to them any more.

[20] For they could not endure what was commanded. And if any beast touched that mountain, it *was to* be stoned or thrust through with a dart. *Exodus 19:12,13*

[21] So terrible was the sight *that* Moses said: I fear and quake exceedingly.

[22] But you have come to Mount Zion,[+] to the city of the living God, the heavenly Jerusalem, and to an innumerable company of angels.

[23] *You have come* to the general assembly and *to the* assembly[+] of the firstborn who are registered[+] in heaven and to God the Judge of all and to the spirits of righteous[+] people made perfect.

[24] *You have come* to Jesus, the Mediator of the new covenant and to the blood of sprinkling that speaks better than Abel.

[25] See that you do not refuse *the one* who speaks *to you*. For if *those* who refused *Jesus* who spoke on earth did not escape, *then* much more *will we not escape* if we turn away from Him who *speaks* from heaven.

[26] *His* voice then shook the earth. But now He has promised, saying: Yet once more I *will* shake not only the earth, but also heaven. *Haggai 2:6*

[27] And this yet once more signifies the removing of the things that *shall be* shaken *apart so* that the things that cannot be shaken *may* remain.

[28] We *will* receive a kingdom which cannot be moved. Therefore, let us have grace by which we may serve God acceptably, with reverence and godly fear.

[29] For our God *is* a consuming fire.

Hebrews Chapter 13

[1] Let brotherly love continue.

[2] Do not be forgetful to entertain strangers. For thereby some have entertained angels unexpectedly.[+]

[3] Remember *those* who are in chains,[+] as *though you were* bound with them. *Remember those* who suffer adversity, as *though* being yourselves also in *their* body.

[4] *Let* marriage *be* honorable in every *way* and the *marriage* bed undefiled. God will judge fornicators[+] and adulterers.

---

[5] *Let your* conversation *and conduct be* without covetousness.
Be content
with such things as you have.
For He has said:
I will never leave you
nor forsake you. *John 14:18*

---

[6] Therefore, we may boldly say: The Lord *is* my helper and I will not fear what mankind[+] will do to me. *Psalm 118:6*

[7] Remember *those* who have the rule over you *and those* who have spoken the Word of God to you. Follow *their* faith, considering the example[+] of *their* conversation *and conduct*.

---

[8] Jesus Christ *is* the same yesterday and today and forever.
Malachi 3:6

---

[9] Do not be carried away[+] with many different[+] and strange doctrines. For *it is* good that the heart be established with grace *and* not with food[+] *laws* that have not benefited[+] *those* who have been preoccupied[+] with them.

[10] We have an altar from which those who serve the tabernacle have no right to eat.

[11] For the bodies of those beasts whose blood is brought into the sanctuary by the high priest for sin, are burned outside[+] the camp.

[12] Therefore Jesus also, *so* that He might sanctify the people with His own blood, suffered outside[+] the gate.

[13] Therefore, let us go forth to Him outside[+] the camp, bearing His reproach.

[14] For here we have no continuing city. But we seek one *that is* to come.

[15] Therefore through Him, let us offer the sacrifice of praise to God continually. That is, the fruit of *our* lips giving thanks to His name.

[16] Do not forget to do good and to share.[+] For with such sacrifices God is well pleased.

17Obey *those* who have the rule over you and submit yourselves *to them*. For they watch *out* for your souls as *those* who must give account. *Obey them so* that they may do it with joy and not with grief. For that *is* not beneficial+ for you.
18Pray for us. For we trust we have a good conscience, in all things willing to live honestly.
19But I urge+ *you* rather to do this *so* that I may be restored to you *all* the sooner.
20Now *may* the God of peace who brought our Lord Jesus *up* from the dead, that great shepherd of the sheep, through the blood of the everlasting covenant,
21make you perfect in every good work to do His will, working in you what is well pleasing in His sight, through Jesus Christ, to whom *be* glory forever and ever. Amen.
22I urge you family+: Endure+ the word of exhortation. For I have written *this letter* to you in few words.
23Know that *our* brother Timothy is released,+ with whom, if he come soon,+ I will see you.
24Greet+ all who have the rule over you and all the saints. Those from Italy greet+ you.
25Grace be with you all. Amen.

This epistle was written by Timothy in Italy.

James Chapter 1

1 *From* James, a servant of God and of the Lord Jesus Christ. To the twelve tribes that are scattered: Greetings.
2 My family,+

> count it all joy
> when you fall into
> many different+ trials.+

3 Know that the testing+ of your faith works patience.
4 And let patience have *its* perfect work *so* that you may be perfect and complete,+ lacking+ in nothing.

5 If any of you lack wisdom, *then* ask God who gives to everyone liberally and does not upbraid, and *it* will be given. *Matthew 7:7*
6 But ask in faith, not wavering. For *those* who waver are like a wave of the sea driven with the wind and tossed.
7 For do not suppose that one+ *who is wavering* will receive anything from the Lord.
8 A double minded person+ *is* unstable in all their ways.

9 Let those+ of low degree rejoice in their elevation,+
10 and *let* the rich *rejoice* in being humbled.+ Because, like the flower *of the* grass, they will pass away.
11For the sun rises with a burning heat and withers the grass, and its flower falls and the grace of the fashion of it perishes. So also will the rich fade away in their ways.
12Blessed *are those* who *patiently* endure trials.+ For when they are proved,+ they will receive the crown of life that the Lord has promised to *those* who love Him.
13Let no one say, when tempted, I am tempted by God. For God cannot be tempted with evil, nor does He tempt anyone.
14But everyone+ is tempted when drawn away by lust and enticed.
15Then when lust has conceived, it brings forth sin. And sin, when it is finished, brings forth death.
16Do not err my beloved.+

> 17 Every good gift and every perfect gift is from above and comes down from the Father of lights with whom *there* is no variableness nor shadow of turning. *Malachi 3:6*

18Of His own will *God* brought+ us *forth* with the Word of Truth *so* that we would be a kind of first fruits of His creatures.
19Therefore my beloved,+ let everyone+

Be swift to hear,
slow to speak,
and slow to anger. +
Matthew 12:36, Proverbs 10:19, Proverbs 14:9

²⁰For anger+ does not produce+ the righteousness of God.

²¹Therefore, put away+ all filthiness and superfluity of naughtiness. *Instead,* receive with meekness, the engrafted Word that is able to save your souls.

²²But *then* be doers of the Word, and not hearers only, deceiving yourselves.

²³For if any are hearers of the Word and not doers, they are like those beholding their natural face in a mirror. +

²⁴For they behold themselves and *then* go away and immediately+ forget what kind+ of person they are.

²⁵But whoever looks into the perfect law of liberty and continues *therein*, not being a forgetful hearer but a doer of the work, shall be blessed in their deeds.

²⁶If any among you seem to be religious and do not bridle their tongue but deceive their own hearts, their religion *is* vain.

²⁷Pure religion, undefiled before God the Father is this: To visit the fatherless and widows in their affliction *and* keep oneself unspotted from the world.

James Chapter 2

¹ My family,+ do not have the faith of our Lord Jesus Christ, *the Lord* of glory, with *deferential* respect of persons.

² For *one* man *may* come into your assembly with gold rings *and wearing* fine+ apparel, and a poor man *may* also come in *wearing* vile clothing. +

³ *If* you look+ *with deferential respect* upon the one who wears fine+ apparel and say to him: Sit here in a good place, *and then* say to the poor: Stand *over* there or sit here under my footstool,

⁴ then are you not *showing* partiality among+ yourselves and becoming judges with evil thoughts?

⁵ Listen+ my beloved+: Has God not chosen the poor of this world *to be* rich in faith and heirs of the kingdom that He has promised to *those* who love Him?

⁶ But *by acting deferentially,* you have despised the poor. Do not rich men oppress you and draw you before the judgment seats?

⁷ Do they not blaspheme that worthy name by which you are called?

⁸ If you fulfill the royal law according to the Scripture: You shall love your neighbor as yourself, *then* you do well. *Matthew 19:19*

⁹ But if you *show* partiality+ to *certain* persons, you commit sin and are convicted+ by the law as transgressors.

¹⁰For whoever keeps the whole law and yet offends in one *point* is guilty of all.

¹¹For He who said: Do not commit adultery, also said: Do not kill. Now if you commit no adultery, yet if you kill, *then* you have become a transgressor of the law.

¹²So speak and do as *those* who shall be judged by the law of liberty.

¹³For there will be judgment without mercy for *those* who have not shown mercy, and rejoicing over merciful judgment.

¹⁴My family, + what *is the* benefit+ if someone says they have faith but *they* do not have works? Can faith save them?

¹⁵If a brother or sister is naked and destitute of daily food,

¹⁶and one of you says to them: Go+ in peace, be warm and filled, but you do not give them those things that are necessary+ for the body, what benefit *are your words*?

¹⁷So faith, if it does not *also* have works, is dead, being alone.

¹⁸Someone+ may say: You have faith and I have works. *But I say,* show me your faith without your works, and I will show you my faith by my works.

¹⁹You believe that *there* is one God *and* you do well *to thus believe*. And the demons+ *also* believe and tremble.

²⁰But will you know *this*, O vain person+: That faith without works is dead.

²¹Was not Abraham our father justified

by works when he had offered his son Isaac upon the altar?

22 See how faith worked [+] with his works, and by works faith was made perfect?

23 *In this,* the Scripture was fulfilled that says: Abraham believed God and it was credited [+] to him as righteousness and he was called the Friend of God. *Genesis 15:6*

24 You see then, that by works a man is justified, and not by faith only.

25 Likewise also was not Rahab the harlot justified by works when she received the messengers and sent *them* out another way?

26 For *just* as the body without the spirit is dead, so also faith without works is dead.

James Chapter 3

1 My family, [+] not many *of you should* be teachers, [+] knowing that we *who are* will receive greater judgment. [+]

2 For in many things we all offend. If anyone does not offend in word, *then* they *are* perfect *and* able also to bridle the whole body. *Proverbs 13:3*

3 Behold, we put bits in the horses' mouths *so* that they will obey us, and *thus* we turn their whole body.

4 Behold the ships, also. Although *they are* so large [+] and driven by fierce winds, yet are they turned with a very small rudder, [+] *to* whatever course [+] *the* one who steers wills *it to go.*

5 Even so, the tongue is a little member and boasts great things. Behold how great a matter a little fire kindles. *Matthew 12:35*

6 The tongue *can set on* fire a *whole* world of iniquity. Thus is the tongue set among our members *so* that it *can* defile the whole body and set on fire the course of nature. And, it is set on fire by Hell. *Proverbs 16:27*

7 For every kind of beast and bird and serpent and *sea* creature can be subdued [+] and has been subdued [+] by mankind.

8 However no one is able to subdue [+] the tongue of an unruly [+] evil [+] person full of deadly poison. *Proverbs 16:28*

9 With *the tongue one can* bless God the Father and with *the tongue one can* curse men who are made in the likeness [+] of God.

10 Out of the same mouth proceed blessing and cursing. My family, [+] these things should not be.

11 Does a fountain send forth sweet and bitter at the same place?

12 Can the fig tree, my family, [+] produce [+] olives? Or *can* a vine *produce* figs? Likewise, [+] no fountain *can* yield both salt water and fresh.

13 Who *is* wise and endowed [+] with knowledge among you? Let them show their works out of a good conversation *and conduct,* with meekness of wisdom.

14 However, if you have bitter envying and strife in your hearts, do not boast [+] and lie against the truth.

15 This *false* wisdom does not descend from above, but *it is* earthly, sensual, *and* devilish.

16 For where *there is* envy and strife, there *is* confusion and every evil work. *Proverbs 10:12*

17 But the wisdom that is from above is first pure, then peaceable, gentle, *and* yielding, [+] full of mercy and good fruits, without partiality, and without hypocrisy.

18 The fruit of righteousness is sown in peace by *those* who make peace.

James Chapter 4

1 From where *do* wars and fighting *arise* among you? *Is it* not [+] from your lusts that war within [+] you?

2 You lust and do not have. You kill and desire to have and cannot obtain. You fight and war, yet you do not have because you do not ask.

3 You ask and do not receive because you ask amiss *so* that you may consume upon your lusts.

4 *You* adulterers and adulteresses: Do you not know that attachment [+] *to the pleasures* of the world is enmity with God? Therefore, whoever chooses [+] to

be attached+ *to the pleasures* of the world is *thereby* made+ an enemy of God.

5 Do you suppose+ that the Scripture says *in* vain: The *natural* spirit that lives+ in us lusts to envy. *Genesis 6:5*

6 But *God* gives more grace. Therefore *it* says: God resists the proud but gives grace to the humble. *Proverbs 4:34*

7 Therefore, submit yourselves to God. Resist the devil and he will flee from you.

8 Draw near to God and He will draw near to you. Cleanse *your* hands, *you* sinners. Purify *your* hearts, *you* double minded.

9 Be afflicted and mourn and weep. Let your laughter be turned to mourning and *your* joy to sorrow.+

10 Humble yourselves in the sight of the Lord and He will lift you up.

11 Do not speak evil about one another, family.+ *Those* who speak evil of *their* family+ and judge their family,+ speak evil of the law and judge the law. But if you judge the law, you are not a doer of the law, but a judge.

12 There is one lawgiver who is able to save and to destroy. Who are you that *you* judge another?

13 Come+ now, you who say: Today or tomorrow we will go into some+ city and continue there a year and buy and sell and get gain.

14 You do not know what *will be* tomorrow, for what *is* your life? It is but a vapor that appears for a little time and then vanishes away.

15 You *ought* to say: If the Lord is willing and we live, *we may* do this or that.

16 But now you rejoice in your boasting, *however* all such rejoicing is evil.

17 Therefore to *those* who know to do good and do not do *it*, to them it is sin.

James Chapter 5

1 Come+ now, *you* rich men: Weep and howl for your miseries that shall come upon *you*.

2 Your riches are corrupted and your garments are moth eaten.

3 Your gold and silver are corroded+ and their rust will be a witness against you and will eat your flesh as *though* it were fire *because* you have *piled up* treasure for the last days.

4 Behold the wages+ of the laborers who harvested+ your fields, which you kept back by fraud, cries *out*, and the cries of *those* who harvested+ have entered the ears of the Lord of Sabaoth.

5 You have lived in pleasure on the earth and been wanton. You have nourished your hearts, as in a day of slaughter.

6 You have condemned *and* killed the just, *and* they have not resisted you.

7 Therefore be patient, family,+ for the coming of the Lord. Behold the grower+ waits for the precious fruit of the earth and has long patience for it until it receives *the* early and *the* latter rain.

8 You be patient also. Strengthen+ your hearts. For the coming of the Lord draws near.

9 Do not complain+ against one another, family,+ lest you be condemned. Behold, the judge stands before the door.

10 My family,+ take the prophets who have spoken in the name of the Lord as an example of suffering affliction and patience.

11 Behold, we count *those* who endure blessed.+ You have heard of the patience of Job and have seen the end of the Lord, that the Lord is full of pity and tender mercy.

12 But above all things, my family,+ do not swear by heaven or by the earth or by any other oath. But let your yes be yes and *your* no, no. Lest you fall into condemnation. *Matthew 5:37*

13 Are any among you suffering+? Let them pray. Are any merry? Let them sing psalms.

14 Are any sick among you? Let them call for the elders of the assembly+ and let *the elders* pray over them, anointing them with oil in the name of the Lord.

15 The prayer of faith will save the sick and the Lord will raise them up. If they have committed sins, they will be forgiven.

16 Confess *your* faults to one another and pray for one another *so* that you may be healed. The effective+ fervent prayer of a righteous person+ avails much. *Proverbs 15:29*

17Elijah was a man subject to passions *just* as we are, and he prayed earnestly that it might not rain and it did not rain on the earth for three years and six months.

18*Then* he prayed again and the heaven gave rain and the earth brought forth her fruit.

19Family, + if any of you do err from the truth, and one convert them,

20know this: that *those* who convert sinners from the error of their ways, save souls from death and cover+ *a* multitude of sins. *Proverbs 11:30*

1 Peter Chapter 1

1 *From* Peter, an apostle of Jesus Christ. To the sojourners+ scattered throughout Pontus, Galatia, Cappadocia, Asia, and Bithynia.

2 *You have been elected* according to the foreknowledge of God *the* Father, through sanctification by the *Holy* Spirit, unto obedience and *the* sprinkling of the blood of Jesus Christ. Grace *to* you and peace *be* multiplied.

3 Blessed *is* the God and Father *of* our Lord Jesus Christ. According to His abundant mercy *He has made us* born+ again to a living+ hope through *the* resurrection of Jesus Christ from the dead,

4 to an inheritance incorruptible, un-defiled, and that does not fade away, reserved in heaven for you

5 who are kept by the power of God through faith unto salvation, ready to be revealed in the last time.

6 In this, you greatly rejoice. Although now, for a season if need be, you are in sorrow+ through *many* different+ trials.+

7 Because+ the proving+ of your faith *is* much more precious than gold that

perishes. Though *it be* tested+ by fire, *may it* be found to praise and honor and glory, at the appearing of Jesus Christ.

8 *Even though you* have not seen *Him*, you love *Him*. *Even* though you do not see *Him* now, yet *you* believe *and* rejoice with unspeakable joy and *expressions* of glory,

9 receiving the end of your faith, the salvation of *your* souls.

10Regarding+ this salvation, the prophets have inquired and searched diligently. *They* prophesied about the grace *that would come* to you,

11searching *by* what *means* or *in* what *season* of time the Spirit of Christ in them was declaring, + when He testified beforehand *about* the sufferings of Christ and the glory that would follow.

12It was revealed to *them*, that *it was* not to themselves, but to us *that* they ministered the things that are now reported to you by *those* who have proclaimed+ the Gospel to you with the Holy Spirit sent down from heaven. *Even* the angels desire to look into *these* things.

13Therefore, gird up the loins of your mind. Be sober. And hope to the end for the grace that is to be brought to you at the revelation of Jesus Christ.

14Be+ obedient children, not fashioning yourselves according to the former lusts in your ignorance.

15But as He who has called you is holy, so you *must* be holy in all kinds+ of conversation *and conduct*.

16Because it is written: Be holy, for I am holy. *Leviticus 11:44*

17If you call on the Father who judges without partiality+ according to everyone's+ work, *then* pass the time of your sojourning *here* in fear.

18For+ you know that *it was* not with corruptible things *like* silver and gold *that* you were redeemed from your vain conversation *and conduct that you re-ceived* by tradition from your fathers.

19But *it was* with the precious blood of Christ, as of a lamb without blemish and without spot.

[20] Truly[+] He was foreordained before the foundation of the world, but was revealed[+] in these last times for you.

[21] Through Him *you* believe in God who raised Him up from the dead and gave Him glory *so* that your faith and hope might be in God.

[22] Your souls are purified by obedience to the truth through the Spirit *and* to sincere[+] affection[+] for the family.[+] Love one another fervently with a pure heart.

[23] Be born again, not of corruptible seed but of incorruptible, by the Word of God who lives and abides forever.

[24] For all flesh *is* like grass, and all the glory of man is like the flower of grass: The grass withers and its flower falls away. *Isaiah 40:7*

[25] But the Word of the Lord endures forever. And this is the Word proclaimed[+] *as Gospel* to you. *Isaiah 40:8*

1 Peter Chapter 2

[1] Therefore, laying aside all malice and all deceitfulness[+] and hypocrisies and envies and all evil speaking,

[2] like newborn babes, desire the sincere milk of the Word *so* that you may grow thereby,

[3] if *you* have tasted that goodness[+] *of* the Lord.

[4] Come to *Jesus as to* a living stone, rejected[+] indeed by men, but chosen by God *and* precious.

[5] You also, as living[+] stones, are *being* built up *as* a spiritual house, a holy priesthood, to offer up spiritual sacrifices, acceptable to God by Jesus Christ.

[6] Therefore also, it is contained in the Scripture: Behold I lay in Zion[+] a chief corner stone, chosen[+] *and* precious, and *those* who believe in Him will not be ashamed.[+] *Isaiah 28:16*

[7] Therefore, to you who believe, *He is* precious. But to *those* who are disobedient: The stone that the builders rejected[+] has become the chief[+] cornerstone,[+] *Psalm 118:22*

[8] a stone of stumbling and a rock of offense. *Those* who stumble at the Word are disobedient to *what* they also were appointed. *Isaiah 8:14*

[9] But you *are* a chosen generation, a royal priesthood, a holy nation, a unique[+] people. You should show forth the praises of Him who has called you out of darkness into His marvelous light.

[10] In time past, *these were* not a people. But now *they* are the people of God. *Previously, they* had not received[+] mercy. But now, *they* have received[+] mercy.

[11] Beloved, I urge[+] *you* as strangers and sojourners[+]: Abstain from fleshly lusts that war against the soul.

[12] Have your conversation *and conduct* honest among the Gentiles *so* that, *even* if they speak against you as evildoers, they may, by *your* good works that they shall behold, glorify God in the day of visitation.

[13] Submit yourselves to every ordinance of mankind[+] for the Lord's sake, whether[+] to the king as *the* supreme *ruler*

[14] or to governors as to *those* who are sent by *the king* for the punishment of evildoers and for the praise of *those* who do well.

[15] For this is the will of God: That by doing well, you may put to silence the ignorance of foolish men.

[16] As free *in the Lord* do not use *your* liberty as a cover[+] for maliciousness, but *use it* as servants of God.

[17] Honor all *people*. Love the family.[+] Fear God. Honor the king.

[18] Servants, *be* subject to *your* masters with all fear. Not only to the good and gentle, but also to the ornery.

[19] For this *is* grace[+]: If a person,[+] for conscience toward God, endures grief *and* wrongful suffering.

[20] For what glory *is it*, if, when you are buffeted for your faults, you take it patiently? But if, when you do well and suffer *for it*, you take it patiently, this *is* acceptable with God.

[21] For even to this you were called. Because Christ also suffered for us, leaving an example *for* us, *so that* you should follow His steps.

22He did not sin, nor was *any* deceitfulness+ found in His mouth. *Isaiah 53:9*
23When He was reviled, He did not revile in return.+ When He suffered, He did not threaten. But *He* committed *Himself* to *the One* who judges righteously.
24*Jesus* Himself bore our sins in His own body on the tree *so* that we, being dead to sins, should live to righteousness. By *His* stripes you were healed. *Isaiah 53:5*
25For you were like sheep going astray. But now *you* are returned to the Shepherd and Bishop of your souls.

1 Peter Chapter 3

1 Likewise, you wives, *be* in subjection to your own husbands *so* that if any do not obey the Word, they may also, *even* without the Word, be won by the conversation *and conduct* of the wives,
2 while they behold your chaste conversation *and conduct coupled* with fear.
3 Do not *stress* the outward adorning of glamorous+ hair and luxurious+ gold and showy+ apparel.
4 But *emphasize* the hidden *qualities* of the heart, in the incorruptible *adornment* of a meek and quiet spirit that is, in the sight of God, of great value.+
5 For in this way,+ the holy women *of long ago* who trusted in God, adorned themselves, being subject to their own husbands,
6 like Sarah obeyed Abraham, calling him lord. You become *like her* children *when you* give honor *in this way and* not *out of* fear+ or terror.+
7 Likewise, you husbands live with your wife with understanding,+ honoring*her* as a delicate+ vessel and as being heirs together of the grace of life,*so* that your prayers *will* not be hindered.
8 Finally, *be* all of one mind, having compassion for one another. *Be* affectionate+ as family.+ *Be* compassionate.+ *Be* courteous.
9 Do not render evil for evil or reviling+ for reviling.+ But instead+ *give* blessing. Know that you are called to this *so* that you should inherit a blessing.

10For *those* who will *their* lives to love and to see good days, *must* refrain their tongue from evil and their lips to not speak deceitfulness.+ *Psalm 34:12-13, Proverbs 21:23*
11Avoid+ evil and do good. Seek peace and follow+ it. *Psalm 34:14*
12For the eyes of the Lord*are* over the righteous and His ears *are open* to their prayers. But the face of the Lord *is* against*those* who do evil. *Psalm 34:15,16 John 9:31*
13Who will harm you if you are followers of what is good?
14But if you suffer for righteousness' sake, *be* blessed.+ Do not be afraid of their terror or be troubled. *Matthew 5:10 Isaiah 8:12*
15But sanctify the Lord God in your hearts. *Be* ready always to *give* an answer to everyone+ who asks you the reason for the hope that is in you. *And do so* with meekness and fear. *Proverbs 15:28*
16Have a good conscience *so* that, *even* though they speak evil about you, as evildoers, *those* who falsely accuse your good conversation *and conduct* in Christ may be ashamed.
17For*it is* better that you suffer for doing well than for doing evil, if that is the will of God.
18For Christ also once suffered for sins: The righteous+ for the unrighteous+ *so* that He might bring us to God, being put to death in the flesh, but given life+ by the Spirit.
19*And* by *the Spirit* He also went to the spirits in prison and proclaimed+ *the Word*.
20When+ *people* were disobedient, when the longsuffering God once waited, in the days of Noah while the ark was being prepared, into it, a few, that is eight souls, were saved by water.
21*That was* an illustration+ of what baptism also does now *to* save us. Not the putting away of the filth of the flesh, but the answer of a good conscience toward God through+ the resurrection of Jesus Christ.
22*Jesus* has gone into heaven and is at the

right hand of God and *all the* angels and authorities and powers are made subject to Him.

1 Peter Chapter 4

[1] Since[+] Christ has suffered for us in the flesh, arm yourselves likewise with the same mind. For *those* who have suffered in the flesh stop[+] sinning,

[2] *so* that they will no longer live the rest of *their* time in the flesh *giving in* to the lusts of men, but to the will of God.

[3] For *in* the past times of *our* life *it may have been* sufficient[+] *for* us to have worked[+] the will of the Gentiles, when we walked in filthiness,[+] lusts, excess of wine, riots,[+] wild parties,[+] and abominable idolatries.

[4] *Those caught* in that think it strange that you do not run with *them* to the same excesses of rioting, *and they* speak evil of *you*.

[5] *They* will give account to Him who is ready to judge the living[+] and the dead.

[6] Because *it was* for this reason[+] the Gospel was proclaimed[+] also to *those* who are dead, *so* that they might be judged according to men in the flesh but live according to God in the spirit.

[7] But the end of all things is *very* near.[+] Therefore, be sober and watch in prayer.

[8] Above all things, have fervent *true* love among yourselves. For *true* love will cover *the* multitude *of* sins. *Proverbs 10:12*

[9] Use hospitality to one another without complaining.[+]

[10] As everyone has received the gift, *even so* minister the same to one another as good stewards of the manifold grace of God.

[11] If anyone speaks, *let them speak* as the oracles of God. If anyone ministers, *let them do it* by the ability that God gives *so* that in all things God may be glorified through Jesus Christ, to whom be praise and dominion forever and ever. Amen.

[12] Beloved, do not think it strange concerning the fiery trial that is to try you, as though some strange thing happened to you.

[13] But rejoice in that you are partakers of Christ's sufferings *so* that, when His glory shall be revealed, you may be glad also with exceeding joy.

[14] If you are reproached for the name of Christ, *be* blessed.[+] For the spirit of glory and of God rests upon you. On their part, He is blasphemed, but on your part He is glorified.

[15] But let none of you suffer as a murderer or *as* a thief or *as* an evildoer or as a busybody in other people's affairs.[+]

[16] Yet if *anyone suffers* as a Christian, let them not be ashamed, but let them glorify God on this behalf.

[17] For the time *is coming* that judgment must begin at the house of God. If *it begins* first with us, what will the end *be* for *those* who do not obey the Gospel of God?

[18] If the righteous scarcely be saved, where will the ungodly and the sinner appear? *Proverbs 11:31*

[19] Therefore, let *those* who suffer according to the will of God commit the keeping of their souls in well doing, as to a faithful Creator.

1 Peter Chapter 5

[1] I exhort the elders who are among you. *I* also am an elder and a witness of the sufferings of Christ and also a partaker of the glory that will be revealed.

[2] Feed the flock of God that is among you. Take responsibility *for it*, not by constraint, but willingly. Not for filthy gain[+] but from a ready mind.

[3] Do not be like lords over *God's* heritage, but be examples to the flock.

[4] When the chief Shepherd appears, you will receive a crown of glory that does not fade away.

[5] Likewise, you younger *ones* submit yourselves to the elders. Yes, all *of you should* be subject to one another and be clothed with humility. For God resists the proud and gives grace to the humble. *Proverbs 3:34*

[6] Therefore, humble yourselves under the mighty hand of God *so* that He may exalt you in due time.

⁷ Cast all your care upon Him, for He cares for you.

⁸ Be sober. Be vigilant. Because your adversary the devil walks around⁺ like⁺ a roaring lion seeking whom he may devour.

⁹ Resist *the devil and be* steadfast in the faith, knowing that the same afflictions are accomplished in your family⁺ that are in the world.

¹⁰But the God of all grace who has called us to His eternal glory by Christ Jesus, *will,* after you have suffered a while, make you perfect. *He will* establish,⁺ strengthen, *and* settle *you.*

¹¹To *God be* glory and dominion forever and ever. Amen.

¹²By *the hand of* Silvanus, a faithful brother to you, as I deduce,⁺ *so* I have written briefly, exhorting and testifying that this is the true grace of God in which you stand.

¹³The *assembly* at Babylon *who were* elected together with *you,* greet⁺ you. *So does* my son Mark.

¹⁴Greet one another with a kiss of *true* love. Peace *be* with you all who are in Christ Jesus. Amen.

2 Peter Chapter 1

¹ *From* Simon Peter, a servant and apostle of Jesus Christ. To *those* who have obtained like precious faith with us through the righteousness of our God and Savior Jesus Christ.

² Grace and peace be multiplied to you in the knowledge of God and Jesus our Lord.

³ By His divine power *He* has given everything⁺ to us that *pertains* to life and godliness, through the knowledge of Him who has called us to glory and virtue.

⁴ By this exceedingly great and precious promises are given to us *so* that by these you might be partakers of the divine nature, having escaped the corruption that is in the world through lust.

⁵ Also by this, giving all diligence, add to your faith virtue *and* to virtue knowledge,

⁶ to knowledge temperance *and* to tem-

perance patience, to patience godliness ⁷ *and* to godliness, brotherly kindness. *And* to brotherly kindness, *add true* love.

⁸ For if these things are in you and abound *in you, then* they *will* not make *you* barren or unfruitful in the knowledge of our Lord Jesus Christ.

⁹ But *those* who lack these things are blind *and* cannot see *and* have forgotten the purging of their old sins.

¹⁰Therefore family,⁺ rather *than this,* be diligent to make your calling and election sure. For if you do these things, you will never fall.

¹¹For *in* this *way* you will be abundantly supplied⁺ an entrance into the everlasting kingdom of our Lord and Savior Jesus Christ.

¹²Therefore, I will not neglect⁺ to remind you about these things, *even* though you *already* know *them* and *have already been* established in the present truth.

¹³*Yes,* I consider⁺ it *proper,* as long as I am in this tabernacle, to stir you up by reminding you,

¹⁴knowing that *very* soon⁺ I must put off *this* my *temporary* tabernacle, as our Lord Jesus Christ has shown me.

¹⁵Moreover, I will endeavor *in this, so* that after my departure⁺ you may be able to always remember these things.

¹⁶For we have not followed cunningly devised fables when we made known to you the power and coming of our Lord Jesus Christ. But *we* were eyewitnesses of His majesty.

¹⁷For He received honor and glory from God the Father when there came such a voice to Him from the *most* excellent glory: This is my beloved Son in whom I am well pleased.

¹⁸We heard this voice from heaven when we were with Him on the holy mountain.

¹⁹We also have a more sure word of prophecy to which you *will* do well to take heed, as to a light that shines in a dark place, until the day dawns and the Day Star arises in your hearts.

²⁰Know this first: That no prophecy in the Scriptures is of any private interpretation.

[21] For *true* prophecy has not come *forth at any* time by the will of man, but holy men of God spoke *as they were* moved by the Holy Spirit.

2 Peter Chapter 2

[1] But there were also false prophets among the people, even as there will be false teachers among you. *They* will privately[+] bring in damnable heresies, even denying the *Lord and* Master who bought them, *thereby* bringing swift destruction upon themselves.

[2] Many will follow their *exceedingly* deadly[+] ways *because* through them, the way of truth will be blasphemed[+] *and slandered*.

[3] Through covetousness *and* with deceptive[+] words they will exploit[+] you. *For* them, the judgment of long ago[+] is not idle.[+] Their damnation does not slumber.

[4] For God did not spare the angels who sinned but cast *them* down to Hell and delivered *them* into chains of darkness to be reserved to judgment.

[5] *He* did not spare the old world, but saved Noah the eighth *from Adam*, a preacher of righteousness, *by* bringing in the flood upon the world of the ungodly.

[6] And *He* turned the cities of Sodom and Gomorrah into ashes *to* condemn *them* with an overthrow. *In doing this, He* made an example to *those* who might later live ungodly *lives*.

[7] *He* delivered righteous[+] Lot *who was* oppressed[+] with the filthy conversation *and conduct* of the wicked.

[8] For *He* saw and heard that righteous *man* living[+] among them, *his* righteous soul tormented[+] day after day with *their* unlawful deeds.

[9] The Lord knows how to deliver the godly out of trials[+] and reserve the unrighteous[+] to the day of judgment to be punished,

[10] but chiefly *those* who walk after the flesh in the lust of uncleanness and despise government. They are presumptuous, selfwilled, *and* not afraid to speak evil of the glory.[+]

[11] Angels, however, who are greater in power and might, do not bring a reviling[+] accusation against them before the Lord.

[12] But these, as natural brute beasts, are made to be taken and destroyed. *They* speak evil about things they do not understand *and they* will utterly perish in their own corruption.

[13] *They* will receive the reward of unrighteousness *as those* who count it pleasure to riot in the daytime. *They are* spots and blemishes, sporting themselves with their own deceitfulness while they feast with you.

[14] *They* have eyes full of adultery and cannot stop[+] sinning, deceiving[+] unstable souls. They have hearts exercised with covetous practices. *They are* cursed children

[15] who have forsaken the right way and are gone astray, following the way of Balaam *the son* of Bosor, who loved the wages of unrighteousness

[16] but was rebuked for his iniquity. The speechless[+] donkey[+] spoke with a man's voice *and* stopped[+] the madness of the *corrupt* prophet.

[17] These are wells without water, clouds that are carried with a storm[+] for whom the mist of darkness is reserved forever.

[18] They speak great swelling *words* of vanity to entice[+] into the lusts of the flesh *by* wantonness *those* who had escaped from *those* who live in error.

[19] While they promise them liberty, they themselves are the servants of corruption. For anyone *who has been* overcome *by sin* is brought in bondage.

[20] For if, after they have escaped the pollutions of the world through the knowledge of the Lord and Savior Jesus Christ, they are again entangled therein and overcome, *then* the latter end is worse for them than the beginning.

[21] For it would have been better for them to have not known the way of righteousness than, after they have known *it*, to turn *away* from the holy commandment delivered to them.

²²But what happens to them is true to the *old* proverb: The dog returns to its own vomit again and the sow that was washed *returns* to wallowing in the mire.

Proverbs 26:11

2 Peter Chapter 3

¹ Now, beloved, I write this second epistle to you, in *both of which* I *hope to* stir you up to remember *to have* a pure mind

² *and so* that you may be mindful of the words that were spoken before by the holy prophets and of the commandments of *our* Lord and Savior *as proclaimed* by us, the apostles.

³ Know this first: That in the last days, there will come scoffers, walking after their own lusts.

⁴ *They will* say: Where is the promise of His coming? For since the fathers fell asleep, everything⁺ continues as *it was* from the beginning of creation.

⁵ For this they are willingly ignorant that the heavens were *made* by the Word of God long ago⁺ and the earth *came forth* out of *the* water and *still* stands in the water.

⁶ And the world *as it was* then, over-flowed with water *and* perished.

⁷ But the Word *of God* has kept the heavens and the earth in store *and they are* reserved *for* fire *until* the day of judgment and damnation⁺ of *all* ungodly people.⁺

⁸ But, beloved, do not be ignorant about this one thing: That with the Lord, one day *is* as a thousand years, and a thousand years as one day.

⁹ The Lord is not slack concerning His promise, as some men count slackness. But *He* is longsuffering toward us, not willing that any should perish, but that all should come to repentance.

¹⁰The day of the Lord will come like a thief in the night in which the heavens will pass away with a great noise and the elements will melt with fervent heat and the earth also and *all* the works therein will be burned up.

¹¹*Seeing* then *that* all these things shall be destroyed,⁺ what manner *of persons* ought you to be in *all* holy conversation *and conduct* and godliness?

¹²*Should you not be* looking for and hastening to the coming of the day of God in which the heavens being on fire will be destroyed⁺ and the elements will melt with fervent heat?

¹³Nevertheless, according to His promise, we look for new heavens and a new earth in which righteousness will live.⁺

¹⁴Therefore beloved, since you look for such things, be diligent *so* that you may be found by Him in peace, without spot and blameless.

¹⁵And *know* that the longsuffering *of* our Lord *is for* salvation, *just* as our beloved brother Paul has also written to you, according to the wisdom given to him.

¹⁶In all *his* epistles, *Paul* also spoke about these things. *Some* things among them are hard to understand, which *cause those* who are uneducated⁺ and unstable *to* wrestle, as *they do* also *with* other Scriptures, to their own destruction.

¹⁷Therefore, beloved, since⁺ you knew *these things* before, beware lest you also, being led away with the error of the wicked, fall from your own steadfastness.

¹⁸Grow in grace and *in* the knowledge of our Lord and Savior Jesus Christ. To Him *be* glory both now and forever. Amen.

1 John Chapter 1

¹ That which was from the beginning, which we have heard, which we have seen with our eyes, which we have looked upon and our hands have touched⁺ *is*⁺ the Word of life.

² For the life was revealed⁺ and we have seen *it* and testify⁺ and *we are now* showing you the eternal life that was with the Father and was revealed⁺ to us.

³ What we have seen and heard we declare to you *so* that you also may have fellowship with us. Truly our fellowship *is* with the Father and with His Son Jesus Christ.

⁴ We write these things to you *so* that your joy may be full.

⁵ This then is the message we have heard from Him and declare to you: That God is light and in Him is no darkness at all.

⁶ If we say that we have fellowship with Him and walk in darkness, *then* we lie and do not live⁺ *by* the truth.

⁷ But if we walk in the light as He is in the light, *then* we have fellowship with one another and the blood of Jesus Christ His Son cleanses us from all sin.

⁸ If we say that we have no sin, we deceive ourselves and the truth is not in us. *Proverbs 28:13*

⁹ *But* if we confess our sins, *then* He is faithful and just to forgive us *for our* sins and to cleanse us from all unrighteousness. *Proverbs 28:13*

¹⁰ If we say that we have not sinned, we make Him a liar and His Word is not in us.

1 John Chapter 2

¹ My little children, I write these things to you *so* that you do not sin. And if anyone sins, we have an advocate with the Father: Jesus Christ the Righteous.

² He is the *means of* reconciliation⁺ for our sins, and not only for ours, but also for *the sins of* the whole world.

³ By this we know that we know Him: If we keep His commandments.

⁴ *Those* who say: I know Him but do not keep His commandments are liars and the truth is not in them.

⁵ But whoever keeps His Word, truly⁺ the love of God is perfected in them, *and* by this⁺ we know that we are in Him.

⁶ *Those* who say *that they* abide in Him should⁺ *also* walk in the same way as He walked.

⁷ Believers,⁺ I do not write a new commandment to you, but an old commandment that you have had from the beginning. The old commandment is the Word that you have heard from the beginning.

⁸ *Then* again, a new commandment I write to you: Which thing is true in Him and in you. Because the darkness is past and the true light now shines.

⁹ *Those* who say they are in the light and *yet* hate others⁺ are still in darkness.

> ¹⁰ *Those* who love *one* another⁺ abide in the light and there is no occasion for stumbling in them.
>
> ¹¹ But *those* who hate *one* another⁺ are in darkness and walk in darkness and do not know where they are going, because darkness has blinded their eyes.

¹²I write to you little children because your sins are forgiven for His name's sake.

¹³I write to you fathers because you have known Him *who is* from the beginning. I write to you young men because you have overcome the wicked. I write to you little children because you have known the Father.

¹⁴I have written to you fathers because you have known Him *who is* from the beginning. I have written to you young men because you are strong and the Word of God abides in you and you have overcome the wicked.

¹⁵Do not love the world or the things *that are* in the world. If anyone loves the world, the love of the Father is not in them.

¹⁶For all that *is* in the world, the lust of the flesh and the lust of the eyes and the pride of life, is not of the Father, but is of the world.

¹⁷The world is passing away, and the lust thereof, but *those* who do the will of God *will* live⁺ forever.

¹⁸Little children, it is the last hour.⁺ As you have heard that antichrist is coming, even now there are many antichrists. And by this we know that it is the last hour.⁺

¹⁹*Many* have gone out from among us, but they were not *a part* of us. For if they had been *a part* of us, *then no doubt* they would have continued with us. But *they went out so* that it might be revealed⁺ that they were not all *a part* of us.

²⁰But you have an anointing⁺ from the Holy One and *therefore* you understand⁺ everything.⁺

²¹I have not written to you because you do not know the truth, but because you *do* know it and *know* that no lie is of the truth.

²²Who is a liar but *one* who denies that Jesus is the Christ? *One* who denies the Father and the Son is antichrist.

²³Whoever denies the Son does not have the Father. *But those who confess the Son have the Father also.*

²⁴Therefore, let what you have heard from the beginning abide in you. If what you have heard from the beginning remains in you, *then* you also will continue in the Son and in the Father.

²⁵And this is the promise: That He has promised us eternal life.

²⁶I have written these *things* to you concerning *those* who *try to* deceive⁺ you.

²⁷But the anointing you have received from Him lives⁺ in you and you do not need anyone *else to* teach you. But as the same anointing teaches you about everything and is truth and is no lie, even as it has taught you, you shall abide in Him.

²⁸Now little children: Abide in Him *so* that when He shall appear we may have confidence and not be ashamed before Him at His coming.

²⁹If you know that He is righteous, *then* you know that everyone who does righteousness is born of Him.

1 John Chapter 3

¹ Behold what manner of love the Father has bestowed upon us, that we should be called the children⁺ of God. Therefore the world does not know us because it did not know Him.

² Beloved, we are now the children⁺ of God and it does not yet appear what we shall become. But we know that when He appears, we will be like Him. For we shall see Him as He is.

³ Everyone⁺ who has this hope in Him purifies themselves, even as He is pure.

⁴ Whoever commits sin, transgresses the law also. For sin is the transgression of the law.

⁵ You know that He was manifested to take away our sins, and in Him *there* is no sin.

⁶ Whoever abides in Him does not sin. Whoever sins has not seen Him or known Him.

⁷ Little children, let no one deceive you. *Those* who do righteousness are righteous, even as He is righteous.

⁸ *Those* who commit sin are of the devil, for the devil sins from the beginning. For this purpose, the Son of God was manifested *so* that He might destroy the works of the devil.

⁹ Whoever is born of God does not commit sin, for His seed remains in them. They cannot sin, because they are born of God.

---

¹⁰ In this the children of God are revealed,⁺ and *also* the children of the devil: Whoever does not do righteousness is not of God, nor *are those* who do not *truly* love others.⁺ ¹¹ For this is the message that you heard from the beginning: That we should love one another.

---

¹²Not like Cain *who* was wicked and killed⁺ his brother. Why did he kill⁺ him? Because his own works were evil and his brother's *were* righteous.

¹³Do not marvel, my family,⁺ if the world hates you.

¹⁴We know that we have passed from death to life because we love others.⁺ *Those* who do not love others⁺ abide in death.

¹⁵Whoever hates their brother is a murderer. You know that no murderer has eternal life abiding in them.

¹⁶By this we perceive the *true* love *of God*, that He laid down His life for us. And we *therefore* ought to *be willing to* lay down *our* lives for others.⁺

¹⁷But whoever has this world's goods and sees others⁺ have needs and *yet*

shuts up their heart+ *of compassion* from them, *then* how does the love of God live in them?

¹⁸My little children, let us not love in word or in tongue *only*, but in deed and in truth.

¹⁹By this, we know that we are of the truth and *by this we* will assure our hearts before Him.

²⁰For if our *own* heart condemns us, God is greater than our heart and *He* knows everything.+

²¹Beloved, if our heart does not condemn us, *then* we *can* have confidence toward God.

²²Whatever we ask, we receive from Him because we keep His commandments and do those things that are pleasing in His sight.

²³This is His commandment: That we should believe in the name of His Son Jesus Christ and love one another, as He gave us *this* commandment.

²⁴*Those* who keep His commandments live in Him and He in them. By this, we know that He abides in us: By the Spirit whom He has given us.

1 John Chapter 4

¹ Beloved, do not believe every spirit, but test+ the spirits *to see* if they are of God. Because many false prophets have gone out into the world.

² By this, you know the Spirit of God: Every spirit that confesses that Jesus Christ has come in the flesh is from God.

³ Every spirit that does not confess that Jesus Christ has come in the flesh is not of God. This is the *spirit* of antichrist that you have heard would come. Even now it is already in the world.

⁴ Little children, you are of God and have overcome them. Because greater is *He* who *is* in you than *he* who *is* in the world.

⁵ They are of the world. Therefore they speak of the world and the world hears them.

⁶ We are of God. *Those* who know God hear us. Anyone who is not of God does not hear us. By this, we know the spirit of truth and the spirit of error.

---

⁷ Beloved, let us love one another.
For *true* love is from God.
Everyone who loves
is born of God and knows God.

---

⁸ *Those* who do not love do not know God, for God is love.

⁹ In this, the love of God was revealed+ to us: That God sent His Only Begotten Son into the world *so* that through Him we might live.

¹⁰Herein is love: Not that we loved God, but that He loved us and sent His Son *to be* the *means of* reconciliation+ for our sins.

¹¹Beloved, if God so loved us, *then* we should+ also love one another.

---

¹² No one has seen God at any time.
But if we love one another,
then God lives in us
and His love is perfected in us.

---

¹³By this we know that we live in Him and He in us: That He has given us His Spirit.

¹⁴We have seen and testify that the Father sent the Son *to be* the Savior of the world.

¹⁵Whoever confesses that Jesus is the Son of God, *reveals that* God lives in them and they *live* in God.

¹⁶We have known and believed the love that God has toward us. God is love. *Those* who abide in love, abide in God and God *is* in them.

¹⁷Herein is our love made perfect, that we may have boldness in the day of judgment. Because, as He is, so are we in this world.

---

¹⁸ There is no fear in love,
but perfect love casts out fear.
Because fear has torment.
Those who fear
are not made perfect in love.

[19] We love Him because He first loved us.
[20] If anyone says: I love God, and hates others,+ they are a liar. For how can *those* who do not love others+ whom they have seen, love God whom they have not seen?
[21] This commandment we have from Him: That *those* who love God love others+ also.

1 John Chapter 5

[1] Whoever believes that Jesus is the Christ is born of God. Everyone who loves *God* who fathered+ *us all* also loves *those* who are fathered+ by Him.
[2] By this we know that we love the children of God: When we love God and keep His commandments.

> [3] For this is the love of God:
> That we keep His commandments.

His commandments are not grievous.
John 14:15
[4] For whatever is born of God overcomes the world. This is the victory that overcomes the world: Our faith.
[5] Who are *those* who overcome the world but *those* who believe that Jesus is the Son of God?
[6] This is *the One* who came by water and blood: Jesus Christ. Not by water only, but by water and blood. And it is the Spirit who bears witness, because the Spirit is truth.
[7] For there are three who bear witness+ in heaven: The Father, the Word, and the Holy Spirit. And these three are one.
[8] There are three who bear witness on earth: The Spirit, the water, and the blood. And these three agree in one.
[9] If we receive the witness of men, the witness of God is greater. For this is the witness of God that He has testified about His Son.
[10] *Those* who believe in the Son of God have the witness within themselves. *Those* who do not believe God, have made Him a liar because they do not believe the record that God gave of His Son.

[11] This is the record: That God has given eternal life to us, and this life is in His Son.
[12] *Those* who have the Son have life. *Those* who do not have the Son of God do not have life.

> [13] I have written these things to you who believe in the name of the Son of God *so* that you may know that you have eternal life and *so* that you may believe in the name of the Son of God.

[14] *Now* this is the confidence that we have in Him: That if we ask anything according to His will, He hears us.
[15] And if we know that He hears us, whatever we ask, *then* we know that we *shall* have the petitions that we desired of Him.
[16] If anyone sees another sin a sin *that is* not unto death, they should ask and He will give life to *those* who do not *commit* sin *that leads* to death. *Yet* there is a sin *that is* to death and I do not say that you shall pray for this.
[17] All unrighteousness is sin, *but* there is sin *that is* not unto death.
[18] We know that whoever is born of God does not sin, but *those* who are fathered+ by God keep themselves and the wicked does not touch them.
[19] *And* we know that we are of God. *But* the whole world lies in wickedness.
[20] We know that the Son of God has come and given us an understanding *so* that we may know Him who is true and *so that* we are in Him who is true, in His Son Jesus Christ. This is the true God and eternal life.
[21] Little children, keep yourselves from idols. Amen.

2 John Chapter 1

[1] *From John* the elder. To the elect lady and her children whom I love in the truth. Not only I but also all who have known the truth.

2 For the sake of the truth that lives in us and shall be with us forever.

3 Grace be with you, mercy, *and* peace, from God the Father and from *the* Lord Jesus Christ, the Son of the Father, in truth and love.

4 I rejoiced greatly that I have found of your children walking in truth as we received commandment from the Father.

5 Now I appeal⁺ *to* you, lady, not as though I wrote a new commandment to you, but *one* we have had from the beginning: *to* love one another.

6 And this is love: That we walk after His commandments. *And* this is the commandment: That as you have heard from the beginning, you should walk in it.

7 For many deceivers have entered the world who do not confess that Jesus Christ has come in the flesh. This is the deceiver and the antichrist.

8 Look to yourselves *so* that we do not lose those things *for* which we have worked,⁺ but *so* that we receive a full reward.

9 *For* everyone who transgresses and does not abide in the doctrine of Christ, does not have God *within them. But those* who abide in the doctrine of Christ have both the Father and the Son.

10 If anyone comes to you and does not bring this doctrine, do not receive them into *your* house or bid them *cordial* greetings.⁺

11 For *those* who bid them *cordial* greetings⁺ are partakers of their evil deeds.

12 *Although I* have many things to write to you, I would not *write* with paper and ink, but I trust to come to you and speak face to face *so* that our joy may be full.

13 The children of your elect sister greet you. Amen.

3 John Chapter 1

1 *From John* the elder. To the beloved Gaius whom I love in the truth.

2 Beloved, I wish above all things that you may prosper and be in health, even as your soul prospers.

3 For I rejoiced greatly when the family⁺ came and testified of the truth that is in you, even as you walk in the truth.

4 I have no greater joy than to hear that my children walk in truth.

5 Beloved, you do faithfully whatever you do for the family⁺ and for strangers.

6 *For they* have testified⁺ of your *true* love before the assembly. ⁺ *If* you bring *them* forward on their journey in a godly way, you will do well.

7 *It was* for *His* name *that* they went forth, taking nothing from the Gentiles.

8 Therefore, we ought to receive such *people so* that we might be *their* fellow helpers for the truth.

9 I wrote to the assembly,⁺ but Diotrephes, who *takes* pleasure⁺ in having preeminence among them, does not receive us.

10 Therefore if I come, I will remember his deeds that he does, babbling⁺ against us with malicious words. And not content with that, neither does he himself receive the family⁺ and *he* forbids *those* who would, and casts *them* out of the assembly. ⁺

11 Beloved, do not follow what is evil, but what is good. *Those* who do good are of God. But *those* who do evil have not seen God.

12 Demetrius has good report from everyone and from the truth itself. Yes, and we *also* testify⁺ and you know that our testimony⁺ is true.

13 I had many things to write, but I will not write to you with pen and ink.

14 But I trust *that* I will see you soon⁺ and we will speak face to face. Peace to you. *Our* friends greet⁺ you. Greet the friends by name.

Jude Chapter 1

1 *From* Jude, the servant of Jesus Christ and brother of James. To *those* who are sanctified by God the Father, preserved in Jesus Christ, *and* called.

2 Mercy to you, and peace and love be multiplied.

3 Beloved, when I gave all diligence to write to you of the common salvation, it was necessary+ for me to write to you and exhort*you* that you should earnestly contend for the faith that was once delivered to the saints.

4 For certain men crept in unexpectedly,+ who were long ago+ written+ *off as* ungodly men, turning the grace of our God into filthiness+ and denying the only Lord God and our Lord Jesus Christ.

5 Therefore I remind you, though you once knew this, that the Lord, having saved the people out of the land of Egypt, afterward destroyed *those* who did not believe.

6 The angels who did not keep their first estate but left their own habitation, He has reserved in everlasting chains under darkness until+ the judgment of the great day.

7 Even as Sodom and Gomorrah and the cities around them in like manner, giving themselves over to fornication and going after strange flesh, are set forth for an example, suffering the vengeance of eternal fire.

8 Likewise also these dreamers defile the flesh, despise the dominion, and speak evil of the glory.+

9 Yet Michael the archangel, when contending with the devil *as* he disputed about the body of Moses, did not dare+ *to* bring a reviling+ accusation against him but said: The Lord rebuke you.

10 But these *ungodly men* speak evil about things that they do not understand,+ but what they understand+ *in a* natural *sense*, as brute beasts, in those things they corrupt themselves.

11 Woe to them. For they have gone in the way of Cain and run greedily after the error of Balaam for reward and perished in the rebellion+ of Korah.

12 These *ungodly men* are spots in your love feasts when they feast with you, feeding themselves without fear. *They are* clouds without water carried about by winds, rotten+ trees without fruit, twice dead *and* uprooted,+

13 raging waves of the sea foaming out their own shame, wandering stars to whom is reserved the blackness of darkness forever.

14 Enoch, the seventh from Adam, also prophesied about them saying: Behold the Lord comes with ten thousands of His saints

15 to execute judgment upon everyone and convict+ all who are ungodly among them for all their ungodly deeds they have ungodly committed and for all the harsh+ *words* that ungodly sinners have spoken against Him.

16 These *ungodly people* are complainers+ *and* faultfinders+ walking after their lusts. Their mouths speak great swelling *words* in admiration of people *to gain* favor+ *and* benefit.+

17 But beloved, remember the words that were spoken before by the apostles of our Lord Jesus Christ.

18 They told you that there would be mockers in the last *of* time who would walk after their own ungodly lusts.

19 These are *the ones* who who set *themselves* apart+ *as* sensual *persons*, not having the Spirit.

20 But you, beloved, building up yourselves on your most holy faith, praying in the Holy Spirit,

21 keep yourselves in the love of God, looking for the mercy of our Lord Jesus Christ to eternal life.

22 On some have compassion, making a difference.

23 Others save with fear, pulling *them* out of the fire, hating even the garment spotted by the flesh.

24 Now to Him who is able to keep you from falling and to present *you* faultless before the presence of His glory with exceeding joy,

25 to the only wise God our Savior *be* glory and majesty, dominion and power, both now and ever. Amen.

The Revelation Chapter 1

¹ *The* Revelation *of* Jesus Christ *that* was given *by the One* who *is* God to show His servants *those* things that must soon⁺ come to pass. He sent *this* communication⁺ through His angel to His servant John.
² *John* testified⁺ *about* the Word of God and the testimony *of* Jesus Christ and *about* all *the* things that he saw.
³ Blessed *are those* who read and who hear the words of this prophecy and keep those things that are written *here*. For the time *is very* near.⁺
⁴ *From* John, to the seven assemblies⁺ *of believers* in Asia. Grace to you and peace from Him who is and who was and who is to come, and from the seven spirits who are before His throne.
⁵ From Jesus Christ *who is* the faithful witness, the firstborn⁺ of the dead, and the prince of the kings of the earth. To Him who loves us and washes us from our sins by His own blood,
⁶ and makes us kings and priests to God and His Father, to Him *be* glory and dominion forever and ever. Amen.
⁷ Behold, He *will* come after⁺ clouds and every eye will see Him, *even* those who pierced Him. All families⁺ of the earth will mourn⁺ because of Him. Even so, Amen.
⁸ I am the Alpha and the Omega: *The* beginning and *the* end, says the Lord who is and who was and who *is* to come, the Almighty.
⁹ I John, your brother and companion in tribulation and in the kingdom and patience of Jesus Christ, was on the island called Patmos because of the Word of God and testimony of Jesus Christ.
¹⁰ *I* became in the Spirit on the Lord's day and heard a great voice behind me, *sounding* like⁺ *that* of a trumpet.
¹¹ *The voice* said: I am Alpha and Omega, the first and the last. What you see, write in a book and send *it* to the seven assemblies⁺ *of believers* in Asia: To Ephesus, to Smyrna, to Pergamos, to Thyatira, to Sardis, to Philadelphia, and to Laodicea.
¹² I turned to see the voice that spoke to me and I saw seven golden candlesticks.
¹³ In the midst of the seven candlesticks *was one* like the Son of man, clothed with a garment down to the foot and belted⁺ about the chest⁺ with a golden belt.⁺
¹⁴ His head and hair *were* white like wool, as white as snow. His eyes *were* like a flame of fire.
¹⁵ His feet *were* like fine brass as though they burned in a furnace. His voice *was* like the sound of many waters.
¹⁶ In His right hand He *held* seven stars. A sharp, two edged sword came *forth* out of His mouth, and His countenance *was like the* sun shine in *its* power.⁺
¹⁷ When I saw Him, I fell at His feet as *though* dead. But *then* He laid His right hand on me, saying to me: Do not be afraid. I Am The First and The Last.
¹⁸ *As one* living, I became dead, and behold I am *now* alive forever and ever. Amen. And *I* have the keys *to* Hell and *to* death.
¹⁹ Write *down* the things that you have *just* seen and the things that are *now* before *you* and *the* things that are about to come to pass.
²⁰ The mystery of the seven stars that you saw in my right hand and the seven golden candlesticks: The seven stars are the angels of the seven assemblies.⁺ The seven candlesticks that you saw are the seven assemblies⁺.

The Revelation Chapter 2

¹ To the angel of the assembly⁺ *of believers* in Ephesus write: These things says He who holds the seven stars in His right hand *and* walks in the midst of the seven golden candlesticks:
² I know your works and your labor and your patience and how you cannot bear *those* who are evil. You have tested⁺ *those* who say they are apostles and are not and have found them *to be* liars..
³ *You* have carried⁺ *the load* and *endured* with patience and for my name's sake *you* have labored and have not fainted.

4 Nevertheless I have *something* against you because you have left your first love.
5 Remember therefore from where you have fallen and repent and do the first works. Or else I will come to you quickly and remove your candlestick out of its place, unless you repent.
6 But you have this *right*: That you hate the deeds of the Nicolaitans *who commit fornication*, which I also hate.
7 *Those* who have an ear, let them hear what the Spirit is saying to the assemblies.+ To *those* who overcome I will give *the reward* to eat from the tree of life that is in the midst of the paradise of God.
8 To the angel of the assembly+ in Smyrna write: The First and The Last who was dead and is *now* alive says these things:
9 I know your works and tribulation and poverty. Yet you are *really* rich. *I know* the blasphemy of *those* who say they are Jews and are not, but *are of* the synagogue of Satan.
10 Do not fear *any* of the things that you *must* suffer. Behold the devil will cast *some* of you into prison *so* that you may be tested+ *and* have tribulation *for* ten days. *But* be faithful *even* to death and I will give you a crown of life.
11 Let *those* who have an ear hear what the Spirit *is* saying to the assemblies.+ *Those* who overcome will not be hurt by the second death.
12 To the angel of the assembly+ in Pergamos write: These things says He who has the sharp sword with two edges.
13 I know your works and where you live, *even* where Satan's throne+ *is*. You hold fast *to* my name and have not denied faith *in* me, even in those days in which my faithful martyr Antipas was slain where Satan lives among you.
14 But I have a few things against you because you have *some* there who hold *to* the doctrine of Balaam who taught Balac to cast a stumbling block before the children of Israel *and* to eat things sacrificed to idols and to commit fornication.

15 You also have *some* who hold the doctrine of the Nicolaitans, which I hate.
16 *Therefore* repent. For if *you* do not, I will come to you quickly and fight against them with the sword of my mouth.
17 Let *those* who have an ear hear what the Spirit *is* saying to the assemblies.+ To *those* who overcome I will give *the reward* to eat of the hidden manna and *I* will give them a white stone and in the stone a new name written that no one knows except+ *those* who receive *it*.
18 To the angel of the assembly+ in Thyatira write: The Son of God who has eyes like a flame of fire and feet like fine brass says these things:
19 I know your works, *your* love and service, your faith and patience, and *that* your last works *are* more than the first.
20 Nevertheless I have a few things against you because you allow+ that woman Jezebel who calls herself a prophetess to teach and seduce my servants to commit fornication and to eat things sacrificed to idols.
21 I gave her time+ to repent of her fornication, but she did not repent.
22 Behold I will cast her into bed and *those* who commit adultery with her into great tribulation unless they repent of their deeds.
23 I will kill her children with death. All the assemblies+ will know that I Am He who searches the reins and hearts. I will give to everyone of you according to your works.
24 But I say to you and to the rest in Thyatira, *to* as many as do not have this doctrine and who have not known the depths of Satan as they speak, I will put no other burden on you.
25 Hold fast what you have until I come.
26 To those who overcome and keep my works to the end I will give authority+ over the nations,
27 to rule them with a rod of iron. *Just* like the vessels *that* the potter breaks, so also *will they* receive *judgment* from+ my Father.

[28] I will give them The Morning Star.
[29] Let *those* who have an ear hear what the Spirit *is* saying to the assemblies[+].

The Revelation Chapter 3

[1] To the angel of the assembly[+] in Sardis write: These things says He who has the seven spirits of God and the seven stars. I know your works, that you have a name that *says that* you *are* alive, but *really, you* are dead.

[2] Be watchful and strengthen the things that remain, that are ready to die. For I have not found your works perfect before God.

[3] Remember therefore what you have received and heard, and hold fast and repent. If you do not watch, I will come upon you like a thief and you will not know *at* what hour I will come upon you.

[4] You have a few names even in Sardis who have not defiled their garments. They shall walk with me in white, for they are worthy.

[5] *Those* who overcome will be clothed in white clothing.[+] I will not blot out their names out of the Book of Life, but I will confess their names before my Father and before His angels.

[6] Let *those* who have an ear hear what the Spirit *is* saying to the assemblies[+].

[7] To the angel of the assembly[+] in Philadelphia write: These things says He who is holy, He who is true, He who has the key of David, He who opens and no one shuts, and shuts and no one opens.

[8] I know your works. Behold I have set before you an open door and no one can shut it. For you have a little strength and have kept my Word and have not denied my name.

[9] Behold I will make those of the synagogue of Satan who say they are Jews and are not, but lie, behold I will make them to come and worship before your feet and to know that I have loved you.

[10] Because you have kept the Word of my patience, I will also keep you from the hour of trials[+] that is about to come upon all the world, to try *those* who live upon the earth.

[11] Behold I *will* come quickly. Hold fast what you have *so* that no one *will* take *away* your crown.

[12] *Those* who overcome I will make a pillar in the temple of my God and they shall go out no longer.[+] I will write upon them the name of my God and the name of the city of my God, *the* new Jerusalem that comes down out of heaven from my God. *I will write upon them* my new name.

[13] Let *those* who have an ear hear what the Spirit *is* saying to the assemblies[+].

[14] To the angel of the assembly[+] of the Laodiceans write: The Amen, The Faithful and True Witness, The Beginning of the Creation of God says these things:

[15] I know your works, that you are neither cold nor hot. I would *prefer that* you were *either* cold or hot.

[16] *However* because you are lukewarm and neither cold nor hot, I will spew you out of my mouth.

[17] Because you say: I am rich and increased with goods and have need of nothing, *you* do not understand[+] that you are wretched and miserable and poor and blind and naked.

[18] I counsel you to buy from me gold tested[+] in the fire, *so* that you may be rich. And *buy from me* white clothing[+] *so* that you may be clothed *properly* and *so that* the shame of your nakedness does not appear. And anoint your eyes with salve[+] *so* that you may see.

[19] For as many as I love, I rebuke and discipline.[+] Therefore be zealous and repent.

---

[20] Behold
I stand at the door and knock.
If anyone *will* hear my voice
and open the door,
I will come in to them
and dine[+] with them
and they with me.

²¹To *those* who overcome I will grant to sit with me in my throne, even as I also overcame and am set down with my Father in His throne.

²²Let *those* who have an ear hear what the Spirit *is* saying to the assemblies⁺.

The Revelation Chapter 4

¹ After this I looked and behold a door *was* opened in heaven. The first voice that I heard *was* like a trumpet speaking with me *and* saying: Come up here and I will show you things *that* must be *fulfilled* after this.

² Immediately, I became⁺ in the spirit and behold, a throne was set in heaven and *one* was sitting on the throne.

³ He who sat *there* was like a jasper and a ruby⁺ stone in appearance. And a rainbow *was all* around⁺ the throne, like an emerald in appearance.

⁴ *All* around⁺ the throne *were* twenty four seats *and* on the seats I saw twenty four elders sitting. *They were* clothed in white clothing⁺ *and* had gold crowns on their heads.

⁵ Lightning, thunder, and voices came forth⁺ out of the throne and seven lamps of fire *representing* the seven spirits of God *were* burning before the throne.

⁶ Before the throne *was* a sea of glass like crystal. In the midst of the throne and *all* around⁺ the throne *were* four beasts full of eyes *both* in front⁺ and behind.

⁷ The first beast *was* like a lion. The second beast like a calf. The third beast had a face like a man. And the fourth beast *was* like a flying eagle.

⁸ The four beasts each had six wings around *them* and *they were* full of eyes within. They did not rest day and night saying: Holy, holy, holy, Lord God Almighty who was and is and is to come.

⁹ When the beasts give glory and honor and thanks to Him who sits upon the throne *and* who lives forever and ever,

¹⁰the twenty four elders fall down before Him who sits upon the throne and *they* worship Him who lives forever and ever and cast their crowns before the throne saying:

¹¹You are worthy, O Lord, to receive glory and honor and power. For you have created all things and for your will⁺ they are and *they* were created.

The Revelation Chapter 5

¹ And then I saw in the right *hand of God* sitting on His throne a scroll written *both* inside and *on the* backside *and* sealed with seven seals.

² And I saw a strong angel proclaiming with a loud voice: Who is worthy to open the scroll and loosen its seals?

³ No one in heaven or on the earth or under the earth was able to open the scroll or look upon it.

⁴ I wept many *tears* because no one was found worthy to open and read the scroll or *even* to look upon it.

⁵ One of the elders said to me: Do not weep. Behold the Lion of the tribe of Judah, the Root of David has prevailed to open the scroll and loosen its seven seals.

⁶ I observed⁺ and saw in the midst of the throne and *among* the four beasts and in the midst of the elders, stood a Lamb that had been slain. *But now He* had seven horns and seven eyes that are the seven spirits of God sent forth into all the earth.

⁷ He came and took the scroll out of the right *hand of the one* who sat upon the throne.

⁸ And when He had taken the scroll, the four beasts and twenty four elders fell down before the Lamb. Each of them had harps and golden vials full of fragrances,⁺ which are the prayers of saints.

⁹ They sang a new song saying: You are worthy to take the scroll and open its seals for you were slain and *thereby* redeemed us to God by your blood out of every family,⁺ tongue, people, and nation.

¹⁰*You* have made us kings and priests to reign upon the earth.

¹¹Then I saw⁺ and heard the voice of many angels *all* around⁺ the throne. The number of beasts and elders was ten thousand times ten thousand, and thousands of thousands.

12 With a loud voice, *they were all* saying: Worthy is the Lamb who was slain to receive power and riches and wisdom and strength and honor and glory and blessing.

13 Every creature in heaven and on the earth and under the earth and such as are in the sea and all who are in them, I heard saying: Blessing and honor and glory and power *be* to Him who *is* upon the throne, and to the Lamb, forever and ever.

14 The four beasts said: Amen. And the twenty four elders fell down and worshiped Him who lives forever and ever.

The Revelation Chapter 6

1 When the Lamb opened one of the seals, I saw and heard, as *though* it were the noise of thunder, one of the four beasts saying: Come and see.

2 *Then I looked* and behold I saw a white horse and He who sat upon it had a bow. A crown was given to Him and He went forth conquering and to conquer.

3 When *the Lamb* opened the second seal, I heard the second beast say: Come and see.

4 *Then* another horse *that was* red went out. *Power* was given to *the one* who sat upon it to take peace from the earth *so* that *people* would kill one another. A great sword was given to him.

5 When *the Lamb* opened the third seal, I heard the third beast say: Come and see. And I observed+ and saw+ a black horse and *the one* who sat upon it had a pair of balances in his hand.

6 Then I heard a voice in the midst of the four beasts say: A measure of wheat for a penny and three measures of barley for a penny. *See that* you do not hurt the oil and the wine.

7 When *the Lamb* opened the fourth seal, I heard the voice of the fourth beast say: Come and see.

8 I looked and behold *I saw* a pale horse and his name who sat upon it was Death, and Hell followed with him. Power was given to them over a fourth of the earth,

to kill with sword and with hunger and with death and with the beasts of the earth.

9 When *the Lamb* opened the fifth seal, I saw under the altar the souls of *those* who had been slain for the Word of God and for the testimony that they held.

10 They cried *out* with a loud voice saying: How long, O Lord, holy and true, will you not judge and avenge our blood upon *those* who live on the earth?

11 White robes were given to everyone of them and it was said to them that they should rest for yet a little season *longer* until their fellow servants and their family+ who would also be killed as they *had been*, should be fulfilled.

12 When *the Lamb* opened the sixth seal, I looked+ and behold there was a great earthquake. The sun became *as* black as sackcloth *made* of hair and the moon became *the color of* blood.

13 The stars of heaven fell to the earth like a fig tree casts *off* untimely figs when shaken by a mighty wind.

14 The heavens disappeared+ like *writing on* a scroll when it is rolled together. All the mountains and islands were moved out of their places.

15 *All* the kings of the earth and *all* the great men and rich men and chief captains and mighty men and every servant+ and free man hid themselves in the dens and in the rocks of the mountains.

16 *They all* said to the mountains and rocks: Fall on us and hide us from the face of Him who sits on the throne and from the wrath of the Lamb.

17 For the great day of His wrath has come *and* who shall be able to stand?

The Revelation Chapter 7

1 After these things, I saw four angels standing at the four corners of the earth, holding *back* the four winds of the earth *so* that the wind would not blow on the earth or on the sea or on any tree.

2 Then I saw another angel with the seal of the living God ascending from the east.

He cried *out* with a loud voice to the four angels who had been given *authority* to hurt the earth and the sea,

³ saying: Do not hurt the earth or the sea or the trees until we have *placed a* seal on the foreheads *of* the servants of our God.

⁴ I heard the number of *those* who were sealed *and there were* a hundred *and* forty four thousand from all the tribes of the children of Israel.

⁵ From the tribe of Judah twelve thousand *were* sealed. From the tribe of Reuben twelve thousand *were* sealed. From the tribe of Gad twelve thousand *were* sealed.

⁶ From the tribe of Asher twelve thousand *were* sealed. From the tribe of Nepthalim twelve thousand*were* sealed. From the tribe of Manasseh twelve thousand *were* sealed.

⁷ From the tribe of Simeon twelve thousand *were* sealed. From the tribe of Levi twelve thousand *were* sealed. From the tribe of Issachar twelve thousand *were* sealed.

⁸ From the tribe of Zabulon twelve thousand *were* sealed. From the tribe of Joseph twelve thousand *were* sealed. From the tribe of Benjamin twelve thousand *were* sealed.

⁹ After this, lo and behold, a great multitude that no one could number of all nations and families⁺ and people and tongues *of the earth* stood before the throne and before the Lamb, clothed with white robes and *with* palms in their hands.

¹⁰*They all* cried *out* with a loud voice saying: Salvation *is by* our God who sits upon the throne, and by the Lamb.

¹¹All the angels stood around⁺ the throne, and the elders and the four beasts fell before the throne on their faces and worshiped God,

¹²saying: Amen. Blessing and glory and wisdom and thanksgiving and honor and power and might *be* to our God forever and ever. Amen.

¹³One of the elders answered, saying to me: Who are these who are arrayed in white robes? And from where did they come?

¹⁴I said to him: Sir, you know. And he said to me: These are the ones who have come out of great tribulation and have washed their robes and made them white by the blood of the Lamb.

¹⁵Therefore, they are before the throne of God and serve Him day and night in His temple. And He who sits on the throne will live among them.

¹⁶They will no longer hunger or thirst anymore. Nor will the sun blaze⁺ on them. Nor *will they suffer* any heat.

¹⁷For the Lamb who is in the midst of the throne will feed them and lead them to fountains of living water *and* God will wipe away all tears from their eyes.

The Revelation Chapter 8

¹ When *the Lamb* opened the seventh seal, there was silence in heaven *for* about half an hour.

² Then I saw the seven angels standing before God *and* seven trumpets were given to them.

³ Another angel came and stood at the altar with a golden censer *and* much incense was given to him *so* that he could offer *it* with the prayers of all saints upon the golden altar that was before the throne.

⁴ The smoke of the incense *that came* with the prayers of the saints ascended up from the angel's hand to God.

⁵ Then the angel filled the censer with fire from the alter and cast *it* onto the earth and there were voices and thunder and lightning and a *great* earthquake.

⁶ The seven angels with the seven trumpets *then* prepared to sound.

⁷ The first angel sounded and hail and fire mingled with blood were cast *down* upon the earth. One third of *all the* trees and all *of* the green grass was burned up.

⁸ The second angel sounded and *it was* as *though* a great mountain burning with fire was cast into the sea and one third of the sea became *like* blood.

⁹ One third of *all* the creatures living in the sea died *and* one third of *all* ships were destroyed.

[10] The third angel sounded and a great star fell from heaven burning like a lamp and falling upon a third of *all* the rivers and fountains of waters.

[11] The name of this star was Wormwood and one third of the waters *that it fell upon* became wormwood *poisoned.* Many people[+] died because the waters were made bitter *with poison.*

[12] The fourth angel sounded and one third of the sun and moon and stars were struck[+] so *that* one third of them were darkened. *Therefore* for one third of *each* day and night *the sun, moon, and stars* did not shine.

[13] *Then* I saw[+] and heard an angel flying through the midst of heaven saying with a loud voice: Woe, woe, woe, to the inhabitants of the earth because[+] of the other voices of the trumpets of the three angels that are yet to sound.

The Revelation Chapter 9

[1] The fifth angel sounded and I saw a star fall from heaven to the earth, and the key to the bottomless pit was given to him.

[2] He opened the bottomless pit and smoke like *that* from a great furnace rose *up* out of the pit, and the sun and air were darkened by the smoke from the pit.

[3] Out of the smoke, locusts *covered* the earth and were given power like the power of scorpions upon the earth.

[4] They were commanded *to* not hurt the earth or any green thing or any tree, but only those people[+] who did not have the seal of God on their foreheads.

[5] *The locusts* were given *instructions* that they should not kill *the* people,[+] but that they should be tormented *for* five months. The torment *was to be* like the torment of a scorpion when it strikes.

[6] In those days, people[+] will seek death, but will not find it. *They* will desire to die, but death will flee from them.

[7] The shapes of the locusts *were* like horses prepared for battle. On their heads were gold crowns and their faces *were* like the faces of men.

[8] They had hair like women's hair and teeth like a lion's.

[9] They had breastplates like iron and the sound of their wings *was* like the sound of chariots with many horses running to battle.

[10] They had tails like scorpions with stingers in their tails to hurt people[+] *for* five months.

[11] They had a king over them, the angel of the bottomless pit, whose name in Hebrew *is* Abaddon and in Greek is Apollyon.

[12] *After all this,* one woe is past and behold, there are two more woes *to come.*

[13] The sixth angel sounded and I heard a voice from the four horns of the golden altar that is before God.

[14] *God* said to the sixth angel with a trumpet: *Let* loose the four angels who are bound in the great river Euphrates.

[15] So the four angels were released.[+] *They* had been prepared for *this* hour and day and month and year to slay one third of *all* mankind.[+]

[16] The number of the army of the horsemen *was* two hundred million[+] and I heard their number.

[17] Then in the vision I saw the horses and *those* who sat on them. *They* had breastplates of fire, hyacinth,[+] and brimstone. The heads of the horses *were* like the heads of lions, and fire, smoke, and brimstone came[+] out of their mouths.

[18] By these three *plagues*, a third of all mankind were killed: by the fire, the smoke, and the brimstone that came out of their mouths.

[19] For their power[+] was in their mouth and in their tails. For their tails *were* like serpents with heads that *caused great* pain.[+]

[20] The rest of mankind[+] that was not killed by these plagues still[+] did not repent of *worshiping* the works of their hands. *They did not stop* worshiping demons[+] and idols of gold, silver, brass, stone, and wood that can neither see nor hear nor walk.

[21] Nor did they repent of their murders, sorceries, fornications, or thefts.

The Revelation Chapter 10

¹ I then saw another mighty angel come down from heaven, clothed with a cloud. There was a rainbow on his head and his face *shone* as *though* it were the sun, and his feet were like pillars of fire.

² He had a little book open in his hand, and he placed⁺ his right foot on the sea and *his* left *foot* on the earth.

³ *He* cried *out* with a loud voice like a lion's roar. When he cried *out*, seven thunders uttered their voices.

⁴ After the seven thunders uttered their voices, I was about to write when I heard a voice from heaven saying to me: Seal up those things that the seven thunders uttered and do not write them.

⁵ Then the angel that I saw standing upon the sea and upon the earth lifted up his hand to heaven.

⁶ He swore by *God* who lives forever and ever and who created heaven and earth and the sea and everything that is in them, that time shall not be *further delayed*.

⁷ But in the days when the voice of the seventh angel shall begin to sound, the mystery of God will be finished, *just* as He declared to His servants the prophets.

⁸ Then the voice that I heard from heaven spoke to me again and said: Go *and* take the little book that is open in the hand of the angel who is standing upon the sea and upon the earth.

⁹ I went to the angel and said to him: Give me the little book. He said to me: Take *it* and eat it up. It will make your belly bitter, but it will be sweet as honey in your mouth.

¹⁰ I took the little book out of the angel's hand and ate it up. It was as sweet as honey in my mouth, but as soon as I had eaten it, my belly was bitter.

¹¹ He said to me: You must prophesy again before many peoples, nations, tongues, and kings.

The Revelation Chapter 11

¹ Then a reed like rod was given to me and the angel standing *there* said: Rise and measure the temple of God and the altar and *those* who worship there.

² But leave out and do not measure the court that is outside⁺ the temple for it is given to the Gentiles and they shall tread the holy city under foot *for* forty two months.

³ I will give *power* to my two witnesses and they shall prophesy for a thousand two hundred and sixty days, clothed in sackcloth.

⁴ These *two witnesses* are *the* two olive trees and two candlesticks standing before the God of the earth. Zechariah 4:2-12

⁵ If anyone *tries to* hurt them, fire will come⁺ out of their mouth and devour their enemies. If anyone *tries to* hurt them, they must be killed in the same way.

⁶ These *two witnesses* have *the* power to shut *up* heaven *so* that it will not rain during the days of their prophecy. *They* have power over *the* waters to turn them to blood and to strike⁺ the earth with all *kinds of* plagues as often as they will *it to be done*.

⁷ When they have finished their testimony, the beast will ascend out of the bottomless pit to make war against them and overcome them and kill them.

⁸ Their dead bodies *will lie* in the street of the great city that is spiritually called Sodom and Egypt, where our Lord was also *in essence* crucified.

⁹ *All* the people and families⁺ and tongues and nations will see their dead bodies *for* three and a half days but will not allow⁺ their bodies to be put into graves.

¹⁰ Then *those* who live on the earth will rejoice and make merry and send gifts to each other because these two prophets tormented *those* who lived⁺ on the earth.

¹¹ After three and a half days, the spirit of life from God entered them and they stood up on their feet, and great fear fell upon *all* who saw them.

¹²Then they *all* they heard a great voice from heaven say to *the two witnesses*: Come up here. And their enemies saw⁺ them *as* they ascended up to heaven in a cloud.

¹³*In* that same hour, there was a great earthquake and a tenth part of the city fell and seven thousand people⁺ were killed.⁺ *Those who* remained⁺ were frightened⁺ and gave glory to the God of heaven.

¹⁴*Now* the second woe is past *and* behold the third woe is quickly coming.

¹⁵The seventh angel sounded and there were great voices in heaven saying: The kingdoms of this world *now* become *the kingdom* of our Lord and of His Christ and He shall reign forever and ever.

¹⁶*Then* the twenty four elders who sat on their seats before God fell face *down* and worshiped God

¹⁷saying: We give you thanks, O Lord God Almighty, who is and was and is to come, because you have *now* taken *up* your great power to reign.

¹⁸The nations were angry, but *now* your wrath has come. And the time *has come* for the dead to be judged and to give rewards to your servants the prophets and to the saints and to *those* who fear your name, great and small, *and* to destroy *those* who have destroyed the earth.

¹⁹Then the temple of God was opened in heaven and the ark of His covenant⁺ appeared⁺ with lightning and voices and thunder and an earthquake and great hail.

The Revelation Chapter 12

¹ Then a great wonder appeared in heaven: A woman clothed with the sun, the moon under her feet, and a crown with twelve stars on her head.

² *Being* in labor⁺ with child, *she* cried *out* in pain to give birth.

³ Then another wonder appeared in heaven: Behold, a great dragon with seven heads, ten horns, and seven crowns upon its heads.

⁴ Its tail drew *together* a third of *all* the stars of heaven and cast them to the earth. Then the dragon stood before the woman who was ready to give birth,⁺ to devour her child as soon as it was born.

⁵ *After the woman* brought *forth* a man child to guide⁺ all *the* nations with a rod of iron, her child was caught up to God and *to* His throne.

⁶ The woman *then* fled into the wilderness *to* a place prepared for her by God *who* would care⁺ for her *there* for a thousand two hundred *and* sixty days.

⁷ *Then* there was a *great* war in heaven. Michael and his angels fought against the dragon *and* the dragon fought *back*, but his angels

⁸ did not prevail. *There was* no place for them in heaven any more.

⁹ The great dragon *known as* the old serpent, the Devil, and Satan, *the* deceiver of the whole world, was cast out onto the earth, and his angels were cast out with him.

¹⁰Then I heard a loud voice in heaven say: Now, salvation and strength and the kingdom of God and the authority⁺ of His Christ have come. For the accuser of our family⁺ who accused them before our God day and night has *now* been cast down.

¹¹*Believers* overcame *Satan* by the blood of the Lamb and by the word of their testimony, not loving their *own* lives to the death.

¹²Therefore rejoice *O* heavens and you who live in them. Woe to the inhabitants of the earth and of the sea. For the devil has come down to you with great wrath, because he knows that he has only⁺ a short time.

¹³When the dragon saw that he was cast *down* to the earth, he persecuted the woman who brought forth the man *child*.

¹⁴But the woman was given two wings of a great eagle *so* that she could fly to the wilderness, to her place where she *she would be* nourished *and protected* from the presence⁺ of the serpent for a time and times and half a time.

¹⁵Then the serpent thrust⁺ water out of

his mouth like a flood after the woman *so* that he might *try to* cause her to be carried away by the flood.

¹⁶But the earth helped the woman. It opened up its mouth and swallowed up the flood that the dragon had thrust out of its mouth.

¹⁷Then the dragon was angry⁺ with the woman and went to make war with the remnant of her seed who keep the commandments of God and have the testimony of Jesus Christ.

The Revelation Chapter 13

¹ Then standing on the sand of the seashore, I saw a beast rise up out of the sea with seven heads and ten horns. On his horns were ten crowns and on his heads a blasphemous name.

² The beast that I saw was like a leopard. His feet were like *those* of a bear and his mouth like a lion's. The dragon gave him his power, his throne,⁺ and great authority.

³ I saw *that* one of his heads *was* mortally⁺ wounded but *then* the wound was healed and all the world marveled⁺ over the beast.

⁴ *So the people* worshiped the dragon that gave authority⁺ to the beast and they worshiped the beast saying: Who *is* like the beast? Who is able to make war with him?

⁵ *The beast* was given a mouth to speak great things and blasphemies, and he was given power to continue *for* forty two months.

⁶ So he opened his mouth in blasphemy against God, to blaspheme His name and His tabernacle and *those* who live in heaven.

⁷ He was given *the ability* to make war with the saints and overcome them *with* power over all families,⁺ tongues, and nations.

⁸ All who live on the earth will worship *the beast*, *except* not *those* whose names *are* written in the Book of Life by the Lamb *who was* slain. *His* from the foundation of the world.

⁹ If anyone has an ear, let them hear.

¹⁰*Those* who lead into captivity shall go into captivity. *Those* who kill by the sword must be killed by the sword. Here is the patience and the faith of the saints.

¹¹Then I saw⁺ another beast coming up out of the earth with two horns like a lamb but speaking like a dragon.

¹²*This beast* exercises all the authority⁺ of the first beast before him, and *he* causes *all* the earth and *those* who live there to worship the first beast whose deadly wound was healed.

¹³He does great wonders, *even* causing⁺ fire to come down from heaven to earth in the sight of men.

¹⁴And *he* deceives *those* who live on the earth by *performing* miracles that he is given⁺ the power to do in the sight of the beast. *Then he* tells *those* who live on the earth that they should make an image to the beast that had been *mortally* wounded by a sword, but *yet* lived.

¹⁵*The second beast* had power to give life to the image of the beast *so that* the image of the beast could both speak and cause all⁺ *who* would not worship the image of the beast to be killed.

¹⁶*This beast* causes all, both small and great, rich and poor, free and bond, to receive a mark in their right hand or in their foreheads,

¹⁷*so* that no one may buy or sell except⁺ *those* who have the mark or the name of the beast or the number of his name.

¹⁸Here is wisdom: Let *those* who have understanding count the number of the beast, for it is the number of a man, and his number *is* six hundred *and* sixty six.

The Revelation Chapter 14

¹ Then I looked and behold, a Lamb stood on Mount Zion,⁺ and with Him a hundred *and* forty four thousand, *all* having His Father's name written in their foreheads.

² I heard a voice from heaven like the sound of many *rushing* waters and like the sound of great thunder. I also heard the sound of harpists playing⁺ their harps.

3 They sang a new song before the throne and before the four beasts and the elders. No one could learn that song but the hundred *and* forty four thousand who were redeemed from the earth.

4 These are the *ones* who were not defiled with women, for they are virgins. These are the *ones* who follow the Lamb wherever He goes. These were redeemed from among men, *being* the first fruits to God and to the Lamb.

5 No deceitfulness+ was found in their mouth for they are without fault before the throne of God.

6 Then I saw another angel flying in the midst of heaven and proclaiming+ the everlasting Gospel to *all* who live on the earth, to every nation, family,+ tongue, and people.

7 With a loud voice, *he* said: Fear God and give glory to Him, for the hour of His judgment has come. Worship *the one* who made heaven and earth and the sea and the fountains of waters.

8 Another angel followed, saying: Babylon has fallen. That great city has fallen because she made all nations drink the wine of wrath *caused by* her fornication.

9 If anyone worships the beast and his image and receives *the beast's* mark in their forehead or in their hand,

10 the same shall drink the wine of God's wrath that will be poured *full* strength+ into the cup of His indignation. They will be tormented with fire and brimstone in the presence of the holy angels and in the presence of the Lamb.

11 The smoke from their torment will ascend up forever and ever. Those who worship the beast and his image and whoever receives the mark of his name will have no rest day or night.

> 12 Here the patience
> of the saints *is revealed*
> in keeping the commandments
> of God and faith *in* Jesus.

13 Then I heard a voice from heaven saying to me: Write *this*: Blessed *are* the dead who die in the Lord from now on. Yes, says the Spirit. *So* that they may rest from their labors, their works follow them.

14 And then I looked and saw a white cloud and the Son of man sitting on the cloud. On His head, he had a golden crown, and in His hand a sharp sickle.

15 Then another angel came out of the temple, crying *out* with a loud voice to *the one* who sat on the cloud: Thrust in your sickle and reap, for the time to reap has come, for the harvest of the earth is ripe.

16 So *the one* who sat on the cloud thrust His sickle across+ the earth and reaped *the harvest from* the earth.

17 Then another angel came out of the temple in heaven. He also had a sharp sickle.

18 And *still* another angel came out from the altar. *This one* had authority+ over fire. *He* cried *out* with a loud cry to the one who had the sharp sickle saying: Thrust in your sharp sickle and gather the clusters of vines from the earth, for her grapes are fully ripe.

19 So the angel thrust his sickle across+ the earth and gathered the vines and cast *them* into the great wine press of the wrath of God.

20 The wine press was *then* trod+ outside+ the city and blood came out of the wine press, even *up* to the horse's bridles for two hundred miles.+

The Revelation Chapter 15

1 Then I saw another great and marvelous sign in heaven: Seven angels *appeared* with the seven last plagues and the wrath of God is fulfilled+ by them.

2 I saw *what appeared to be* a sea of glass mingled with fire. *Those* who overcame+ the beast, his image, his mark, *and* the number of his name, stand on the sea of glass with harps from God.

3 They sing the song of Moses, the servant of God, and the song of the Lamb saying: Great and marvelous *are* your works, Lord God Almighty. Just

and true *are* your ways *O* King of *all that is* holy.[+]

[4] Who shall not fear you, O Lord, and glorify your name? For *only you* alone[+] *are* holy. All nations will come and worship before you. for your righteous-ness[+] is *clearly* seen.[+]

[5] After that, I saw[+] *that* the temple of the tabernacle of the testimony in heaven was opened.

[6] The seven angels clothed in pure white and girded with golden belts[+] came out of the temple with the seven plagues.

[7] One of the four beasts gave to the seven angels the seven golden vials filled with the wrath of God who lives forever and ever.

[8] The temple was filled with smoke from the glory of God and from His power. No one was able to enter into the temple until the seven plagues of the seven angels were fulfilled.

The Revelation Chapter 16

[1] Then I heard a great voice out of the temple saying to the seven angels: Go and pour out the vials of the wrath of God upon the earth.

[2] The first *angel* poured out his vial on the earth and an evil[+] and grievious sore fell on *those* who had the mark of the beast and *on those* who worshiped his image.

[3] The second angel poured out his vial on the sea and it became like the blood of a dead *man* and every soul living in the sea died.

[4] The third angel poured out his vial on the rivers and fountains of waters and they became blood.

[5] I heard the angel of the waters say: You are righteous, O Lord, who is and was and shall be, because you have judged *in this* manner.[+]

[6] For they have shed the blood of saints and prophets, and you have given them blood to drink, *which is* a worthy *judgment*.

[7] Then I heard another *voice* from the altar say: So *be it* Lord God Almighty,

your judgments *are* true and righteous.

[8] The fourth angel poured out his vial on the sun and it was given power to scorch mankind[+] with fire.

[9] *Therefore* great heat scorched mankind[+] and *they* cursed[+] the name of God who has authority[+] over these plagues, but they did not repent to give Him glory.

[10] The fifth angel poured out his vial on the throne[+] of the beast and his kingdom was filled with darkness and they gnawed their tongues with pain.

[11] *They* cursed[+] the God of heaven because of their pain and sores, and *they* did not repent of their deeds.

[12] The sixth angel poured out his vial on the great river Euphrates and its water was dried up *so* that the way for the kings of the east would be prepared.

[13] Then I saw three unclean spirits like frogs *come* out of the mouth of the dragon, out of the mouth of the beast, and out of the mouth of the false prophet.

[14] These are the spirits of demons[+] work-ing *pretended* miracles. *They* go to *all* the kings of the earth and of the whole world to gather them *together* for the *final* battle of that great day of God the Almighty.

[15] *The Lord said:* Behold I will come like a thief, *unexpected*. Blessed *are those* who watch and keep their garments *ready*, lest they walk naked and in shame. *Matthew 25:13*

[16] Then *the spirits* gathered them together to a place called Armageddon in Hebrew.

[17] The seventh angel poured out his vial into the air and a great voice came out of the temple in heaven from the throne saying: It is done.

[18] Then there were voices, thunder, light-ning and a great earthquake. Such a great *and* mighty earthquake had not *previously occurred* since mankind[+] *came* upon the earth.

[19] The great city was *broken* into three parts and the cities of the nations fell. And *then* God remembered to give the great Babylon the cup *filled with* the wine of the fierceness of His wrath.

[20] Every island fled away and mountains *just* disappeared.[+]

²¹Great hail with *stones* the weight of a talent fell from heaven onto mankind.⁺ People⁺ cursed⁺ God because the plague of hail was *so* exceedingly great.

The Revelation Chapter 17

¹ Then one of the seven angels who had the seven vials came and talked with me. He said: Come here and I will show you the judgment of the great whore who sits on many waters.

² Kings of the earth have committed fornication with her and the inhabitants of the earth have been made drunk with the wine of her fornication.

³ *The angel* then carried me away in the spirit into the wilderness. There, I saw a woman sitting on a scarlet colored beast with seven heads and ten horns and filled with blasphemous names.

⁴ The woman was arrayed in purple and scarlet color, and decked with gold and precious stones and pearls. She had a golden cup in her hand full of abominations and filth from her fornication.

⁵ The name written on her forehead *was*: Mystery Babylon the great, the mother of harlots and abominations of the earth.

⁶ I saw *that* the woman *was* drunk with the blood of the saints and with the blood of Jesus' martyrs and I wondered with great amazement.⁺

⁷ The angel said to me: Why did you marvel? I will tell you the mystery of the woman and of the beast with seven heads and ten horns that carries her.

⁸ The beast that you saw was *of one kind*, is not *now the same*, but will *again* ascend from the bottomless pit and go into damnation.⁺ *Those* who live on the earth whose names were not written in the Book of Life from the foundation of the world will wonder when they behold the beast that was *of one kind*, is not *now the same*, and yet is.

⁹ Here, the mind must⁺ have understanding⁺: The seven heads are the seven mountains on which the woman sits.

¹⁰There are seven kings. Five have fallen, one is *still there*, *and* the other has not yet come. When he comes, he must continue *for* a short time.⁺

¹¹The beast that was *of one kind*, and is not *now the same*, will also *become an* eighth after⁺ the seven, and *then he will go* into damnation.⁺

¹²The ten horns that you saw are ten kings who have received no kingdom yet, but *they* have received authority⁺ as kings *for* one hour with the beast.

¹³They are of one mind and *therefore* give their authority⁺ and strength to the beast.

¹⁴These *kings* will make war with the Lamb, but the Lamb will overcome them. For He is Lord of lords and King of kings. *Those* who are with Him *are* called and chosen and faithful.

¹⁵Then *the angel* said to me: The waters that you saw where the whore sits are peoples and multitudes and nations and tongues.

¹⁶The ten horns that you saw on the beast will hate the whore and will make her desolate and naked and will eat her flesh and burn her with fire.

¹⁷For God has put *it* in their hearts to fulfill His will and to agree to give their kingdoms to the beast until *all of* God's words are fulfilled.

¹⁸The woman you saw is that great city that reigns over the kings of the earth.

The Revelation Chapter 18

¹ After *all* these things, I saw *another* angel come down from heaven with *such* great power that the earth was illuminated⁺ with his glory.

² He cried *out* mightily with a strong voice saying: Babylon the great has fallen, *yes* fallen. *It* has become the habitation of demons⁺ and prison⁺ *for* every unclean⁺ spirit and prison⁺ *for* every unclean and hated bird. *Isaiah 21:9*

³ For all nations have drunk of the wine of the wrath of her fornication. The kings of the earth have committed fornication with her and the merchants

of the earth have grown[+] rich through the abundance of her delicacies.

[4] Then I heard another voice from heaven saying: Come *away* from her my people *so* that you will not be partakers of her sins and *so* that you will not receive her plagues.

[5] For her sins have reached to heaven and God has remembered her iniquities.

[6] Reward her even as she rewarded you and double to her. *Give her* double according to her works in the cup *that she has* filled, fill her double.

[7] *Consider* how much she has glorified herself and lived deliciously, *and* give her that much torment and sorrow. For she said in her heart: I sit *as* a queen. I am no widow. I shall see no sorrow.

[8] Therefore, *all* her plagues shall come in one day: death, mourning, and famine. She shall be utterly burned with fire. For the Lord God who judges her *is* strong.

[9] The kings of the earth who have committed fornication and lived deliciously with her will wail and mourn[+] for her when they see the smoke from her burning.

[10] *They will* stand a far *distance away* for fear of her torment saying: Alas, alas that great city Babylon, that mighty city. In one hour, your judgment has come.

[11] The merchants of the earth will weep and mourn over her, for no one buys their merchandise any more.

[12] *Their* merchandise *included* gold and silver, precious stones and pearls, fine linen in purple, silk and scarlet, all *kinds of* fragrant[+] wood, all kinds[+] of ivory vessels, all kinds[+] *of* vessels in precious wood, brass, iron, and marble,

[13] cinnamon, fragrances,[+] ointments, frankincense, wine, oil, fine flour, wheat, beasts, sheep, horses, chariots, slaves, and people's *very* souls.

[14] The fruits that your soul lusted after are gone[+] from you. All *the* things that were dainty and fine[+] are gone[+] from you. You shall no longer find them at all.

[15] The merchants of *all* these things who were made rich by her will stand a far *distance away* for fear of her torment, weeping, and wailing.

[16] *They will* say: Alas, alas, *for* that great city that was clothed in fine linen, purple and scarlet, and decked with gold, precious stones, and pearls.

[17] For in one hour such[+] great riches have come to nothing. Every ship master and all the company in ships and sailors and all[+] *who* trade by sea, stood at a far *distance away*.

[18] *They all* cried *out* when they saw the smoke from her burning, saying: What *city is* like this great city.

[19] They threw[+] dust on their heads and cried *out*, weeping and wailing, saying: Alas, alas, that great city in which all who had ships in the sea were made rich by her wealth,[+] in one hour she is made desolate.

[20] Rejoice over her *demise*, *O* heaven and holy apostles and prophets. For God has avenged you on her.

[21] Then a mighty angel took up a stone like a great millstone and cast *it* into the sea saying: Thus with violence that great city Babylon *is* thrown down, no longer[+] to be found at all.

[22] The voices of harpists, musicians, pipers, and trumpeters will no longer[+] be heard in you at all. No craftsman of any *kind of* craft will be found in you any more. The sound of a millstone will no longer[+] be heard in you at all.

[23] The light of a candle will no longer[+] shine in you at all. The voices of brides and grooms will no longer[+] be heard in you at all. Your merchants were the great men of the earth, *but* all *the* nations were deceived by your sorceries.

[24] *The* blood of prophets, saints, and all *who have been* slain on the earth *by her order is* found in *Babylon*.

The Revelation Chapter 19

[1] After these things, I heard a great voice of many people in heaven saying: Alleluia. Salvation, glory, honor, and

power *belong* to the Lord our God.

² His judgments *are* true and righteous. For He has judged the great whore who corrupted the earth with her fornication, and *He* has avenged the blood of His servants at her hand.

³ Again they said: Alleluia. And her smoke rose up forever and ever.

⁴ The twenty four elders and the four beasts fell down and worshiped God who sat on the throne saying: Amen. Alleluia.

⁵ Then a voice came from the throne saying: Praise our God all *of* you *who are* His servants and you who fear Him, both small and great.

⁶ I heard the voice of a great multitude like the voice of many waters and like the voice of mighty thunder saying: Alleluia, for the Lord God omnipotent reigns.

⁷ Let us be glad and rejoice and give honor to Him, for the marriage of the Lamb has come and His wife has made herself ready.

⁸ To her was granted that she should be arrayed in fine linen, clean and white. For fine linen is *to affirm* the righteousness of saints.

⁹ *The angel* said to me: Write *this*: Blessed *are those* who are called to the marriage supper of the Lamb. And *then* he said to me: These are the true sayings of God.

¹⁰ I fell *down* at *the angel's* feet to worship him, but he said to me: See *that you do* not, *for* I am your fellow servant and *one* of your family⁺ who has the testimony of Jesus. Worship *only* God. For the testimony of Jesus is the spirit of prophecy.

¹¹ Then I saw heaven open and behold, *I saw* a white horse and *the one* who sat on it called Faithful and True. In righteousness, He judges and makes war.

¹² His eyes *were* like a flame of fire and on His head *were* many crowns. *And* He had a name written *on Himself* that no one but He Himself knew.

¹³ He *was* clothed with a robe⁺ dipped in blood, and

> His name is called
> The Word of God.

¹⁴ The armies in heaven followed Him on white horses, clothed in fine linen, white and clean.

¹⁵ Out of His mouth, a sharp sword *came forth* to strike⁺ the nations. He will rule them with a rod of iron and tread the wine press with the fierceness and wrath of Almighty God.

¹⁶ On *His* robe⁺ and on His thigh He has *this* name written: King of kings and Lord of lords.

¹⁷ Then I saw an angel standing in the sun. He cried *out* with a loud voice to all the birds⁺ that fly in the midst of heaven: Come and gather yourselves together for the supper of the great God.

¹⁸ Thus *the birds shall* eat the flesh of kings and the flesh of captains and the flesh of mighty men and the flesh of horses and of *those* who sit on them and the flesh of all *men, both* free and bond, both small and great.

¹⁹ Then I saw the beast and the kings of the earth and their armies gathered together to make war against *the Lord* who sat on the *white* horse and against His army.

²⁰ The beast was taken *captive* and with him the false prophet who worked⁺ *pretended* miracles. By them, *the false prophet* deceived *those* who had received the mark of the beast and *those* who worshiped his image. Therefore, these two were *both* cast alive into the lake of fire burning with brimstone.

²¹ The rest⁺ were killed⁺ by the sword of *the Lord* who sat on the *white* horse, whose *sword* came⁺ *forth* out of His mouth. And all the birds⁺ were filled with their flesh.

The Revelation Chapter 20

¹ I then saw an angel come down from heaven with the key to the bottomless pit and a great chain in his hand.

² He laid hold on the dragon, that old

serpent who is the Devil or Satan, and bound him *for* a thousand years.

³ *Then the Lord* cast *Satan* into the bottomless pit and shut him up and set a seal on him *so* that he could no longer⁺ deceive the nations until the thousand years would be fulfilled. After that, *Satan* must be loosed *again for* a short⁺ time.

⁴ Then I saw thrones and sitting on them and giving judgment were those souls *who had been* beheaded for their testimony⁺ *for* Jesus and for the Word of God. They had not worshiped the beast or his image nor received *his* mark on their foreheads or in their hands, *and therefore* they *would* live and reign with Christ *for* a thousand years.

⁵ But the rest of the dead would not live again until the thousand years were finished. This *is* the first resurrection.

⁶ Blessed and holy *are those* who have a part in the first resurrection. The second death will have no authority⁺ over them, but they shall be priests of God and of Christ and shall reign with Him *for* a thousand years.

⁷ When the thousand years have expired, Satan will be released⁺ from his prison.

⁸ *He* will go out to deceive *all* the nations in the four corners⁺ of the earth, Gog and Magog, to gather them together for battle. The number of them *is* like *grains of* sand on the seashore.⁺

⁹ The *enemy* went across⁺ the breadth of the earth and surrounded⁺ the camp of the saints and the beloved city. And then fire came down from God in heaven and consumed⁺ them.

¹⁰The devil who had deceived them was cast into the lake of fire and brimstone where the beast and the false prophet *are*, and *where they* will be tormented day and night forever and ever.

¹¹Then I saw a great white throne and *the Lord* who sat on it. Heaven and earth fled away from *His* face and no place was found for them.

¹²I saw the dead, small and great, stand before God and the books were opened. Then another *book called* the Book of Life was opened and the dead were judged out of those things that were written in the books, according to their works.

¹³The sea gave up the dead that were in it. Death and Hell delivered up the dead that were in them. Everyone⁺ was judged according to their works.

¹⁴Then death and Hell were cast into the lake of fire, *and* this is the second death.

> ¹⁵ Anyone *whose name was* not found written in the Book of Life was cast into the lake of fire.

The Revelation Chapter 21

¹ Now I saw a new heaven and a new earth. For the first heaven and the first earth had passed away and there was no more sea.

² Then I John saw the holy city, the new Jerusalem, coming down from God out of heaven, prepared as a bride adorned for her husband.

³ I heard a great voice out of heaven saying: Behold the tabernacle of God *is* with men and He will live with them and they shall be His people and God Himself will be with them *and be* their God.

⁴ And God will wipe away all tears from their eyes. There will be no more death nor sorrow nor crying nor any more pain. For the former things are *now* passed away.

⁵ Then *the Lord God* who sat upon the throne said: Behold, I make everything new. And He said to me: Write *this down*, for these words are true and faithful.

⁶ And He said to me: It is done. I am Alpha and Omega, the beginning and the end. I will give to *those* who are thirsty from the fountain of the water of life freely.

⁷ *Those* who overcome will inherit everything. I will be their God and they will be my children.

8 But the fearful and unbelieving and the abominable and murderers and fornicators[+] and sorcerers and idolaters and all liars will have their part in the lake that burns with fire and brimstone. *For* that is the second death.

9 Then one of the seven angels who had the seven vials filled with the seven last plagues came to me and talked with me saying: Come here, I will show you the bride, the wife *of* the Lamb.

10 He carried me away in the spirit to a great and high mountain and showed me that great city, the holy Jerusalem, descending out of heaven from God.

11 Its light *radiated* with the glory of God like a most precious stone, like crystal clear jasper.

12 *It* had a great, high wall *with* twelve gates and twelve angels at the gates and *the names* of the twelve tribes of the children of Israel written on them.

13 *There were* three gates on the east, three gates on the north, three gates on the south, *and* three gates on the west.

14 The wall of the city had twelve foundations and on them *were* the names of the twelve apostles of the Lamb.

15 *The angel* who talked with me had a golden reed to measure the city and its gates and its walls.

16 The city lay foursquare with its length *equally* as long as its breadth. He measured the city with the reed, *and it was* fifteen hundred miles.[+] Its length, breadth, and height *were all* equal.

17 He measured the wall *as one* hundred *and* forty four cubits, *or 216 feet, according to the* human[+] measure *used by* the angel.

18 The wall was made[+] *of* jasper and the city *was* pure gold as clear as glass.

19 The foundations of the wall of the city *were* adorned[+] with all kinds[+] of precious stones. The first foundation *was* jasper, the second sapphire, the third quartz,[+] the fourth an emerald,

20 the fifth onyx,[+] the sixth ruby,[+] the seventh golden topaz[+] the eighth beryl, the ninth green topaz, the tenth *green* agate,[+] the eleventh *blue* hyacinth,[+] *and* the twelfth an amethyst.

21 The twelve gates *were* twelve pearls. Each gate was *made* of one pearl. And the street of the city *was* pure gold as *though* it were transparent glass.

22 But no temple could be seen there, for the Lord God Almighty Himself is the temple and the Lamb.

23 The city had no need for the sun or the moon to shine there, for the glory of God illuminated[+] it, and the Lamb *is* its light.

24 The nations of *those* who are saved will walk in this light and the kings of the earth will bring their glory and honor into it.

25 Its gates will not be shut *any* day and there will not be *any* night there.

26 And *the Lord* will bring the glory and honor of the nations, *all true believers*, into it.

27 But none[+] who defile or work abominations or lie shall enter into it. Only *those* whose *names* are written in the Lamb's Book of Life *shall enter*.

The Revelation Chapter 22

1 *The angel* then showed me a river of the pure water of life as bright[+] as crystal, *flowing* forth[+] from the throne of God and the Lamb.

2 In the midst *between* the street *on* this[+] side and the river *on* that[+] side *was a* tree of life producing[+] twelve fruits, yielding fruit each month, and the leaves of the tree *were* for the healing the nations.

3 All curses will no longer exist[+] *there*. But the throne of God and of the Lamb will exist[+] there and His servants will serve Him.

4 *True believers* will see His face and His name *will be* on their foreheads.

5 There will be no night there and no need for any lamp[+] or sunlight. Because the Lord God will enlighten[+] them and they will reign forever and ever.

6 *The angel* said to me: These sayings *are* faithful and true. The Lord God of the holy prophets sent His angel to show to His servants the things that must soon[+] be done.

[7] *And the Lord said:* Behold I am coming quickly. Blessed *are those* who keep the words[+] of the prophecy of this book.
[8] I John saw *all* these things and heard *them*. And when I had heard and seen, I fell down to worship before the feet of the angel who showed these things to me.
[9] But he said to me: See *that you do* not *do this*. For I am your fellow servant and of your family[+] the prophets and of *those* who keep the words of this book*to* worship God.
[10]He said to me: Do not seal *up* the words of the prophecy of this book, for the time is *very* near.[+]
[11]*Those* who are unjust, let them be unjust still. *Those* who are filthy, let them be filthy still. *Those* who are righteous, let them be righteous still. *Those* who are holy, let them be holy still.
[12]*And the Lord said:*

> Behold I am coming quickly
> and my reward *is* with me
> to give *to* everyone[+]
> according *to* their work.

[13]I am Alpha and Omega, The Beginning and The End, The First and The Last.
[14]Blessed *are those* who do His commandments *so* that they may have *the* right to the tree of life and *to* enter into the city through the gates.

[15]For outside[+] *are* dogs and sorcerers and fornicators[+] and murderers and idolaters and everyone who delights[+] *in* and commits[+] a lie.
[16]*Then the Lord said:* I Jesus have sent my angel to testify to you these things in the assemblies.[+] I am the Root and the offspring of David, The Bright and Morning Star.
[17]The Spirit and the bride say: Come. Let *those* who hear say: Come.

> Let *those* who are thirsty come.
> And whoever will, let them take
> *from* the water of life freely.

[18] For I testify to everyone[+] who hears the words of the prophecy of this book: If anyone shall add to these things, God will add to them the plagues that are written in this book.
[19] And if anyone takes away words from this book *of* prophecy, God will take away their part from the Book of Life and *from* the holy city and *from* the *rewards* written in this book.
[20]*The Lord* who testifies *to* these things says: Surely I come quickly. Amen. Even so, come Lord Jesus.
[21]The grace of our Lord Jesus Christ *be* with you all. Amen.

What choice have you made?

Do you realize that your eternal destiny will be determined by whatever choice you make? You have the option to choose to believe in God *and* believe His Word and follow Him...or to just go your own way and do your own thing, disregarding God's Word. Whatever you choose will determine the consequences and the reward that you will receive for all of eternity.

God loves you. He wants your life to be filled with love, joy, peace, and all the fruit of the Spirit here and now during your brief journey through this temporary life. And, He wants to give you the gift of eternal life. It's up to you to decide if you want to accept His offer, or reject it. On the last page of this book is an invitation that you can accept or reject. The choice is yours.

A Treasure of Old Testament Wisdom

The Old Testament is a treasure of history and prophecy, all of which points forward to that day when the Word of God Himself appeared in the flesh to speak directly to mankind.

The Old Testament describes God's creation of the world, declares His sovereignty, and documents His interaction with the human race from the creation of the first man and woman through the accounts of each individual that God appointed to communicate His messages to various target audiences over many centuries of human history.

While there is much wisdom encompassed within the 610,000 words in the Old Testament, most of it is revealed through illustrative case histories rather than by direct statements of declarative instructions and declarations of universal truth.

Other than the Ten Commandments, most of the other "commandments," "statutes," "ordinances," "laws," and "decrees" that the prophets declared as God's spokesmen were clearly intended for very specific target audiences and for very specific times, places, and circumstances.

Following is a representative selection of Old Testament verses that are featured in the book, *The Most Essential Truth in the Bible*.

---

¹ **Genesis**

1:1 In the beginning God created the heaven and the earth.

1:27 God *also* created mankind⁺ in His *own* image … He created them *as* male and female.

2:2 On the seventh day, God ended His work that He had made, and He rested on the seventh day from all His work that He had made.

2:7 *When* the Lord formed man *from* the dust of the ground, *He* breathed the breath of life into his nostrils and man became a living soul.

2:15-17 The Lord put man into the Garden of Eden to dress it and to keep it. ¹⁶ And He commanded the man, saying: Of every tree in the garden you may freely eat, ¹⁷ but from the tree of the knowledge of good and evil, you shall not eat. For in the day that you eat of it, you will surely die.

2:18 The Lord God said: *It is* not good that a man should be alone. I will make a help meet for him.

2:24 Therefore shall a man leave his father and his mother and be joined⁺ to his wife and they shall be one flesh.

3:1-5 Now the serpent was more subtle than any beast of the field that the Lord God had made, and he said to the woman: Has God said you shall not eat of every tree of the garden? ² The woman said to the serpent: We may eat from the fruit of the trees of the garden, ³ except from the fruit of the tree in the midst of the garden, *for* God said: You shall not eat from it nor shall you touch it, or else you will die.

⁴ The serpent said to the woman: You will not die, ⁵ for God knows that in the day *that* you eat from it, your eyes will be opened and you *yourselves* will be like gods, knowing good and evil.

3:6-7 *Therefore,* when the woman saw that the tree *was* good for food and pleasing to the eyes and desired to make *one* wise, she took *some* of the fruit and ate and gave *it* to her husband with her and he ate; ⁷ and their eyes were opened and they knew that they *were* naked. *So* they knit⁺ fig leaves together and made aprons *to cover* themselves.

3:8-13 When Adam and his wife heard the voice of the Lord God walking in the garden, they hid themselves from *His* presence ... ¹¹ *God said:* Have you *disobeyed me and* eaten from the tree that I commanded that you should not eat? ¹² *Adam* said: The woman that you gave me, gave me *fruit from* the tree and I did eat. ¹³ The Lord God said to the woman: What have you done? The woman said: The serpent beguiled me and I did eat.

3:16-17 *The Lord* said to the woman: *Because you have done this,* I will greatly multiply your sorrow in your conception. In sorrow you shall bring forth children and your desire *shall be* to your husband and he shall rule over you. ¹⁷ *Then* to Adam He said: Because you have listened⁺ to the voice of your wife and have eaten from the tree that I commanded you saying: You shall not eat from it, cursed *is* the ground for your sake. In sorrow shall you eat *from* it all the days of your life.

3:23 Therefore the Lord banished⁺ mankind⁺ out of the garden of Eden ...

6:5-7 *Later, when* God saw *all* the wickedness *on the earth* ... ⁶ He regretted⁺ that He had made mankind⁺ ... *all the rebellion* grieved Him ... ⁷ and the Lord said, I will destroy mankind⁺ from the face of the earth.

6:8 However, *one righteous man,* Noah,

found grace in the eyes of the Lord ... *and God saved Noah and his family* ...

9:1 God blessed Noah and his sons and said to them: Be fruitful and multiply and replenish the earth.

17:2-21 *Later still, God said to another righteous man, Abraham:* I will make my covenant between me and you and will multiply you exceedingly. ⁴ My covenant *is* with you and you shall be a father of many nations. ⁷ I will establish my covenant between me and you and your descendants⁺ after you for an everlasting covenant, to be God to you and to your descendants after you.

18:18 Abraham will surely become a great and mighty nation and all the nations of the earth will be blessed through him.

21:5 Abraham was a hundred years old when his son Isaac was born.

22:18 In your descendants, ⁺ all nations of the earth will be blessed because you have obeyed my voice.

24:1-4 *When* Abraham was old ... ² *he* said to his eldest servant ... ⁴ go to my country, to my kindred, and take a wife for my son Isaac.

24:67 Isaac took Rebekah into his mother's tent and she became his wife ... and he loved her ...

25:23 The Lord said to *Rebekah*: Two nations *are* in your womb and two kinds⁺ of people shall be separated from your bowels, and *one* people shall be stronger than *the other* people, and the elder shall serve the younger.

² Exodus

20:1-17 *The Ten Commandments as found in these verses are presented on page 5 of this book.*

34:14 You shall worship no other god because the Lord, whose name *is* Jealous, *is* a jealous God.

3 **Leviticus**

18:5 You shall keep my statutes and my judgments: which, if anyone does, they shall live in them: I *am* the Lord.

19:18 You shall not avenge nor bear any grudge against the children of your people, but *rather* you shall love your neighbor as yourself: I *am* the Lord.

4 **Numbers**

6:24-26 The Lord bless you and keep you. The Lord make his face shine upon you and be gracious to you. The Lord lift up His countenance upon you and give you peace.

5 **Deuteronomy**

1:11 The Lord God of your fathers *will* make you a thousand times as many more as you *are now*, and *He will* bless you *just* as He has promised.

4:2 You shall not add to the word which I command you, neither diminish *anything* from it, so that you may keep the commandments of the Lord your God which I command you.

6:5-7 You shall love the Lord your God with all your heart and with all your soul and with all your might. 6 These words which I command you shall be in your heart. 7 You shall teach them diligently ... and shall talk of them *daily* ...

6:16 You shall not tempt the Lord your God ...

8:3 ... mankind+ does not live by bread only, but by every *word*+ that proceeds out of the mouth of the Lord does mankind+ live.

10:12 What does the Lord require of you, but to fear the Lord your God, to walk in all His ways, and to love Him and to serve the Lord your God with all your heart and with all your soul ...

10:20 You shall fear the Lord your God. You shall serve Him and to Him shall you cleave and swear by His name.

6 **Joshua**

1:8 ... you shall meditate *in the Word* day and night+ ...

22:5 ... love the Lord your God and walk in all His ways and keep His commandments and cleave to Him and serve Him with all your heart and with all your soul.

24:15 ... as for me and my house, we will serve the Lord.

7 **Judges**

8:23 Gideon said, I will not rule over you and neither shall my son rule over you, but the Lord shall rule over you.

8 **Ruth**

2:12 *May* the Lord repay+ you and a full reward be given to you by the Lord God of Israel under whose wing you trust.

9 **1 Samuel**

15:22-23 Does the Lord have *as great a* delight in burnt offerings and sacrifices, as in obeying the voice of the Lord? Behold, to obey *is* better than sacrifice, *and* to hearken *is better* than the fat of rams. 23 For rebellion *is as bad as* the sin of witchcraft, and stubbornness *as bad as* iniquity and idolatry. Because you have rejected the Word of the Lord, He has also rejected you ...

16:7 *The Lord* does not *see things* as man sees things. For man looks at the outward appearance, but the Lord looks at the heart.

10 **2 Samuel**

22:4 I will call upon the Lord *who is* worthy to be praised. So shall I be saved from my enemies.

11 **1 Kings**

3:9 Give your servant an understanding heart to judge your people, so that I may discern between good and evil ...

¹² 2 Kings

19:15 ... You are God *and* you alone of all the kingdoms of the earth. *For* you have made the heavens and the earth.

¹³ 1 Chronicles

16:8 Give thanks unto the Lord. Call upon His name. Make known His deeds among the people.

16:10-12 Glory in the holy name of the Lord. Let the heart of *those* who seek the Lord rejoice. ¹¹ Seek the Lord and His strength *and* seek His face continually. ¹² Remember the marvelous works that He has done, His wonders and the judgments of His mouth.

29:12 *All* riches and honor *come* from the Lord. He reigns over everything. *All* power and might are in His hand *alone* and *it is* in His hand *alone* to make greatness and to give strength.

¹⁴ 2 Chronicles

7:14 If my people who are called by my name will humble themselves and pray and seek my face and turn from their wicked ways, then I will hear from heaven and *I* will forgive their sin and heal their land.

14:11 ... Help us, O Lord our God, for we rest on you and in your name we go against the multitude. O Lord, you *are* our God. Do not let *evil* men prevail against you.

36:16 They mocked the messengers of God and despised His words and misused his prophets until the wrath of the Lord arose against His people until *there was* no remedy.

¹⁵ Ezra

7:10 Ezra prepared his heart to seek the law of the Lord, and to do *it*, and to teach statutes and judgments in Israel.

¹⁶ Nehemiah

8:10 ... the joy of the Lord is your strength.

¹⁷ Esther

1:19-20 Let there be a royal commandment from the king ... that *if the* queen⁺ refuses⁺ to come before the king, then let the king give her royal estate to another who is better than she. ²⁰ And when the king's decree is published throughout his empire, all the wives shall give their husbands honor, both to great and small.

4:16 Gather *everyone* together *to* fast *and pray* for me *for* three days ... and *then* if I perish, I perish.

¹⁸ Job

22:22 Receive the law from His mouth and lay up His words in your heart.

¹⁹ Psalms

1:1-6 Blessed *is* the man who does not walk in the counsel of the ungodly or stand in the way of sinners or sit in the seat of the scornful. ² But his delight *is* in the law of the Lord and in His law does he meditate day and night. ³ He shall be like a tree planted by the rivers of water that brings forth fruit in its season. His leaf shall not wither and whatever he does shall prosper. ⁴ The ungodly *are* not like that, but *rather they are* like chaff that the wind blows⁺ away. ⁵ Therefore the ungodly shall not stand in the judgment, nor *shall* sinners *stand* in the congregation of the righteous. ⁶ For the Lord knows the ways of the righteous, but the ways of the ungodly shall perish.

18:2 The Lord *is* my rock and my fortress, my deliverer, my God *and* my strength in whom I will trust. *He is* my buckler, the horn of my salvation *and* my high tower.

19:14 Let the words of my mouth and the meditation of my heart be acceptable in your sight, O Lord, my strength, and my redeemer.

23:1-6 The Lord *is* my shepherd, I shall not want. ² He makes me to lie down in green pastures. He leads me beside the still waters. ³ He restores my soul. He leads me in the paths of righteousness for His name's sake. ⁴ Yes, *even* though I walk through the valley of the shadow of death, I will fear no evil. For you *are* with me. Your rod and your staff comfort me. ⁵ You prepare a table before me in the presence of my enemies. You anoint my head with oil. My cup overflows⁺. ⁶ Surely goodness and mercy will follow me all the days of my life, and I will dwell in the house of the Lord forever.

27:4 One *thing* I have desired of the Lord that will I seek after: that I may dwell in the house of the Lord all the days of my life, to behold the beauty of the Lord and to inquire in His temple.

31:23 Love the Lord, all you His saints, *for* the Lord preserves the faithful ...

34:3 O magnify the Lord with me and let us exalt His name together.

34:4 Delight yourself in the Lord and He will give you the desires of your heart.

37:11 The meek shall inherit the earth and delight themselves in the abundance of peace.

27:14 Wait on the Lord. Be of good courage and He will strengthen your heart.

46:1 God *is* our refuge and strength, a very present help in trouble.

46:10 *The Lord God has said:* Be still and know that I am God.

51:10 Create in me a clean heart O God and renew a right spirit within me.

61:2 From the ends of the earth, when my heart is overwhelmed, I will cry *out* to you: Lead me to the rock *that* is higher than I.

62:5 My soul waits only upon God, for my expectation *is* from Him.

62:11 God has spoken once *and* twice I have heard this: that *all* power *belongs* to God.

84:5 Blessed *are all*⁺ whose strength *is* in God ...

84:11 The Lord God *is* a sun and *a* shield. He gives grace and glory. No good *thing* will He withhold from those who walk uprightly.

107:9 He satisfies the longing soul and fills the hungry soul with goodness.

119:11 I have hid your Word in my heart so that I might not sin against you.

119:105 Your Word *is* a lamp unto my feet and a light unto my path.

145:20 The Lord preserves all who love Him, but He will destroy all the wicked.

147:3-5 He heals the broken in heart and binds up their wounds. ⁴ He tells the number of the stars. He calls them all by name. ⁵ Great *is* our Lord and of great power. His understanding *is* infinite.

20 Proverbs

1:7 The fear of the Lord *is* the beginning of knowledge. But fools despise wisdom and instruction.

3:5-6 Trust in the Lord with all your heart and do not lean on your own understanding. ⁶ In all your ways acknowledge Him and He will direct your paths.

3:12 *Those* whom the Lord loves, He corrects ...

6:16-19 Six *things* the Lord hates ... seven are an abomination to Him ...

17 a proud look, a lying tongue, hands that shed innocent blood,

18 a heart devising wicked imaginations, swift running to mischief,

19 a false witness ... and one who sows discord among the family⁺.

Proverbs *(continued)*

8:17 I love those who love me, and those who seek me early will find me.

8:32-33 Listen+ ... for blessed *are those who* keep my ways. 33 Listen to instruction and be wise and do not refuse it.

9:9-10 Give *instruction* to the wise and they will be wiser. Teach the just and they will increase in learning. 10 The fear of the Lord *is* the beginning of wisdom ...

10:11-12 The mouth of a righteous *person is* a well of life. But violence covers the mouths of the wicked. 12 Hatred stirs up strifes, but love covers all sins.

10:19 In a multitude of words, sin is not absent+. But those who refrain their lips *are* wise.

10:27-28 The fear of the Lord prolongs days, but the years of the wicked shall be shortened. 28 The hope of the righteous *shall be* gladness, but the expectation of the wicked shall perish.

11:13 A talebearer reveals secrets, but one who is of a faithful spirit conceals the matter.

11:14 Where no counsel *is*, the people fall, but in the multitude of counselors *there is* safety.

11:17 The merciful do good to their own soul. But *those who are* cruel trouble their own flesh.

11:19 Righteousness *is* to life. *Those* who pursue evil *pursue it* to their own death.

11:22 A pretty+ woman without discretion *is like* a jewel of gold in a pig's+ snout.

11:23 The desire of the righteous *is* good. The expectation of the wicked *is* wrath.

11:28 *Those* who trust in riches will fall, but the righteous will flourish ...

11:29 *Those* who trouble their own house will inherit the wind. The fool *will become a* servant to the wise of heart.

11:30 The fruit of the righteous *is* a tree of life. One who wins souls *is* wise.

12:2 A good *person* obtains *the* favor of the Lord, but *the Lord* will condemn those of wicked devices.

12:4 A virtuous woman *is* a crown to her husband, but one who makes ashamed *is* like rottenness in the bones.

12:15 The way of fools *is* right in their own eyes, but one who heeds+ counsel *is* wise.

12:16 A fool's wrath is quickly+ known, but a prudent *person* covers shame.

12:22 Lying lips *are an* abomination to the Lord, but those who deal truly *are* His delight.

12:25 Heaviness in the heart makes one stoop, but a good word makes one glad.

13:7 There are *some* who make themselves rich yet *have* nothing, and *some* who make themselves poor who *have* great riches.

13:10 Contention comes from pride, but from the well advised *comes* wisdom.

13:11 Wealth *gotten* by vanity will diminish, but one who gathers by labor will increase.

13:13 Whoever despises the Word will be destroyed, but one who fears the commandment will be rewarded.

13:18 Poverty and shame *come to* those who refuse instruction, but those who regard reproof will be honored.

14:9 Fools mock at sin. But among the righteous *there is* favor.

14:29 *One who is* slow to wrath *is* of great understanding, but *one who is* hasty of spirit exalts folly.

15:1 A soft answer turns away wrath, but grievous words stir up anger.

15:2 The tongue of the wise use knowledge rightly, but the mouths of fools pour out foolishness.

15:3 The eyes of the Lord *are* in every place, beholding the evil and the good.

15:22 Without counsel purposes are disappointed. But in the multitude of counselors *purposes* are established.

15:29 The Lord *is* far from the wicked. But He hears the prayers of the righteous.

15:31-33 The ear that hears the reproof of life abides among the wise. 32 *Those* who refuse instruction despise their own soul. But *those* who hear *and heed* reproof gain+ understanding. 33 The fear of the Lord *is* the instruction of wisdom and before honor *is* humility.

16:3 Commit your work to the Lord and your thoughts will be established.

16:7 When *one's* ways please the Lord, they make even their enemies to be at peace with them.

16:18 Pride *goes* before destruction and a haughty spirit before a fall.

16:20 One who handles a matter wisely will find good, and whoever trusts in the Lord *will be* blessed+.

16:27 An ungodly person+ digs up evil and in their lips *are* like a burning fire.

16:28 A contrary+ person+ sows strife and a whisperer separates chief friends.

16:32 *One who is* slow to anger *is* better than the mighty ...

17:9 Those who cover a transgression seek love, but those who repeat a matter separate friends.

17:17 A friend loves at all times ...

17:22 A merry heart does good *like* a medicine, but a broken spirit dries the bones.

17:27-28 Those who have knowledge spare their words. A man of understanding is of an excellent spirit. 28 Even a fool is considered wise when he remains silent.+ Those who keep their mouths closed *are esteemed* to have understanding.

18:10 The name of the Lord *is* a strong tower. The righteous run into it and are safe.

18:21 Death and life *are* in the power of the tongue ...

18:22 *Whoever* finds a wife finds *something* good and obtains *the* favor of the Lord.

19:5 A false witness will not be unpunished. *One who* speaks lies will not escape.

19:11 Discretion defers anger. *It is to one's* credit+ to pass over a transgression.

19:20 Hear counsel and receive instruction *so* that you may be wise in the latter end.

20:3 *It is* an honor to cease from strife, but every fool will *continue* meddling.

20:18 *Every* purpose is established by *wise* counsel ...

21:19 It is better to dwell in the wilderness than with a contentious, angry woman

21:23 Whoever keeps the mouth and the tongue *still* keeps the soul from trouble.

22:1 A *good* name *is* better+ to be chosen than great riches ...

22:6 Train up children in the way they should go and when they are old, they will not depart from it.

22:24 Do not make make a friendship with an angry person+.

22:26 Do not be a cosigner+ for the debts of others.

23:7 For as one thinks in their heart, so *are* they. Eat and drink, one *may* say to you. But their heart *is* not with you.

23:9 Do not speak in the ears of fools, for they will despise the wisdom ...

24:11 If you forbear to deliver *those who are* drawn to death and *those who are* ready to be slain.

24:26 ... kiss *the* lips that give a right answer *or a forthright response*.

25:6 Do not put yourself forth in the presence of the king and do not stand in the place of *those who are* great.

25:11 A word fitly spoken *is like* apples of gold in pictures of silver.

25:21-22 If your enemy is hungry, give them bread to eat. If they are thirsty, give them water to drink. 22 For *thereby* you heap coals of fire upon their head, and the Lord will reward you.

26:4 Do not answer a fool according to his folly, lest you also be like them.

26:20 Where no wood is, the fire goes out, so where *there is* no talebearer, strife ceases.

27:2 Let others praise you, not your own mouth ...

27:5 Open rebuke *is* better than secret love.

27:12 A prudent *person* foresees the evil *and* hides. The simple continue+ on *and* are punished.

27:15 A continual dropping in a very rainy day and a contentious woman are alike.

27:17 Iron sharpens iron. So *also* a friend+ sharpens the countenance of a friend.

28:6 Better *are* the poor who walk in uprightness than *those* perverse *in their* ways, *even if they are* rich.

28:25 Those who are of a proud heart stir up strife, but those who put their trust in the Lord shall be made whole+.

28:26 Those who trust in their own hearts are fools ...

29:18 Where *there is* no vision, people perish. But one who keeps the law *is* blessed+.

29:23 A person's pride will bring them low, but honor will uphold the humble in spirit.

> 30:5 Every Word of God *is* pure. He *is* a shield to those who put their trust in Him.

21 Ecclesiastes

8:11 *The* sentence against an evil work is not executed speedily, therefore the hearts of the sons of men is fully set in them to do evil.

9:9 Live joyfully with the wife whom you love all the days of *your* life …

10:1 Dead flies cause the ointment of the apothecary to send forth a stinking smell.+ *So does* a little folly *to one who* has a reputation for wisdom *and* honor.

22 Song of Solomon

8:7 Many waters cannot quench love, neither can the floods drown it …

23 Isaiah

8:12 … do not fear nor be afraid.

26:3 You *Lord,* will keep in perfect peace *the* mind stayed on you *by* trusting in you …

30:18 … The Lord *is* a God of judgment. Blessed *are* all who wait for Him.

32:17 The work of righteousness shall be peace, and the effect of righteousness *will be* quietness and assurance forever.

40:8 The grass withers, the flower fades, but the Word of God will stand forever.

40:31 Those who wait upon the Lord shall renew *their* strength. They shall mount up with wings like eagles. They shall run and not be weary. They shall walk and not faint.

41:10 Do not be afraid for I *am* with you. Do not be dismayed for I *am* your God. I will strengthen you. Yes, I will help you. Yes, I will uphold you with the right hand of my righteousness.

49:15-16 … *Others* may forget *you* but will I not forget you. 16 I have engraved you upon the palms of *my* hands.

53:5 He *was* wounded for our transgressions. *He was* bruised for our iniquities. The chastisement of our peace *was* upon Him. And with His stripes we are healed.

55:11 So shall my Word be that goes forth out of my mouth. It will not return to me void, but it will accomplish that which I please and it will prosper *in those purposes* to which I send it.

61:3 *I will give to them* beauty for ashes, the oil of joy for mourning, *and* the garment of praise for the spirit of heaviness *so* that they might be called trees of righteousness, the planting of the Lord, *so* that He might be glorified.

63:9 In all their affliction He was afflicted and the angel of His presence saved them. In His love and in His pity He redeemed them and He bore them and carried them all the days of old.

24 Jeremiah

3:1 If a man *shall* put away his wife … and she becomes another man's, shall he *ever* return to her again? Is that land not greatly polluted?

15:16 I found your words and consumed+ them and your Word became+ the joy and rejoicing of my heart. For *now* I am called by your name, O Lord God of hosts.

29:8 For thus says the Lord of hosts, the God of Israel: Do not let prophets and diviners among you deceive you …

29:11 For I know the thoughts that I think toward you, saith the Lord, thoughts of peace, and not of evil, to give you an expected end.

29:13 You shall seek me and find *me* when you search for me with all your heart.

31:3 The Lord has appeared to me *saying*, I have loved you with an everlasting love. Therefore, with lovingkindness have I drawn you.

31:25 I have satiated the weary soul and replenished every sorrowful soul.

32:17 Ah Lord God. Behold, you have made the heaven and the earth by your great power and your outstretched arm. There is nothing too hard for you.

25 Lamentations

3:22-23 *It is because of* the Lord's mercies that we are not consumed, because His compassions do not fail. 23 *They are* new every morning. Great *is* your faithfulness.

3:25 The Lord *is* good to those who wait for Him, to the soul *that* seeks Him.

26 Ezekiel

36:26 I will give you a new heart and I will put a new spirit in you.

27 Daniel

9:4 ... God keeps the covenant and *shows* mercy to those who love Him and to those who keep His commandments.

28 Hosea

2:19 I will betroth you to me forever ... in righteousness and in judgment and in loving kindness and in mercies.

6:6 I desire mercy and not sacrifice and knowledge of God more than burnt offerings.

29 Joel

2:32 Whoever shall call upon the name of the Lord shall be delivered ...

30 Amos

5:15 Hate the evil and love the good

31 Obadiah

1:12 You should not look *down* on your brother, neither should you rejoice ... in their destruction ...

32 Jonah

2:2 I cried *out* to the Lord because[+] of my affliction and He heard me

33 Micah

6:8 He has shown you what *is* good. And what does the Lord require of you, but to do justly and to love mercy and to walk humbly with your God?

34 Nahum

1:7 The Lord *is* good, a strong hold in the day of trouble, and He knows those who trust in Him.

35 Habakkuk

2:4 *The* souls *of those who* are lifted up are not upright in them. But the just shall live by faith.

3:19 The Lord is my strength ... He will make me to walk in high places ...

36 Zephaniah

3:17 The Lord your God in the midst of you *is* mighty. He will save you. He will rejoice over you with joy

37 Haggai

2:8 The silver *is* mine and the gold *is* mine, says the Lord of hosts.

38 Zechariah

4:6 Not by might nor by power but by my spirit, says the Lord of hosts.

39 Malachi

2:16 The Lord ... hates divorce[+] ... therefore take heed... *so* that you do not deal treacherously.

3:6 I *am* the Lord. I do not change ...

AV7
Features & Benefits

AV7 is an accurate literal translation, not a paraphrase. This is important because non-literal Bible versions often incorporate interpretive words and paraphrasing that may not be accurate but may instead reflect subjective ideas, opinions, and doctrinal distinctives.

AV7 uses easy-to-read present-day English. It was compiled by a computerized system that uses seven levels of processing to translate original language sources into grammatically correct English, preserving the literal translation accuracy of the trustworthy sources.

AV7 replaces the obsolete and archaic words and phrases that are used in the traditional 1611 English text with direct-equivalent present-day English words and phrases, using translation tables that identify and explain compilation details, word-for-word and phrase by phrase.

AV7 corrects previous grammatical and translation errors and provides exhaustive documentation to explain the corrections.

AV7 uses *reduced-size italics* to identify words that have been added interpolatively to improve the readability and clarity of the text.

AV7 uses superscript pluses⁺ as key-word flags to unobtrusively identify significant word revisions and to prompt readers to investigate corresponding word-studies.

AV7 replaces non-essential masculine gender presentation style with more accurate gender-inclusive wording. For example, inaccurate wording such as "he that" is revised to "those who" where applicable.

AV7 uses identity clarification revision to replace confusing pronoun sequences with proper nouns or descriptive titles in italics to clarify who is speaking with whom: For example, "he said to him" might be replaced by "*Jesus* said to him" where applicable.

AV7 is supported by exhaustive documentation to explain every aspect and detail of its compilation and presentation.

How the **AV7** *text was compiled*

AV7 = **A**uthorized **V**ersion + 7

AV7 is a computer-generated, updated, and enhanced presentation of the Bible that closely follows the traditional 1611 English text commonly known as "The Authorized Version" or "King James Version" or "KJV" but with acknowledged errors corrected and with thousands of archaic words and phrases replaced by their direct equivalent, present-day English words and phrasing.

The 1611 English compilation stood, virtually unchallenged, as the most widely accepted English translation of the Bible for more than 300 years. It acquired the title "Authorized Version" by acclaim, although it was never formally authorized by any official body. Today, the 1611 text continues to be a valuable benchmark against which to test and compare the accuracy of other versions of the Bible.

AV7 gives new meaning to the title "Authorized Version" because, unlike the many "All Rights Reserved" copyright restricted Bible versions and paraphrases in print today, **AV7** is authorized to be freely copied and distributed for any non-commercial purpose.

AV7 is compiled without using any paraphrasing or so-called "dynamic-equivalent" or "thought-for-thought" renderings such as have become common in many Bible versions. Instead ...

AV7 is compiled by an automated system that is able to perform translations directly from Greek and Hebrew original language sources into word-for-word, direct equivalent English. The resulting literal translation is then fine-tuned through seven levels of processing to produce an accurate yet easy-to-read, present-day English text.

In the example below, on line 1 is the Greek source text for John 3:8. On line 2 is an interlinear transliterated representation of the Greek. On line 3 is a literal, word-for-word English translation of each Greek word using mostly 1611 English words and spellings:

```
1. το    πνευμα οπου    θελει      πνει     και  την  φωνην    αυτου
2. to    pneuma opou    qelei      pnei     kai  thn  fwnhn    autou
3. the   wind   where [it] will*   bloweth and  the  sound [of] it*

1. ακουεις αλλ  ουκ  οιδας    ποθεν    ερχεται και  που   υπαγει
2. akoueiV all  ouk  oidaV    poqen    ercetai kai  pou   upagei
3. hearest but  not  know*    whence   cometh  and  where goeth

1. ουτως   εστιν πας         ο        γεγεννημενος  εκ  του  πνευματος
2. outwV   estin paV         o        gegennhmenoV  ek  tou  pneumatoV
3. so      is    every[one] who [is]  born              of  the  spirit
```

Limited space here does not permit a complete explanation of all of the sophisticated processing used in *AV7* compilation. The words shown with asterisks in the example above have alternate renderings that *AV7* processing uses to replicate the following *traditional* "KJV" text:

> The wind bloweth where it listeth, and thou hearest the sound thereof, but canst not tell whence it cometh, and whither it goeth: so is every one that is born of the Spirit.

Multiple additional translation tables include the following:

BEFORE	....	AFTER
bloweth	....	blows
listeth	....	will+
thou	....	you
hearest	....	hear
thereof	....	of it
canst not	....	[you] cannot
whence	....	from where
cometh	....	comes
whither	....	where
goeth	....	goes
so is	....	So [it] is [with]
every one that	....	everyone who

When all seven *AV7* translation tables are applied, this is the result:

> The wind blows where it will+ and you hear the sound of it, but *you* cannot tell from where it comes and where it goes. So *it* is *with* everyone who is born of the Spirit.

AV7 compilation is much more complex than indicated in this overview, but this provides a brief description of the process. Following are the seven stages of computer processing *AV7* uses to convert the Bible's original language source texts into the result shown above:

Stage 1 translates Greek and Hebrew to the literal English equivalent
Stage 2 converts literal English to a traditional 1611 English equivalent
Stage 3 converts archaic Olde English text to present-day English, replacing obsolete and archaic words, spelling, and syntax
Stage 4 corrects known grammatical and translation errors
Stage 5 adds technical enhancements into the master source files
Stage 6 incorporates many textual refinements to fine-tune the presentation
Stage 7 encodes the text for print font styles, sizes, and custom features

Additional information about the *AV7* translation and compilation system can be found at this Internet address: www.*AV7*.org

The case for literal accuracy.

Prove all things.
Hold fast what is good.
1 Thessalonians 5:21

People often ask: "Why are there so many different versions of the Bible, and which one is the best and most trustworthy?"

There are four basic answers to the first part of this question — two good reasons and two reasons that can be a cause for concern.

Reason #1: To translate the Bible into common languages. Since the Bible was originally written in Hebrew and Greek, it has been necessary to translate it into contemporary languages that people understand. The Bible has been translated into more languages than any other book.

Reason #2: To update obsolete and archaic language. The English language has undergone significant changes over centuries of time, and so it is beneficial to replace outdated words, grammar, and phrasing with literally accurate, direct equivalent words and grammatically correct phrasing in order to make the Bible easier to read and understand.

Reason #3: To promote private interpretations. Regrettably, some versions of the Bible have been compiled to promote the private interpretations and doctrines of various groups.

Reason #4: For commercial objectives. Some proprietary versions of the Bible have been sponsored and published by various commercial firms.

Since there can never be more than one version of the truth, ideally there should be only one version of the Bible in any given language. And yet, non-literal-translation paraphrases of the Bible can sometimes be helpful to first time readers. Any version of the Bible that helps people to know God and encourages them to learn and understand more about God's purpose and plan for their lives, serves a useful purpose.

However, it is important to make a very clear distinction between literal truth and subjective interpretation. Everyone who would like to understand God's Word better and grow in faith will do well to compare whatever version they consider using to an accurate literal translation.

Just as a ship or airplane that is only a fraction of a degree off course can end up hundreds of miles away from its intended destination, so also following interpretations that are not literally accurate can lead to serious error. The following explanation includes a few examples:

First, it is important to note that *AV7* is *not* a new version of the Bible. Rather, *AV7* is a new *presentation* of the traditional English translation that has stood the test of time for nearly 400 years.

The first English translation of the Bible began with work done by William Wycliffe in 1385 A.D. and by William Tyndale in 1536 A.D. Between 1603 and 1611 A.D., a team of 50 scholars compiled a further developed English text based largely on Wycliffe and Tyndale's work. But even after that, the English text first published in 1611 was further revised and improved many times between 1611 and 1769 A.D. That text became almost universally recognized as the most trustworthy English translation.

Even so, while there are few significant errors in this traditional English text, there are some renderings that are curious and not literally accurate. For example, in Acts 12:4, the Greek word πασχα, which is correctly translated as "passover" in 26 other places, is incorrectly translated as "Easter" in this verse. Another translation error is the colloquial expression "God forbid" that appears, incorrectly, 15 times in the traditional English text. The correct translation of the Greek source, μη γενοιτο, is "not be" or "*may it* not be." So, these are a just a few examples of errors in the traditional English translation that are corrected in *AV7*.

More serious problems occur when paraphrases take great liberty in changing the literal Word of God to say something quite different than an accurate literal translation. Compare the Greek, literal, 1611, *AV7*, and three currently popular versions below for the verse Luke 21:19:

Greek	εν	τη	υπομονη	υμων	κτησασθε	τας	ψυχας	υμων
literal	in	the	patience	you	possess	the	souls	you
1611	In		your patience		possess ye	your	souls	
AV7	In		your patience,		possess	your	souls	
(x)	By standing firm you will save yourselves							
(y)	By standing firm you will gain life							
(z)	By your endurance you will gain your lives							

As you can see, the *AV7* rendering exactly follows the literal word-for-word and the traditional 1611 English translation. Version "x" is a radically different interpretation. One must ask, is it really possible for anyone to "save themselves"? Versions "y" and "z" are paraphrases that suggest a very different interpretation and understanding than the literal. These same versions (x, y, and z) all translate υπομονη as "patience" in dozens of other places, but here change the meaning to "endurance" or "standing firm." One must question why.

Study to show yourself approved to God,
a worker+ who does not need to be ashamed,
rightly dividing the Word of Truth.
2 Timothy 2:15

317

A Cordial Invitation
to join the family of God

Do you know that *God loves you*
and that He wants you and everyone you care about
to be filled with love, joy, peace,
patience, gentleness, goodness,
and faith that will encourage and inspire you?

All you need to do
to become a member of God's family
is *read or listen* to the Word of God and *believe* Him.

That is all... He will do the rest.

You do not have to join any particular church
or follow any special religious doctrine
based on man-made rules.
You do not have to pay any dues or fees.
And you do not have to participate
in any special ceremonies or secret rituals.

If you will *just read the most essential truths* in the Bible
you will see how easy it is to receive the free gifts
of abundant life for today and eternal life
after your temporary life on earth comes to an end.

But you must understand
that God's greatest blessings are given
only to those who *choose* to believe in Him
and believe Him *(believe His Word)*
and who make a resolute decision
to join His family and follow Him.

The good news is that this is very easy to do.
God never intended for reading and believing His Word
to be confusing or complicated.

Repent. For the kingdom of heaven is very near.
Matthew 4:17

Those who believe and are baptized will be saved,
but those who do not believe will be damned.
Mark 16:16